CLYMER®

HONDA

CBR600F4 • 1999-2006

CLYMER®

P.O. Box 12901, Overland Park, Kansas 66282-2901

Copyright ©2006 Prism Business Media Inc.

FIRST EDITION
First Printing January, 2003

SECOND EDITION
First Printing September, 2006

Printed in U.S.A.

CLYMER and colophon are registered trademarks of Prism Business Media Inc.

ISBN-10: 1-59969-082-9

ISBN-13: 978-1-59969-082-7

Library of Congress: 2006931684

AUTHOR: Ed Scott.

TECHNICAL PHOTOGRAPHY: Ed Scott with assistance from Jordan Engineering Oceanside, CA. Motorcycles courtesy of Nathan White (CBR600F4i) and Michael Miller (CBR600F4). U.K. technical assistance courtesy of David Gath of Motohaus Marketing. Tire photos in Chapter Twelve courtesy of Avon Tyres.

TECHNICAL ILLUSTRATIONS: Errol McCarthy.

WIRING DIAGRAMS: Bob Meyer.

EDITOR: James Grooms.

PRODUCTION: Darin Watson.

TOOLS AND EQUIPMENT: K and L Supply @ www.klsupply.com

COVER: Photographed by Mark Clifford Photography, Los Angeles, California. 2002 CBR600F4i courtesy of Rice Motorsports, La Puenta, CA.

Publisher Shawn Etheridge

EDITORIAL	MARKETING/SALES AND ADMINISTRATION
Managing Editor James Grooms	*Sales Channel & Brand Marketing Coordinator* Melissa Abbott Mudd
Associate Editors Richard Arens Steven Thomas	*Art Director* Chris Paxton
Authors Jay Bogart Jon Engleman Michael Morlan George Parise Mark Rolling Ed Scott Ron Wright	*Sales Managers* Justin Henton Dutch Sadler Matt Tusken *Business Manager* Ron Rogers *Customer Service Manager* Terri Cannon
Illustrators Steve Amos Errol McCarthy Mitzi McCarthy	*Customer Service Representatives* Felicia Dickerson Courtney Hollars April LeBlond
Group Production Manager Dylan Goodwin	*Warehouse & Inventory Manager* Leah Hicks
Senior Production Editors Greg Araujo Darin Watson	
Production Editors Julie Jantzer-Ward Justin Marciniak Holly Messinger	
Associate Production Editor Susan Hartington	
Technical Illustrator Bob Meyer	

PRISM
BUSINESS MEDIA™
P.O. Box 12901, Overland Park, KS 66282-2901 • 800-262-1954 • 913-967-1719

The following books and guides are published by Prism Business Media

More information available at *clymer.com*

CONTENTS

QUICK REFERENCE DATA

MOTORCYCLE INFORMATION

MODEL: _CBR 600 F4i_ YEAR: _2002_

VIN NUMBER: _____

ENGINE SERIAL NUMBER: _____

CARBURETOR SERIAL NUMBER OR I.D. MARK: _____

TIRE INFLATION PRESSURE*

	Front kPa (psi)	Rear kPa (psi)
Up to 90 kg (200 lbs.) load	250 (36)	290 (42)
Up to maximum weight capacity	250 (36)	290 (42)

* Tire inflation pressure is for OE tires. Aftermarket tires may require different inflation pressure. The use of tires other than those specified by Honda may cause instability.

Battery: YTZ 10S

RECOMMENDED LUBRICANTS AND FLUIDS AND CAPACITIES

Brake fluid	DOT 4
Cooling system	
Coolant type	Honda HP coolant or an equivalent*
Coolant capacity	
Radiator and engine	2.7 L (2.9 U.S. qt., 2.4 Imp. qt.)
Reserve tank	0.31 L (0.33 U.S. qt., 0.27 Imp. qt.)
Drive chain	SAE 80 or SAE 90 gear oil
Engine oil	
Grade	API SF or SG
Viscosity	SAE 10W/40
Capacity	
Oil change only	3.0 L (3.2 U.S. qt., 2.6 Imp. qt.)
Oil and filter change	3.3 L (3.5 U.S. qt., 2.9 Imp. qt.)
After disassembly (engine dry)	3.7 L (3.9 U.S. qt., 3.3 Imp. qt.)
Fuel	
Type	Unleaded
Octane	Pump research octane of 86 or higher
Fuel tank capacity, including reserve	
U.S. and Canada models	
1999-2000 models	17.0 L (4.49 U.S. gal, 3.74 Imp gal)
2001-on models	18.0 L (4.76 U.S. gal, 3.96 Imp gal)
Other than U.S. and Canada models	18.0 L (4.76 U.S. gal, 3.96 Imp gal)

* Use a high quality ethylene glycol coolant that does not contain silicate inhibitors as they can case premature wear to the water pump seals and cause blockage of radiator passages. See text for further information.

MAINTENANCE AND TUNE-UP SPECIFICATIONS

Brake pedal height	Rider preference
Clutch lever free play	10-20 mm (3/8-13/16 in.)
Carburetor synchronizing difference	30 mm (1.2 in. Hg)
Starter valve synchronizing difference	20 mm (0.8 in. Hg)
Compression pressure at 350 rpm	
(at sea level)	1226 kPa (178 psi)
Drive chain free play	25-35 mm (1-1 3/8 in.)
Engine oil pressure (at oil pressure switch)	
at 80° C (176° F)	490 kPa (71 psi) at 6000 rpm
Idle speed (U.S. and Canada models)	
1999-2000 models	
49 states and Canada models	1200-1400 rpm
California models	1300-1500 rpm
2001-on models	1200-1400 rpm
Idle speed (Other than U.S. and Canada models)	
1999-2000 models	
Switzerland models	1150-1250
Other than Switzerland models	1100-1300
2001-on models	1200-1400 rpm
Spark plug types (U.S. and Canada models)	
1999-2000 models	
49 states and Canada models	CR9EH-9 (NGK) or U27FER-9 (Denso)
California models	CR9EHVX-9 (NGK)
2001-on models	IMR9A-9H (NGK) or IUH27D (Denso)
Spark plug types (Other than U.S. and Canada models)	
1999-2000 models	
Standard	CR9EH-9 (NGK) or U27FER-9 (Denso)
For cold climates	
(below 41° F/5° C)	CR8EH-9 (NGK) or U24FER-9 (Denso)
2001-on models	IMR9A-9H (NGK) or IUH27D (Denso)
Spark plug gap	
1999-2000 models	0.8-0.9 mm (0.031-0.035 in.)
2001-on models*	1.0 mm (0.040 in.)
Throttle cable free play	2-6 mm (3/32-1/4 in.)
Valve clearance (cold engine)	
Intake	0.17-0.23 mm (0.007-0.009 in.)
Exhaust	0.25-0.31 mm (0.010-0.012 in.)

*Gap is not adjustable. See text.

MAINTENANCE AND TUNE UP TORQUE SPECIFICATIONS

Item	N•m	in.-lb.	ft.-lb.
Brake hose banjo bolt	34	–	25
Crankcase timing hole cap	18	–	13
Cylinder head cover bolt	12	106	–
Driven sprocket nuts	88	–	65
Front axle bolt	59	–	43
Front axle pinch bolt	22	–	16
Oil drain bolt	29	–	21
Oil filter cartridge	26	–	19
Oil pressure main oil			
gallery plug	29	–	21
Rear axle nut	93	–	69
Spark plug	12	106	–

CHAPTER ONE

GENERAL INFORMATION

This detailed and comprehensive manual covers the Honda CBR600F4 and CBR600F4i U.S. models and the CBR600F and CBR600F Sport U.K. models from 1999-2006. The text provides complete information on maintenance, tune-up, repair and overhaul. Hundreds of photos and drawings guide the reader through every job.

A shop manual is a reference tool and as in all Clymer manuals, the chapters are thumb tabbed for easy reference. Important items are indexed at the end of the book. All procedures, tables and figures are designed for the reader who may be working on the motorcycle for the first time. Frequently used specifications and capacities from individual chapters are summarized in the *Quick Reference Data* at the front of the book.

Tables 1-10 are at the end of this chapter.

Table 1 lists engine and frame serial numbers (U.S. models).

Table 2 lists engine and frame serial numbers (other than U.S. models).

Table 3 lists motorcycle dimensions.

Table 4 lists motorcycle weight.

Table 5 lists fuel tank capacity.

Table 6 lists Honda general torque specifications.

Table 7 lists conversion formulas.

Table 8 lists technical abbreviations.

Table 9 lists metric tap and drill sizes.

Table 10 lists metric, inch and fractional equivalents.

MANUAL ORGANIZATION

All dimensions and capacities are expressed in metric and U.S. standard units of measurement.

This chapter provides general information on shop safety, tool use, service fundamentals and shop supplies. The tables at the end of the chapter include general motorcycle information.

Chapter Two provides methods for quick and accurate diagnosis of problems. Troubleshooting procedures present typical symptoms and logical methods to pinpoint and repair the problem.

Chapter Three explains all routine maintenance necessary to keep the motorcycle running well. Chapter Three also includes recommended tune-up procedures, eliminating the need to constantly consult the chapters on the various assemblies.

Subsequent chapters describe specific systems such as engine, transmission, clutch, drive system, fuel and exhaust systems, suspension and brakes. Each disassembly, repair and assembly procedure is discussed in step-by-step form.

Color wiring diagrams are at the back of the manual.

Some of the procedures in this manual specify special tools. In most cases, the tool is illustrated in use. Well-equipped mechanics may be able to substitute similar tools or fabricate a suitable replacement. However, in some cases, the specialized equipment or expertise may make it impractical for the home mechanic to attempt the procedure. When necessary, such operations are identified in the text with the recommendation to have a dealership or specialist perform the task. It may be less expensive to have a professional perform these jobs, especially when considering the cost of the equipment.

WARNINGS, CAUTIONS AND NOTES

The terms WARNING, CAUTION and NOTE have specific meanings in this manual.

A WARNING emphasizes areas where injury or even death could result from negligence. Mechanical damage may also occur. WARNINGS *are to be taken seriously.*

A CAUTION emphasizes areas where equipment damage could result. Disregarding a CAUTION could cause permanent mechanical damage, though injury is unlikely.

A NOTE provides additional information to make a step or procedure easier or clearer. Disregarding a NOTE could cause inconvenience, but would not cause equipment damage or personal injury.

SAFETY

Professional mechanics can work for years and never sustain a serious injury or mishap. Follow these guidelines and practice common sense to safely service the motorcycle.

1. Do not operate the motorcycle in an enclosed area. The exhaust gasses contain carbon monoxide, an odorless, colorless, and tasteless poisonous gas. Carbon monoxide levels build quickly in small enclosed areas and can cause unconsciousness and death in a short time. Make sure the work area is properly ventilated or operate the motorcycle outside.

2. *Never* use gasoline or any extremely flammable liquid to clean parts. Refer to *Cleaning Parts* and *Handling Gasoline Safely* in this chapter.

3. *Never* smoke or use a torch in the vicinity of flammable liquids, such as gasoline or cleaning solvent.

4. If welding or brazing on the motorcycle, remove the fuel tank, carburetor and shocks to a safe distance at least 50 ft. (15 m) away.

5. Use the correct type and size of tools to avoid damaging fasteners.

6. Keep tools clean and in good condition. Replace or repair worn or damaged equipment.

7. When loosening a tight fastener, be guided by what would happen if the tool slips.

8. When replacing fasteners, make sure the new fasteners are of the same size and strength as the original ones.

9. Keep the work area clean and organized.

10. Wear eye protection *anytime* the safety of the eyes is in question. This includes procedures involving drilling, grinding, hammering, compressed air and chemicals.

11. Wear the correct clothing for the job. Tie up or cover long hair so it cannot get caught in moving equipment.

12. Do not carry sharp tools in clothing pockets.

13. Always have an approved fire extinguisher available. Make sure it is rated for gasoline (Class B) and electrical (Class C) fires.

14. Do not use compressed air to clean clothes, the motorcycle or the work area. Debris may be blown into the eyes or skin. *Never* direct compressed air at anyone. Do not allow children to use or play with any compressed air equipment.

15. When using compressed air to dry rotating parts, hold the part so it cannot rotate. Do not allow the force of the air to spin the part. The air jet is capable of rotating parts at extreme speed. The part may be damaged or disintegrate, causing serious injury.

16. Do not inhale the dust created by brake pad and clutch wear. These particles may contain asbestos. In addition, some types of insulating materials and gaskets may contain asbestos. Inhaling asbestos particles is hazardous to health.

17. Never work on the motorcycle while someone is working under it.

18. When placing the motorcycle on a stand, make sure it is secure before walking away.

Handling Gasoline Safely

Gasoline is a volatile flammable liquid and is one of the most dangerous items in the shop. Because gasoline is used so often, many people forget that it is hazardous. Only use gasoline as fuel for gasoline internal combustion engines. Keep in mind, when working on a motorcycle, that gasoline is always present in the fuel tank, fuel line and carburetor. To avoid a disastrous accident when working around the fuel system, carefully observe the following precautions:

1. *Never* use gasoline to clean parts. See *Cleaning Parts* in this chapter.

2. When working on the fuel system, work outside or in a well-ventilated area.

3. Do not add fuel to the fuel tank or service the fuel system while the motorcycle is near open flames, sparks or where someone is smoking. Gasoline vapor is heavier than air, it collects in low areas and is more easily ignited than liquid gasoline.

4. Allow the engine to cool completely before working on any fuel system component.

5. On carburetted models, when draining the carburetor, catch the fuel in a plastic container and then pour it into an approved gasoline storage device.

6. Do not store gasoline in glass containers. If the glass breaks, a serious explosion or fire may occur.

7. Immediately wipe up spilled gasoline with rags. Store the rags in a metal container with a lid until they can be properly disposed of, or place them outside in a safe place for the fuel to evaporate.

8. Do not pour water on a gasoline fire. Water spreads the fire and makes it more difficult to put out. Use a class B, BC or ABC fire extinguisher to extinguish the fire.

9. Always turn off the engine before refueling. Do not spill fuel onto the engine or exhaust system. Do not overfill the fuel tank. Leave an air space at the top of the tank to allow room for the fuel to expand due to temperature fluctuations.

Cleaning Parts

Cleaning parts is one of the more tedious and difficult service jobs performed in the home garage. There are many types of chemical cleaners and solvents available for shop use. Most are poisonous and extremely flammable. To prevent chemical exposure, vapor buildup, fire and serious injury, observe each product warning label and note the following:

1. Read and observe the entire product label before using any chemical. Always know what type of chemical is being used and whether it is poisonous and/or flammable.

2. Do not use more than one type of cleaning solvent at a time. If mixing chemicals is called for, measure the proper amounts according to the manufacturer.

3. Work in a well-ventilated area.

4. Wear chemical-resistant gloves.

5. Wear safety glasses.

6. Wear a vapor respirator if the instructions call for it.

7. Wash hands and arms thoroughly after cleaning parts.

8. Keep chemical products away from children and pets.

9. Thoroughly clean all oil, grease and cleaner residue from any part that must be heated.

10. Use a nylon brush when cleaning parts. Metal brushes may cause a spark.

11. When using a parts washer, only use the solvent recommended by the manufacturer. Make sure the parts washer is equipped with a metal lid that will lower in case of fire.

Warning Labels

Most manufacturers attach information and warning labels to the motorcycle. These labels contain instructions that are important to personal safety when operating, servicing, transporting and storing the motorcycle. Refer to the owner's manual for the description and location of labels. Order replacement labels from the manufacturer if they are missing or damaged.

SERIAL NUMBERS

Serial numbers are stamped on various locations on the frame, engine, transmission and carburetor. Record these numbers in the *Quick Reference Data* section in the front of the book. Have these numbers available when ordering parts.

The frame serial number (**Figure 1**) is stamped on the right side of the steering head.

The VIN number label (**Figure 2**) is located on the left side of the frame adjacent to the steering head.

The engine serial number is stamped on a pad at the rear upper surface of the upper crankcase. Refer to **Figure 3** and **Figure 4**.

The carburetor serial number (**Figure 5**) is located on the intake side of the carburetor body above the float bowl.

The fuel injection throttle body serial number (**Figure 6**) is located on the intake side of the throttle body.

The color label (**Figure 7**) is located on the rear fender under the seat.

FASTENERS

Proper fastener selection and installation is important to ensure that the motorcycle operates as designed and can be serviced efficiently. The choice of original equipment fasteners is not arrived at by chance. Make sure that replacement fasteners meet all the same requirements as the originals.

Threaded Fasteners

Threaded fasteners secure most of the components on the motorcycle. Most are tightened by turning them clockwise (right-hand threads). If the normal rotation of the component being tightened would loosen the fastener, it may have left-hand threads. If a left-hand threaded fastener is used, it is noted in the text.

Two dimensions are required to match the thread size of the fastener: the number of threads in a given distance and the outside diameter of the threads.

Two systems are currently used to specify threaded fastener dimensions: the U.S. Standard system and the metric system (**Figure 8**). Pay particular attention when working with unidentified fasteners; mismatching thread types can damage threads.

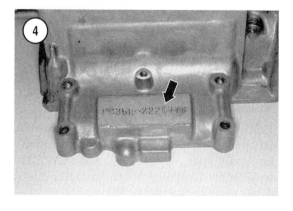

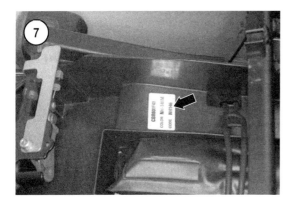

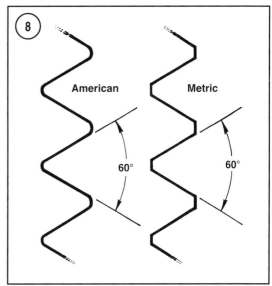

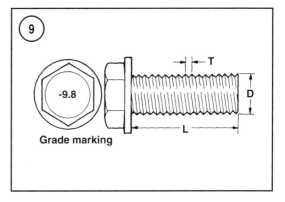

NOTE
To ensure that the fastener threads are not mismatched or cross-threaded, start all fasteners by hand. If a fastener is hard to start or turn, determine the cause before tightening with a wrench.

The length (L, **Figure 9**), diameter (D) and distance between thread crests (pitch) (T) classify metric screws and bolts. A typical bolt may be identified by the numbers, 8—1.25 × 130. This indi-

cates the bolt has diameter of 8 mm, the distance between thread crests is 1.25 mm and the length is 130 mm. Always measure bolt length as shown in L, **Figure 9** to avoid purchasing replacements of the wrong length.

The numbers located on the top of the fastener (**Figure 9**) indicate the strength of metric screws and bolts. The higher the number, the stronger the fastener is. Unnumbered fasteners are the weakest.

Many screws, bolts and studs are combined with nuts to secure particular components. To indicate the size of a nut, manufacturers specify the internal diameter and the thread pitch.

The measurement across two flats on a nut or bolt indicates the wrench size.

WARNING
Do not install fasteners with a strength classification lower than

what was originally installed by the manufacturer. Doing so may cause equipment failure and/or damage.

Torque Specifications

The materials used in the manufacture of the motorcycle may be subjected to uneven stresses if the fasteners of the various subassemblies are not installed and tightened correctly. Fasteners that are improperly installed or work loose can cause extensive damage. It is essential to use an accurate torque wrench, described in this chapter, with the torque specifications in this manual.

Specifications for torque are provided in Newton-meters (N•m), foot-pounds (ft.-lb.) and inch-pounds (in.-lb.). Refer to **Table 6** for Honda general torque specifications. To use **Table 6**, first determine the size of the fastener as described in *Fasteners* in this chapter. Torque specifications for specific components are at the end of the appropriate chapters. Torque wrenches are covered in the *Basic Tools* section.

Self-Locking Fasteners

Several types of bolts, screws and nuts incorporate a system that creates interference between the two fasteners. Interference is achieved in various ways. The most common type is the nylon insert nut and a dry adhesive coating on the threads of a bolt.

Self-locking fasteners offer greater holding strength than standard fasteners, which improves their resistance to vibration. Self-locking fasteners cannot be reused. The materials used to form the lock become distorted after the initial installation and removal. It is a good practice to discard and replace self-locking fasteners after their removal. Do not replace self-locking fasteners with standard fasteners.

Washers

There are two basic types of washers: flat washers and lockwashers. Flat washers are simple discs with a hole to fit a screw or bolt. Lockwashers are used to prevent a fastener from working loose. Washers can be used as spacers and seals, or to help distribute fastener load and to prevent the fastener from damaging the component.

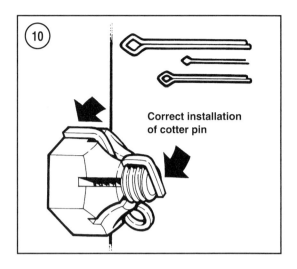

Correct installation of cotter pin

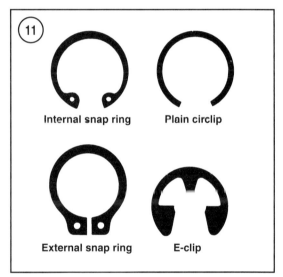

Internal snap ring   Plain circlip

External snap ring   E-clip

As with fasteners, make sure replacement washers are of the same design and quality as the originals.

Cotter Pins

A cotter pin is a split metal pin inserted into a hole or slot to prevent a fastener from loosening. In certain applications, such as the rear axle on an ATV or motorcycle, the fastener must be secured in this way. For these applications, a cotter pin and castellated (slotted) nut is used.

To use a cotter pin, first make sure the diameter is correct for the hole in the fastener. After correctly tightening the fastener and aligning the holes, insert the cotter pin through the hole and bend the ends

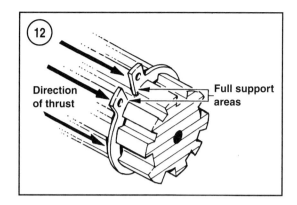

Direction of thrust

Full support areas

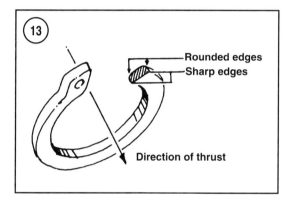

Rounded edges

Sharp edges

Direction of thrust

over the fastener (**Figure 10**). Unless instructed to do so, never loosen a tightened fastener to align the holes. If the holes do not align, tighten the fastener just enough to achieve alignment.

Cotter pins are available in various diameters and lengths. Measure length from the bottom of the head to the tip of the shortest pin.

Snap Rings and E-clips

Snap rings (**Figure 11**) are circular-shaped metal retaining clips. They are required to secure parts and gears in place on parts such as shafts, pins or rods. External-type snap rings are used to retain items on shafts. Internal-type snap rings secure parts within housing bores. In some applications, in addition to securing the component(s), snap rings of varying thickness also determine endplay. These are usually called selective snap rings.

Two basic types of snap rings are used: machined and stamped. Machined snap rings (**Figure 12**) can be installed in either direction, since both faces have sharp edges. Stamped snap rings (**Figure 13**) are manufactured with a sharp edge and a round edge.

When installing a stamped snap ring in a thrust application, install the sharp edge facing away from the part producing the thrust.

E-clips are used when it is not practical to use a snap ring. Remove E-clips with a flat blade screwdriver by prying between the shaft and E-clip. To install an E-clip, center it over the shaft groove and push or tap it into place.

Observe the following when installing snap rings:
1. Remove and install snap rings with snap ring pliers. See *Snap Ring Pliers* in this chapter.
2. In some applications, it may be necessary to replace snap rings after removing them.
3. Compress or expand snap rings only enough to install them. If overly expanded, they lose their retaining ability.
4. After installing a snap ring, make sure it seats completely.
5. Wear eye protection when removing and installing snap rings.

SHOP SUPPLIES

Lubricants and Fluids

Periodic lubrication helps ensure a long service life for any type of equipment. Using the correct type of lubricant is as important as performing the lubrication service, although in an emergency the wrong type is better than not using one. The following section describes the types of lubricants most often required. Make sure to follow the manufacturer's recommendations for lubricant types.

Engine oils

Engine oil is classified by two standards: the American Petroleum Institute (API) service classification and the Society of Automotive Engineers (SAE) viscosity rating. This information is on the oil container label. Two letters indicate the API service classification. The number or sequence of numbers and letter (10W-40, for example) is the oil's viscosity rating. The API service classification and the SAE viscosity index are not indications of oil quality.

The service classification indicates that the oil meets specific lubrication standards. The first letter in the classification (*S*) indicates that the oil is for gasoline engines. The second letter indicates the standard the oil satisfies.

Always use an oil with a classification recommended by the manufacturer. Using an oil with a different classification can cause engine damage.

Viscosity is an indication of the oil's thickness. Thin oils have a lower number, while thick oils have a higher number. Engine oils fall into the 5- to 50-weight range for single-grade oils.

Most manufacturers recommend multi-grade oil. These oils perform efficiently across a wide range of operating conditions. Multi-grade oils are identified by a *W* after the first number, which indicates the low-temperature viscosity.

Engine oils are most commonly mineral (petroleum) based; however, synthetic and semi-synthetic types are used more frequently. When selecting engine oil, follow the manufacturer's recommendation for type, classification and viscosity.

Greases

Grease is lubricating oil with thickening agents added to it. The National Lubricating Grease Institute (NLGI) grades grease. Grades range from No. 000 to No. 6, with No. 6 being the thickest. Typical multipurpose grease is NLGI No. 2. For specific applications, manufacturers may recommend water-resistant type grease or one with an additive such as molybdenum disulfide (MoS_2).

Brake fluid

Brake fluid is the hydraulic fluid used to transmit hydraulic pressure (force) to the wheel brakes. Brake fluid is classified by the Department of Transportation (DOT). Current designations for brake fluid are DOT 3, DOT 4 and DOT 5. This classification appears on the fluid container.

Each type of brake fluid has its own definite characteristics. Do not intermix different types of brake fluid, as this may cause brake system failure. DOT 5 brake fluid is silicone based. DOT 5 is not compatible with other brake fluids or in systems for which it was not designed. Mixing DOT 5 fluid with other fluids may cause brake system failure. When adding brake fluid, *only* use the fluid recommended by the manufacturer.

Brake fluid will damage any plastic, painted or plated surface it contacts. Use extreme care when working with brake fluid and remove any spills immediately with soap and water.

Hydraulic brake systems require clean and moisture-free brake fluid. Never reuse brake fluid. Keep containers and reservoirs properly sealed.

> *WARNING*
> *Never put a mineral-based (petroleum) oil into the brake system. Mineral oil will cause rubber parts in the system to swell and break apart, resulting in complete brake failure.*

> *NOTE*
> *DOT 4 brake fluid is used in the hydraulic-actuated clutch system.*

Coolant

Coolant is a mixture of water and antifreeze used to dissipate engine heat. Ethylene glycol is the most common form of antifreeze used. Check the motorcycle manufacturer's recommendations when selecting antifreeze; most require one specifically designed for use in aluminum engines. These types of antifreeze have additives that inhibit corrosion.

Only mix distilled water with antifreeze. Impurities in tap water may damage internal cooling system passages.

Drive chain lubricant

There are many types of chain lubricants available. Which type of drive chain lubricant to use depends on the type of chain.

On O-ring (sealed) chains, the lubricant keeps the O-rings pliable and prevents corrosion. The actual chain lubricant is enclosed in the chain by the O-rings. Recommended types include aerosol sprays specifically designed for O-ring chains, and conventional engine and gear oils. When using a spray lubricant, make sure it is suitable for O-ring chains.

Do not use high-pressure washer, solvents or gasoline to clean an O-ring chain. Only use kerosene to clean O-ring chains.

Cleaners, Degreasers and Solvents

Many chemicals are available to remove oil, grease and other residue from the motorcycle. Before using cleaning solvents, consider how they will be used and disposed of, particularly if they are not water-soluble. Local ordinances may require special procedures for the disposal of many types of cleaning chemicals. Refer to *Cleaning Parts* in this chapter for more information on their use.

Use brake parts cleaner to clean brake system components when contact with petroleum-based products will damage seals. Brake parts cleaner leaves no residue. Use electrical contact cleaner to clean electrical connections and components without leaving any residue. Carburetor cleaner is a powerful solvent used to remove fuel deposits and varnish from fuel system components. Use this cleaner carefully, as it may damage finishes.

Generally, degreasers are strong cleaners used to remove heavy accumulations of grease from engine and frame components.

Most solvents are designed to be used with a parts washing cabinet for individual component cleaning. For safety, use only nonflammable or high flash point solvents.

Gasket Sealant

Sealants are used in combination with a gasket or seal and are occasionally alone. Follow the manufacturer's recommendation when using sealants. Use extreme care when choosing a sealant different from the type originally recommended. Choose sealants based on their resistance to heat, various fluids and their sealing capabilities.

One of the most common sealants is RTV, or room temperature vulcanizing sealant. This sealant cures at room temperature over a specific time period. This allows the repositioning of components without damaging gaskets.

Moisture in the air causes the RTV sealant to cure. Always install the tube cap as soon as possible after applying RTV sealant. RTV sealant has a limited shelf life and will not cure properly if the shelf life has expired. Keep partial tubes sealed and discard them if they have surpassed the expiration date.

Applying RTV sealant

Clean all old gasket residue from the mating surfaces. Remove all gasket material from blind threaded holes; it can cause inaccurate bolt torque.

Spray the mating surfaces with aerosol parts cleaner and then wipe with a lint-free cloth. The area must be clean for the sealant to adhere.

Apply RTV sealant in a continuous bead 2-3 mm (0.08-0.12 in.) thick. Circle all the fastener holes unless otherwise specified. Do not allow any sealant to enter these holes. Assemble and tighten the fasteners to the specified torque within the time frame recommended by the RTV sealant manufacturer.

Gasket Remover

Aerosol gasket remover can help remove stubborn gaskets. This product can speed up the removal process and prevent damage to the mating surface that may be caused by using a scraping tool. Most of these types of products are very caustic. Follow the gasket remover manufacturer's instructions for use.

Threadlocking Compound

A threadlocking compound is a fluid applied to the threads of fasteners. After tightening the fastener, the fluid dries and becomes a solid filler between the threads. This makes it difficult for the fastener to work loose from vibration, or heat expansion and contraction. Some threadlocking compounds also provide a seal against fluid leakage.

Before applying threadlocking compound, remove any old compound from both thread areas and clean them with aerosol parts cleaner. Use the compound sparingly. Excess fluid can run into adjoining parts.

Threadlocking compounds are available in different strengths. Follow the particular manufacturer's recommendations regarding compound selection. Two manufacturers of threadlocking compound are ThreeBond and Loctite. They both offer a wide range of compounds for various strength, temperature and repair applications.

BASIC TOOLS

Most of the procedures in this manual can be carried out with simple hand tools and test equipment familiar to the home mechanic. Always use the correct tools for the job at hand. Keep tools organized and clean. Store them in a tool chest with related tools organized together.

Quality tools are essential. The best are constructed of high-strength alloy steel. These tools are light, easy to use and resistant to wear. Their working surface is devoid of sharp edges and the tool is carefully polished. They have an easy-to-clean finish and are comfortable to use. Quality tools are a good investment.

When purchasing tools to perform the procedures covered in this manual, consider the tool's potential frequency of use. If a tool kit is just now being started, consider purchasing a basic tool set from a quality tool supplier. These sets are available in many tool combinations and offer substantial savings when compared to individually purchased tools. As work experience grows and tasks become more complicated, specialized tools can be added.

Screwdrivers

Screwdrivers of various lengths and types are mandatory for the simplest tool kit. The two basic types are the slotted tip (flat blade) and the Phillips tip. These are available in sets that often include an assortment of tip sizes and shaft lengths.

As with all tools, use a screwdriver designed for the job. Make sure the size of the tip conforms to the size and shape of the fastener. Use them only for driving screws. Never use a screwdriver for prying or chiseling metal. Repair or replace worn or damaged screwdrivers. A worn tip may damage the fastener, making it difficult to remove.

Wrenches

Open-end, box-end and combination wrenches (**Figure 14**) are available in a variety of types and sizes.

The number stamped on the wrench refers to the distance between the work areas. This size must match the size of the fastener head.

The box-end wrench is an excellent tool because it grips the fastener on all sides. This reduces the chance of the tool slipping. The box-end wrench is designed with either a 6- or 12-point opening. For stubborn or damaged fasteners, the 6-point provides superior holding ability by contacting the fastener

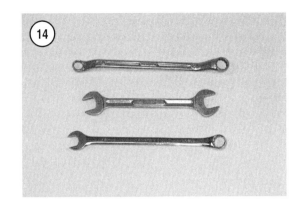

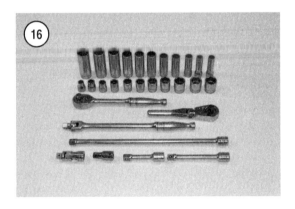

across a wider area at all six edges. For general use, the 12-point works well. It allows the wrench to be removed and reinstalled without moving the handle over such a wide arc.

An open-end wrench is fast and works best in areas with limited overhead access. It contacts the fastener at only two points, and is subject to slipping under heavy force, or if the tool or fastener is worn. A box-end wrench is preferred in most instances, especially when breaking loose and applying the final tightness to a fastener.

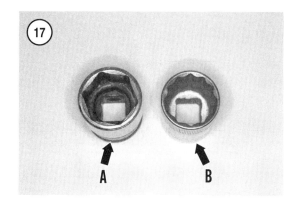

17

A   B

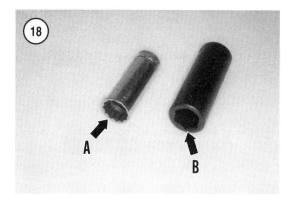

18

A

B

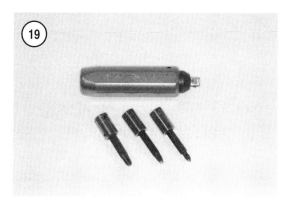

19

The combination wrench has a box end on one end and an open end on the other. This combination makes it a very convenient tool.

Adjustable Wrenches

An adjustable wrench or Crescent wrench (**Figure 15**) can fit nearly any nut or bolt head that has clear access around its entire perimeter. Adjustable wrenches are best used as a backup wrench to keep a large nut or bolt from turning while the other end

is being loosened or tightened with a box-end or socket wrench.

Adjustable wrenches contact the fastener at only two points, which makes them more subject to slipping off the fastener. The fact that one jaw is adjustable and may loosen only aggravates this shortcoming. Make certain the solid jaw is the one transmitting the force.

Socket Wrenches, Ratchets and Handles

Sockets that attach to a ratchet handle (**Figure 16**) are available with 6-point (A) or 12-point (B) openings (**Figure 17**) and different drive sizes. The drive size indicates the size of the square hole that the ratchet handle fits. The number stamped on the socket is the size of the work area and must match the fastener head.

As with wrenches, a 6-point socket provides superior-holding ability, while a 12-point socket needs to be moved only half as far to reposition it on the fastener.

Sockets are designated for either hand or impact use. Impact sockets are made of thicker material for more durability. Compare the size and wall thickness of a 19-mm hand socket (A, **Figure 18**) and the 19-mm impact socket (B). Use impact sockets when using an impact driver or air tools. Use hand sockets with hand-driven attachments.

> *WARNING*
> *Do not use hand sockets with air or impact tools, as they may shatter and cause injury. Always wear eye protection when using impact or air tools.*

Various handles are available for sockets. The speed handle is used for fast operation. Flexible ratchet heads in varying lengths allow the socket to be turned with varying force, and at odd angles. Extension bars allow the socket setup to reach difficult areas. The ratchet is the most versatile. It allows the user to install or remove the nut without removing the socket.

Sockets combined with any number of drivers make them undoubtedly the fastest, safest and most convenient tool for fastener removal and installation.

Impact Driver

An impact driver provides extra force for removing fasteners, by converting the impact of a hammer into a turning motion. This makes it possible to remove stubborn fasteners without damaging them. Impact drivers and interchangeable bits (**Figure 19**) are available from most tool suppliers. When using a socket with an impact driver, make sure the socket is designed for impact use. Refer to *Socket Wrenches, Ratchets and Handles* in this section.

> *WARNING*
> *Do not use hand sockets with air or impact tools, as they may shatter and cause injury. Always wear eye protection when using impact or air tools.*

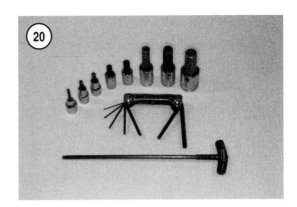

Allen Wrenches

Allen or setscrew wrenches (**Figure 20**) are used on fasteners with hexagonal recesses in the fastener head. These wrenches are available in L-shaped bar, socket and T-handle types. A metric set is required when working on most motorcycles. Allen bolts are sometimes called socket bolts.

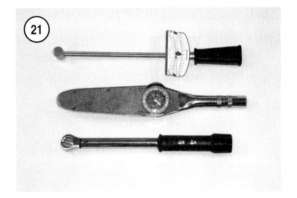

Torque Wrenches

A torque wrench is used with a socket, torque adapter or similar extension to tighten a fastener to a measured torque. Torque wrenches come in several drive sizes (1/4, 3/8, 1/2 and 3/4) and have various methods of reading the torque value. The drive size indicates the size of the square drive that accepts the socket, adapter or extension. Common methods of reading the torque value are the deflecting beam, the dial indicator and the audible click (**Figure 21**). When choosing a torque wrench, consider the torque range, drive size and accuracy. The torque specifications in this manual provide an indication of the range required.

A torque wrench is a precision tool that must be properly cared for to remain accurate. Store torque wrenches in cases or separate padded drawers within a toolbox. Follow the manufacturer's instructions for their care and calibration.

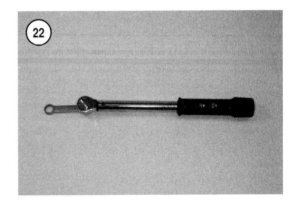

Torque Adapters

Torque adapters or extensions extend or reduce the reach of a torque wrench. The torque adapter shown in **Figure 22** is used to tighten a fastener that cannot be reached due to the size of the torque wrench head, drive, and socket. If a torque adapter changes the effective lever length (**Figure 23**), the torque reading on the wrench will not equal the actual torque applied to the fastener. It is necessary to recalibrate the torque setting on the wrench to compensate for the change of lever length. When a torque adapter is used at a right angle to the drive head, calibration is not required, since the effective length has not changed.

To recalculate a torque reading when using a torque adapter, use the following formula, and refer to **Figure 23**.

$$TW = \frac{TA \times L}{L + A}$$

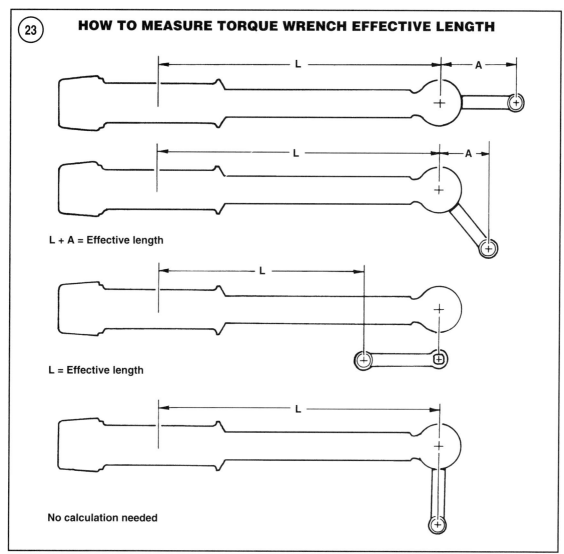

23 **HOW TO MEASURE TORQUE WRENCH EFFECTIVE LENGTH**

L + A = Effective length

L = Effective length

No calculation needed

TW is the torque setting or dial reading on the wrench.

TA is the torque specification and the actual amount of torque that will be applied to the fastener.

A is the amount that the adapter increases (or in some cases reduces) the effective lever length as measured along the centerline of the torque wrench (**Figure 23**).

L is the lever length of the wrench as measured from the center of the drive to the center of the grip.

The effective length is the sum of L and A (**Figure 23**).

Example:

TA = 20 ft.-lb.

A = 3 in.

L = 14 in.

$$TW = \frac{20 \times 14}{14 + 3} = \frac{280}{17} = 16.5 \text{ ft. lb.}$$

In this example, the torque wrench would be set to the recalculated torque value (TW = 16.5 ft.-lb.). When using a beam-type wrench, tighten the fastener until the pointer aligns with 16.5 ft.-lb. In this example, although the torque wrench is preset to 16.5 ft.-lb., the actual torque is 20 ft.-lb.

Pliers

Pliers come in a wide range of types and sizes. Pliers are useful for holding, cutting, bending, and crimping. Do not use them to turn fasteners. **Figure**

24 and **Figure 25** show several types of useful pliers. Each design has a specialized function. Slip-joint pliers are general-purpose pliers used for gripping and bending. Diagonal cutting pliers are needed to cut wire and can be used to remove cotter pins. Needlenose pliers are used to hold or bend small objects. Locking pliers (**Figure 25**), sometimes called Vise-grips, are used to hold objects very tightly. They have many uses, ranging from holding two parts together to gripping the end of a broken stud. Use caution when using locking pliers, as the sharp jaws will damage the objects they hold.

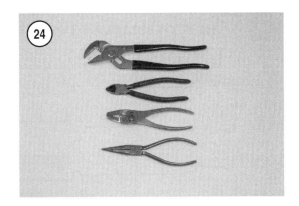

Snap Ring Pliers

Snap ring pliers are specialized pliers with tips that fit into the ends of snap rings to remove and install them.

Snap ring pliers are available with a fixed action (either internal or external) or convertible (one tool works on both internal and external snap rings). They may have fixed tips or interchangeable ones of various sizes and angles. For general use, select convertible-type pliers with interchangeable tips.

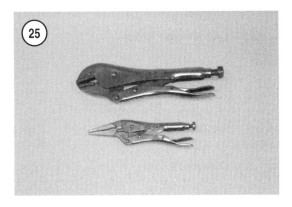

> *WARNING*
> *Snap rings can slip and fly off when removing and installing them. Also, the snap ring pliers tips may break. Always wear eye protection when using snap ring pliers.*

Hammers

Various types of hammers (**Figure 26**) are available to fit a number of applications. A ball-peen hammer is used to strike another tool, such as a punch or chisel. Soft-faced hammers are required when a metal object must be struck without damaging it. *Never* use a metal-faced hammer on engine and suspension components, as damage will occur in most cases.

Always wear eye protection when using hammers. Make sure the hammer face is in good condition and the handle is not cracked. Select the correct hammer for the job and make sure to strike the object squarely. Do not use the handle or the side of the hammer to strike an object.

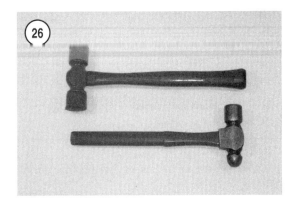

PRECISION MEASURING TOOLS

The ability to accurately measure components is essential to successfully rebuild an engine. Equipment is manufactured to close tolerances, and obtaining consistently accurate measurements is essential to determining which components require replacement or further service.

Each type of measuring instrument is designed to measure a dimension with a certain degree of accuracy and within a certain range. When selecting the

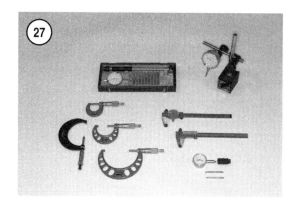

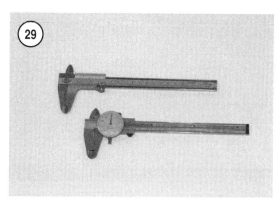

dure. Accurate results are only possible if the mechanic possesses a feel for using the tool. Heavy-handed use of measuring tools will produce less accurate results. Hold the tool gently by the fingertips so the point at which the tool contacts the object is easily felt. This feel for the equipment will produce more accurate measurements and reduce the risk of damaging the tool or component. Refer to the following sections for specific measuring tools.

Feeler Gauge

The feeler or thickness gauge (**Figure 28**) is used for measuring the distance between two surfaces.

A feeler gauge set consists of an assortment of steel strips of graduated thickness. Each blade is marked with its thickness. Blades can be of various lengths and angles for different procedures.

A common use for a feeler gauge is to measure valve clearance. Wire (round) type gauges are used to measure spark plug gap.

Calipers

Calipers (**Figure 29**) are excellent tools for obtaining inside, outside and depth measurements. Although not as precise as a micrometer, they allow reasonable precision, typically to within 0.05 mm (0.001 in.). Most calipers have a range up to 150 mm (6 in.).

Calipers are available in dial, vernier or digital versions. Dial calipers have a dial readout that provides convenient reading. Vernier calipers have marked scales that must be compared to determine the measurement. The digital caliper uses a LCD to show the measurement.

Properly maintain the measuring surfaces of the caliper. There must not be any dirt or burrs between the tool and the object being measured. Never force the caliper closed around an object; close the caliper around the highest point so it can be removed with a slight drag. Some calipers require calibration. Always refer to the manufacturer's instructions when using a new or unfamiliar caliper.

To read a vernier caliper, refer to **Figure 30**. The fixed scale is marked in 1.0 mm and .025 inch increments. In this example, refer to the mm scale. Ten individual lines on the fixed scale equal 1

measuring tool, make sure it is applicable to the task. Refer to **Figure 27** for a basic measuring set.

As with all tools, measuring tools provide the best results if cared for properly. Improper use can damage the tool and result in inaccurate results. If any measurement is questionable, verify the measurement using another tool. A standard gauge is usually provided with measuring tools to check accuracy and calibrate the tool if necessary.

Precision measurements can vary according to the experience of the person performing the proce-

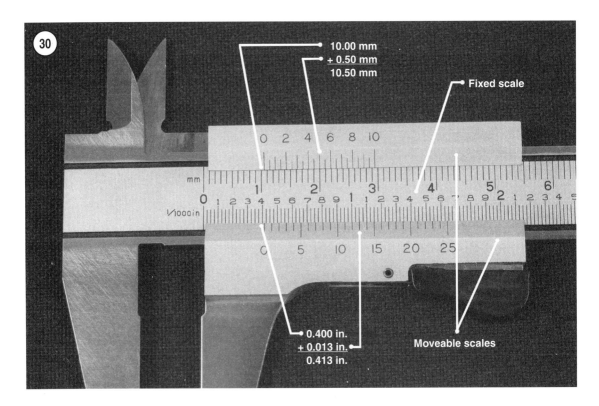

10.00 mm
+ 0.50 mm
10.50 mm

Fixed scale

0.400 in.
+ 0.013 in.
0.413 in.

Moveable scales

DECIMAL PLACE VALUES*

0.100	Indicates 1/10 (one tenth of an inch or millimeter)
0.010	Indicates 1/100 (one one-hundreth of an inch or millimeter)
0.001	Indicates 1/1,000 (one one-thousandth of an inch or millimeter)

*This chart represents the values of figures placed to the right of the decimal point. Use it when reading decimals from one-tenth to one one-thousandth of an inch or millimeter. It is not a conversion chart (for example: 0.001 in. is not equal to 0.001 mm).

cm. The movable scale is marked in 0.05 mm (hundredth) increments. To obtain a reading, establish the first number by the location of the 0 line on the movable scale in relation to the first line to the left on the fixed scale. In this example, the number is 10 mm. To determine the next number, note which of the lines on the movable scale align with a mark on the fixed scale. A number of lines will seem close, but only one will align exactly. In this case, 0.50 mm is the reading to add to the first number. The result of adding 10 mm and 0.50 mm is a measurement of 10.50 mm.

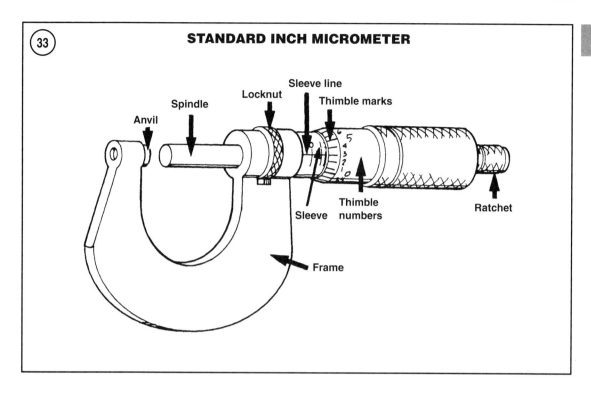

33 **STANDARD INCH MICROMETER**

Anvil — Spindle — Locknut — Sleeve line — Thimble marks — Sleeve — Thimble numbers — Ratchet — Frame

Micrometers

A micrometer is an instrument designed for linear measurement using the decimal divisions of the inch or meter (**Figure 31**). While there are many types and styles of micrometers, most of the procedures in this manual call for an outside micrometer. The outside micrometer is used to measure the outside diameter of cylindrical forms and the thickness of materials.

A micrometer's size indicates the minimum and maximum size of a part that it can measure. The usual sizes (**Figure 32**) are 0-1 in. (0-25 mm), 1-2 in. (25-50 mm), 2-3 in. (50-75 mm) and 3-4 in. (75-100 mm).

Micrometers that cover a wider range of measurements are available. These use a large frame with interchangeable anvils of various lengths. This type of micrometer offers a cost savings; however, its overall size may make it less convenient.

Reading a Micrometer

When reading a micrometer, numbers are taken from different scales and added together. The fol-lowing sections describe how to read the measurements of various types of outside micrometers.

For accurate results, properly maintain the measuring surfaces of the micrometer. There can not be any dirt or burrs between the tool and the measured object. Never force the micrometer closed around an object. Close the micrometer around the highest point so it can be removed with a slight drag. **Figure 33** shows the markings and parts of a standard inch micrometer. Be familiar with these terms before using a micrometer in the follow sections.

Standard inch micrometer

The standard inch micrometer is accurate to one-thousandth of an inch or 0.001. The sleeve is marked in 0.025 in. increments. Every fourth sleeve mark is numbered 1, 2, 3, 4, 5, 6, 7, 8, 9. These numbers indicate 0.100, 0.200, 0.300, and so on.

The tapered end of the thimble has twenty-five lines marked around it. Each mark equals 0.001 in. One complete turn of the thimble will align its zero mark with the first mark on the sleeve or 0.025 in.

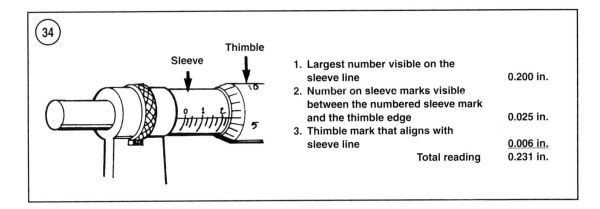

1. Largest number visible on the sleeve line   0.200 in.
2. Number on sleeve marks visible between the numbered sleeve mark and the thimble edge   0.025 in.
3. Thimble mark that aligns with sleeve line   <u>0.006 in.</u>
                         Total reading   0.231 in.

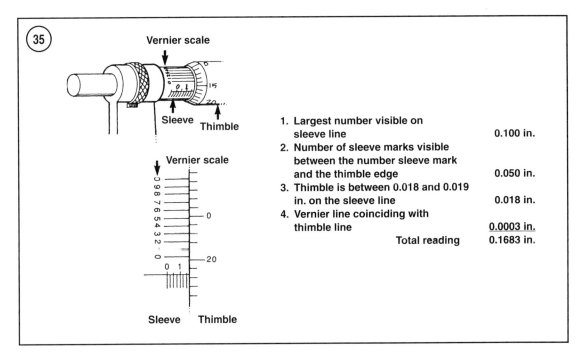

1. Largest number visible on sleeve line   0.100 in.
2. Number of sleeve marks visible between the number sleeve mark and the thimble edge   0.050 in.
3. Thimble is between 0.018 and 0.019 in. on the sleeve line   0.018 in.
4. Vernier line coinciding with thimble line   <u>0.0003 in.</u>
                         Total reading   0.1683 in.

When reading a standard inch micrometer, perform the following steps while referring to **Figure 34**.

1. Read the sleeve and find the largest number visible. Each sleeve number equals 0.100 in.

2. Count the number of lines between the numbered sleeve mark and the edge of the thimble. Each sleeve mark equals 0.025 in.

3. Read the thimble mark that aligns with the sleeve line. Each thimble mark equals 0.001 in.

NOTE
If a thimble mark does not align exactly with the sleeve line, estimate the amount between the lines. For accurate readings in ten-thousandths of an inch (0.0001 in.), use a vernier inch micrometer.

4. Add the readings from Steps 1-3.

Vernier inch micrometer

A vernier inch micrometer is accurate to one ten-thousandth of an inch or 0.0001 in. It has the same marking as a standard inch micrometer with an additional vernier scale on the sleeve. The vernier scale consists of 11 lines marked 1-9 with a 0 on each end. These lines run parallel to the thimble lines and represent 0.0001 in. increments.

When reading a vernier inch micrometer, perform the following steps while referring to **Figure 35**.

1. Read the micrometer in the same way as a standard micrometer. This is the initial reading.

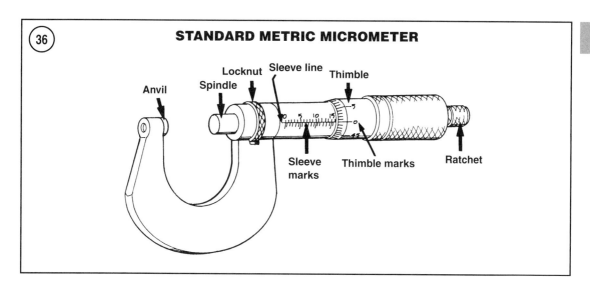

STANDARD METRIC MICROMETER

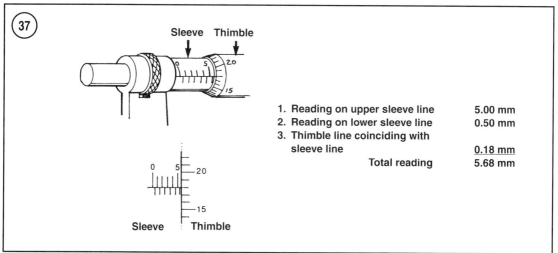

1. Reading on upper sleeve line — 5.00 mm
2. Reading on lower sleeve line — 0.50 mm
3. Thimble line coinciding with sleeve line — 0.18 mm
Total reading — 5.68 mm

2. If a thimble mark aligns exactly with the sleeve line, reading the vernier scale is not necessary. If they do not align, read the vernier scale in Step 3.

3. Determine which vernier scale mark aligns with one thimble mark. The vernier scale number is the amount in ten-thousandths of an inch to add to the initial reading from Step 1.

Metric micrometer

The standard metric micrometer (**Figure 36**) is accurate to one one-hundredth of a millimeter (0.01 mm). The sleeve line is graduated in millimeter and half millimeter increments. The marks on the upper half of the sleeve line equal 1.00 mm. Each fifth mark above the sleeve line is identified with a number. The

number sequence depends on the size of the micrometer. A 0-25 mm micrometer, for example, will have sleeve marks numbered 0 through 25 in 5 mm increments. This numbering sequence continues with larger micrometers. On all metric micrometers, each mark on the lower half of the sleeve equals 0.50 mm.

The tapered end of the thimble has fifty lines marked around it. Each mark equals 0.01 mm. One complete turn of the thimble aligns its 0 mark with the first line on the lower half of the sleeve line or 0.50 mm.

When reading a metric micrometer, add the number of millimeters and half-millimeters on the sleeve line to the number of one one-hundredth millimeters on the thimble. Perform the following steps while referring to **Figure 37**.

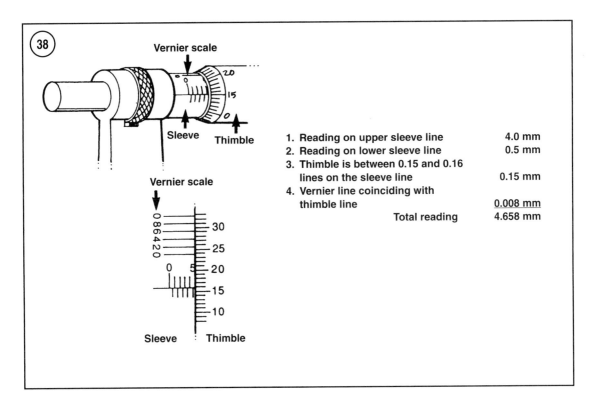

1. Reading on upper sleeve line	4.0 mm
2. Reading on lower sleeve line	0.5 mm
3. Thimble is between 0.15 and 0.16 lines on the sleeve line	0.15 mm
4. Vernier line coinciding with thimble line	0.008 mm
Total reading	4.658 mm

1. Read the upper half of the sleeve line and count the number of lines visible. Each upper line equals 1 mm.

2. See if the half-millimeter line is visible on the lower sleeve line. If so, add 0.50 mm to the reading in Step 1.

3. Read the thimble mark that aligns with the sleeve line. Each thimble mark equals 0.01 mm.

NOTE
If a thimble mark does not align exactly with the sleeve line, estimate the amount between the lines. For accurate readings in two-thousandths of a millimeter (0.002 mm), use a metric vernier micrometer.

4. Add the readings from Steps 1-3.

Metric vernier micrometer

A metric vernier micrometer is accurate to two-thousandths of a millimeter (0.002-mm). It has the same markings as a standard metric micrometer with the addition of a vernier scale on the sleeve. The vernier scale consists of five lines marked 0, 2,

4, 6, and 8. These lines run parallel to the thimble lines and represent 0.002-mm increments.

When reading a metric vernier micrometer, perform the following steps and refer to **Figure 38**.

1. Read the micrometer in the same way as a standard metric micrometer. This is the initial reading.

2. If a thimble mark aligns exactly with the sleeve line, reading the vernier scale is not necessary. If they do not align, read the vernier scale in Step 3.

3. Determine which vernier scale mark aligns exactly with one thimble mark. The vernier scale number is the amount in two-thousandths of a millimeter to add to the initial reading from Step 1.

Micrometer Adjustment

Before using a micrometer, check its adjustment as follows.

1. Clean the anvil and spindle faces.

2A. To check a 0-1 in. or 0-25 mm micrometer:

    a. Turn the thimble until the spindle contacts the anvil. If the micrometer has a ratchet stop, use it to ensure that the proper amount of pressure is applied.

    b. If the adjustment is correct, the 0 mark on the thimble will align exactly with the 0 mark on

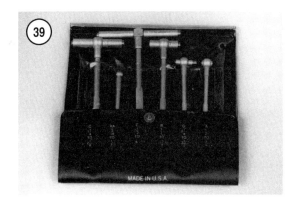

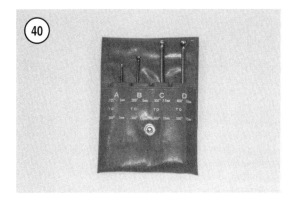

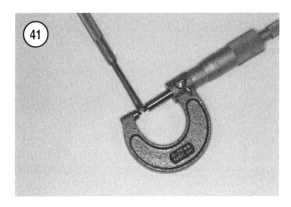

use it to ensure that the proper amount of pressure is applied.

  b. If the adjustment is correct, the 0 mark on the thimble will align exactly with the 0 mark on the sleeve line. If the marks do not align, the micrometer is out of adjustment.

  c. Follow the manufacturer's instructions to adjust the micrometer.

Micrometer Care

Micrometers are precision instruments. They must be used and maintained with great care. Note the following:

1. Store micrometers in protective cases or separate padded drawers in a toolbox.

2. When in storage, make sure the spindle and anvil faces do not contact each other or another object. If they do, temperature changes and corrosion may damage the contact faces.

3. Do not clean a micrometer with compressed air. Dirt forced into the tool will cause wear.

4. Lubricate micrometers with WD-40 to prevent corrosion.

Telescoping and Small Bore Gauges

Use telescoping gauges (**Figure 39**) and small hole gauges (**Figure 40**) to measure bores. Neither gauge has a scale for direct readings. An outside micrometer must be used to determine the reading.

To use a telescoping gauge, select the correct size gauge for the bore. Compress the movable post and carefully insert the gauge into the bore. Carefully move the gauge in the bore to make sure it is centered. Tighten the knurled end of the gauge to hold the movable post in position. Remove the gauge and measure the length of the posts. Telescoping gauges are typically used to measure cylinder bores.

To use a small-bore gauge, select the correct size gauge for the bore. Carefully insert the gauge into the bore. Tighten the knurled end of the gauge to carefully expand the gauge fingers to the limit within the bore. Do not overtighten the gauge, as there is no built-in release. Excessive tightening can damage the bore surface and damage the tool. Remove the gauge and measure the outside dimension (**Figure 41**). Small hole gauges are typically used to measure valve guides.

the sleeve line. If the marks do not align, the micrometer is out of adjustment.

  c. Follow the manufacturer's instructions to adjust the micrometer.

2B. To check a micrometer larger than 1 in. or 25 mm use the standard gauge supplied by the manufacturer. A standard gauge is a steel block, disc or rod that is machined to an exact size.

  a. Place the standard gauge between the spindle and anvil, and measure its outside diameter or length. If the micrometer has a ratchet stop,

Dial Indicator

A dial indicator (**Figure 42**) is a gauge with a dial face and needle used to measure variations in dimensions and movements. Measuring brake rotor runout is a typical use for a dial indicator.

Dial indicators are available in various ranges and graduations and with three basic types of mounting bases: magnetic, clamp, or screw-in stud. When purchasing a dial indicator, select the magnetic stand (**Figure 42**) type with a continuous dial.

Cylinder Bore Gauge

A cylinder bore gauge is similar to a dial indicator. The gauge set shown in **Figure 43** consists of a dial indicator, handle, and different length adapters (anvils) to fit the gauge to various bore sizes. The bore gauge is used to measure bore size, taper and out-of-round. When using a bore gauge, follow the manufacturer's instructions.

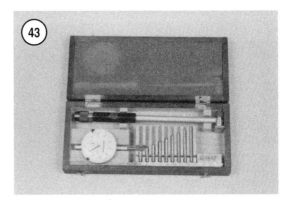

Compression Gauge

A compression gauge (**Figure 44**) measures combustion chamber (cylinder) pressure, usually in psi or kg/cm^2. The gauge adapter is either inserted or screwed into the spark plug hole to obtain the reading. Disable the engine so it will not start and hold the throttle in the wide-open position when performing a compression test. An engine that does not have adequate compression cannot be properly tuned. See Chapter Three.

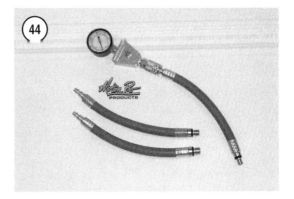

Multimeter

A multimeter (**Figure 45**) is an essential tool for electrical system diagnosis. The voltage function indicates the voltage applied or available to various electrical components. The ohmmeter function tests circuits for continuity, or lack of continuity, and measures the resistance of a circuit.

Some manufacturers' specifications for electrical components are based on results using a specific test meter. Results may vary if a meter not recommended by the manufacturer is used. Such requirements are noted when applicable.

Ohmmeter (analog) calibration

Each time an analog ohmmeter is used or if the scale is changed, the ohmmeter must be calibrated.

Digital ohmmeters do not require calibration.

1. Make sure the meter battery is in good condition.
2. Make sure the meter probes are in good condition.
3. Touch the two probes together and observe the needle location on the ohms scale. The needle must align with the 0 mark to obtain accurate measurements.
4. If necessary, rotate the meter ohms adjust knob until the needle and 0 mark align.

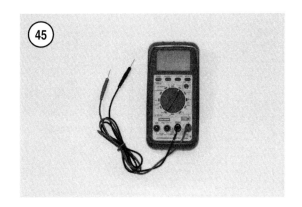

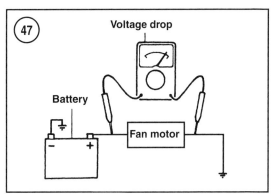

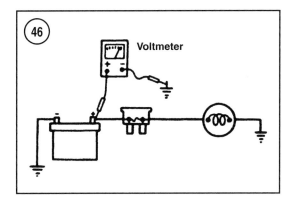

Measuring voltage

Unless otherwise specified, perform all voltage tests with the electrical connectors attached. When measuring voltage, select the meter range that is one scale higher than the expected voltage of the circuit to prevent damage to the meter. To determine the actual voltage in a circuit, use a voltmeter. To simply check if voltage is present, use a test light.

NOTE
When using a test light, either lead can be attached to ground.

1. Attach the negative meter test lead to a good ground (bare metal). Make sure the ground is not insulated with a rubber gasket or grommet.
2. Attach the positive meter test lead to the point being checked for voltage (**Figure 46**).
3. Turn on the ignition switch. The test light should light or the meter should display a reading. The reading should be within one volt of battery voltage. If the voltage is less, there is a problem in the circuit.

ELECTRICAL SYSTEM FUNDAMENTALS

A thorough study of the many types of electrical systems used in today's motorcycles is beyond the scope of this manual. However, a basic understanding of electrical fundamentals is necessary to perform simple diagnostic tests.

Voltage

Voltage is the electrical potential or pressure in an electrical circuit and is expressed in volts. The more pressure (voltage) in a circuit, the more work the circuit can perform.

Direct current (DC) voltage means the electricity flows in one direction. All circuits powered by a battery are DC circuits.

Alternating current (AC) means that the electricity flows in one direction momentarily then switches to the opposite direction. Alternator output is an example of AC voltage. This voltage must be changed or rectified to direct current to operate in a battery powered system.

Voltage drop test

Resistance causes voltage to drop. This resistance can be measured in an active circuit by using a voltmeter to perform a voltage drop test, which compares the difference between the voltage available at the start of a circuit to the voltage at the end of the circuit while the circuit is operational. If the circuit has no resistance, there will be no voltage drop. The greater the resistance, the greater the voltage drop will be. A voltage drop of one volt or more indicates excessive resistance.
1. Connect the positive meter test lead to the electrical source (where electricity is coming from).
2. Connect the negative meter test lead to the electrical load (where electricity is going). See **Figure 47**.

3. If necessary, activate the component(s) in the circuit.

4. A voltage reading of 1 volt or more indicates excessive resistance in the circuit. A reading equal to battery voltage indicates an open circuit.

Resistance

Resistance is the opposition to the flow of electricity within a circuit or component and is measured in ohms. Resistance causes a reduction in available current and voltage.

Resistance is measured in a inactive circuit with an ohmmeter. The ohmmeter sends a small amount of current into the circuit and measures how difficult it is to push the current through the circuit.

An ohmmeter, although useful, is not always a good indicator of a circuit's actual ability under operating conditions. This is due to the low voltage (6-9 volts) that the meter uses to test the circuit. The voltage in an ignition coil secondary winding can be several thousand volts. Such high voltage can cause the coil to malfunction, even though it tests acceptable during a resistance test.

Resistance generally increases with temperature. Perform all testing with the component or circuit at room temperature. Resistance tests performed at high temperatures may indicate high resistance readings and result in the unnecessary replacement of a component.

Measuring resistance and continuity testing

> *CAUTION*
> *Only use an ohmmeter on a circuit that has no voltage present. The meter will be damaged if it is connected to a live circuit. An analog meter must be calibrated each time it is used or the scale is changed. See **Multimeter** in this chapter.*

A continuity test can determine if the circuit is complete. This type of test is performed with an ohmmeter or a self-powered test lamp.

1. Disconnect the negative battery cable.

2. Attach one test lead (ohmmeter or test light) to one end of the component or circuit.

3. Attach the other test lead to the opposite end of the component or circuit (**Figure 48**).

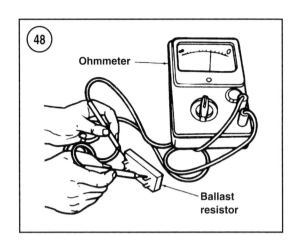

4. A self-powered test light will come on if the circuit has continuity or is complete. An ohmmeter will indicate either low or no resistance if the circuit has continuity. An open circuit is indicated if the meter displays infinite resistance.

Amperage

Amperage is the unit of measure for the amount of current within a circuit. Current is the actual flow of electricity. The higher the current, the more work that can be performed up to a given point. If the current flow exceeds the circuit or component capacity, the system will be damaged.

Measuring amps

An ammeter measures the current flow or amps of a circuit (**Figure 49**). Amperage measurement requires that the circuit be disconnected and the ammeter be connected in series to the circuit. Always use an ammeter that can read higher than the anticipated current flow to prevent damage to the meter. Connect the red test lead to the electrical source and the black test lead to the electrical load.

SPECIAL TOOLS

Some of the procedures in this manual require special tools. These are described in the appropriate chapter and are available from either the manufacturer or a tool supplier.

In many cases, an acceptable substitute may be found in an existing tool kit. Another alternative is to make the tool. Many schools with a machine shop

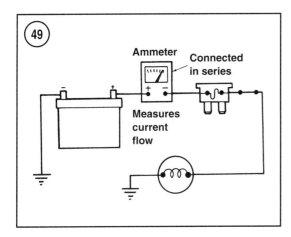

49

Ammeter
Connected
in series

Measures
current
flow

1

curriculum welcome outside work that can be used as practical shop applications for students.

BASIC SERVICE METHODS

Most of the procedures in this manual are straightforward and can be performed by anyone reasonably competent with tools. However, consider personal capabilities carefully before attempting any operation involving major disassembly of the engine.

1. Front, in this manual, refers to the front of the motorcycle. The front of any component is the end closest to the front of the motorcycle. The left and right sides refer to the position of the parts as viewed by the rider sitting on the seat facing forward.

2. Whenever servicing an engine or suspension component, secure the motorcycle in a safe manner.

3. Tag all similar parts for location and mark all mating parts for position. Record the number and thickness of any shims as they are removed. Identify parts by placing them in sealed and labeled plastic sandwich bags.

4. Tag disconnected wires and connectors with masking tape and a marking pen. Do not rely on memory alone.

5. Protect finished surfaces from physical damage or corrosion. Keep gasoline and other chemicals off painted surfaces.

6. Use penetrating oil on frozen or tight bolts. Avoid using heat where possible. Heat can warp, melt or affect the temper of parts. Heat also damages the finish of paint and plastics.

7. When a part is a press fit or requires a special tool for removal, the information or type of tool is identified in the text. Otherwise, if a part is difficult to remove or install, determine the cause before proceeding.

8. To prevent objects or debris from falling into the engine, cover all openings.

9. Read each procedure thoroughly and compare the illustrations to the actual components before starting the procedure. Perform the procedure in sequence.

10. Recommendations are occasionally made to refer service to a dealership or specialist. In these cases, the work can be performed more economically by the specialist than by the home mechanic.

11. The term *replace* means to discard a defective part and replace it with a new part. *Overhaul* means to remove, disassemble, inspect, measure, repair and/or replace parts as required to recondition an assembly.

12. Some operations require the use of a hydraulic press. If a press is not available, have these operations performed by a shop equipped with the necessary equipment. Do not use makeshift equipment that may damage the motorcycle.

13. Repairs are much faster and easier if the motorcycle is clean before starting work. Degrease the motorcycle with a commercial degreaser; follow the directions on the container for the best results. Clean all parts with cleaning solvent as they are removed.

CAUTION
Do not direct high-pressure water at steering bearings, carburetor hoses, wheel bearings, suspension and electrical components. The water will force the grease out of the bearings and possibly damage the seals.

14. If special tools are required, have them available before starting the procedure. When special tools are required, they will be described at the beginning of the procedure.

15. Make diagrams of similar-appearing parts. For instance, crankcase bolts are often not the same lengths. Do not rely on memory alone. It is possible that carefully laid out parts will become disturbed, making it difficult to reassemble the components correctly without a diagram.

16. Make sure all shims and washers are reinstalled in the same location and position.

17. Whenever rotating parts contact a stationary part, look for a shim or washer.

18. Use new gaskets if there is any doubt about the condition of old ones.

19. If self-locking fasteners are used, replace them with new ones. Do not install standard fasteners in place of self-locking ones.

20. Use grease to hold small parts in place if they tend to fall out during assembly. Do not apply grease to electrical or brake components.

Removing Frozen Fasteners

If a fastener cannot be removed, several methods may be used to loosen it. First, apply penetrating oil such as Liquid Wrench or WD-40. Apply it liberally and let it penetrate for 10 to 15 minutes. Rap the fastener several times with a small hammer. Do not hit it hard enough to cause damage. Reapply the penetrating oil if necessary.

For frozen screws, apply penetrating oil as described, then insert a screwdriver in the slot and rap the top of the screwdriver with a hammer. This loosens the rust so the screw can be removed in the normal way. If the screw head is too damaged to use this method, grip the head with locking pliers and twist the screw out.

Avoid applying heat unless specifically instructed, as it may melt, warp or remove the temper from parts.

Removing Broken Fasteners

If the head breaks off a screw or bolt, several methods are available for removing the remaining portion. If a large portion of the remainder projects out, try gripping it with locking pliers. If the projecting portion is too small, file it to fit a wrench or cut a slot in it to fit a screwdriver (**Figure 50**).

If the head breaks off flush, use a screw extractor. To do this, centerpunch the exact center of the remaining portion of the screw or bolt. Drill a small hole in the screw and tap the extractor into the hole. Back the screw out with a wrench on the extractor (**Figure 51**).

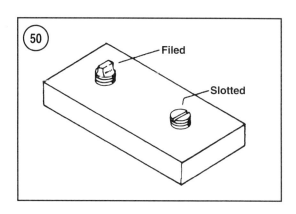

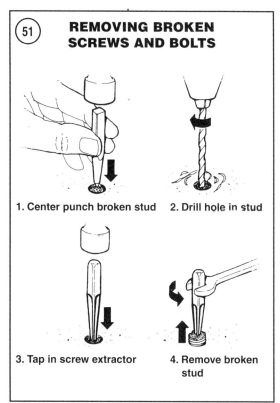

REMOVING BROKEN SCREWS AND BOLTS

1. Center punch broken stud
2. Drill hole in stud
3. Tap in screw extractor
4. Remove broken stud

Repairing Damaged Threads

Occasionally, threads are stripped through carelessness or impact damage. Often the threads can be repaired by running a tap (for internal threads on nuts) or die (for external threads on bolts) through the threads (**Figure 52**). To clean or repair spark plug threads, use a spark plug tap.

If an internal thread is damaged, it may be necessary to install a Helicoil or some other type of thread insert. Follow the manufacturer's instructions when installing their insert.

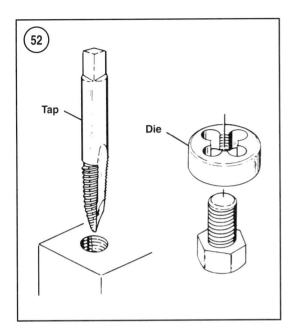

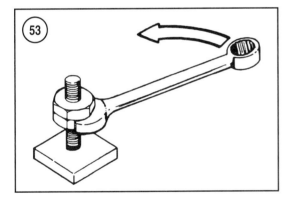

If it is necessary to drill and tap a hole, refer to **Table 9** for metric tap and drill sizes.

Stud Removal/Installation

A stud removal tool is available from most tool suppliers. This tool makes the removal and installation of studs easier. If one is not available, thread two nuts onto the stud and tighten them against each other. Remove the stud by turning the lower nut (**Figure 53**).

1. Measure the height of the stud above the surface.

2. Thread the stud removal tool onto the stud and tighten it, or thread two nuts onto the stud.

3. Remove the stud by turning the stud remover or the lower nut.

4. Remove any threadlocking compound from the threaded hole. Clean the threads with an aerosol parts cleaner.

5. Install the stud removal tool onto the new stud or thread two nuts onto the stud.

6. Apply threadlocking compound to the threads of the stud.

7. Install the stud and tighten with the stud removal tool or the top nut.

8. Install the stud to the height noted in Step 1 or its torque specification.

9. Remove the stud removal tool or the two nuts.

Removing Hoses

When removing stubborn hoses, do not exert excessive force on the hose or fitting. Remove the hose clamp and carefully insert a small screwdriver or pick tool between the fitting and hose. Apply a spray lubricant under the hose and carefully twist the hose off the fitting. Clean the fitting of any corrosion or rubber hose material with a wire brush. Clean the inside of the hose thoroughly. Do not use any lubricant when installing the hose (new or old). The lubricant may allow the hose to come off the fitting, even with the clamp secure.

Bearings

Bearings are used in the engine and transmission assembly to reduce power loss, heat and noise resulting from friction. Because bearings are precision parts, they must be maintained with proper lubrication and maintenance. If a bearing is damaged, replace it immediately. When installing a new bearing, take care to prevent damaging it. Bearing replacement procedures are included in the individual chapters where applicable; however, use the following sections as a guideline.

NOTE
Unless otherwise specified, install bearings with the manufacturer's mark or number facing outward.

Removal

While bearings are normally removed only when damaged, there may be times when it is necessary to remove a bearing that is in good condition. However, improper bearing removal will damage the bearing and maybe the shaft or case half. Note the following when removing bearings.

1. When using a puller to remove a bearing from a shaft, take care that the shaft is not damaged. Always place a piece of metal between the end of the shaft and the puller screw. In addition, place the puller arms next to the inner bearing race. See **Figure 54**.

2. When using a hammer to remove a bearing from a shaft, do not strike the hammer directly against the shaft. Instead, use a brass or aluminum rod between the hammer and shaft (**Figure 55**) and make sure to support both bearing races with wooden blocks as shown.

3. The ideal method of bearing removal is with a hydraulic press. Note the following when using a press:

   a. Always support the inner and outer bearing races with a suitable size wooden or aluminum ring (**Figure 56**). If only the outer race is supported, pressure applied against the balls and/or the inner race will damage them.

   b. Always make sure the press arm (**Figure 56**) aligns with the center of the shaft. If the arm is not centered, it may damage the bearing and/or shaft.

   c. The moment the shaft is free of the bearing, it will drop to the floor. Secure or hold the shaft to prevent it from falling.

Installation

1. When installing a bearing in a housing, apply pressure to the *outer* bearing race (**Figure 57**). When installing a bearing on a shaft, apply pressure to the *inner* bearing race (**Figure 58**).

2. When installing a bearing as described in Step 1, some type of driver is required. Never strike the bearing directly with a hammer or the bearing will be damaged. When installing a bearing, use a piece of pipe or a driver with a diameter that matches the bearing inner race. **Figure 59** shows the correct way to use a driver and hammer to install a bearing.

3. Step 1 describes how to install a bearing in a case half or over a shaft. However, when installing a bearing over a shaft and into the housing at the same time, a tight fit will be required for both outer and inner bearing races. In this situation, install a spacer underneath the driver tool so that pressure is applied

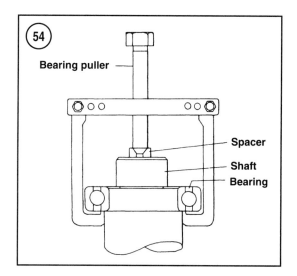

(54) Bearing puller — Spacer / Shaft / Bearing

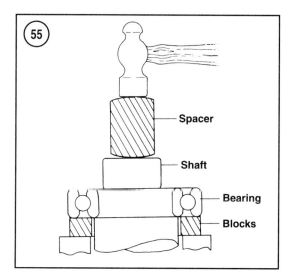

(55) Spacer / Shaft / Bearing / Blocks

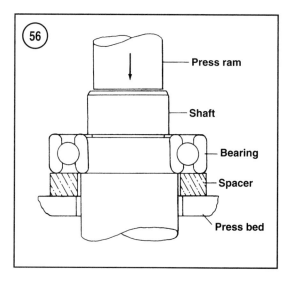

(56) Press ram / Shaft / Bearing / Spacer / Press bed

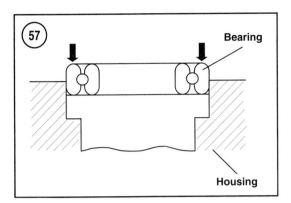

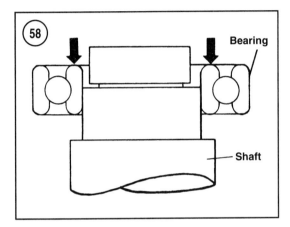

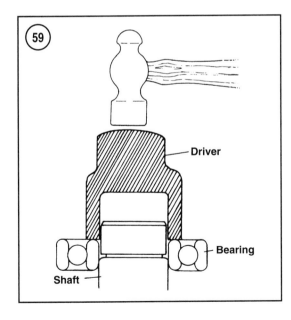

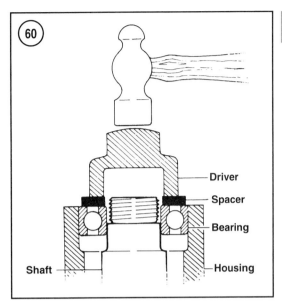

Interference fit

1. Follow this procedure when installing a bearing over a shaft. When a tight fit is required, the bearing inside diameter will be smaller than the shaft. In this case, driving the bearing on the shaft using normal methods may cause bearing damage. Instead, heat the bearing before installation. Note the following:

   a. Secure the shaft so it is ready for bearing installation.

   b. Clean all residues from the bearing surface of the shaft. Remove burrs with a file or sandpaper.

   c. Fill a suitable pot or beaker with clean mineral oil. Place a thermometer rated above 120° C (248° F) in the oil. Support the thermometer so that it does not rest on the bottom or side of the pot.

   d. Remove the bearing from its wrapper and secure it with a piece of heavy wire bent to hold it in the pot. Hang the bearing in the pot so it does not touch the bottom or sides of the pot.

   e. Turn the heat on and monitor the thermometer. When the oil temperature rises to approximately 120° C (248° F), remove the bearing from the pot and quickly install it. If necessary, place a socket on the inner bearing race and tap the bearing into place. As the bearing chills, it will tighten on the shaft, so installation must be done quickly. Make sure the bearing is installed completely.

evenly across both races. See **Figure 60**. If the outer race is not supported as shown in **Figure 60**, the balls will push against the outer bearing race and damage it.

2. Follow this step when installing a bearing in a housing. Bearings are generally installed in a housing with a slight interference fit. Driving the bearing into the housing using normal methods may damage the housing or cause bearing damage. Instead, heat the housing before the bearing is installed. Note the following:

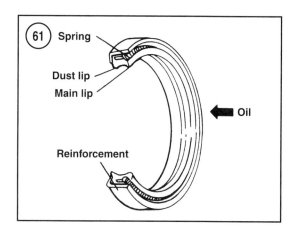

CAUTION
Before heating the housing in this procedure, wash the housing thoroughly with detergent and water. Rinse and rewash the cases as required to remove all traces of oil and other chemical deposits.

  a. Heat the housing to approximately 212° F (100° C) in an oven or on a hot plate. An easy way to check that it is the proper temperature is to place tiny drops of water on the housing; if they sizzle and evaporate immediately, the temperature is correct. Heat only one housing at a time.

CAUTION
Do not heat the housing with a propane or acetylene torch. Never bring a flame into contact with the bearing or housing. The direct heat will destroy the case hardening of the bearing and will likely warp the housing.

  b. Remove the housing from the oven or hot plate, and hold onto the housing with a kitchen potholder, heavy gloves or heavy shop cloth. It is hot!

NOTE
Remove and install the bearings with a suitable size socket and extension.

  c. Hold the housing with the bearing side down and tap the bearing out. Repeat for all bearings in the housing.
  d. Before heating the bearing housing, place the new bearing in a freezer if possible. Chilling a bearing slightly reduces its outside diameter while the heated bearing housing assembly is slightly larger due to heat expansion. This will make bearing installation easier.

NOTE
Always install bearings with the manufacturer's mark or number facing outward.

  e. While the housing is still hot, install the new bearing(s) into the housing. Install the bearings by hand, if possible. If necessary, lightly tap the bearing(s) into the housing with a socket placed on the outer bearing race (**Figure 57**). Do not install new bearings by driving on the inner-bearing race. Install the bearing(s) until it seats completely.

Seal Replacement

Seals (**Figure 61**) are used to contain oil, water, grease or combustion gasses in a housing or shaft. Improper removal of a seal can damage the housing or shaft. Improper installation of the seal can damage the seal. Note the following:

1. Prying is generally the easiest and most effective method of removing a seal from the housing. However, always place a rag underneath the pry tool (**Figure 62**) to prevent damage to the housing.

2. Pack waterproof grease in the seal lips before the seal is installed.

3. In most cases, install seals with the manufacturer's numbers or marks face out.

4. Install seals with a socket placed on the outside of the seal as shown in **Figure 63**. Drive the seal squarely into the housing until it is flush (**Figure 64**). Never install a seal by hitting against the top of the seal with a hammer.

STORAGE

Several months of non-use can cause a general deterioration of the motorcycle. This is especially true in areas of extreme temperature variations. This deterioration can be minimized with careful preparation for storage. A properly stored motorcycle will be much easier to return to service.

Storage Area Selection

When selecting a storage area, consider the following:

1. The storage area must be dry. A heated area is best, but not necessary. It should be insulated to minimize extreme temperature variations.

2. If the building has large window areas, mask them to keep sunlight off the motorcycle.

3. Avoid buildings in industrial areas where corrosive emissions may be present. Avoid areas close to saltwater.

4. Consider the area's risk of fire, theft or vandalism. Check with an insurer regarding motorcycle coverage while in storage.

Preparing the Motorcycle for Storage

The amount of preparation a motorcycle should undergo before storage depends on the expected length of non-use, storage area conditions and personal preference. Consider the following list the minimum requirement:

1. Wash the motorcycle thoroughly. Make sure all dirt, mud and road debris are removed.

2. Start the engine and allow it to reach operating temperature. Drain the engine oil, regardless of the riding time since the last service. Fill the engine with the recommended type of oil.

3. Drain all fuel from the fuel tank and run the engine until all the fuel is consumed from the lines and carburetors.

4. Remove the spark plugs and pour a teaspoon of engine oil into the cylinders. Place a rag over the openings and slowly turn the engine over to distribute the oil. Reinstall the spark plugs.

5. Remove the battery. Store the battery in a cool, dry location.

6. Cover the exhaust and intake openings.

7. Reduce the normal tire pressure by 20%.

8. Apply a protective substance to the plastic and rubber components, including the tires. Make sure to follow the manufacturer's instructions for each type of product being used.

9. Place the motorcycle on a stand or wooden blocks so the wheels are off the ground. If this is not possible, place a piece of plywood between the tires and the ground. Inflate the tires to the recommended pressure if the motorcycle cannot be elevated.

10. Cover the motorcycle with old bed sheets or something similar. Do not cover it with any plastic material that will trap moisture.

Returning the Motorcycle to Service

The amount of service required when returning a motorcycle to service after storage depends on the length of non-use and storage conditions. In addition to performing the reverse of the above procedure, make sure the brakes, clutch, throttle and engine stop switch work properly before operating the motorcycle. Refer to Chapter Three and evaluate the service intervals to determine which areas require service.

Table 1 ENGINE AND FRAME SERIAL NUMBERS (U.S. MODELS)

Model	Engine serial number (start to end)	Frame serial number (start to end)
1999		
49 states	PC35E-2000001-2028238	JH2PC350-XM000001-XM007194
California	PC35E-2000001-2027371	JH2PC351-XM000001-XM000837
2000		
49 states	PC35E-2100001-2122225	JH2PC350-YM000001-YM106777
California	PC35E-2100001-2221005	JH2PC351-YM000001-
2001		
49 states	PC35E-2200001-on	JH2PC350-1M000001-on
California	PC35E-2200001-on	JH2PC351-1M000001-on
2002		
49 states	PC35E-2300001-on	JH2PC350-2M000001-on
California	PC35E-2300001-on	JH2PC351-2M000001-on
2003-2006	N/A	N/A

Table 2 ENGINE AND FRAME SERIAL NUMBERS (OTHER THAN U.S. MODELS)

Model	Engine serial number (start to end)	Frame serial number (start to end)
1999 CBR600Fx carbureted		
Brazil	PC35E-2000103-on	JH2PC353-WM900001-on
	PC35E-2014728-on	JH2PC353-XM900001-on
Denmark, England and France	PC35E-2000001-on	JH2PC35A-XM000001-on
ED[1]	PC35E-2000001-on	JH2PC35A-XM000001-on
Korea and Mexico	PC35E-2000001-on	JH2PC359-XM000001-on
Switzerland	PC35E-2000001-on	JH2PC35C-XM000001-on
Austria	PC35E-2000001-on	JH2PC35U-XM000001-on
IIED[2]	PC35E-3000001-on	JH2PC35D-XM000001-on
CBR600F4x		
Canada	PC35E-2000001-on	JH2PC352-XM000001-on
2000 CBR600Fy carbureted		
Brazil	PC35E-2100101-on	JH2PC353-YM100001-on
Denmark, England and France	PC35E-2100001-on	JH2PC35A-YM000001-on
ED[1]	PC35E-2100001-on	JH2PC35A-YM000001-on
Korea and Mexico	PC35E-2100001-on	JH2PC359-YM100001-on
Switzerland	PC35E-2100001-on	JH2PC35C-YM000001-on
Austria	PC35E-2100001-on	JH2PC35U-YM100001-on
IIED[2]	PC35E-3100001-on	JH2PC35D-YM100001-on
	(continued)	

Table 2 ENGINE AND FRAME SERIAL NUMBERS (OTHER THAN U.S. MODELS) (continued)

Model	Engine serial number (start to end)	Frame serial number (start to end)
CBR600F4y		
Canada	PC35E-2100001-on	JH2PC352-YM100001-on
2001-on CBR699F sport fuel injected		
England	PC35E-2200001-on	JH2PC35E-1M200001-on
ED[3]	PC35E-2200001-on	JH2PC35E-1M200001-on
France	PC35E-2200001-on	JH2PC35A-1M200001-on
Germany	PC35E-2200001-on	JH2PC35F-1M200001-on
IIED[4]	PC35E-2200001-on	JH2PC35D-1M200001-on

1. ED (carbureted models)—European direct sales include Germany, Belgium, Holland, Portugal, Greece, Italy, Spain, Norway, Sweden, Finland and Austria.
2. IIEd (carbureted models)—European direct sales (Type II) include Germany, Belgium, Holland, Portugal and Spain.
3. ED (fuel injected models)—European direct sales include Netherlands, Denmark, Spain, Greece, Belgium, Portugal, Italy, Switzerland, Austria, Sweden, Norway, and Finland.
4. IIED (fuel injected models)—European direct sales include Germany, Netherlands, Spain, Belgium and Portugal.

Table 3 MOTORCYCLE DIMENSIONS

Overall length (U.S. models)	
1999-2000 models	2060 mm (81.1 in.)
2001-on models	2041 mm (80.4 in.)
Overall length (U.K. models)	
CBR600Fx models	
Switzerland and Denmark models	2145 mm (84.4 in.)
Other than Switzerland and Denmark models	2060 mm (81.1 in.)
CBR600F1 models	2065 mm (81.3 in.)
Overall width	685 mm (27.0 in.)
Overall height	
1999-2000 models	1130 mm (44.5 in.)
2001-on models	1135 mm (44.7 in.)
Wheelbase (U.S. models)	
1999-2000 models	1390 mm (54.7 in.)
2001-on models	1386 mm (54.6 in.)
Wheelbase (U.K. models)	
CBR600Fx models	1395 mm (54.9 in.)
CBR600F1 models	1390 mm (54.7 in.)
Seat height (U.S. models)	810 mm (31.9 in.)
Seat height (U.K. models)	
CBR600Fx models	810 mm (31.9 in.)
CBR600F1 models	805 mm (31.7 in.)
Footpeg height	360 mm (14.2 in.)
Ground clearance	135 mm (5.3 in.)

Table 4 MOTORCYCLE WEIGHT

Dry weight (U.S. and Canada models)	
California models	
1999-2000 models	170 kg (375 lbs.)
2001-on models	169 kg (373 lbs.)

(continued)

Table 4 MOTORCYCLE WEIGHT (continued)

Dry weight (U.S. and Canada models) (continued)	
49 states and Canada models	
1999-2000 models	169 kg (373 lbs.)
2001-on models	168 kg (370 lbs.)
Dry weight (U.K. models)	170 kg (375 lbs.)
Curb weight (U.S. and Canada models)	
California models	
1999-2000 models	198 kg (437 lbs.)
2001-on models	197 kg (434 lbs.)
49 states and Canada models	
1999-2000 models	197 kg (434 lbs.)
2001-on models	196 kg (432 lbs.)
Curb weight (U.K. models)	198 kg (437 lbs.)
Maximum weight capacity (U.S. and Canada models)	
1999-2000 models	
49 states and California models	175 kg (386 lbs.)
Canada models	179 kg (395 lbs.)
2001-on models	175 kg (386 lbs.)
Maximum weight capacity (U.K. models)	189 kg (417 lbs.)
Maximum weight capacity (Mexico models)	175 kg (386 lbs.)

Table 5 FUEL TANK CAPACITY

U.S. and Canada models	
1999-2000 models	17.0 liters (4.49 U.S. gal./3.74 Imp. gal.)
2001-on models	18.0 liters (4.76 U.S. gal./3.96 Imp. gal.)
U.K. models	18.0 liters (4.76 U.S. gal./3.96 Imp. gal.)

Table 6 HONDA GENERAL TORQUE SPECIFICATIONS

Fastener size or type	N•m	in.-lb.	ft.lb.
5 mm screw	4	35	–
5 mm bolt and nut	5	44	–
6 mm screw	9	80	–
6 mm bolt and nut	10	88	–
6 mm flange bolt (8 mm head, small flange)	9	80	–
6 mm flange bolt (10 mm head) and nut	12	106	–
8 mm bolt and nut	22	–	16
8 mm flange bolt and nut	27	–	20
10 mm bolt and nut	35	–	26
10 mm flange bolt and nut	40	–	29
12 mm bolt and nut	55	–	40

Table 7 CONVERSION FORMULAS

Multiply:	By:	To get the equivalent of:
Length		
Inches	25.4	Millimeter
Inches	2.54	Centimeter
	(continued)	

Table 7 CONVERSION FORMULAS (continued)

Multiply:	By:	To get the equivalent of:
Length (continued)		
Miles	1.609	Kilometer
Feet	0.3048	Meter
Millimeter	0.03937	Inches
Centimeter	0.3937	Inches
Kilometer	0.6214	Mile
Meter	3.281	Feet
Fluid volume		
U.S. quarts	0.9463	Liters
U.S. gallons	3.785	Liters
U.S. ounces	29.573529	Milliliters
Imperial gallons	4.54609	Liters
Imperial quarts	1.1365	Liters
Liters	0.2641721	U.S. gallons
Liters	1.0566882	U.S. quarts
Liters	33.814023	U.S. ounces
Liters	0.22	Imperial gallons
Liters	0.8799	Imperial quarts
Milliliters	0.033814	U.S. ounces
Milliliters	1.0	Cubic centimeters
Milliliters	0.001	Liters
Torque		
Foot-pounds	1.3558	Newton-meters
Foot-pounds	0.138255	Meters-kilograms
Inch-pounds	0.11299	Newton-meters
Newton-meters	0.7375622	Foot-pounds
Newton-meters	8.8507	Inch-pounds
Meters-kilograms	7.2330139	Foot-pounds
Volume		
Cubic inches	16.387064	Cubic centimeters
Cubic centimeters	0.0610237	Cubic inches
Temperature		
Fahrenheit	$(°F - 32) \times 0.556$	Centigrade
Centigrade	$(°C \times 1.8) + 32$	Fahrenheit
Weight		
Ounces	28.3495	Grams
Pounds	0.4535924	Kilograms
Grams	0.035274	Ounces
Kilograms	2.2046224	Pounds
Pressure		
Pounds per square inch	0.070307	Kilograms per square centimeter
Kilograms per square centimeter	14.223343	Pounds per square inch
Kilopascals	0.1450	Pounds per square inch
Pounds per square inch	6.895	Kilopascals
Speed		
Miles per hour	1.609344	Kilometers per hour
Kilometers per hour	0.6213712	Miles per hour

Table 8 TECHNICAL ABBREVIATIONS

ABDC	After bottom dead center
ATDC	After top dead center
BBDC	Before bottom dead center

(continued)

Table 8 TECHNICAL ABBREVIATIONS (continued)

BDC	Bottom dead center
BTDC	Before top dead center
C	Celsius (centigrade)
cc	Cubic centimeters
cid	Cubic inch displacement
CDI	Capacitor discharge ignition
cu. in.	Cubic inches
DAI	Direct air induction
ECM	Engine control module
ECT	Engine coolant temperature sensor
EFI	Electronic fuel injection
F	Fahrenheit
ft.	Feet
ft.-lb.	Foot-pounds
gal.	Gallons
H/A	High altitude
hp	Horsepower
IAT	Intake air temperature sensor
ICM	Ignition control module
in.	Inches
in.-lb.	Inch-pounds
I.D.	Inside diameter
kg	Kilograms
kgm	Kilogram meters
km	Kilometer
kPa	Kilopascals
L	Liter
m	Meter
MAG	Magneto
ml	Milliliter
mm	Millimeter
N•m	Newton-meters
O2	Oxygen
O.D.	Outside diameter
oz.	Ounces
PAIR	Pulsed secondary air injection system
PGM-FI	Programmed fuel injection
psi	Pounds per square inch
PTO	Power take off
pt.	Pint
qt.	Quart
rpm	Revolutions per minute
TP	Throttle position sensor

Table 9 METRIC TAP AND DRILL SIZES

Metric size	Drill equivalent	Decimal fraction	Nearest fraction
3 × 0.50	No. 39	0.0995	3/32
3 × 0.60	3/32	0.0937	3/32
4 × 0.70	No. 30	0.1285	1/8
4 × 0.75	1/8	0.125	1/8
5 × 0.80	No. 19	0.166	11/64
5 × 0.90	No. 20	0.161	5/32
6 × 1.00	No. 9	0.196	13/64
7 × 1.00	16/64	0.234	15/64

(continued)

Table 9 METRIC TAP AND DRILL SIZES (continued)

Metric size	Drill equivalent	Decimal fraction	Nearest fraction
8 × 1.00	J	0.277	9/32
8 × 1.25	17/64	0.265	17/64
9 × 1.00	5/16	0.3125	5/16
9 × 1.25	5/16	0.3125	5/16
10 × 1.25	11/32	0.3437	11/32
10 × 1.50	R	0.339	11/32
11 × 1.50	3/8	0.375	3/8
12 × 1.50	13/32	0.406	13/32
12 × 1.75	13/32	0.406	13/32

Table 10 METRIC, INCH AND FRACTIONAL EQUIVALENTS

mm	in.	Nearest fraction	mm	in.	Nearest fraction
1	0.0394	1/32	26	1.0236	1 1/32
2	0.0787	3/32	27	1.0630	1 1/16
3	0.1181	1/8	28	1.1024	1 3/32
4	0.1575	5/32	29	1.1417	1 5/32
5	0.1969	3/16	30	1.1811	1 3/16
6	0.2362	1/4	31	1.2205	1 7/32
7	0.2756	9/32	32	1.2598	1 1/4
8	0.3150	5/16	33	1.2992	1 5/16
9	0.3543	11/32	34	1.3386	1 11/32
10	0.3937	13/32	35	1.3780	1 3/8
11	0.4331	7/16	36	1.4173	1 13/32
12	0.4724	15/32	37	1.4567	1 15/32
13	0.5118	1/2	38	1.4961	1 1/2
14	0.5512	9/16	39	1.5354	1 17/32
15	0.5906	19/32	40	1.5748	1 9/16
16	0.6299	5/8	41	1.6142	1 5/8
17	0.6693	21/32	42	1.6535	1 21/32
18	0.7087	23/32	43	1.6929	1 11/16
19	0.7480	3/4	44	1.7323	1 23/32
20	0.7874	25/32	45	1.7717	1 25/32
21	0.8268	13/16	46	1.8110	1 13/16
22	0.8661	7/8	47	1.8504	1 27/32
23	0.9055	29/32	48	1.8898	1 7/8
24	0.9449	15/16	49	1.9291	1 15/16
25	0.9843	31/32	50	1.9685	1 31/32

CHAPTER TWO

TROUBLESHOOTING

The troubleshooting procedures described in this chapter provide typical symptoms and logical methods for isolating the cause(s). There may be several ways to solve a problem, but only a systematic approach will be successful in avoiding wasted time and possibly unnecessary parts replacement.

Gather as much information as possible to aid in diagnosis. Never assume anything and do not overlook the obvious. Make sure the start switch is in the run position and there is fuel in the tank. Learning to recognize symptoms will make troubleshooting easier. In most cases, expensive and complicated test equipment is not needed to determine whether repairs can be performed at home. On the other hand, be realistic and do not start procedures that are beyond the experience and equipment available. Many service departments will not take work that involves the reassembly of damaged or abused equipment; if they do, expect the cost to be high. If the motorcycle does require the attention of a professional, describe symptoms and conditions accu-

rately and fully. The more information a technician has available, the easier it will be to diagnose the problem.

Proper lubrication, maintenance and periodic tune-ups reduce the chance that problems will occur. However, even with the best of care, the motorcycle may require troubleshooting.

OPERATING REQUIREMENTS

An engine needs three basics to run properly: correct air/fuel mixture, compression and a spark at the right time. If one basic requirement is missing, the engine will not run. Four-stroke engine operating principles are described in Chapter Four.

If the motorcycle has not been used for any length of time and refuses to start, check and clean the spark plugs. If the plugs are not fouled, inspect the fuel system. This includes the fuel tank, fuel and vacuum hoses, fuel pump, and the carburetor as-

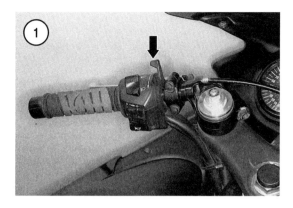

sembly or the fuel injection system. Gasoline tends to lose its potency after standing for long periods; as it evaporates, the mixture becomes richer. Condensation may contaminate gasoline with water. Drain the old gas and try starting with a fresh tankful.

STARTING THE ENGINE (CARBURETED MODELS)

When experiencing engine starting troubles, it is easy to work out of sequence and forget basic engine starting procedures. The following sections list recommended starting procedures for carbureted models at the various ambient temperatures and engine conditions.

Starting Notes

1. All models are equipped with a sidestand ignition cut-off system. The position of the sidestand will affect engine starting. Note the following:
   a. The engine cannot start when the sidestand is down and the transmission is in gear.
   b. The engine can start when the sidestand is down and the transmission is in neutral. The engine will stop if the transmission is put in gear with the sidestand down.
   c. The engine can be started when the sidestand is up and the transmission is in neutral or in gear with the clutch lever pulled in.
2. Before starting the engine, shift the transmission into NEUTRAL and place the engine stop switch in the RUN position.
3. Turn the ignition switch to the ON position and confirm the following:
   a. The neutral indicator light is on (when the transmission is in neutral).

b. The engine oil pressure warning light is on.
4. The engine is now ready to start. Refer to the starting procedure that best describes the conditions.
5. If the engine idle speed is high for more than five minutes and/or the throttle is snapped on and off repeatedly at normal air temperature, the exhaust pipe may discolor.
6. Excessive choke can cause an excessively rich fuel mixture. This condition can wash oil off of the pistons and cylinder walls, causing piston and cylinder scuffing.

CAUTION
*Once the engine starts, the red oil pressure warning light should go off in a few seconds. If the light stays on longer than a few seconds, stop the engine immediately. Check the oil level as described in Chapter Three. If the oil level is good, the oil pressure may be too low or the oil pressure switch may be shorted. Check the lubrication system and correct the problem before restarting the engine. If the oil pressure switch is good, some type of stoppage has occurred in the lubrication system and oil is not being delivered to engine components. Severe engine damage will occur if the engine is run with low oil pressure. Refer to **Engine Lubrication** in this chapter.*

CAUTION
Do not operate the starter for more than five seconds at a time. Wait for approximately ten seconds between starting attempts.

Starting Procedures

Engine cold with air temperature between 50-95° F (10-35° C)

1. Review the *Starting Notes* section.
2. Turn the ignition switch ON.
3. Place the engine stop switch in the RUN position.
4. Pull the choke lever to the fully ON position (**Figure 1**).
5. Operate the starter button and start the engine. Do not open the throttle.

NOTE
When the engine is started with the throttle open and the choke on, a lean

mixture will result and cause hard starting.

6. With the engine running, operate the choke lever as required to keep the engine idle between 1500-2500 rpm.

7. After approximately 30 seconds, push the choke lever to the fully OFF position (**Figure 2**). If the idle is rough, open the throttle slightly until the engine warms up.

Cold engine with air temperature of 50° F (10° C) or lower

1. Review the *Starting Notes* section.
2. Turn the ignition switch ON.
3. Place the engine stop switch in the RUN position.
4. Pull the choke lever to the fully ON position (**Figure 1**).
5. Operate the starter button and start the engine. Do not open the throttle when pressing the starter button.
6. Once the engine is running, open the throttle slightly to help warm the engine. Operate the engine until the choke can be turned to the fully off position (**Figure 2**) and the engine responds to the throttle cleanly.

Warm engine and/or air temperature 95° F (35° C) or higher

1. Review the *Starting Notes* section.
2. Turn the ignition switch ON.
3. Place the engine stop switch in the RUN position.
4. Open the throttle slightly and push the starter button. Do not operate the choke.

Engine flooded

If the engine will not start after a few attempts, it may be flooded. If a gasoline smell is present after attempting to start the engine and the engine will not start, the engine is probably flooded. To start a flooded engine, perform the following:

1. Turn the ignition key switch ON.
2. Turn the engine stop switch to the OFF position.
3. Push the choke lever to the OFF position (**Figure 2**).

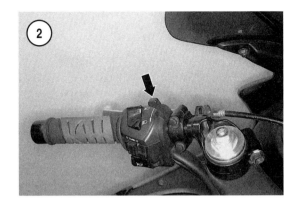

4. Open the throttle completely and operate the starter for five seconds.
5. Wait ten seconds, then continue with Step 6.
6. Place the engine stop switch in the RUN position.
7. Open the throttle slightly and push the starter button to start the engine. Do not use the choke.

STARTING THE ENGINE (FUEL INJECTED MODELS)

When experiencing engine-starting troubles, it is easy to work out of sequence and forget basic starting procedures. The following sections describe the recommended starting procedures for fuel injected models.

Starting Notes

1. All models are equipped with a sidestand ignition cut-off system. The position of the sidestand will affect engine starting. Note the following:
   a. The engine cannot start when the sidestand is down and the transmission is in gear.
   b. The engine can start when the sidestand is down and the transmission is in neutral. The engine will stop if the transmission is put in gear with the sidestand down.
   c. The engine can be started when the sidestand is up and the transmission is in neutral or in gear with the clutch lever pulled in.
2. Before starting the engine, shift the transmission into NEUTRAL and confirm that the engine stop switch is in the RUN position.
3. Turn the ignition switch to the ON position and confirm the following:

a. The neutral indicator light is on (when the transmission is in neutral).

b. The engine oil pressure warning light is flashing. The warning light should go off a few seconds after the engine starts. If the light stays on, turn the engine off and check the oil level as described in Chapter Three.

c. The malfunction indicator light (**Figure 3**) is on. The indicator light should go off a few seconds after the engine starts. If the light stays on, turn the engine off and check the oil level as described in Chapter Three.

4. The engine is now ready to start. The motorcycle's fuel-injection system is fitted with an automatic fast idle system. Refer to the following starting procedures.

CAUTION
*Once the engine starts, the red oil pressure warning light should go off in a few seconds. If the light stays on longer than a few seconds, stop the engine immediately. Check the oil level as described in Chapter Three. If the oil level is good, the oil filter or oil cooler may be plugged, the oil pressure may be too low, or the oil pressure switch may be shorted. Check the lubrication system and correct the problem before restarting the engine. If the oil pressure switch is good, some type of stoppage has occurred in the lubrication system and oil is not being delivered to engine components. Severe engine damage will occur if the engine is run with low oil pressure. Refer to **Engine Lubrication** in this chapter.*

NOTE
The CBR600F4i and CBR600 Sport models are equipped with a bank angle (lean angle) sensor system that turns the engine and fuel pump off if the motorcycle falls on its side with the engine running. After the motorcycle is returned to the upright position, the ignition switch must be turned OFF, then turned back ON before the engine will restart.

Starting Procedure

All ambient and engine temperatures

1. Review the *Starting Notes* section.
2. Turn the ignition switch ON.
3. Place the engine stop switch in the RUN position.
4. Depress the starter button and start the engine. Do not open the throttle when pressing the starter button.

NOTE
*To prevent the engine from starting with the throttle in the wide-open position, the electronic control module (ECM) interrupts the fuel supply if the throttle is in this position while the engine is cranking. The only time it would be necessary to open the throttle all the way is when attempting to start a flooded engine. See **Engine Flooded** in this section.*

Engine flooded

If the engine will not start after a few attempts, it may be flooded. If a gasoline smell is present after attempting to start the engine, the engine is probably flooded. To start a flooded engine:
1. Turn the engine stop switch to the OFF position.
2. Open the throttle fully.
3. Turn the ignition switch ON and operate the starter button for five seconds.
4. Follow the *All ambient and engine temperatures* starting procedure. Note the following:
   a. If the engine starts but idles roughly, vary the throttle position slightly until the engine idles and responds smoothly.

b. If the engine does not start, turn the ignition switch OFF and wait approximately ten seconds. Then repeat Steps 1-4. If the engine still will not start, refer to *Starting Difficulties* in this chapter.

STARTING DIFFICULTIES

If the engine does not start, perform the following procedure in sequence while remembering the *Operating Requirements* described in this chapter. If the engine fails to start after performing these checks, refer to the troubleshooting procedures indicated in the steps.

1. Refer to *Starting the Engine* in this chapter to make sure all switches and starting procedures are correct.

2. If the starter does not operate, refer to *Starting System* in this chapter.

3. If the starter operates, and the engine seems flooded, refer to *Engine Flooded* in this chapter. If the engine is not flooded, continue with Step 4.

4. On fuel injected models, turn the ignition switch ON and check the fuel gauge. If the E segment on the display is flashing, the fuel level in the tank is low. The amount of fuel remaining in the tank when the E segment first starts to flash is less than one gallon (0.92 U.S. gal./3.4 liters/0.77 imp. gal.).

5. If there is sufficient fuel in the fuel tank, remove one of the spark plugs immediately after attempting to start the engine. The plug's insulator should be wet, indicating that fuel is reaching the engine. If the plug tip is dry, fuel is not reaching the engine. Confirm this condition by checking another spark plug. A faulty fuel pump or a clogged fuel filter can cause this condition. Refer to *Fuel System* in this chapter. If there is fuel on the spark plug and the engine will not start, the engine may not have adequate spark. Continue with Step 6.

6. Make sure each spark plug wire is secure. Push on the two-pin electrical connector on the top of each direct ignition coil (**Figure 4**). If necessary, carefully push and slightly rotate the direct ignition coil on the top of the spark plug(s). If the engine does not start, continue with Step 7.

7. Perform the *Spark Test* described in this chapter. If there is a strong spark, perform Step 8. If there is

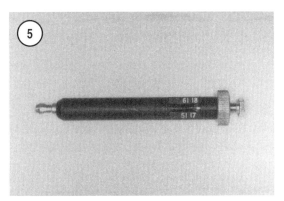

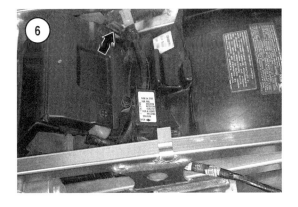

no spark or if the spark is very weak, refer to *Ignition System* in this chapter.

8. Check cylinder compression as described in Chapter Three.

Spark Test

Perform a spark test to determine if the ignition system is producing adequate spark. This test can be performed with a spark plug or a spark tester. A spark tester (**Figure 5**) is used as a substitute for the spark plug and

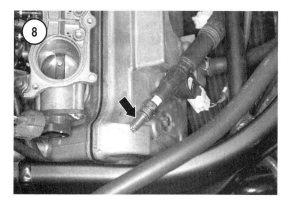

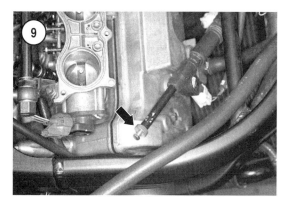

allows the spark to be more easily observed between the adjustable air gap. The tool shown is available from Motion Pro (part No. 08-0122). If a spark tester is not available, always use a new spark plug.

> *WARNING*
> *Step 1 must be performed to disable the fuel system. Otherwise, fuel will enter into the cylinders when the engine is turned over during the spark test, flooding the cylinders and creating explosive fuel vapors.*

1A. On carbureted models, perform the following:
   a. Remove the seat as described in Chapter Sixteen.
   b. Disconnect the fuel pump 2P (black) electrical connector (**Figure 6**).
1B. On fuel injected models, perform the following:
   a. Raise and secure the fuel tank as described in Chapter Nine.
   b. On the left side, disconnect the fuel pump 3P (black) electrical connector (**Figure 7**).

> *CAUTION*
> *After removing the spark plug caps, clean the area around each spark plug with compressed air. Dirt that falls into the cylinder will cause rapid piston, piston ring and cylinder wear.*

2. Remove the spark plugs as described in Chapter Three.
3. Connect each spark plug wire and connector to a *new* spark plug (**Figure 8**), or tester (**Figure 9**), and touch each spark plug base or tester to a good engine ground. Position the spark plugs or tester so the electrodes are visible.

> *WARNING*
> *Mount the spark plugs, or spark tester, away from the spark plug holes in the cylinder head so the spark plugs or tester cannot ignite the gasoline vapors in the cylinder. If the engine is flooded, do not perform this test. The firing of the spark plugs or spark tester can ignite fuel that is ejected through the spark plug holes.*

4. Shift the transmission to NEUTRAL, turn the ignition system ON and place the engine stop switch in the RUN position.

> *WARNING*
> *Do not hold the spark plugs, tester, wire or connector, or a serious electrical shock may result.*

5. Operate the starter button to turn the engine over. A fat blue spark must be evident across the spark plug electrodes or between the tester terminals. Repeat for each cylinder.
6. If the spark is good at each spark plug, the ignition system is functioning properly. Check for one or more of the following possible malfunctions:

a. Faulty fuel system component. See *Fuel System* in this chapter.

b. Engine damage (low compression).

c. Engine flooded.

7. If the spark was weak or if there was no spark at one or more plugs, note the following:

  a. If there is no spark on all of the plugs, check for a problem on the input side of the ignition system or the ignition control module (ICM) or engine control module (ECM), as described in *Ignition System* in this chapter.

  b. If there is no spark at one spark plug only, the spark plug is probably faulty or there is a problem with the spark plug wire or plug cap. Retest with a spark tester, or use a new spark plug. If there is still no spark at that one plug, make sure the spark plug cap is installed correctly.

  c. If there is no spark, the ignition coil is faulty.

  d. Troubleshoot the ignition system as described under *Ignition System* in this chapter.

8. Install the spark plugs as described in Chapter Three.

9A. On carbureted models, perform the following:

  a. Connect the fuel pump 2P (black) electrical connector (**Figure 6**).

  b. Install the seat as described in Chapter Sixteen.

9B. On fuel injected models, perform the following:

  a. Connect the fuel pump 3P (black) electrical connector (**Figure 7**).

  b. Lower and secure the fuel tank as described in Chapter Seven.

Engine is Difficult to Start

1. After attempting to start the engine, remove one of the spark plugs as described in Chapter Three and check for the presence of fuel on the plug tip. Note the following:

  a. If there is no fuel visible on the plug, remove another spark plug. If there is no fuel on this plug, perform Step 2.

  b. If there is fuel present on the plug tip, go to Step 5.

  c. If there is an excessive amount of fuel on the plug, check for a clogged or plugged air filter, incorrect choke operation and adjustment (carbureted models) or incorrect throttle valve operation (stuck open) (fuel injected models).

2. Perform the *Fuel Pump Operation Check* in Chapter Seven. Note the following:

  a. If the fuel pump operation is correct, go to Step 4.

  b. If the fuel pump operation is faulty, replace the fuel pump and retest the fuel system.

3A. On carbureted models, perform the *Fuel Flow Test* in Chapter Eight. Note the following:

  a. If the fuel flow is normal, go to Step 5.

  b. If there is no fuel flow, replace the fuel pump as described in Chapter Seven.

  c. If there is fuel flow but the volume is less than specified, check for a clogged fuel line.

3B. On fuel injected models, perform the *Fuel Flow Test* in Chapter Nine. Note the following:

  a. If the fuel flow is normal, go to Step 5.

  b. If there is no fuel flow, replace the pressure regulator as described in Chapter Nine.

  c. If there is fuel flow but the volume is less than specified, check for a clogged fuel tube and fuel return tube. Then check for a clogged fuel filter, damaged pressure regulator or damaged fuel pump.

4. On fuel injected models, inspect the fuel injectors as described in Chapter Nine.

5. Perform the spark test as described in this chapter. Note the following:

  a. If the spark is weak or if there is no spark, go to Step 6.

  b. If the spark is good, go to Step 7.

6. If the spark is weak or if there is no spark, check the following:

  a. Fouled spark plug(s).

  b. Damaged spark plug(s).

  c. Loose or damaged spark plug wire(s).

  d. Loose or damaged spark plug cap(s).

  e. Damaged ignition control module (ICM) or engine control module (ECM).

  f. Damaged ignition pulse generator.

  g. Damaged ignition coil(s).

  h. Damaged engine stop switch.

  i. Damaged ignition switch.

  j. Dirty or loose-fitting terminals.

7. If the engine turns over but does not start, the engine compression is probably low. Check for the following possible malfunctions:

a. Leaking cylinder head gasket.

b. Valve clearance too tight.

c. Bent or stuck valve.

d. Incorrect valve timing. Worn cylinders and/or pistons rings.

8. If the spark is good, try starting the engine by following normal starting procedures. If the engine starts but then stops, check for the following conditions:

a. Incorrect choke operation on carbureted models.

b. Leaking or damaged intake manifold.

c. Contaminated fuel.

d. Incorrect ignition timing due to a damaged ignition coil(s) or ignition pulse generator.

Engine Will Not Crank

If the engine will not turn over, check for one or more of the following possible malfunctions:

1. Blown fuse.

2. Discharged battery.

3. Defective starter motor or starter relay switch.

4. Seized piston(s).

5. Seized crankshaft bearings.

6. Broken connecting rod(s).

7. Locked-up transmission or clutch assembly.

8. Defective starter clutch.

ENGINE PERFORMANCE

If the engine runs, but performance is unsatisfactory, refer to the following procedure(s) that best describes the symptom(s).

NOTE
The ignition timing is not adjustable. If incorrect ignition timing is suspected as being the cause of a malfunction, check the timing as described in Chapter Three. If the timing is incorrect, a defective ignition system component is indicated. Refer to **Ignition System** *in this chapter.*

Engine Will Not Idle

1. Clogged air filter element.

2. Poor fuel flow.

3A. On carbureted models, incorrect carburetor synchronization.

3B. On fuel injected models, incorrect starter valve synchronization.

4. Fouled or improperly gapped spark plug(s).

5. Leaking head gasket or vacuum leak.

6. Leaking or damaged intake manifolds.

7. Incorrect ignition timing. Defective ignition control module (ICM), or engine control module (ECM), or ignition pulse generator.

8. Obstructed or defective carburetor(s) or fuel injector(s).

9. Low engine compression.

Poor Overall Performance

1. Support the motorcycle with the rear wheel off the ground, then spin the rear wheel by hand. If the wheel spins freely, perform Step 2. If the wheel does not spin freely, check for the following conditions:

a. Dragging rear brake.

b. Damaged rear axle/bearing holder assembly.

c. Damaged drive chain (swollen O-rings).

2. Check the clutch adjustment and operation. If the clutch slips, refer to *Clutch* in this chapter.

3. If Step 1 and Step 2 did not locate the problem, test ride the motorcycle and accelerate lightly. If the engine speed increased according to throttle position, perform Step 4. If the engine speed did not increase, check for one or more of the following problems:

a. Clogged air filter.

b. Restricted fuel flow.

c. Pinched fuel tank breather hose.

d. Clogged or damaged muffler.

4. Check for one or more of the following problems:

a. Low engine compression.

b. Worn spark plugs.

c. Fouled spark plug(s).

d. Incorrect spark plug heat range.

e. Clogged or defective fuel injector(s).

f. Incorrect ignition timing. Defective ignition control module (ICM), or engine control module (ECM), or ignition pulse generator.

g. Incorrect oil level (too high or too low).

h. Contaminated oil.

i. Worn or damaged valve train assembly.

j. Engine overheating. See *Engine Overheating* in this section.

5. If the engine knocks when it is accelerated or when running at high speed, check for one or more of the following possible malfunctions:
 a. Incorrect type of fuel.
 b. Lean fuel mixture.
 c. Advanced ignition timing. Defective ignition control module (ICM), or engine control module (ECM), or ignition pulse generator.
 d. Excessive carbon buildup in combustion chamber.
 e. Worn pistons and/or cylinder bores.

Poor Idle or Low Speed Performance

1. Check the starter valve synchronization (Chapter Three).
2. Check for damaged intake manifolds or loose throttle body and air filter housing hose clamps.
3. Check the fuel flow and the carburetors or fuel injectors (Chapter Eight or Nine).
4. Perform the spark test in this section. Note the following:
 a. If the spark is good, go to Step 5.
 b. If the spark is weak, test the ignition system as described in this chapter.
5. Check the ignition timing as described in Chapter Three. Note the following:
 a. If the ignition timing is incorrect, the ignition control module (ICM), or engine control module (ECM) is probable defective.
 b. If the ignition timing is correct, recheck the fuel system.

Poor High Speed Performance

1. Check the fuel flow and the carburetors or the fuel injectors (Chapters Eight or Nine).
2. Check ignition timing as described in Chapter Three. If ignition timing is correct, perform Step 3.
3. If the timing is incorrect, test the following ignition system components as described in Chapter Ten:
 a. Ignition control module (ICM), or engine control module (ECM).
 b. Pulse generators.
 c. Ignition coils.
4. Check the valve clearance as described in Chapter Three. Note the following:
 a. If the valve clearance is correct, perform Step 5.

 b. If the clearance is incorrect, readjust the valves.
5. Incorrect valve timing and worn or damaged valve springs can cause poor high-speed performance. If the camshafts were timed just prior to the motorcycle experiencing this type of problem, the cam timing may be incorrect. If the cam timing was not set or changed, and all of the other inspection procedures in this section failed to locate the problem, remove the cylinder heads and inspect the camshafts and valve assembly.

Engine Overheating

Cooling system malfunction

1. Low coolant level.
2. Air in cooling system.
3. Clogged radiator, hose or engine coolant passages.
4. Thermostat stuck closed.
5. Worn or damaged radiator cap.
6. Damaged water pump.
7. Damaged fan motor switch.
8. Damaged fan motor.
9. Damaged temperature gauge.
10. Damaged coolant temperature sensor.

Other causes

1. Incorrect carburetor jet selection or throttle body adjustment.
2. Improper spark plug heat range.
3. Low oil level.
4. Oil not circulating properly.
5. Valves leaking.
6. Heavy engine carbon deposits in combustion chamber.
7. Dragging brake(s).
8. Clutch slipping.

Engine Not Reaching Operating Temperature

1. Thermostat stuck open.
2. Defective fan motor switch.
3. Inaccurate temperature gauge.
4. Defective coolant temperature sensor.

Engine Backfires

1. Incorrect ignition timing (due to loose or defective ignition system component).
2. Incorrect carburetor jet selection or throttle body adjustment.

Engine Misfires During Acceleration

1. Incorrect ignition timing (due to loose or defective ignition system component).
2. Incorrect carburetor jet selection or throttle body adjustment.

ENGINE NOISES

Unusual noises are often the first indication of a developing problem. Investigate any new noises as soon as possible. Something that may be a minor problem, if corrected, could prevent the possibility of more extensive damage.

Use a special mechanic's stethoscope or a small section of hose held near the ear (not directly on the ear) with the other end close to the source of the noise to isolate the location. Determining the exact cause of a noise can be difficult. If this is the case, consult with a professional mechanic to determine the cause. Do not disassemble major components until all other possibilities have been eliminated.

Consider the following when troubleshooting engine noises:

1. *Knocking or pinging during acceleration*—Caused by using a lower octane fuel than recommended. May also be caused by poor fuel. Pinging can also be caused by an incorrect spark plug heat range or carbon build-up in the combustion chamber. Refer to *Spark Plug Heat Range* and *Compression Test* in Chapter Three.

2. *Slapping or rattling noises at low speed or during acceleration*—May be caused by excessive piston-to-cylinder wall clearance (piston slap).

NOTE
Piston slap is easier to detect when the engine is cold and before the pistons have expanded. Once the engine has warmed up, piston expansion reduces piston-to-cylinder clearance.

3. *Knocking or rapping while decelerating*—Usually caused by excessive rod bearing clearance.
4. *Persistent knocking and vibration occurring every crankshaft rotation*—Usually caused by worn rod or main bearing(s). Can also be caused by broken piston rings or damaged piston pins.
5. *Rapid on-off squeal*—Compression leak around cylinder head gasket or spark plug(s).
6. *Valve train noise*—Check for the following:
    a. Valve clearance excessive.
    b. Worn or damaged camshaft.
    c. Damaged camshaft, camshaft drive chain and guides.
    d. Worn or damaged valve lifters and/or shims.
    e. Damaged valve lifter bore(s).
    f. Valve sticking in guide(s).
    g. Broken valve spring(s).
    h. Low oil pressure.
    i. Clogged cylinder oil hole or oil passage.

ENGINE LUBRICATION

An improperly operating engine lubrication system will quickly lead to engine seizure. Check the engine oil level before each ride, and top off as described in Chapter Three. Oil pump service is described in Chapter Five.

High Oil Consumption or Excessive Exhaust Smoke

1. Worn valve guides.
2. Worn or damaged piston rings.

Oil Leaks

1. Clogged air filter breather hose.
2. Loose engine parts.
3. Damaged gasket sealing surfaces.

High Oil Pressure

1. Clogged oil filter.
2. Clogged oil gallery or metering orifices.
3. Incorrect type of engine oil.

Low Oil Pressure

1. Low oil level.
2. Worn or damaged oil pump.
3. Clogged oil strainer screen.
4. Clogged oil filter.
5. Internal oil leakage.
6. Incorrect type of engine oil.

No Oil Pressure

1. Damaged oil pump.
2. Low oil level.
3. Damaged oil pump drive shaft.
4. Damaged oil pump drive sprocket.
5. Incorrect oil pump installation.

Oil Pressure Warning Light Stays On

1. Low oil pressure.
2. No oil pressure.
3. Damaged oil pressure switch.
4. Short circuit in warning light circuit.

Oil Level Too Low

1. Oil level not maintained at correct level.
2. Worn piston rings.
3. Worn cylinder(s).
4. Worn valve guides.
5. Worn valve stem seals.
6. Piston rings incorrectly installed during engine overhaul.
7. External oil leakage.
8. Oil leaking into the cooling system.

Oil Contamination

1. Blown head gasket allowing coolant to leak into the engine.
2. Water contamination.
3. Oil and filter not changed at specified intervals or when operating conditions demand more frequent changes.

CYLINDER LEAKDOWN TEST

A cylinder leakdown test can locate engine problems from leaking valves, blown head gasket or

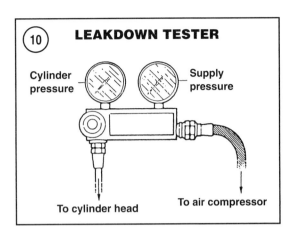

(10) **LEAKDOWN TESTER**

Cylinder pressure
Supply pressure

To cylinder head
To air compressor

broken, worn or stuck piston rings. To perform this test, apply compressed air to the cylinder and then measuring the percent of leakage. Use a cylinder leakdown tester (**Figure 10**) and an air compressor to perform this test.

Follow the manufacturer's directions along with the following information when performing a cylinder leakdown test.

1. Start and run the engine until it is warm. Turn off the engine.
2. Remove the fuel tank as described in Chapter Eight or Nine.
3. Remove the No. 1 cylinder spark plug as described in Chapter Three.
4. Set the No. 1 piston to TDC on its compression stroke as described under *Valve Clearance* in Chapter Three.

> *WARNING*
> *The crankshaft may rotate when compressed air is applied to the cylinder. Remove any tools attached to the end of the crankshaft.*

> *NOTE*
> *To prevent the engine from turning over as compressed air is applied to the cylinder, shift the transmission into sixth gear and then have an assistant apply the rear brake.*

5. Thread the 10 mm test adapter into the No. 1 spark plug hole and make the hose connections following the manufacturer's instructions.
6. Apply compressed air to the leakdown tester and make a cylinder leakage test following the manufacturer's instructions. Read the percent of leakage

on the gauge, following the manufacturer's instructions. Note the following:

a. For a new or rebuilt engine, a leakage rate of 0 to 5 percent per cylinder is desired. A leakage rate of 6 to 14 percent is acceptable and means the engine is in good condition.

b. If testing a used engine, the critical rate is not the percent of leakage for each cylinder, but instead, the difference between the cylinders. On a used engine, a leakage rate of 10 percent or less between cylinders is satisfactory.

c. A leakage rate exceeding 10 percent between cylinders points to an engine that is in poor condition and requires further inspection and possible repair.

7. After checking the percent of leakage, and with air pressure still applied to the combustion chamber, listen for air escaping from the following areas. If necessary, use a mechanic's stethoscope to pinpoint the source.

a. Air leaking through the exhaust pipe indicates a leaking exhaust valve.

b. Air leaking through the carburetors or the throttle body indicates a leaking intake valve.

c. Air leaking through the crankcase breather tube suggests worn piston rings or a worn cylinder bore.

d. Air leaking into the cooling system will cause the coolant to bubble in the radiator. When this condition is indicated, check for a damaged cylinder head gasket and warped cylinder head or cylinder block surfaces.

8. Remove the leakdown tester and repeat these steps for each cylinder.

9. After testing each cylinder, reverse Step 2 and Step 3 to complete installation.

CLUTCH

Excessive Clutch Lever Operation

If the clutch lever is too hard to pull in, check the following:

1. Dry and/or dirty clutch cable.
2. Kinked or damaged clutch cable.
3. Damaged clutch lifter bearing.

Rough Clutch Operation

This condition can be caused by excessively worn, grooved or damaged clutch housing slots.

Clutch Slippage

If the engine speed increases without an increase in motorcycle speed, the clutch is probably slipping. The main causes of clutch slippage are:
1. Worn clutch plates.
2. Weak clutch springs.
3. Insufficient clutch lever free play.
4. Loose clutch lifter bolts.
5. Damaged clutch lifter.
6. Clutch plates contaminated by engine oil additive.

Clutch Drag

If the clutch will not disengage or if the motorcycle creeps with the transmission in gear and the clutch disengaged, the clutch is dragging. Some main causes of clutch drag are:
1. Excessive clutch lever free play.
2. Warped clutch plates.
3. Damaged clutch lifter assembly.
4. Loose clutch housing locknut.
5. Engine oil level too high.
6. Incorrect oil viscosity.
7. Engine oil additive being used.
8. Damaged clutch hub and clutch housing splines.

GEARSHIFT LINKAGE

The gearshift linkage assembly connects the gearshift pedal (external shift mechanism) to the shift drum (internal shift mechanism).

The external shift mechanism can be examined after removing the clutch assembly. The internal shift mechanism can be examined after disassembling the crankcase.

Transmission Jumps Out of Gear

1. Loose stopper arm mounting bolt.
2. Damaged stopper arm.
3. Weak or damaged stopper arm spring.
4. Loose or damaged shift drum.
5. Loose stopper plate bolt.

6. Bent shift fork shaft.
7. Bent or damaged shift fork(s).
8. Worn gear dogs or slots.
9. Damaged shift drum grooves.
10. Weak or damaged gearshift linkage springs.

Difficult Shifting

1. Incorrect clutch operation.
2. Incorrect engine oil viscosity.
3. Loose or damaged stopper arm assembly.
4. Loose stopper plate bolt.
5. Loose stopper plate and pin.
6. Bent shift fork shaft.
7. Bent or damaged shift fork(s).
8. Worn gear dogs or slots.
9. Damaged shift drum grooves.
10. Weak or damaged gearshift linkage springs.
11. Incorrect gearshift linkage installation.

Shift Pedal Does Not Return

1. Bent shift shaft.
2. Weak or damaged shift shaft spindle return spring.
3. Shift shaft incorrectly installed (return spring incorrectly indexed around pin).

TRANSMISSION

Transmission symptoms are sometimes hard to distinguish from clutch symptoms. Prior to working on the transmission, make sure the clutch and gearshift linkage assemblies are not causing the problem.

Difficult Shifting

1. Incorrect clutch operation.
2. Bent shift fork(s).
3. Damaged shift fork guide pin(s).
4. Bent shift fork shaft.
5. Bent shift spindle.
6. Damaged shift drum grooves.

Jumps Out of Gear

1. Loose or damaged shift drum stopper arm.
2. Bent or damaged shift fork(s).

3. Bent shift fork shaft.
4. Damaged shift drum grooves.
5. Worn gear dogs or slots.
6. Broken shift shaft return springs.

Incorrect Shift Lever Operation

1. Bent shift pedal or linkage.
2. Stripped shift pedal splines.
3. Damaged shift pedal linkage.

Excessive Gear Noise

1. Worn or damaged transmission bearings.
2. Worn or damaged gears.
3. Excessive gear backlash.

FUEL SYSTEM
(CARBURETED MODELS)

Many riders automatically assume that the carburetors are at fault when the engine does not run properly. While fuel system problems are not uncommon, carburetor adjustment is seldom the answer. In many cases, adjusting will only compound the problem by making the engine run worse.

Begin fuel system troubleshooting with the fuel tank and work through the system, reserving the carburetors as the final point. Most fuel system problems result from an empty fuel tank, a plugged fuel filter or fuel valve, sour fuel, a dirty air filter or clogged carburetor jets.

Identifying Carburetor Conditions

Refer to the following conditions to identify whether the engine is running lean or rich.

Rich

1. Fouled spark plugs.
2. Engine misfires and runs rough under load.
3. Excessive exhaust smoke as the throttle is increased.
4. An extreme rich condition results in a choked or dull sound from the exhaust and an inability to clear the exhaust with the throttle held wide open.

Lean

1. Blistered or very white spark plug electrodes.
2. Engine overheats.
3. Slow acceleration, engine power is reduced.
4. Flat spots on acceleration that are similar in feel to when the engine starts to run out of gas.
5. Engine speed fluctuates at full throttle.

Troubleshooting

Isolate fuel system problems to the fuel tank, fuel shutoff valve and filter, fuel pump, fuel hoses, external fuel filter or the carburetors. The following procedures assume that the ignition system is working properly and is correctly adjusted.

Fuel Level System

Proper carburetor operation depends on a constant and correct carburetor fuel level. As fuel is drawn from the float bowl during engine operation, the float level in the bowl drops. As the float drops, the fuel valve moves away from its seat and allows fuel to flow through the seat into the float bowl. Fuel entering the float bowl will cause the float to rise and push against the fuel valve. When the fuel level reaches a predetermined level, the fuel valve is pushed against the seat to prevent the float bowl from overfilling.

If the fuel valve fails to close, the engine will run too rich or flood with fuel. Symptoms of this problem are rough running, excessive black smoke and poor acceleration. This condition will sometimes clear up when the engine is run at wide-open throttle, as the fuel is being drawn into the engine before the float bowl can overfill. As the engine speed is reduced, however, the rich running condition returns.

Several things can cause fuel overflow. In most instances, it can be as simple as a small piece of dirt trapped between the fuel valve and seat or an incorrect float level.

Starting Enrichment (Choke) System

A cold engine requires a rich mixture to start and run properly. A cable-actuated starting enrichment (choke) lever (**Figure 1**) located on the left side handlebar and the valve on each carburetor are used for cold starting.

If the engine is difficult to start when cold, check the starting enrichment (choke) cable operation. If necessary, lubricate the cable assembly as described in Chapter Three.

FUEL SYSTEM
(FUEL INJECTION MODELS)

The following section isolates common fuel system problems under specific complaints.

Engine Will Not Start

If the engine will not start and the electrical and mechanical systems are operating correctly, check the following:
1. Intake air leak at the intake manifold, air filter or throttle body assembly.
2. Contaminated or old fuel.
3. Clogged fuel tube.
4. Clogged fuel injector filter.
5. Sticking or damaged fuel injector needle.
6. Damaged fuel pump.
7. Faulty fuel pump system.

Engine Starts but Idles and
Runs Poorly or Stalls

An engine that idles roughly or stalls may have one or more of the following problems:
1. Intake air leak at the intake manifold, air filter or throttle body assembly.
2. Contaminated or old fuel.
3. Clogged fuel tube.
4. Clogged fuel injector filter.
5. Sticking or damaged fuel injector needle.
6. Incorrect idle speed.
7. Incorrect starter valve synchronization.
8. Restricted low-pressure fuel return hose causing a rich condition.

Poor Fuel Mileage and Engine Performance

1. Infrequent tune-ups.
2. Clogged air filter.
3. Clogged fuel system.
4. Damaged pressure regulator.

Engine Backfires or Misfires
During Acceleration

1. Lean fuel mixture.
2. Incorrect throttle body adjustment.
3. Ignition system malfunction.
4. Ignition is intermittently stopped by ECM rpm limiter circuit.
5. Faulty vacuum hoses.
6. Vacuum leaks at the throttle body and/or intake manifold(s).
7. Fouled spark plug(s).

ELECTRICAL TROUBLESHOOTING

This section describes basic electrical troubleshooting and test equipment use.

Electrical troubleshooting can be very time-consuming and frustrating without proper knowledge and a suitable plan. Refer to the wiring diagrams at the end of the manual for component and connector identification. Use the wiring diagrams to help determine how the circuit works by tracing the current paths from the power source through the circuit components to ground. Also check any circuits that share the same fuse, ground or switch. If the other circuits work properly and the shared wiring is in good condition, the cause must be in the wiring used only by the suspect circuit. If all related circuits are faulty at the same time, the probable cause is a poor ground connection or a blown fuse(s).

As with all troubleshooting procedures, analyze typical symptoms in a systematic process. Never assume anything and do not overlook the obvious like a blown fuse or an electrical connector that has separated. Test the simplest and most obvious cause first and try to make tests at easily accessible points on the motorcycle.

Preliminary Checks and Precautions

Prior to starting any electrical troubleshooting procedure, perform the following:
1. Check the main fuse (Chapter Ten). If the fuse is blown, replace it.
2. Check the individual fuses mounted in the fuse box (Chapter Ten). Remove the suspected fuse and replace if blown.

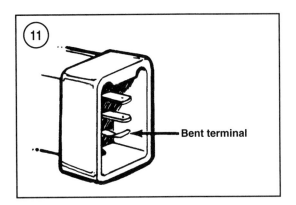

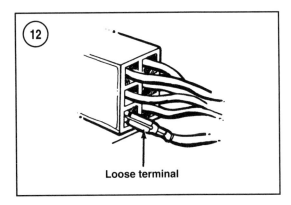

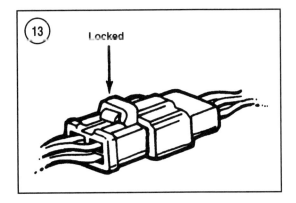

3. Inspect the battery. Make sure it is fully charged, and that the battery leads are clean and securely attached to the battery terminals. Refer to *Battery* in Chapter Ten.

NOTE
Always consider electrical connectors the weak link in the electrical system. Dirty, loose fitting and corroded connectors cause numerous electrical related problems, especially on high-mileage motorcycles. When

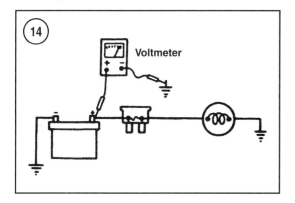

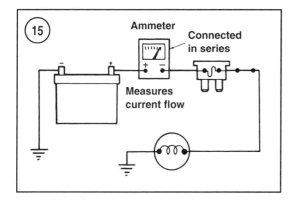

8. Push the connectors together and make sure they are fully engaged and locked together (**Figure 13**).

9. Never pull on the electrical wires when disconnecting an electrical connector—pull only on the connector plastic housing.

10. Never use a self-powered test light on circuits that contain solid-state devices. The solid-state devices may be damaged.

TROUBLESHOOTING TEST EQUIPMENT

Test Light or Voltmeter

A test light can be constructed of a 12-volt light bulb with a pair of test leads carefully soldered to the bulb. To check for battery voltage (12 volts) in a circuit, attach one lead to ground and the other lead to various points along the circuit. Where battery voltage is present, the light bulb will light.

A voltmeter is used in the same manner as the test light to determine if battery voltage is present in any given circuit. The voltmeter, unlike the test light, will also indicate how much voltage is present at each test point. When using a voltmeter, attach the positive lead to the component or wire to be checked and the negative lead to a good ground (**Figure 14**).

Ammeter

An ammeter measures the flow of current (amps) in a circuit (**Figure 15**). When connected in series in the circuit, the ammeter determines whether current is flowing in the circuit, and whether the current flow is excessive because of a short in the circuit. This current flow is usually referred to as current draw. Comparing actual current draw in the circuit or component to the manufacturer's specified current draw rating provides useful diagnostic information.

Self-Powered Test Light

A self-powered test light can be constructed of a 12-volt light bulb, a pair of test leads and a 12-volt battery. When the test leads are touched together, the light bulb illuminates.

Use a self-powered test light as follows:

troubleshooting an electrical problem, carefully inspect the connectors and wiring harness.

4. Disconnect each electrical connector in the suspect circuit and check that there are no bent metal terminals (male or female) (**Figure 11**) inside the connectors. Bent terminals will not connect, causing an open circuit.

5. Make sure the metal terminals on the end of each wire (**Figure 12**) are pushed all the way into the plastic connector. If not, carefully push them in with a narrow blade screwdriver.

6. Check the wires where they enter the individual connectors.

7. Make sure all electrical terminals within the connector are clean and free of corrosion. Clean, if necessary, and pack the connectors with dielectric grease.

NOTE
Dielectric grease is used as an insulator on electrical components such as connectors and battery connections. Dielectric grease can be purchased at automotive part stores.

1. Touch the test leads together to make sure the light bulb goes on. If not, correct the problem prior to using it in a test procedure.

2. Disconnect the motorcycle's battery or remove the fuse(s) that protects the circuit to be tested. Refer to Chapter Ten.

3. Select two points within the circuit that should have continuity.

4. Attach one lead of the self-powered test light to each point.

5. If there is continuity, the self-powered test light bulb will come on.

6. If there is no continuity, the self-powered test light bulb will not come on. This indicates an open circuit.

Ohmmeter

The ohmmeter reads resistance in ohms. Like the self-powered test light, an ohmmeter contains its own power source and should not be connected to a live circuit.

Ohmmeters may be an analog type (needle scale) or a digital type (LCD or LED readout). Both types of ohmmeters have a switch that allows the selection of different ranges of resistance for accurate readings. The analog ohmmeter also has a set-adjust control which is used to zero or calibrate the meter needle for accurate adjustments. Digital ohmmeters do not require calibration.

An ohmmeter is used by connecting its test leads to the terminals or leads of the circuit or component being tested (**Figure 16**). If an analog meter is used, it should be calibrated by crossing the test leads and adjusting the meter needle until it reads zero. When the leads are uncrossed, the needle should move to the other end of the scale, indicating infinite resistance.

The infinite reading indicates an open in the circuit or component; a reading of zero indicates continuity. If the meter needle falls between these two points on the scale, it indicates the actual resistance to current flow that is present. To determine the resistance, multiply the meter reading by the ohmmeter scale. For example, a meter reading of 5 ohms multiplied by the R × 1000 scale is 5000 ohms of resistance.

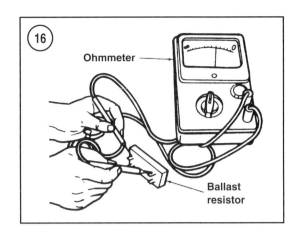

CAUTION
Never connect an ohmmeter to a circuit that has power applied to it. Always disconnect the negative battery cable before using the ohmmeter.

Jumper Wire

When using a jumper wire, always install an inline fuse/fuse holder (available at most auto supply stores or electronic supply stores) to the jumper wire. Never use a jumper wire across any load (a component that is connected and turned on). This would result in a direct short and will blow the fuse(s).

BASIC TEST PROCEDURES

Voltage Testing

Unless otherwise specified, all voltage tests are made with the electrical connectors still connected. Insert the test leads into the backside of the connector and make sure the test lead touches the wire or metal terminal within the connector. If the test lead only touches the wire insulation, a false reading will result.

Always check both sides of the connector, as one side may be loose or corroded. This prevents electrical flow through the connector. This type of test can be performed with a test light or a voltmeter. A voltmeter gives the best results.

NOTE
If using a test lamp, it does not make any difference which test lead is attached to ground.

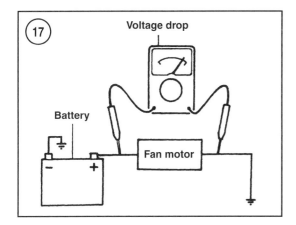

1. Attach the negative test lead (if using a voltmeter) to a good ground (bare metal). Make sure the part used for ground is not insulated with a rubber gasket or rubber grommet.
2. Attach the positive test lead (if using a voltmeter) to the point being checked.
3. Turn the ignition switch ON. If using a test light, the test light will come on if voltage is present. If using a voltmeter, note the voltage reading. The reading should be within 1 volt of battery voltage. If the voltage is less, there is a problem in the circuit.

Voltage Drop Test

Resistance causes voltage to drop. This resistance can be measured in an active circuit by using a voltmeter to perform a voltage drop test. A voltage drop test compares the difference between the voltage available at the start of a circuit to the voltage at the end of the circuit while the circuit is operational. If the circuit has no resistance, there will be no voltage drop. The greater the resistance, the greater the voltage drop will be. A voltage drop of one volt or more indicates excessive resistance in the circuit. It is important to remember that a 0 reading on a voltage drop test is good; a battery voltage reading indicates an open circuit. A voltage drop test is an excellent way to check the condition of relays, battery cables and other high-current electrical loads.
1. Connect the positive meter test lead to the electrical source (where electricity is coming from).
2. Connect the negative meter test lead to the electrical load (where electricity is going). See **Figure 17**.
3. If necessary, activate the component(s) in the circuit.

4. A voltage reading of 1 volt or more indicates excessive resistance in the circuit. A reading equal to battery voltage indicates an open circuit.

Continuity Test

A continuity test is made to determine if the circuit is complete with no opens in either the electrical wires or components within that circuit.

Unless otherwise specified, all continuity tests are made with the electrical connector still connected. Insert the test leads into the backside of the connector and make sure the test lead touches the wire or metal terminal within the connector. If the test lead only touches the wire insulation, a false reading will result. Always check both sides of the connectors as one side may be loose or corroded. This prevents electrical flow through the connector.

This type of test can be performed with a self-powered test light or an ohmmeter. An ohmmeter will give the best results. If using an analog ohmmeter, calibrate the meter by touching the leads together and turning the ohms calibration knob until the meter reads zero.
1. Disconnect the negative battery cable.
2. Attach one test lead, the test light or ohmmeter, to one end of the part of the circuit to be tested.
3. Attach the other test lead to the other end of the part of the circuit to be tested.
4. If the circuit has continuity, a self-powered test lamp will illuminate and an ohmmeter will indicate low or no resistance. If the circuit is open, a self-powered test lamp will not illuminate and an ohmmeter will indicate infinite resistance.

Testing for a Short With a Self-Powered Test Light or Ohmmeter

This test can be performed with either a self-powered test light or an ohmmeter.
1. Disconnect the battery negative lead from the battery.
2. Remove the blown fuse from the fuse panel.
3. Connect one test lead of the test light or ohmmeter to the load side or battery side of the fuse terminal in the fuse panel.
4. Connect the other test lead to a good ground (bare metal). Make sure the part used for a ground is not insulated with a rubber gasket or rubber grommet.

5. With the self-powered test light or ohmmeter attached to the fuse terminal and ground, wiggle the wiring harness relating to the suspect circuit at 6 in. (15.2 cm) intervals. Start next to the fuse panel and work away from the fuse panel. Watch the self-powered test light or ohmmeter while moving along the harness.

6. If the test light blinks or the needle on the ohmmeter moves, there is a short-to-ground at that point in the harness.

Testing For a Short with a Test Light or Voltmeter

1. Remove the blown fuse from the fuse panel.

2. Connect the test light or voltmeter across the fuse terminals in the fuse panel. Turn the ignition switch ON and check for battery voltage.

3. With the test light or voltmeter attached to the fuse terminals, wiggle the wiring harness relating to the suspect circuit at 6 in. (15.2 cm) intervals. Start next to the fuse panel and work away from the fuse panel. Watch the test light or voltmeter while moving along the harness.

4. If the test light blinks or the needle on the voltmeter moves, there is a short-to-ground at that point in the harness.

LIGHTING SYSTEM

If bulbs burn out frequently, the cause may be excessive vibration, loose connections that permit sudden current surges or the installation of the wrong type of bulb. Most light and ignition problems are caused by loose or corroded ground connections. Check these prior to replacing a bulb or electrical component.

CHARGING SYSTEM

The charging system consists of the battery, alternator and a voltage regulator/rectifier. A 30 amp main fuse protects the circuit.

Alternating current generated by the alternator is rectified to direct current. The voltage regulator maintains the voltage to the battery and additional electrical loads at a constant voltage regardless of variations in engine speed and load.

Battery Discharging

Before testing the charging system, the battery must be fully charged. If necessary, inspect and charge the battery as described in Chapter Ten.

1. Check all of the connections. Make sure they are tight and free of corrosion.

2. Perform the *Regulated Voltage Test* in Chapter Ten.

    a. If the voltage reading is 14.0-14.8 volts at 5000 rpm, continue at Step 3.

    b. If the voltage reading is incorrect, go to Step 5.

    c. If the regulated voltage exceeds 15.5 volts, refer to *Battery Overcharging* in this section.

3. Perform the *Current Leakage (Draw) Test* as described in Chapter Ten.

    a. If the current leakage is 1.2 mA or less, continue at Step 6.

    b. If the current leakage exceeds 1.2 mA, continue at Step 4.

4. Disconnect the regulator/rectifier (**Figure 18**, typical) connector and repeat Step 3.

    a. If the current leakage reading is correct (1.2 mA or less), the regulator/rectifier is defective. Replace the regulator/rectifier (Chapter Ten) and retest.

    b. Moisture or electrolyte on the top of the battery can create a path for current to flow from the battery. Clean the top of the battery and repeat the current drain test. If the drain is still excessive, check the wiring harness for a short circuit. If the wiring harness is in good condition, test the ignition switch as described in Chapter Ten. If the ignition switch is in good condition, the battery is probably defective. Test the battery as described in Chapter Ten.

5. Perform the battery charging circuit and ground voltage test as described under *Regulator/Rectifier Unit Resistance Test* in Chapter Ten.

   a. If the resistance readings are correct, continue at Step 6.

   b. If the test results are incorrect, check for a short circuit or a loose or corroded connection in the charging circuit wiring harness. Also check for damaged or blown fuses.

6. Perform the charging coil circuit resistance test as described under *Regulator/Rectifier Wiring Harness Test* in Chapter Ten.

   a. If the charging coil circuit resistance is as specified in Chapter Ten, replace the voltage regulator/rectifier.

   b. If the charging coil circuit resistance is not as specified, check the stator resistance as described in Step 7.

7. Perform the *Stator Coil Resistance Test* as described in Chapter Ten.

   a. If the stator resistance is not as specified, replace the stator coil and retest.

   b. If the resistance is correct, check for an open circuit, loose or corroded connections or damaged wiring and repair or replace the harness as required.

Battery Overcharging

If the regulated voltage exceeds 15.5 volts at 5000 rpm, perform the following test. Prior to testing, make sure the battery is in serviceable condition.

1. Check all connections for loose or corroded connections.

2. Perform the *Regulated Voltage Test* in Chapter Ten.

   a. If the voltage reading is correct, the battery is damaged. Replace the battery.

   b. If the regulated voltage exceeds the 15.5 volts, perform Step 3.

3. Perform the ground circuit test as described under *Regulator/Rectifier Wiring Harness Test* in Chapter Ten.

   a. If the test readings are incorrect, check for dirty or loose-fitting terminals. Then check for an open circuit in the wiring harness.

   b. If the test readings are correct, check the regulator/rectifier connector for dirty or loose-fitting terminals. If the battery continues to

overcharge after cleaning or repairing these connectors, the regulator/rectifier (**Figure 18**, typical) is defective. Replace it and retest.

IGNITION SYSTEM

This section covers the most common ignition system problems, which are: no spark at all four spark plugs, no spark at one direct ignition coil, and sidestand related malfunctions.

The procedures describe the use of a peak voltage tester. Refer to *Peak Voltage Tests and Equipment* in Chapter Ten.

Refer to Chapter Ten for component location and the appropriate wiring diagram at the end of the manual.

Prior to troubleshooting the ignition system, perform the following:

1. Make sure the battery is fully charged and in good condition. A weak battery will result in slow engine cranking speed.

2. Perform the *Spark Test* described in this chapter. Then refer to the appropriate ignition system complaint.

3. Check for dirty or loose-fitting connector terminals. Refer to *Electrical Troubleshooting* in this chapter for additional information.

No Spark at All Four Spark Plugs

> *WARNING*
> *High voltage is present during ignition system operation. Do not touch ignition components, wires or test leads while cranking or running the engine.*

1. Check for dirty or loose-fitting connector terminals as previously described. Clean and repair as required.

2. Perform the *Ignition Coil Primary Peak Voltage Test* in Chapter Ten. After recording the test results, note the following before continuing with the diagnosis:

   a. If there is no initial voltage with the ignition and engine stop switch on, go to Step 3.

   b. If the initial voltage is normal, but then drops to 2-4 volts while cranking the engine, go to Step 4.

c. If the initial voltage reading is correct, but there is no peak voltage while cranking the engine, go to Step 5.

d. If the initial and peak voltage readings are correct, but there is no spark, go to Step 6.

e. If the initial voltage reading is correct, but the peak voltage is lower than specified, go to Step 7.

3. If there is no initial voltage with the ignition and engine stop switch on, check for one or more of the following conditions in the order given:

a. Defective engine stop switch (test as described in Chapter Ten).

b. An open circuit in the ignition coil (black/white wire) and engine stop switch.

c. Defective ignition control module (ICM) or engine control module (ECM) unit.

4. If the initial voltage is normal, but then drops to 2-4 volts while cranking the engine, check for one or more of the following conditions in the order given:

a. Incorrect peak voltage adapter connections.

b. Battery undercharged.

c. Loose ICM or ECM connection.

d. No voltage between the black/white (+) and green (–) side of the ICM or ECM connector. Check for voltage with a voltmeter.

e. A loose or damaged ICM or ECM green wire.

f. Loose connection or open circuit between the ICM or ECM and ignition coil(s) blue/black, yellow/white, red/blue and red/yellow wires.

g. Short circuit in the direct ignition coil (primary side).

h. Defective sidestand switch.

i. Defective neutral switch.

j. Loose connection or open circuit between the sidestand switch green/white and green wires.

k. Loose connection or open circuit between the clutch diode light green and light green/red wires.

l. Damaged ignition pulse generator. Confirm by performing the *Ignition Pulse Generator Peak Voltage Test* in Chapter Ten.

m. If a problem cannot be found with one of the above listed items, the ICM or ECM is probably faulty.

5. If the initial voltage reading is correct, but there is no peak voltage while the engine is cranked, check for one or more of the following conditions in the order given:

a. Incorrect peak voltage adapter connections.

b. Damaged peak voltage adapter.

c. If a problem cannot be found with one of the above listed items, the ICM or ECM is probably faulty.

6. If the initial and peak voltage readings are correct, but there is no spark, check for one or more of the following conditions in the order given:

a. Defective spark plug.

b. Defective spark plug wire.

c. Defective direct ignition coil.

7. If the initial voltage reading is correct, but the peak voltage is lower than specified, check the following:

a. The impedance of the digital multimeter is below 10 M ohms/DCV.

b. The battery charge is low, causing a low engine cranking speed.

c. The multimeter and peak voltage adapter components are not working properly.

d. If a problem cannot be found with one of the above listed items, the ICM or ECM is probably faulty.

NOTE
If the spark problem could not be found after performing Steps 2-7, continue with Step 8.

8. Perform the *Ignition Pulse Generator Peak Voltage Test* in Chapter Ten. After recording the test results, note the following before continuing with the diagnosis:

a. If the peak voltage reading is lower than 100 volts, go to Step 9.

b. If there is no peak voltage reading, go to Step 10.

9. If the peak voltage reading was lower than 100 volts, check for one or more of the following conditions in the order given:

a. The impedance of the digital multimeter is below 10 M ohms/DCV.

b. The battery charge is low, causing a low engine cranking speed.

c. The multimeter and peak voltage adapter components are not working properly.

d. If the problem cannot be found with one of the above listed items, the ICM or ECM is probably faulty.

10. If there is no peak voltage reading, check for one or more of the following conditions in the order given:

    a. The peak voltage adapter connection is incorrect.

    b. The peak voltage adapter is damaged.

    c. The ignition pulse generator is damaged.

Engine Starts and Runs but Sidestand Switch Does Not Operate

If the engine runs with the transmission in neutral, it should continue to run when the sidestand is moved down. When the engine is running and the transmission is in gear, the engine should stop when the sidestand is moved down. If the engine does not perform as described, test the sidestand switch as described in Chapter Ten.

> *WARNING*
> *Before riding the motorcycle, make sure the sidestand switch and its indicator light work properly. Riding the motorcycle with the sidestand down can cause loss of control.*

STARTING SYSTEM

The starting system consists of the starter motor, starter gears, starter relay switch, starter switch button, ignition switch, engine stop switch, clutch switch, clutch diode, neutral switch, main and auxiliary fuses and battery.

When the starter switch button is pressed, it allows current to flow through the starter relay switch coil. This will cause the coil contacts to close, allowing electricity to flow from the battery to the starter motor.

> *CAUTION*
> *Do not operate the starter for more than five seconds at a time. Wait approximately 10 seconds between starting attempts.*

The starter should turn when the starter switch button is depressed and the transmission is in neutral and/or the clutch lever pulled in. If the starter does not operate properly, perform the following preliminary checks.

1. Check the battery to make sure it is fully charged. Refer to Chapter Ten for battery service.

2. Check the starter cables for loose or damaged connections.

3. Check the battery cables for loose or damaged connections. Then check the battery state of charge as described under *Battery Testing* in Chapter Ten.

4. If the starter does not operate correctly after making these checks, perform the test procedure that best describes the starting malfunction.

Starter Inoperative

1. Check for a blown main fuse or sub-fuse (Chapter Ten). If the fuses are good, continue with Step 2.

2. Check the starter motor cable for an open circuit or dirty or loose-fitting terminals.

3. Check the starter relay switch connectors for dirty or loose-fitting terminals. Clean and repair as required.

4. Check the starter relay switch (**Figure 19**, typical) as follows. Turn the ignition switch ON and depress the starter switch button. When the starter switch button is depressed, the starter relay switch should click once.

    a. If the relay clicks, continue with Step 5.

    b. If the relay does not click, go to Step 6.

> *CAUTION*
> *Because of the large amount of current that flows from the battery to the starter in Step 5, use large diameter cables when making the connection.*

5. Remove the starter from the motorcycle as described in Chapter Ten. Using an auxiliary battery and cables, apply battery voltage directly to the starter. The starter should turn when battery voltage is applied directly.

    a. If the starter motor did not turn, disassemble and inspect the starter motor as described in

Chapter Ten. Test the starter components and replace worn or damaged parts as required.

   b. If the starter motor turned, check for loose or damaged starter motor cables. If the cables are good, check the starter relay switch as described in Chapter Ten. Replace the starter relay switch if necessary.

6. Check the starter relay switch (**Figure 19**, typical) ground circuit as described under *Starter Relay Switch Testing* in Chapter Ten.

   a. If there is continuity, continue with Step 7.

   b. If there is no continuity reading (high resistance), check for a loose or damaged connector or an open circuit in the wiring harness. If these items are in good condition, test the neutral switch, sidestand switch and clutch diode as described in Chapter Ten.

   c. Reconnect the starter relay switch electrical connector (**Figure 19**, typical).

7. Check the starter relay voltage as described under *Starter Relay Switch Testing* in Chapter Ten.

   a. If battery voltage is indicated, continue with Step 8.

   b. If there is no battery voltage reading, check for a blown main or sub-fuse (Chapter Ten). If the fuses are good, check for an open circuit in the wiring harness or for dirty or loose-fitting terminals. If the wiring and connectors are in good condition, check for a defective ignition and/or starter switch (Chapter Ten).

8. Perform the starter relay switch operational check as described under *Starter Relay Switch Testing* in Chapter Ten.

   a. If the starter relay switch is normal, check for dirty or loose-fitting terminals in its connector block.

   b. If the starter relay switch is defective, replace it and retest.

Starter Operates Slowly

If the starter motor turns slowly and all engine components and systems are normal, perform the following:

1. Test the battery as described in Chapter Ten.

2. Check for the following:

   a. Loose or corroded battery terminals.

   b. Loose or corroded battery ground cable.

   c. Loose starter motor cable.

3. Remove, disassemble and bench test the starter as described in Chapter Ten.

4. Check the starter for binding during operation. Disassemble the starter and check the armature shafts for bending or damage. Also check the starter clutch as described in Chapter Ten.

Starter Operates but Engine Does Not Turn Over

1. If the starter motor is running backward and the starter was just reassembled, or if the starter motor cables were disconnected and then reconnected to the starter:

   a. The starter motor is reassembled incorrectly.

   b. The starter motor cables are incorrectly installed.

2. Check for a damaged starter clutch (Chapter Ten).

3. Check for a damaged or faulty starter drive gears (Chapter Ten).

Starter Relay Switch Clicks but Engine Does Not Turn

Crankshaft cannot turn because of mechanical failure.

Starter Operates With the Transmission in Neutral but Does Not With the Transmission in Gear With the Clutch Lever Pulled In and the Sidestand Up

1. Turn the ignition switch ON and move the sidestand UP and DOWN while watching the sidestand switch indicator light.

   a. If the indicator light works properly, perform Step 2.

   b. If the indicator light does not work, check for a blown bulb, damaged sidestand switch (Chapter Ten) or an open circuit in the wiring harness.

2. Test the clutch switch as described in Chapter Ten. Note the following:

   a. If the clutch switch is good, perform Step 3.

   b. If the clutch switch is defective, replace the switch and retest.

3. Test the sidestand switch as described in Chapter Ten. Note the following:

a. If the sidestand switch is good, perform Step 4.

b. If the sidestand switch is defective, replace switch and retest.

4. Check for an open circuit in the wiring harness. Check for a loose or damaged electrical connector.

WARNING
Before riding the motorcycle, make sure the sidestand switch and its indicator light work properly. Riding the motorcycle with the sidestand down can cause loss of control.

FRONT SUSPENSION AND STEERING

Steering is Sluggish

1. Incorrect steering stem adjustment (too tight).
2. Damaged steering head bearings.
3. Tire pressure too low.

Motorcycle Steers to One Side

1. Bent axle.
2. Bent frame.
3. Worn or damaged wheel bearings.
4. Worn or damaged swing arm pivot bearings.
5. Damaged steering head bearings.
6. Bent swing arm.
7. Incorrectly installed wheels.
8. Front and rear wheels are not aligned.
9. Front fork legs positioned unevenly in steering stem.
10. Incorrect drive chain adjustment.

Front Suspension Noise

1. Loose mounting fasteners.
2. Damaged fork(s) or rear shock absorber.
3. Low fork oil capacity.
4. Loose or damaged fairing mounts.

Front Wheel Wobble/Vibration

1. Loose front wheel axle.
2. Loose or damaged wheel bearing(s).
3. Damaged wheel rim(s).
4. Damaged tire(s).
5. Unbalanced tire and wheel assembly.

Hard Suspension (Front Fork)

1. Incorrectly adjusted fork.
2. Excessive tire pressure.
3. Damaged steering head bearings.
4. Incorrect steering head bearing adjustment.
5. Bent fork tubes.
6. Binding slider.
7. Incorrect weight fork oil.
8. Plugged fork oil passage.

Hard Suspension (Rear Shock Absorber)

1. Incorrectly adjuster rear shock.
2. Excessive rear tire pressure.
3. Bent damper rod.
4. Incorrect shock adjustment.
5. Damaged shock absorber bushing(s).
6. Damaged shock absorber bearing.
7. Damaged swing arm pivot bearings.

Soft Suspension (Front Fork)

1. Incorrectly adjusted fork.
2. Insufficient tire pressure.
3. Insufficient fork oil level or fluid capacity.
4. Incorrect oil viscosity.
5. Weak or damaged fork springs.

Soft Suspension (Rear Shock Absorber)

1. Incorrectly adjusted rear shock.
2. Insufficient rear tire pressure.
3. Weak or damaged shock absorber spring.
4. Damaged shock absorber.
5. Incorrect shock absorber adjustment.
6. Leaking damper unit.

BRAKE SYSTEM

The front and rear brake units are critical to riding performance and safety. Inspect the front and rear brakes frequently and repair any problem immediately. When replacing or refilling the disc brake fluid, use only DOT 4 brake fluid from a closed container. See Chapter Fifteen for additional information on brake fluid selection and disc brake service.

When checking brake pad wear, check that the brake pads in each caliper contact the disc squarely.

If one of the brake pads is wearing unevenly, suspect a warped or bent brake disc or damaged caliper.

Always check the brake operation before riding the motorcycle.

Soft or Spongy Brake Lever or Pedal

When the front brake lever or rear brake pedal travel increases, the brake system is not capable of producing sufficient brake force. When an increase in lever/pedal travel is noticed or when the brake feels soft or spongy, check the following possible causes:

1. Air in system.

NOTE
If the brake level in the reservoir drops too low, air can enter the hydraulic system through the master cylinder. Air can also enter the system from loose or damaged hose fittings. Air in the hydraulic system results in a soft or spongy brake lever or pedal action. This condition is noticeable and reduces brake performance. When it is suspected that air has entered the hydraulic system, flush the brake system and bleed the brakes as described in Chapter Fifteen.

2. Low brake fluid level.

NOTE
As the brake pads wear, the brake fluid level in the master cylinder reservoir drops. Whenever adding brake fluid to the reservoirs, visually check the brake pads for wear. If there does not appear to be an increase in pad wear, check the brake hoses and banjo bolts for leaks.

3. Leak in the brake system.
4. Contaminated brake fluid.
5. Plugged brake fluid passages.
6. Damaged brake lever or pedal assembly.
7. Worn or damaged brake pads.
8. Worn or damaged brake disc.
9. Warped brake disc.
10. Contaminated brake pads and disc.

NOTE
A leaking fork seal can allow oil to contaminate the brake pads and disc.

11. Worn or damaged master cylinder cups and/or cylinder bore.
12. Worn or damaged brake caliper piston seals.
13. Contaminated master cylinder assembly.
14. Contaminated brake caliper assembly.
15. Brake caliper not sliding correctly on slide pins.
16. Sticking master cylinder piston assembly.
17. Sticking brake caliper pistons.

Brake Drag

When the brakes drag, the brake pads are not capable of moving away from the brake disc when the brake lever or pedal is released. Any of the following causes, if they occur, would prevent correct brake pad movement and cause brake drag.

1. Warped or damaged brake disc.
2. Brake caliper not sliding correctly on slide pins.
3. Sticking or damaged brake caliper pistons.
4. Contaminated brake pads and disc.
5. Plugged master cylinder port.
6. Contaminated brake fluid and hydraulic passages.
7. Restricted brake hose joint.
8. Loose brake disc mounting bolts.
9. Damaged or misaligned wheel.
10. Incorrect wheel alignment.
11. Incorrectly installed brake caliper.

Hard Brake Lever or Pedal Operation

When the brakes are applied and there is sufficient brake performance but the operation of brake lever or pedal feels excessively hard, check for the following possible causes:

1. Clogged brake hydraulic system.
2. Sticking caliper piston.
3. Sticking master cylinder piston.
4. Glazed or worn brake pads.
5. Mismatched brake pads.
6. Damaged front brake lever.
7. Damaged rear brake pedal.
8. Brake caliper not sliding correctly on slide pins.
9. Worn or damaged brake caliper seals.

Brakes Grab

1. Damaged brake pad pin bolt. Look for steps or cracks along the pad pin bolt surface.
2. Contaminated brake pads and disc.
3. Incorrect wheel alignment.
4. Warped brake disc.
5. Loose brake disc mounting bolts.
6. Brake caliper not sliding correctly on slide pins.
7. Mismatched brake pads.
8. Damaged wheel bearings.

Brake Squeal or Chatter

1. Contaminated brake pads and disc.
2. Incorrectly installed brake caliper.
3. Warped brake disc.
4. Incorrect wheel alignment.
5. Mismatched brake pads.
6. Incorrectly installed brake pads.

Leaking Brake Caliper

1. Damaged dust and piston seals.
2. Damaged cylinder bore.
3. Loose caliper body bolts.
4. Loose banjo bolt.
5. Damaged banjo bolt washers.
6. Damaged banjo bolt threads in caliper body.

Leaking Master Cylinder

1. Damaged piston secondary seal.
2. Damaged piston snap ring/snap ring groove.
3. Worn or damaged master cylinder bore.
4. Loose banjo bolt.
5. Damaged banjo bolt washers.
6. Damaged banjo bolt threads in master cylinder body.
7. Loose or damaged reservoir cap.

2

CHAPTER THREE

LUBRICATION, MAINTENANCE AND TUNE-UP

This chapter describes lubrication, maintenance and tune-up procedures. Procedures that require more than minor disassembly or adjustment are covered in the appropriate subsequent chapter. Specifications are listed in **Tables 1-5** at the end of the chapter.

To maximize the service life of the motorcycle and gain the utmost in safety and performance, it is necessary to perform periodic inspections and maintenance. Minor problems found during routine service can be corrected before they develop into major ones. A neglected motorcycle will be unreliable and may be dangerous to ride.

Table 1 lists the recommended lubrication, maintenance and tune-up intervals. If the motorcycle is operated in extreme conditions, it may be appropriate to reduce the interval between some maintenance items.

Before servicing the motorcycle, make sure the procedures and the required skills are thoroughly understood. If experience and equipment are lim-

ited, start by performing basic procedures, and perform more involved tasks as further experience is gained and the necessary tools are acquired.

FUEL TYPE

All models covered in this manual require fuel with a pump octane number of 86 or higher. Using fuel with a lower octane number can cause pinging or spark knock, and lead to engine damage.

When choosing gasoline and filling the fuel tank, note the following:

1. When filling the tank, do not overfill it. There should be no fuel in the filler neck (tube located between the fuel cap and tank).

2. Because oxygenated fuels can damage plastic and paint, make sure not to spill fuel onto the fuel tank during filling.

3. Ethanol (ethyl or grain alcohol) fuels that contain more than 10 percent ethanol by volume may cause engine starting and performance related problems.

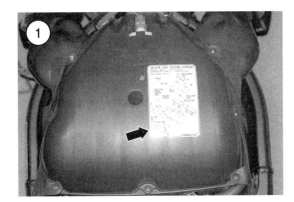

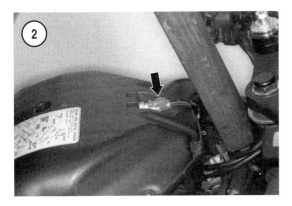

4. Methanol (methyl or wood alcohol) fuels that contain more than 5 percent methanol by volume may cause engine starting and performance related problems. Fuel that contains methanol must have corrosion inhibitors to protect the metal, plastic and rubber parts in the fuel system from damage. In some areas of the United States and Canada, oxygenated fuels are being used to reduce exhaust emissions. If using oxygenated fuel, make sure it meets the minimum octane requirements.

TUNE-UP PROCEDURES

A complete tune-up restores performance lost due to normal wear and deterioration of engine parts. Perform the engine tune-up procedures at the intervals specified in **Table 1**. More frequent tune-ups may be required if the motorcycle is operated primarily in stop-and-go traffic or in areas where there is a large amount of blowing dirt and dust.

The Vehicle Emission Control Information labels are attached to the inside of the pillion seat storage compartment and on top of the air filter case (**Figure 1**). Refer to **Table 2** for tune-up specifications.

> *NOTE*
> *If the specifications on the **Vehicle Emission Control Information** label differ from those in **Table 2**, use those on the label.*

To perform a tune-up, service the following items as described in this chapter:
1. Air filter.
2. Spark plugs.
3. Engine compression.
4. Ignition timing inspection.
5. Valve clearance and adjustment.
6A. Carburetor synchronization (carbureted models).
6B. EFI starter valve synchronization (fuel injected models).
7. Engine oil and filter.
8. Drive chain.
9. Brake system.
10. Tires.
11. Suspension components.
12. Fasteners.

AIR FILTER

Replacement

The air filter removes dust and abrasive particles from the air before the air enters the engine. A clogged air filter element will decrease the efficiency and life of the engine. With a damaged air filter, very fine particles could enter the engine and cause rapid wear of the piston rings, cylinder and bearings. Never run the motorcycle without the air filter element installed. Replace the air filter element at the service intervals specified in **Table 1**.

> *NOTE*
> *The service intervals specified in **Table 1** should be followed with general use. However, replace the air filter more often if dusty areas are frequently encountered.*

1. Open and support the fuel tank as described in Chapter Eight or Nine.
2. On fuel injected models, perform the following:
   a. Disconnect the electrical connector from the IAT sensor (**Figure 2**).

b. Remove the rubber heat shield (A, **Figure 3**).

3. Remove the air filter housing cover screws and lift the cover (B, **Figure 3**) off the housing.

4. Lift the air filter element (**Figure 4**) out of the housing.

5A. On carbureted models, cover the exposed carburetor inlets to prevent objects from entering the carburetors.

5B. On fuel injected models, cover the exposed throttle body air funnels to prevent objects from entering the throttle bodies (**Figure 5**).

6. At the specified service intervals in **Table 1**, replace the air filter element. If the motorcycle has not yet reached the mileage interval for replacement, check the element for damage or dirt buildup. **Figure 6** shows a clean air filter element, while **Figure 7** shows a dirty, clogged element. Replace the element if necessary.

7. Check the inside of the air filter air box and cover for dust and other contamination.

8. Wipe out the interior of the air box with a damp cloth. Remove any debris that may have passed through a broken element.

9. Remove the covering installed in Step 5.

10. Install the air filter element into the housing (**Figure 4**).

11. Install the air filter housing cover (B, **Figure 3**) and its screws; tighten the screws securely. Make sure the housing cover is seated around the lower housing.

12. On fuel injected models, perform the following:

a. Install the rubber heat shield (A, **Figure 3**).

b. Connect the electrical connector onto the IAT sensor (**Figure 2**).

13. Lower and secure the fuel tank as described in Chapter Eight or Nine.

ENGINE COMPRESSION TEST

A cranking compression test is one of the quickest ways to check the internal condition of the engine (piston rings, pistons, head gasket, valves and cylinders). It is a good idea to check compression at each tune-up, record it in the maintenance log at the back of the manual, and compare it with subsequent readings.

Use the spark plug tool included in the motorcycle's tool kit and a screw-in type compression gauge with a flexible adapter (**Figure 8**). Before using the

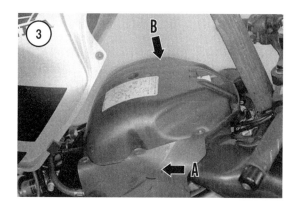

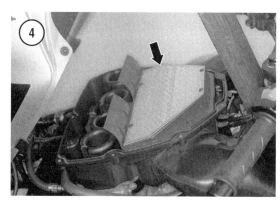

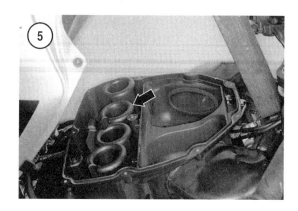

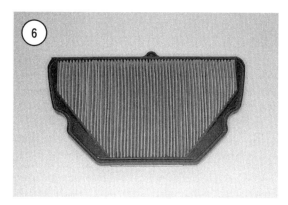

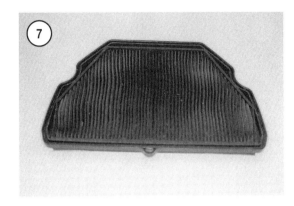

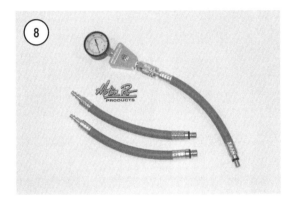

gauge, check that the rubber gasket on the end of the adapter is not cracked or damaged; this gasket seals the cylinder to ensure accurate compression readings.

NOTE
*The compression gauge in **Figure 8** is made by Motion Pro and includes flexible adapters for each spark plug thread size.*

NOTE
Make sure the socket used to remove the spark plugs is equipped with a rubber insert that secures the spark plug. This type of socket is included in the standard tool kit and is necessary for both removal and installation, since the spark plugs are located in the cylinder head receptacles. It is not possible to remove or install the spark plugs by hand.

1. Make sure the battery is fully charged to ensure proper engine cranking speed.

2. Run the engine until it reaches normal operating temperature, then turn it off.

3. Remove the spark plug/ignition coils as described under *Spark Plug Removal* in this chapter.

WARNING
Step 4 must be performed to disable the fuel system. Otherwise, fuel will enter the cylinders when the engine is turned over during the compression test, flooding the cylinders and creating explosive fuel vapors.

4A. On 1999-2000 models, disconnect the fuel pump 2P (black) electrical connector (**Figure 9**).

4B. On 2001-on models, disconnect the fuel pump 3P (black) electrical connector (**Figure 10**).

5. Lubricate the threads of the compression gauge adapter with a *small* amount of antiseize compound and carefully thread the gauge into one of the spark plug holes.

CAUTION
Do not crank the engine more than is absolutely necessary. When the spark plug direct ignition coil leads are disconnected, the electronic ignition will produce the highest voltage possible

and the coils may overheat and be damaged.

6. Move the engine stop switch to the RUN position, then turn the ignition switch to the ON position. *Open the throttle completely* and using the starter, crank the engine over until there is no further rise in pressure. Maximum pressure is usually reached within 4-7 seconds of engine cranking. Record the reading and the cylinder number. The number one cylinder is on the left side.

7. Repeat Step 5 and Step 6 for the other cylinders.

8. When interpreting the results, actual readings are not as important as the difference between the readings. Standard compression pressure is specified in **Table 2**. Low compression indicates worn or broken rings, leaky or sticky valves, blown head gasket or a combination of all three.

    a. If the compression reading does not differ between cylinders by more than 10 percent, the rings and valves are in good condition.

    b. If a low reading (10 percent or more) is obtained on one of the cylinders, it indicates valve or ring trouble. To determine which, pour about a teaspoon of engine oil into the spark plug hole. Turn the engine over once to distribute the oil, then take another compression test and record the reading. If the compression increases significantly, the valves are good but the rings are defective on that cylinder. If compression does not increase, the valves require servicing.

NOTE
If the compression is low, the engine cannot be tuned to maximum performance.

9. Reverse Steps 1-5 to complete installation. Reinstall the spark plug/ignition coils as described under *Spark Plug Installation* in this chapter.

SPARK PLUGS

Inspect and replace the spark plugs at the service intervals specified in **Table 1**.

Spark Plug Removal

When properly read, a spark plug can reveal the operating condition of its cylinder. As each spark plug is removed, label it with its cylinder number. The num-

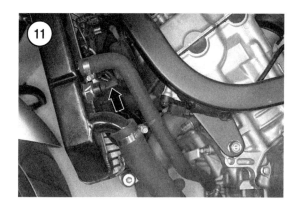

ber one cylinder is on the left side. Use the spark plug tools included in the motorcycle's tool kit.

NOTE
Make sure the socket used to remove the spark plugs is equipped with a rubber insert that secures the spark plug. This type of socket is included in the standard tool kit and is necessary for both removal and installation. The spark plugs are located deep within the cylinder head receptacles and cannot be reached by hand.

1. Remove both side fairing panels and the front inner faring as described in Chapter Sixteen.

2. Disconnect the cooling fan motor two-pin black electrical connector (**Figure 11**).

3. On 1999-2000 models, disconnect the electrical connector from the horn. Remove the mounting bolt and remove the horn.

4. Partially remove the radiator from the engine as follows:

a. Remove the lower bolt, nut and washer (**Figure 12**) securing the bottom of the radiator to the lower frame bracket.

b. On the left side, remove the upper bolt and washer (**Figure 13**) securing the top of the radiator to the frame.

c. On 2001-on models, remove the radiator upper mount grommet from the frame boss.

d. Cover the radiator with a towel to prevent damage to the cooling fins.

e. Swing the radiator forward so the lower mounting stay will not interfere with the radiator.

f. Slide the radiator to the right side and remove it from the frame boss.

g. Move the radiator forward and secure it to the front fork. Do not disconnect any of the coolant hoses from the radiator.

NOTE
Figure 14 is shown with the air filter housing removed to better illustrate this step.

5. Carefully disconnect the two-pin electrical connector from the top of each direct ignition coil (**Figure 14**).

6. Clean the cylinder head cover and frame surfaces with compressed air. Check for and remove all loose debris or small parts that could fall into the spark plug receptacles in the cylinder head cover.

7. Carefully pull straight up on the direct ignition coil and disengage it from the top of the spark plug. Remove it from the cylinder head cover and spark plug.

8. Once again, clean the cylinder head cover surfaces and spark plug receptacles with compressed air. Check for and remove all loose debris or small parts that could fall through the spark plug holes and into the engine.

CAUTION
Whenever the spark plugs are removed, dirt around them can fall into the spark plug hole. This can cause serious engine damage.

9. Install the spark plug socket onto the spark plug. Make sure it is correctly seated, then loosen and remove the spark plug. Mark the spark plug as to which cylinder it was removed from.

10. Repeat Steps 7-9 for the remaining spark plugs.

11. Inspect the spark plugs carefully. Look for plugs with broken center porcelain, excessively eroded electrodes and excessive carbon or oil fouling (**Figure 15**). Replace such plugs.

12. Also inspect the spark plug direct ignition coil for external wear or damage. Inspect the two-pin electrical connector for corrosion or damage. To service the spark plug direct ignition coils, refer to *Direct Ignition Coil* in Chapter Ten.

Spark Plug Gap

1999-2000 models

Carefully gap new plugs to ensure a reliable, consistent spark. To do this, use a spark plug gapping tool with a wire gauge.

1. Remove the new plugs from the box. If installed, unscrew the terminal nut (A, **Figure 16**) from the end of the spark plug. It is not used with this ignition system.

SPARK PLUG CONDITIONS

⑮

NORMAL

GAP BRIDGED

CARBON FOULED

OVERHEATED

OIL FOULED

SUSTAINED PREIGNITION

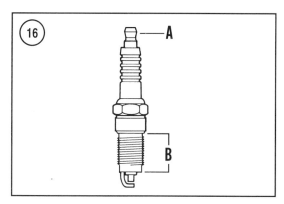

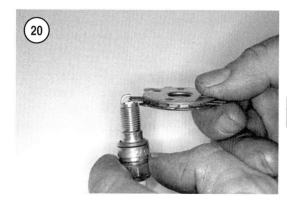

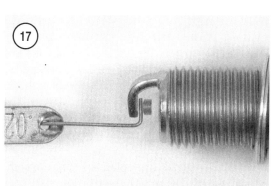

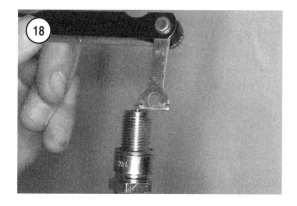

2. Insert a round feeler gauge between the center and the side electrode of the plug (**Figure 17**). The correct gap is listed in **Table 2**. If the gap is correct, a slight drag should be felt as the gauge is pulled through. If there is no drag, or if the gauge will not pass through, bend the side electrode with the gapping tool (**Figure 18**) to set the proper gap listed in **Table 2**.

3. Repeat for all four spark plugs.

2001-on models

The spark plugs used on these models are equipped with an iridium center electrode as shown in **Figure 19**. The center electrode is very small with a fine needle-like point. The gap on this type of spark plug *cannot be adjusted*; it can only be inspected.

1. Remove the spark plug from the engine as described in this section.

2. Insert a 1.0 mm (0.04 in.) round feeler gauge between the center and the side electrode of the plug (**Figure 20**). Make sure a 1.0 mm (0.04 in.) wire gauge *cannot* pass between the gap. If this thickness wire gauge can pass through, the spark plug is worn and must be replaced.

3. Inspect the electrode for wear, burning condition or damage. If the electrode is contaminated with an accumulation of dirt, replace the spark plug.

4. Replace the spark plug if the center electrode is worn off. It must have a sharp pointed end.

5. Inspect the insulator for damage.

6. Repeat for all four spark plugs.

Spark Plug Installation

1. Apply a *light* coat of antiseize compound onto the threads of the spark plug before installing it. Re-

move any compound that contacts the plug's firing tip. Do not use engine oil on the plug threads.

CAUTION
The cylinder head is aluminum. If the spark plug is cross-threaded into the cylinder head, the internal threads will be damaged.

2. The spark plugs are recessed into the cylinder head and cannot be started by hand. Install the spark plug into the spark plug socket. Make sure it is properly seated in the socket so it will not fall out during installation. Carefully screw the spark plug in by hand until it seats. Very little effort is required. If force is necessary, the plug may be cross-threaded. Unscrew it and try again.

3. Tighten the spark plug to 12 N•m (106 in.-lb.). If a torque wrench is not available, tighten it 1/2 turn after the gasket contacts the head.

CAUTION
Do not overtighten the spark plug. This will crush the gasket and destroy its sealing ability. It may also damage the spark plug threads in the cylinder head.

4. Carefully push straight down on the direct ignition coil and engage it onto the top of the spark plug. Push it down until it seats completely on the spark plug and the cylinder head cover.

5. Connect the two-pin electrical connector onto the top of each direct ignition coil (**Figure 14**).

6. Repeat for each spark plug.

7. Install the partially removed radiator onto the engine as follows:
   a. Disconnect the radiator from the front fork.
   b. Carefully move the radiator to the left side and onto the frame boss.
   c. Move the radiator toward the rear, making sure not to interfere with the lower mounting stay.
   d. Remove the protective cover from the radiator.
   e. On 2001-on models, install the radiator upper mount grommet onto the frame boss.
   f. On the left side, install the upper bolt and washer (**Figure 13**) securing the top of the radiator to the frame.
   g. Install the lower bolt, nut and washer (**Figure 12**) securing the bottom of the radiator to the lower frame bracket.

8. On 1999-2000 models, install the horn and mounting bolt. Connect the electrical connector onto it.

9. Connect the cooling fan motor two-pin black electrical connector (**Figure 11**).

10. Install both side fairing panels and the front inner fairing as described in Chapter Sixteen.

Spark Plug Heat Range

Spark plugs are available in various heat ranges, hotter or colder than the plugs originally installed by the manufacturer.

Select a plug with a heat range designed for the loads and conditions under which the motorcycle will be operated. A plug with an incorrect heat range can foul, overheat and cause piston damage.

In general, use a hot plug for low speeds and low temperatures. Use a cold plug for high speeds, high engine loads and high temperatures. The plug should operate hot enough to burn off unwanted deposits, but not so hot that it is damaged or causes preignition. To determine if plug heat range is correct, remove each spark plug and examine the insulator.

Do not change the spark plug heat range to compensate for adverse engine or air/fuel mixture conditions. Compare the insulator to those in **Figure 15** when reading plugs.

When replacing plugs, make sure the reach (B, **Figure 16**) is correct. A longer than standard plug could interfere with the piston, causing engine damage. Refer to **Table 2** for recommended spark plugs.

Spark Plug Inspection

Inspecting or reading the spark plugs can provide a significant amount of information regarding engine performance. Reading plugs that have been in use will give an indication of spark plug operation, air/fuel mixture composition and engine conditions (such as oil consumption or piston wear). Before checking new spark plugs, operate the motorcycle under a medium load for approximately 6 miles (10 km). Avoid prolonged idling before shutting off the engine. Remove the spark plugs as described in this chapter. Examine each plug and compare it to those in **Figure 15**.

Normal condition

If the plug has a light tan- or gray-colored deposit and no abnormal gap wear or erosion, good engine, fuel system and ignition conditions are indicated.

The plug in use is of the proper heat range and may be serviced and returned to use.

Carbon fouled

Soft, dry, sooty deposits covering the entire firing end of the plug are evidence of incomplete combustion. Even though the firing end of the plug is dry, the plug's insulation decreases when in this condition. The carbon forms an electrical path that bypasses the spark plug electrodes, resulting in a misfire condition. One or more of the following can cause carbon fouling:
1. Rich fuel mixture.
2. Cold spark plug heat range.
3. Clogged air filter.
4. Improperly operating ignition component.
5. Ignition component failure.
6. Low engine compression.
7. Prolonged idling.

Oil fouled

The tip of an oil fouled plug has a black insulator tip, a damp oily film over the firing end and a carbon layer over the entire nose. The electrodes are not worn. Oil fouled spark plugs may be cleaned in an emergency, but it is better to replace them. It is important to correct the cause of the fouling before the engine is returned to service. Common causes for this condition are:
1. Incorrect air/fuel mixture.
2. Faulty fuel injection system (fuel injected models).
3. Low idle speed or prolonged idling.
4. Ignition component failure.
5. Cold spark plug heat range.
6. Engine still being broken in.
7. Valve guides worn.
8. Piston rings worn or broken.

Gap bridging

Plugs with this condition exhibit gaps shorted out by combustion deposits between the electrodes. If this condition is encountered, check for excessive carbon or oil in the combustion chamber. Be sure to locate and correct the cause of this condition.

Overheating

Badly worn electrodes and premature gap wear are signs of overheating, along with a gray or white blistered porcelain insulator surface. The most common cause for this condition is using a spark plug of the wrong heat range (too hot). If the spark plug is in the correct heat range and is overheating, consider the following causes:
1. Lean air/fuel mixture.
2. Faulty fuel injection operation (fuel injected models).
3. Improperly operating ignition component.
4. Cooling system malfunction.
5. Engine lubrication system malfunction.
6. Engine air leak.
7. Improper spark plug installation.
8. No spark plug gasket.

Worn out

Corrosive gases formed by combustion and high voltage sparks have eroded the electrodes. A spark plug in this condition requires more voltage to fire under hard acceleration. Replace with a new spark plug.

Preignition

If the electrodes are melted, preignition is almost certainly the cause. Check for intake air leaks at the manifolds and carburetors, or throttle bodies, and advanced ignition timing. It is also possible that a plug of the wrong heat range (too hot) is being used. Find the cause of the preignition before returning the engine into service.

IGNITION TIMING INSPECTION

The engine is equipped with a non-adjustable transistorized ignition system. However, periodically check the timing to make sure all ignition components are operating correctly. Incorrect ignition timing can cause a drastic loss of engine performance. It may also cause overheating, detonation and engine damage.

Before starting this procedure, check all electrical connections related to the ignition system. Make sure all connections are tight and free of corrosion. Refer to *Ignition System* in Chapter Ten.

> *WARNING*
> *Do not start and run the motorcycle in an enclosed area. The exhaust gasses contain carbon monoxide, a colorless, odorless, poisonous gas. The carbon monoxide levels build quickly in an en-*

closed area and can cause uncon-sciousness and death in a short time.

1. Remove the right side fairing as described in Chapter Sixteen.

2. Start the engine and let it reach normal operating temperature. Shut off the engine.

3. Remove the timing hole cap and its O-ring (**Figure 21**).

4. Connect the timing light to the No. 1 spark plug wire, following the manufacturer's instructions.

5. Start the engine and set the idle speed as described in this chapter.

6A. On 1999-2000 models, check the ignition timing as follows:

   a. Aim the timing light at the timing hole and pull the trigger.

   b. On 49-state, Canada and U.K. models, the ignition timing is correct if the pulse generator rotor *three punch marks* align with the index notch on the right crankcase rotor cover (**Figure 22**).

   c. On California models, the ignition timing is correct if the pulse generator rotor *two punch marks* align with the index notch on the right crankcase rotor cover (**Figure 23**).

6B. On 2001-on models, check the ignition timing as follows:

   a. Aim the timing light at the timing hole and pull the trigger.

   b. The ignition timing is correct if the index notch on the right crankcase rotor cover aligns between the *three punch marks* and the *F* mark on the pulse generator rotor (**Figure 24**).

7. Turn off the engine and disconnect the timing light.

8. If the timing is incorrect, there is a problem with one or more ignition system components; refer to *Ignition System* in Chapter Two. There is no method of adjusting ignition timing.

9. Apply engine oil onto the timing hole cap O-ring and molybdenum disulfide grease onto the cap's threads. Then install the cap and tighten to 18 N•m (13 ft.-lb.).

10. Install the right side fairing as described in Chapter Sixteen.

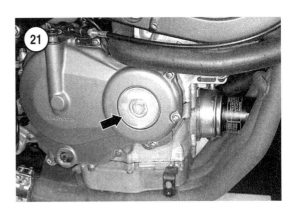

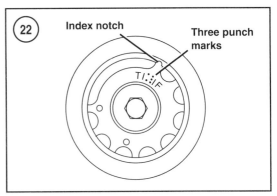

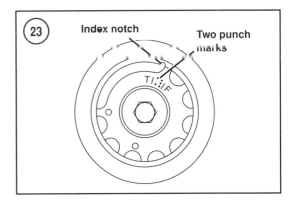

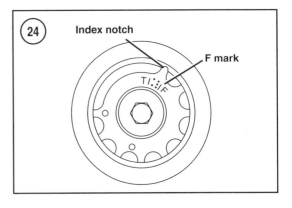

3

| ㉕ | CAMSHAFT SHIM CHART | | | | | | | | ↑ FRONT | |

EXHAUST								
	Cyl. No. 1		Cyl. No. 2		Cyl. No. 3		Cyl. No. 4	
Clearance								
Shim No.								

INTAKE								
	Cyl. No. 1		Cyl. No. 2		Cyl. No. 3		Cyl. No. 4	
Clearance								
Shim No.								

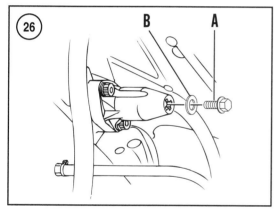

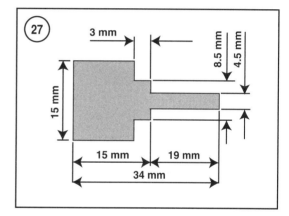

VALVE CLEARANCE

The correct valve clearances for all models are listed in **Table 2**.

Measurement

In this procedure, the engine is shown removed from the frame. Do not remove the engine to perform this procedure. Use the chart shown in **Figure 25** to keep track of the valve clearance measurements and the associated shims in relation to the cylinder number and note if it is an intake or exhaust valve.

NOTE
Valve clearance measurement and adjustment must be performed with the engine cold (below 35° C [95° F]).

1. Remove the cylinder cover as described in Chapter Four.
2. Loosen and remove the timing hole cap and O-ring (**Figure 21**).
3. Remove all of the spark plugs as described in this chapter. This will make it easier to turn the engine by hand.
4. On 2001-on models, perform the following:
   a. Remove the camshaft drive chain tensioner sealing bolt (A, **Figure 26**) and washer (B).

   NOTE
   *Refer to **Figure 27** and fabricate the special tool from a piece of 1.0 mm thick steel.*

   b. Using the special tool (**Figure 28**), rotate the tensioner lifter shaft *clockwise* to the fully retracted position and lock the tensioner in this position with the special tool.

5. Correctly position the engine for measuring valve clearances:

   a. Using the bolt on the pulse generator rotor (**Figure 29**), rotate the engine *clockwise*, as viewed from the right side of the motorcycle, until the pulse generator rotor *T* mark aligns with the index notch on the right crankcase cover (**Figure 30**).

   b. The camshaft driven sprocket *IN* and *EX* timing marks must be flush with the top surface of the cylinder head and must face outward (**Figure 31**).

NOTE
*If the sprocket IN and EX timing marks face inward, the engine is positioned incorrectly. If this condition exists, rotate the engine **clockwise**, as viewed from the right side of the motorcycle, 360° (one full turn) and realign the pulse generator rotor T mark with the index notch on the right crankcase cover (**Figure 30**).*

6. With the engine in this position, measure the clearance of the No. 1 and No. 3 cylinders' intake valves (**Figure 32**) as described in Step 7.

7. Check the clearance by inserting a flat feeler gauge between the cam and the valve lifter (**Figure 33**). When the clearance is correct, there will be a slight drag on the feeler gauge when it is inserted and withdrawn. Record the clearance and cylinder number and whether it is an intake or exhaust valve. The clearance dimensions will be used during the adjustment procedure if valve adjustment is necessary.

8. Rotate the crankshaft clockwise 180° (1/2 turn) until the pulse generator rotor *punch* mark aligns with the index notch on the right crankcase cover (**Figure 34**). With the engine in this position, measure the clearance of the No. 2 and No. 4 cylinders' exhaust valves (**Figure 35**) as described in Step 7.

9. Rotate the crankshaft clockwise 180° (1/2 turn) until the pulse generator rotor *T* mark aligns with the index notch on the right crankcase cover (**Figure 30**). With the engine in this position, measure the clearance of the No. 2 and No. 4 cylinders' intake valves (**Figure 36**) as described in Step 7.

10. Rotate the crankshaft clockwise 180° (1/2 turn) until the pulse generator rotor *punch* mark aligns

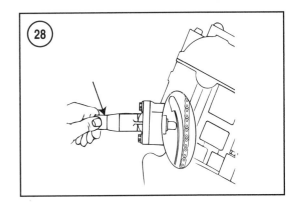

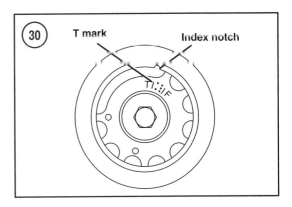

T mark   Index notch

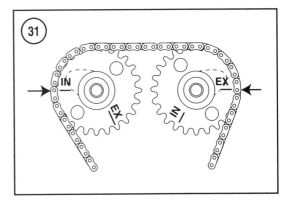

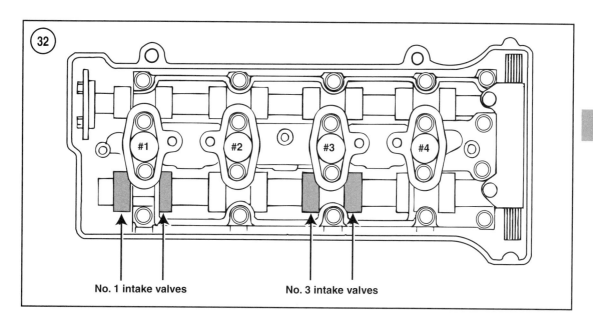

No. 1 intake valves   No. 3 intake valves

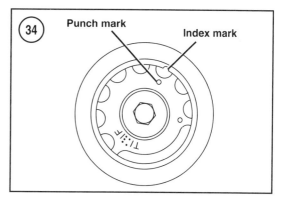

Punch mark   Index mark

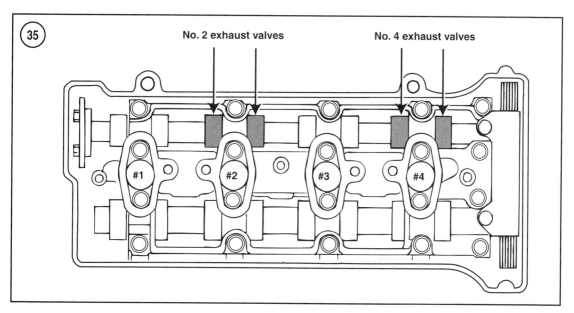

No. 2 exhaust valves   No. 4 exhaust valves

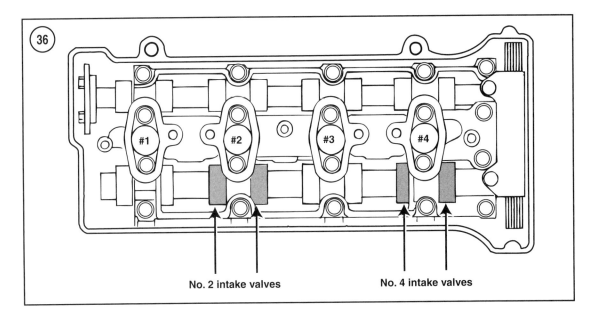

No. 2 intake valves   No. 4 intake valves

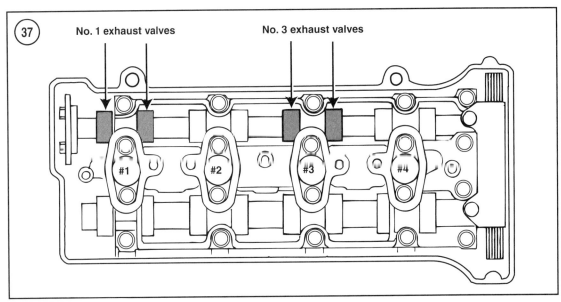

No. 1 exhaust valves   No. 3 exhaust valves

with the index notch on the right crankcase cover (**Figure 34**). With the engine in this position, measure the clearance of the No. 1 and No. 3 cylinders' exhaust valves (**Figure 37**) as described in Step 7.

11. If any of the valve clearance dimensions are incorrect, replace the shim installed on top of the valve keeper with a shim of a different thickness. The shims are available from a Honda dealership in 0.025 mm increments that range from 1.200 to 2.800 mm in thickness. To adjust the valve clearance, refer to *Adjustment* in the following procedure.

12. If all of the valve clearances are correct, continue with Step 13.

13. On 2001-on models, perform the following:

   a. Remove the stopper tool from the camshaft chain tensioner.

   b. Install the sealing washer and bolt onto the camshaft chain tensioner and tighten securely.

14. Reinstall the spark plugs as described in this chapter.

15. Install the cylinder head cover as described in Chapter Four.

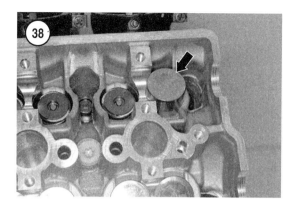

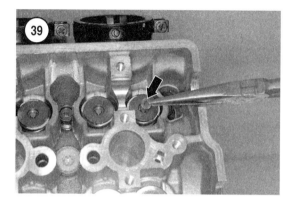

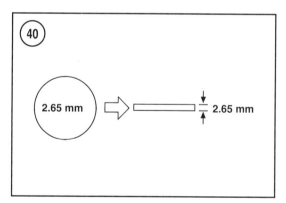

2.65 mm ⟹ ▭ 2.65 mm

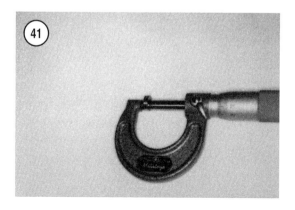

16. Apply engine oil onto the timing cap O-ring and molybdenum disulfide grease onto the cap's threads. Then install the cap and tighten to 18 N•m (13 ft.-lb.).

Adjustment

1. Remove the camshafts as described under *Camshaft Removal* in Chapter Four.
2. When removing the valve lifters and shims, note the following:
   a. Identify and store valve lifters and shims so they can be installed in their original locations. This step is critical to ensure correct valve clearance adjustment and assembly.
   b. The shims are located under the valve lifters and may stick to the valve lifters when the lifter is removed. Remove the lifter carefully to avoid dropping the shim into the crankcase. Use a magnet to remove the lifter. The shims can be removed with a magnet or tweezers.
   c. Clean the valve lifters and shims in solvent and dry with compressed air.
3. Remove the valve lifter (**Figure 38**) and shim (**Figure 39**) for each valve to be adjusted. Label and store each lifter and shim assembly in the marked container.

> *NOTE*
> *Always measure the thickness of the old shim with a micrometer to make sure of the exact thickness of the shim. If the shim is worn to less than the indicated thickness marked on it (**Figure 40**), the calculations for a new shim will be inaccurate. Measure the new shim to make sure it is marked correctly and not worn.*

4. Measure the thickness of the old shim with a micrometer (**Figure 41**).
5. Using the recorded valve clearance, the specified valve clearance listed in **Table 2** and the old shim thickness, determine the new shim thickness with the following equation:
   a = (b - c) + d
   where:
   a is the new shim thickness.
   b is the measured valve clearance.
   c is the specified valve clearance.
   d is the old shim thickness.

> *NOTE*
> *The following numbers are for example only. Use the numbers recorded*

*during the **Valve Clearance Measurement** procedure.*

For example: If the measured intake valve clearance is 0.26 mm, the old shim thickness is 1.870 mm and the specified valve clearance is 0.20 mm (midpoint of specification), then: a = (0.26 - 0.20) + 1.870, a = 1.930 (new shim thickness).

NOTE
If the required shim thickness exceeds 2.800 mm, the valve seat is heavily carboned and must be cleaned or refaced.

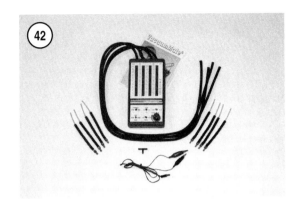

6. Apply clean engine oil to both sides of the new shim.
7. Install the new shim (**Figure 39**) and the valve lifter (**Figure 38**).
8. Repeat for each valve to be adjusted.
9. Install the camshafts as described under *Camshaft Installation* in Chapter Four.
10. Rotate the crankshaft clockwise several times to turn the camshafts and seat the new shims.
11. Recheck the valve clearances as described in the preceding procedure. Repeat this procedure until all valve clearances are correct.
12. Reinstall the spark plugs as described in this chapter.
13. Install the cylinder head cover as described in Chapter Four.
14. Apply engine oil onto the timing hole cap O-ring and molybdenum disulfide grease onto the cap's threads. Then install the cap and tighten to 18 N•m (13 ft.-lb.).

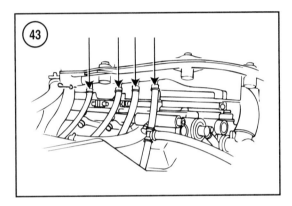

CARBURETOR SYNCHRONIZATION (1999-2000 MODELS)

WARNING
Do not start and run the motorcycle in an enclosed area. The exhaust gasses contain carbon monoxide, a colorless, tasteless, poisonous gas. Carbon monoxide levels build quickly in a small enclosed area and can cause unconsciousness and death in a short time.

Correct carburetor synchronization ensures that each cylinder receives the same air/fuel mixture by synchronizing the vacuum in each carburetor. When the synchronization is correct, the engine

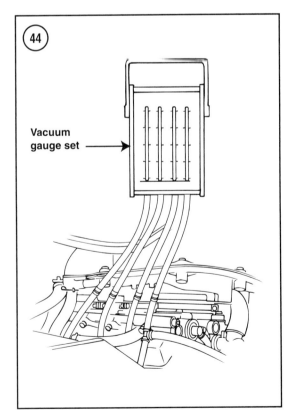

Vacuum gauge set

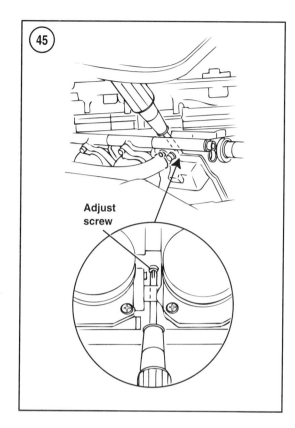

Adjust screw

warms up faster and throttle response, performance and mileage are improved.

Prior to synchronizing the carburetors, make sure the air filter element is clean and that the valve clearances are correct. Also ensure the ignition system is operating correctly by checking the ignition timing.

A vacuum gauge set (**Figure 42**) that can measure the vacuum in each cylinder simultaneously is required to synchronize the starter valves. The Motion Pro vacuum gauge used in this procedure can

be purchased through most motorcycle dealers and parts suppliers.

1. Start the engine and let it reach normal operating temperature.

2. Install the portable tachometer following the manufacturer's instructions.

3. Make sure the idle speed is within the range specified in Table 2. If necessary, adjust the idle speed as described in this chapter. Shut off the engine.

4. Remove the fuel tank as described in Chapter Eight.

WARNING
When using an auxiliary fuel tank, make sure the tank is secure and that all fuel lines are tight to prevent leaks.

NOTE
Fuel tanks from small displacement motorcycles, ATV's and lawn mowers make excellent auxiliary fuel tanks. Make sure the tank is mounted securely and positioned so that the connecting fuel hose is not kinked or obstructed.

5. Install an auxiliary fuel tank onto the motorcycle, and attach its fuel hose to the carburetor assembly.

6. Label and disconnect the four vacuum hoses from the air filter housing (**Figure 43**).

7. Balance the vacuum gauge set, following the manufacturer's instructions, prior to using it in this procedure.

8. Connect the vacuum gauge set to the vacuum hoses, following the manufacturer's instructions (**Figure 44**).

9. Start the engine and let it idle.

10. If the carburetors are correctly balanced, the vacuum gauges will all be at the same level or within 30 mm Hg (1.2 in. Hg) of the No. 4 carburetor.

NOTE
The No. 4 carburetor is the base carburetor. It has no synchronizing screw. The other carburetors must be synchronized to the No. 4 carburetor.

11. Turn the synchronizing screws (**Figure 45** and **Figure 46**) and adjust the No. 1, 2 and 3 carburetors so each have the same gauge reading as the No. 4 carburetor. Snap the throttle a few times and re-

check the synchronization readings. Readjust synchronization if required.

12. If necessary, adjust the idle speed to the specification in **Table 2**.

13. Shut off the engine.

14. Disconnect the auxiliary fuel tank and the vacuum gauge set from the carburetors.

15. Connect the four vacuum hoses onto the fittings on the air filter housing (**Figure 47**). Make sure they are correctly seated to avoid a vacuum leak.

16. Install the fuel tank as described in Chapter Eight.

17. Restart the engine and check the engine idle speed.

FUEL INJECTION STARTER VALVE SYNCHRONIZATION (2001-ON MODELS)

WARNING
Do not start and run the motorcycle in an enclosed area. The exhaust gasses contain carbon monoxide, a colorless, tasteless, poisonous gas. Carbon monoxide levels build quickly in a small enclosed area and can cause unconsciousness and death in a short time.

Correct starter valve synchronization ensures that each cylinder receives the same air/fuel mixture by synchronizing the vacuum in each throttle intake port. When the synchronization is correct, the engine warms up faster and throttle response, performance and mileage are improved.

Prior to synchronizing the starter valves, make sure the air filter element is clean and that the valve clearances are correct. Also ensure the ignition system is operating correctly by checking the ignition timing.

A vacuum gauge set (**Figure 42**) that can measure the vacuum in each cylinder simultaneously is required to synchronize the starter valves. The Motion Pro vacuum gauge used in this procedure can be purchased through most motorcycle dealers and parts suppliers.

1. Start the engine and warm it up fully.

2. Connect the tachometer to the engine following the manufacturer's instructions.

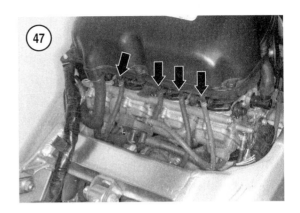

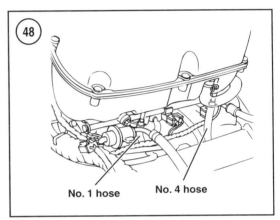

No. 1 hose   No. 4 hose

3. Adjust the idle speed as described in this chapter, then turn the engine off.

4. Raise and support the fuel tank as described in Chapter Nine.

CAUTION
When removing the vacuum caps in the following steps, pinch the end of the cap to remove it. Pinching the rubber cap body and then trying to remove it can damage the cap.

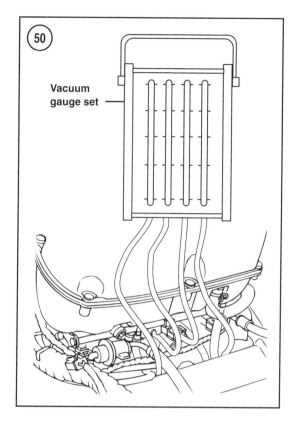

Vacuum gauge set

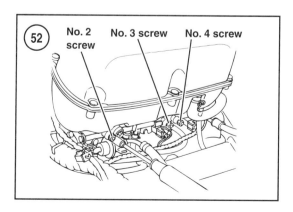

No. 2 screw   No. 3 screw   No. 4 screw

NOTE
Some of the following steps are shown with the throttle body removed to better show the location of the vacuum inlet fittings. Do not remove the throttle body for this procedure.

NOTE
Label the vacuum hoses before disconnecting them in the following steps.

5. Disconnect the No. 1 and 4 vacuum hoses from the air filter housing (**Figure 48**). Disconnect the vacuum hose from the pressure regulator (**Figure 49**). Disconnect the No. 2 vacuum hose from the 5-way joint. Connect the four hoses to the vacuum gauge, following its manufacturer's instructions (**Figure 50**).

6. Balance the vacuum gauge set, following its manufacturer's instructions, prior to using it in this procedure.

7. Disconnect the PAIR air tube (**Figure 51**) from both tube fittings on the reed valve covers on the cylinder head cover. Plug the reed valve covers' tube fittings.

8. Start the engine and let it idle at the speed specified in **Table 2**. If necessary, adjust the idle speed as described in this chapter.

9. If the starter valves are correctly balanced, the vacuum gauges will all be at the same level or within 20 mm (0.8 in.) Hg of the No. 1 (base) starter valve.

NOTE
The No. 1 throttle valve is the base throttle valve and has no synchronization screw; the other three throttle valves must be synchronized to it.

10. Adjust the No. 2, No. 3 and No. 4 (**Figure 52**) screws until they have the same gauge readings as the No. 1 throttle valve.

11. Snap the throttle a few times and recheck the synchronization readings. The vacuum gauges must all be at the same level or within 20 mm (0.8 in.) Hg of the No. 1 starter valve. Readjust the idle speed and synchronization if required. Repeat until all adjustments remain the same.

12. Disconnect the plugs from the tube fitting on the reed valve covers on the cylinder head cover. Connect the PAIR air tubes (**Figure 51**) onto the fit-

tings. Make sure the hoses and air tube are tight to prevent vacuum leaks.

13. Disconnect the vacuum gauge set.

14. Connect the vacuum hose onto the pressure regulator (A, **Figure 53**).

15. Connect the No. 1 (B, **Figure 53**) and No. 4 (C) vacuum hoses onto the air filter housing fittings. Make sure they are properly seated to avoid a vacuum leak.

16. Lower and secure the fuel tank as described in Chapter Nine.

17. Restart the engine and reset the engine idle speed, if necessary.

18. Shut off the engine.

IDLE SPEED ADJUSTMENT (ALL MODELS)

Prior to adjusting the idle speed, make sure the air filter element is clean, the valve clearances are correct and the carburetors or fuel injector starter valves are synchronized.

1. Make sure the throttle cable free play is adjusted correctly. Check and adjust as described in this chapter.

2. On fuel injected models, remove the left side fairing panel as described in Chapter Sixteen.

3. Start the engine and warm it to its normal operating temperature.

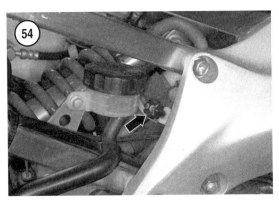

NOTE
The engine must be at normal operating temperature for the idle speed adjustment to be accurate.

4A. On carbureted models, on the right side, turn the idle speed knob (**Figure 54**) in or out to adjust the idle speed. The correct idle speed is listed in **Table 2**.

4B. On fuel injected models, on the left side, turn the idle speed knob (**Figure 55**) in or out to adjust the idle speed. The correct idle speed is listed in **Table 2**.

5. Open and close the throttle a couple of times and check for variations in idle speed. Readjust if necessary.

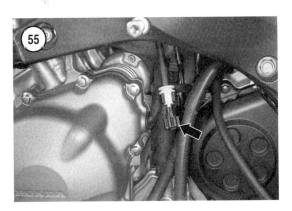

WARNING
With the engine running at idle speed, move the handlebars from side to side. If the idle speed increases during this movement, either the throttle cables need adjusting or they may be incorrectly routed through the frame. Correct this problem immediately. Do not ride the motorcycle in this unsafe condition.

6. On fuel injected models, install the left side fairing panel as described in Chapter Sixteen.

FUEL HOSE INSPECTION

Inspect the fuel hoses at the intervals specified in **Table 1**.

1. Raise and support the fuel tank as described in Chapter Eight.

2. Inspect the fuel hoses for leakage, hardness, age deterioration or other damage.

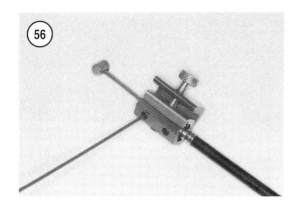

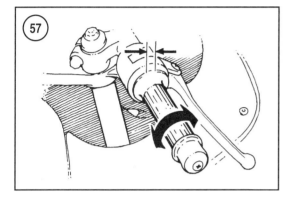

3. Replace damaged fuel hoses as described in Chapter Seven.

4. Lower and secure the fuel tank.

CONTROL CABLE LUBRICATION (NON-NYLON LINED CABLES ONLY)

Lubricate the non-nylon lined control cables with a cable lubricant and cable lubricator (**Figure 56**) during cable adjustment or if they become stiff or sluggish. The main cause of cable breakage or stiffness is improper lubrication. Periodic lubrication ensures a long service life. Inspect the cables for fraying, and check the sheath for chafing. Replace any defective cables.

CAUTION
When servicing nylon-lined and other aftermarket cables, follow the cable manufacturer's instructions.

1. Disconnect each throttle cable as described under *Throttle Cable Replacement* in Chapter Eight or Nine.

2. On carbureted models, disconnect the choke cable at both ends as described under *Choke Cable Replacement* in Chapter Eight.

3. Disconnect the clutch cable as described under *Clutch Cable Replacement* in Chapter Six.

4. Attach a cable lubricator (**Figure 56**) to each cable, following the manufacturer's instructions.

5. Insert the nozzle of the lubricant can into the lubricator, press the button on the can and hold it down until the lubricant begins to flow out of the other end of the cable. If the lubricant flows out from the cable lubricator, the lubricator is not installed properly onto the end of the cable. The lubricator may have to be installed a few times to get it to seal properly. Place a shop cloth at the end of the cable(s) to catch all excess lubricant that flows out.

NOTE
If lubricant does not flow out the end of the cable, check the entire cable for fraying, bending or other damage.

6. Remove the lubricator and wipe off all excess lubricant from the cable. Place a dab of grease onto the cable barrel before reconnecting it.

7. Reverse Step 1 and Step 2 to install the cables.

8. Adjust the throttle cables and clutch cable as described in this chapter. There is no adjustment procedure for the choke cable.

THROTTLE CABLE (ALL MODELS)

Throttle Operation Inspection

Check the throttle operation at the intervals specified in **Table 1**.

Check for smooth throttle operation from the fully closed to fully open positions. Check at various steering positions. The throttle lever must return to the fully closed position without any hesitation.

Check the throttle cables for damage, wear or deterioration. Make sure the throttle cables are not kinked at any place.

If the throttle lever does not return to the fully closed position smoothly and the cables do not appear to be damaged, lubricate the throttle cables as described in this chapter. At the same time, clean and lubricate the throttle grip housing with a lightweight oil. If the throttle still does not return properly, the cables are probably kinked or routed incorrectly. Replace the throttle cables as described in Chapter Eight or Nine.

Check free play at the throttle grip flange (**Figure 57**). The free play specification is 2-6 mm (3/32-1/4 in.). If adjustment is required, perform the following procedure.

**Throttle Cable Adjustment
(Carbureted Models)**

> *WARNING*
> *If idle speed increases when the handlebar is turned, check the throttle cable routing. Correct this problem immediately. Do not ride the motorcycle in this unsafe condition.*

1. If minor adjustment is required, perform the following at the throttle grip:

   a. Loosen the locknut (A, **Figure 58**) and turn the adjuster (B) in or out to achieve 2-6 mm (3/32-1/4 in.) free play rotation.

   b. Tighten the locknut and recheck the adjustment.

2. If major adjustment is necessary, perform the following at the carburetor assembly:

   a. Raise and support the fuel tank as described in Chapter Eight.

   b. Loosen the cable locknut (A, **Figure 59**) at the throttle valve and turn the cable adjuster (B) to achieve proper free play rotation at the throttle grip. Tighten the locknut securely.

   c. Recheck free play. If necessary, readjust the upper cable adjuster as described in Step 1.

3. Operate the throttle a few times. The throttle grip should now be adjusted correctly. If not, the throttle cables may have stretched. Replace cables in this condition.

4. Lower and secure the fuel tank as described in Chapter Eight.

5. Sit on the seat and start the engine with the transmission in NEUTRAL. Turn the handlebars from lock to lock to check for idle speed variances due to improper cable routing or damage.

> *WARNING*
> *If idle speed increases when the handlebar is turned, check the throttle cable routing. Do not ride the motorcycle in this unsafe condition.*

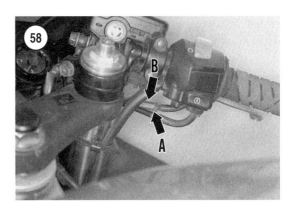

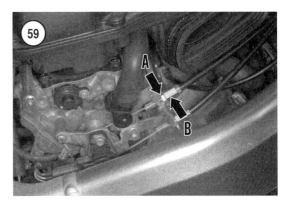

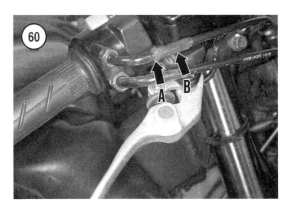

6. Test ride the motorcycle, slowly at first, to make sure the throttle cables are operating correctly. Readjust if necessary.

**Throttle Cable Adjustment
(Fuel Injected Models)**

> *WARNING*
> *If idle speed increases when the handlebar is turned, check the throttle cable routing. Correct this problem*

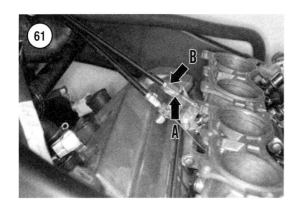

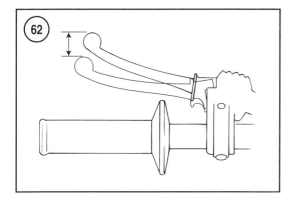

immediately. Do not ride the motorcycle in this unsafe condition.

1. If minor adjustment is required, perform the following at the throttle grip:
   a. On the throttle pull cable, loosen the locknut (A, **Figure 60**) and turn the adjuster (B) in or out to achieve 2-6 mm (3/32-1/4 in.) free play rotation.
   b. Tighten the locknut and recheck the adjustment.
2. If major adjustment is necessary, perform the following at the throttle body assembly:
   a. Raise and support the fuel tank as described in Chapter Nine.
   b. Loosen the cable locknut (A, **Figure 61**) at the throttle valve and turn cable adjuster (B) to achieve proper free play rotation at the throttle grip. Tighten the locknut securely.
   c. Recheck free play. If necessary, readjust the upper cable adjuster as described in Step 1.
3. Operate the throttle a few times. The throttle grip should now be adjusted correctly. If not, the throttle

cables may have stretched. Replace cables in this condition.
4. Lower and secure the fuel tank as described in Chapter Nine.
5. Sit on the seat and start the engine with the transmission in NEUTRAL. Turn the handlebars from lock to lock to check for idle speed variances due to improper cable routing or damage.

> *WARNING*
> *If idle speed increases when the handlebar is turned, check the throttle cable routing. Do not ride the motorcycle in this unsafe condition.*

6. Test ride the motorcycle, slowly at first, to make sure the throttle cables are operating correctly. Readjust if necessary.

STARTING ENRICHMENT (CHOKE) CABLE

Inspect the starting enrichment (choke) cable (carbureted models only) at both ends for fraying or other damage.

The choke lever mounted on the left handlebar should move smoothly between its fully open and fully closed positions. If the choke lever moves roughly, lubricate the choke cable as described in this section. Then check the cable for any kinks or other damage.

There is no adjustment procedure for the starting enrichment (choke) cable.

CLUTCH CABLE ADJUSTMENT

Check the clutch adjustment frequently and adjust it, if necessary, to compensate for clutch cable stretch and clutch plate wear. Excessive clutch lever play prevents the clutch from disengaging and causes clutch drag. Too little or no clutch lever free play does not allow the clutch to fully engage, resulting in clutch slippage. Both conditions cause unnecessary clutch wear.

The specified clutch lever free play is 10-20 mm (3/8-13/16 in.).
1. With the engine turned OFF, pull the clutch lever toward the handlebar until resistance is felt, then stop and measure the free play at the end of the clutch lever (**Figure 62**).

2. Minor adjustments can be made at the clutch hand lever adjuster. Loosen the locknut (A, **Figure 63**) and turn the clutch cable adjuster (B) in or out to obtain the correct amount of free play. Tighten the locknut.

NOTE
If sufficient free play cannot be obtained at the clutch hand lever, or if there is minimal thread engagement on the clutch adjuster, additional adjustment must be made at the opposite end of the clutch cable.

3. If the proper amount of free play cannot be achieved at the clutch hand lever adjuster, perform the following:
   a. Remove the right side faring panel as described in Chapter Sixteen.
   b. At the clutch hand lever on the handlebar, turn the adjuster (B, **Figure 63**) all the way in, then back it out one full turn. Tighten the locknut (A, **Figure 63**).
   c. At the clutch release lever, loosen the locknut (A, **Figure 64**) and turn the adjust nut (B) until the correct amount of free play is achieved at the clutch lever on the handlebar.
   d. Hold onto the adjust nut (B, **Figure 64**) and securely tighten the locknut (A).
   e. If necessary, fine-tune the adjustment at the clutch hand lever adjuster.
4. Make sure all locknuts are tight.
5. Start the engine and make sure the clutch operates correctly.
6. Install the right side faring panel as described in Chapter Sixteen.
7. If the proper amount of free play cannot be achieved by using this adjustment procedure, either the cable has stretched to the point that it needs to be replaced or the friction discs inside the clutch assembly are worn and need replacing. Refer to Chapter Six for clutch cable and clutch component service.

ENGINE OIL AND FILTER

Engine Oil Level Check

Check the engine oil level at the oil level gauge located on the bottom of the right crankcase cover.

NOTE
This procedure is shown with the right side faring panel removed to better illustrate the steps.

1. Park the motorcycle on level ground on the sidestand.
2. Start the engine and let it idle for 2-3 minutes.
3. Shut OFF the engine and let the oil settle for 3 minutes.

CAUTION
Do not check the oil level with the motorcycle on its sidestand; the oil will flow away from the gauge and result in a false reading.

4. Support the motorcycle upright on a level surface.
5. Check the engine oil level on the oil level gauge (A, **Figure 65**). The oil level must be between the upper and lower level lines.
6. If the oil level is low, remove the oil fill cap (B, **Figure 65**). Add the recommended oil (**Table 4**) to correct the level. Add oil slowly to avoid overfilling.

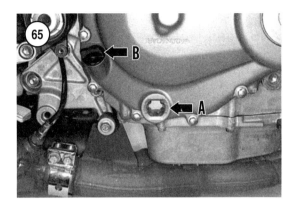

NOTE
*Refer to **Engine Oil and Filter Change** in this section for additional information on oil selection.*

7. Inspect the O-ring on the oil fill cap. Replace it if it is starting to deteriorate or harden.

8. Install the oil fill cap (B, **Figure 65**) and tighten securely.

9. If the oil level is too high, perform the following:

a. Remove the oil fill cap (B, **Figure 65**) and draw out the excess oil using a syringe or suitable pump.

b. Recheck the oil level and adjust if necessary.

c. Install the oil fill cap and tighten securely.

Engine Oil and Filter Change

Regular oil and filter changes contribute more to engine longevity than any other maintenance. The recommended oil and filter change interval is listed in **Table 1**. This assumes that the motorcycle is operated in moderate climates. If the motorcycle is not operated on a regular basis, consider using a time interval for oil changes. Combustion acids, formed by gasoline and water vapor, contaminate the oil even if the motorcycle is not run for several months. If a motorcycle is operated under dusty conditions, the oil gets dirty more quickly and should be changed more frequently than recommended.

Use only high-quality motorcycle oil with an API classification of SF or SG. The classification is printed on the container. Try always to use the same brand of oil. Honda recommends SAE 10W-40 oil under normal conditions.

CAUTION
Only use oils with an API classification of SF or SG. Other oils may contain friction modifiers that reduce frictional losses on engine components. Oil specifically designed for automotive engines can damage motorcycle engines and clutches.

NOTE
A socket-type oil filter wrench must be used when removing the oil filter because of the small working area between the oil filter and exhaust pipes.

NOTE
*Never dispose of motor oil in the trash, on the ground or down a storm drain. Many service stations and oil retailers will accept used oil and filters for recycling. Do not combine other fluids with motor oil to be recycled. To locate a recycler, contact the American Petroleum Institute (API) at **www.recycleoil.org**.*

NOTE
Warming the engine allows the oil to heat up; thus it flows freely and carries more contamination and sludge out with it.

1. Start the engine and run it until it is at normal operating temperature, then turn it off.
2. Remove both side fairing panels and the front inner faring panel as described in Chapter Sixteen.
3. Support the motorcycle on level ground on the sidestand when draining the engine oil. This ensures complete draining.

WARNING
The engine, exhaust pipes and oil are hot! Work quickly and carefully when removing the oil drain bolt and oil filter to avoid contacting the oil.

4. Clean the area around the oil drain bolt and oil filter.
5. Place a clean drip pan under the crankcase and remove the oil drain bolt (**Figure 66**) and washer.
6. Remove the oil filler cap (B, **Figure 65**), as this helps speed up the flow of oil.

7. Allow the oil to drain completely.

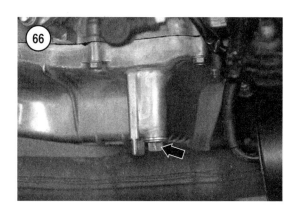

CAUTION
*Install the correct oil filter onto the motorcycle being worked on. For 1999-2000 models, use the longer oil filter (A, Figure 67) and for 2001-on models, use the shorter oil filter (B). Do **not** intermix these two different size filters.*

8. To replace the oil filter, perform the following:
   a. Temporarily install the oil drain bolt (**Figure 66**) and washer and tighten finger-tight. Then move the drain pan underneath the oil filter.
   b. Install a socket-type oil filter wrench squarely onto the oil filter (**Figure 68**) and turn the filter counterclockwise until oil begins to run out, then remove the oil filter.
   c. Hold the filter over the drain pan and pour out any remaining oil, then place the old filter in a plastic bag, seal it and discard it properly.
   d. Carefully clean the sealing surface on the crankcase for the oil filter. Do not allow any dirt or other debris to enter the engine.
   e. Lubricate the rubber seal on the new filter with engine oil.
   f. Install the new oil filter onto the threaded fitting on the crankcase.
   g. Tighten the filter by hand until it contacts the crankcase. Then tighten it an additional 3/4 turn. If using the oil filter socket, tighten to 26 N•m (19 ft.-lb.).

CAUTION
Overtightening the filter will cause it to leak.

9. Move the drain pan back underneath the oil drain bolt, then remove the bolt and its washer. Allow any remaining oil to drain into the pan.

10. Inspect the oil drain bolt gasket. Install a *new* gasket at every other oil change.

11. Install the oil drain bolt (**Figure 66**) and its gasket and tighten to 29 N•m (21 ft.-lb.).

12. Use a funnel and fill the engine with the correct weight and quantity of oil (**Table 4**).

13. Remove the funnel and install the oil fill cap (B, **Figure 65**) and its O-ring. Tighten it securely.

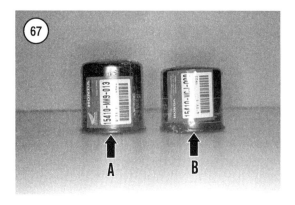

NOTE
*If a new oil pump has been installed or the engine has been rebuilt, check the engine oil pressure as described under **Engine Oil Pressure Test** in this section.*

14. Start the engine and allow it to idle.

NOTE
The oil pressure warning light should go out within 1-3 seconds. If it stays on, shut off the engine immediately and locate the problem. Do not run the engine with the oil pressure warning light on.

15. Check the oil filter and drain bolt for leaks.

16. Turn the engine off after 2-3 minutes and check the oil level as described in this chapter. Adjust the oil level if necessary.

WARNING
Prolonged contact with oil may cause skin cancer. Wash hands thoroughly with soap and water after contacting engine oil.

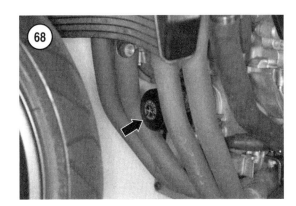

17. Install both side fairing panels and the front inner fairing panel as described in Chapter Sixteen.

Engine Oil Pressure Test

Check the engine oil pressure after installing a new oil pump, reassembling the engine or when troubleshooting the lubrication system.

An oil pressure gauge (Honda part No. 07506-3000000, or an equivalent) and an oil pressure gauge attachment (07510-MJ10100, or an equivalent) are required to test the oil pressure.

1. Park the motorcycle on level ground. Support the motorcycle securely on a swing arm stand (or centerstand on U.K. models) with the rear wheel off the ground.

2. Start the engine and run it until it is at normal operating temperature, then turn it off.

3. Remove the right side fairing panel as described in Chapter Sixteen.

4. Place a drain pan underneath the main oil gallery plug on the right side.

5. Remove the main oil gallery plug (**Figure 69**). Thoroughly clean off all threadlocking agent from

the oil gallery plug threads in the crankcase. Do not allow any debris to enter the engine during this test.

6. Lubricate the oil pressure gauge attachment O-ring with engine oil.

7. Install the oil pressure gauge attachment onto the engine. Tighten the attachment nut securely.

8. Install the oil pressure gauge onto the oil pressure gauge attachment. Make sure the fitting is tight to prevent oil leakage.

CAUTION
Secure the gauge hose away from the exhaust pipe during this test.

9. Recheck the engine oil level.

10. Start the engine and allow it to reach normal operating temperature.

11. Increase engine speed to 6000 rpm and read the oil pressure on the gauge. The correct reading is 490 kPa (71 psi) with the oil temperature at 80° C (176° F).

12. Allow the engine to return to idle, then shut it off.

13. If the oil pressure readings are lower or higher than specified, refer to *Engine Lubrication* in Chapter Two.

14. Remove the test equipment from the engine.

15. Clean off all old threadlocking compound from main oil gallery plug.

16. Apply a medium strength threadlocking compound to the main oil gallery plug.

17. Install the main oil gallery plug (**Figure 69**) and tighten to 29 N•m (21 ft.-lb.).

18. Start the engine and check for leaks.

19. Install the right side fairing panel as described in Chapter Sixteen.

COOLING SYSTEM

Check, inspect and service the cooling system at the intervals specified in **Table 1**.

WARNING
*When performing any service work on the engine or cooling system, **never** remove the radiator cap, coolant drain bolt or disconnect any coolant hose while the engine and radiator are hot. Scalding fluid and steam may be blown out under pressure and cause serious injury.*

Coolant Type

If adding coolant to the cooling system, use Pro Honda HP Coolant. This is a ready-to-use 50:50 antifreeze/purified, de-ionized water coolant blend. If mixing antifreeze and water, use a 50:50 mixture of distilled water and antifreeze that does not contain silicate inhibitors. Use only soft or distilled water. Never use tap water, as this will damage engine parts. Distilled, or purified, water can be purchased at supermarkets or drug stores in gallon containers. Never use alcohol-based antifreeze.

> *CAUTION*
> *Many antifreeze solutions contain silicate inhibitors to protect aluminum parts from corrosion damage. However, these silicate inhibitors can cause premature wear to water pump seals. When selecting an antifreeze, make sure it does not contain silicate inhibitors.*

Coolant Test

> *WARNING*
> *Do not remove the radiator cap when the engine is hot.*

1. Remove the right side fairing panel as described in Chapter Sixteen.
2. Remove the radiator cap (**Figure 70**).
3. Test the specific gravity of the coolant with an antifreeze tester to ensure adequate temperature and corrosion protection. A 50:50 mixture is recommended. Never allow the mixture to become less than 40 percent antifreeze. See *Coolant* in this section.
4. Reinstall the radiator cap (**Figure 70**).
5. Install the right side air duct as described in Chapter Sixteen.

Coolant Level

1. Park the motorcycle on level ground.
2. Start the engine and allow it to idle until it reaches normal operating temperature. Shut off the engine.
3A. On 1999-2000 models, perform the following:
   a. On the right side, check the coolant level in the reserve tank. It should be between the

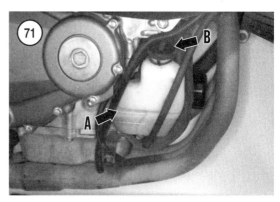

UPPER and LOWER level marks (A, **Figure 71**).
   b. If necessary, remove the coolant reserve tank cap (B, **Figure 71**) and add coolant into the reserve tank (not the radiator) to bring the level to the upper mark. See *Coolant Type* in this section.
   c. Reinstall the reserve tank cap.
3B. On 2001-on models, perform the following:
   a. On the right side, check the coolant level in the reserve tank. It should be between the UPPER and LOWER level marks (A, **Figure 72**).
   b. If necessary, remove the coolant reserve tank cap (B, **Figure 72**) and add coolant into the reserve tank (not the radiator) to bring the level to the upper mark. See *Coolant Type* in this section.
   c. Reinstall the reserve tank cap.

Cooling System Inspection

1. Remove both side fairing panels as described in Chapter Sixteen.

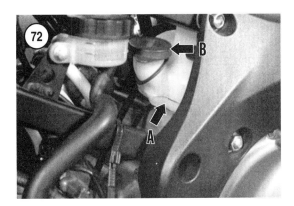

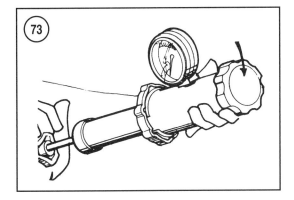

2. Check all cooling system hoses for damage or deterioration. Replace any hose that is questionable. Make sure all hose clamps are tight.

3. Carefully clean any dirt and debris from the radiator core. Use a whiskbroom, compressed air or low-pressure water. If an object has hit the radiator, carefully straighten the fins with a screwdriver.

Pressure test

A cooling system tester is required to make the following tests.

WARNING
Do not remove the radiator cap when the engine is hot.

1. Remove the right side fairing panel as described in Chapter Sixteen.

2. Remove the radiator cap (**Figure 70**).

3. Pressure test the radiator cap (**Figure 73**) using a cooling system tester. Refer to the manufacturer's instructions when making the tests. The specified radiator cap pressure is 108-137 kPa (16-20 psi).

Replace the radiator cap if it does not hold pressure or if the relief pressure is too high or too low.

CAUTION
Excessive pressure can damage the radiator or other cooling system component. Do not exceed the pressure specified in Step 3.

4. Leave the radiator cap off and pressure test the cooling system up to 137 kPa (20 psi). The cooling system must be able to hold this pressure. If there is a leak, locate and replace the damaged component.

5. Reinstall the radiator cap (**Figure 70**).

6. Install the right side fairing panel as described in Chapter Sixteen.

Coolant Change and Air Bleeding

Drain and refill the cooling system at the intervals listed in **Table 1**.

It is sometimes necessary to drain the cooling system when performing a service on some part of the engine. If the coolant is still in good condition, the coolant can be reused if it is not contaminated. Drain the coolant into a clean pan and pour the coolant into a clean container for storage.

WARNING
Waste antifreeze is toxic and may never be discharged into storm sewers, septic systems, waterways, or onto the ground. Place used antifreeze in the original container and dispose of it according to local regulations. Do not store coolant where it is accessible to children or pets.

WARNING
*Do not remove the radiator cap (**Figure 70**) if the engine is hot. The coolant is very hot and is under pressure. Severe scalding will result if hot coolant contacts skin.*

CAUTION
Be careful not to spill antifreeze on painted surfaces, as it will damage the surface. Wash immediately with soapy water and rinse thoroughly.

Perform the following procedure when the engine is cold.

1. Park the motorcycle on level ground.

2. Remove both side fairings as described in Chapter Sixteen.

3. On the left side, place a drain pan under the water pump. Remove the drain bolt (**Figure 74**) and sealing washer from the water pump cover. Allow the coolant to drain into the pan.

NOTE
*When the radiator cap is removed in the next step, the coolant will spray from the drain bolt hole (**Figure 74**) with considerable force. Hold the drain pan near and in front of the drain bolt hole, then have an assistant loosen and remove the radiator cap.*

4. Slowly remove the radiator cap (**Figure 70**) and allow the coolant to drain completely through the water pump drain hole. Reinstall the drain bolt and sealing washer on the water pump cover (**Figure 74**). Replace the sealing washer if it is leaking or damaged. Tighten the coolant drain bolt securely.

5. Refer to *Radiator Removal/Installation* in Chapter Eleven and partially remove the radiator to gain access to the cylinder drain plug . Do not disconnect any of the coolant hoses from the radiator.

6. Remove the cylinder block drain bolt and washer (**Figure 75**) and drain the cylinder block. Replace the sealing washer if it is leaking or damaged. Install the drain bolt and washer and tighten the cylinder drain bolt securely.

7. Drain the coolant reserve tank as follows:

   a. Place a drain pan underneath the coolant reserve tank.

   b. Remove the reserve tank cap. Refer to B, **Figure 71** or B, **Figure 72**.

   c. Disconnect the radiator siphon tube from the reserve tank and drain the coolant into the drain pan.

   d. Rinse the inside of the coolant reserve tank with water and allow to drain.

   e. Reconnect the siphon tube and secure it with its clamp.

CAUTION
*Do not use a higher percentage of antifreeze-to-water solution than is recommended under **Coolant Type** in this section. A higher concentration of coolant will actually decrease the performance of the cooling system.*

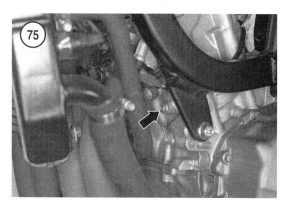

8. Place a funnel in the radiator filler neck and slowly refill the radiator and engine with a mixture of 50% antifreeze and 50% distilled water. Add the mixture slowly so it will expel as much air as possible from the cooling system. See *Coolant Type* in this section before purchasing and mixing coolant. **Table 4** lists engine coolant capacity.

9. Sit on the motorcycle and slowly rock it from side to side to help expel air bubbles from the engine and coolant hoses.

10. Fill the coolant reserve tank to the UPPER level line. Refer to A, **Figure 71** or A, **Figure 72**.

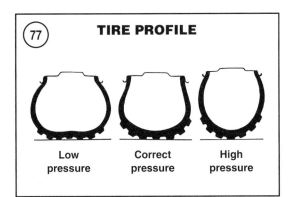

TIRE PROFILE

Low pressure | Correct pressure | High pressure

WARNING
Do not start and run the motorcycle in an enclosed area. The exhaust gasses contain carbon monoxide, a colorless, odorless, poisonous gas. Carbon monoxide levels build quickly in a small enclosed area and can cause unconsciousness and death in a short time.

11. After filling the radiator, leave the radiator cap off and bleed the cooling system as follows:

   a. Start the engine and allow it to idle for two to three minutes.

   b. Snap the throttle a few times to bleed air from the cooling system. When the coolant level drops in the radiator, add coolant to bring the level to the bottom of the filler neck.

   c. When the radiator coolant level has stabilized, perform Step 12.

12. Install the radiator cap (**Figure 70**). Turn the radiator cap clockwise to the first stop. Then push the cap down and turn it clockwise until it stops.

13. Start the engine and let it run at idle speed until the engine reaches normal operating temperature.

Make sure there are no air bubbles in the coolant and that the coolant level in the coolant reserve tank stabilizes at the correct level. Add coolant to the coolant reserve tank, as necessary.

14. Install the side fairings as described in Chapter Sixteen.

15. Test ride the motorcycle and readjust the coolant level in the reserve tank as required.

EMISSION CONTROL SYSTEMS

Inspection

Models sold in California and some European countries are equipped with a secondary air supply and evaporative emission control systems. A vacuum hose routing diagram label is attached to the air filter cover (**Figure 76**). At the intervals specified in **Table 1**, check all emission control hoses for deterioration, damage or loose connections. Also check the charcoal canister housing for damage. Replace any parts or hoses as required. Refer to the emission control sections in Chapter Eight for additional information for both carbureted and fuel injected models.

BATTERY

The original equipment battery is a maintenance-free type. Maintenance-free batteries do not require periodic electrolyte inspection and water cannot be added. Refer to Chapter Ten for battery service, testing and replacement procedures.

TIRES AND WHEELS

Tire Inspection

1. Check and adjust the tire pressure (**Table 5**) to maintain the tire profile (**Figure 77**), good traction and handling and to get the maximum life out of the tire. Check tire pressure when the tires are cold. Never release air pressure from a warm or hot tire to match the recommended tire pressure; doing so causes the tire to be underinflated. Use an accurate tire pressure gauge and reinstall the air valve cap (A, **Figure 78**).

2. Periodically inspect the tires for the following:

   a. Deep cuts and imbedded objects, such as nails and stones. If a nail or other object is in a tire, mark its location with a light crayon prior to removing it. This helps to locate the hole for repair. Refer to Chapter Twelve for tire changing and repair information.

b. Flat spots.

c. Cracks.

d. Separating plies.

e. Sidewall damage.

NOTE
If a small object has punctured the tire, air leakage may be very slow due to the tendency of tubeless tires to self-seal when punctured. Check the tires carefully.

Tire Wear Analysis

Analyze abnormal tire wear to determine the cause. Common causes are:

1. Incorrect tire pressure. Check the tire pressure and examine the tire tread as follows:

   a. Measure the tread depth (**Figure 79**) in the center of the tire using a small ruler or a tread depth gauge. Honda recommends replacing the original equipment tires before the center tread depth has worn to 1.5 mm (0.06 in.) for the front tire and 2.0 mm (0.08 in.) for the rear tire.

   b. Compare the wear in the center of the contact patch with the wear at the edge of the contact patch.

   c. If the tire shows excessive wear at the edge of the contact patch, but the wear at the center of the contact patch is normal, the tire has been underinflated. Underinflated tires result in higher tire temperatures, hard or imprecise steering and abnormal wear.

   d. If the tires shows excessive wear in the center of the contact patch, but wear at the edge of the contact patch is normal, the tire has been overinflated. Overinflated tires result in a hard ride and abnormal wear.

   e. The tires are also designed with tread wear indicators that appear when the tires are worn out. When these are visible, the tires are no longer safe and must be replaced.

2. Overloading.

3. Incorrect wheel alignment.

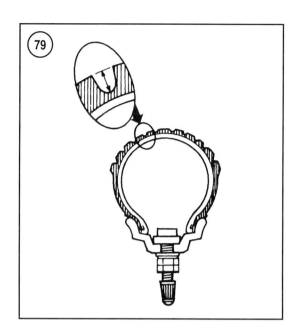

4. Incorrect wheel balance. Balance the tire/wheel assembly when installing a new tire, and then rebalance each time the tire is removed.

5. Worn or damaged wheel bearings.

Wheel Inspection

Frequently inspect the wheel (B, **Figure 78**) for cracks, warp or dents. A damaged wheel may cause an air leak or steering vibration.

Wheel rim runout is the amount of wobble a wheel shows as it rotates. Check runout with the wheels on the motorcycle. See *Wheel Runout and Balance* in Chapter Twelve for service procedures.

FRONT FORK OIL CHANGE

All models are equipped with cartridge forks. This type of fork must be partially disassembled for fork oil replacement and oil level adjustment. Refer to *Front Fork Disassembly and Assembly* in Chapter Thirteen.

DRIVE CHAIN

Drive Chain Lubrication

Lubricate the drive chain at the interval indicated in **Table 1**. A properly maintained drive chain will provide maximum service life and reliability.

Honda recommends SAE 80 or 90 gear oil or Pro Honda Chain Lube designed for O-ring chains.

NOTE
On an O-ring type drive chain, the chain lubrication described in this procedure is used mainly to keep the O-rings pliable and to prevent the side plates and rollers from rusting. The actual chain lubrication is enclosed within the chain by the O-rings.

1. Ride the motorcycle a few miles to warm the drive chain. A warm chain increases lubricant penetration.
2. Park the motorcycle on level ground. Support the motorcycle securely on a swing arm stand (or centerstand on U.K. models) with the rear wheel off the ground.
3. Oil the bottom chain run with SAE 80 or 90 gear oil or a commercial chain lubricant recommended for use on O-ring equipped drive chains. Concentrate on getting the oil down between the side plates on both sides of the chain. Do not overlubricate.

CAUTION
Not all commercial chain lubricants are recommended for use on O-ring drive chains. Read the product label to be sure it is formulated for O-ring chains.

4. Rotate the chain and continue lubricating until the entire chain has been lubricated.
5. Turn the rear wheel slowly and wipe off excess oil from the chain with a shop cloth. Also wipe off lubricant from the rear hub, wheel and tire.
6. Remove the auxiliary stand.

Drive Chain Cleaning

Clean the drive chain after riding over dusty or sandy conditions. A properly maintained chain provides maximum service life and reliability.

CAUTION
All models are equipped with an O-ring drive chain. Clean the chain with kerosene only. Solvents and gasoline cause the rubber O-rings to swell. The drive chain then becomes so stiff it cannot move or flex. If this

happens, the drive chain must be replaced. High pressure washers and steam cleaning can also damage the O-rings.

Because all models are equipped with an endless drive chain, it is not practical to break the chain in order to clean it. This section describes how to clean the drive chain while it is mounted on the motorcycle.
1. Ride the motorcycle a few miles to warm the drive chain. A warm chain increases lubricant penetration.
2. Park the motorcycle on level ground. Support the motorcycle securely on a swing arm stand (or centerstand on U.K. models) with the rear wheel off the ground.
3. Place some stiff cardboard and a drain pan underneath the drive chain.

NOTE
Wear rubber gloves when cleaning the drive chain in the following steps.

NOTE
Do not splash the kerosene when cleaning the drive chain in the following steps. Make sure to keep the kerosene off of the rear tire and other parts as much as possible.

4. Soak a thick rag in kerosene, then wipe it against the section of chain that is exposed on the lower chain run. When this section of the chain is clean, turn the rear wheel to expose the next section and clean it. Repeat until all of the chain is clean. To remove stubborn dirt, scrub the rollers and side plates with a soft brush. To avoid catching fingers and rag between the chain and sprocket, do not rotate the rear wheel when cleaning the chain. Clean one section of the chain at a time.
5. Turn the rear wheel slowly and wipe the drive chain dry with a thick shop cloth.
6. Clean the rear swing arm, driven sprocket, chain guard, wheel and tire of all kerosene residue.
7. Lubricate the drive chain as previously described in this section.

Drive Chain and Sprocket Inspection

Frequently check the chain and both sprockets for excessive wear and damage.

1. Clean the drive chain as described in this chapter.

2. Park the motorcycle on level ground. Support the motorcycle securely on a swing arm stand (or centerstand on U.K. models) with the rear wheel off the ground.

3. Turn the rear wheel and inspect both sides of the chain for missing or damaged O-rings.

4. At the rear sprocket, pull one of the links away from the driven sprocket. If the link pulls away more than 1/2 the height of the sprocket tooth (**Figure 80**), the chain is excessively worn. Also refer to *Drive Chain Wear Inspection* in this section.

5. Inspect the inner plate chain faces (**Figure 81**). They should be polished on both sides. If they show considerable uneven wear on one side, the sprockets are not aligned properly. Severe wear requires replacement of not only the drive chain but also the drive and driven sprockets.

6. Inspect the drive and driven sprockets for the following defects:

    a. Undercutting or sharp teeth (**Figure 82**).

    b. Broken teeth.

7. Check the drive sprocket bolt and the driven sprocket nuts for looseness. If loose, tighten to 55 N•m (41 ft.-lb.) and 88 N•m (65 ft.-lb.), respectively.

8. If excessive chain or sprocket wear is evident, replace the drive chain and both sprockets as a complete set. If only the drive chain is replaced, the worn sprockets will cause rapid chain wear.

Drive Chain Wear Inspection

A drive chain wear label is mounted on the drive chain adjuster. Determine chain wear as follows:

1. Check the chain adjustment and adjust if necessary as described in this chapter.

2. If any part of the red zone on the label aligns with the index mark on the swing arm (**Figure 83**), and the chain free play is correct, the drive chain is excessively worn and must be replaced.

Drive Chain Adjustment

Check and adjust the drive chain at the intervals specified in **Table 1**. If the motorcycle is operated at sustained high speeds or if it is repeatedly accelerated very hard, check the drive chain adjustment more often. A properly lubricated and adjusted

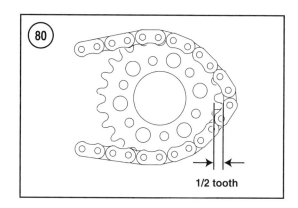
1/2 tooth

drive chain will provide maximum service life and reliability. The correct amount of drive chain free play (**Figure 84**), when pushed up midway on the lower chain run, is listed in **Table 2**.

CAUTION
Excessive drive chain slack of 50 mm (2.0 in.) or more may cause damage to the frame.

When adjusting the chain, check the free play at several places along its length by rotating the rear wheel. The chain will rarely wear uniformly and as a result will be tighter at some places than others. Measure the chain free play halfway between the sprockets (**Figure 84**). Make sure the chain free play at the tightest place on the chain is not less than the specification in **Table 2**.

1. Turn the engine off and shift the transmission into NEUTRAL.

2. Park the motorcycle on level ground. Support the motorcycle securely on a swing arm stand (or centerstand on U.K. models) with the rear wheel off the ground.

NOTE
As drive chains stretch and wear in use, the chain will become tighter at one point. The chain must be checked and adjusted at this point.

3. Turn the rear wheel slowly, then stop it and check the chain tightness. Continue until the tightest point is located. Mark this spot with chalk and turn the wheel so that the mark is located on the lower chain run, midway between both drive sprockets. Check and adjust the drive chain as follows.

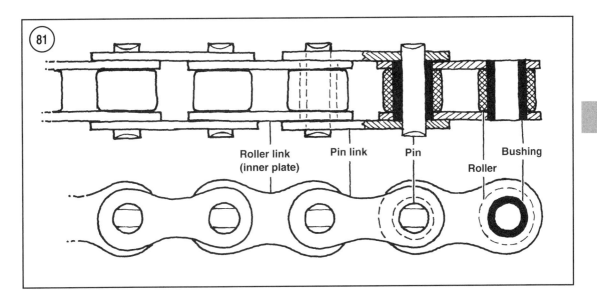

Roller link (inner plate)   Pin link   Pin   Bushing   Roller

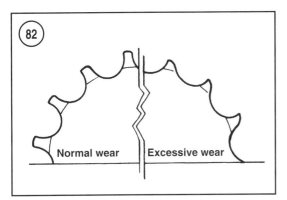

Normal wear   Excessive wear

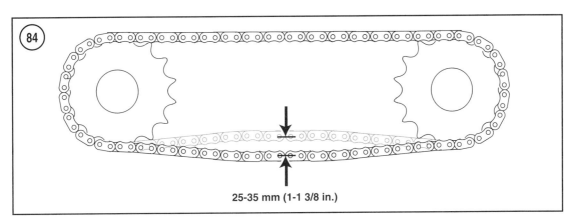

25-35 mm (1-1 3/8 in.)

NOTE
If the drive chain is kinked or feels tight, it may require cleaning and lubrication. Clean and lubricate the drive chain as described in this chapter.

4. Lower the motorcycle so the rear wheel is on the ground, then support it on its sidestand.

5. Loosen the rear axle nut (A, **Figure 85**) and turn both adjuster bolts (B) an equal number of turns to obtain the correct drive chain free play. Check that

the same adjuster marks on both the right and left side are aligned with the index mark on the swing arm (**Figure 83**).

6. Recheck chain free play.

7. Check the chain wear indicator as described under *Drive Chain Wear Inspection* in this section.

8. To verify the swing arm adjuster marks, remove the drive chain guard and check rear wheel alignment by sighting along the drive chain as it runs over the rear driven sprocket. It should leave the driven sprocket in a straight line as shown in A, **Figure 86**. If it is cocked to one side or the other (B or C, **Figure 86**), perform the following:

    a. Check that the adjusters are set to the same index mark position on the swing arm.

    b. If not, readjust the drive chain to achieve the same position on both sides as well as maintaining the correct free play.

9. Tighten the rear axle nut to 93 N•m (69 ft.-lb.).

Swing Arm Slider Inspection

A slider is installed on the left side of the swing arm (**Figure 87**) to protect the swing arm from chain damage. Inspect the slider frequently for advanced wear or damage that would allow the chain to contact and damage the swing arm. Replace the slider (**Figure 88**) if it is worn to the wear limit line on the slider. Replace the slider after removing the swing arm as described under *Swing Arm Removal/Installation* in Chapter Fourteen.

BRAKE SYSTEM

Check the brake fluid in each brake master cylinder at the intervals listed in **Table 1**. At the same time, inspect the brake pads for wear. Brake bleeding, servicing the brake components and replacing the brake pads are covered in Chapter Fifteen.

Brake Hose Inspection

Check the brake hoses between the front and rear master cylinders and the brake calipers. If there is any leakage, tighten the banjo bolt or hose and then bleed the brake as described in Chapter Fifteen. If this does not stop the leak or if a brake line is obviously damaged, cracked or chafed, replace the brake hose and bleed the system.

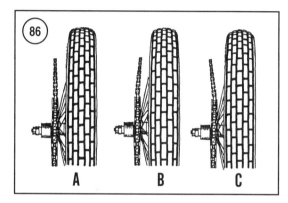

A   B   C

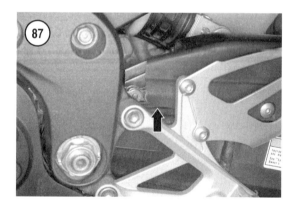

Brake Fluid Type

Use DOT 4 brake fluid in the front and rear master cylinder reservoirs.

> *WARNING*
> *Use brake fluid clearly marked DOT 4. Others may cause brake failure. Do not intermix different brands or types of brake fluid as they may not be compatible. Do not intermix silicone-based (DOT 5) brake fluid, as it*

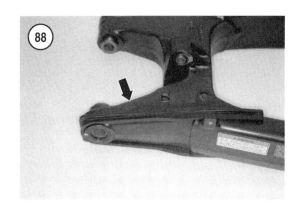

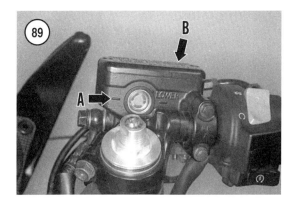

can cause brake component damage,
leading to brake system failure.

CAUTION
Handle brake fluid carefully. Do not
spill it on painted or plastic sur-
faces, as it will damage the surface.
Wash the area immediately with
soap and water and thoroughly rinse
it off.

Brake Fluid Change

Every time the reservoir cap is removed, a
small amount of dirt and moisture enters the
brake fluid. The same thing happens if a leak occurs or when a brake hose is loosened. Dirt can
clog the system and cause unnecessary wear. Water in the brake fluid will vaporize at high brake
system temperatures, impairing the hydraulic action and reducing the brake's stopping ability. To
maintain peak performance, change the brake
fluid at the interval in **Table 1** or whenever the
caliper or master cylinder is overhauled. To

change brake fluid, follow the brake bleeding procedure in Chapter Fifteen.

Front Brake Fluid Level Inspection

1. Turn the handlebar to the left side so the front
master cylinder is level.
2. The brake fluid level must be above the lower
level line (A, **Figure 89**) in the master cylinder window. If the brake fluid level is at or below the lower
level line, continue with Step 3.

NOTE
If the reservoir is empty, air has prob-
ably entered the brake system. Bleed
the front brakes as described in Chap-
ter Fifteen.

3. Wipe clean the master cylinder cover and remove the cover screws. Then remove the cover (B,
Figure 89), set plate and diaphragm.
4. Add fresh DOT 4 brake fluid to fill the reservoir
to the upper level mark in the reservoir.
5. Install the diaphragm, set plate and cover. Install
and tighten the cover screws.
6. If the brake fluid level was low, check the brake
pads for excessive wear as described in this section.

NOTE
A low brake fluid level usually indi-
cates brake pad wear. As the pads
wear and become thinner, the brake
caliper pistons automatically extend
farther out of their bores. As the cali-
per pistons move outward, the brake
fluid level drops in the system. How-
ever, if the brake fluid level is low and
the brake pads are not worn exces-
sively, check all of the brake hoses for
leaks.

Rear Brake Fluid Level Inspection

1. Park the motorcycle on level ground and support
it vertically.

WARNING
Do not check the rear brake fluid
level with the motorcycle resting on
its sidestand. A false reading will re-
sult.

2. The brake fluid level must be between the upper and lower level marks (A, **Figure 90**) on the reservoir housing. If the brake fluid level is at or below the lower level line, continue with Step 3.

NOTE
If the reservoir is empty, air has probably entered the brake system. Bleed the rear brake as described in Chapter Thirteen.

3. Remove the bolt and nut (B, **Figure 90**) securing the reservoir to the frame.

4. Wipe all debris from the master cylinder cover and move the reservoir partially out from the frame.

5. Unscrew the cover (C, **Figure 90**). Then remove the cover and diaphragm.

6. Add fresh DOT 4 brake fluid to fill the reservoir to the upper level mark on the reservoir.

7. Install the diaphragm and cover. Tighten the cover securely.

8. Reposition the reservoir and tighten the mounting bolt and nut securely.

9. If the brake fluid level was low, check the brake pads for excessive wear as described in this section.

NOTE
A low brake fluid level usually indicates brake pad wear. As the pads wear and become thinner, the brake caliper pistons automatically extend farther out of their bores. As the caliper pistons move outward, the brake fluid level drops in the system. However, if the brake fluid level is low and the brake pads are not worn excessively, check all of the brake hoses and lines for leaks.

Brake Pad Wear Inspection

Inspect the brake pads for wear at the intervals specified in **Table 1**.

1. Inspect the front (**Figure 91**) and rear (**Figure 92**) brake pads for uneven wear, scoring, oil contamination or other damage. If there is no visible brake pad damage or contamination, perform Step 2.

2. Replace the brake pads as a set if either pad is worn to the bottom of the wear groove. Refer to **Fig-**

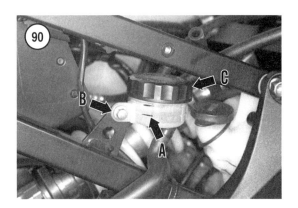

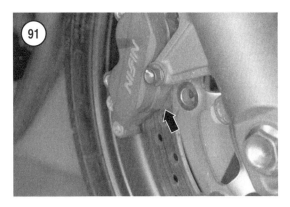

ure 93 for the front brake pads or **Figure 94** for the rear brake pads.

3. If either set of pads is worn to the wear groove, the pads must be replaced as described in Chapter Fifteen.

NOTE
Always replace both pads in each caliper at the same time. On the front brakes, replace the brake pads in both calipers at the same time to maintain even braking.

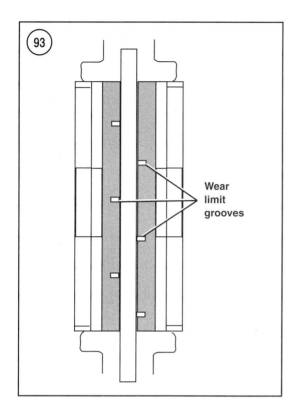

Wear limit grooves

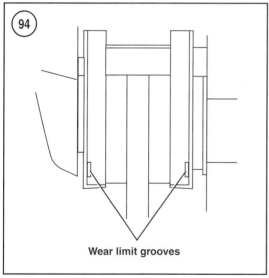

Wear limit grooves

NOTE
Because the thickness of riding gloves can affect the feel of the front brake lever, wear riding gloves when adjusting the brake lever's operating position. If you change gloves, recheck the brake lever operating position.

2. Support the motorcycle with the front wheel off the ground. Then spin the front wheel by hand and apply the front brake several times. Make sure the front wheel turns without any brake drag and that the front brakes work correctly.

Rear Brake Pedal Height Adjustment

The rear brake pedal height can be adjusted to suit rider preference.

1. At the rear brake master cylinder, loosen the locknut (A, **Figure 96**) and turn the pushrod (B) until the correct pedal height is achieved.

2. Tighten the locknut (A, **Figure 96**) and recheck the adjustment.

Front Brake Lever Adjustment

The distance between the front brake lever and throttle grip can be adjusted to suit rider preference.

1. Turn the adjuster (A, **Figure 95**) and align one of the index marks on the adjuster with the arrow on the brake lever pivot bolt (B).

3. Park the motorcycle on level ground. Support the motorcycle securely on a swing arm stand (or centerstand on U.K. models) with the rear wheel off the ground.

4. Spin the rear wheel by hand and apply the rear brake several times. Make sure the rear wheel turns without any brake drag and that the rear brake works correctly.

Front Brake Light Switch Adjustment

There is no adjustment for the front brake light switch.

Rear Brake Light Switch Adjustment

Check the rear brake light switch adjustment at the intervals specified in **Table 1**.

> *NOTE*
> *This procedure is shown with the brake pedal assembly removed from the frame and partially disassembled to better illustrate this step.*

1. Turn the ignition switch on.

2. Depress the brake pedal. The brake light must come on just before the brake begins to work.

3. If the brake light comes on too late, perform the following:

    a. Hold the brake light switch body (A, **Figure 97**).

    b. Turn the adjuster nut (B, **Figure 97**) as required to make the brake light come on earlier.

> *NOTE*
> *Do not turn the switch body when adjusting the rear brake light switch.*

    c. Recheck the rear brake light switch adjustment.

4. Turn the ignition switch off.

HEADLIGHT AIM INSPECTION

Check the headlight aim at the intervals specified in **Table 1**. Refer to *Headlight* in Chapter Ten.

SIDESTAND AND IGNITION CUT-OFF SWITCH INSPECTION

Check the sidestand and the ignition cut-off system operation at the intervals specified in **Table 1**.

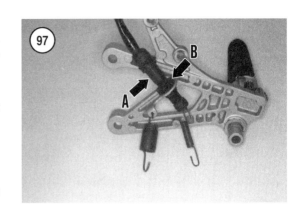

1. Park the motorcycle on level ground. Support the motorcycle securely on a swing arm stand (or centerstand on U.K. models) with the rear wheel off the ground.

2. Operate the sidestand and check its movement and spring tension. Replace the spring if it is weak or damaged.

3. Lubricate the sidestand pivot bolt if necessary.

4. Check the sidestand ignition cut-off system as follows:

    a. Park the motorcycle so both wheels are on the ground.

    b. Sit on the motorcycle and raise the sidestand.

    c. Shift the transmission into NEUTRAL.

    d. Start the engine, then squeeze the clutch lever and shift the transmission into gear.

    e. Move the sidestand down. When doing so, the engine should stop.

    f. If the engine did not stop as the sidestand was lowered, inspect the sidestand switch as described under *Switches* in Chapter Eight.

STEERING BEARING INSPECTION

Inspect the steering head adjustment at the intervals specified in **Table 1**.

1. Support the motorcycle on a stand with the front wheel off the ground.

> *NOTE*
> *When performing Step 2, make sure the control cables do not interfere with handlebar movement.*

2. Hold onto the handlebars and move them from side to side. Note any binding or roughness.

3. Support the motorcycle so that both wheels are on the ground.

4. Sit on the motorcycle and hold on to the handlebars. Apply the front brake lever and try to push the front fork forward. Try to detect any movement in the steering head area. If so, the bearing adjustment is loose and requires adjustment.

5. If any roughness, binding or looseness was detected when performing Step 2 or Step 4, service the steering bearings as described in Chapter Thirteen.

FRONT SUSPENSION INSPECTION

Inspect the front suspension at the intervals specified in **Table 1**.

1. Use a soft wet cloth to wipe the fork tubes to remove any dirt and debris. As this debris passes against the fork seals, it will eventually damage the seals and cause an oil leak.

2. Check the fork for any oil seal leaks or damage.

3. Apply the front brake and pump the fork up and down as vigorously as possible. Check for smooth operation.

4. Make sure the upper and lower fork tube pinch bolts are tight.

5. Check that the handlebar mounting bolts are tight.

6. Make sure the front axle is tight.

7. To adjust the front fork settings, refer to Chapter Thirteen.

> *CAUTION*
> *If any of the previously mentioned fasteners are loose, refer to Chapter Thirteen for procedures and torque specifications.*

REAR SUSPENSION INSPECTION

Inspect the rear suspension at the intervals specified in **Table 1**.

1. With both wheels on the ground, check the shock absorber by bouncing on the seat several times.

2. Park the motorcycle on level ground. Support the motorcycle securely on a swing arm stand (or centerstand on U.K. models) with the rear wheel off the ground.

3. With an assistant steadying the motorcycle, push hard on the rear wheel (sideways) to check for side play in the rear swing arm bearings.

4. Check the shock absorber for signs of oil leakage, loose mounting fasteners or other damage.

5. Check for loose or missing suspension fasteners.

6. Make sure the rear axle nut is tight.

7. Check the drive chain guard for loose or missing fasteners.

8. To adjust the rear shock absorber settings, refer to Chapter Fourteen.

> *CAUTION*
> *If any of the previously mentioned fasteners are loose, refer to Chapter Fourteen for procedures and torque specifications.*

FASTENER INSPECTION

Constant vibration can loosen many fasteners on a motorcycle.

1. Check the tightness of all exposed fasteners. Refer to the appropriate chapter for torque specifications.

2. Check that all hose clamps, cable stays and safety clips are properly installed. Replace missing or damaged items.

WHEEL BEARING INSPECTION

Inspect the wheel bearings at the interval specified in **Table 1**. Check the wheel bearings whenever the wheels are removed or whenever there is the likelihood of water or other contamination. See Chapter Twelve for service procedures.

LIGHTS AND HORN INSPECTION

With the engine running, check the following.

1. Pull the front brake lever and check that the brake light comes on.

2. Push the rear brake pedal and check that the brake light comes on.

3. Move the dimmer switch up and down between the high and low positions, and check to see that both headlight elements are working.

4. Move the turn signal switch to the left position and then to the right position and check that all four turn signal lights are working.

5. Operate the horn button and make sure that the horn sounds loudly.

6. If the horn or any light failed to work properly, refer to Chapter Ten.

Table 1 MAINTENANCE SCHEDULE[1]

Every 500 miles (800 km)
Lubricate drive chain[2]
Check drive chain tension and adjustment[2]
Initial 600 miles (1000 km)
Replace engine oil and filter
Check idle speed
Check carburetor synchronization (1999-2000 models)
Check brake system
Check clutch release system
Check steering play
Check fasteners
Every 4000 miles (6400 km)
Check spark plugs
Check engine idle speed
Check brake fluid levels
Check brake pad wear
Check clutch system
Every 8000 miles (12,800 km)
Check all fuel system hoses for leakage
Check throttle operation and adjustment
Check enrichment valve (choke) operation and adjustment (1999-2000 models)
Check carburetor synchronization (1999-2000 models)
Replace spark plugs
Replace engine oil and filter
Check idle speed
Check cooling system
Check coolant level
Check secondary air supply system
Check drive chain slider
Check brake pad wear
Check brake fluid level
Check brake light operation
Check headlight aim
Check clutch release system
Check side stand operation
Check front and rear suspension
Check tires, wheels and wheel bearings
Check steering head adjustment
Check fasteners
Every 12,000 miles (19,200 km)
Replace air filter element[2]
Check spark plugs
Check evaporative emission control system[3]
Check idle speed
Replace brake fluid
Check brake pad wear
Check clutch release system
Every 16,000 miles (25,600 km)
Check valve clearance
Every 20,000 miles (32,000 km)
Check spark plugs
Check idle speed
Check brake fluid levels
Check brake pad wear
Check clutch release system
Every 24,000 miles (38,400 km)
Check all fuel systems hoses for leakage
Check throttle operation and adjustment
(continued)

Table 1 MAINTENANCE SCHEDULE[1] (continued)

Every 24,000 miles (38,400 km) (continued)
  Check enrichment valve (choke) operation and adjustment (1999-2000 models)
  Check carburetor synchronization (1999-2000 models)
  Replace spark plugs
  Replace engine oil and filter
  Replace air filter element
  Check idle speed
  Replace coolant
  Check coolant level
  Check secondary air supply system
  Check evaporative emission control system[3]
  Check drive chain slider
  Check brake pad wear
  Replace brake fluid
  Check brake light operation
  Check headlight operation
  Check headlight aim
  Check clutch release system
  Check sidestand/ignition cut-off system operation
  Check front and rear suspension
  Check tires, wheels and wheel bearings
  Check steering head adjustment and lubricate bearings
  Check fasteners

1. Consider this maintenance schedule as a guide to general maintenance and lubrication intervals. Harder than normal use (stop-and-go traffic) and exposure to wet or dusty conditions may require more frequent attention to some maintenance items.
2. Increase service intervals when riding in wet or dusty areas.
3. California and other non-U.S. models.

Table 2 MAINTENANCE AND TUNE-UP SPECIFICATIONS

Brake pedal height	Rider preference
Clutch lever free play	10-20 mm (3/8-13/16 in.)
Carburetor synchronizing level difference	30 mm (1.2 in. Hg)
Starter valve synchronizing difference	20 mm (0.8 in. Hg)
Compression pressure at 350 rpm	
(at sea level)	1226 kPa (178 psi)
Drive chain free play	25-35 mm (1-1 3/8 in.)
Engine oil pressure (at oil pressure switch)	
at 80° C (176° F)	490 kPa (71 psi) at 6000 rpm
Idle speed (U.S. and Canada models)	
1999-2000 models	
49 states and Canada models	1200-1400 rpm
California models	1300-1500 rpm
2001-on models	1200-1400 rpm
Idle speed (other than U.S. and Canada models)	
1999-2000 models	
Switzerland models	1150-1250 rpm
Other than Switzerland models	1100-1300 rpm
2001-on models	1200-1400 rpm
Spark plug types (U.S. and Canada models)	
1999-2000 models	
49 states and Canada models	CR9EH-9 (NGK) or U27FER-9 (Denso)
California models	CR9EHVX-9 (NGK)
2001-on models	IMR9A-9H (NGK) or IUH27D (Denso)

(continued)

Table 2 MAINTENANCE AND TUNE-UP SPECIFICATIONS (continued)

Spark plug types (other than U.S. and Canada models)	
1999-2000 models	
Standard	CR9EH-9 (NGK) or U27FER-9 (Denso)
For cold climates	
(below 41° F [5° C])	CR8EH-9 (NGK) or U24FER-9 (Denso)
2001-on models	IMR9A-9H (NGK) or IUH27D (Denso)
Spark plug gap	
1999-2000 models	0.8-0.9 mm (0.031-0.035 in.)
2001-on models*	1.0 mm (0.040 in.)
Starter valve vacuum	
synchronization difference	20 mm Hg
Base throttle valve	No. 1 throttle body
Throttle cable free play	2-6 mm (3/32-1/4 in.)
Valve clearance (cold engine)	
Intake	0.17-0.23 mm (0.007-0.009 in.)
Exhaust	0.25-0.31 mm (0.010-0.012 in.)

*Gap is not adjustable. See text.

Table 3 MAINTENANCE AND TUNE UP TORQUE SPECIFICATIONS

Item	N•m	in.-lb.	ft.-lb.
Brake hose banjo bolt	34	–	25
Cylinder head cover bolt	12	106	–
Drive sprocket bolt	55	–	41
Driven sprocket nuts	88	–	65
Front axle bolt	59	–	43
Front axle pinch bolt	22	–	16
Oil drain bolt	29	–	21
Oil filter cartridge	26	–	19
Oil pressure main oil			
gallery plug	29	–	21
Rear axle nut	93	–	69
Spark plugs	12	106	–
Timing hole cap	18	–	13

Table 4 RECOMMENDED LUBRICANTS AND FLUIDS AND CAPACITIES

Brake fluid	DOT 4
Cooling system	
Coolant type	Honda HP coolant or an equivalent*
Coolant capacity	
Radiator and engine	2.7 L (2.9 U.S. qt., 2.4 Imp. qt.)
Reserve tank	0.31 L (0.33 U.S. qt., 0.27 Imp. qt.)
Drive chain	SAE 80 or SAE 90 gear oil
Engine oil	
Grade	API SF or SG
Viscosity	SAE 10W-40
Capacity	
Oil change only	3.0 L (3.2 U.S. qt., 2.6 Imp. qt.)
Oil and filter change	3.3 L (3.5 U.S. qt., 2.9 Imp. qt.)
After disassembly (engine dry)	3.7 L (3.9 U.S. qt., 3.3 Imp. qt.)

(continued)

Table 4 RECOMMENDED LUBRICANTS AND FLUIDS AND CAPACITIES (continued)

Fuel	
Type	Unleaded
Octane	Pump research octane of 86 or higher
Fuel tank capacity, including reserve	
U.S. and Canada models	
1999-2000 models	17.0 L (4.49 U.S. gal., 3.74 Imp. gal.)
2001-on models	18.0 L (4.76 U.S. gal., 3.96 Imp. gal.)
Other than U.S. and Canada models	18.0 L (4.76 U.S. gal., 3.96 Imp. gal.)

*Use a high quality ethylene glycol coolant that does not contain silicate inhibitors as they can case premature wear to the water pump seals and cause blockage of radiator passages. See text for further information.

Table 5 TIRE AND WHEEL SPECIFICATIONS

Item	Front	Rear
Tire type	Tubeless	Tubeless
Size	120/70 ZR17 (58W)	180/55 ZR17 (73W)
Minimum tread depth	1.5 mm (0.06 in.)	2.0 mm (0.08 in.)
Inflation pressure (cold)*	250 kPa (36 psi)	290 kPa (42 psi)

*Tire inflation pressure is for original equipment tires. Aftermarket tires may require different inflation pressure. The use of tires other than those specified by Honda may cause instability.

CHAPTER FOUR

ENGINE TOP END AND EXHAUST

This chapter provides complete service and overhaul procedures, including information for disassembly, removal, inspection, service and assembly of the engine top end. The lower end of the engine is covered in Chapter Five, while clutch procedures are in Chapter Six and the transmission procedures are in Chapter Seven.

Engine specifications are in **Tables 1-3** at the end of the chapter.

The CBR600 is a liquid-cooled inline four cylinder engine with double overhead camshafts. The crankshaft is supported by five main bearings and the camshafts are chain driven by the timing gear on the crankshaft. The camshafts operate directly on top of the valve lifters. Shims under the valve lifters determine valve clearance.

The cylinders are an integral part of the upper crankcase, which is referred to in this manual as the upper crankcase/cylinder block and is covered in Chapter Five.

The lubrication system is a wet sump type with the oil supply housed in the lower crankcase. The chain-driven oil pump delivers oil directly to the oil cooler. These components are covered in Chapter Five.

ENGINE SERVICE NOTES

An important part of successful engine service is preparation. Before servicing the engine, note the following:

1. Review the information in Chapter One, especially the *Basic Service Methods* and *Precision Measuring Tools* sections. Accurate measurements are critical to a successful engine rebuild.

2. Clean the entire engine and frame with a commercial degreaser before removing engine components. A clean motorcycle is easier to work on and this will help prevent the possibility of dirt and debris falling into the open engine.

3. Cover the O-ring chain before degreasing the engine. The chemicals in the degreaser will cause the O-rings to swell, permanently damaging the chain.

4. Have all the necessary tools and parts on hand before starting the procedure(s). Store parts in boxes, plastic bags and containers. Use masking tape and a permanent, waterproof marking pen to label parts. Record the location, position and thickness of all shims and washers as they are removed.

5. Use a box of assorted size and color vacuum hose identifiers (Lisle part No. 74600) for identifying hoses and fittings during engine services.

6. Throughout the text there are references to the left and right side of the engine. This refers to the engine as it is mounted in the frame, not how it may sit on the workbench.

7. When inspecting components described in this chapter, compare the measurements to the service specifications listed in **Table 2**. Replace any part that is out of specification, worn to the service limit or damaged.

8. Always replace worn or damaged fasteners with those of the same size, type and torque requirements. If a specific torque value is not listed in the text or in **Table 3**, refer to the general torque specification table in Chapter One.

9. Use a vise with protective jaws to hold parts.

10. Use a press or special tools when force is required to remove and install parts. Do not try to pry, hammer or otherwise force them on or off.

11. Replace all O-rings and seals with *new* ones during assembly. Set aside old seals and O-rings so they can be compared with the new ones if necessary. Apply a small amount of grease to the inner lips of each *new* oil seal to prevent damage when the engine is first started.

ENGINE PRINCIPLES

Refer to **Figure 1** for basic four-stroke engine operation. This information is helpful when troubleshooting or repairing the engine.

EXHAUST SYSTEM

The exhaust system (**Figure 2**) is vital to engine performance. Check the exhaust system for deep dents and fractures and repair or replace them im-

mediately. Check the muffler-to-frame mounting flanges for fractures and loose bolts. Check the cylinder head mounting flanges for tightness. A loose exhaust pipe connection can reduce engine performance.

Removal

WARNING
*Do not remove or service the exhaust system when it is **hot**.*

1. Park the motorcycle on level ground. Support the motorcycle securely on a swing arm stand (or centerstand on U.K. models) with the rear wheel off the ground.

2. Remove both side fairing panels and front inner panel as described in Chapter Sixteen.

3. On 2001-on California models, perform the following:

   a. Remove the seat as described in Chapter Sixteen.

   b. Disconnect the four-pin (natural color) electrical connector for the oxygen sensor located next to the shock absorber upper mount (**Figure 3**).

   c. Carefully pull the electrical cable and connector out through the frame.

4. Loosen the muffler-to-exhaust pipe clamp bolts (A, **Figure 4**).

5. Remove the bolt, washer and nut (**Figure 5**) securing the muffler to the rear footpeg bracket.

6A. On 2001-on California models, carefully pull the muffler free from the exhaust pipe assembly and remove the muffler and the oxygen sensor (B, **Figure 4**) electrical cable and connector.

6B. On all other models, carefully pull the muffler free from the exhaust pipe assembly and remove the muffler.

7. Remove the radiator as described in Chapter Eleven.

8. Remove the bolt, washer and nut (**Figure 6**) securing the exhaust pipe to the frame mount.

9. Remove the front exhaust pipe nuts at the cylinder head and remove the exhaust pipe assembly (**Figure 7**).

10. Remove the exhaust pipe gaskets at each cylinder head exhaust port. Discard the gaskets.

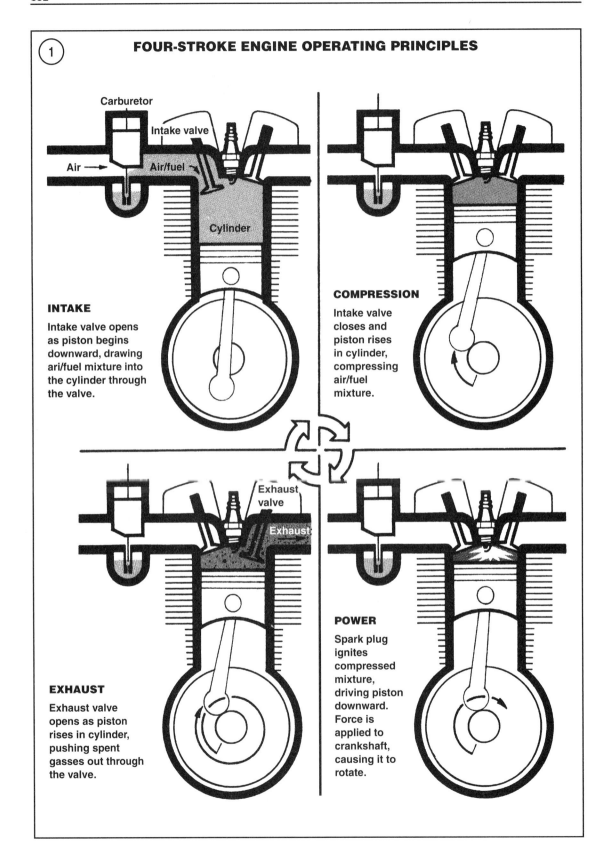

FOUR-STROKE ENGINE OPERATING PRINCIPLES

①

Carburetor

Intake valve

Air →

Air/fuel

Cylinder

INTAKE

Intake valve opens
as piston begins
downward, drawing
ari/fuel mixture into
the cylinder through
the valve.

COMPRESSION

Intake valve
closes and
piston rises
in cylinder,
compressing
air/fuel
mixture.

Exhaust
valve

Exhaust

EXHAUST

Exhaust valve
opens as piston
rises in cylinder,
pushing spent
gasses out through
the valve.

POWER

Spark plug
ignites
compressed
mixture,
driving piston
downward.
Force is
applied to
crankshaft,
causing it to
rotate.

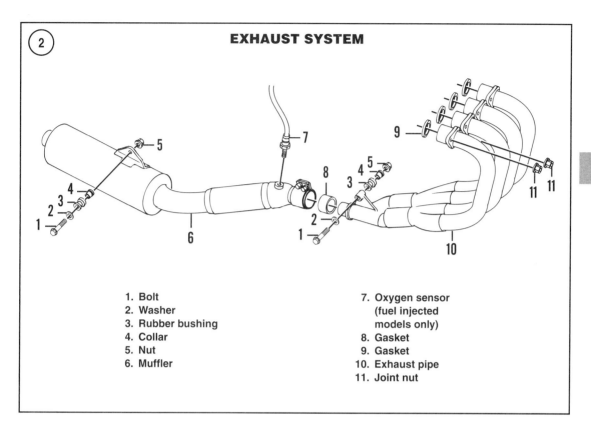

EXHAUST SYSTEM

1. Bolt
2. Washer
3. Rubber bushing
4. Collar
5. Nut
6. Muffler
7. Oxygen sensor (fuel injected models only)
8. Gasket
9. Gasket
10. Exhaust pipe
11. Joint nut

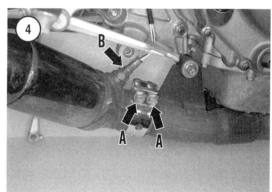

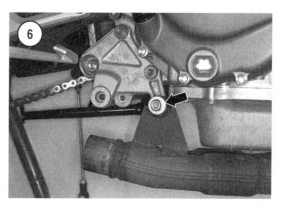

Inspection

1. Inspect the muffler mounting bracket for cracks or damage.

2. Inspect the exhaust pipe-to-cylinder head flanges (**Figure 8**) for corrosion, burned areas or damage.

3. Inspect all welds (**Figure 9**) for leakage or corrosion.

4. Inspect the rubber grommet and collar (**Figure 10**) on the exhaust pipe mount. Replace the rubber grommet if it is starting to harden or deteriorate.

5. Check the muffler mounting rubber grommet and collar on the rear footpeg mounting bracket. Replace the rubber grommet if it is starting to harden or deteriorate.

6. On 2001-on California models, inspect the oxygen sensor (A, **Figure 11**), electrical cable and connector for damage.

7. If any of the areas of black paint are worn off the exhaust pipe assembly, clean off the old paint and repaint with a *heat-resistant* flat black paint.

Installation

1. Make sure the rubber bushing and collar are in place on the exhaust pipe mount and the muffler mount on the rear footpeg bracket.

2. Install *new* exhaust pipe gaskets (**Figure 12**) into each cylinder head exhaust port. Apply grease to the gaskets to prevent them from falling out of place.

3. Install the exhaust pipe assembly (**Figure 7**) onto the cylinder head and install the nuts. Tighten finger-tight at this time.

4. Install the bolt, washer and nut (**Figure 6**) securing the exhaust pipe to the frame mount. Tighten finger-tight at this time.

5. Install a *new* gasket (B, **Figure 11**) into the muffler inlet port.

6A. On 2001-on California models, move the muffler into position and connect it onto the exhaust pipe. Position the oxygen sensor (B, **Figure 4**) electrical cable and connector into the frame area.

6B. On all other models, move the muffler into position and connect it onto the exhaust pipe.

7. Push the muffler in until it bottoms. Tighten the muffler-to-exhaust pipe clamp bolts (A, **Figure 4**) finger-tight at this time.

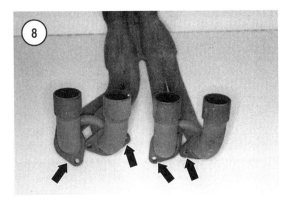
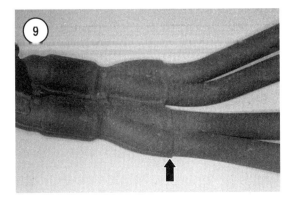
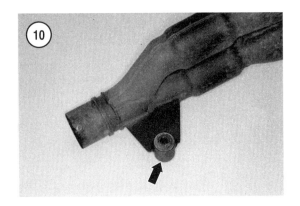

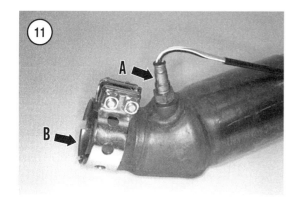

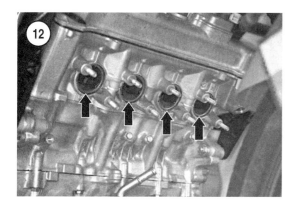

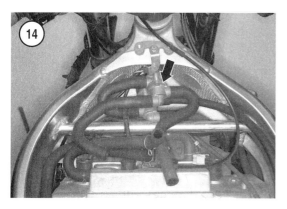

8. Install the bolt, washer and nut (**Figure 5**) securing the muffler to the rear footpeg bracket. Tighten finger-tight at this time.

9. Tighten all bolts and nuts to the specifications in **Table 3**.

10. Install the radiator as described in Chapter Eleven.

11. Refill the cooling system as described in Chapter Three.

12. On 2001-on California models, perform the following:

    a. Carefully route the oxygen sensor electrical cable and connector up through the frame.

    b. Connect the oxygen sensor four-pin electrical connector (**Figure 3**).

    c. Install the seat as described in Chapter Sixteen.

13. After installation is complete, start the engine and make sure there are no exhaust leaks.

14. Install both side fairings and the inner front fairing as described in this chapter.

CYLINDER HEAD COVER

The cylinder head cover can be removed with the engine mounted in the frame. This procedure is shown with the engine removed to better illustrate the steps.

Removal

1. Park the motorcycle on level ground. Support the motorcycle securely on a swing arm stand (or centerstand on U.K. models) with the rear wheel off the ground.

2. Remove both side fairing panels as described in Chapter Sixteen.

3A. On 1999-2000 models, remove the carburetor assembly as described in Chapter Eight.

3B. On 2001-on models, remove the throttle body assembly as described in Chapter Nine.

4. Disconnect and remove the spark plug cap/direct ignition coils from the spark plugs as described in Chapter Three.

5. Disconnect the crankcase breather hose (**Figure 13**) from the cylinder head cover.

6A. On 1999-2000 models, perform the following:

    a. Disconnect the air supply hoses and the vacuum tube, then remove the bolt securing the direct air induction solenoid valve (**Figure 14**).

b. Disconnect the air supply hoses and the vacuum tube, then remove the pulse secondary air injection control valve (PAIR) and hoses from the cylinder head cover.

6B. On 2001-on models, disconnect the PAIR air suction hoses from the PAIR reed valve covers (**Figure 15**).

7. Use compressed air to clean debris from the area above and around the cylinder head cover to prevent dirt from falling into the cylinder head after removing the cylinder head cover.

8. Remove the cylinder head cover bolts and rubber seals (A, **Figure 16**).

9. Lift up on the cylinder head cover and pull it toward the rear to clear the frame cross bracket.

10. Remove the cylinder head cover (B, **Figure 16**) and gasket.

11. Inspect the cylinder head cover as described in this section.

Installation

1. Apply a light coat of gasket sealer to the semi-circular cutouts (**Figure 17**) on the left side of the cylinder head to provide a leak-free seal, following the sealant manufacturer's instructions.

2. Install the cylinder head cover (B, **Figure 16**) onto the cylinder head while noting the following:

   a. Make sure the cylinder head cover gasket is correctly positioned around the perimeter (A, **Figure 18**) and around each spark plug hole (B).

   b. Confirm that the gasket seats squarely into the cylinder head semi-circular cutouts.

   c. Carefully install the cylinder head cover under the frame cross bracket and into position on the cylinder head (B, **Figure 16**). Push it down until it seats.

3. Install the rubber seals (**Figure 19**) with their UP mark facing up.

4. Install the cylinder head cover bolts (**Figure 20**) and tighten to 10 N•m (88 in.-lb.).

5A. On 1999-2000 models, install the pulse secondary air injection control valve (PAIR) (**Figure 14**) and connect the air supply hoses and the vacuum tube.

5B. On 2001-on models, connect the PAIR air suction hoses onto the PAIR reed valve covers (**Figure 15**).

6. Connect the crankcase breather hose (**Figure 13**) onto the cylinder head cover.

7. Connect the spark plug cap/direct ignition coils onto the spark plugs as described in Chapter Three.

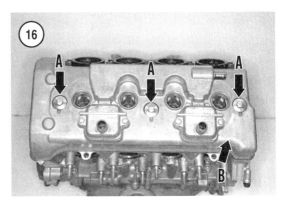

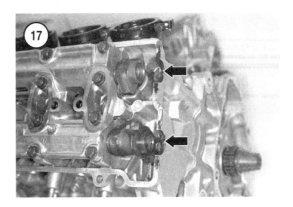

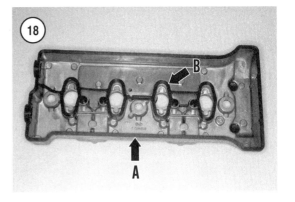

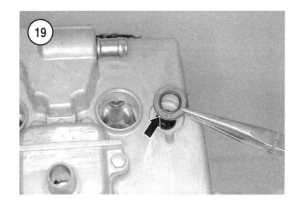

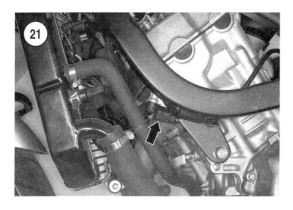

8A. On 1999-2000 models, install the carburetor assembly as described in Chapter Eight.

8B. On 2001-on models, install the throttle body assembly as described in Chapter Nine.

9. Install both side fairing panels as described in Chapter Sixteen.

Inspection

1. Clean the cover in solvent and dry with compressed air.

2. Inspect the rubber gasket assembly around the perimeter of the cylinder head cover (A, **Figure 18**) and each spark plug hole (B). Replace the gasket if it is starting to deteriorate or harden.

3. If necessary, replace the cylinder head cover gasket or reinstall the original gasket as follows:

   a. Remove the old gasket and thoroughly clean any debris or oil residue from the gasket groove around the perimeter of the cover and around the spark plug holes.

   b. Clean the grooves with solvent and dry with compressed air.

> *NOTE*
> *Honda does not recommend the use of any type of gasket sealer to secure the gasket in place on the cylinder head cover.*

   c. Install the gasket into the grooves in the cylinder head cover.

CAMSHAFTS

The camshafts can be serviced with the engine installed in the frame. They are shown with the engine removed to better illustrate the steps.

Camshaft Removal

1. Remove the cylinder head cover as described in this chapter.

2. Remove the spark plugs as described in Chapter Three. This makes it easier to rotate the engine.

3. On 2001-on models, remove the mounting bolt and the camshaft pulse generator (**Figure 21**) from the left side of the cylinder head.

4. Remove the timing hole cap and its O-ring (**Figure 22**) and perform the following:

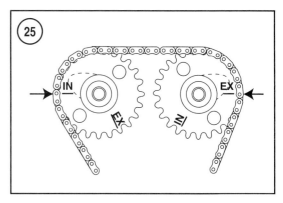

a. Using the bolt on the pulse generator rotor
(**Figure 23**), rotate the engine *clockwise*, as
viewed from the right side of the motorcycle,
until the pulse generator rotor *T* mark aligns
with the index notch on the right crankcase
cover (**Figure 24**).

b. The camshaft driven sprocket *IN* and *EX* timing marks must be flush with the top surface
of the cylinder head and must face out (**Figure 25**).

> *NOTE*
> *If the sprocket **IN** and **EX** timing
> marks face inward, the engine is po-
> sitioned incorrectly. If this condi-
> tion exists, rotate the engine
> **clockwise**, as viewed from the right
> side of the motorcycle, 360° (one
> full turn) and realign the pulse gen-
> erator rotor T mark with the index
> notch on the right crankcase cover
> (**Figure 24**).*

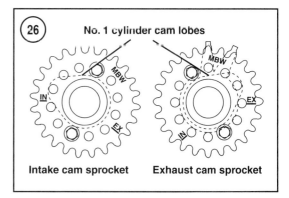

> *NOTE*
> *A cylinder at TDC on its compression
> stroke will have both camshaft lobes
> facing away from the valve lifter sur-
> face, indicating both pairs of intake
> and exhaust valves are closed (**Figure
> 26**).*

5. Remove the camshaft drive chain tensioner sealing bolt (A, **Figure 27**) and washer (B).

> *NOTE*
> *Refer to **Figure 28** and fabricate the
> special tool from a piece of 1.0 mm
> thick steel.*

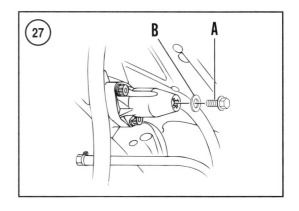

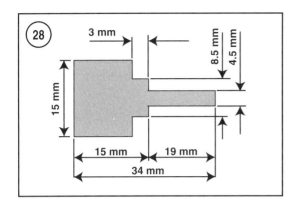

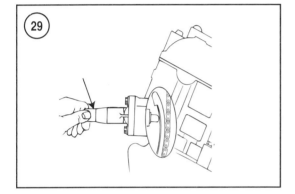

6. Using the special tool (**Figure 29**), rotate the tensioner lifter shaft *clockwise* to the fully retracted position and lock the tensioner in this position.

CAUTION
Due to the valve spring pressure applied against the camshaft holder, failure to loosen the camshaft holder bolts as described in Step 7 and Step 8 may cause the camshaft holder to distort or break. Because the camshaft holder and cylinder head are matched units, a broken camshaft holder also requires replacement of the cylinder head.

7. Remove the bolts securing the camshaft chain guide *B* (**Figure 30**) and remove the guide.

NOTE
*The center eight bolts (**Figure 31**) are equipped with a sealing washer. These sealing washers must be installed along with these eight bolts during installation.*

8. Loosen the camshaft holder bolts gradually and in a crisscross pattern in two to three stages. Continue until all 20 bolts are loose, and then remove the bolts, eight sealing washers, and the camshaft holder (**Figure 32**). Do not lose the four locating dowels installed between the camshaft holder and the cylinder head.

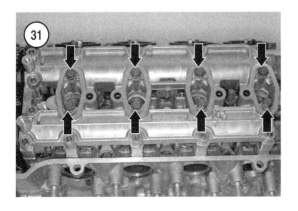

9. Disengage the camshaft chain from the sprockets and remove the intake (A, **Figure 33**) and exhaust (B) camshafts. Secure the camshaft chain to the exterior of the engine to prevent it from falling into the engine.

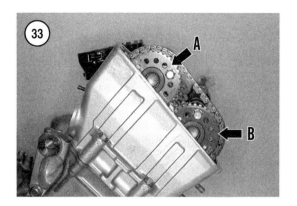

Camshaft Inspection

When measuring the camshafts, compare the measurements to the specifications in **Table 2**. Replace worn or damaged parts as described in this section.

1. Clean the camshafts in solvent and dry thoroughly before inspecting and measuring them.

2. Check the cam lobes (A, **Figure 34**) for wear. The lobes should not be scored and the edges should be square. Replace the camshaft if the lobes are scored, worn or damaged.

3. Check the camshaft bearing journals (B, **Figure 34**) for wear or scoring. Replace the camshaft if the journals are scored, worn or damaged.

> *NOTE*
> *If the camshaft lobes and journals exhibit lubrication wear, check the camshaft holder oil passages for contamination.*

4. Measure each cam lobe height with a micrometer (**Figure 35**).

5A. Support the camshaft journals on a set of V-blocks or crankshaft truing stand and measure runout with a dial indicator.

> *NOTE*
> *In the following step, the camshaft is sitting freely on the cylinder head bearing journals. It is not secured, as it must rotate freely.*

5B. An alternate way to measure runout is to install the camshaft onto the cylinder head bearing journals and measure runout with a dial indicator (**Figure 36**).

> *NOTE*
> *Do not remove the camshaft sprockets from the camshafts to inspect them.*

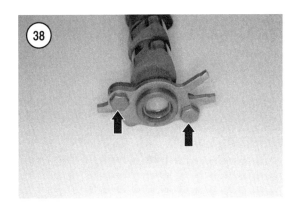

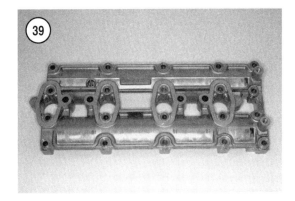

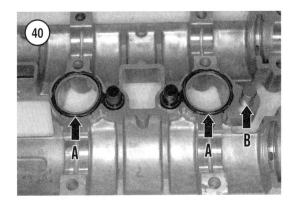

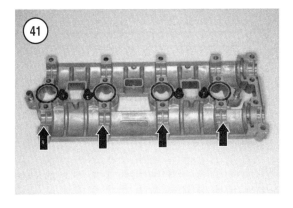

6. Inspect the camshaft sprockets (A, **Figure 37**).

    a. Damaged gear teeth.

    b. Excessive wear.

NOTE
If the camshaft sprockets are worn, also check the camshaft chain, chain guides and chain tensioner for wear or damage.

7. Check the tightness of the sprocket mounting bolts (B, **Figure 37**). If loose, remove the bolt(s), apply a medium strength threadlocking compound to the threads and tighten to 20 N•m (15 ft.-lb.).

8. On the exhaust camshaft of 2001-on models, check the tightness of the camshaft pulse generator rotor (**Figure 38**). If loose, remove the bolt(s), apply a medium strength threadlocking compound to the threads and tighten to 12 N•m (106 in.-lb.).

Camshaft Holder Inspection

1. Before cleaning the camshaft holder, inspect the oil lubrication holes for contamination. Small passages and holes in the camshaft holder provide pressure lubrication for the camshaft journals. Make sure these passages and holes are clean and open.

NOTE
Infrequent oil and filter changes may be indicated if the camshaft holder passages are dirty. Contaminated oil passages can result in camshaft failure.

2. Thoroughly clean the camshaft holder (**Figure 39**) in solvent and dry with compressed air.

3. Remove the spark plug hole gaskets (A, **Figure 40**) from the under side of the camshaft holder.

4. Check the camshaft holder (**Figure 39**) for stress cracks and other damage.

5. Check the camshaft bearing journals in the camshaft holder (**Figure 41**) and cylinder head (**Figure 42**) for wear and scoring. If damage is present, replace the cylinder head and camshaft holder as a set. To determine operational clearance, perform the *Camshaft Oil Clearance Measurement* procedure in this section.

6. Check the camshaft holder mounting bolts for hex-head or thread damage.

Camshaft Journal Oil Clearance Measurement

This section describes how to measure the bearing clearance between the camshaft, the camshaft holders and cylinder head journal using Plastigauge. Plastigauge is a material that flattens when pressure is applied to it. The marked bands on the envelope are then used to measure the width of the flattened Plastigauge. The camshafts and camshaft holder must be installed on the cylinder head when performing this procedure. Plastigauge is available from automotive parts stores in different clearance ranges.

1. Wipe all oil residue from each cam bearing journal on the camshafts, the camshaft holder and the cylinder head.

2A. On 1999-2000 models, the original equipment camshafts are identified for correct placement in the cylinder head (**Figure 43**) as follows:

    a. IN: intake camshaft.

    b. EX: exhaust camshaft

2B. On 2001-on models, the exhaust camshaft is equipped with the camshaft pulse generator rotor (**Figure 44**), but the intake camshaft is not.

> *NOTE*
> *It is not necessary to install the camshaft chain onto the sprockets for this procedure.*

3. Install the exhaust and intake camshafts into the cylinder head. Position the cam lobes so the majority of the valves will not be pressed open when the camshaft is installed. See *Camshaft Installation* in this chapter.

4. Wipe all oil from the cam bearing journals before applying the Plastigauge material.

5. Place a strip of Plastigauge material on the top of each camshaft bearing journal (**Figure 45**), parallel to the camshaft.

6. Install and tighten the camshaft holder as described under *Camshaft Installation* in this section.

> *CAUTION*
> *Do not rotate the camshafts with the Plastigauge in place.*

> *CAUTION*
> *Loosen the camshaft holder bolts as described or the camshaft holder may be damaged.*

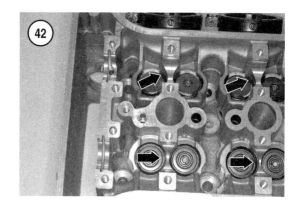

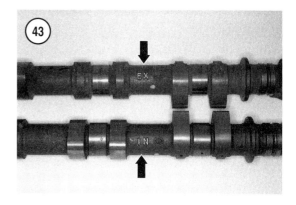

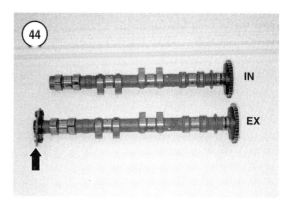

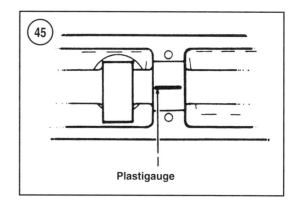

Plastigauge

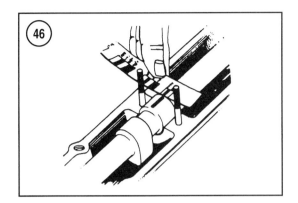

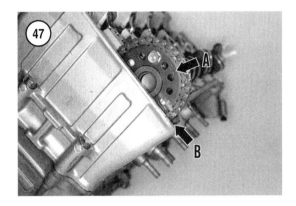

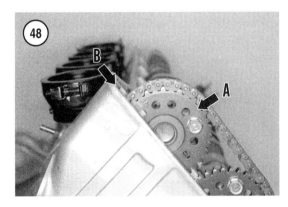

7. Loosen and remove the camshaft holder mounting bolts as described under *Camshaft Removal* in this section.

8. Remove the camshaft holder carefully, making sure the camshafts do not rotate.

9. Measure the width of the flattened Plastigauge (**Figure 46**) according to the manufacturer's instructions and compare to the camshaft journal oil clearance specification in **Table 2**. Note the following:

    a. If all the measurements are within specification, the cylinder head, camshaft and camshaft holder can be reused.

    b. If any measurement exceeds the service limit, replace the camshaft(s) and recheck the oil clearance.

    c. If the new measurement exceeds the service limit with the new camshaft, replace the camshaft holder and the cylinder head as a set.

10. Remove all Plastigauge material from the camshafts, the camshaft holder and the cylinder head.

Camshaft Installation

1. If removed, install the valve shims and lifters into the cylinder head as described in this chapter.

NOTE
*In the following steps, rotate the engine with a socket on the pulse generator bolt (**Figure 23**).*

2. Using the bolt on the pulse generator rotor (**Figure 23**), rotate the engine *clockwise*, as viewed from the right side of the motorcycle, until the pulse generator rotor *T* mark aligns with the index notch on the right crankcase cover (**Figure 24**). Verify that the No. 1 piston is at TDC.

CAUTION
In the following step, do not get the molybdenum disulfide grease on the camshaft holder mating surfaces and bolt holes. If applied to these areas, it may interfere with the torque values of the mounting bolts, allowing the bolts to be incorrectly tightened.

3. Apply molybdenum disulfide grease to the camshaft holder and cylinder head camshaft bearing journals.

4A. On 1999-2000 models, the original equipment camshafts are identified for correct placement in the cylinder head (**Figure 43**) as follows:

    a. IN: intake camshaft.

    b. EX: exhaust camshaft.

4B. On 2001-on models, the exhaust camshaft is equipped with the camshaft pulse generator rotor (**Figure 44**), and the intake camshaft is not.

5. Install the exhaust (A, **Figure 47**) camshaft into the cylinder head and mesh it with the camshaft chain. Position the camshaft sprocket so the *EX* index line (**Figure 26**) faces toward the front of the

engine and is aligned with the top surface of the cylinder head (B, **Figure 47**).

6. Install the intake camshaft into the cylinder head and mesh it with the camshaft chain (A, **Figure 48**). Position the camshaft sprocket so the *IN* index line (**Figure 26**) faces toward the rear of the engine and is aligned with the top surface of the cylinder head (B, **Figure 48**).

7. Recheck that the *IN* and *EX* marks are still aligned with the top surface of the cylinder head.

8. Install *new* O-ring seals (A, **Figure 40**) to the spark plug holes in the camshaft holder. Apply clean engine oil to the O-rings.

9. If removed, install the locating dowels (B, **Figure 40**) into the camshaft holder or cylinder head.

10. Install the camshaft holder (A, **Figure 49**) on the camshafts and cylinder head. Make sure the camshaft holder is correctly aligned with all locating dowels.

11. Install and tighten the camshaft holder mounting bolts as follows:

   a. Lubricate all camshaft holder mounting bolt threads and head seating surfaces with clean engine oil.

   b. Install *new* washers (B, **Figure 49**) onto the eight center bolts (A, **Figure 50**) and install the bolts, but do not tighten them.

   c. Install the remaining ten bolts (B, **Figure 50**), but do not tighten them.

CAUTION
The camshaft holder must be tightened in such a manner that the holder moves evenly against the cylinder head surface. Tightening only one side of a holder or overtightening the bolts may break the camshaft holder or camshaft. Make sure to tighten the camshaft holder mounting bolts as described in the following steps.

NOTE
*The camshaft holder bolt tightening sequence numbers are cast into the holder as shown in C, **Figure 49** and are numbered from 1-20.*

NOTE
The next step seats the camshaft holder against the cylinder head gasket surface. Final tightening will occur after seating the holder. Read this

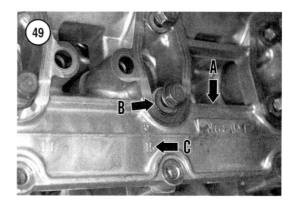

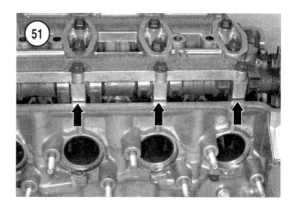

step through once before actually installing and tightening the bolts.

   d. *In this order,* gradually tighten the No. 6, No. 5, No. 8 and No. 7 bolts 1/4 to 1/2 turn at a time to draw the camshaft holder down evenly against the cylinder head until the clearance between the holder and the cylinder head is 2-3 mm (0.08-0.12 in.) around the entire perimeter (**Figure 51**). If the holder tilts toward the No. 1 cylinder during this procedure, readjust the No. 6, No. 5, No. 8 and No.

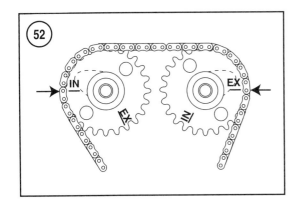

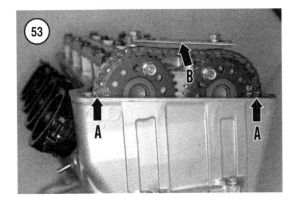

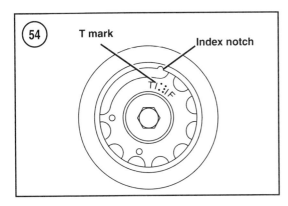

12. Insert a finger into the camshaft chain tensioner hole in the cylinder and apply pressure against the chain. Check that the *IN* and *EX* index lines on the camshaft sprockets (**Figure 52**) are still aligned with the cylinder head gasket surface as shown in A, **Figure 53**. Also make sure the pulse generator rotor *T* mark still aligns with the index mark on the right crankcase cover (**Figure 54**).

CAUTION
The index lines in Step 12 must be aligned correctly at this time; otherwise, camshaft timing will be incorrect. Do not proceed if the camshaft sprocket index lines are positioned incorrectly. Readjust the camshafts at this time if necessary.

13. Install the camshaft chain guide *B* (**Figure 53**) and tighten the bolts to 12 N•m (106 in.-lb.).

14. Remove the stopper tool from the camshaft chain tensioner.

15. Install the sealing washer and bolt onto the camshaft chain tensioner and tighten to 10 N•m (88 in.-lb.). Once again, check that camshaft timing is correct as noted in Step 12.

16. Install the timing hole cap and O-ring (**Figure 22**) and tighten to 18 N•m (13 ft.-lb.).

17. On 2001-on models, apply clean engine oil to the O-ring seal and install the camshaft pulse generator (**Figure 21**) into the left side of the cylinder head. Tighten the mounting bolt to 12 N•m (106 in.-lb.).

18. Install the cylinder head cover as described in this chapter.

19. Install the spark plugs as described in Chapter Three.

CAMSHAFT CHAIN TENSIONER

Removal/Installation

1. Park the motorcycle on level ground. Support the motorcycle securely on a swing arm stand (or centerstand on U.K. models) with the rear wheel off the ground.

2. Remove both side fairing panels as described in Chapter Sixteen.

3A. On 1999-2000 models, remove the carburetor assembly as described in Chapter Eight.

3B. On 2001-on models, remove the throttle body assembly as described in Chapter Nine.

7 bolts as necessary to keep the holder parallel to the cylinder head and with this clearance.

e. When the camshaft holder is parallel to the cylinder head, with a 2 to 3 mm (0.080-0.12 in.) clearance around the entire perimeter, continue to tighten all 20 bolts in numerical order (No. 1, No. 2, No. 3 through No. 20). Tighten the bolts 1/4 turn at a time until the camshaft holder is fully seated against the cylinder head. Tighten the bolts to the final torque of 12 N•m (106 in.-lb.).

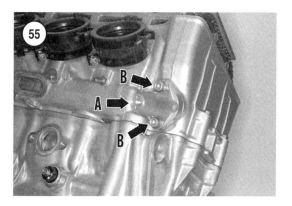

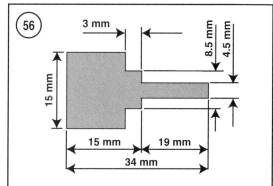

4. Remove the camshaft drive chain tensioner sealing bolt (A, **Figure 55**) and washer.

NOTE
*Refer to **Figure 56** and fabricate the special tool from a piece of 1.0 mm thick steel.*

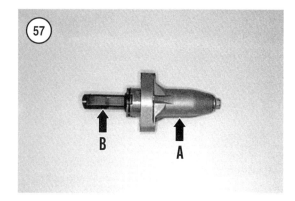

5. Using the special tool (**Figure 56**), rotate the tensioner lifter shaft *clockwise* to the fully retracted position and lock the tensioner in this position with the special tool.

6. Remove the bolts and washers (B, **Figure 55**) securing the tensioner to the cylinder head. Remove the tensioner and gasket.

7. Install by reversing these removal steps while noting the following:

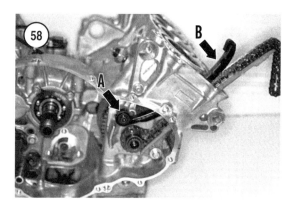

   a. Install a *new* gasket.

   b. There are two different length bolts. Install the longer bolt in the bottom hole.

   c. Tighten the bolts to 10 N•m (88 in.-lb.).

Inspection

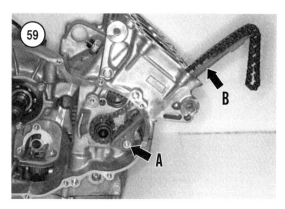

   The camshaft chain tensioner (A, **Figure 57**) cannot be rebuilt or serviced.

1. Move the tensioner pushrod (B, **Figure 57**) in and out by hand. The pushrod must move smoothly with no roughness or binding. Replace the camshaft chain tensioner if necessary.

2. Remove all gasket residue from the tensioner housing.

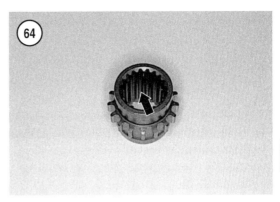

CAMSHAFT CHAIN, TIMING SPROCKET AND CHAIN GUIDES

Removal

1. Remove the cylinder head as described in this chapter.

2. Remove the right crankcase cover and ignition pulse generator rotor as described under *Pulse Generator Rotor Removal/Installation* in Chapter Ten.

3. Remove the Allen pivot bolt and washer (A, **Figure 58**) securing the camshaft chain tensioner guide (B). Remove the guide from the crankcase post and the chain.

4. Remove the shoulder bolt (A, **Figure 59**) securing the camshaft chain guide (B). Remove the guide and the washer behind it.

5. Disengage the camshaft chain (**Figure 60**) from the timing sprocket and remove the chain.

6. Note the installed direction and slide the sprocket (**Figure 61**) off the crankshaft.

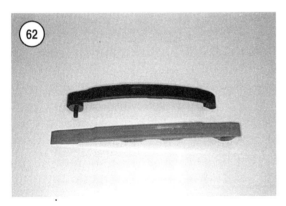

Inspection

1. Wash all parts in solvent and dry with compressed air.

2. Inspect the guides (**Figure 62**) for wear, chipping or other damage.

3. Inspect the mounting bolts for thread and/or other damage.

4. Inspect the timing sprocket (**Figure 63**) and internal splines (**Figure 64**) for wear or damage. If damaged, check the camshaft chain and camshaft sprockets for wear. See *Camshaft Inspection* in this chapter.

5. Inspect the chain (**Figure 65**) for wear or damage. If damaged, check the camshaft sprockets for wear. See *Camshaft Inspection* in this chapter.

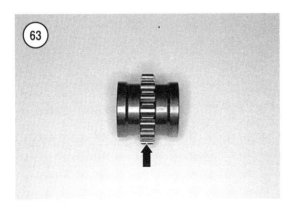

Installation

NOTE
The timing sprocket is symmetrical
*(**Figure 63**) and can be installed onto*
the crankshaft either way.

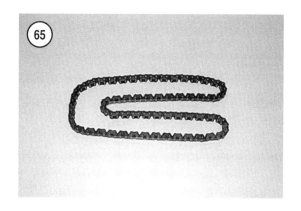

1. Align the timing sprocket wide spline groove (A, **Figure 66**) with the crankshaft wide spline (B) and install the timing sprocket.
2. Install the chain down through the chain cavity in the cylinder block and mesh it with the timing sprocket (**Figure 60**).
3. Mesh the chain with the camshaft chain guide (A, **Figure 67**) and move it into position on the crankcase post. Install the bolt (B, **Figure 67**) and tighten to 12 N•m (106 in.-lb.).
4. Apply a medium strength threadlocking compound to the camshaft chain tensioner guide Allen pivot bolt threads prior to installation.
5. Position the washer (A, **Figure 68**) behind the camshaft chain tensioner guide and install both parts onto the crankcase (B). Align the holes in the guide and washer and install the Allen pivot bolt (C, **Figure 68**).
6. Tighten the bolts to 10 N•m (88 in.-lb.).
7. Install the ignition pulse generator rotor and the right crankcase cover as described under *Pulse Generator Rotor Removal/Installation* in Chapter Ten.
8. Install the cylinder head as described in this chapter.

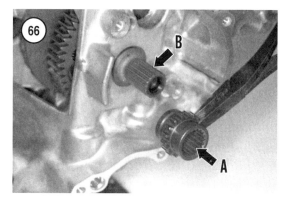

CYLINDER HEAD

The cylinder head can be removed with the engine mounted in the frame. This procedure is shown with the engine removed from the frame to better illustrate the steps.

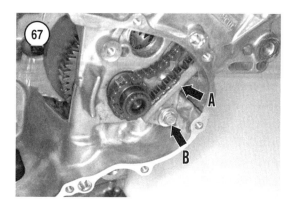

Removal

1. Drain the engine coolant as described in Chapter Three.
2. Remove the cylinder head cover and camshafts (A, **Figure 69**) as described in this chapter.
3. Remove the cylinder block coolant drain bolt and washer (**Figure 70**).
4. Remove the thermostat housing from the cylinder head as described in Chapter Eleven.
5. Remove the camshaft chain tensioner as described in this chapter.

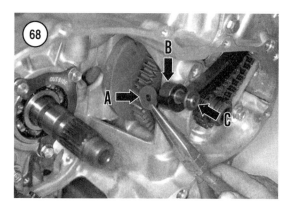

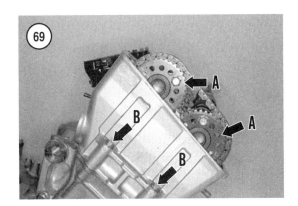

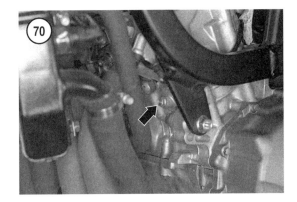

6. Remove the camshaft chain, timing sprocket and chain guides as described in this chapter.

CAUTION
Do not remove the cylinder head mounting bolts or remove the cylinder head when the engine is hot. Doing so could cause the cylinder head to warp, requiring its replacement.

7. Remove the two 6 mm bolts (B, **Figure 69**) from the right side of the cylinder head.

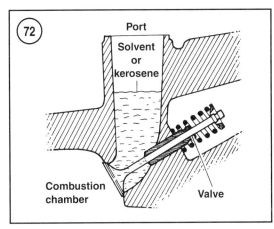

8. Loosen the ten 9 mm cylinder head bolts (**Figure 71**) in a crisscross pattern in two to three steps. Remove the ten bolts and washers.
9. Loosen the cylinder head by tapping around the perimeter with a rubber or plastic mallet.
10. When the cylinder head is free, pull it up and off the crankcase/cylinder block assembly.
11. Place the cylinder head on wooden blocks to avoid damaging the gasket surfaces.
12. Remove the cylinder head gasket and locating dowels.

NOTE
After removing the cylinder head, check the top and bottom gasket surfaces for any indications of coolant leakage. Also check the head gasket for signs of leakage. A blown gasket could indicate a warped cylinder head or other damage.

13. If the cylinder head is not going to be serviced, place it in a strong cardboard box and cover it to keep the valve lifters in place and keep the cylinder head clean.
14. If necessary, remove the valve lifters and shims as described in this chapter.

Solvent Test for Valve Seat Seal

Before removing the valves from the cylinder head, perform a solvent test to check the valve face-to-valve seat seal.
1. Remove the cylinder head as described in this chapter.
2. Support the cylinder head with the exhaust ports facing up (**Figure 72**). Then pour solvent or kero-

sene into the ports. Immediately check the combustion chambers for fluid leaking past the exhaust valves.

3. Repeat Step 2 for the intake valves.

4. If there is fluid leakage around one or both sets of valves, the valve(s) is not seating correctly. The following conditions will cause poor valve seating:

    a. A bent valve stem.

    b. A worn or damaged valve seat.

    c. A worn or damaged valve face.

    d. A crack in the combustion chamber.

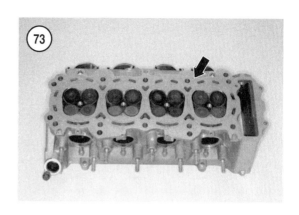

Inspection

1. Perform the *Solvent Test* before cleaning or servicing the cylinder head.

2. Remove all traces of gasket residue from the cylinder head (**Figure 73**) and cylinder block (A, **Figure 74**) surfaces. Do not scratch the gasket surface.

3. Before removing the valves, remove all carbon deposits from the combustion chambers (A, **Figure 75**) with a wire brush or wooden scraper. Take care not to damage the head, valves or spark plug threads.

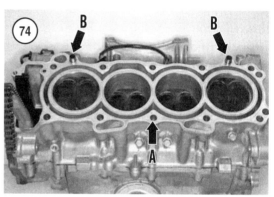

> *CAUTION*
> *If the combustion chambers are cleaned with the valves removed, it is easy to damage a valve seat. A damaged or even slightly scratched valve seat causes poor valve sealing.*

4. Examine the spark plug threads (B, **Figure 75**) in the cylinder head for damage. If damage is minor or if the threads are contaminated with carbon, use a spark plug thread tap to clean the threads, following the manufacturer's instructions. If thread damage is severe, repair the head by installing a steel thread insert. Purchase thread insert kits at an automotive supply store, or have the inserts installed by a Honda dealership or machine shop.

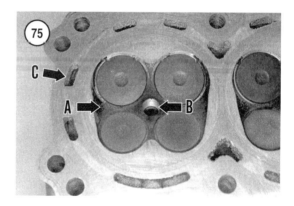

> *CAUTION*
> *Aluminum spark plug threads are commonly damaged due to galling, cross-threading and overtightening. It is easy to cross thread spark plugs on this engine because the plug holes are recessed deep within the cylinder head and are hard to access. To prevent galling, apply an antiseize compound on the plug threads before*

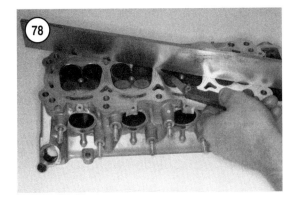

*installation and do not overtighten. Do **not** lubricate the spark plug threads with engine oil.*

NOTE
When using a tap to clean spark plug threads, lubricate the tap with aluminum tap cutting fluid or kerosene.

5. Make sure the coolant passages (C, **Figure 75**) are clear. Clean out with low air pressure if necessary.

6. Clean the entire head in solvent and dry with compressed air.

NOTE
If the cylinder head was bead-blasted, make sure to clean the head thoroughly with solvent. Residual grit seats in small crevices and other areas and can be hard to remove. Chase each exposed thread with a tap to remove grit from the threads. Residual grit left in the engine will cause premature piston, ring and bearing wear.

7. Check for cracks in the combustion chamber, intake ports (**Figure 76**) and exhaust ports (**Figure 77**). A cracked head must be replaced.

8. Examine the piston crowns. The crowns should show no signs of wear or damage. If the crown appears pecked or spongy-looking, check the spark plug, valves and combustion chamber for aluminum deposits. If these deposits are found, the cylinder is overheating due to a lean fuel mixture or preignition.

CAUTION
Do not clean the piston crowns while the pistons are installed in the cylinder block. Carbon scraped from the tops of the pistons will fall between the cylinder wall and piston and onto the piston rings. Because carbon grit is very abrasive, premature cylinder, piston and ring wear will occur. If the piston crowns have heavy deposits of carbon, remove the pistons as described in Chapter Five and clean them. Excessive carbon buildup on the piston crowns reduces piston cooling, raises engine compression and causes overheating.

9. Place a straightedge across the gasket surface at several points. Measure warp by inserting a feeler gauge between the straightedge and cylinder head at each location (**Figure 78**). Maximum allowable warp is listed in **Table 2**. If warp exceeds this limit, the cylinder head must be resurfaced or replaced. Distortion or nicks in the cylinder head surface could cause an air leak and result in overheating.

10. Check the exhaust pipe studs (**Figure 79**) for looseness or thread damage. Slight thread damage can be repaired with a thread file or die. If thread

damage is severe, replace the damaged stud(s) as described in Chapter One.

11. Check the valves and valve guides as described under *Valves and Valve Components* in this chapter.

12. Inspect the valve lifters and valve lifter bores in the cylinder head as described under *Valve Lifters and Shims* in this chapter.

Installation

1. If removed, install the camshaft chain and guides as described in this chapter.

2. Clean the cylinder head and cylinder gasket surfaces of all gasket residue.

3. If removed, install the two dowel pins (B, **Figure 74**).

4. Install a *new* cylinder head gasket (**Figure 80**) over the dowel pins and seat it against the cylinder block.

5. Position the cylinder head over the cylinder block and both dowel pins, seating it against the gasket. Check that the cylinder head is sitting flush against the head gasket around the entire perimeter.

6. Lubricate the 9 mm cylinder head bolt threads and washer seating surfaces with molybdenum oil or clean engine oil. Then install a *new* washer onto each bolt.

> *NOTE*
> *Do not lubricate the 6 mm bolt threads.*

7. Install the cylinder head 9 mm mounting bolts and washers (**Figure 71**). Tighten the bolts in a crisscross pattern in two to three stages. Tighten the bolts to 47 N•m (35 ft.-lb.).

8. Install the two 6 mm bolts (B, **Figure 69**) and tighten them securely.

9. Install the camshaft chain tensioner as described in this chapter.

10. Install the thermostat housing onto the cylinder head as described in Chapter Eleven.

11. Install a *new* sealing washer and the coolant drain bolt (**Figure 70**) onto the cylinder block. Tighten the drain bolt securely.

12. Install the camshafts and the cylinder head cover as described in this chapter.

13. Refill the engine coolant as described in Chapter Three.

14. Start the engine and check for leaks. While doing so, bleed the cooling system as described in Chapter Three.

VALVE LIFTERS AND SHIMS

Removal

1. Remove the cylinder head cover and camshafts as described in this chapter.

2. Before removing the valve lifters and shims, note the following:

  a. Temporarily install the spark plugs to close off the openings into the cylinder block.

  b. Use a divided container to store the valve lifters and shims so they will be installed in their original mounting positions. This will make valve clearance adjustment much easier after the cylinder head and camshaft have been installed.

  c. The shims may stick to the bottom of the valve lifter. Remove the valve lifters carefully to prevent a shim from falling into the engine.

  d. Remove the valve lifters carefully to avoid damaging the lifter bores in the cylinder head.

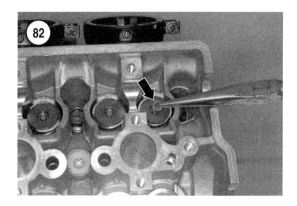

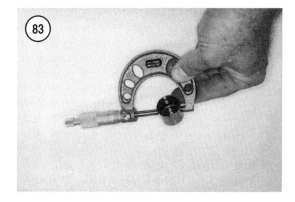

3. Remove one of the valve lifters (**Figure 81**) and its respective shim (**Figure 82**) and place both of them in the correct location in the holder.
4. Repeat Step 3 for all of the valve lifters and shims.

Inspection

Maintain the correct alignment of the valve lifters and shims when inspecting them.
1. Inspect the valve lifters and shims for wear and damage.
2. Check each valve lifter for any scoring or other damage. The lifter must operate in its cylinder head bore with no binding or chatter. If the side of a lifter is damaged, replace it.
3. Measure the valve lifter outside diameter (**Figure 83**) and compare to the specifications in **Table 2**.
4. Check the valve lifter bores in the cylinder head for any scoring or damage. These surfaces must be smooth.
5. Measure the valve lifter bore inside diameter and compare to the specification in **Table 2**.

6. Check the shims for stress cracks and other damage.

Installation

The shims and valve lifters must be installed in their original operating positions as noted during removal.

NOTE
If the shims and valve lifters were not stored in a marked divided container, the valve clearance will be more time consuming after installing the camshafts and camshaft holder.

1. Lubricate the valve lifters and shims with clean engine oil.
2. Install a shim into the valve retainer bore (**Figure 82**) with its thickness number facing down. Make sure it is seated correctly.
3. Install the valve lifter (**Figure 81**) over the shim and into the cylinder head bore. Push the lifter down until it seats against the shim.
4. Repeat for each shim and valve lifter.

VALVES AND VALVE COMPONENTS

Due to the number of special tools and the skills required to use them, it is general practice for those who perform their own service to remove the cylinder head and entrust valve service to a Honda dealership or machine shop. The following procedures describe how to check for valve component wear and to determine what type of service is required.

Valve Service Tools

To remove and install the valves in this section, the following tools are required:
1. Valve spring compressor.
2. Valve lifter bore protector. This tool is used to protect the valve lifter bore when removing and installing the valves. This tool can be made from a 35 mm film container cut to the dimensions shown in **Figure 84**.

Valve Removal

Refer to **Figure 85** and **Figure 86**.

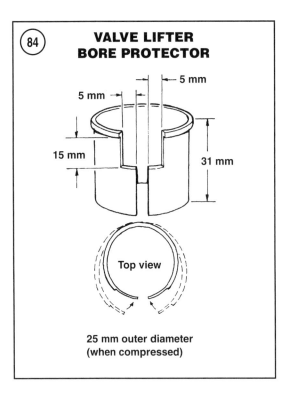

(84) VALVE LIFTER
BORE PROTECTOR

Top view

25 mm outer diameter
(when compressed)

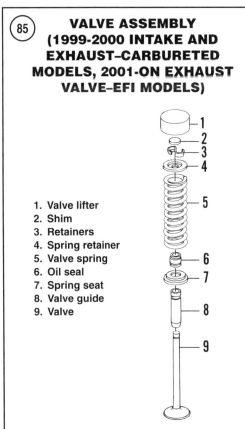

(85) VALVE ASSEMBLY
(1999-2000 INTAKE AND
EXHAUST–CARBURETED
MODELS, 2001-ON EXHAUST
VALVE–EFI MODELS)

1. Valve lifter
2. Shim
3. Retainers
4. Spring retainer
5. Valve spring
6. Oil seal
7. Spring seat
8. Valve guide
9. Valve

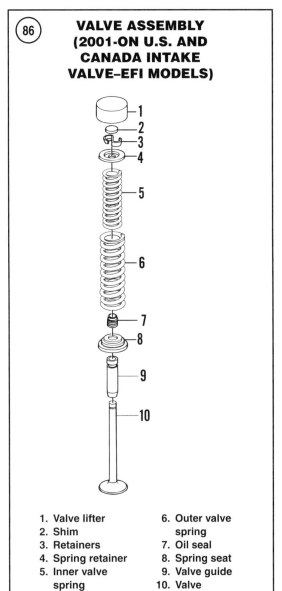

(86) VALVE ASSEMBLY
(2001-ON U.S. AND
CANADA INTAKE
VALVE–EFI MODELS)

1. Valve lifter
2. Shim
3. Retainers
4. Spring retainer
5. Inner valve
   spring
6. Outer valve
   spring
7. Oil seal
8. Spring seat
9. Valve guide
10. Valve

(87)

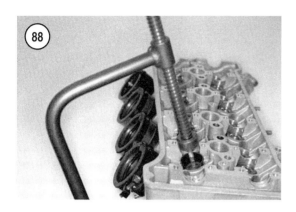

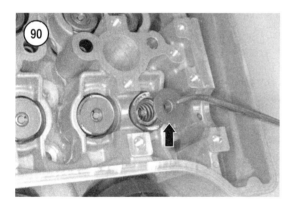

NOTE
The 2001-on intake valves on U.S. and Canada models are equipped with an inner and outer valve spring. The exhaust valves on these models are equipped with a single valve spring. All other models and years are equipped with a single spring on both the intake and exhaust valves.

1. Remove the camshafts, valve lifters and shims as described in this chapter.

2. Remove the cylinder head as described in this chapter.

3. Install the protector into the valve lifter bore (**Figure 87**) of the valve being removed.

4. Install a valve spring compressor squarely over the upper retainer with the other end of the tool placed against the valve head (**Figure 88**).

5. Tighten the valve spring compressor until the valve keepers separate. Lift the valve keepers out through the valve spring compressor with needlenose pliers or tweezers (**Figure 89**).

6. Gradually loosen the valve spring compressor and remove it from the head.

7. Remove the protector from the valve lifter bore.

8. Remove the retainer (**Figure 90**).

9A. On 2001-on intake valves on U.S. and Canada fuel injected models, remove the outer (**Figure 91**) and inner (**Figure 92**) valve springs.

9B. On all other years and models, remove the single valve spring (**Figure 93**).

CAUTION
*Remove any burrs from the valve stem grooves (**Figure 94**) before removing the valve; otherwise, the valve guides will be damaged.*

10. Turn the cylinder head over and remove the valve (**Figure 95**).

> *NOTE*
> *If a valve is difficult to remove, it may be bent, causing it to stick in its valve guide. This condition will require valve and valve guide replacement.*

11. Pull the oil seal (**Figure 96**) off of the valve guide and discard it.
12. Remove the spring seat (**Figure 97**).

> *NOTE*
> *All components of each valve assembly must be kept together. Refer to **Figure 98** and **Figure 99**. Place each set in a plastic bag, a divided carton or into separate small boxes. Label the sets as to which cylinder and either intake or exhaust valves. This will keep them from getting mixed up and will make installation simpler. Do not intermix components from the valves, or excessive wear may result.*

13. Mark all parts as they are removed so that they will be installed in their same locations.
14. Repeat for the remaining intake and exhaust valves as necessary.

> *NOTE*
> *Do not remove the valve guides unless they require replacement.*

Valve Component Inspection

When measuring the valve components, compare the actual measurements to the specifications in **Table 2**. Replace parts that are damaged or out of specification as described in this section.

1. Clean the valve components in solvent. Do not damage the valve seating surface.
2. Inspect the valve face (**Figure 100**) for burning, pitting or other signs of wear. Unevenness of the valve face is an indication that the valve is not serviceable. If the wear on a valve is too extensive to be corrected by hand-lapping the valve into its seat, replace the valve. The face on the valve cannot be ground. Replace the valve if defective.
3. Inspect the valve stems for wear and roughness. Check the valve keeper grooves for damage.
4. Measure each valve stem outside diameter with a micrometer (**Figure 101**). Note the following:

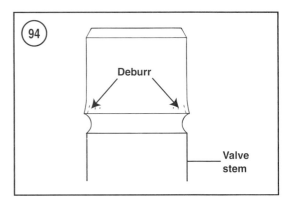

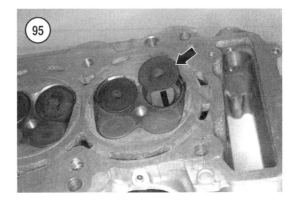

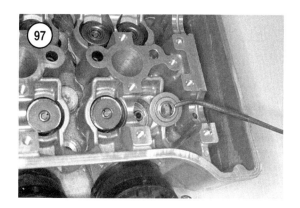

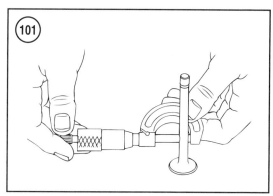

a. If a valve stem is out of specification, discard the valve.

b. If a valve stem is within specification, record the measurement so it can be used to determine the valve stem-to-guide clearance in Step 7.

NOTE
Honda recommends reaming the valve guides to remove any carbon buildup before checking and measuring the guides in the following steps. For the home mechanic it is more practical to remove carbon and varnish from the valve guides with a stiff spiral wire brush. Then clean the valve guides with solvent to wash out all debris. Dry with compressed air.

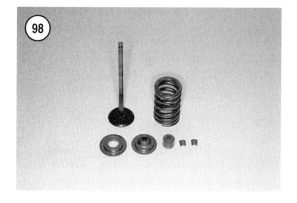

5. Insert each valve into its respective valve guide and move it up and down by hand. The valve should move smoothly.

6. Measure each valve guide inside diameter with a small hole gauge and record the measurements. Note the following:

NOTE
Because valve guides wear unevenly (oval shape), measure each guide at different positions. Use the largest bore diameter measurement when determining its size.

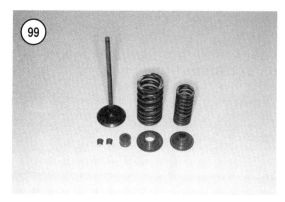

a. If a valve guide is out of specification, replace it as described in this section.

b. If a valve guide is within specification, record the measurement so it can be used to determine the valve stem-to-guide clearance in Step 7.

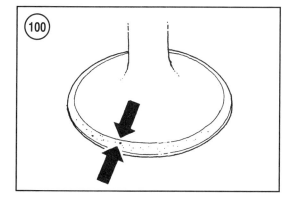

7. Subtract the measurement made in Step 4 from the measurement made in Step 6 to determine the valve stem-to-guide clearance. Note the following:

   a. If the clearance is out of specification, determine if a new guide would bring the clearance within specification.

   b. If the clearance would be out of specification with a new guide, replace the valve and valve guide as a set.

8. If a small hole gauge or inside micrometer is not available, insert each valve into it guide. Hold the valve just slightly off its seat and rock it sideways or use a dial indicator with its plunger against the valve head (**Figure 102**). If the valve rocks more than slightly, the guide is probably worn and should be replaced. As a final check, take the cylinder head and valve assemblies to a Honda dealership or machine shop and have the valve guides accurately measured.

9. Inspect the valve springs as follows:

   a. Inspect each spring for any cracks, distortion or other damage.

   b. Measure the free length of each valve spring with a vernier caliper (**Figure 103**).

   c. Replace the defective spring(s). On 2001-on U.S. and Canada intake valves, replace defective springs in pairs (both inner and outer).

10. Check the upper retainer and valve keepers. If they are in good condition, they may be reused; replace in pairs as necessary.

11. Inspect the valve seats as described under *Valve Seat Inspection* in this chapter.

Valve Guide Replacement

Special tools and considerable experience are required to properly replace the valve guides in the cylinder head. If these tools are unavailable, have a Honda dealership or machine shop perform this procedure. Removing the cylinder head, then taking it to a dealership or machine shop to have the valves guides replaced, can save a considerable amount of money. The following procedure is provided for those who choose to perform this task. When a valve guide is replaced, also replace the valve.

1. Remove the securing screws and remove all four intake manifolds (**Figure 104**) from the cylinder head.

2. Place the new valve guides in a freezer for approximately one hour prior to heating the cylinder head. Chilling them will slightly reduce the outside

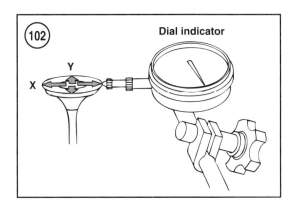

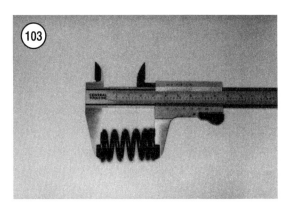

diameter, while the hot cylinder head is slightly larger due to heat expansion. This will make valve guide installation much easier.

NOTE
Because flangeless valve guides are used, the measurements required in Step 3 are critical for proper valve guide and valve operation.

3. Measure the height of the valve guide that is above the cylinder head surface with a vernier cali-

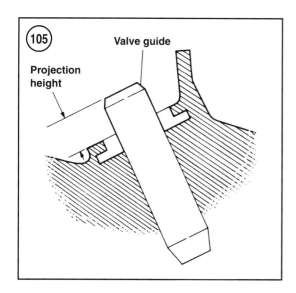

105

Projection height

Valve guide

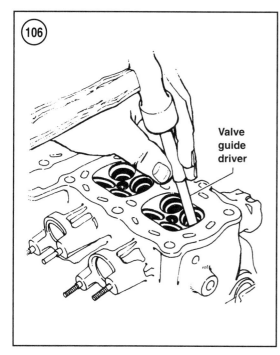

106

Valve guide driver

per. This measurement is the projection height (**Figure 105**). Record the projection height for each valve guide. The valve guide projection height specifications for intake and exhaust valves are listed in **Table 2**.

NOTE
To monitor the cylinder head temperature when heating it in Step 4, use heat indicator sticks, available at welding supply stores. Follow the

manufacturer's directions when using the sticks.

4. The valve guides are installed with a slight interference fit. Heat the cylinder head in a shop oven or on a hot plate. Heat the cylinder head to a temperature of 100-150° C (212-300° F).

WARNING
*Wear insulated or welding gloves when performing the following procedure. The cylinder head will be very **hot**.*

CAUTION
Do not heat the cylinder head with a torch (propane or acetylene); never bring a flame into contact with the cylinder head or valve guide. The direct heat will destroy the case hardening of the valve guide and may cause warpage of the cylinder head.

5. Remove the cylinder head from the oven or hot plate. Place it on wooden blocks with the combustion chambers facing *up*. Make sure the cylinder head is properly supported on the wooden blocks.

CAUTION
Do not attempt to remove the valve guides if the head is not hot enough. Doing so may damage the valve guide bore.

6. From the combustion side of the cylinder head, drive out the old valve guide with a hammer and the Honda valve guide driver (part No. 07JMD-KY20100) or an equivalent (**Figure 106**). Discard the valve guides after removing them. Never reinstall a valve guide that has been removed, as it is no longer within tolerances.

7. Reheat the cylinder head as described in Step 4, then remove it from the heat source and install it onto the wooden blocks with the valve spring side facing *up*.

8. Remove a *new* valve guide from the freezer.

NOTE
The same Honda valve guide driver tool is used for both removal and installation of the valve guide.

9. Using the valve guide driver tool, from the topside (valve spring side) of the cylinder head, drive in the

valve guide (**Figure 107**) until the projection height of the valve guide is within the specifications in **Table 2** (**Figure 105**). Note that the projection height measurements for the intake and exhaust valves are different.

10. Repeat for each valve guide.

11. After the cylinder head has cooled to room temperature, ream the *new* valve guide as follows:

    a. Use the Honda valve guide reamer, 4.008 mm (part No. 07MMH-MV90100) and a tap wrench.

    b. Apply cutting oil to both the *new* valve guide and the valve guide reamer.

> *CAUTION*
> *Always rotate the reamer **clockwise** when installing and removing it in the valve guides. If the reamer is rotated counterclockwise, it will dull its cutting surfaces and damage the guide.*

    c. Insert the reamer from the combustion chamber side and rotate it *clockwise* through the valve guide (**Figure 108**). Continue to rotate the reamer and work it down through the entire length of the *new* valve guide. Apply additional cutting oil during this procedure.

    d. While rotating the reamer *clockwise*, withdraw the reamer from the valve guide.

12. If necessary, repeat for any other valve guide.

13. Thoroughly clean the cylinder head and valve guides with solvent to remove all metal particles. Clean the cylinder head with hot soapy water, rinse the cylinder head completely and thoroughly dry it with compressed air.

14. Measure the valve guide inside diameter with a small hole gauge. This measurement must be within the specification listed in **Table 2**.

15. Lubricate the valve guides with engine oil.

16. Recondition the valve seats as described in this chapter.

17. Install the intake manifolds in their original locations on the cylinder head.

Valve Seat Inspection

The most accurate method for checking the valve seat surface is to use a marking compound (machinist's dye), available from auto parts and tool stores. Marking compound is used to locate high or irregular spots when checking or making close fits. Follow the manufacturer's directions.

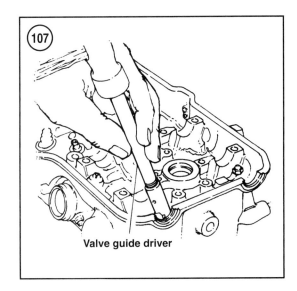

Valve guide driver

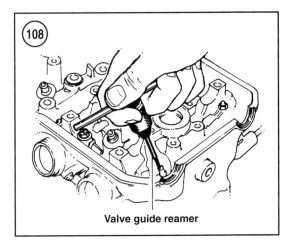

Valve guide reamer

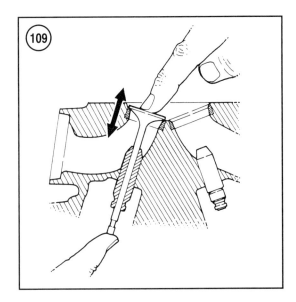

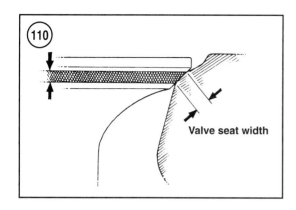

Valve seat width

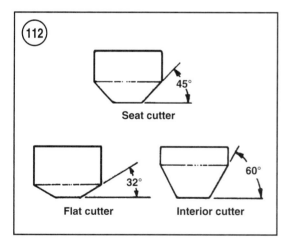

Seat cutter — 45°

Flat cutter — 32°   **Interior cutter** — 60°

NOTE
*Because of the close operating toler-
ances within the valve assembly, the
valve stem and guide must be within
tolerance; otherwise, the inspection
results will be inaccurate.*

1. Remove the valves as described in this chapter.
2. Clean the valve seat in the cylinder head and
valve mating areas with contact cleaner.

3. Thoroughly clean all carbon deposits from the
valve face with solvent and dry thoroughly.
4. Spread a thin layer of marking compound evenly
on the valve face.
5. Slowly insert the valve into its guide.
6. Support the valve with two fingers (**Figure 109**)
and tap the valve up and down in the cylinder head.
Do *not* rotate the valve or a false reading will result.
7. Remove the valve and examine the impression left
by the marking compound. If the impression on the
valve or in the cylinder head is not even and continuous and the valve seat width (**Figure 110**) is not within
the specified tolerance listed in **Table 2**, the valve seat
in the cylinder head must be reconditioned.
8. Closely examine the valve seat in the cylinder
head (**Figure 111**). It should be smooth and even
with a polished seating surface.
9. If the valve seat is not in good condition, recondition the valve seat as described in this chapter.
10. Repeat for the other valves.

Valve Seat Reconditioning

Tools

Special valve cutters and considerable experience
are required to properly recondition the valve seats
in the cylinder head. If these tools are unavailable,
have a Honda dealership or machine shop perform
this procedure. Removing the cylinder head, then
taking it to a dealership or machine shop to have the
valve seats reconditioned, can save a considerable
amount of money. The following procedure is provided for those who choose to perform this task.

While the valve seat for both the intake and exhaust valves are machined to the same angles, different cutter sizes are required. The following
Honda valve seat cutters (**Figure 112**) are required:
1. 24.5 mm valve seat cutter (EX 45°).
2. 27.5 mm valve seat cutter (IN 45°).
3. 24 mm valve seat cutter (EX 32°).
4. 27 mm valve seat cutter (IN 32°).
5. 22 mm valve seat cutter (EX 60°).
6. 26 mm valve seat cutter (IN 60°).
7. 4.0 mm cutter holder.

Procedure

NOTE
*Follow the manufacturer's instructions
when using the valve facing equipment.*

1. Carefully rotate and insert the solid pilot into the valve guide. Be sure the pilot is correctly seated.

2. Install the 45° cutter and T-handle onto the solid pilot.

3. Using the 45° cutter, de-scale and clean the valve seat with one or two turns (**Figure 113**).

> *CAUTION*
> *When cutting valve seats, work slowly. Measure the valve seat contact area in the cylinder head (**Figure 110**) after each cut to make sure the contact area is correct and to avoid removing too much material. Overgrinding will sink the valves too far into the cylinder head, requiring its replacement.*

4. If the seat is still pitted or burned, turn the 45° cutter additional turns until the surface is clean. Refer to the previous CAUTION to avoid removing too much material from the cylinder head.

5. Measure the valve seat with a vernier caliper (**Figure 110**). Record the measurement to use as a reference point when performing the following.

> *CAUTION*
> *The 32° cutter removes material quickly. Work carefully and check the progress often.*

6. Install the 32° cutter onto the solid pilot and lightly cut the seat to remove 1/4 of the existing valve seat (**Figure 114**).

7. Install the 60° cutter onto the solid pilot and lightly cut the seat to remove 1/4 of the existing valve seat (**Figure 115**).

8. Measure the valve seat with a vernier caliper (**Figure 110**). Then fit the 45° cutter onto the solid pilot and cut the valve seat to the specified width (**Figure 116**) listed in **Table 2**.

9. When the valve seat width is correct, check valve seating as follows:

   a. Clean the valve seat with contact cleaner.

   b. Spread a thin layer of marking compound evenly on the valve face.

   c. Slowly insert the valve into its guide.

   d. Support the valve with two fingers (**Figure 109**) and tap the valve up and down in the cylinder head. Do *not* rotate the valve or a false reading will result.

   e. Remove the valve and examine the impression left by the marking compound.

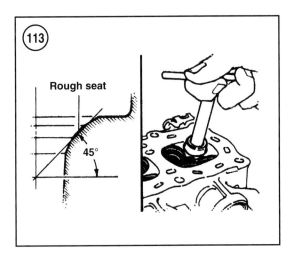

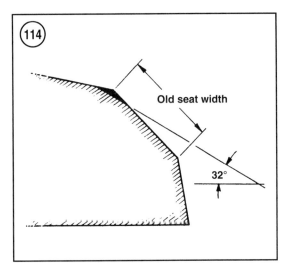

   f. Measure the valve seat width as shown in **Figure 110**. Refer to **Table 2** for specified valve width.

   g. The valve contact should be approximately in the center of the valve seat area.

10. If the contact area is too *high* on the valve, or if it is too wide, use the 32° cutter and remove a portion of the top area of the valve seat material to lower and narrow the contact area on the valve (**Figure 114**).

11. If the contact area is too *low* on the valve, or too wide, use the 60° cutter and remove a portion of the lower area of the valve seat material to raise and narrow the contact area on the valve.

12. After the desired valve seat position and width is obtained, use the 45° cutter to lightly clean off any burrs that may have been caused by previous cuts.

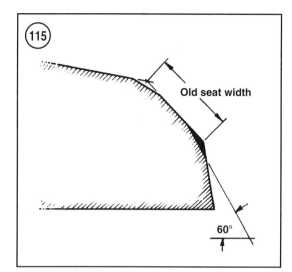

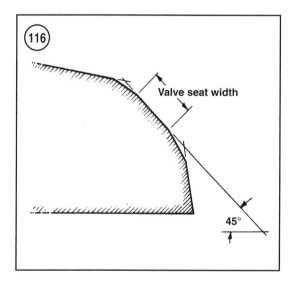

This procedure should only be performed after determining that the valve seat width is within specifications.

1. Smear a light coating of fine grade valve lapping compound on the valve face seating surface.

2. Insert the valve into the head.

3. Wet the suction cup of the lapping stick and stick it onto the head of the valve. Spin the tool in both directions while pressing it against the valve seat, and lap the valve to the seat. Every 5 to 10 seconds, lift and rotate the valve 180° in the valve seat. Continue until the mating surfaces on the valve and seat are smooth and equal in size.

4. Closely examine the valve seat in the cylinder head (**Figure 111**). It should be smooth and even with a smooth, polished seating *ring*.

5. Repeat Steps 1-4 for the other valves.

6. Thoroughly clean the valves and cylinder head in solvent and then with hot soapy water to remove all valve grinding compound. Dry thoroughly.

> *CAUTION*
> *Any compound left on the valves or in the cylinder head causes excessive wear to the engine components.*

7. Install the valve assemblies as described in this chapter.

8. After the lapping is completed and the valves are reinstalled in the head, perform the *Solvent Test* described in this chapter. There should be no leakage past the seat. If leakage occurs, the combustion chamber appears wet. If fluid leaks past any of the seats, disassemble that valve assembly and repeat the lapping procedure until there is no leakage.

> *NOTE*
> *This solvent test does not ensure long-term durability or maximum power. It merely ensures maximum compression will be available on initial start-up after assembly.*

9. If the cylinder head and valve components are cleaned in detergent and hot water, apply a light coat of engine oil to all bare metal surfaces to prevent rust formation.

13. When the contact area is correct, lap the valve as described in this chapter.

14. Repeat Steps 1-13 for all remaining valve seats.

15. Thoroughly clean the cylinder head and all valve components in solvent, then with detergent and hot water. Rinse in cold water. Dry with compressed air. Then apply a light coat of clean engine oil to all non-aluminum surfaces to prevent any rust accumulation.

Valve Lapping

Valve lapping is a simple operation which can restore the valve seat without machining if the amount of wear or distortion is not too great.

Valve Installation

Refer to **Figure 85** and **Figure 86**.

NOTE
The 2001-on intake valves on U.S. and
Canada models are equipped with inner
and outer valve springs. The exhaust
valves on these models are equipped
with a single valve spring. All other
models are equipped with a single spring
on both the intake and exhaust valves.

Following the reference marks made during removal, install the valves in their original locations.

1. Install the valve as follows;

   a. Turn the cylinder head over.

   b. Coat a valve stem with molybdenum disulfide
   oil.

   c. Install the valve partway into its guide (**Figure
   95**); then, slowly turn the valve as it enters the
   valve stem seal and continue turning it until the
   valve is installed all the way. To avoid damage,
   rotate and push the valve through its valve guide.

2. Install the spring seat and make sure it is seated
squarely on the cylinder head surface (**Figure 117**).

NOTE
The intake and exhaust valve seals are
identical.

3. Lubricate the inside of a new oil seal with engine
oil. Install the oil seal (**Figure 118**). Then push the
seal straight down the valve guide until it snaps into
the groove in the top of the guide (**Figure 119**).
Check that the oil seal is centered and seats squarely
on top of the guide. If the seal is cocked to one side,
oil will leak past the seal during engine operation.

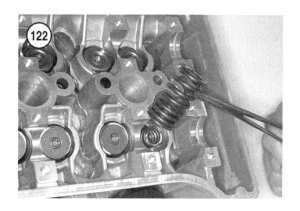

4

NOTE
The oil seals must be replaced when-
ever the valves are removed. Also, if
the new seal was installed and then
removed, do not reuse it.

4. On all models and years, position the valve springs with the tightly wound springs facing the combustion chamber (**Figure 120**).

5A. On 2001-on intake valves on U.S. and Canada models, install the inner (**Figure 121**) and outer (**Figure 122**) valve springs. Make sure the springs are seated correctly (**Figure 123**).

5B. On all other years and models, install the valve spring (**Figure 124**). Make sure the spring is seated correctly (**Figure 125**).

6. Install the retainer (**Figure 126**) on top of the valve spring(s).

7. Install the protector (**Figure 127**), used during removal, into the valve lifter bore.

CAUTION
To avoid loss of spring tension, do not
compress the spring(s) any more than
necessary when installing the valve
keepers.

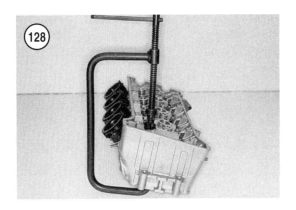

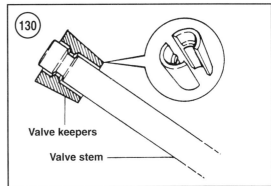

Valve keepers

Valve stem

8. Compress the valve spring(s) with a valve spring compressor tool (**Figure 128**) and install the valve keepers (**Figure 129**). Make sure the keepers fit into the rounded groove in the valve stem (**Figure 130**).

9. Remove the valve spring compressor tool.

CAUTION
If Step 10 is not performed, the valve keepers may pop out of the valve stem groove after the cylinder head has been installed and the engine is started. This may result in engine damage.

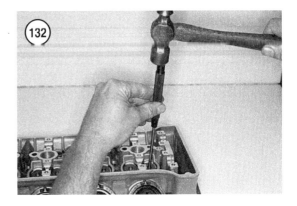

10. Place a drift onto the top of the valve stem (**Figure 131**) and tap on the end with a hammer (**Figure 132**) to ensure the keepers are seated correctly. If the keepers are not installed correctly, they will pop out at this time.

11. Repeat Steps 1-10 for the remaining valves.

12. Install the cylinder head as described in this chapter.

13. Install the shims and valve lifters and camshafts as described under *Camshaft Installation* in this chapter.

14. After installing the cylinder head, camshafts and camshaft holder on the engine, check and adjust the valve clearance as described in Chapter Three.

Table 1 GENERAL ENGINE SPECIFICATIONS

Item	Specification
Cylinder arrangement	In-line four cylinder inclined 31° from vertical
Engine type	Four-stroke, DOHC, four-valve head
Bore × stroke	67.0 × 42.5 mm (2.64 1.67 in.)
Displacement	599 cc (36.5 cu. in.)
Compression ratio	12.0:1
Compression pressure at 350 rpm (at sea level)	1226 kPa (178 psi)
Firing order	1-2-4-3
Ignition type	Electronic (fully transistorized)
Valve timing	
Intake valve opens at 1 mm (0.04 in.) lift	22° BTDC
Intake valve closes at 1 mm (0.04 in.) lift	43° ABDC
Exhaust valve opens at 1 mm (0.04 in.) lift	38° BBDC
Exhaust valve closes at 1 mm (0.04 in.) lift	7° ATDC
Cooling system	Liquid cooled
Lubrication system	
Type	Wet sump, forced pressure
Oil pump	Trochoid
Oil pressure (at oil pressure switch) at 80° C (176° F)	490 kPa (71 psi) at 6000 rpm
Engine dry weight	59 kg (130 lbs.)

Table 2 ENGINE TOP END SPECIFICATIONS

Item	Standard mm (in.)	Wear limit mm (in.)
Camshaft (49-state, Canada carbureted models)		
Cam lobe height		
Intake	36.60-36.76 (1.4409-1.4472)	36.57 (1.440)
Exhaust	35.38-35.54 (1.3929-1.3992)	35.35 (1.392)
Journal oil clearance		
(bearing clearance)	0.020-0.062 (0.0008-0.0024)	0.10 (0.004)
Camshaft runout	–	0.05 mm (0.002)
Camshaft (California carbureted models)		
Cam lobe height		
Intake	34.64-34.72 (1.3638-1.3669)	34.61 (1.363)
Exhaust	33.92-34.00 (1.3354-1.3386)	33.89 (1.334)
Journal oil clearance		
(bearing clearance)	0.020-0.062 (0.0008-0.0024)	0.10 (0.004)
Camshaft runout	–	0.05 mm (0.002)
Camshaft (U.K. carbureted models)		
Cam lobe height		
Intake	36.60-36.76 (1.4409-1.4472)	36.57 (1.440)
Exhaust	35.38-35.54 (1.3929-1.3992)	35.35 (1.392)
Journal oil clearance		
(bearing clearance)	0.020-0.062 (0.0008-0.0024)	0.10 (0.004)
Camshaft runout	–	0.05 mm (0.002)
Camshaft (All fuel-injected models)		
Cam lobe height		
Intake	36.56-36.80 (1.4390-1.4490)	36.50 (1.437)
Exhaust	35.34-35.58 (1.3910-1.4010)	35.35 (1.392)
Journal oil clearance		
(bearing clearance)	0.020-0.062 (0.0008-0.0024)	0.10 (0.004)
Camshaft runout	–	0.05 mm (0.002)

(continued)

Table 2 ENGINE TOP END SPECIFICATIONS (continued)

Item	Standard mm (in.)	Wear limit mm (in.)
Cylinder head warp	–	0.10 (0.004)
Valve lifter		
Outside diameter	25.978-25.993 (1.0228-1.0233)	25.97 (1.022)
Lifter bore inside diameter	26.010-26.026 (1.0240-1.0246)	26.04 (1.025)
Valves and valve springs		
Valve clearance (cold engine)		
Intake	0.17-0.23 (0.007-0.009)	–
Exhaust	0.25-0.31 (0.010-0.012)	–
Valve stem outside diameter		
Intake	3.975-3.990 (0.1565-0.1571)	3.965 (0.1561)
Exhaust	3.965-3.980 (0.1561-0.1567)	3.955 (0.1557)
Valve stem-to-guide clearance		
Intake	0.010-0.037 (0.0004-0.0015)	0.075 (0.0030)
Exhaust	0.020-0.047 (0.0008-0.0018)	0.085 (0.0033)
Valve guide		
Inside diameter	4.000-4.012 (0.1575-0.1580)	4.040 (0.159)
Projection height		
Intake	16.1-16.4 (0.63-0.65)	–
Exhaust	14.3-14.6 (0.56-0.57)	
Valve seat width		
Intake and exhaust	0.90-1.10 (0.035-0.043)	1.5 (0.06)
Valve spring free length		
(1999-2000 U.S. and Canada models)		
Intake	39.87 (1.570)	38.27 (1.507)
Exhaust	36.23 (1.426)	34.73 (1.367)
Valve spring free length		
(2001-on U.S. and Canada models)		
Intake		
Inner	36.40 (1.430)	35.57 (1.400)
Outer	42.20 (1.660)	41.36 (1.628)
Exhaust	36.30 (1.429)	35.75 (1.400)
Valve spring free length		
(U.K. carbureted models)		
Intake	39.87 (1.570)	38.27 (1.507)
Exhaust	36.23 (1.426)	34.73 (1.367)
Valve spring free length		
(U.K. fuel-injected models)		
Intake	39.50 (1.555)	38.71 (1.524)
Exhaust	36.30 (1.430)	35.57 (1.400)

Table 3 ENGINE TOP END TORQUE SPECIFICATIONS

Item	N•m	in.-lb.	ft.-lb.
Camshaft chain tensioner mounting bolt	10	88	–
Camshaft chain tensioner guide Allen pivot bolt[1]	10	88	–
Camshaft chain guide socket bolt	12	106	–
Camshaft holder bolts[3]	12	106	–
Camshaft pulse generator rotor bolt	12	106	
Camshaft sprocket bolt[1]	20	–	15

(continued)

Table 3 ENGINE TOP END TORQUE SPECIFICATIONS (continued)

Item	N•m	in.-lb.	ft.-lb.
Cylinder head cover bolts	10	88	–
Cylinder head bolts[2][3]	47	–	35
Cylinder head sealing bolt[1]	32	–	24
Exhaust pipe			
To cylinder head nuts	12	106	–
To muffler clamp bolts	23	–	17
PAIR reed valve cover bolt	12	106	–
Spark plugs	14	124	–
Timing hole cap	18	–	13

1. Apply a medium strength threadlock to threads.
2. Apply molybdenum disulfide oil to the threads and seating surfaces.
3. See text.

4

CHAPTER FIVE

ENGINE LOWER END

This chapter describes service procedure for lower end engine components. Engine removal and installation procedures are also described. Specifications and bearing selection tables are in **Tables 1-10** at the end of the chapter.

SERVICING ENGINE IN FRAME

The following components can be serviced while the engine is installed in the frame:

1. Camshafts.

2. Cylinder head.

3. Clutch.

4. Gearshift mechanism.

5. Oil pump.

6. Alternator.

7. Pulse generator.

8. Starter motor.

9. Carburetor assembly or the throttle body.

10. Water pump.

11. Oil cooler.

ENGINE SERVICE NOTES

Before removing and installing the engine in the frame, note the following:

1. A hydraulic floor jack is required to support the engine.

2. Because the swing arm is mounted onto the engine, a separate stand must be used to support the rear of the motorcycle before removing and installing the engine. A typical stand is shown in the service procedure. The U.S. and Canada models are not equipped with a centerstand, but U.K. models are equipped with a centerstand.

3. The engine dry weight is 59 kg (130 lbs.). Due to its weight and bulk, it is essential that a minimum of two, preferably three, people perform engine removal and installation.

4. Cover the O-ring drive chain before degreasing the engine. The chemicals in the degreaser will cause the O-rings to swell, permanently damaging the chain.

5. Label electrical connectors and hoses with tape and a permanent pen.

6. The engine mounting hardware components are very complicated. It is advisable to make notes or

take photographs of the bolts, adjusting bolts and various locknuts during the removal procedure. Keep these components separated and note their location to assist during installation.

ENGINE

Removal

1. Support the motorcycle on a swing arm safety stand. Block the front wheel so the motorcycle will not roll in either direction while on the safety stand (or centerstand on U.K. models).

2. Remove the following as described in Chapter Sixteen:
   a. Seat.
   b. Front fairing and air ducts.
   c. Both side fairings and front inner fairing.
   d. Rear cowl.

3. Disconnect the negative battery cable as described in Chapter Ten.

4. Remove the following as described in Chapter Eight or Nine:
   a. Fuel tank.
   b. Air filter housing assembly.
   c. Carburetor assembly or throttle body assembly.

NOTE
Plug the cylinder head intake openings with rubber plugs or clean shop rags.

5. Drain the cooling system as described in Chapter Three.

6. Remove the radiator and coolant hoses as described in Chapter Eleven. Also remove the mounting bolts and the radiator lower mounting bracket (**Figure 1**).

7. Remove the muffler and exhaust pipe as described in Chapter Four.

8. On California models, remove the EVAP canister and EVAP purge control valve as described in Chapter Eight.

9. Drain the engine oil as described in Chapter Three.

10. Remove the oil filter as described in Chapter Three.

11. Remove the oil cooler as described in this chapter.

12. Remove the drive sprocket.

NOTE
*After removing the drive sprocket, pull the drive chain back onto the driven sprocket to take out the slack and move the loose end of the chain out of the way. Use a tie-wrap and secure the loop of chain together (**Figure 2**) on the driven sprocket.*

13. Disconnect the PAIR hoses (A, **Figure 3**) from the cylinder head cover.

14. Remove the direct ignition coils (B, **Figure 3**) as described in Chapter Three. Do not remove the spark plugs from the cylinder head.

15. Remove the thermostat housing as described in Chapter Eleven.

16. Disconnect the clutch cable from the clutch arm (**Figure 4**) and the cable bracket on the clutch cover.

17. Remove the starter motor as described in Chapter Ten.

18A. On 1999-2000 models, label and disconnect the following electrical connectors:

    a. Ignition pulse generator two-pin electrical connector.

    b. Speed sensor three-pin black electrical connector.

    c. Oil pressure switch wire connector.

    d. Thermosensor connector.

    e. Alternator three-pin white electrical connector.

    f. Sidestand two-pin electrical connector.

18B. On 2001-on models, label and disconnect the following electrical connectors:

    a. Engine sub-harness twelve-pin gray electrical connector.

    b. Camshaft pulse generator two-pin electrical connector.

    c. Alternator three-pin white electrical connector.

    d. Sidestand two-pin electrical connector.

19. Loosen the clamp bolt and disconnect the gearshift lever arm (**Figure 5**) from the shift shaft.

20. Disconnect the neutral position switch (**Figure 6**).

21. Remove the camshaft chain tensioner as described in Chapter Four.

22. On the right side, remove the bolt and nuts securing the shock link bracket (**Figure 7**) and remove the bracket.

23. On the left side, perform the following:

    a. Remove the bolts (**Figure 8**) securing the sidestand assembly to the shock link/sidestand bracket and remove the assembly.

    b. Remove the bolt and nuts securing the shock link/sidestand bracket (**Figure 9**) and remove the bracket assembly.

24. If the engine is going to be disassembled, remove the following parts while the engine is still in the frame.

    a. Right crankcase cover (Chapter Six).

    b. Starter clutch (Chapter Ten).

    c. Clutch assembly (Chapter Six).

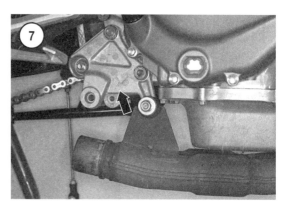

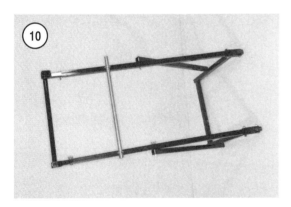

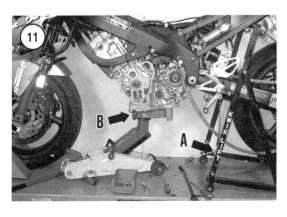

d. Water pump (Chapter Eleven).

e. Alternator stator and flywheel (Chapter Ten).

f. External gearshift linkage assembly (Chapter Six).

NOTE
Use a helper when supporting the motorcycle with the frame stand. If a stand is being constructed or modified for use on these models, construct it so that when it is supporting the motorcycle, all weight is removed from the rear wheel. The frame stand shown in **Figure 10** *is a modified Kwik Lift front end stand sold through motorcycle dealerships. This allows easy removal of the engine and/or the rear swing arm assembly.*

25. With one or more assistants lifting the rear of the motorcycle, support the motorcycle with a frame stand installed at the seat rail assembly (A, **Figure 11**).

CAUTION
Do not work on the motorcycle until it is supported securely on the stand.

26. Secure the engine with a hydraulic jack. Place a wooden block between the engine and jack support (B, **Figure 11**). Operate the jack to place tension against the engine and to help with engine mounting bolt removal.

27. Check the engine to make sure all electrical connectors and hoses are disconnected and will not interfere with engine removal.

28. Refer to **Figures 12-14** and remove the following engine mounting components in the following order:

CAUTION
Continually adjust the jack height during engine removal and installation to prevent damage to the mounting bolt threads and hardware. Ideally, the jack should support the engine so its mounting bolts can be easily removed or installed.

NOTE
There are many different sizes and lengths of bolts, adjusting bolts and various locknuts and fasteners used to secure the engine. As each set of bolts, adjust bolts and nuts are removed,

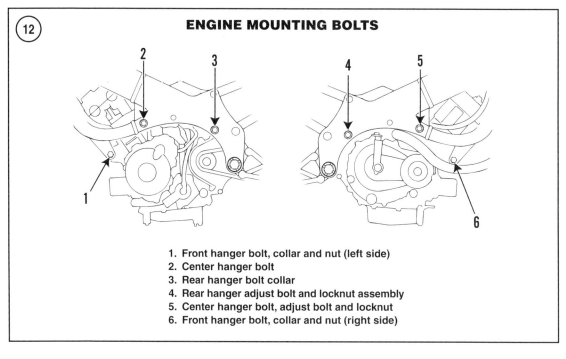

ENGINE MOUNTING BOLTS

1. Front hanger bolt, collar and nut (left side)
2. Center hanger bolt
3. Rear hanger bolt collar
4. Rear hanger adjust bolt and locknut assembly
5. Center hanger bolt, adjust bolt and locknut
6. Front hanger bolt, collar and nut (right side)

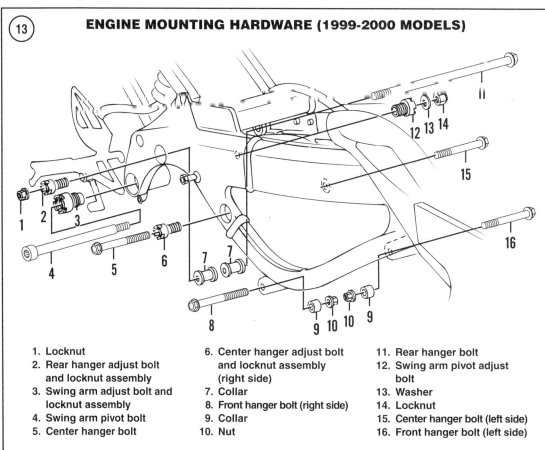

ENGINE MOUNTING HARDWARE (1999-2000 MODELS)

1. Locknut
2. Rear hanger adjust bolt and locknut assembly
3. Swing arm adjust bolt and locknut assembly
4. Swing arm pivot bolt
5. Center hanger bolt
6. Center hanger adjust bolt and locknut assembly (right side)
7. Collar
8. Front hanger bolt (right side)
9. Collar
10. Nut
11. Rear hanger bolt
12. Swing arm pivot adjust bolt
13. Washer
14. Locknut
15. Center hanger bolt (left side)
16. Front hanger bolt (left side)

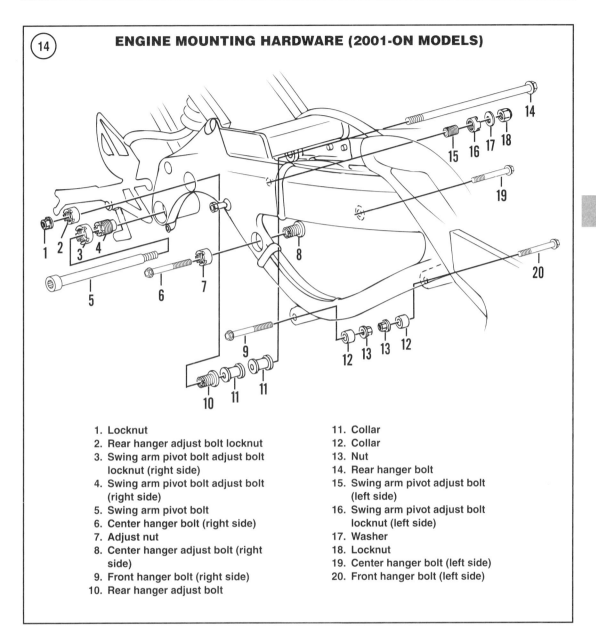

ENGINE MOUNTING HARDWARE (2001-ON MODELS)

14

1. Locknut
2. Rear hanger adjust bolt locknut
3. Swing arm pivot bolt adjust bolt locknut (right side)
4. Swing arm pivot bolt adjust bolt (right side)
5. Swing arm pivot bolt
6. Center hanger bolt (right side)
7. Adjust nut
8. Center hanger adjust bolt (right side)
9. Front hanger bolt (right side)
10. Rear hanger adjust bolt
11. Collar
12. Collar
13. Nut
14. Rear hanger bolt
15. Swing arm pivot adjust bolt (left side)
16. Swing arm pivot adjust bolt locknut (left side)
17. Washer
18. Locknut
19. Center hanger bolt (left side)
20. Front hanger bolt (left side)

15

place each individual set in a separate plastic bag or box. This will help when installing the engine.

NOTE
In this procedure, two Honda special locknut wrenches are used to loosen the adjusting bolt locknuts. These tools are also used during engine installation.

a. On the left side, remove the swing arm pivot bolt locknut and washer (**Figure 15**).

b. On the right side, withdraw the swing arm pivot bolt (A, **Figure 16**).

c. On both the right and left side, use the Honda special locknut wrench (part No. 07908-4690003) and loosen the swing arm pivot adjust bolt locknut (**Figure 17**).

d. On both the right and left side, loosen the swing arm pivot bolt adjust bolt (**Figure 18**).

e. On the right side, remove the center hanger bolt (B, **Figure 16**).

f. On the right side, remove the rear hanger adjust bolt locknut (C, **Figure 16**).

g. On the right side, use the Honda special locknut wrench (part No. 07VMA-MBB0100) and loosen the center hanger adjust bolt locknut (A, **Figure 19**).

h. On the right side, use the Honda special locknut wrench (part No. 07VMA-MBB0100) and loosen the rear hanger adjust bolt locknut (B, **Figure 19**).

i. On the left side, remove the center hanger bolt (A, **Figure 20**).

j. On the right side, push the rear hanger bolt out sufficiently to access the adjust bolt.

k. Loosen the rear hanger adjust bolt (B, **Figure 19**).

l. On the right side, loosen the center hanger adjust bolt (A, **Figure 19**).

m. On both sides, remove the front hanger bolts, nuts and collars (C, **Figure 19**).

NOTE
Have an assistant steady the engine on the jack when removing the last bolt.

n. On the left side, remove the rear hanger bolt and collars (B, **Figure 20**).

o. Completely loosen the swing arm adjust bolt on both sides.

CAUTION
The following steps require the aid of an assistant to safely remove the engine assembly from the frame. Due to the weight of the engine, it is suggested that at least one helper, preferably two, assist in engine removal.

p. Gradually lower the engine assembly to clear the frame members and maneuver the engine out of the frame. The engine can be removed through either side of the frame. Take the en-

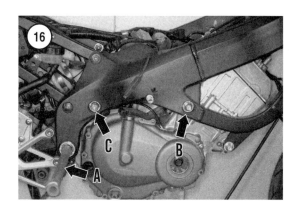

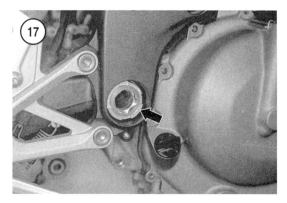

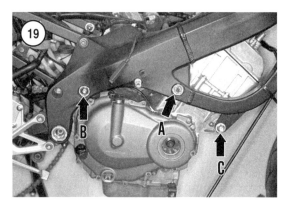

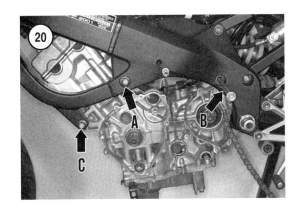

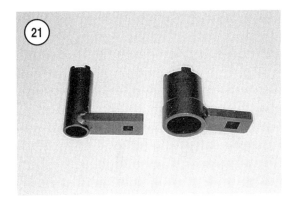

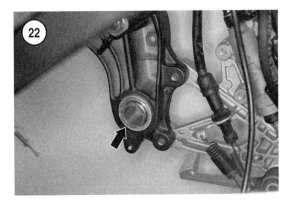

gine to a workbench or engine stand for further disassembly.

    q. Reinstall the swing arm pivot bolt and nut to hold the swing arm securely in place.

29. Refer to *Cleaning and Inspection* in this chapter.

Installation

In this procedure, two Honda special locknut wrenches (**Figure 21**) are used to tighten the adjusting bolt locknuts. The locknut wrench increases the torque wrench's leverage so the torque wrench reading (*indicated*) will be less than the torque actually applied to the locknut (*actual*). Refer to *Torque Adapters* in Chapter One for information on how changes in torque wrench length affect torque readings.

1. Check the coolant hoses, vacuum hoses and fuel lines, spark plug cables and electrical wires and connectors throughout the frame. If necessary, reposition them so that they will not interfere or be damaged when installing the engine.

> *CAUTION*
> *The following steps require the aid of a helper, preferably two, to safely install the engine in the frame.*

2. With one or more assistants, carefully transfer the engine from the workbench or engine stand to the floor directly below the frame. Install the engine on a floor jack and steady the engine by hand.

3. Secure the swing arm, then remove the swing arm pivot bolt.

4. If removed, install the engine hanger and swing arm adjust bolts (**Figure 22**) and screw them in fully so they will be flush with the inner surface of the frame to allow engine installation.

5. Slowly maneuver the engine and center it between the sides of the frame (**Figure 23**).

> *CAUTION*
> *Before installing the mounting bolts that pass through the frame and engine, make sure the engine is square and level with the frame. Attempting to install the bolts with the engine misaligned can damage the various fasteners.*

6. Slowly apply jack pressure and raise the engine into position. Pivot the front portion (cylinder head assembly) up into the frame, then the rear portion into position. Align all of the mounting bolt holes (**Figure 24**).

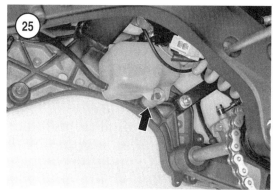

7. Refer to **Figures 12-14** for the following steps:

a. On the left side, install the center hanger bolt (A, **Figure 20**).

b. Correctly position and install the collars on the right and left side front hanger bolts and nuts (C, **Figure 19** and **Figure 20**). Tighten the nuts finger-tight at this time.

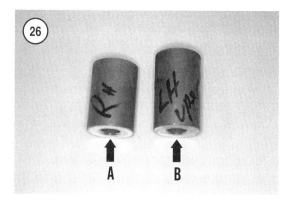

NOTE
*On 2001-on models, the coolant reserve tank secures the right side collar (**Figure 25**).*

NOTE
*The collars are different in length and must be installed on the correct side of the engine bosses. The right side collar (A, **Figure 26**) is shorter than the left side (B).*

c. On the left side, install the rear hanger bolt (B, **Figure 20**) and both collars. Push the rear hanger bolt all the way through.

d. On the left side, install and tighten the left side center hanger bolt (A, **Figure 20**) to 39 N•m (29 ft.-lb.).

e. On the left side, tighten the left side front hanger bolt (C, **Figure 20**) to 39 N•m (29 ft.-lb.).

f. On the right side, tighten the right side front hanger bolt (C, **Figure 19**) to 39 N•m (29 ft.-lb.).

g. On the right side, tighten the right side center hanger adjust bolt (A, **Figure 27**) to 39 N•m (29 ft.-lb.). Unscrew the bolt 1/2 turn (180°) so there is minimal clearance between the engine and the frame (B, **Figure 27**).

h. On the right side, tighten the right side rear hanger adjust bolt (**Figure 28**) to 39 N•m (29 ft.-lb.). Then, unscrew the bolt 1/2 turn (180°)

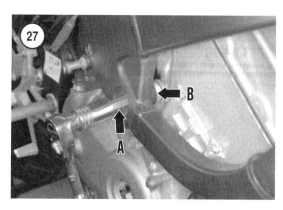

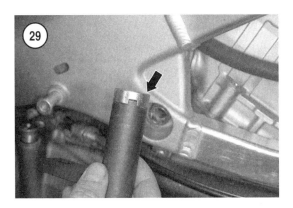

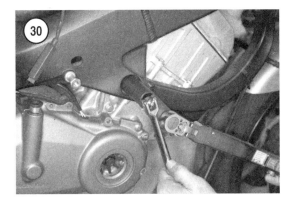

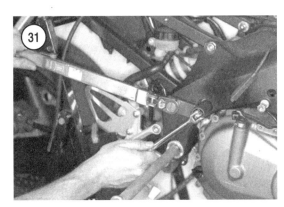

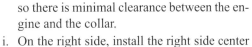

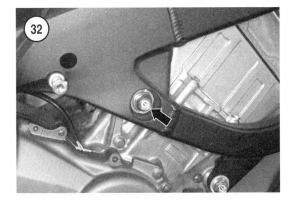

so there is minimal clearance between the engine and the collar.

i. On the right side, install the right side center hanger adjust bolt locknut (**Figure 29**). Secure the center hanger adjust bolt and use the Honda special locknut wrench (part No. 077VMA-MBB0100) and tighten the right side center hanger adjust bolt locknut (**Figure 30**) to 49 N•m (36 ft.-lb.).

j. On the right side, install the right side rear hanger adjust bolt locknut. Secure the rear hanger adjust bolt and use the Honda special locknut wrench (part No. 077VMA-MBB0100) and tighten the right side rear hanger adjust bolt locknut (**Figure 31**) to 49 N•m (36 ft.-lb.).

k. On the right side, install the right side center hanger bolt (**Figure 32**) and tighten (**Figure 33**) to 39 N•m (29 ft.-lb.).

l. On the right side, install the engine rear hanger bolt locknut and tighten (**Figure 34**) 39 N•m (29 ft.-lb.).

NOTE
It is difficult to install the standard swing arm pivot bolt after the engine

*has been removed and installed due to the partial misalignment of the various spacers within the swing arm and engine pivot areas. The shoulder at the end of the threaded portion (**Figure 35**) will catch on the spacers and make installation difficult. Obtain an additional swing arm pivot bolt and modify it. Remove the threaded end and grind a slight chamfer on the end as shown in **Figure 36**. The chamfered end will then make it easier for the pivot bolt to pass through the spacers and align them. This modified bolt is also used for swing arm removal and installation in Chapter Fourteen.*

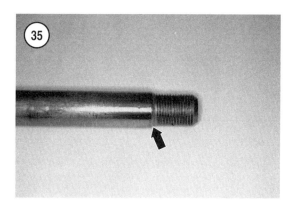

8. Refer to *Swing Arm Installation* in Chapter Fourteen and complete the installation and adjustment of the swing arm pivot bolt.

9. If the engine was disassembled, install the following parts:

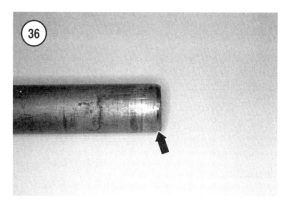

   a. External gearshift linkage assembly (Chapter Six).
   b. Alternator stator and flywheel (Chapter Ten).
   c. Water pump (Chapter Eleven).
   d. Clutch assembly (Chapter Six).
   e. Starter clutch (Chapter Ten).
   f. Right crankcase cover (Chapter Six).

10. Install the camshaft chain tensioner as described in Chapter Four.

11. Connect the neutral position switch (**Figure 37**).

12. Connect the gearshift lever arm (**Figure 38**) onto the shift shaft. Tighten the clamp bolt securely.

13A. On 1999-2000 models, connect the following electrical connectors:

   a. Sidestand two-pin electrical connector.
   b. Alternator three-pin white electrical connector.
   c. Thermosensor connector.
   d. Oil pressure switch wire connector.
   e. Speed sensor three-pin black electrical connector.
   f. Ignition pulse generator two-pin electrical connector.

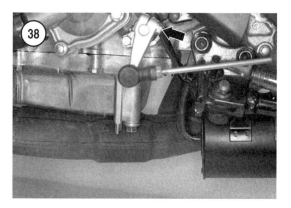

13B. On 2001-on models, connect the following electrical connectors:

   a. Sidestand two-pin electrical connector.
   b. Alternator three-pin white electrical connector.
   c. Camshaft pulse generator two-pin natural electrical connector.

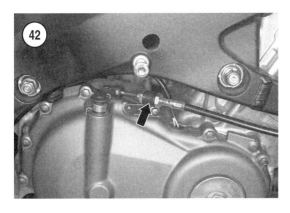

d. Engine sub-harness twelve-pin gray electrical connector.

14. On the left side, perform the following:

a. Install the shock link/sidestand bracket (**Figure 39**) onto the crankcase. Tighten the bolts to 39 N•m (29 ft.-lb.) and the nut to 44 N•m (32 ft.-lb.).

b. Install the sidestand assembly onto the shock link/sidestand bracket (**Figure 40**). Install the bolts and tighten to 44 N•m (32 ft.-lb.).

15. On the right side, install the shock link bracket (**Figure 41**). Tighten the bolt to 39 N•m (29 ft.-lb.) and the nuts to 44 N•m (32 ft.-lb.).

16. Install the camshaft chain tensioner as described in Chapter Four.

17. Install the starter motor as described in Chapter Ten.

18. Connect the clutch cable onto the clutch arm (**Figure 42**).

19. Install the thermostat housing as described in Chapter Eleven.

20. Install the direct ignition coils as described in Chapter Three. Do not remove the spark plugs from the cylinder head.

21. Connect the PAIR hoses onto the cylinder head cover.

22. Install the drive sprocket.

23. Install the oil cooler as described in this chapter.

24. Install the oil filter as described in Chapter Three.

25. Refill the engine oil as described in Chapter Three.

26. On California models, install the EVAP purge control valve and EVAP canister as described in Chapter Eight.

27. Install the muffler and exhaust pipe as described in Chapter Four.

28. Install the radiator lower mounting bracket and bolts. Tighten the bolts securely.

29. Install the radiator and coolant hoses as described in Chapter Eleven.

30. Refill the cooling system as described in Chapter Three.

31. With one or more assistants, lift the rear of the motorcycle and remove the frame stand from under the seat rail assembly.

32. Support the motorcycle on a swing arm safety stand (or centerstand on U.K. models).

33. Block the front wheel so the motorcycle will not roll in either direction while on the safety stand (or centerstand on U.K. models).

34. Install the following as described in Chapter Eight or Nine:

    a. Carburetor assembly or throttle body assembly.

    b. Air filter housing assembly.

    c. Fuel tank.

35. Connect the negative battery cable as described in Chapter Ten.

NOTE
Do not install the fairing assembly until after starting the engine and checking for leaks.

36. Start the engine and check for oil and coolant leaks. At the same time the engine is running, bleed the cooling system as described in Chapter Three.

37. Install the following as described in Chapter Sixteen:

    a. Rear cowl.

    b. Front center and both fairing panels.

    c. Upper fairing.

    d. Seat.

38. Operate the clutch lever, making sure there is resistance at the lever when operated. If necessary, adjust the clutch as described in Chapter Three.

39. Shift the transmission into gear and check clutch and transmission operation.

40. Slowly test-ride the motorcycle to ensure all systems are operating correctly.

Cleaning and Inspection

1. Remove any corrosion from the engine mount bolts with a wire wheel.

2. Clean and dry the engine mount bolts, nuts adjust bolts, locknuts and collars.

3. Clean the engine hanger adjust bolt threads in the frame for damage.

4. Replace damaged fasteners.

5. Inspect the shock link/sidestand bracket for cracks and fractures.

6. Check the coolant hoses for cracks, leakage or other damage. Replace if necessary.

7. Check the wire harness routing in the frame. Check the harness cover and wires for chafing or other damage. Replace harness cable guides and clips as required.

8. Clean the electrical connectors with contact cleaner.

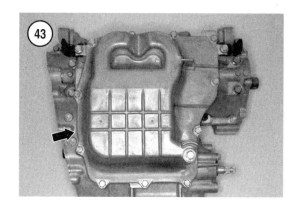

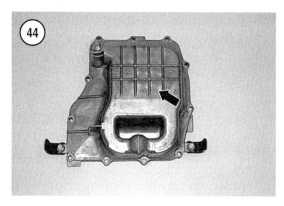

OIL PAN, OIL STRAINER AND PRESSURE RELIEF VALVE

The oil pan can be removed with the engine installed in the frame. The following procedure is shown with the engine removed to better illustrate the steps.

Oil Pan Removal/Installation

1. Support the motorcycle on a swing arm safety stand (or centerstand on U.K. models).

2. Block the front wheel so the motorcycle will not roll in either direction while on the safety stand (or centerstand on U.K. models).

3. Remove the front inner fairing panel and both side fairing panels as described in Chapter Sixteen.

4. Remove the exhaust system as described in Chapter Four.

5. Drain the engine oil as described in Chapter Three.

6. Thoroughly clean the oil pan and lower crankcase of all dirt and debris.

7. If compressed air is available, clean dirt and debris off the oil pan, frame and other parts to prevent particles from entering the exposed engine crankcase.

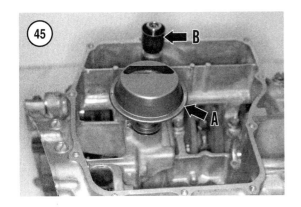

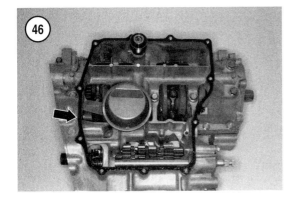

NOTE
Place an empty oil drain pan underneath the engine when performing Step 7.

8. Using a crisscross pattern, loosen the bolts securing the oil pan (**Figure 43**) to the lower crankcase; allow residual oil to drain into the drain pan. If the oil pan is stuck to the crankcase, tap it with a plastic mallet; do not pry the oil pan away from the crankcase.

9. Remove the oil pan mounting bolts and remove the oil pan.

10. Check the inside of the oil pan for aluminum or metal debris, which indicates engine, clutch or transmission damage.

11. Remove all sealer residue from the oil pan and lower crankcase mating surfaces.

12. Thoroughly clean the oil pan in solvent and then dry with compressed air. Remove all solvent residue and any oil sludge left in the pan.

13. Inspect the bottom surface of the oil pan (**Figure 44**) for cracks or damage from road debris.

14. Make sure the oil strainer (A, **Figure 45**) and pressure relief valve (B) are properly installed; refer to the appropriate procedure in this section.

15. Apply a thin bead of ThreeBond 1207B or an equivalent RTV silicone onto the oil pan mating surface (**Figure 46**).

NOTE
If using RTV silicone, allow it to set for 10-15 minutes before installing the oil pan.

16. Align the holes in the oil pan with the threaded holes in the lower crankcase and install the oil pan (**Figure 43**). Install the bolts finger-tight to seat the oil pan against the lower crankcase sealing surface. Tighten all of the bolts securely in a crisscross pattern and in two or three steps.

17. Fill the engine with the correct type and quantity of oil as described in Chapter Three.

18. Install the exhaust system as described in Chapter Four.

19. Start the engine and check the oil pan for leaks.

20. Install the front inner fairing panel and both side fairing panels as described in Chapter Sixteen.

Oil Strainer Removal/Installation

1. Remove the oil pan as described in this chapter.

2. Remove the oil strainer (A, **Figure 45**) and gasket.

3. Check the oil strainer screen (**Figure 47**) for clogging or damage. If the screen is clogged, clean it in solvent and thoroughly dry. If the screen cannot be cleaned or if it is damaged, replace the oil strainer assembly.

4. Lubricate a new oil strainer gasket with engine oil and install it onto the oil strainer as shown in **Figure 48**.

5. Align the oil strainer groove with the crankcase boss (**Figure 49**) and push the oil strainer into the crankcase until it bottoms.

6. Install the oil pan as described in this chapter.

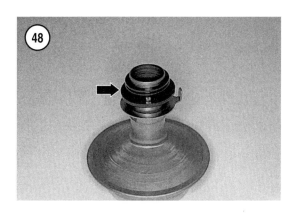

**Oil Pressure Relief Valve
Removal/Inspection/Installation**

1. Remove the oil pan as described in this chapter.
2. Pull straight up and remove the oil pressure relief valve (**Figure 50**) from the lower crankcase and place it on a clean, lint-free cloth. If the valve is not going to be serviced, store it in a sealed plastic bag until it is installed.

> *CAUTION*
> *Handle the oil pressure relief valve carefully to prevent dirt from entering the valve and scoring the piston and cylinder.*

3. Remove the O-ring seal from the body and discard it.
4. Service the oil pressure relief valve as follows:
   a. Remove the snap ring from the end of the valve (**Figure 51**). Then remove the washer, spring and piston.
   b. Clean and dry all parts.
   c. Check the piston and piston pin for scoring, scratches or other damage.
   d. Inspect the spring for cracks, stretched coils or other damage.
   e. If any part shows severe wear or damage, replace the pressure relief valve assembly.

> *NOTE*
> *The relief valve spring tension helps control oil pressure. A weak or damaged spring can reduce oil pressure and cause engine damage. The piston will be forced open at a lower oil pressure, reducing the amount of oil the engine receives. Likewise, a damaged or stuck piston can reduce oil pressure.*

   f. Reverse these steps to assemble the pressure relief valve assembly. Make sure the piston seats against the stop pin. Install a *new* snap ring with its flat side facing out. Make sure the snap ring seats in the groove completely (**Figure 51**).

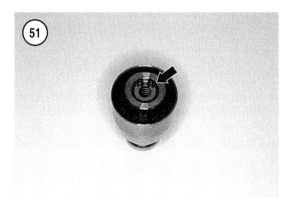

5. Install a *new* O-ring seal (**Figure 52**) into the relief valve groove.
6. Install and push the pressure relief valve into the crankcase until it bottoms (**Figure 50**).
7. Install the oil pan as described in this chapter.

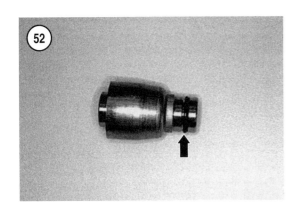

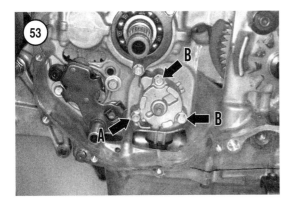

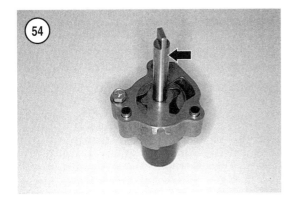

OIL PUMP

The oil pump is located behind the clutch assembly on the right side and can be removed with the engine installed in the frame.

Removal/Installation

1. Remove the clutch assembly, oil pump drive sprocket, driven sprocket and drive chain as described under *Clutch Removal* in Chapter Six.

> *NOTE*
> *There are two different length flange bolts securing the oil pump to the lower crankcase.*

2. Remove the single short flange bolt (A, **Figure 53**) and two long flange bolts (B) securing the oil pump to the lower crankcase.

3. Pull straight out and remove the oil pump from the lower crankcase. Do not lose the two dowel pins. The dowel pins will either stay with the oil pump or on the lower crankcase.

4. If necessary, inspect the oil pump as described in this chapter.

5. Inspect the oil pump driven sprocket assembly as described in Chapter Six.

6. Rotate the oil pump drive shaft (**Figure 54**) by hand. If there is any binding or roughness, service the oil pump as described in this chapter.

7. If the oil pump is not going to be disassembled, place it in a clean plastic bag until it is installed.

8. Install the two dowel pins (**Figure 55**).

9. Turn the oil pump drive shaft (**Figure 56**) until it is positioned to engage the notch in the end of the water pump drive shaft. Then install the oil pump and push it against the lower crankcase. If neces-

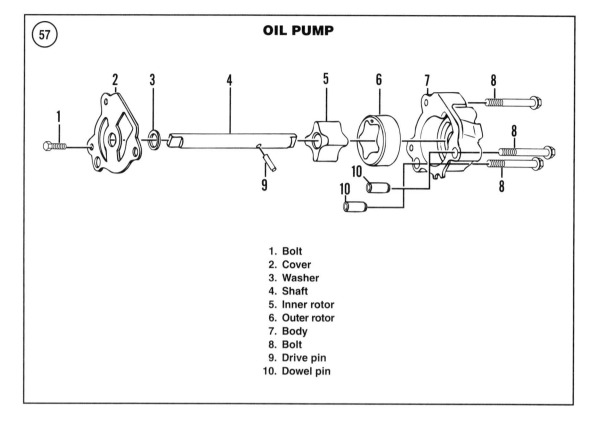

OIL PUMP

1. Bolt
2. Cover
3. Washer
4. Shaft
5. Inner rotor
6. Outer rotor
7. Body
8. Bolt
9. Drive pin
10. Dowel pin

sary, slowly rotate the drive shaft back and forth until it correctly aligns with the water pump drive shaft.

NOTE
If the oil pump does not fit flush against the crankcase and the water pump is installed on the engine, the oil pump and water pump shafts are not properly engaged.

10. Ensure that the oil pump is seated correctly against the lower crankcase surface. Apply a low strength threadlocking compound to the oil pump mounting bolt threads prior to installation. Install the single short flange bolt (A, **Figure 53**) and two long flange bolts (B) securing the oil pump and tighten the flange bolts to 9.5 N•m (84 in.-lb.).

11. Install the oil pump drive sprocket, driven sprocket, drive chain and clutch assembly as described in Chapter Six.

Disassembly

Refer to **Figure 57**.

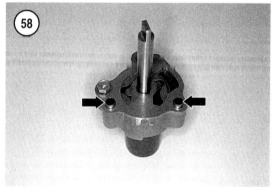

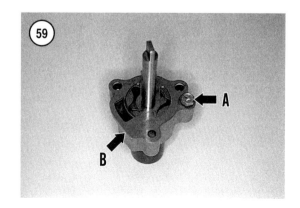

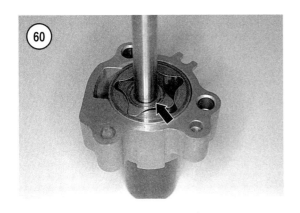

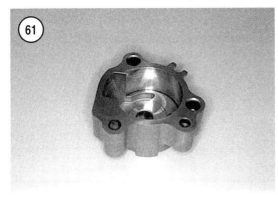

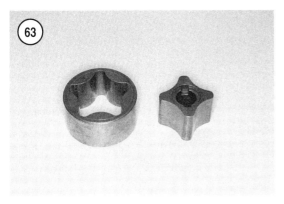

NOTE
When disassembling the oil pump, place the parts on a clean, lint-free cloth or towel.

1. Remove the oil pump as described in this chapter.

2. If still in place, remove the locating dowels (**Figure 58**).

3. Remove the assembly bolt (A, **Figure 59**) and remove the cover (B).

4. Remove the thrust washer and drive pin (**Figure 60**) from the drive shaft.

5. Remove the drive shaft.

NOTE
Prior to removing the rotors, check for a punch mark on the outer surface. If there is no mark, make one with a scribe or punch. The rotors must be reinstalled into the body in the same direction.

6. Remove the inner and outer rotors.

Inspection

When measuring the oil pump components, compare the actual measurements to the specifications in **Table 1**. If any part is damaged or out of specification, replace the oil pump as an assembly. Replacement parts are not available for the oil pump.

1. Clean all parts in solvent and dry with compressed air.

2. Inspect the body (**Figure 61** and **Figure 62**) and the inner and outer rotor set (**Figure 63**) for wear, cracks or other damage.

3. Inspect the cover for wear, stress cracks and other damage.

4. Roll the oil pump drive shaft on a piece of glass and check it for flatness. Check the drive pin hole in the shaft for cracks or other damage.

NOTE
Proceed with Step 5 only if the previous visual inspection confirms that all parts are good. If any component is worn or damaged, replace the oil pump as an assembly.

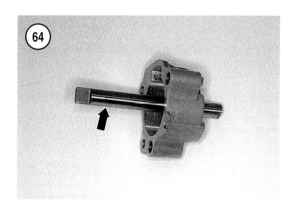

5. Position the drive shaft with the long side (**Figure 64**) (away from the drive pin hole) going in last and install the drive shaft into the body.

6. Position the outer rotor with the punch mark facing out and install the outer rotor (**Figure 65**).

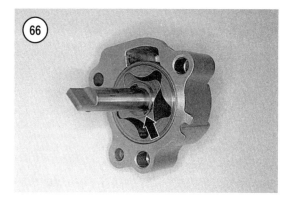

7. Position the inner rotor with the drive pin groove facing out and install the inner rotor (**Figure 66**).

8. Install the drive pin through the oil pump shaft and seat it into the inner rotor groove (**Figure 67**).

9. Measure the tip clearance between the inner rotor tip and the outer rotor with a flat feeler gauge (**Figure 68**).

10. Measure the body clearance between the outer rotor and housing with a flat feeler gauge (**Figure 69**).

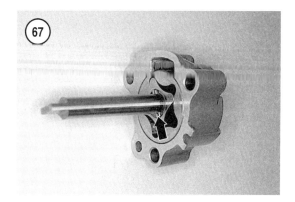

11. Measure the end clearance with a straightedge and flat feeler gauge (**Figure 70**).

12. Replace the oil pump assembly if any clearance is out of specification.

13. Remove all parts from the oil pump body.

Assembly

1. Lubricate all components with clean engine oil.

2. Position the drive shaft with the long side (**Figure 64**) (away from the drive pin hole) going in last and install the drive shaft into the body.

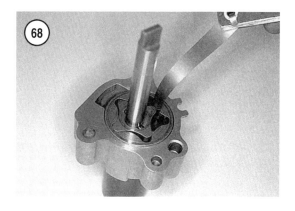

3. Position the outer rotor with the punch mark facing out and install the outer rotor (**Figure 65**).

4. Position the inner rotor with the drive pin groove facing out and install the inner rotor (**Figure 66**).

5. Install the drive pin through the oil pump shaft and seat it into the inner rotor groove (**Figure 67**).

6. Install the thrust washer onto the drive shaft.

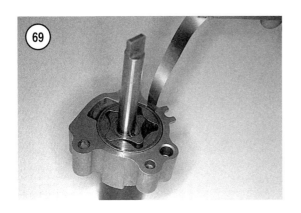

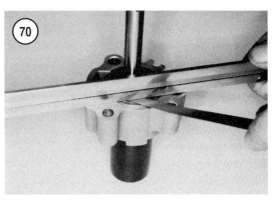

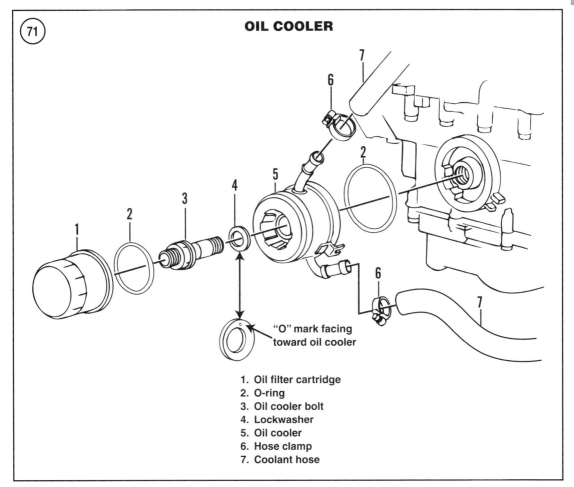

OIL COOLER

"O" mark facing toward oil cooler

1. Oil filter cartridge
2. O-ring
3. Oil cooler bolt
4. Lockwasher
5. Oil cooler
6. Hose clamp
7. Coolant hose

7. Install the cover (B, **Figure 59**) and the assembly bolt (A), then tighten securely.

8. Install the two locating dowels (**Figure 58**).

9. Rotate the drive shaft by hand. If there is any binding or roughness, disassemble the oil pump and check the parts for correct alignment.

10. Install the oil pump as described in this chapter.

11. Check the oil pressure (Chapter Three).

OIL COOLER

The oil cooler is mounted on the front of the lower crankcase. Refer to **Figure 71**.

Removal

1. Support the motorcycle on a swing arm safety stand (or centerstand on U.K. models).
2. Block the front wheel so the motorcycle will not roll in either direction while on the safety stand (or centerstand on U.K. models).
3. Remove the front inner fairing and both of the side fairing panels as described in Chapter Sixteen.
4. Drain the cooling system as described in Chapter Three.
5. Loosen the hose clamps and disconnect the upper (**Figure 72**) and lower (**Figure 73**) coolant hoses from the oil cooler.
6. Remove the exhaust system as described in Chapter Four.
7. Drain the engine oil and remove the oil filter from the oil cooler as described in Chapter Three.
8. Plug the oil cooler hose openings.
9. Unscrew and remove the oil cooler bolt and lockwasher (A, **Figure 74**).
10. Remove the oil cooler (B, **Figure 74**) from the lower crankcase. Discard the O-ring seal.

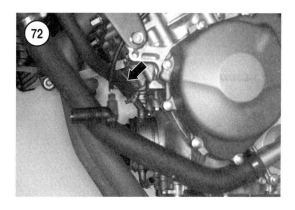

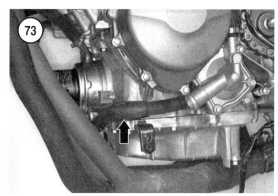

Inspection

1. Clean the oil cooler and dry with compressed air. Apply *low* pressure air to the coolant inlet or outlet fitting (**Figure 75**) to ensure that the cooler is not clogged.
2. Remove the large O-ring seal (**Figure 76**) and discard it.
3. Inspect the oil cooler bolt threads (**Figure 77**) for damage. Repair if necessary.
4. Check the oil cooler hoses for leakage and damage.

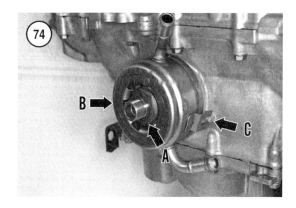

Installation

1. Install a *new* large O-ring seal (**Figure 76**) onto the backside of the oil cooler. Apply a light coat of clean engine oil to it.
2. Position the lockwasher with the *O* mark facing the oil cooler.
3. Apply a medium strength threadlock to the oil cooler bolt threads prior to installation.
4. Align the oil cooler guide groove (C, **Figure 74**) with the raised boss on the lower crankcase and install the oil cooler.

5. Install and tighten the oil cooler bolt (A, **Figure 74**) to 64 N•m (47 ft.-lb.).
6. Connect the upper (**Figure 72**) and lower (**Figure 73**) coolant hoses onto the oil cooler. Tighten the hose clamps securely.
7. Install the exhaust system as described in Chapter Four.
8. Refill the cooling system as described in Chapter Three.
9. Install a *new* oil filter and refill the engine oil as described in Chapter Three.

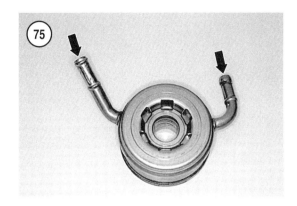

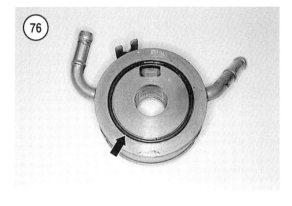

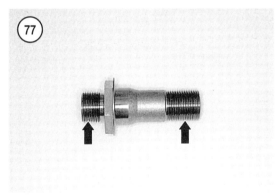

10. Start the engine and check for oil and coolant leaks.

11. Install the front inner fairing and both of the side fairing panels as described in Chapter Sixteen.

STARTER CLUTCH

The starter clutch is mounted onto the back of the flywheel. To service the starter clutch, refer to *Charging System* in Chapter Ten.

CRANKCASE

The crankcase halves are made of die-cast aluminum and matched as a set. The mating of the halves is a precision fit with no gasket at the joint, only a thin layer of gasket sealer. Handle the crankcase carefully during all service procedures to avoid damaging the bearing and mating surfaces.

The cylinder block is an integral part of the upper crankcase. To remove the pistons, the engine must be removed from the frame and the crankcase halves split.

Crankcase Mounting Bolts

Honda specifies that *new* 8 mm lower crankcase mounting bolts *must be installed* during engine assembly. Refer to *Crankcase Assembly* in this section for information on these bolts.

Crankcase Disassembly

1. While the engine is still in the frame, remove the following components as described in this and other related chapters:
   a. Cylinder head assembly (Chapter Four).
   b. Starter motor (Chapter Ten).
   c. Water pump (Chapter Eleven).
   d. Clutch (Chapter Five).
   e. External gearshift linkage (Chapter Six).
   f. Flywheel (Chapter Ten).
2. Remove the engine as described under *Engine Removal/Installation* as described in this chapter.

NOTE
When servicing the engine on a workbench, support it on a rubber mat and/or wooden blocks to protect the gasket surfaces from damage.

3. Remove the oil pan, oil strainer and pressure relief valve as described in this chapter.
4. Set the engine on the workbench so the *upper* crankcase half faces up.
5. Remove the mounting bolts (**Figure 78**) and the mainshaft bearing set plate.
6. Before removing the crankcase mounting bolts, draw an outline of each crankcase half on a piece of thick cardboard. Then punch holes along the outline for the placement of each mounting bolt.

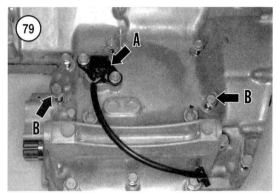

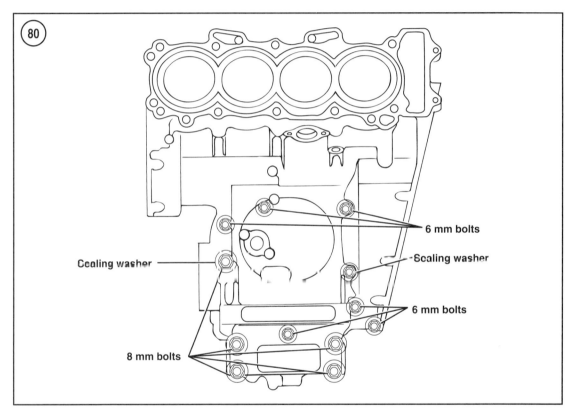

6 mm bolts

Sealing washer

6 mm bolts

8 mm bolts

Sealing washer

7. If still in place, remove the bolts and the speed sensor (A, **Figure 79**).

8. Refer to **Figure 80** and perform the following:

a. Using two to three steps in a crisscross pattern, loosen and remove the upper crankcase 6 mm and 8 mm bolts.

b. Note the location of the two bolts (B, **Figure 79**) equipped with a sealing washer.

9. Turn the engine over so the *lower* crankcase side faces up.

10. Refer to **Figure 81** and perform the following:

a. Loosen and remove the 10 mm bolt.

b. Loosen and remove the lower crankcase 6 mm bolts.

c. Loosen and remove the lower crankcase 7 mm bolts.

d. Starting outside and working in (**Figure 82**), loosen the 8 mm main journal bolts in two to three steps in a crisscross pattern. Remove all ten bolts.

NOTE
*These 8 mm main journal bolts cannot be reused. **New** bolts must be installed*

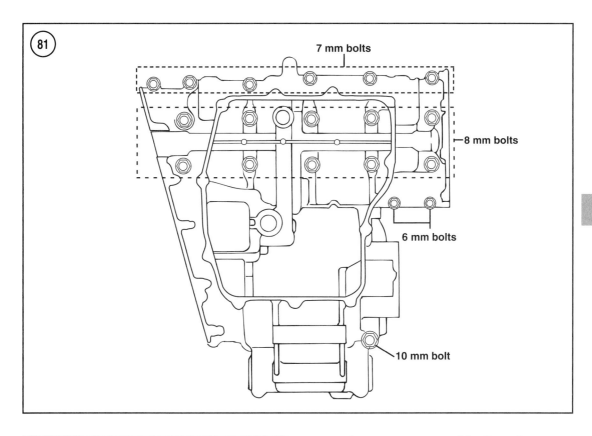

during engine assembly. Save these used bolts as they will be used in **Crankshaft Main Bearing Clearance Measurement** *later in this chapter.*

11. Verify that all the upper and lower crankcase bolts have been removed. See **Figure 80** and **Figure 81**.

12. Tap the lower crankcase with a plastic mallet and separate the case halves.

CAUTION
Do not pry the crankcase halves apart. The crankcases are machined as a set. If one is damaged, both will require replacement. If the halves will not separate, check for an unloosened bolt.

NOTE
When separating the crankcase halves, the crankshaft and transmission shafts will remain in the upper crankcase. The shift drum and shift fork assembly are installed in the lower crankcase.

13. Lift the lower crankcase (**Figure 83**) off the upper crankcase. Turn the lower crankcase over im-

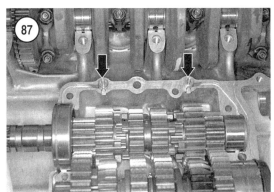

mediately and be careful that the crankshaft main bearing inserts do not fall out. If any do, reinstall them immediately into their original position, if possible.

14. Remove the three dowel pins. Refer to **Figures 84-86**.

15. Remove the two oil orifices (**Figure 87**).

16. Remove the transmission shafts (**Figure 88**) as described in Chapter Seven.

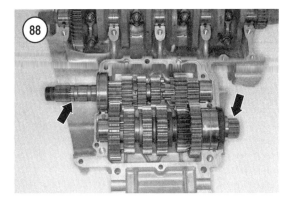

17. Remove the internal shift mechanism as described in Chapter Seven.

18. Remove the crankshaft as described under *Crankshaft* in this chapter.

19. Remove the main bearing inserts as described under *Crankshaft* in this chapter.

20. Remove the piston/connecting rod assemblies as described under *Piston and Connecting Rod Assembly* in this chapter.

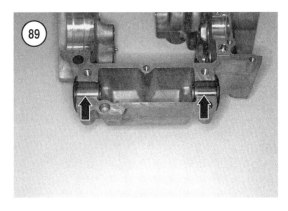

21. If loose, remove the swing arm pivot collars (**Figure 89**).

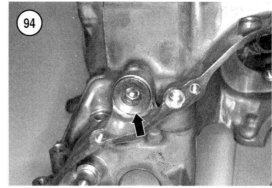

5

Crankcase Cleaning

NOTE
Place the crankcase halves on wooden blocks or rubber mats and handle them carefully to avoid damaging the numerous machined gasket surfaces.

1. If still in place, unscrew and remove the oil pressure switch (**Figure 90**) and the bolts securing the speed sensor and O-ring (**Figure 91**) from the upper crankcase.

2. If still in place, unscrew and remove the neutral switch and washer (**Figure 92**) from the lower crankcase.

3. Remove the main bearing inserts as described under *Crankshaft* in this chapter.

NOTE
To ensure thorough cleaning of the crankcase, the oil passage sealing plugs must be removed.

4. Remove the oil passageway sealing plugs from each side of the lower crankcase. Refer to **Figure 93** and **Figure 94**.

5. Remove all sealer and gasket residue material from all crankcase gasket surfaces.

6. Remove all threadlocking compound from the crankcase threaded holes, where used.

7. Check all bolts and threaded holes for stripping, cross-threading or deposit buildup. Clean out threaded holes with compressed air. Dirt buildup in the bottom of a hole may prevent the bolt from being accurately tightened to the correct torque specification. Replace damaged bolts and washers.

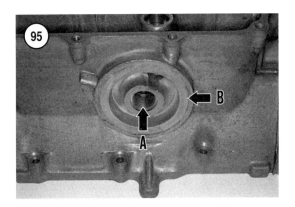

8. Inspect the crankcase threads for the oil cooler bolt (A, **Figure 95**) for damage.

9. Inspect machined surfaces for burrs, cracks or other damage. Repair minor damage with a fine-cut file or oilstone.

10. Inspect the crankcase oil cooler sealing surface (B, **Figure 95**) for burrs, cracks or other damage. This surface must provide a smooth surface for the oil cooler O-ring seal.

11. Thoroughly clean the inside and outside of both crankcase halves and all oil passages with solvent. Refer to **Figure 96** and **Figure 97**.

12. Clean and dry the oil passages with compressed air. Refer to **Figure 98** and **Figure 99**. Make sure there is no sealer residue left in any of the oil passages especially next to the oil control orifices (**Figure 100**). Use a small flashlight and visually check the oil passages for contamination.

13. Dry the case halves with compressed air. Make sure there is no solvent residue remaining in the cases, as it will contaminate the new engine oil.

14. Install the crankcase oil passage sealing plugs as follows:

    a. Apply a medium grade threadlocking compound onto the plug threads.

    b. Install the crankcase oil passage sealing plugs and tighten to 29 N•m (21 ft.-lb.). Refer to **Figure 93** and **Figure 94**.

15. Install the oil pressure switch as follows:

    a. Remove all sealer residue from the switch threads.

    b. Apply ThreeBond 1207B or an equivalent RTV sealer onto the oil pressure switch threads as shown in **Figure 101**. Do not apply sealer within 3-4 mm (0.1-0.2 in.) from the end of the switch threads.

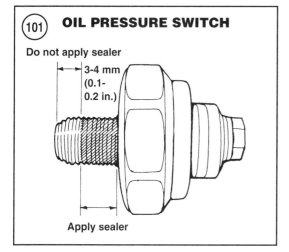

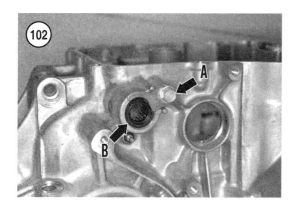

5

speed sensor (**Figure 91**) and tighten the mounting bolts securely.

17. Apply a light coat of clean engine oil to the cylinder walls to prevent any rust formation.

Gearshift Shaft Oil Seal Replacement

Replace the gearshift shaft oil seal whenever the engine is disassembled.

1. Remove the bolt and retainer (A, **Figure 102**) securing the oil seal.

2. Carefully pry the oil seal (B, **Figure 102**) out of the crankcase with a wide-blade screwdriver. Pad the side of the screwdriver to avoid damage to the lower crankcase.

3. Pack the lips of the *new* oil seal with a waterproof bearing grease.

4. Position the *new* oil seal with the manufacturer's marks facing out. Install the oil seal with a suitable size socket.

5. Install the bolt and retainer (A, **Figure 102**) securing the oil seal and tighten securely.

Upper Crankcase/Cylinder Block Inspection

The cylinder block is an integral part of the upper crankcase half. When measuring the cylinder block, compare the actual measurements to the specifications in **Table 3**. Replace or bore the cylinder block if damaged or out of specification as described in this section.

1. Check the cylinder block surface for cracks and damage (A, **Figure 103**).

2. Check the top surface cylinder block for warp with a straightedge and flat feeler gauge (**Figure**

NOTE
If using silicone, allow it to set for 10-15 minutes before installing the oil pressure switch.

   c. Install the oil pressure switch (**Figure 90**) and tighten to 12 N•m (106 in.-lb.).

16. Install a new O-ring seal on the speed sensor and apply clean engine oil to the O-ring. Install the

104). Check at different spots across the cylinder block.

> *NOTE*
> *If the cylinder block is warped beyond the specification, refer service to a Honda dealership.*

3. Check the cylinder walls (**Figure 105**) for deep scratches or signs of seizure or other damage.

4. Measure the cylinder bores with a cylinder gauge (**Figure 106**) or inside micrometer at the points shown in **Figure 107**. Measure in two axes-aligned with the piston pin and at 90° to the pin. If the bore diameter, taper or out-of-round for any cylinder exceeds the specifications in **Table 3**, all four cylinders must be bored to the next oversize and new pistons and rings installed.

5. Make sure all of the coolant passages (B, **Figure 103**) surrounding the cylinders are clear. Clean out any debris or residue from the base of the coolant passages.

> *NOTE*
> *Purchase the new pistons before the cylinders are bored so the pistons can be measured; each cylinder must be bored to match one piston only. Piston-to-cylinder clearance is specified in Table 3.*

6. Wash each cylinder bore in hot soapy water and rinse completely. This is the only way to clean the cylinder walls of the fine grit material left from the bore or honing job. After washing the cylinder walls, run a clean white cloth through each cylinder; the cloth should show no traces of grit or other debris. If the cloth is dirty, the cylinder wall is not clean and must be re-washed. After the cylinder walls are cleaned, lubricate each cylinder wall with clean engine oil to prevent the cylinder liners from rusting.

Crankcase Assembly

> *NOTE*
> *When servicing the engine on a workbench, support it on a rubber mat and/or wooden blocks to protect the gasket surfaces from damage.*

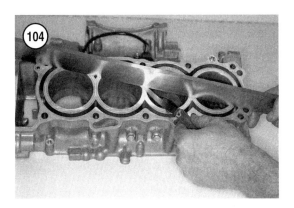

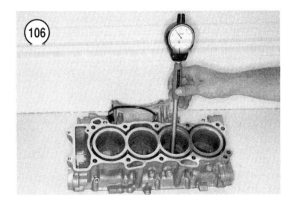

> *NOTE*
> *Purchase ten **new** 8 mm main journal bolts that secure the crankcase halves together. The old bolts **cannot be reused**, as they have stretched.*

1. Clean and dry all of the crankcase mounting bolts.

2. Prior to assembly, coat all parts with assembly oil or engine oil.

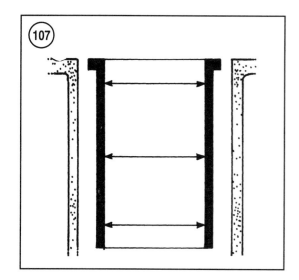

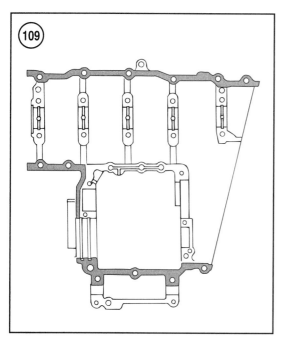

3. If removed, install the swing arm pivot collars (**Figure 89**). Lubricate the inner surface of the swing arm pivot collars with waterproof grease.

4. Install the crankshaft bearing inserts as described under *Crankshaft Removal/Installation* in this chapter. If reusing old bearings, make sure that they are installed in the same location as noted during removal.

5. Install the pistons and connecting rods as described under *Piston/Connecting Rod Installation* in this chapter.

6. Install the crankshaft as described under *Crankshaft Removal/Installation* in this chapter.

7. Install the transmission shaft assemblies as described under *Transmission Installation* in Chapter Seven.

8. Install the internal shift mechanism as described in Chapter Seven.

9. Shift the transmission into NEUTRAL and spin the shafts by hand.

10. Install the two oil orifices. Refer to **Figure 108** and **Figure 87**.

11. Install the three dowel pins. Refer to **Figures 84-86**.

12. Make sure both crankcase half sealing surfaces are clean and dry. Clean with aerosol contact cleaner and allow to dry.

> *NOTE*
> *Use a semi-drying liquid gasket sealer (ThreeBond Silicone Liquid Gasket 1207D or equivalent) to seal the crankcase. When selecting an equivalent, avoid thick and hard-setting materials.*

13. Apply a thin coating of gasket sealer to the lower crankcase sealing surfaces indicated in **Figure 109**.

> *CAUTION*
> *Do not apply sealer to the curved bearing surfaces or oil passage areas, as it will restrict oil flow. Applying sealer to the bearing surfaces will change bearing clearance and cause crankshaft seizure.*

14. Position the shift fork pins into the shift drum grooves (**Figure 110**).

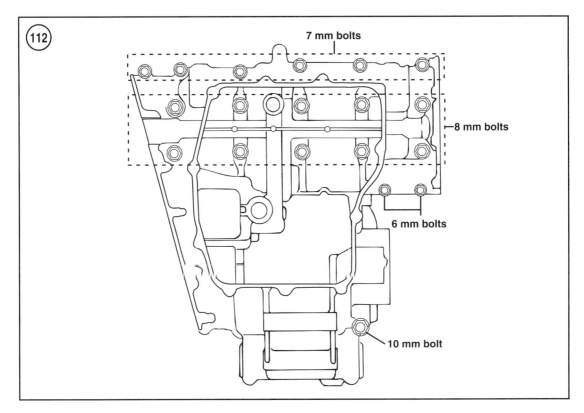

7 mm bolts

8 mm bolts

6 mm bolts

10 mm bolt

15. Position the lower crankcase (**Figure 83**) onto the upper crankcase. Set the front portion down first and lower the rear while making sure the shift forks engage properly into the transmission assemblies (**Figure 110**).

16. Join both halves and tap them together lightly with a plastic mallet. Check the gasket surface around the entire perimeter for any gaps. Note the following:

 a. Check that the countershaft and mainshaft seals are seated properly.

 b. Make sure the swing arm pivot collars are seated fully in the crankcase bore.

17. If the crankcase halves do not fit together completely, note the following:

 a. First check that the transmission shafts are properly installed. Make sure the countershaft oil seal is properly installed and seated.

 b. If the transmission is not the problem, separate the crankcase halves and investigate the cause of the interference.

CAUTION
Crankcase halves should fit together
without force. If the crankcase halves
do not fit together completely, do not

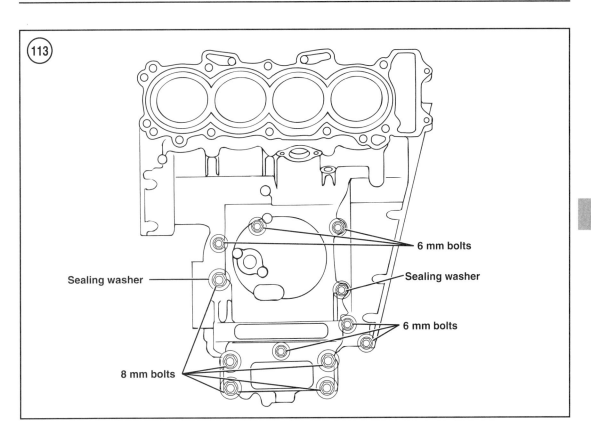

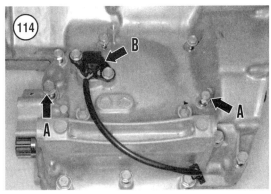

attempt to pull them together with the crankcase bolts. Do not risk damage by trying to force the cases together.

NOTE
Different size and length crankcase mounting bolts are used. When installing the mounting bolts, refer to the identification marks made during disassembly.

NOTE
***New** 8 mm bolts must be installed during engine assembly. The old bolts can-*

not be reused, as they have stretched. Thoroughly clean the new bolts with solvent and dry with compressed air.

18. Apply clean engine oil to the bolt threads and to the bolt head seating surfaces.

19. Install and tighten the *new* 8 mm main journal bolts (**Figure 111**) in two to three steps in a crisscross pattern. Start with the center two bolts and work to the outside and tighten to 25 N•m (18 ft.-lb.).

20. Install the lower crankcase 6 mm, 7 mm and 10 mm bolts (**Figure 112**) and tighten finger-tight. Then tighten these bolts in two to three steps and in a crisscross pattern. Tighten the 6 mm bolts securely. Tighten the 7 mm and 10 mm bolts to 18 N•m (13 ft.-lb.) and 39 N•m (29 ft.-lb.), respectively.

21. Turn the engine over so the upper crankcase faces up.

22. Install and tighten the upper crankcase 6 mm and 8 mm mounting bolts (**Figure 113**) as follows:

   a. Install a *new* sealing washer on the 6 mm bolt and 8 mm bolt installed adjacent to the raised triangle mark cast into the upper case half (A, **Figure 114**). Tighten the bolts finger-tight.

b. Tighten the 8 mm mounting bolts in two to three steps and in a crisscross pattern to 25 N•m (18 ft.-lb.).

c. Install the remaining 6 mm mounting bolts and tighten securely in two to three steps and in a crisscross pattern.

23. Install the speed sensor (B, **Figure 114**) and the mounting bolts. Tighten the bolts securely.

24. Clean the bearing set plate bolt threads, then apply a medium-strength threadlock to the threads.

25. Position the transmission mainshaft bearing set plate with the OUTSIDE mark facing away from the engine. Install the bearing set plate and mounting bolts (**Figure 115**). Tighten the mounting bolts to 12 N•m (106 in.-lb.).

26. Install the oil strainer and pressure relief valve and oil pan as described in this chapter.

27. Install the engine in the frame as described under *Engine Removal/Installation* in this chapter.

28. Reverse Step 1 under *Crankcase Disassembly* and install all engine assemblies that were removed.

PISTON AND CONNECTING ROD ASSEMBLY

The crankcase must be separated to remove the pistons and connecting rods.

Piston/Connecting Rod Removal

The pistons, connecting rods and bearing inserts must be reinstalled in their original locations. Mark all parts as they are removed and store them in individual parts boxes or containers. Mark the parts with a *1*, *2*, *3* and *4* starting from the left side of the engine. The No. 1 cylinder is on the left side (**Figure 116**). The No. 1-4 marks relate to the left and right side of the engine as it sits in the frame, not as it sits on the workbench.

The pistons and connecting rods are removed as an assembly from the cylinder block.

1. Mark the cylinder number on the crown of each piston.

2. Measure the connecting rod big end side clearance. Insert a flat feeler gauge between a connecting rod big end and either crankshaft machined web (**Figure 117**). Record the clearance for each connecting rod and compare to the specification in **Table 4**. Note the following:

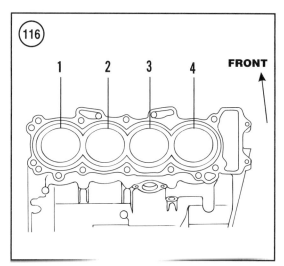

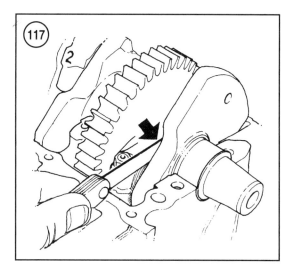

a. If the clearance is greater than specified, replace the connecting rods and re-measure.

b. If the clearance is greater than specified with the new connecting rods, replace the crankshaft.

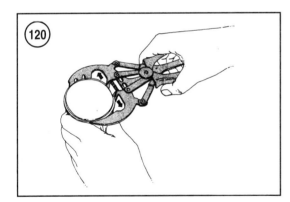

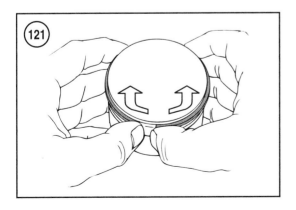

3. Remove the connecting rod cap nuts (**Figure 118**).

NOTE
Keep each bearing insert in its original place in the crankcase, rod or rod cap. If reusing the original inserts, they must be installed exactly as removed to prevent rapid wear or bearing seizure.

4. Remove the connecting rod caps and bearing inserts.

5. Lift the crankshaft out of the upper crankcase half and remove it. Support the crankshaft on the workbench so that it cannot roll off.

6. Reinstall the connecting rod caps and bearing inserts onto the connecting rods.

7. Place a strip of duct tape onto the outer side of the connecting rods (**Figure 119**) to prevent the rods from damaging the cylinder bore surfaces when removing the piston/connecting rod assembly.

CAUTION
Do not remove the connecting rod/piston assembly through the bottom of the cylinder. Doing so will allow the oil ring to expand into the gap between the cylinder liner and upper crankcase, which prevents piston removal without damaging the engine.

8. Remove the piston through the *top* of the cylinder.

WARNING
The edges of all piston rings are very sharp. Be careful when handling them to avoid cutting fingers.

NOTE
*There are two ways to remove the rings: with a ring expander tool (**Figure 120**) or by hand (**Figure 121**). The ring expander tool is useful because it removes the rings without damaging them or scratching the piston. If this tool is not available, remove the rings by carefully spreading their end gaps with two thumbs and sliding them off the top of the piston.*

NOTE
The top and second rings have identification marks near their end gaps

(Figure 122). These marks are not always visible on used rings. If the rings are going to be reused, mark them for location and direction during disassembly. On original equipment pistons and rings, the top ring is narrower than the second ring.

9. Remove the piston rings from the piston, starting with the top ring and working down (**Figure 122**).
10. Repeat to remove the remaining piston/connecting rod assemblies.

> *NOTE*
> *If necessary, remove the pistons from the connecting rods as described in Steps 11-14.*

11. Before removing the piston, hold the rod tightly and rock the piston. Any rocking motion (do not confuse with the normal sliding motion) indicates wear on the piston pin, rod bushing, pin bore or, more likely, a combination of all three.
12. Mark the piston, pin and connecting rod with its cylinder number so they will be reassembled into the same set.

> *WARNING*
> *The piston pin clips are under spring tension and can fly out. Wear safety glasses when removing them in the following steps.*

13. Remove the clip from each side of the piston pin bore (**Figure 123**) with a small screwdriver or small scribe. Hold a thumb over one edge of the clip when removing it to prevent the clip from springing out.

> *CAUTION*
> *Discard the piston circlips. New circlips must be installed during assembly.*

14. Push the piston pin out of the piston by hand. If the pin is tight, make the tool shown in **Figure 124** to remove it. Do not drive the piston pin out, as this may damage the piston pin, connecting rod or piston.
15. Lift the piston off the connecting rod.
16. Repeat Steps 12-15 for the remaining pistons.
17. Inspect the piston and connecting rod assemblies (**Figure 125**) as described in this chapter.

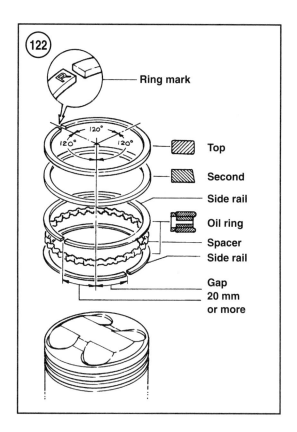

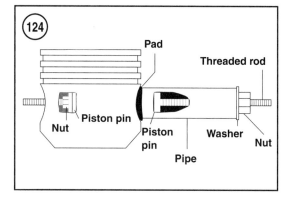

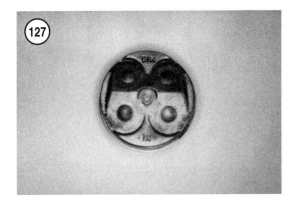

Piston Inspection

When measuring the piston components, compare the actual measurements to the specifications in **Table 3**. Replace worn or damaged parts as described in this section.

1. Carefully clean the carbon from the piston crown (**Figure 126**) with a soft scraper or wire wheel. Large carbon accumulations reduce piston cooling and result in detonation and piston damage. Do not remove or damage the carbon ridge around the circumference of the piston above the top ring. If the pistons, rings and cylinders are found to be dimensionally correct and can be reused, removal of the carbon ring from the top of the piston or the carbon ridges from the cylinders will promote excessive oil consumption.

> *CAUTION*
> *Do not use a wire brush on piston skirts or ring lands. The wire brush removes aluminum and increases piston clearance. It also rounds the corners of the ring lands, which results in decreased support for the piston rings.*

> *NOTE*
> *Make sure to renumber the piston crowns after performing Step 1. Used pistons must be reinstalled in their original cylinder.*

2. After cleaning the piston, examine the crown (**Figure 127**). There should be no wear or damage. If the crown appears pecked or spongy-looking, also check the spark plug, valves and combustion chamber for aluminum deposits. If these deposits are found, the cylinder(s) is overheating due to a lean fuel mixture or preignition.

3. Examine each ring groove (**Figure 128**) for burrs, dented edges and excessive wear. Pay particular attention to the top compression ring groove, as it usually wears more than the other grooves. Because the oil rings are constantly exposed to oil, these rings and grooves wear little compared to compression rings and their grooves. If there is evidence of oil ring groove wear or if the oil ring assembly is tight and difficult to remove, the piston skirt may have collapsed due to excessive heat and is permanently deformed. Replace the pistons.

5

4. Check the oil control holes (**Figure 129**) in the piston for carbon or oil sludge buildup. Clean the holes by hand using a small diameter drill bit.

> *CAUTION*
> *The piston skirts have a special coating (**Figure 130**). Do not scrape or use any type of abrasive on this surface, as it will be damaged.*

5. Check the piston skirts (**Figure 130**) for cracks or other damage. If a piston(s) shows signs of partial seizure (bits of aluminum build-up on the piston skirts), replace the pistons and bore the cylinders, if necessary, to reduce the possibility of engine noise and further piston seizure.

> *NOTE*
> *If the piston skirts are worn or scuffed unevenly from side to side, the connecting rod may be bent or twisted.*

6. Inspect the piston pin circlip grooves (**Figure 131**) in each piston for cracks, metal fatigue or other damage.

7. Measure the piston-to-cylinder clearance as described under *Piston Clearance* in this chapter.

8. If damage or wear indicates piston replacement, select new pistons as described under *Piston Clearance* in this chapter.

Piston Pin Inspection

When measuring the piston pins, compare the actual measurements to the specifications in **Table 3**. Replace the piston pins if worn or damaged as described in this section.

1. Clean and dry the piston pins.

2. Inspect the piston pin for chrome flaking or cracks (**Figure 132**). Replace if necessary.

3. Measure the piston pin bore inside diameter (**Figure 133**) with a telescoping gauge.

4. Measure the piston pin outside diameter (**Figure 134**) with a micrometer.

5. Subtract the measurement made in Step 4 from the measurement made in Step 3 to determine piston pin oil clearance.

6. Repeat for each piston pin and piston.

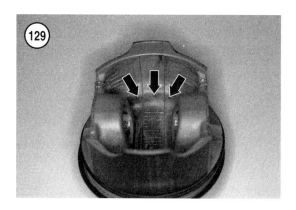

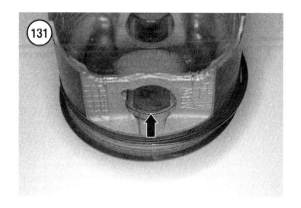

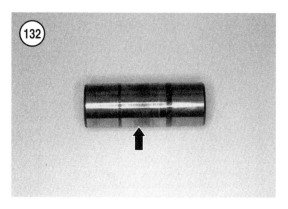

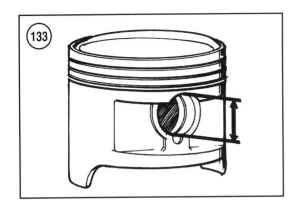

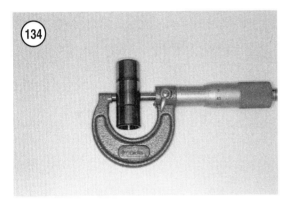

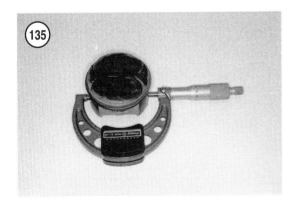

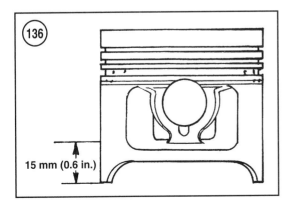

15 mm (0.6 in.)

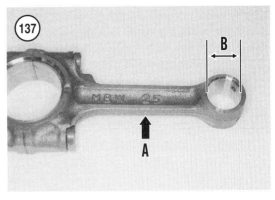

5

Piston Clearance

1. Make sure the piston and cylinder walls are clean and dry.
2. Measure the cylinder bore inside diameter as described under *Cylinder Block Inspection* in this chapter. Record the largest bore diameter obtained.
3. Measure the piston outside diameter (**Figure 135**) at right angles to the piston pin with a micrometer. Measure at a distance 15 mm (0.6 in.) up from the bottom of the piston skirt (**Figure 136**).
4. Piston clearance is the difference between maximum piston diameter and minimum cylinder diameter. Subtract the largest piston diameter from the largest bore diameter to determine piston-to-cylinder clearance. If the piston clearance exceeds the service limit in **Table 3**, note the following:
   a. If the bore diameter is still within specification, the pistons are worn. It may be possible to install new pistons (same size) to decrease the excessive piston-to-cylinder clearance. However, check carefully before deciding to use new pistons.
   b. If the bore diameter is out of specification, bore the cylinder oversize and install oversized new pistons. Honda offers one 0.25 mm oversize piston.
5. Repeat for the other pistons and cylinders.

Connecting Rod Inspection

When measuring the connecting rods, compare the actual measurements to the specifications in **Table 4**. Replace connecting rods that are worn or damaged as described in this section.
1. Check each connecting rod (A, **Figure 137**) for obvious damage such as cracks and burns.
2. Check the piston pin bore for wear or scoring.

3. Measure the connecting rod piston pin bore inside diameter (B, **Figure 137**) with a snap gauge. Then measure the snap gauge with a micrometer and check against the service limit.

4. If the connecting rod straightness is in question, take the connecting rods to a Honda dealership or machine shop and have them checked for twisting and bending.

5. Examine the bearing inserts for excessive wear, scoring or burning (**Figure 138**). They are reusable if in good condition. Make a note of the bearing color (if any) marked on the side of the insert if the bearing is to be discarded.

6. Remove the connecting rod bearing bolts (**Figure 139**) and check them for cracks or twisting. Replace bolts and nuts in pairs.

7. Check bearing clearance as described in this chapter.

Connecting Rod Bearing Clearance Measurement

This section describes how to measure the connecting rod bearing clearance using Plastigauge (**Figure 140**). Plastigauge is a material that flattens when pressure is applied to it. The marked bands on the envelope are then used to measure the width of the flattened Plastigauge. Plastigauge is available in different clearance ranges (www.plastigauge.co.uk).

1. Clean and dry the crankshaft crankpins.

2. Before measuring the connecting rod bearing clearance, measure the outside diameter, taper and out-of-roundness of each crankpin with a micrometer (**Figure 141**). Note the following:

    a. To check for taper, measure at several places in a line along the crankpin. Record the measurements for each crankpin.

    b. To check for out-of-roundness, measure the crankpin diameter all the way around the crankpin. Record the measurements for each crankpin.

    c. If the crankpins are tapered or out-of-round by more than 0.025 mm (0.001 in.), the crankshaft may have to be replaced. However, before doing so, consult with a Honda dealership on the appropriate service.

3. Install the crankshaft into the upper crankcase. Turn the crankshaft so that none of the crankpin oil holes face up.

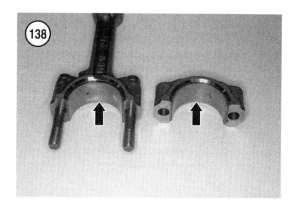

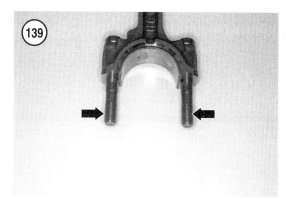

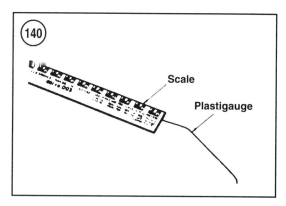

Scale

Plastigauge

4. Check each rod bearing insert (**Figure 138**) for uneven wear, nicks, seizure and scoring. If the bearings do not show any visible wear, they can be used with the Plastigauge to check the bearing clearance. If the crankpins are in good condition but the bearing inserts are too worn or damaged to be used with the Plastigauge, refer to *Connecting Rod Bearing Selection* in this section.

5. Clean the connecting rod and cap bearing surfaces and bearings inserts.

6. Install the rod bearing inserts in the connecting rod and bearing cap. Make sure the anti-rotation

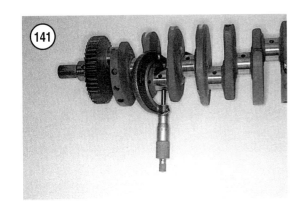

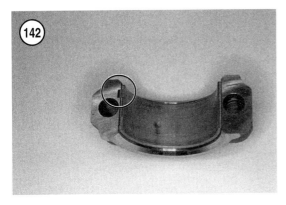

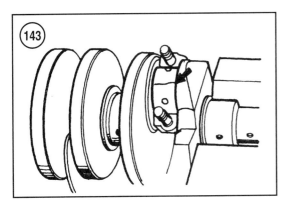

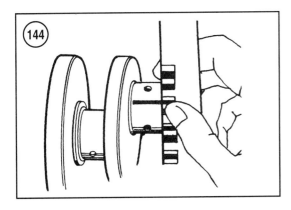

tabs on the bearing inserts lock into the rod and cap notches correctly (**Figure 142**).

CAUTION
Install the used bearing inserts in their original locations.

7. Install all of the pistons and connecting rods as described in this section.

8. Slide the piston down its bore and install the connecting rod onto the crankshaft, being careful not to damage the crankpin surface with the rod bolts.

9. Place a piece of Plastigauge (**Figure 140**) over the connecting rod bearing journal parallel to the crankshaft (**Figure 143**). Do not place the Plastigauge material over an oil hole in the crankshaft.

CAUTION
Do not rotate the crankshaft while the Plastigauge is in place. This will spread the Plastigauge and cause an inaccurate reading.

10. Match the identification code number on the end of the cap with the mark on the rod and install the cap.

11. Apply a light coat of oil on the connecting rod bolt threads and install the cap nuts. Tighten the cap nuts in two to three stages to 25 N•m (18 ft.-lb.).

12. Loosen the nuts and carefully remove the cap from the connecting rod.

13. Place the envelope scale over the flattened Plastigauge (**Figure 144**) to measure it. Compare the different marked bands on the envelope and find one that is closest to the width of the flattened Plastigauge. The number adjacent to that band is the oil clearance indicated in millimeters or inches. Then measure the Plastigauge at both ends of the strip. If the width of the Plastigauge varies from one end to the other, the crankpin is tapered. Confirm with a micrometer. See **Table 4** for the correct connecting rod bearing oil clearance. Record the clearance for each crankpin.

14. Remove the Plastigauge strips from the main bearing journals with solvent or contact cleaner. Do not scrape the Plastigauge off.

15. If the bearing oil clearance is greater than specified, select new bearings as described in the next section.

Connecting Rod Bearing Selection

Due to manufacturing tolerances, the connecting rod inside diameters (without bearing inserts) and the crankpin outside diameters are identified in two size groups. These size groups are listed in **Table 5**.

The connecting rod journal inside diameter code number (1 or 2) is marked on the side of each connecting rod and cap (**Figure 145**). The numbers correspond to the numbers listed under the connecting rod journal inside diameter code number and dimension in **Table 5**.

The crankshaft weights are marked with a series of two letters (A or B) that represents the outside diameter of each crankpin (Nos. 1-4) reading from left to right (**Figure 146**). These letters correspond to the letters listed under crankpin outside diameter code letter and dimension in **Table 5**.

> *NOTE*
> *The letter on the left-hand end relates to the bearing insert in the left side (No. 1 cylinder) and so on, working across from left to right. Remember, the left side relates to the engine as it sits in the motorcycle's frame, not as it sits on the workbench. See* ***Figure 147*** *for cylinder numbers.*

1A. To select new bearings with a new crankshaft, perform the following:
   a. Select new main bearings by cross-referencing the connecting rod journal code letter (**Figure 146**) with the connecting rod number (**Figure 148**) in **Table 5**.
   b. Where the two columns intersect, the new bearing insert color is indicated. **Table 6** gives the bearing color and thickness.

1B. To select new bearings with the original crankshaft, perform the following:

> *NOTE*
> *Because of crankpin wear, the original code numbers marked on the crankshaft may no longer represent the actual crankpin outside diameter sizes.*

   a. Measure the crankpin outside diameters (**Figure 141**) with a micrometer. Record the measurement for each crankpin.
   b. Select the crankpin outside diameter dimension in **Table 5** that best matches the crankpin's original measurement determined in Step 1. Cross-reference that crankpin code

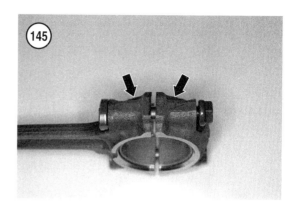

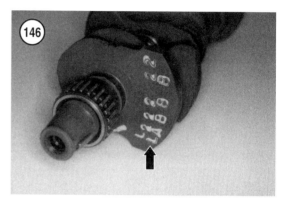

with the connecting rod number (**Figure 148**) in **Table 5**. Where the two columns intersect, the new bearing insert color is indicated. **Table 6** gives the bearing color and thickness.

1C. If the bearing inserts installed in the connecting rod are too worn or damaged for measurement with Plastigauge, determine connecting rod size as follows:
   a. Remove the bearing inserts from the connecting rod and its cap.
   b. Install the bearing cap onto its connecting rod and secure it with its two cap nuts. Tighten the nuts securely.

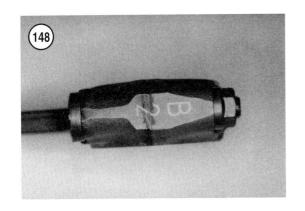

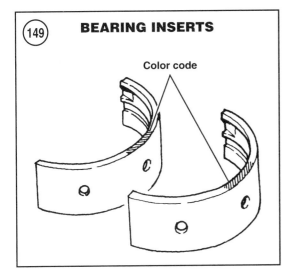

BEARING INSERTS

Color code

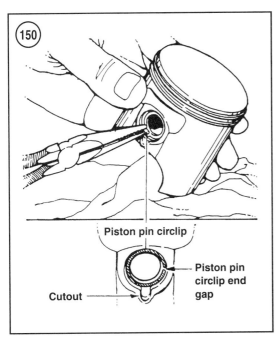

Piston pin circlip

Cutout

Piston pin circlip end gap

c. Measure the connecting rod inside diameter with a bore gauge or snap gauge. Record the measurement for each connecting rod.

d. Select the connecting rod journal inside diameter in **Table 5** that best matches the connecting rod inside diameter determined in substep c. Then cross-reference that connecting rod code letter with the crankpin outside diameter code letter or measurement in **Table 5**. Where the two columns intersect, the new bearing insert color is indicated. **Table 6** gives the bearing color and thickness.

2. The connecting rod bearing inserts are color-coded on the side of the bearing insert (**Figure 149**).

3. After new bearings have been installed, recheck clearance by repeating this procedure. If a clearance is incorrect, remeasure the crankpin diameter with a micrometer (**Figure 141**). Replace the crankshaft whenever a crankpin outside diameter (**Table 5**) is beyond the specified range of the stamped letter code (**Figure 146**).

4. Clean and oil the main bearing journals and insert faces.

Connecting Rod Selection

An alphabetical weight code (A or B) is marked on the side of the connecting rod and cap (**Figure 146**). When replacing a connecting rod, replace it with the same weight code as the original connecting rod.

Piston/Connecting Rod Assembly

1. Thoroughly clean the piston, piston pin and connecting rod assemblies. Dry with compressed air and place on a clean lint-free cloth until assembly.

> *CAUTION*
> *Do not install used piston pin clips during assembly. Piston pin clips are not designed to be reused. A weak clip that pops from its groove will cause severe cylinder damage.*

2. Install one piston pin clip in one piston pin bore groove of each piston. The circlip ends must not align with the cutout in the piston pin bore (**Figure 150**).

3. Apply molybdenum disulfide grease to the inside surface of the connecting rod's small end and to the piston pin outside surface.

4. Install the piston pin in the piston until its end extends slightly beyond the inside of the boss (**Figure 151**).

5. Install the pistons onto the connecting rods as follows:

   a. Refer to the reference numbers marked on the pistons and connecting rods during removal and install the pistons on their original connecting rods. If the cylinders were bored, match each piston with the correct cylinder.

   b. Install the pistons so the IN mark on each piston crown is on the same side as the oil hole in the connecting rod (**Figure 152**).

   c. The *IN* mark will face toward the intake side when the piston is properly installed in the cylinder block.

6. Line up the piston pin with the hole in the connecting rod. Push the piston pin into the connecting rod. Do not use force during installation or damage may occur. Push the piston pin in until it clears the circlip groove or until it touches the circlip on the other side of the piston.

7. After the piston is installed, recheck and make sure the piston and connecting rod are aligned as described in Step 5.

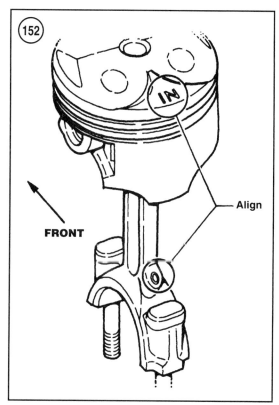

Align

FRONT

NOTE
In the next step, install the second circlip with the gap away from the notch in the piston. The first circlip was installed during Step 2.

8. Install the second piston pin circlip (**Figure 153**) in the groove in the piston. Make sure both piston pin clips are correctly seated in the piston pin grooves.

9. Repeat Steps 1-8 for the remaining three pistons.

10. Install the piston rings as described in this chapter.

11. Install the piston/connecting rod assemblies as described in this chapter.

Piston Ring Inspection

Refer to **Figure 154**.

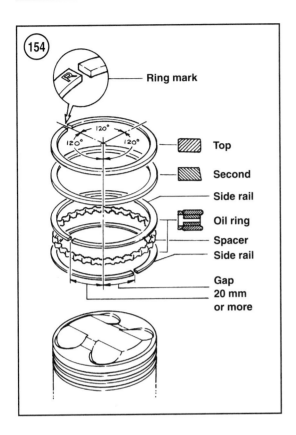

Ring mark

120°
120° 120°

Top
Second
Side rail
Oil ring
Spacer
Side rail
Gap
20 mm
or more

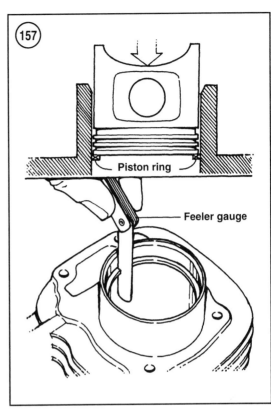

Piston ring

Feeler gauge

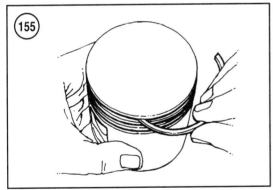

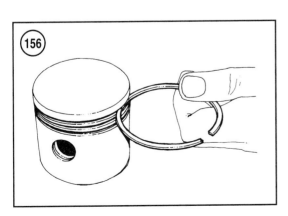

WARNING
The piston ring edges are sharp. Be careful when handling them.

1. Carefully remove all carbon buildup from the ring grooves with a broken piston ring (**Figure 155**). Do not gouge the groove or remove any aluminum. Inspect the grooves carefully for burrs, nicks or broken and cracked lands. Replace the piston if necessary.

CAUTION
Do not use a wire brush on piston skirts or ring lands. The wire brush removes aluminum and increases piston clearance. It also rounds the corners of the ring lands, which results in decreased support for the piston rings.

2. Roll each ring around its piston groove as shown in **Figure 156** to check for binding. If there is any binding, check the ring groove and piston for damage.

3. Place each piston ring, one at a time, into the bottom of its cylinder, and square it in the bore with the piston. Measure the gap with a flat feeler gauge (**Figure 157**) and compare it to the specifications in

Table 3. If the gap is greater than specified, replace the piston rings.

> *NOTE*
> *When checking the oil ring assembly, measure the end gap of the upper and lower side rails. Do not measure the oil spacer.*

4. When installing new rings, measure their end gap as described in Step 3 and compare to the specifications in **Table 3**. If the end gap is greater than specified, the cylinder may be worn excessively. Check the cylinder inside diameter as described under *Cylinder Block Inspection* in this chapter.

5. Measure piston ring side clearance as follows:

   a. Install the top and second compression rings as described under *Piston Ring Installation* in this chapter.

   b. Push the ring until its outer surface is flush with the piston and measure the clearance with a flat feeler gauge (**Figure 158**).

   c. Compare the clearance to the specifications in **Table 3**. If the clearance is greater than specified, replace the piston rings.

   d. If using new rings, measure the side clearance of the rings and compare to the specifications in **Table 3**. If the clearance is greater than specified, the piston ring lands are worn excessively. Replace the pistons.

   e. Repeat for each piston and compression ring.

6. If new rings are installed, the cylinders must be deglazed or honed for the new rings to seat. Refer honing service to a Honda dealership or a motorcycle service shop. After honing, measure the end gap of each ring (Step 3) and compare to the specifications in **Table 3**.

Piston Ring Installation

1. Thoroughly clean the pistons and piston rings and dry with compressed air.

2. When installing the piston rings, note the following:

   a. When installing the original piston rings, refer to the reference numbers marked on the piston rings during removal and install the piston rings in their original positions.

   b. When installing new piston rings, identify the rings as shown in **Figure 154**.

   c. The top and second rings have identification marks near the end gap (**Figure 154**). These

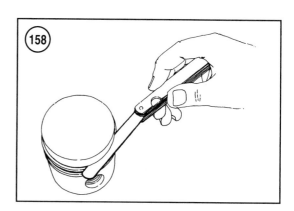

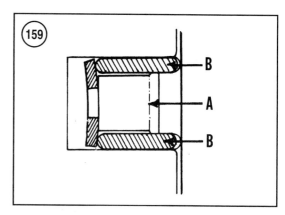

marks must face up when the rings are installed on the piston. On original equipment piston rings, the top ring is narrower than the second.

> *NOTE*
> *When installing aftermarket piston rings, follow the manufacturer's directions regarding ring identification and installation.*

   d. If installing oversized compression rings, check the ring number to make sure the correct rings are being installed. The ring oversize number must be the same as the piston oversize number.

3. Install the oil spacer first (A, **Figure 159**), then both side rails (B). The original equipment oil ring side rails do not have top and bottom designations and can be installed either way. If reassembling used parts, install the side rails as they were removed.

> *NOTE*
> *There are two ways to install the rings: with a ring expander tool (**Figure 120**) or by hand (**Figure 121**).*

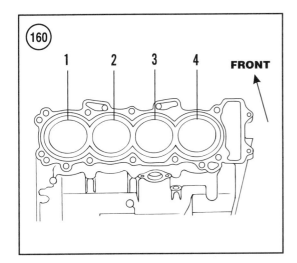

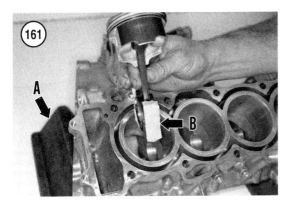

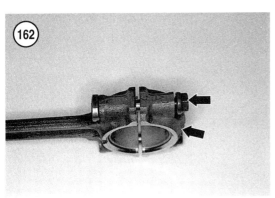

The ring expander tool is useful because it installs the rings without damaging them or scratching the piston. If this tool is not available, install the rings by carefully spreading their end gaps by hand and sliding them on the top of the piston.

4. Install the second and top compression rings.

NOTE
The top compression ring is narrower than the second compression ring.

5. Make sure the rings are seated completely in their grooves all the way around the piston and that the end gaps are distributed around the piston, as shown in **Figure 154**. It is important that the ring gaps are not aligned with each other when installed to prevent compression pressures from escaping past them during initial start-up.

Piston/Connecting Rod Installation

The pistons, connecting rods and bearing inserts must be reinstalled in their original cylinder number locations. Refer to **Figure 160** for cylinder numbers.
1. Clean the cylinder bores as described under *Cylinder Block Inspection* in this chapter. Apply clean engine oil to the cylinder walls.
2. Place the upper crankcase on supports to allow room for the connecting rods to protrude through the bottom of the crankcase (A, **Figure 161**).
3. Clean and assemble the piston/connecting rod assemblies as described in this chapter.
4. Install the rod bearing inserts in the connecting rod and bearing cap (**Figure 138**). Make sure the anti-rotation tabs on the bearing inserts lock into the rod and cap notches correctly (**Figure 142**).
5. Temporarily install the rod caps and nuts (**Figure 162**) onto the connecting rods.
6. Install the piston rings onto the pistons as described in this chapter.
7. Place a strip of duct tape onto the intake side of the connecting rod assembly (B, **Figure 161**). This will prevent the connecting rods from damaging the cylinder bore surfaces when installing the piston/connecting rod assembly.

CAUTION
Do not install the connecting rod/piston assembly through the bottom of the cylinder. Doing so will allow the oil ring to expand into the gap between the cylinder liner and upper crankcase, which prevents piston installation without damaging the engine.

8. Make sure the piston ring end gaps are not lined up with each other. They must be staggered, as shown in **Figure 154**.
9. Lightly oil the piston rings with clean engine oil.

10. Install the pistons as follows:

   a. Lubricate the piston and the inside of a piston ring compressor with engine oil.

> *NOTE*
> *It does not matter in which order the pistons are installed. In the following steps, the No. 1 piston is installed first.*

   b. Align the piston assembly with the cylinder bore so the IN mark on the piston crown faces toward the intake side of the engine.

   c. Install the piston ring compressor on the piston and compress the piston rings (**Figure 163**) following the manufacturer's instructions.

   d. Install the piston into the top of the cylinder bore (**Figure 164**).

> *NOTE*
> *The piston ring compressor must seat flush against the top surface of the upper crankcase bore when moving the piston through it. If there is a gap between the ring compressor and top surface, a ring will push out and catch on top of the cylinder. If the piston becomes tight when installing it, stop and inspect the piston rings. More than likely, one ring is caught between the ring compressor and cylinder block. If this happens, remove the piston assembly and reinstall the ring compressor onto it.*

   e. With the ring compressor located flush on top of the cylinder bore, slowly push the piston into the cylinder with a hammer handle until it is slightly below the top of the cylinder bore.

   f. Remove the piston ring compressor and push the piston into the cylinder bore until it is flush with the top surface of the cylinder bore (**Figure 165**).

11. Repeat Step 10 for the remaining three pistons.

12. Remove the connecting rod cap nuts and the caps from all four connecting rods.

13. Place a piece of hose onto each of the connecting rod bolts (**Figure 166**) to prevent the bolts from damaging the crankshaft journals when installing the crankshaft.

14. Move the No. 1 and No. 4 pistons to top dead center (TDC).

15. Move the No. 2 and No. 3 pistons at bottom dead center (BDC) (A, **Figure 167**).

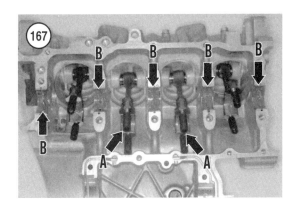

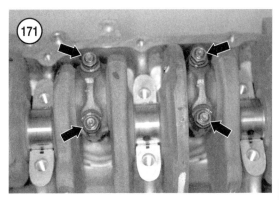

16. Apply a light, even coating of molybdenum disulfide grease to the connecting rod and cap bearing inserts and to the main bearing inserts (B, **Figure 167**) in the crankcase.

17. Carefully install the crankshaft past the connecting rod bolts (**Figure 168**) and into position in the upper crankcase (**Figure 169**).

18. Remove the pieces of hose from the No. 2 and No. 3 connecting rod bolts.

19. Match the identification code number on the end of the cap with the mark on the rod (**Figure 148**) and install the caps (**Figure 170**).

20. Apply a light coat of oil to the connecting rod cap nut threads and seating surfaces and install the cap nuts (**Figure 171**). Tighten the cap nuts in two to three stages to 25 N•m (18 ft.-lb.).

21. Carefully move the No. 1 and No. 4 piston and connecting rods into position on the crankshaft.

22. Repeat Steps 18-20 for the No. 1 and No. 4 connecting rods.

23. When all the pistons and rods are installed and the nuts tightened to the specified torque, rotate the crankshaft several complete revolutions to make sure it turns smoothly.

24. Recheck the connecting rod side clearance as described under *Piston/Connecting Rod Removal* in this chapter.

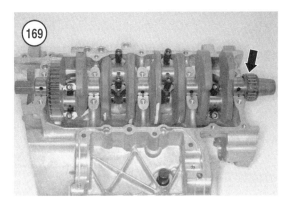

CRANKSHAFT

Crankshaft Removal

1. Disassemble the crankcase as described under *Crankcase* in this chapter.

CAUTION
Keep each bearing insert in its original place in the crankcase, rod or rod

cap. If the engine is reassembled with the original inserts, they must be installed exactly as removed to prevent rapid wear or engine seizure.

2. Remove the connecting rod cap nuts (**Figure 171**).

3. Remove the connecting rod cap and bearing insert.

4. Lift the crankshaft (**Figure 169**) out of the upper crankcase half and remove it. Support the crankshaft on the workbench so that it cannot roll off.

5. Install a piece of hose over the connecting rod bolts (**Figure 166**) to prevent the rod bolts from damaging the crankshaft journal and cylinder bore surfaces when removing the crankshaft assembly.

6. Repeat for each piston/rod assembly.

7. If necessary, remove the pistons and connecting rods as described under *Piston and Connecting Rod Assembly* in this chapter.

NOTE
In Step 8, the bearings are identified as Nos. 1-5 from left to right. The left side of the engine refers to it as it sits in the frame, not as it sits on the workbench.

8. Remove the bearing inserts as follows:
   a. Remove the main bearing inserts from the upper (**Figure 172**) and lower (**Figure 173**) crankcase halves.
   b. Mark the backs of the bearing inserts from left to right with a 1, 2, 3, 4 or 5 and U (upper) or L (lower).

9. Inspect the crankshaft and main bearings as described in this chapter.

Crankshaft Inspection

1. Clean the crankshaft thoroughly with solvent. Clean the oil holes (**Figure 174**, typical) with rifle cleaning brushes; flush thoroughly and dry with compressed air. Lightly oil all oil journal surfaces immediately to prevent rust.

2. Inspect each main bearing journal (A, **Figure 175**) for scratches, ridges, scoring, nicks and other damage.

3. Inspect the primary drive gear teeth (B, **Figure 175**). If damaged, the crankshaft must be replaced. Also check the clutch outer housing gear teeth (**Figure 176**), as they may also be damaged.

4. Inspect the clutch center outer splines (C, **Figure 175**). If damaged, the crankshaft must be replaced. Also check the clutch center inner splines (**Figure 177**), as they may also be damaged.

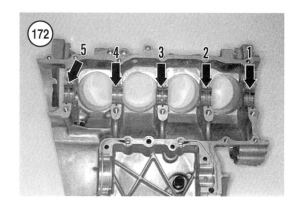

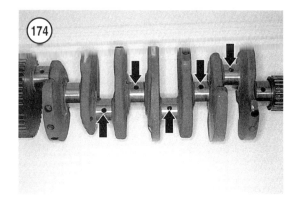

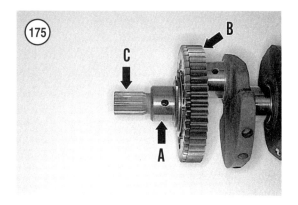

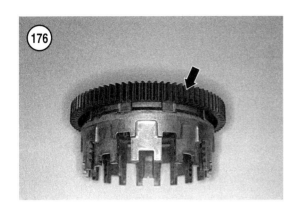

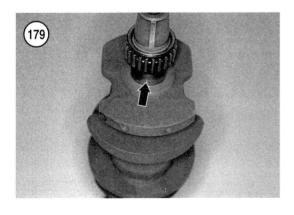

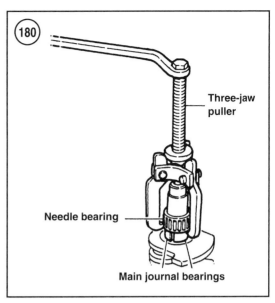

5. Inspect the starter clutch needle bearing (A, **Figure 178**) for wear, damaged needles or a loose fit on the crankshaft. If necessary, replace the bearing as described in this chapter.

6. Inspect the crankshaft flywheel taper (B, **Figure 178**) for scoring or damage.

7. Check the crankshaft for bending. Mount the crankshaft between accurate centers (lathe or crankshaft truing stand) and rotate it one full turn with a dial gauge contacting the center journal. Actual runout is half the reading shown on the gauge. If the runout exceeds the service limit in **Table 4**, replace the crankshaft.

Starter Clutch Needle Bearing Replacement

1. Remove the crankshaft as described in this chapter.

2. If still in place, remove the Woodruff key from the crankshaft.

3. Wrap the crankshaft directly below the bearing (**Figure 179**) with shim stock, or use two worn main bearing inserts. This is to protect the bearing journal from damage when using the puller in Step 4.

4. Use a universal three-jaw puller (**Figure 180**) and remove the starter clutch needle bearing (A, **Figure 178**).

5. Press the new bearing onto the crankshaft with the Honda inner driver C (part No. 07746-0030100) and 30 mm I.D. attachment (part No. 07746-0030300). Press the new bearing on until its edge is flush with the groove in the crankshaft. Check that the outer

surface of the bearing is 27.2-27.9 mm (1.07-1.10 in.) from the end of the crankshaft (**Figure 181**).

6. Spin the bearing (A, **Figure 178**), checking that it turns smoothly with no roughness or other damage.

> *CAUTION*
> *Whenever the starter clutch needle bearing is removed, a new bearing must be installed. Do not install a used bearing, as it is no longer true.*

Primary Drive Sub-Gear Replacement

1. Remove the crankshaft as described in this chapter.
2. Remove the snap ring (A, **Figure 182**) and friction spring (B).
3. Slide the primary drive sub-gear (C, **Figure 182**) off the end of the crankshaft.
4. Remove the springs and stopper pins from the recesses in the primary drive gear.
5. Install the stopper pins to the right side of the recess, then install the spring next to it. Make sure the stopper pins and springs are properly seated.
6. Apply molybdenum disulfide grease to the sub-gear sliding surface and to the friction spring sliding surface.
7. Align the sub-gear punch mark with the hole in the primary drive gear (**Figure 183**) and install the sub-gear (C, **Figure 182**).
8. Position the spring washer with the dished side facing out and install the spring washer (B, **Figure 182**).
9. Use a 5 mm pick or narrow screwdriver and position the stoppers on the backside of the sub-gear push against the springs in the gear.
10. Install a *new* snap ring (A, **Figure 182**) with the large tab on the right side. Align the snap ring end gap at a right angle to the cutouts in the crankshaft (**Figure 184**). Make sure the snap ring is correctly seated in the crankshaft groove.

> *NOTE*
> *The sub-gear will only move a minimal amount in the Step 11, but it must move smoothly.*

11. Use a flat-tip screwdriver and move the sub-gear (A, **Figure 185**) back and forth on the primary drive gear (B). The sub-gear must move smoothly back and forth with no binding.

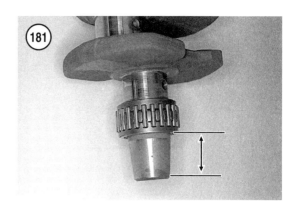

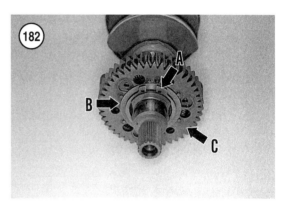

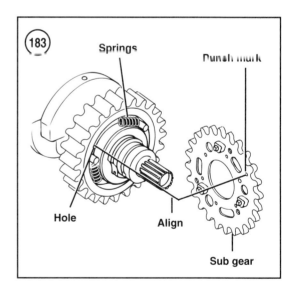

Crankshaft Main Bearing Clearance Measurement

This section describes how to measure crankshaft main bearing clearance using Plastigauge. Plastigauge is a material that flattens when pressure is applied to it. The marked bands on the envelope

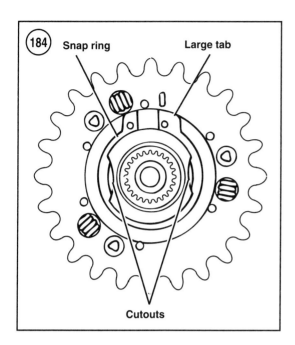

(184) Snap ring   Large tab

Cutouts

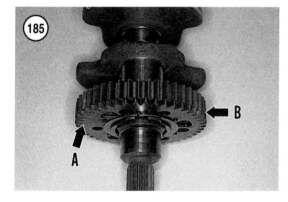

(185)

← B

A

(186)

2. Before measuring the crankshaft main bearing clearance, measure the outside diameter, taper and out-of-roundness of each main bearing journal (**Figure 186**) with a micrometer. Note the following:

    a. To check the main bearing journal for wear, measure the journal at several places with a micrometer. Subtract the largest diameter from the standard diameter to determine the minimum amount of wear.

    b. To check for taper, measure at both ends of a main bearing journal. Do not measure where the radius connects the crank web to the main bearing journal. Subtract the smallest diameter from the largest diameter to obtain the maximum amount of taper. Record the measurements for each main bearing journal.

    c. To check for out-of-roundness, measure the main bearing journal diameter at different places around the journal. Record the different measurements for each crankpin. Subtract the smallest diameter from the largest diameter to determine the maximum out-of-round.

    d. If the main bearing journal is tapered or out-of-round by more than 0.025 mm (0.001 in.), the crankshaft may have to be replaced. However, before doing so, consult with a Honda dealership on the appropriate service.

3. Clean all of the bearing surfaces of the insert in the upper and lower crankcases.

4. Clean and dry each main bearing insert.

CAUTION
There must be no dirt, lint or other material on the bearing bores or bearing inserts. If these parts are not clean, an incorrect bearing clearance reading may be obtained. This may result in the installation of the incorrect size bearings, leading to bearing seizure and engine damage.

5. Check each main bearing insert for uneven wear, nicks, seizure and scoring. If the bearings do not show any visible wear, they can be used with the Plastigauge to check the main bearing clearance. If the main bearing journals are in good condition but the bearing inserts are too worn to be used with the Plastigauge, refer to *Crankshaft Main Bearing Selection* in this section.

NOTE
The bearing inserts must be installed in their original operating position.

are used to measure the width of the flattened Plastigauge. Plastigauge is available from automotive parts stores in different clearance ranges.

1. Clean and dry the crankshaft main bearing journals.

6. Install the upper (**Figure 172**) and lower (**Figure 171**) main bearing inserts into the upper and lower crankcase halves. Make sure the anti-rotation tabs on the bearing inserts lock into the case notches correctly (**Figure 187**).

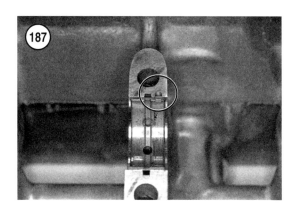

7. Place the upper and lower crankcase halves upside down on a workbench.

> *NOTE*
> *If the piston/connecting rod assemblies are installed, make sure hose guides are placed over the connecting rod bolts. The hose guides will prevent the connecting rod bolts from damaging the main bearing journals when installing the crankshaft.*

8. Install the crankshaft (**Figure 169**) into the upper crankcase.

9. Place a piece of Plastigauge over each main bearing journal parallel to the crankshaft (**Figure 188**). Do not place the Plastigauge over an oil hole in the crankshaft.

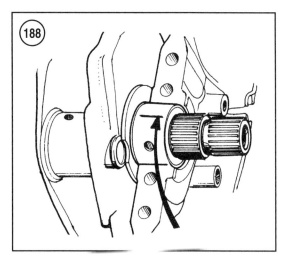

> *CAUTION*
> *Do not rotate the crankshaft while the Plastigauge is in place. This will spread the Plastigauge and cause an inaccurate reading (reduced oil clearance measurement).*

10. Position the lower crankcase onto the upper crankcase. Set the front portion down first and lower the rear. Join both halves and tap them together lightly with a plastic mallet. Do not use a metal hammer, as it will damage the case.

> *CAUTION*
> *Crankcase halves should fit together without force. If the crankcase halves do not fit together completely, do not attempt to pull them together with the crankcase bolts. Separate the crankcase halves and investigate the cause of the interference. Do not risk damage by trying to force the cases together.*

> *NOTE*
> *Use the original 8 mm main bearing bolts in Step 11. During final engine assembly, new main bearing bolts must be installed. See **Crankcase Assembly** in this chapter.*

11. Apply clean engine oil to the original 8 mm bolt threads and to the bolt head seating surface.

12. Install and tighten the original 8 mm crankcase mounting bolts (**Figure 189**) in two to three steps in a crisscross pattern to 25 N•m (18 ft.-lb.). Start with the center two bolts and work to the outside.

13. Starting at the outside and working in, loosen the lower crankcase 8 mm bolts in two to three

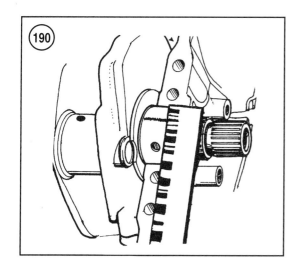

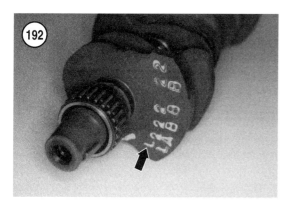

oil clearance. Then measure the Plastigauge at both ends of the strip. If the width of the Plastigauge varies from one end to the other, the main bearing journal is tapered. Confirm with a micrometer. See **Table 4** for the main bearing oil clearance specification. Record the clearance for each journal.

16. Remove the Plastigauge strips from the main bearing journals with solvent or contact cleaner. Do not scrape the Plastigauge off.

17. If the bearing oil clearance is greater than specified, select new bearings as described in the next section.

Crankshaft Main Bearing Selection

1. The upper crankcase is marked with a series of letters (A, B or C) that represent the inside diameter of each crankcase main bearing bore (Nos. 1-5) from left to right (**Figure 191**). These letters correspond to the letters listed under crankcase inside diameter code letter in **Table 7**.

2. The crankshaft weights are marked with a series of numbers (1, 2 or 3) that represent the outside diameter of each crankshaft main bearing journal from left to right (**Figure 192**). These numbers correspond to the numbers listed under crankshaft outside diameter code number and dimension in **Table 7**.

NOTE
The letter on the left-hand end relates to the bearing insert in the left side and so on, working across from left to right. Remember, the left side relates to the engine as it sits in the motorcycle frame, not how it may sit on the workbench.

3. Select new main bearings by cross-referencing the crankshaft outside diameter code number and journal diameter (**Figure 192**) with the crankcase inside diameter code letter and dimension (**Figure 191**) in **Table 7**. Where the two columns intersect, the new bearing insert color is indicated. **Table 8** gives the bearing insert color and thickness.

NOTE
*Main bearings are color-coded as shown in **Figure 193**.*

4. After new bearings have been installed, recheck clearance by repeating this procedure. If a clearance

stages in a crisscross pattern. Then remove the bolts starting from the inside and working out.

14. Carefully remove the lower crankcase half.

15. Place the envelope scale over the flattened Plastigauge (**Figure 190**). Compare the different marked bands with the flattened Plastigauge. Find the band that is closest to the width of the flattened Plastigauge. The number adjacent to that band is the

is incorrect, measure the crankshaft journal with a micrometer. Replace the crankshaft if a crankshaft outside diameter dimension (**Table 7**) is beyond the specified range of the stamped number code. If the crankshaft is within specification, the crankcase is worn and requires replacement.

5. Clean and oil the main bearing journals and bearing inserts.

Crankshaft Installation

1. Clean the crankshaft in solvent and dry it thoroughly with compressed air. Make sure to remove all solvent residue from the oil holes.

2. Place the upper crankcase half upside down on a workbench.

> *NOTE*
> *If the piston/connecting rod assemblies are installed, install a hose guide over each connecting rod bolt, or place a piece of duct tape on the rod bolt, to prevent them from damaging the crankpin journals.*

3. Install the upper (**Figure 172**) main bearing inserts in the upper crankcase case half. Make sure the anti-rotation tabs on the bearing inserts lock into the case notches correctly (**Figure 194**).

4. Install the lower (**Figure 171**) main bearing inserts in the lower crankcase case half. Make sure the anti-rotation tabs on the bearing inserts lock into the case notches correctly (**Figure 187**).

> *NOTE*
> *Used bearing inserts must be installed in their original locations.*

5. Install the crankshaft (**Figure 169**) into the upper crankcase.

6. Install the connecting rods onto the crankshaft as described in this chapter.

7. Assemble the crankcase as described in this chapter.

BREAK-IN PROCEDURE

If the rings were replaced, new pistons installed, the cylinders bored or honed or major lower end work performed, break in the engine just as though it were new. The performance and service life of the engine depends greatly on a careful and sensible break-in.

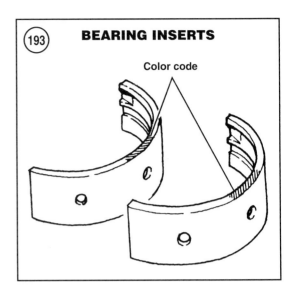

BEARING INSERTS

Color code

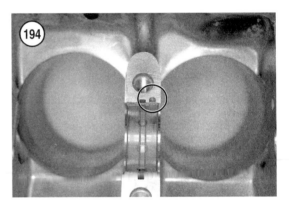

For the first 600 miles (1000 km), engine rpm should not exceed 4000 rpm. Prolonged steady running at one speed, no matter how moderate, is to be avoided, as well as hard acceleration.

Increase engine speed by 1000 rpm between 600 miles (1000 km) and 1000 miles (1600 km). Engine speed should be frequently varied during this mileage interval. Do not exceed 5000 rpm.

At 1000 miles (1600 km), full throttle operation can be used. However, never exceed the tachometer redline zone at any time, as this may damage the engine.

During engine break-in, oil consumption will be higher than normal. It is therefore important to frequently check and correct oil level. At no time during the break-in or later should the oil level be allowed to drop below the lower line on the oil level window. If the oil level is low, the oil will become overheated, resulting in insufficient lubrication and increased wear.

600 Mile (1000 km) Service

It is essential that the oil and oil filter be changed after the first 600 miles (1000 km). In addition, it is a good ideal to change the oil and filter at the completion of the break-in (about 1500 miles/2414 km) to ensure that all of the particles produced during the break-in are removed from the lubrication system. The minimal added expense may be considered a small investment that will pay off in increased engine life.

Table 1 OIL PUMP SERVICE SPECIFICATIONS

Item	Standard mm (in.)	Wear limit mm (in.)
Body clearance	0.15-0.22 (0.006-0.009)	0.35 (0.014)
Side clearance	0.02-0.07 (0.001-0.003)	0.10 (0.004)
Tip clearance	0.15 (0.006)	0.20 (0.008)

Table 2 STARTER DRIVEN GEAR SPECIFICATIONS

Item	Standard mm (in.)	Wear limit mm (in.)
Starter driven gear boss outside diameter	51.699-51.718 (2.0354-2.0361)	51.684 (2.0348)

Table 3 CYLINDER, PISTON AND PISTON RING SPECIFICATIONS

Item	Standard mm (in.)	Wear limit mm (in.)
Cylinder		
Bore	67.000-67.015 (2.6378-2.6384)	67.10 (2.642)
Taper and out of round	–	0.10 (0.004)
Warp	–	0.10 (0.004)
Piston		
Outside diameter*	66.965-66.985 (2.6364-2.6372)	66.90 (2.634)
Piston-to-cylinder clearance	0.015-0.050 (0.0006-0.0020)	0.10 (0.004)
Piston oversize	0.25 mm	–
Piston-pin bore		
inside diameter	17.002-17.008 (0.6694-0.6696)	17.02 (0.670)
Piston pin outside diameter	16.994-17.000 (0.6691 0.6693)	16.98 (0.669)
Piston pin oil clearance	0.002-0.014 (0.0001-0.0006)	0.04 (0.002)
Piston rings		
Ring-to-groove clearance		
Top	0.020-0.050 (0.0008-0.0020)	0.08 (0.003)
Second	0.015-0.050 (0.0006-0.0020)	0.08 (0.003)
Ring end gap (installed)		
Top	0.10-0.20 (0.004-0.008)	0.40 (0.016)
Second	0.18-0.30 (0.007-0.012)	0.50 (0.020)
Oil ring side rail	0.20-0.70 (0.008-0.028)	1.00 (0.039)

*Measured at a point 15 mm (0.6 in.) from the bottom of the piston shirt. See text for information.

Table 4 CRANKSHAFT AND CONNECTING RODS SPECIFICATIONS

Item	Standard mm (in.)	Wear limit mm (in.)
Connecting rod		
Small end inside diameter	17.016-17.034 (0.6699-0.6706)	17.04 (0.671)
Big end side clearance	0.10-0.25 (0.004-0.010)	0.30 (0.012)
Clearance to piston pin	0.016-0.040 (0.006-0.0016)	0.06 (0.002)
	(continued)	

Table 4 CRANKSHAFT AND CONNECTING RODS SPECIFICATIONS (continued)

Item	Standard mm (in.)	Wear limit mm (in.)
Connecting rod bearing oil clearance	0.028-0.052 (0.0011-0.0020)	0.06 (0.002)
Crankshaft main bearing oil clearance	0.020-0.038 (0.0008-0.0015)	0.05 (0.002)
Crankshaft runout	–	0.05 (0.002)

Table 5 CONNECTING ROD BEARING INSERT SELECTION

Crankpin outside diameter size code letter	Connecting rod inside diameter size code number	
	Number 1 34.000-34.008 mm (1.3386-1.3389 in.)	Number 2 34.008-34.016 mm (1.3389-1.3392 in.)
Letter A 31.492-31.500 mm (1.2398-1.2402 in.)	Yellow	Green
Letter B 31.484-31.492 mm (1.2395-1.2398 in.)	Green	Brown

Table 6 CONNECTING ROD BEARING INSERT THICKNESS

Color	mm	in.
Brown	1.244-1.248	0.0490-0.0491
Green	1.240-1.244	0.0488-0.0490
Yellow	1.236-1.240	0.0487-0.0488

Table 7 CRANKSHAFT MAIN BEARING INSERT SELECTION

Crankshaft outside diameter code number	Crankcase inside diameter code letter		
	Letter A 33.000-33.006 mm (1.2992-1.2994 in.)	Letter B 33.006-33.012 (1.2994-1.2997 in.)	Letter C 33.012-33.018 mm (1.2997-1.2999 in.)
Letter 1 30.000-30.006 mm (1.1811-1.1813 in.)	Pink	Yellow	Green
Letter 2 29.994-30.000 mm (1.1809-1.1811 in.)	Yellow	Green	Brown
Letter 3 29.988-29.994 mm (1.1806-1.1809 in.)	Green	Brown	Black

Table 8 MAIN BEARING INSERT THICKNESS

Color	mm	in.
Black	1.506-1.509	0.0593-0.0594
Brown	1.503-1.506	0.0592-0.0593
Green	1.500-1.503	0.0591-0.0592
Yellow	1.497-1.500	0.0598-0.0591
Pink	1.494-1.497	0.0588-0.0589

Table 9 ENGINE MOUNTING FASTENER TORQUE SPECIFICATIONS

Item	N•m	in.-lb.	ft.-lb.
Front engine hanger bolt			
Right and left side	39	–	29
Left side center engine			
hanger bolt	39	–	29
Right side center engine hanger			
Adjust bolt locknut*			
Actual	54	–	40
Indicated	49	–	36
Bolt	39	–	29
Right side rear engine hanger			
Adjust bolt locknut*			
Actual	54	–	40
Indicated	49	–	36
Bolt	39	–	29
Shock link/sidestand			
Bracket bolts	39	–	29
Bracket nuts	44	–	32
Sidestand bolts	44	–	32

*See text.

Table 10 ENGINE LOWER END TORQUE SPECIFICATIONS

Item	N•m	in.-lb.	ft.-lb.
Connecting rod cap nuts	25	–	18
Crankcase bolts			
Lower crankcase bolts[1]			
8 mm main journal	25	–	18
10 mm	39	–	29
7 mm	18	–	13
Upper crankcase bolts[1]			
8 mm	25	–	18
Crankcase oil passageway			
sealing plugs[2]	29	–	21
Transmission mainshaft			
bearing set plate bolts	12	106	–
Gearshift drum bearing and			
shift shaft set bolt	12	106	–
Camshaft chain tensioner			
pivot bolt	10	88	–
Camshaft chain guide			
washer bolt	12	106	–
Ignition pulse generator bolt	59	–	44
Oil drain plug	29	–	21
Oil pump cover bolt	8	71	–
Oil pump mounting flange bolts	9.5	84	–
Oil pressure switch	12	106	–
Oil cooler bolt (filter boss)[2]	64	–	47

1. Lubricate fasteners threads and head seating surface with engine oil.
2. Apply a medium strength threadlock to fastener threads.

CHAPTER SIX

CLUTCH AND EXTERNAL SHIFT MECHANISM

This chapter contains service procedures for the following components:
1. Right crankcase cover.
2. Clutch assembly.
3. Clutch cable.
4. External shift mechanism.

Specifications are in **Table 1** and **Table 2** at the end of the chapter.

RIGHT CRANKCASE COVER

Removal/Installation

1. Remove the right side fairing panel as described in Chapter Sixteen.
2. Drain the engine oil as described under *Engine Oil and Filter Change* in Chapter Three.
3. Disconnect the ignition pulse generator two-pin (red) electrical connector (A, **Figure 1**).

4. Remove the bolts securing the clutch cable bracket and disconnect the clutch cable from the clutch lifter lever (B, **Figure 1**).
5. Using a crisscross pattern, loosen and then remove the bolts securing the right crankcase cover.
6. Remove the right crankcase cover (**Figure 2**).
7. If loose, remove the four dowel pins (**Figure 3**).
8. Remove all gasket sealer residue from the crankcase and cover mating surfaces.
9. Apply a light coat of gasket sealer to the crankcase in the areas shown in **Figure 4**. Apply the gasket sealer 10-15 mm (0.4-0.6 in.) above and below the crankcase halves' mating surface.
10. Apply a light coat of gasket sealer to the entire perimeter of the crankcase cover.
11. If removed, install the four dowel pins (**Figure 3**).

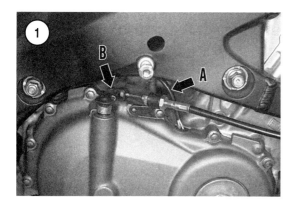

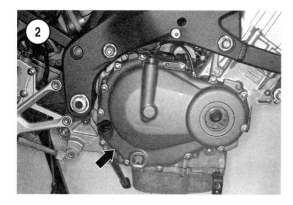

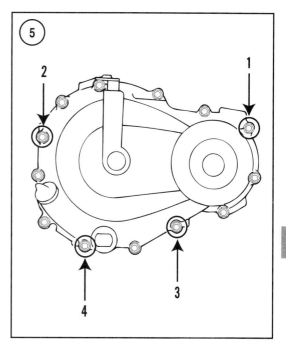

6

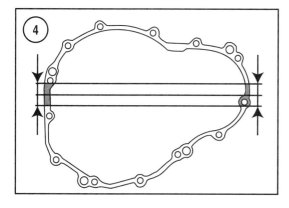

12. Install the right crankcase cover while turning the clutch lifter arm clockwise to engage the lifter arm groove with the lifter piece flange.

13. Push the right crankcase cover up against the crankcase until it bottoms.

14. Install all bolts securing the right crankcase cover and tighten securely.

15. Connect the clutch cable onto the clutch lifter lever (B, **Figure 1**). Install the clutch cable bracket and mounting bolts.

16. Refer to **Figure 5** and tighten the four bolts in two to three steps in the order shown. Tighten to 12 N•m (106 in.-lb.). Tighten the remaining bolts in two to three steps in a crisscross pattern to 12 N•m (106 in.-lb.).

17. Connect the ignition pulse generator two-pin (red) electrical connector (A, **Figure 1**).

NOTE
Debris generated by burnt clutch plates contaminates the engine oil. If the clutch plates are burnt or damaged, replace them and change the engine oil and filter. This step is important, even though the engine may be between oil changes, to remove contaminants from the lubrication system.

18. Refill the engine with oil as described in Chapter Three.

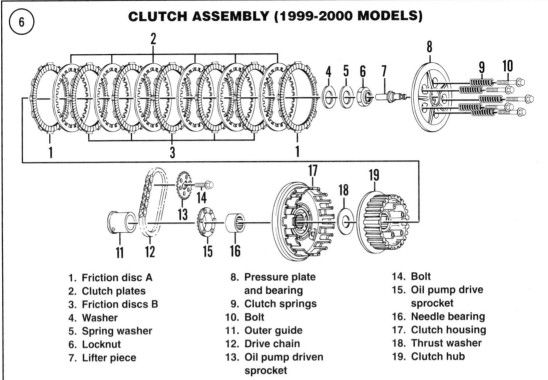

CLUTCH ASSEMBLY (1999-2000 MODELS)

1. Friction disc A
2. Clutch plates
3. Friction discs B
4. Washer
5. Spring washer
6. Locknut
7. Lifter piece
8. Pressure plate and bearing
9. Clutch springs
10. Bolt
11. Outer guide
12. Drive chain
13. Oil pump driven sprocket
14. Bolt
15. Oil pump drive sprocket
16. Needle bearing
17. Clutch housing
18. Thrust washer
19. Clutch hub

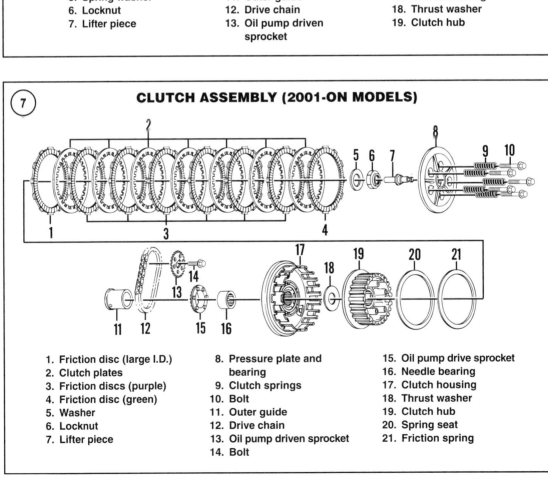

CLUTCH ASSEMBLY (2001-ON MODELS)

1. Friction disc (large I.D.)
2. Clutch plates
3. Friction discs (purple)
4. Friction disc (green)
5. Washer
6. Locknut
7. Lifter piece
8. Pressure plate and bearing
9. Clutch springs
10. Bolt
11. Outer guide
12. Drive chain
13. Oil pump driven sprocket
14. Bolt
15. Oil pump drive sprocket
16. Needle bearing
17. Clutch housing
18. Thrust washer
19. Clutch hub
20. Spring seat
21. Friction spring

CLUTCH

Refer to **Figure 6** and **Figure 7**.

Removal

1. Remove the right crankcase cover as described in this chapter.

2. Shift the transmission into gear.

3. Loosen the clutch spring bolts (**Figure 8**), following a crisscross pattern. Then remove the bolts and springs (**Figure 9**).

4. Remove the pressure plate (**Figure 10**) and clutch lifter piece (**Figure 11**).

> *NOTE*
> *On 1999-2000 models, the first and last friction discs A must be installed in the same location during assembly.*

5. Remove the clutch plates and friction discs (**Figure 12**) from the clutch hub and clutch housing. Keep the parts in the order removed.

6. On 2001-on models, remove the friction spring and the spring seat from the clutch hub.

> *CAUTION*
> *Unstake the clutch locknut before loosening it from the mainshaft, or the nut may damage the mainshaft threads.*

7. Unstake the clutch locknut (**Figure 13**) from the groove in the mainshaft. Use a small grinding stone in a rotary grinding tool to partially grind and weaken the staked part of the locknut. Do not grind through the locknut, or the stone will contact and damage the mainshaft. When the staked part of the locknut is sufficiently weakened, pry it away from the mainshaft with a small, flat tool.

CAUTION
When using the clutch holder in Step 8, make sure to secure it squarely onto the clutch hub splines. If the clutch holder slips, release pressure from the clutch locknut and reposition the clutch holder. If the clutch holder slips, it may damage the clutch hub splines.

8. Secure the clutch hub with a clutch holder, then loosen and remove the clutch locknut (**Figure 14**).

9A. On 1999-2000 models, remove the spring washer (**Figure 15**) and washer (**Figure 16**).

9B. On 2001-on models, remove the washer (**Figure 17**).

10. Remove the clutch hub (**Figure 18**).

11. Remove the thrust washer (**Figure 19**) from the clutch housing.

12. Loosen the camshaft chain tensioner as described under *Camshaft Chain Tensioner* in Chapter Five.

NOTE
The primary drive gear on the crank-shaft is equipped with a spring-loaded sub-gear. The gear teeth on the pri-mary drive gear and this sub-gear

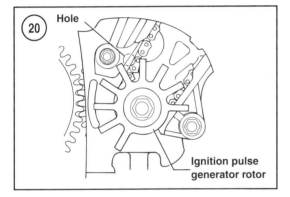

Hole

Ignition pulse
generator rotor

6

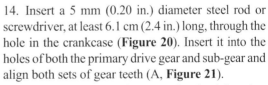

must be aligned correctly in order to disengage the clutch housing gear teeth from these two gears.

13. Align the ignition pulse generator rotor teeth with the hole in the crankcase.

CAUTION
In Step 14, do not damage the ignition pulse generator rotor teeth while inserting the steel pin or screwdriver into the primary drive gear.

14. Insert a 5 mm (0.20 in.) diameter steel rod or screwdriver, at least 6.1 cm (2.4 in.) long, through the hole in the crankcase (**Figure 20**). Insert it into the holes of both the primary drive gear and sub-gear and align both sets of gear teeth (A, **Figure 21**).

15. Pull straight out and remove the clutch housing (B, **Figure 21**).

16. Hold the oil pump driven sprocket with a screwdriver (A, **Figure 22**), then loosen the bolt and washer (B). Remove the bolt and washer (**Figure 23**).

17. Remove the oil pump drive sprocket, driven sprocket, clutch outer and chain as an assembly (**Figure 24**).

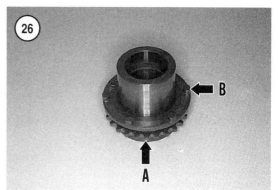

18. Inspect the clutch assembly as described in this chapter.

Installation

1. Coat all clutch parts with engine oil before assembly.
2. Position the outer guide with the flange side (**Figure 25**) facing down on the workbench.
3. Position the oil pump drive sprocket with the chain sprocket side (A, **Figure 26**) going on first and install it onto the clutch outer. The six posts (B, **Figure 26**) on the drive sprocket must face up.
4. Position the drive sprocket face with the OUT mark facing up.
5. Install the drive chain over the oil pump drive and driven sprockets (**Figure 27**).

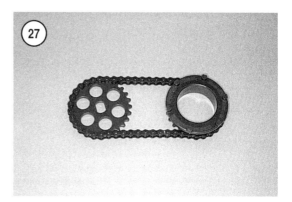

> *CAUTION*
> *Make sure the six posts on the drive sprocket face out and the OUT mark on the driven sprocket faces out. This is necessary so the six posts will engage with the clutch housing receptacles and drive the oil pump.*

6. Pick the assembly up off the workbench and install the oil pump sprockets and drive chain as an assembly (**Figure 24**) onto the transmission shaft. Make sure to align and install the driven sprocket (**Figure 28**) over the oil pump shaft.
7. Apply a threadlocking compound onto the oil pump driven sprocket bolt threads. Install the bolt and washer (**Figure 23**). Secure the driven sprocket with a screwdriver (A, **Figure 22**) and tighten the bolt (B) to 15 N•m (133 in.-lb.).
8. Align the ignition pulse generator rotor teeth with the hole in the crankcase.

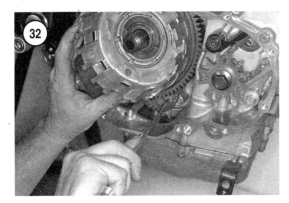

CAUTION
In Step 9, do not damage the ignition pulse generator rotor teeth while inserting the screwdriver into the primary drive gear.

9. Insert a 5 mm (0.20 in.) diameter screwdriver, at least 6.1 cm (2.4 in.) long, through the hole in the crankcase (A, **Figure 29**). Insert it into the holes of both the primary drive gear and sub-gear and align both sets of gear teeth (B, **Figure 29**). Keep the screwdriver in place (A, **Figure 30**) during Step 10.

10. Install the clutch housing as follows:
   a. Align the three holes (A, **Figure 31**) and slots (B) in the back of the clutch housing with the three pins and slots on the oil pump drive sprocket and install the clutch housing over (B, **Figure 30**) the mainshaft.
   b. At the same time, mesh the clutch housing gear with the primary drive gear and sub-gear teeth. Use a screwdriver and turn the driven sprocket to help align the pins and holes (**Figure 32**).
   c. Push the clutch housing on until it bottoms and both sets of gears are aligned (**Figure 33**).
   d. Remove the screwdriver.

CAUTION
Make sure the clutch housing holes engage properly with the oil pump drive sprocket pins. If necessary, slightly rotate the oil pump driven gear back and forth to ensure correct alignment of the drive gear.

11. Install the thrust washer (**Figure 34**).
12. Install the clutch hub (**Figure 18**).
13A. On 1999-2000 models, perform the following:
   a. Install the washer (**Figure 16**) onto the mainshaft.

b. Position the spring washer (**Figure 15**) with its dished side facing out and install it onto the mainshaft.

13B. On 2001-on models, install the washer (**Figure 17**).

14. Install a *new* clutch locknut (**Figure 14**) and tighten finger-tight at this time.

CAUTION
When using the clutch holder in Step 15, make sure to secure it squarely onto the clutch hub splines. If the clutch holder starts to slip, stop tightening the clutch locknut and reposition the clutch holder. If the clutch holder slips, it may damage the clutch hub splines.

15. Hold the clutch hub with the same clutch holder tool (A, **Figure 35**) used during disassembly, then tighten the clutch locknut (B) to 127 N•m (94 ft.-lb.). Remove the clutch holder tool.

NOTE
Check the clutch hub splines for any burrs caused by the clutch holder. Remove burrs with a file, and then clean the area of all aluminum debris.

16. Stake the locknut shoulder into the mainshaft notch (**Figure 36**).

17. On 2001-on models, install the spring seat (**Figure 37**) and the friction spring (**Figure 38**) over the clutch hub. Install the friction spring with its convex side facing in toward the spring seat (**Figure 39**). Push the spring seat and friction spring on and seat against the clutch hub shoulder.

18A. On 1999-2000 models, perform the following:

   a. Lubricate the clutch plates with engine oil.

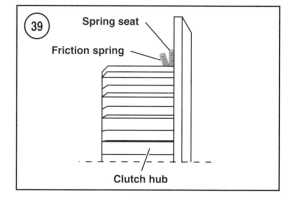

Spring seat

Friction spring

Clutch hub

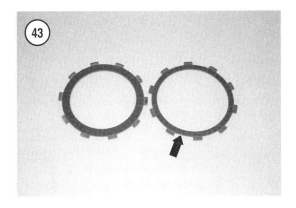

NOTE
One, or more, of the tabs on the friction disc A is colored green. These two friction discs are unique and must be installed first and last as noted in this step.

b. Install the first friction disc *A*.

c. Install a clutch plate (**Figure 40**), then a friction disc *B* (**Figure 41**).

d. Continue to alternately install the clutch plates and the friction discs *B*.

e. The last plate installed must be the friction disc *A*. It must be installed into the narrow slot in the clutch housing (**Figure 42**).

18B. On 2001-on models, perform the following:

a. Lubricate the clutch plates with engine oil.

b. Install the first friction disc with the larger inside diameter and seat it over the spring seat and friction spring. Refer to **Figure 43** and **Figure 44**.

NOTE
If the first friction disc installed contacts the spring seat and friction spring, the incorrect friction disc has been installed.

NOTE
One, or more, of the tabs on the friction discs are colored purple or green. These friction discs are unique and must be installed in the following order.

c. Install a clutch plate (**Figure 45**), then a friction disc (purple) (**Figure 46**).

d. Continue to alternately install the clutch plates and the friction discs (purple).

e. The last plate installed must be the friction disc (green). It must be installed into the narrow slot in the clutch housing (**Figure 47**).

19. If removed, install the bearing into the pressure plate.

20. Install the clutch lifter piece (**Figure 48**) through the backside of the pressure plate.

21. Align the pressure plate and clutch hub, then install the pressure plate (**Figure 49**) over the clutch hub. Make sure the pressure plate seats flush against the outer friction disc.

22. Install the clutch springs (**Figure 50**) and clutch spring bolts (**Figure 51**). Tighten the clutch spring bolts securely in two or three steps, following a crisscross pattern.

23. Shift the transmission into gear.

24. Using a crisscross pattern, tighten the clutch spring bolts to 12 N•m (106 in.-lb.).

25. Install the right crankcase cover as described in this chapter.

26. Refill the engine with the correct type and quantity of oil (Chapter Three).

27. Shift the transmission into NEUTRAL and start the engine. After the engine warms up, pull the clutch in and shift the transmission into first gear. Note the following:

a. If there is a loud grinding and spinning noise coming from the clutch immediately after starting the engine, the engine was not filled with oil or new clutch plates were installed and not lubricated with oil. Once the engine oil lubricates the new plates, the noise will stop.

b. If the motorcycle jumps forward and stalls or creeps with the transmission in gear and the

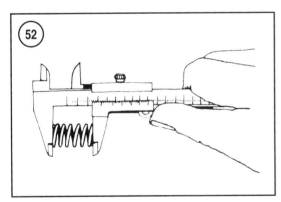

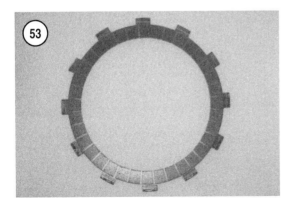

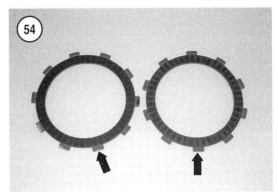

clutch pulled in, check for improper clutch cable adjustment. Refer to Chapter Three.

c. For additional information, refer to *Clutch Troubleshooting* in Chapter Two.

Inspection

When measuring the clutch components, compare the actual measurements to the specifications in **Table 1**. Replace worn or damaged parts as described in this section.

1. Clean and dry all parts.

2. Measure the free length of each clutch spring (**Figure 52**) with a vernier caliper. Replace the springs as a set if any one spring is less than the service limit in **Table 1**.

3. Inspect the friction discs (**Figure 53**) as follows:

NOTE
If any friction disc is damaged or out of specification as described in the following steps, replace all of the friction discs as a set.

a. The friction material used on the friction discs (**Figure 53**) is bonded onto an aluminum plate. Inspect the friction material for excessive or uneven wear, cracks and other damage. Check the disc tangs (**Figure 54**) for surface damage. The sides of the disc tangs must be smooth where they contact the clutch housing fingers; otherwise, the discs cannot engage and disengage correctly.

NOTE
If the disc tangs are damaged, inspect the clutch housing fingers carefully as described in this section.

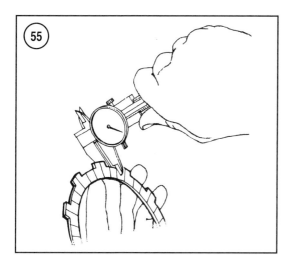

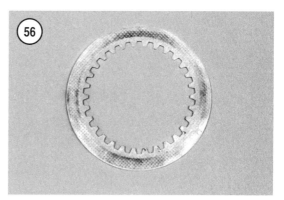

b. Measure the thickness of each friction disc with a vernier caliper (**Figure 55**). Measure at several places around the disc.

4. Inspect the steel clutch plates (**Figure 56**) as follows:

a. Inspect the clutch plates for cracks, damage or color change. Overheated clutch plates will have a blue discoloration.

b. Check the clutch plates for an oil glaze buildup. Remove buildup by lightly sanding both sides of each plate with 400 grit sandpaper placed on a surface plate or piece of glass.

c. Place each clutch plate on a surface plate or piece of glass and check for warp with a feeler gauge (**Figure 57**). If the clutch plates are warped, compare the measurement to the service limit in **Table 1**. If any are warped beyond the specification, replace the entire set.

d. The clutch plate inner teeth mesh with the clutch hub splines. Check the clutch plate teeth for any roughness or damage. The teeth contact surfaces must be smooth; otherwise, the plates cannot engage and disengage correctly.

NOTE
If the clutch plate teeth are damaged, inspect the clutch hub splines carefully as described in this section.

5. Inspect the clutch hub for the following conditions:

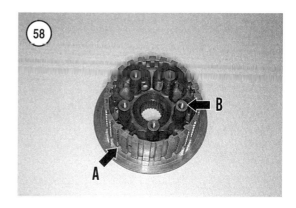

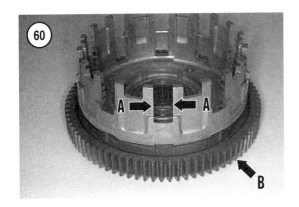

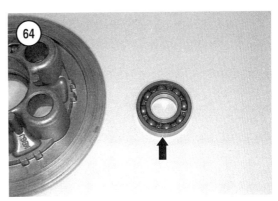

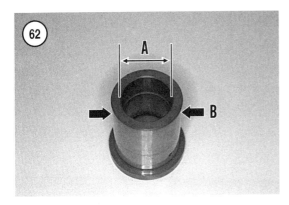

a. The clutch plate teeth slide in the clutch hub splines (A, **Figure 58**). Inspect the splines for rough spots, grooves or other damage. Repair minor damage with a file or oil stone. If the damage is excessive, replace the clutch hub.

b. Damaged spring towers and threads (B, **Figure 58**).

c. Inspect the inner splines (**Figure 59**) for damage.

6. Check the clutch housing for the following conditions:

a. The friction disc tangs slide in the clutch housing grooves. Inspect the grooves (A, **Figure 60**) for cracks or galling. Repair minor damage with a file. If the damage is excessive, replace the clutch housing.

b. Check the clutch housing gear (B, **Figure 60**) for excessive wear, pitting, chipped gear teeth or other damage.

NOTE
If the clutch housing gear is excessively worn or damaged, check the primary drive gear assembly for the same wear conditions.

c. Check the clutch housing needle bearing (**Figure 61**) for cracks or other damage. If damaged, the needle bearing must be pressed out.

7. Measure the clutch outer guide inside diameter (A, **Figure 62**) and outside diameter (B).

8. Inspect the pressure plate (**Figure 63**) for cracks or other damage.

9. Slowly turn the ball bearing (**Figure 64**) by hand. If any roughness or binding is noted, replace the bearing.

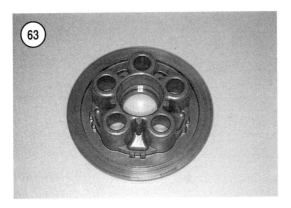

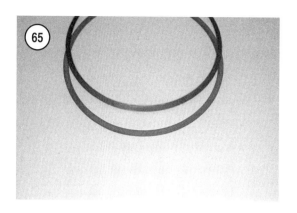

10. On 2001-on models, inspect the spring seat and friction spring (**Figure 65**) for cracks, warp or other damage.

11. Inspect the teeth on the oil pump drive (**Figure 66**) and driven sprockets (**Figure 67**). Replace the sprockets and chain as a set if the teeth are damaged or any are missing.

12. Check the oil pump drive chain (**Figure 68**) for cracks and other damage.

13. Install the drive sprocket onto the clutch outer guide (A, **Figure 69**) and make sure it rotates freely.

14. Inspect the drive sprocket engagement dogs (B, **Figure 69**) and the dog engagement holes (A, **Figure 70**) and receptacles (B) in the backside of the clutch outer for wear or damage.

15. Check the push piece for straightness and damage (A, **Figure 71**). Inspect the end (B, **Figure 71**) where it contacts the lifter lever for abnormal wear.

16. Install the push piece into the bearing (**Figure 72**). It must rotate freely with no binding.

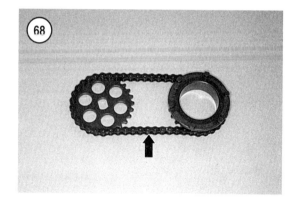

EXTERNAL SHIFT MECHANISM

The external shift mechanism consists of the shift shaft, shift drum cam and stopper arm assembly. The external shift mechanism can be serviced with the engine in the frame.

Troubleshooting

If the motorcycle is experiencing shifting problems, refer to *Gearshift Linkage* and *Transmission* in Chapter Two before removing the shift mechanism in this section.

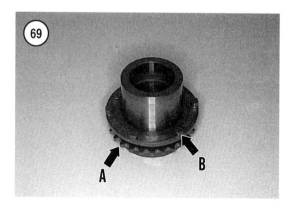

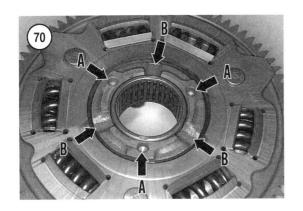

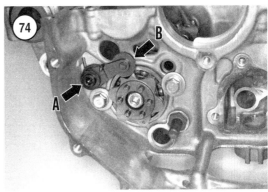

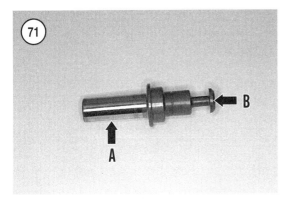

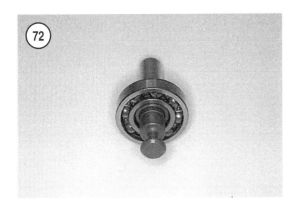

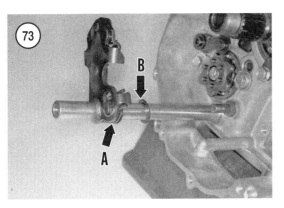

Removal

1. Remove the clutch assembly as described in this chapter.

2. Withdraw the shift shaft (A, **Figure 73**) and the thrust washer (B).

3. Remove the Allen bolt (A, **Figure 74**) securing the stopper arm (B).

4. Disengage the stopper arm, washer and return spring (**Figure 75**) from the shift drum gearshift cam.

> *NOTE*
> *The shift drum gearshift cam mounting bolt was installed with a threadlocking compound. It may be necessary to use an impact driver to loosen this bolt.*

5. Remove the shift drum gearshift cam as follows:
   a. Turn the gearshift drum cam counterclockwise until it stops.
   b. Remove the Allen bolt (A, **Figure 76**), the gearshift drum cam (B) and the dowel pin from the shift drum.

6. Inspect all parts as described in this section.

Installation

1. If removed, install the shift drum cam as follows:
    a. Install the dowel pin into the shift drum hole.
    b. Align the notched hole in the back of the shift drum cam with the dowel pin and install the shift drum cam.
    c. Apply a threadlocking compound onto the shift drum cam Allen bolt threads. Then install the Allen bolt (A, **Figure 76**) and tighten to 23 N•m (17 ft.-lb.).

2. Install the stopper arm, washer and return spring (**Figure 75**) and tighten the bolt securely.

3. Lift up and engage the stopper arm, washer and return spring onto the shift drum gearshift cam (B, **Figure 74**).

4. Install the shift shaft as follows:
    a. Install the thrust washer onto the shift shaft (B, **Figure 73**).
    b. Install the shift shaft (A, **Figure 73**) by centering the return spring on the shift spring with the pin in the crankcase (**Figure 77**). Push the shift shaft in until it bottoms.

5. Install the clutch assembly as described in this chapter.

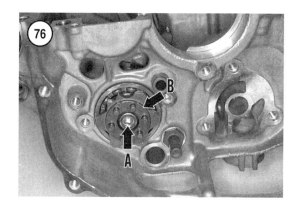

Inspection

Replace worn or damaged parts as described in this section.

1. Clean and dry all parts. Remove all threadlocking residue from the shift drum cam Allen bolt threads.

2. Inspect the shift shaft (A, **Figure 78**) for the following:
    a. Bent shaft.
    b. Damaged splines (**Figure 79**).
    c. Weak or damaged return spring (A, **Figure 80**).
    d. Stuck or damaged shift arm (B, **Figure 80**).

3. To replace the return spring, perform the following:
    a. Remove the washer and snap ring (B, **Figure 78**).
    b. Remove the return spring (C, **Figure 78**).
    c. Slide on the new spring, then spread the spring arms and fit the spring over the shift shaft arm.
    d. Install the snap ring and washer.

4. Inspect the stopper arm assembly (**Figure 81**) for:
    a. Damaged socket bolt shoulder. Remove any burrs or rough spots from the bolt shoulder.

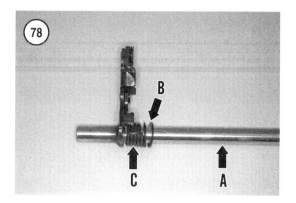

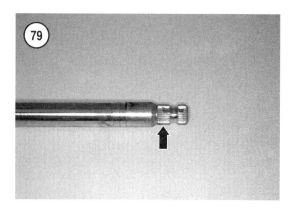

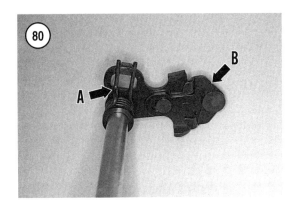

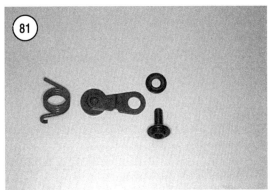

b. Damaged stopper arm. Check stopper arm for a damaged pivot hole or stuck or binding rollers.

c. Bent or damaged washer. A damaged washer can prevent the stopper arm from moving correctly.

d. Weak or damaged return spring.

5. Check the shifter cam ramps for rough spots, burrs or other damage. Repair minor damage with fine emery cloth.

Table 1 CLUTCH SPECIFICATIONS

Item	Standard	Wear limit
Friction disc		
Quantity	7	–
Thickness	2.92-3.08 mm (0.115-0.121 in.)	2.6 mm (0.10 in.)
Clutch plate		
Quantity	6	–
Warp	–	0.30 mm (0.012 in.)
Clutch spring free length		
1999-2000 models	46.5 mm (1.83 in.)	45.2 mm (1.78 in.)
2001-on models	44.7 mm (1.76 in.)	43.4 mm (1.71 in.)
Clutch outer guide		
Inside diameter	25.000-25.021 mm (0.9843-0.9851 in.)	25.03 mm (0.985 in.)
Outside diameter	34.975-34.991 mm (1.3770-1.3776 in.)	34.97 mm (1.377 in.)
Transmission mainshaft		
at clutch outer guide	24.980-24.993 mm (0.9835-0.9840 in.)	24.96 mm (0.9828 in.)

Table 2 CLUTCH TORQUE SPECIFICATIONS

Item	N•m	in.-lb.	ft.-lb.
Clutch hub locknut[1]	127	–	94
Clutch lever pivot nut	6	53	–
Clutch slave cylinder			
bleed screw	9	79	–
Clutch spring bolts	12	106	–
Crankcase (right) cover bolts	12	106	–
Gearshift drum cam bolt	23	–	17
Gearshift stopper arm bolt	12	106	–
Oil pump driven			
sprocket bolt[2]	15	133	–
Stopper arm socket bolt	12	106	–

1. Apply oil to the threads and seating surface and stake.
2. Apply a medium strength locking agent onto fastener threads.

CHAPTER SEVEN

TRANSMISSION AND
INTERNAL GEARSHIFT MECHANISM

This chapter covers service for the transmission and internal shift mechanism. The external shift mechanism is covered in Chapter Six. Transmission and internal shift mechanism service requires crankcase disassembly as described in Chapter Five.

Transmission specifications are listed in **Table 1**. **Tables 1-4** are at the end of the chapter.

TRANSMISSION

Removal

1. Remove the engine and split the crankcase as described under *Crankcase Disassembly* in Chapter Five. The transmission shaft assemblies are installed in the upper crankcase.
2. Remove the mainshaft (A, **Figure 1**) and countershaft (B) assemblies.
3. Remove the countershaft set ring (A, **Figure 2**).
4. If loose, remove the transmission locating dowel pins (B, **Figure 2**) from the upper crankcase.
5. If necessary, service the transmission shafts as described in this chapter. If the shafts are not going to be serviced, make sure the needle bearing housing is in place on both shafts. Wrap the shafts in clean shop cloths and store in a box to avoid damage.
6. Perform the *Preliminary Inspection* prior to shaft disassembly. Perform this even though the shafts may not be intended for service.
7. After disassembly, inspect the transmission shafts as described in this section.

Installation

1. If necessary, replace the countershaft oil seal as follows:
   a. Slide the old seal off of the shaft and discard it.
   b. Pack the lips of the *new* oil seal with a waterproof bearing grease prior to installation.
   c. Position the *new* oil seal with the manufacturer's marks facing out and install the oil seal. Push it on until it bottoms.
2. Prior to installing any components, apply clean engine oil to all bearing surfaces.

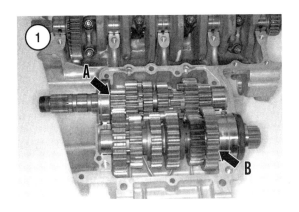

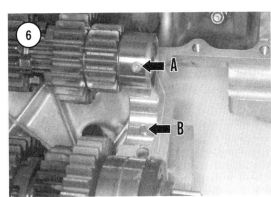

7

3. If removed, install the countershaft set ring (A, **Figure 2**).

4. If removed, install the transmission locating dowel pins (B, **Figure 2**) into the upper crankcase. Press the dowel pins down until they bottom.

5. Make sure the needle bearing housing is in place on both transmission shafts.

6. Install the countershaft into the upper crankcase while noting the following:

    a. Align the hole in the needle bearing housing (A, **Figure 3**) with the locating dowel (B).

    b. Turn the countershaft bearing so the bearing set pin (A, **Figure 4**) is located in the notch in the upper crankcase half and install the shaft.

    c. Make sure the oil seal lip is located in the bearing bore groove (B, **Figure 4**) in the upper crankcase half.

    d. Hold onto the bearing (A, **Figure 5**) and spin the countershaft (B) by hand. It must rotate freely without any play or noise.

7. Install the mainshaft into the upper crankcase while noting the following:

    a. Align the hole in the needle bearing housing (A, **Figure 6**) with the locating dowel (B).

b. Mesh the gears on both shafts together and install the shaft.

c. Properly mesh the shaft assembly together in the NEUTRAL position.

d. Hold onto the bearing (A, **Figure 7**) and spin the mainshaft (B) by hand. Both shafts must rotate freely without any play or noise.

8. Assemble the crankcase and install the engine as described under *Crankcase Assembly* in Chapter Five.

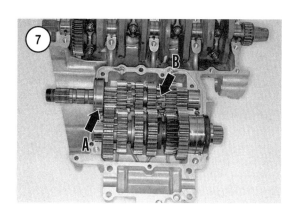

Preliminary Inspection

1. Clean and inspect the assemblies prior to disassembling them. Place the assembled shaft into a large can or plastic bucket and thoroughly clean the assembly with a petroleum-based solvent, such as kerosene, and a stiff brush. Dry the assembly with compressed air or let it sit on rags to drip dry. Do this for both shaft assemblies.

2. Visually inspect the components for excessive wear. Check the gear teeth for chips, burrs or pitting. Clean up damage with an oilstone. Replace any components with damage that cannot be cleaned up.

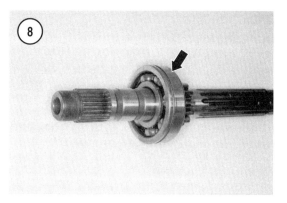

> *NOTE*
> *Replace defective gears and their mating gear on the other shaft as well, even though it may not show as much wear or damage.*

3. Carefully check the engagement dogs. If any are chipped, worn, rounded or missing, the affected gear must be replaced.

4. Rotate the transmission bearings by hand. Refer to mainshaft, **Figure 8** and countershaft, **Figure 9**. Check for roughness, noise and radial play. Replace any bearing that is suspect.

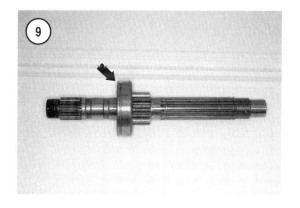

5. If the transmission shafts are satisfactory and are not going to be disassembled, apply assembly oil or engine oil to all components and reinstall them into the crankcase as described in Chapter Five.

> *NOTE*
> *If disassembling a used, high-mileage transmission for the first time, pay particular attention to any additional shims not shown in the illustrations or photographs. To compensate for wear, additional shims may have been installed during the previous repair. If the transmission is being reassembled*

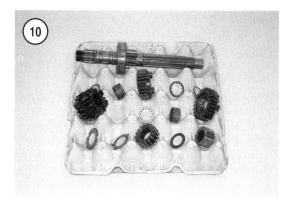

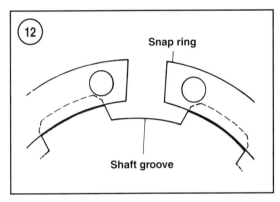

Snap ring

Shaft groove

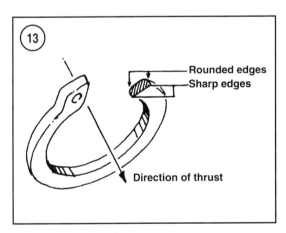

Rounded edges
Sharp edges

Direction of thrust

with the old parts, install these shims in their original locations since the shims have developed a wear pattern. If new parts are being used, discard the additional shims.

Transmission Service Notes

1. Parts with two different sides, such as gears, snap rings and shift forks, can be installed back-

ward. To maintain the correct alignment and position of the parts during disassembly, store each part in order and in a divided container (**Figure 10**).

2. The snap rings are a tight fit on the transmission shafts and will bend and twist during removal. Install *new* snap rings during transmission assembly.

3. To avoid bending and twisting the new snap rings during installation, use the following installation technique:

  a. Open the new snap ring with a pair of snap ring pliers while holding the back of the snap ring with a pair of pliers (**Figure 11**).

  b. Then slide the snap ring down the shaft and seat it into its correct transmission groove. Check the snap ring to make sure it seats in its groove completely.

4. When installing snap rings, align the snap ring opening with the shaft groove as shown in **Figure 12**.

5. Snap rings and flat washers have one sharp edge and one rounded edge (**Figure 13**). Install the snap rings with the sharp edge facing away from the gear producing the thrust.

Mainshaft Disassembly

Refer to **Figure 14**.

1. Clean the assembled mainshaft in solvent, then dry with compressed air.

2. Slide off the needle bearing housing, needle bearing and thrust washer.

3. Slide off the second gear and lockwasher. Rotate the notched spline washer to clear the spline groove and remove it.

4. Slide off the sixth gear, sixth gear splined bushing and spline washer.

5. Remove the snap ring.

6. Slide off the third/fourth combination gear.

7. Remove the snap ring and spline washer.

8. Slide off the fifth gear, fifth gear bushing and thrust washer.

NOTE
*Mainshaft first gear (A, **Figure 15**) is an integral part of the mainshaft.*

NOTE
*Do not remove the bearing (B, **Figure 15**) unless it is going to be replaced.*

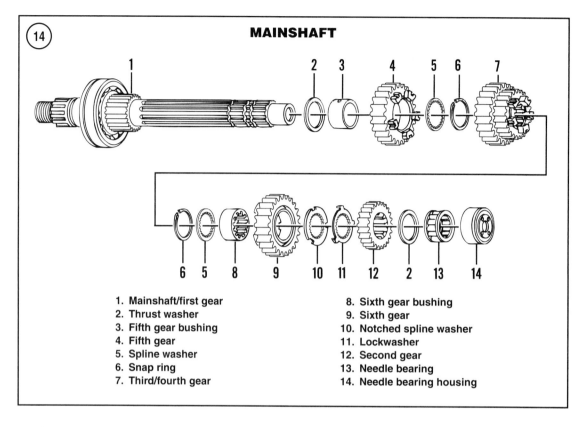

MAINSHAFT

1. Mainshaft/first gear
2. Thrust washer
3. Fifth gear bushing
4. Fifth gear
5. Spline washer
6. Snap ring
7. Third/fourth gear

8. Sixth gear bushing
9. Sixth gear
10. Notched spline washer
11. Lockwasher
12. Second gear
13. Needle bearing
14. Needle bearing housing

9. If necessary, press off the mainshaft ball bearing (B, **Figure 15**) as described under *Bearing Replacement* in Chapter One.

10. Inspect the mainshaft assembly as described under *Transmission Inspection* in this chapter.

Mainshaft Assembly

Refer to **Figure 14**.

1. Prior to mainshaft assembly, note the following:
   a. The mainshaft uses two snap rings. Both of these snap rings are identical, having the same part number.
   b. Install *new* snap rings.
   c. Install the snap rings and thrust washers with their chamfered edge facing away from the thrust load. Refer to **Figure 13** and **Figure 16**.
   d. Align the snap ring gap with the transmission shaft groove as shown in **Figure 12**.

2. If the mainshaft bearing (A, **Figure 17**) was removed, install the new bearing as follows:
   a. The new bearing must be installed so that the groove in the outer race faces toward the outside of the shaft as shown in B, **Figure 17**.

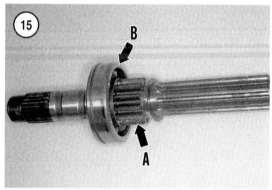

b. Being careful not to damage the first gear or the mainshaft splines, support the shaft and first gear with a bearing splitter in a press and press on the bearing. Use a tool that will apply force only to the mainshaft bearing's inner race as described under *Bearing Replacement* in Chapter One.

CAUTION
If pressure is applied to the bearing's outer race, the bearing will be damaged.

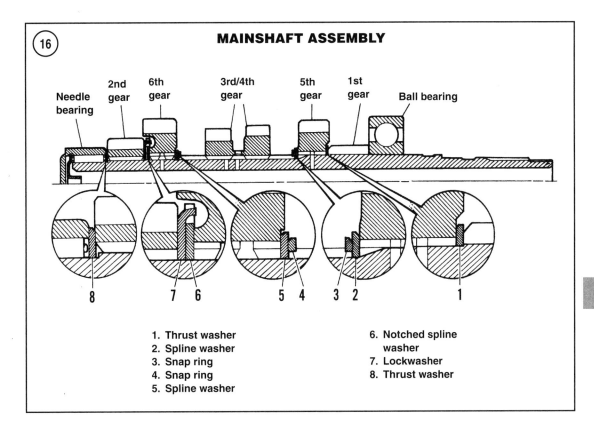

MAINSHAFT ASSEMBLY

Needle bearing | 2nd gear | 6th gear | 3rd/4th gear | 5th gear | 1st gear | Ball bearing

1. Thrust washer
2. Spline washer
3. Snap ring
4. Snap ring
5. Spline washer
6. Notched spline washer
7. Lockwasher
8. Thrust washer

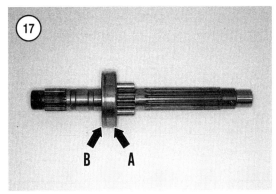

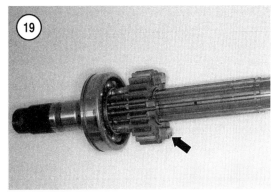

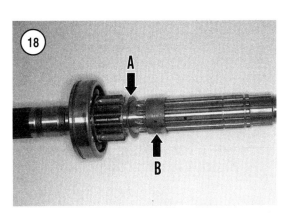

c. Press the bearing (A, **Figure 17**) onto the mainshaft until it bottoms.

3. Apply a light coat of clean engine oil to all sliding surfaces prior to installing any parts.

4. Position the thrust washer with the chamfered side going on last and install the thrust washer (A, **Figure 18**).

5. Slide on the fifth gear bushing (B, **Figure 18**).

6. Position the fifth gear with the dog side going on last (**Figure 19**) and install the fifth gear onto the bushing.

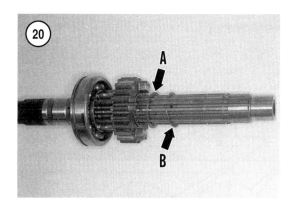

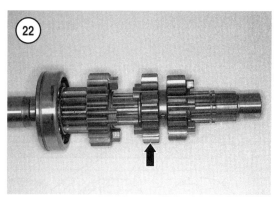

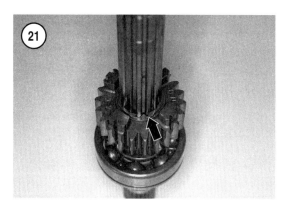

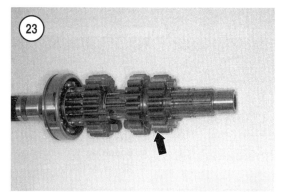

7. Position the thrust washer with the chamfered side going on last. Install the thrust washer (A, **Figure 20**).

8. Install a *new* snap ring (B, **Figure 20**). Make sure the snap ring is correctly seated in the groove (**Figure 21**).

9. Install the third/fourth combination gear as follows:

   a. Position the third/fourth combination gear with the larger fourth gear side (**Figure 22**) going on first.

   b. Slide on the third/fourth combination gear (**Figure 23**).

10. Install a *new* snap ring. Make sure the snap ring is correctly seated in the groove (**Figure 24**).

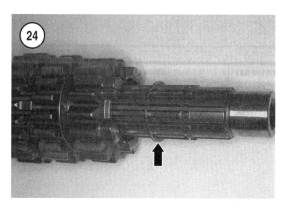

11. Position the spline washer with the chamfered side going on last and install the splined washer (A, **Figure 25**).

12. Align the oil hole in the sixth gear bushing with the mainshaft oil hole and slide on the sixth gear bushing (B, **Figure 25**).

13. Position the sixth gear with the dog side going on first (**Figure 26**) and install the sixth gear onto the bushing (**Figure 27**).

14. Slide on the notched spline washer (**Figure 28**). This washer is symmetrical (both sides are flat).

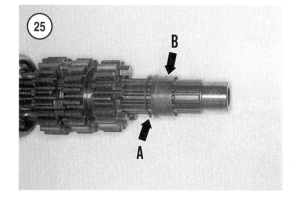

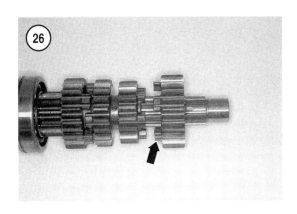

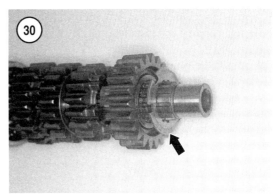

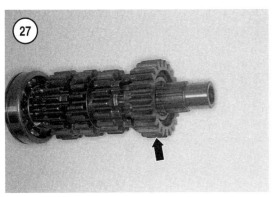

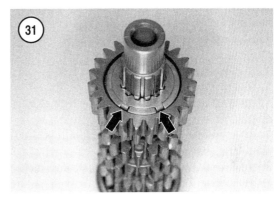

7

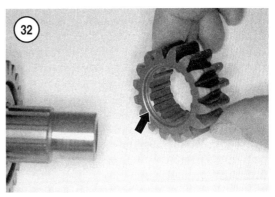

Slightly rotate the splined washer so it is locked in the mainshaft groove (**Figure 29**) and is held in place by the splines.

15. Position the lockwasher with the locking arms facing the notched splined washer installed in Step 14.

16. Slide on the lockwasher (**Figure 30**) and insert the locking arms into the notches in the spline washer as shown in **Figure 31**.

17. Position the second gear with the small chamfered side (**Figure 32**) going on first and slide on the second gear (A, **Figure 33**).

18. Position the thrust washer with the chamfered side going on first and install the splined washer (B, **Figure 33**).

19. Install the needle bearing (**Figure 34**) and its housing (**Figure 35**).

20. Refer to **Figure 36** for the correct placement of the mainshaft gears. Make sure each gear engages properly to the adjoining gear where applicable.

Countershaft Disassembly

Refer to **Figure 37**.

1. Clean the assembled countershaft in solvent, then dry with compressed air.

2. Slide off the needle bearing housing and the needle bearing.

3. Slide off the thrust washer.

4. Slide off the first gear and needle bearing.

5. Slide off the thrust washer and the fifth gear.

6. Remove the snap ring.

7. Slide off the spline washer, the fourth gear and the fourth gear splined bushing.

8. Remove the tab lockwasher. Rotate the notched spline washer to clear the spline groove and remove it.

9. Slide off the third gear and third gear bushing.

10. Slide off the spline washer and remove the snap ring.

11. Slide off the sixth gear.

12. Remove the snap ring and slide off the spline washer.

13. Slide off the second gear and second gear bushing.

> *NOTE*
> *The ball bearing is an integral part of the countershaft. If the bearing is damaged, the countershaft must be replaced. Do not attempt to remove the bearing from the countershaft.*

14. Inspect the countershaft assembly as described under *Transmission Inspection* in this chapter.

Countershaft Assembly

1. Prior to countershaft assembly, note the following:

   a. The countershaft uses three snap rings. Each snap ring is identical, having the same part number.

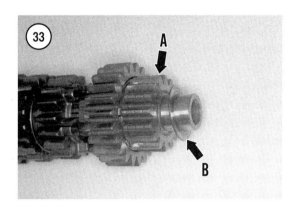

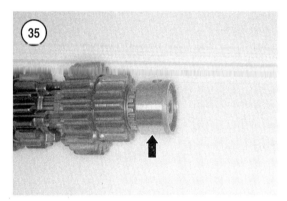

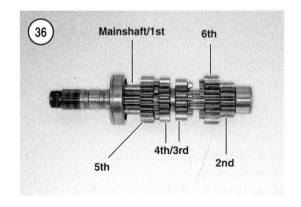

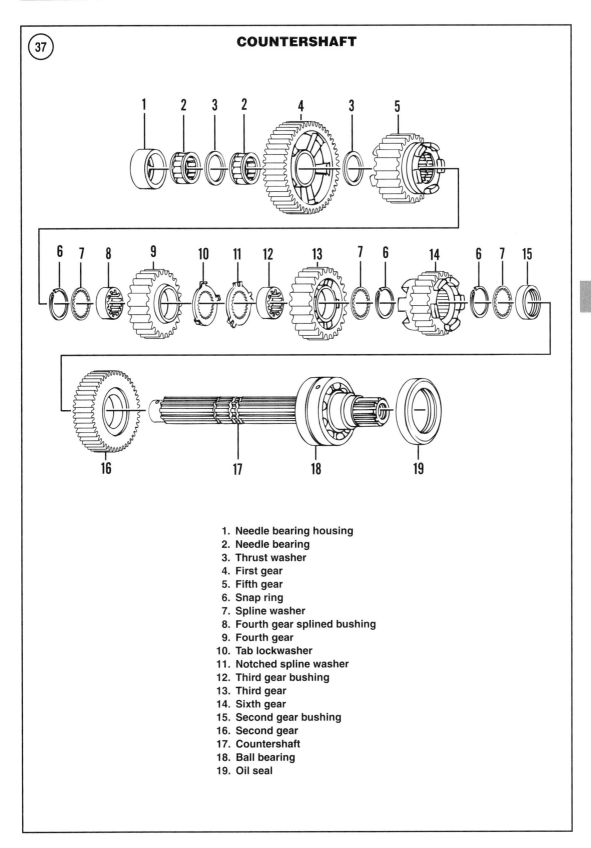

COUNTERSHAFT

1. Needle bearing housing
2. Needle bearing
3. Thrust washer
4. First gear
5. Fifth gear
6. Snap ring
7. Spline washer
8. Fourth gear splined bushing
9. Fourth gear
10. Tab lockwasher
11. Notched spline washer
12. Third gear bushing
13. Third gear
14. Sixth gear
15. Second gear bushing
16. Second gear
17. Countershaft
18. Ball bearing
19. Oil seal

7

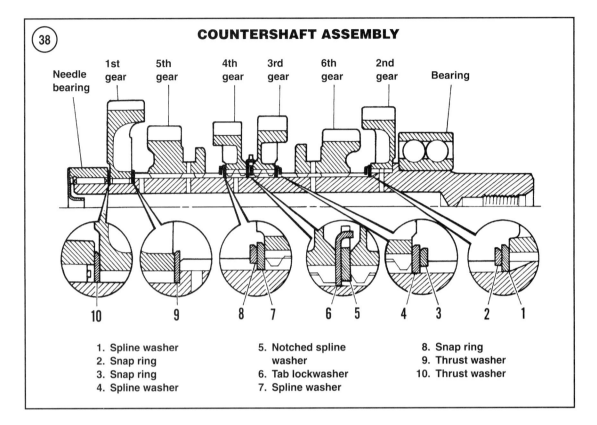

COUNTERSHAFT ASSEMBLY

38

Needle bearing — 1st gear — 5th gear — 4th gear — 3rd gear — 6th gear — 2nd gear — Bearing

10   9   8   7   6   5   4   3   2   1

1. Spline washer
2. Snap ring
3. Snap ring
4. Spline washer
5. Notched spline washer
6. Tab lockwasher
7. Spline washer
8. Snap ring
9. Thrust washer
10. Thrust washer

b. Install *new* snap rings.

c. The countershaft uses three splined washers. Each washer is identical, having the same part number. When reusing the spline washers, install them in their original mounting position.

d. Install the snap rings and thrust washers with their chamfered edge facing away from the thrust load. Refer to **Figure 13** and **Figure 38**.

e. Align the snap ring gap with the transmission shaft groove as shown in **Figure 12**.

2. Apply a light coat of clean engine oil to all sliding surfaces prior to installing any parts.

3. Slide on the second gear bushing (**Figure 39**).

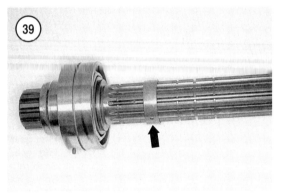

4. Position the second gear with the smooth side going on first (**Figure 40**) and install the second gear onto the bushing (**Figure 41**).

5. Position the spline washer with the chamfered side going on first and install the spline washer (**Figure 42**).

6. Install a *new* snap ring. Make sure the snap ring is correctly seated in the groove (**Figure 43**).

7. Install the sixth gear as follows:

a. Position the sixth gear with the shift fork groove side going on last (**Figure 44**).

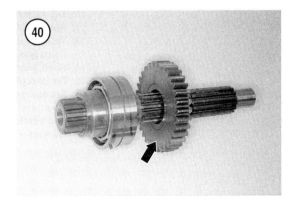

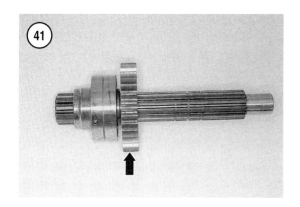

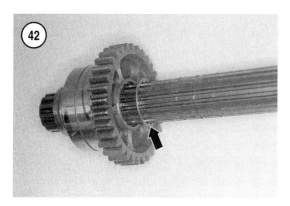

7

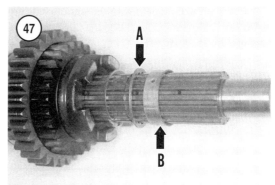

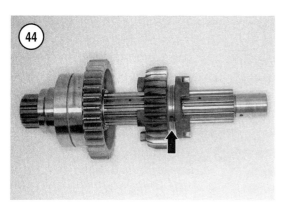

b. Align the oil hole in the gear with the countershaft oil hole.

c. Slide on the sixth gear (A, **Figure 45**).

8. Install a *new* snap ring (B, **Figure 45**). Make sure the snap ring is correctly seated in the groove (**Figure 46**).

9. Position the spline washer with the chamfered side going on last. Install the spline washer (A, **Figure 47**).

10. Align the oil hole in the third gear bushing with the countershaft oil hole and slide on the third gear bushing (B, **Figure 47**).

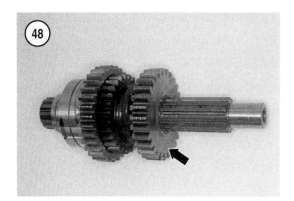

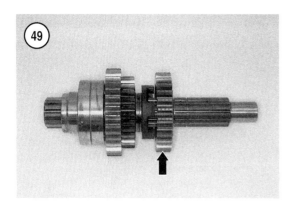

11. Position the third gear with the smooth side going on last (**Figure 48**) and slide the third gear onto the bushing (**Figure 49**).

12. Slide on the notched spline washer (A, **Figure 50**). This washer is symmetrical (both sides are flat). Slightly rotate the splined washer so it is locked in the countershaft groove and held in place by the splines.

13. Position the tab lockwasher with the locking arms facing toward the notched splined washer installed in Step 12.

14. Slide on the tab lockwasher (B, **Figure 50**) and insert the locking arms into the notches in the spline washer as shown in **Figure 51**.

15. Align the oil hole in the fourth gear bushing with the countershaft oil hole and slide on the fourth gear bushing.

16. Position the fourth gear with the shift dog side going on last (**Figure 52**) and install the fourth gear onto the bushing.

17. Position the spline washer with the chamfered side going on first and install the spline washer (**Figure 53**).

7

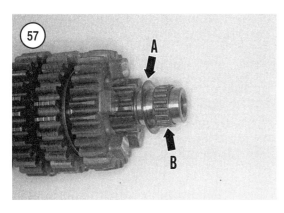

18. Install a *new* snap ring (**Figure 54**). Make sure the snap ring is correctly seated in the groove (**Figure 55**).

19. Install the fifth gear as follows:
   a. Position the fifth gear with the shift fork groove side going on first (**Figure 56**).
   b. Align the oil hole in the gear's shift fork groove with the countershaft oil hole.
   c. Slide on the fifth gear.

20. Position the thrust washer with the chamfered side going on last and install the thrust washer (A, **Figure 57**).

21. Install the needle bearing (B, **Figure 57**).

22. Position the first gear with the smooth side going on last (A, **Figure 58**) and slide the first gear onto the needle bearing.

23. Position the thrust washer with the chamfered side going on first and install the thrust washer (B, **Figure 58**).

24. Install the needle bearing (**Figure 59**) and its housing (**Figure 60**).

25. Refer to **Figure 61** for the correct placement of the countershaft gears. Make sure each gear engages properly to the adjoining gear where applicable.

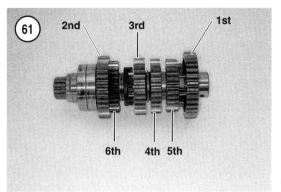

26. After both transmission shafts have been assembled, mesh the two assemblies together in the correct position (**Figure 62**). Check that the gear engages properly with the adjoining gear where applicable. This is the last check prior to installing the shaft assemblies in the lower crankcase; make sure they are correctly assembled.

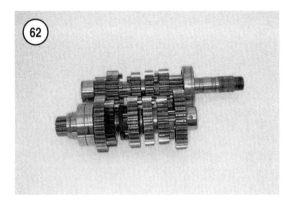

TRANSMISSION INSPECTION

Mainshaft Cleaning and Inspection

When measuring the mainshaft components, compare the actual measurements to the specifications in **Table 2**. Replace worn or damaged parts as described in this section.

Maintain the alignment of the mainshaft components when cleaning and inspecting the parts in this section.

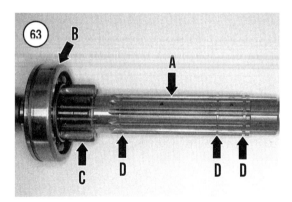

> *NOTE*
> *When cleaning the transmission components, make sure to keep all of the parts in their exact order of disassembly.*

1. Clean the mainshaft (A, **Figure 63**) and bearing assembly (B) in solvent and dry with compressed air.
2. Flush the oil control holes through the mainshaft with compressed air.
3. Inspect the mainshaft (A, **Figure 63**) for:
   a. Worn or damages splines.
   b. Missing, broken or chipped first gear teeth (C, **Figure 63**).
   c. Excessively worn or damaged bearing surfaces.

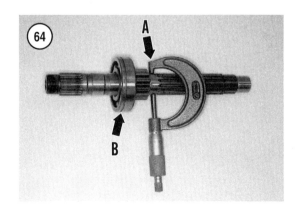

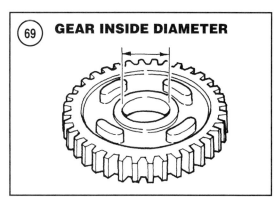

d. Cracked or rounded-off snap ring grooves (D, **Figure 63**).

4. Measure the mainshaft outside diameter at its fifth gear (A, **Figure 64**) operating position.

5. Hold the mainshaft and turn the bearing outer race (B, **Figure 64**) by hand. The bearing should turn smoothly. Then check if the bearing is a tight fit on the mainshaft. If the bearing is loose, turns roughly or is damaged, replace it. Refer to *Bearing Replacement* in Chapter One.

NOTE
If the mainshaft bearing is a loose fit on the shaft, check the bearing's mounting position on the shaft carefully for any cracks, excessive wear or other damage. The mainshaft may require replacement at the same time.

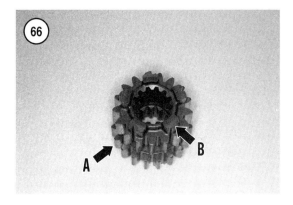

6. Check the needle bearing and housing (**Figure 65**). The bearing should turn smoothly within the housing. If it turns roughly or is damaged, or if the bearing needles are loose, replace the needle bearing and housing assembly.

7. Check each mainshaft gear for:
   a. Missing, broken or chipped teeth (A, **Figure 66**).
   b. Worn, damaged, or rounded-off gear dogs (B, **Figure 66**).
   c. Worn or damaged splines (**Figure 67**).
   d. Cracked or scored gear bore.
   e. Worn shift fork groove (**Figure 68**).
   f. Clear oil holes.

8. Check the mainshaft bushings for:
   a. Severely worn or damaged bearing surface.
   b. Worn or damaged splines.
   c. Cracked or scored bore.

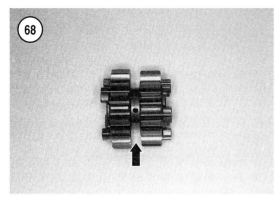

9. Measure the mainshaft fifth and sixth gear inside diameters (**Figure 69**).

10. Measure the mainshaft fifth and sixth gear bushing outside diameters (**Figure 70**).

11. Measure the mainshaft fifth gear bushing inside diameter.

12. Using the measurements recorded in the previous steps, determine the bushing-to-shaft and gear-to-bushing clearances. Replace worn parts to bring the clearances within service limit specifications in **Table 2**.

13. Make sure each mainshaft gear slides or turns on the mainshaft without any binding or roughness.

14. Check the washers, tab lockwasher and notched spline washer (**Figure 71**) for burn marks, excessive wear or other damage.

Countershaft Cleaning and Inspection

When measuring the countershaft components in this section, compare the actual measurements to the specifications in **Table 3**. Replace worn or damaged parts as described in this section.

NOTE
When cleaning the transmission components, make sure to keep all of the parts in their exact order of disassembly.

1. Clean the countershaft (A, **Figure 72**) and bearing assembly (B) in solvent and dry with compressed air.

2. Flush the oil control holes through the countershaft with compressed air.

3. Inspect the countershaft for:
   a. Worn or damaged splines (A, **Figure 72**).
   b. Severely worn or damaged bearing surfaces.
   c. Cracked or rounded-off snap ring grooves (C, **Figure 72**).
   d. Clear oil holes.

4. Measure the countershaft outside diameter at the second gear operating position (A, **Figure 73**).

5. Hold the countershaft and turn the countershaft outer bearing race (B, **Figure 73**) by hand. The bearing should turn smoothly. Then check if the bearing is a tight fit on the countershaft. If the bearing is loose, turns roughly or is damaged, replace the countershaft.

NOTE
The countershaft bearing is not available separately. If the countershaft or

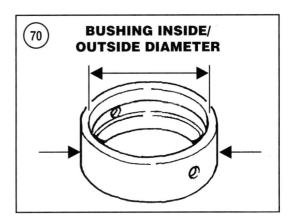

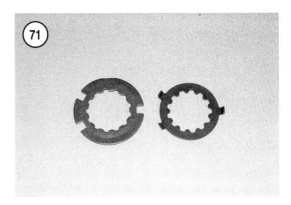

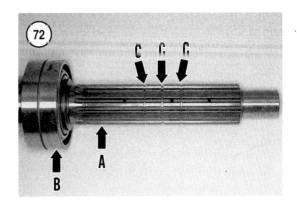

bearing is damaged, replace both parts as an assembly.

6. Check the needle bearing and race (**Figure 65**). The bearing should turn smoothly within the race. If it turns roughly or is damaged, or if the bearing needles are loose, replace the needle bearing and race assembly.

7. Check each countershaft gear for:
   a. Missing, broken or chipped teeth (A, **Figure 74**).

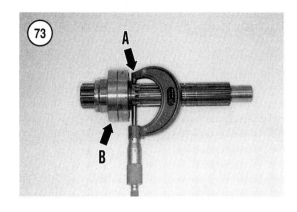

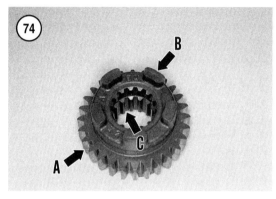

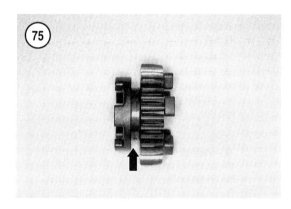

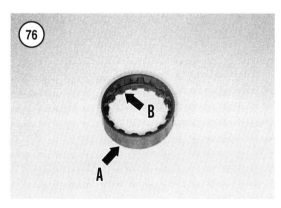

b. Worn, damaged, or rounded-off gear dogs (B, **Figure 74**).

c. Worn or damaged splines (C, **Figure 74**).

d. Cracked or scored gear bore.

e. Worn shift fork groove (**Figure 75**).

8. Check the countershaft bushings for:

a. Severely worn or damaged bearing surface (A, **Figure 76**).

b. Worn or damaged splines (B, **Figure 76**).

c. Cracked or scored bore.

9. Measure the countershaft second, third and fourth gears' inside diameters (**Figure 69**).

10. Measure the countershaft second, third and fourth gears bushings' outside diameters (A, **Figure 76**).

11. Measure the countershaft second gear bushing inside diameter.

12. Using the measurements recorded in the previous steps, determine the bushing-to-shaft and gear-to-bushing clearances specified in **Table 3**. Replace worn parts to bring the clearances within service limit specification.

13. Make sure each countershaft gear slides or turns on the countershaft without any binding or roughness.

14. Check the washers for burn marks, excessive wear or other damage.

15. Check the needle bearings for damaged needles and age. Check the bearing housing for damage.

INTERNAL SHIFT MECHANISM

Refer to **Figure 77**.

Removal

1. Disassemble the crankcase as described in Chapter Five.

2. Remove the Allen bolt (A, **Figure 78**) securing the stopper arm (B).

3. Disengage the stopper arm, washer and return spring (**Figure 79**) from the shift drum gearshift cam.

4. Remove the bolts and washers (**Figure 80**) securing the shift drum.

NOTE
The right and left side shift forks are identical with the same part number. On a high-mileage engine, refer to

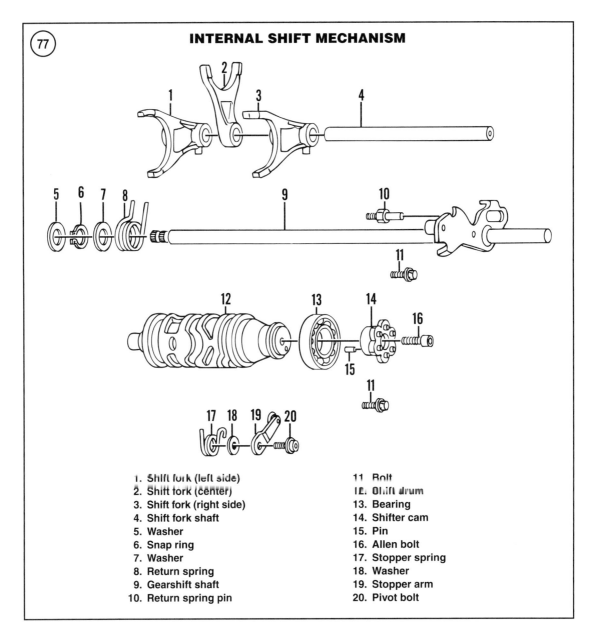

INTERNAL SHIFT MECHANISM

1. Shift fork (left side)
2. Shift fork (center)
3. Shift fork (right side)
4. Shift fork shaft
5. Washer
6. Snap ring
7. Washer
8. Return spring
9. Gearshift shaft
10. Return spring pin
11. Bolt
12. Shift drum
13. Bearing
14. Shifter cam
15. Pin
16. Allen bolt
17. Stopper spring
18. Washer
19. Stopper arm
20. Pivot bolt

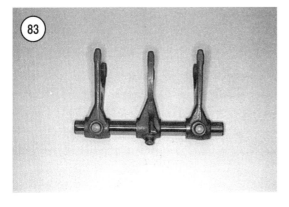

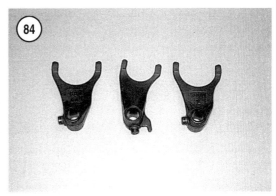

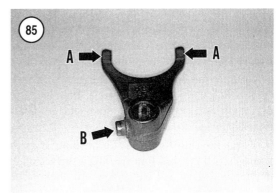

Figure 81 and mark the right **R** and left **L** shift forks to ensure they will be reinstalled in the original location.

5. Withdraw the shift fork shaft from the right side and remove the three shift forks.

6. Withdraw the shift drum and bearing (**Figure 82**) from the right side.

Inspection

When measuring the shift forks and shaft, compare the actual measurements to the specifications in **Table 4**. Replace worn or damaged parts as described in this section.

1. Clean and dry the shift forks and shaft (**Figure 83**).

2. Inspect each shift fork (**Figure 84**) for signs of wear or damage. Examine the shift forks at the points where they contact the slider gear (A, **Figure 85**). These surfaces must be smooth with no signs of wear, bending, cracks, heat discoloration or other damage.

3. Check each shift fork pin (B, **Figure 85**) for cracks, excessive wear or other damage. If damage

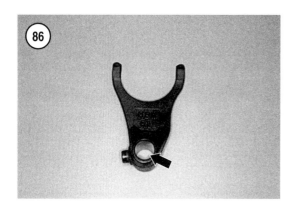

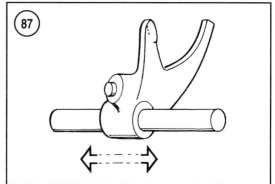

or wear is noted, check the corresponding shift drum groove for damage.

4. Measure the thickness of each shift fork claw (A, **Figure 85**).

5. Measure the inside diameter of each shift fork (**Figure 86**) with a small hole gauge. Then measure the small hole gauge with a micrometer to determine the inside diameter.

6. Check the shift fork shaft for bending or other damage. Roll the shift fork shaft on a surface plate or piece of glass and check for any clicking or other conditions that indicate a bent shaft. Install each shift fork on the shaft and slide it back and forth (**Figure 87**). Each shift fork should slide smoothly with no binding or tight spots. If binding is noticed with all three shift forks, inspect for a bent shaft. If a binding condition is noticed with one shift fork only, check that shift fork for a damaged bore.

7. Measure the shift fork shaft outside diameter at each of the three shift fork operating positions.

8. Clean and dry the shift drum.

9. Check the shift drum for:

   a. Severely worn or damaged cam grooves (A, **Figure 88**).

   b. Severely worn or damaged bearing surfaces.

10. Spin the shift drum bearing (B, **Figure 88**) by hand. The bearing should turn smoothly. If the bearing turns roughly of if there is any catching or other damage, replace it.

11. Check the ramps on the gearshift cam (A, **Figure 89**) for wear or damage. If necessary, remove the mounting Allen bolt (B, **Figure 89**) and remove the cam. Apply a medium strength threadlocking compound to the bolt threads prior to installation and tighten to 23 N•m (17 ft.-lb.).

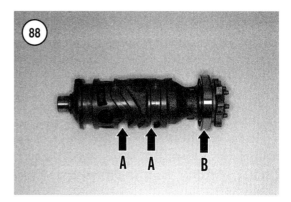

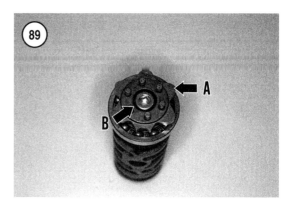

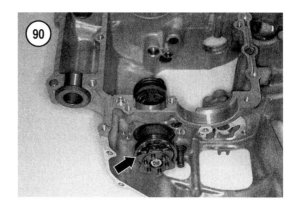

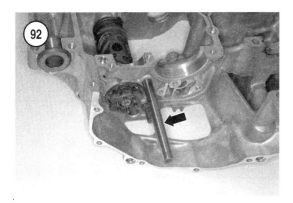

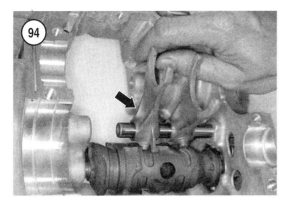

Installation

1. Apply clean engine oil to the shift drum grooves prior to installation.
2. Apply clean engine oil to the shift forks and shaft prior to installation.
3. Install the shift drum and bearing into the lower crankcase (**Figure 90**) from the right side and into the receptacle on the left side (**Figure 91**). Push it in until it bottoms.

> *NOTE*
> *The shift forks are marked with a **R** (right) **L** (left) and **C** (center). These marks relate to the engine as it sits in the frame. These marks must face the clutch (right side of the engine). Refer to the **R** and **L** marks made during removal.*

> *NOTE*
> *When installing the shift forks in the following steps, engage the pin on the fork with the corresponding groove in the shift drum.*

4. Partially install the shift fork shaft into the crankcase (**Figure 92**) and correctly position the *R* shift fork (**Figure 93**) pin into the shift drum groove. Push the shift fork shaft through the shift fork.
5. Correctly position the *C* shift fork (**Figure 94**) pin into the shift drum groove and push the shift fork shaft through that shift fork.
6. Correctly position the remaining *L* shift fork (**Figure 95**) pin into the shift drum groove and push the shift fork shaft through that shift fork. Push the shift fork shaft in until it bottoms.
7. Check that all of the shift fork pins are correctly located in the shift drum grooves.
8. Apply a medium strength thread locking compound to the bolt threads prior to installation. Install

the bolts and washers (**Figure 80**) securing the shift drum and tighten securely.

9. Install the stopper arm, washer and return spring (**Figure 79**). Tighten the bolt securely (A, **Figure 78**).

10. Lift up and engage the stopper arm, washer and return spring onto the shift drum gearshift cam (B, **Figure 78**).

11. Assemble the crankcase as described in Chapter Five.

Table 1 TRANSMISSION SPECIFICATIONS

Transmission	Constant mesh, 6-speed
Shift pattern	1-N-2-3-4-5-6
Primary reduction ratio	1.822 (82/45)
Final reduction ratio	2.812 (45/16)
Transmission gear ratios	
First gear	2.833 (34/12)
Second gear	2.062 (33/16)
Third gear	1.647 (28/17)
Fourth gear	1.421 (27/19)
Fifth gear	1.250 (25/20)
Sixth gear	1.130 (26/23)

Table 2 MAINSHAFT SPECIFICATIONS

Item	Standard mm (in.)	Wear limit mm (in.)
Bushing inside diameter		
Fifth gear	24.985-25.006 (0.9837-0.9845)	25.016 (0.9849)
Bushing outside diameter		
Fifth and sixth gear	27.959-27.980 (1.1007-1.1016)	27.94 (1.100)
Bushing-to-shaft clearance		
Fifth gear	0.005-0.030 (0.0002-0.0012)	0.00 (0.002)
Gear inside diameter		
Fifth and sixth gear	28.000-28.021 (1.1024-1.1032)	28.04 (1.104)
Gear-to-bushing clearance		
Fifth and sixth gear	0.020-0.062 (0.0008-0.0024)	0.10 (0.004)
Mainshaft outside diameter at fifth gear operating position	24.967-24.980 (0.9830-0.9835)	24.96 (0.983)

Table 3 COUNTERSHAFT SPECIFICATIONS

Item	Standard mm (in.)	Wear limit mm (in.)
Bushing inside diameter		
Second	27.985-28.006 (1.1018-1.1026)	28.021 (1.1032)
Bushing outside diameter		
Second	30.955-30.980 (1.2187-1.2197)	30.94 (1.218)
Third and fourth	30.950-30.975 (1.2185-1.2195)	30.93 (1.218)
Bushing-to-shaft clearance		
Second gear	0.005-0.039 (0.0002-0.0015)	0.06 (0.002)
Gear inside diameter		
Second, third and fourth	31.000-31.025 (1.2205-1.2215)	31.04 (1.222)

(continued)

Table 3 COUNTERSHAFT SPECIFICATIONS (continued)

Item	Standard mm (in.)	Wear limit mm (in.)
Gear-to-bushing clearance		
Second gear	0.020-0.070 (0.0008-0.0028)	0.10 (0.004)
Third and fourth gear	0.025-0.075 (0.0010-0.0030)	0.11 (0.004)
Gear bushing inside diameter		
Second gear	29.985-30.006 (1.1805-1.1813)	30.02 (1.182)
Countershaft outside diameter at		
second gear operating position	27.967-27.980 (1.1011-1.1016)	27.96 (1.101)

Table 4 SHIFT FORK AND SHAFT SPECIFICATIONS

Item	Standard mm (in.)	Wear limit mm (in.)
Shift fork		
Bore inside diameter	12.000-12.021 (0.4724-0.4733)	12.03 (0.474)
Claw thickness	5.93-6.00 (0.233-0.236)	5.9 (0.23)
Shift fork shaft		
Outside diameter	11.957-11.968 (0.4707-0.4712)	11.95 (0.470)

7

CHAPTER EIGHT

FUEL, CARBURETORS AND EMISSION CONTROL SYSTEMS

This chapter describes service procedures for the fuel system on carbureted models as well as the emission control systems for both the carbureted and fuel injected models. Specifications are in **Table 1** and **Table 2** at the end of the chapter.

FUEL TANK

Open and Secure Fuel Tank

The fuel tank can be opened and secured in a raised position to access the air filter and fuel hoses.

1. Remove the seat as described in Chapter Sixteen.

2. Remove the air duct cover mounting screws (A, **Figure 1**), and pull the rear of the cover up and off the locating boss (**Figure 2**) on the frame. Pull the cover toward the rear, disconnect the front tab from the front fairing, and remove the cover (B, **Figure 1**). Repeat for the cover on the other side.

3. Remove the front two fuel tank mounting bolts and washers (**Figure 3**). Remove the collar from each mounting rubber grommet.

4. Remove the rear two fuel tank mounting bolts and washers (**Figure 4**). Remove the seat bracket, then remove the collar from each mounting rubber grommet.

5. Place a shop rag at the rear of the fuel tank mounting area to protect the finish.

> *CAUTION*
> *In Step 4, lift the fuel tank slowly, being careful not to overextend the fuel hose.*

6. Lift the fuel tank all the way and support it with a piece of wood. Secure the wood to the front tank mount with a wood screw and washer.

7. Reverse the previous steps to close the fuel tank while noting the following:
   a. Make sure not to pinch or damage the overflow and air vent hoses when closing the fuel tank.

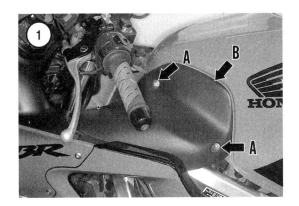

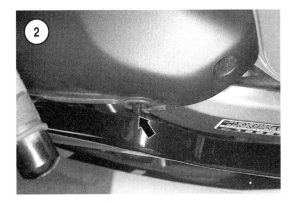

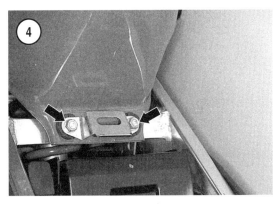

b. Tighten the four fuel tank mounting bolts securely.

Removal/Installation

Refer to **Figure 5**.

Read this procedure through before starting work. Make sure all of the necessary equipment is on hand to keep from damaging the fuel tank.

> *WARNING*
> *Some fuel may spill and fuel vapors will be present when removing the fuel tank. Because gasoline is extremely flammable, perform this procedure away from all open flames, including appliance pilot lights and sparks. Do not smoke or allow someone who is smoking in the work area, as an explosion and fire may occur. Always work in a well-ventilated area. Wipe up spills immediately.*

> *WARNING*
> *Gasoline is extremely flammable and must not be stored in an open container. Store gasoline in a sealed gasoline storage container, away from heat, sparks or flames.*

1. Remove the seat as described in Chapter Sixteen.
2. Remove the air duct cover mounting screws (A, **Figure 1**), and pull the rear of the cover up and off the locating boss (**Figure 2**) on the frame. Pull the cover toward the rear, disconnect the front tab from the front fairing, and remove the cover (B, **Figure 1**). Repeat for the cover on the other side.
3. If the fuel tank is more than one-quarter full, siphon the fuel into a container approved for gasoline storage. This reduces the weight of the tank before having to remove and turn the tank over when disconnecting the fuel hoses later in this procedure. To do this, perform the following:

   a. Open the fuel cap.
   b. Place a siphon hose into the fuel tank. Place the other end of the siphon hose into a fuel storage can.
   c. Operate the siphon to drain as much fuel from the tank as possible.
   d. When the siphon shuts off, remove it from the fuel tank and storage can. Close the fuel cap and place the storage can in a safe place, away

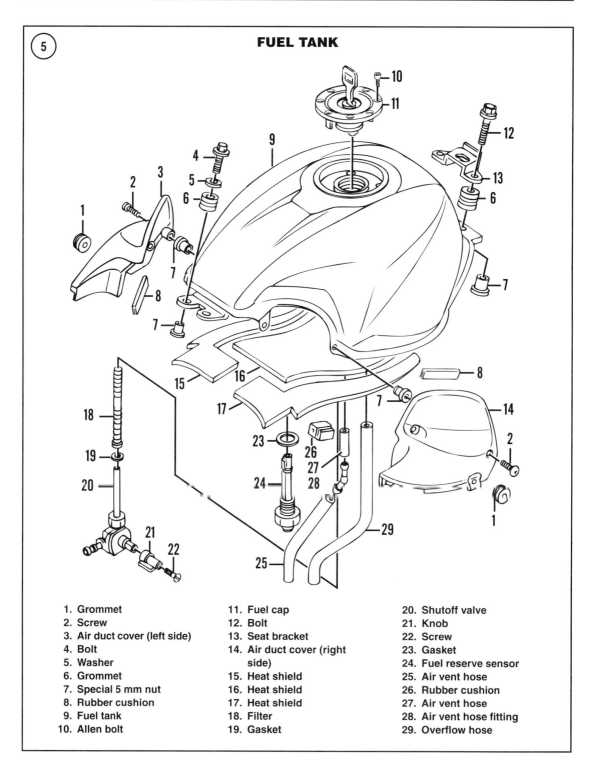

FUEL TANK

1. Grommet
2. Screw
3. Air duct cover (left side)
4. Bolt
5. Washer
6. Grommet
7. Special 5 mm nut
8. Rubber cushion
9. Fuel tank
10. Allen bolt
11. Fuel cap
12. Bolt
13. Seat bracket
14. Air duct cover (right side)
15. Heat shield
16. Heat shield
17. Heat shield
18. Filter
19. Gasket
20. Shutoff valve
21. Knob
22. Screw
23. Gasket
24. Fuel reserve sensor
25. Air vent hose
26. Rubber cushion
27. Air vent hose
28. Air vent hose fitting
29. Overflow hose

from all flames and sparks. Drain the siphon of all gasoline before putting it away.

4. Open and secure the fuel tank in the raised position as described in this section.

NOTE
Place several shop cloths under the fuel hose to catch any fuel remaining in the hose. After the fuel hose is dis-

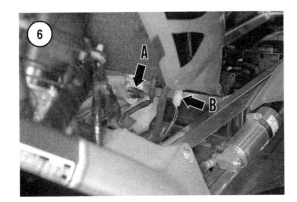

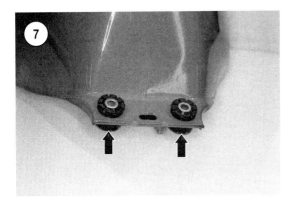

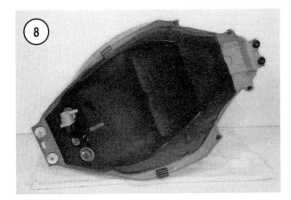

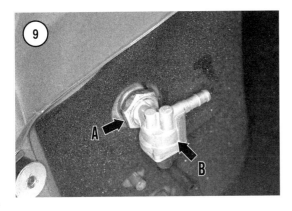

connected, plug the end. Properly discard the shop cloths.

5. Turn the fuel shutoff valve (A, **Figure 6**) to the OFF position. Label, then disconnect the following hoses from the valve:

    a. Fuel hose.

    b. Drain hose.

    c. Breather hose (California models).

6. Disconnect the electrical connector from the fuel level sensor (B, **Figure 6**).

7. Remove the piece of wood installed in Step 4 of *Open and Secure Fuel Tank* in the previous procedure. Lower the fuel tank onto the frame, then remove the fuel tank.

8. Install the fuel tank by reversing these removal steps while noting the following:

    a. First tighten the front fuel tank mounting bolts securely, then tighten the rear mounting bolts (including the seat bracket) securely.

    b. Turn the ignition switch to the ON position and allow the fuel pump to pressurize the system. Check the fuel tank hoses for leaks.

8

Inspection

1. Inspect all of the hoses for cracks, deterioration and other damage. Replace damaged hoses with the same Honda type and size materials. The hoses must be flexible and strong enough to withstand fuel pressure, engine heat and vibration.

2. Inspect the front, side and rear rubber grommets (**Figure 7**) for deterioration or other damage. Replace if necessary. Make sure the metal collars are in place within the rubber grommets.

3. Use the ignition key and open the fuel filler cap. Inspect the fuel filler cap gaskets. If the gaskets are damaged or starting to deteriorate, replace the filler cap assembly.

Fuel Shutoff Valve Removal/Installation

1. Remove the fuel tank as described in this chapter.

2. Place several heavy towels on the workbench to protect the fuel tank finish.

3. Turn the fuel tank on its side on the workbench (**Figure 8**).

4. Loosen the fuel shutoff valve (A, **Figure 9**) and remove the shutoff valve (B) from the fuel tank.

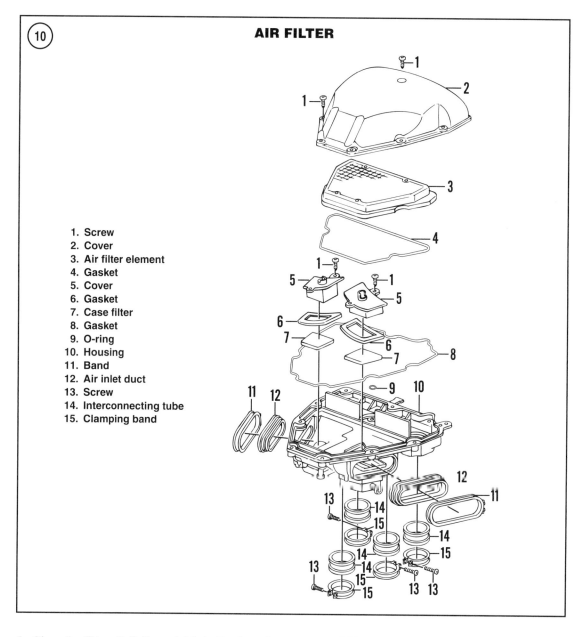

AIR FILTER (10)

1. Screw
2. Cover
3. Air filter element
4. Gasket
5. Cover
6. Gasket
7. Case filter
8. Gasket
9. O-ring
10. Housing
11. Band
12. Air inlet duct
13. Screw
14. Interconnecting tube
15. Clamping band

5. Clean the filter of all dirt and debris. Replace the fuel shutoff valve filter and O-ring if worn or damaged.

6. Install by reversing these removal steps. Check for fuel leakage after the fuel tank is installed and the fuel pump has been turned on.

AIR FILTER HOUSING

Removal/Installation

Refer to **Figure 10**.

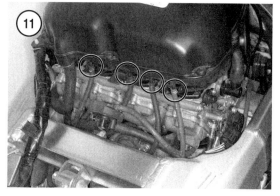

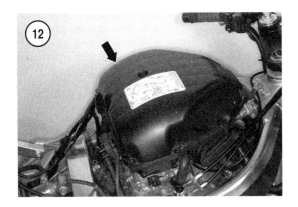

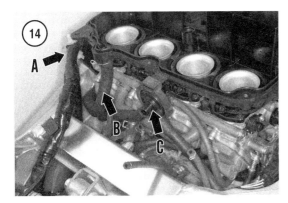

A

B

C

1. Remove the fuel tank as described in this chapter.
2. Disconnect the four vacuum hoses from the air filter housing (**Figure 11**).
3. Remove the screws securing the air filter cover and remove the cover (**Figure 12**).
4. Remove the air filter element (**Figure 13**) from the housing.
5. On the left side, disconnect the wire harness clip (A, **Figure 14**) from the housing.

NOTE
Identify the hoses when disconnecting them from the air filter housing in the following steps. Refer to **Hose And Wiring Harness Identification** *in Chapter Nine.*

NOTE
Hoses can be difficult to remove, especially when they have become bonded to their fittings. If a hose is stuck, twist the hose to break its seating bond. Pulling hard against a stuck hose may damage the hose or fitting end.

6. On California models, perform the following:
   a. Disconnect the No. 15 secondary air supply hose (B, **Figure 14**) from the housing.
   b. Disconnect the evaporative emission (EVAP) purge control valve from housing (C, **Figure 14**).
7. Insert a long Phillips screwdriver and loosen the clamp screw on the four clamps securing the housing to the carburetors.
8. At the front left corner of the housing, disconnect the crankcase breather hose from the housing.
9. Lift the housing up and partially off the carburetors.
10. Disconnect the float chamber inner air vent hose and the vacuum chamber air vent hose (**Figure 15**) from the housing and remove the housing.
11. Cover each carburetor intake opening to prevent contamination or small parts from entering the throttle bores.
12. While the air filter housing is off the engine, visually check all of the exposed vacuum hoses for damage that may have occurred when disconnecting them. Replace damaged hoses with the correct size replacement hose.
13. Install the air filter assembly by reversing these removal steps while noting the following:

8

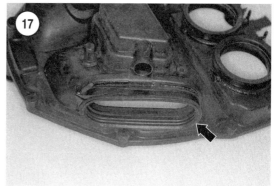

a. Inspect the housing and its gaskets; replace if necessary. Refer to **Figure 16** and **Figure 17**.

b. Route and connect all of the hoses correctly. Make sure all hose clamps, where used, are positioned correctly on the hose ends.

CARBURETOR OPERATION

For proper operation, a gasoline engine must be supplied with air and fuel mixed in proper proportions by weight. A mixture with an excessive amount of fuel is said to be rich. A lean mixture is one that contains insufficient fuel. The properly adjusted carburetors supply the proper air/fuel mixture under all operating conditions.

Each carburetor consists of several major systems. A float and float valve mechanism maintain a constant fuel level in the float bowls. The pilot system supplies fuel at low speeds. The main fuel system supplies fuel at medium and high speeds. A starter (choke) system supplies the very rich mixture needed to start a cold engine.

CARBURETOR SERVICE

If poor engine performance, hesitation and little or no response to mixture adjustment are observed, and if all other factors that could affect performance are correct, perform major carburetor service (removal and cleaning) as described in this chapter. Alterations in jet size, throttle slide cutaway and jet needle position should only be attempted by those experienced in this type of tuning work. Do not adjust or modify the carburetors in an attempt to fix a driveability problem caused by another system.

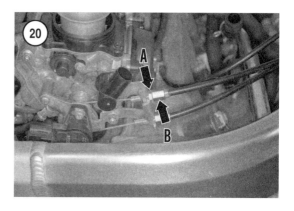

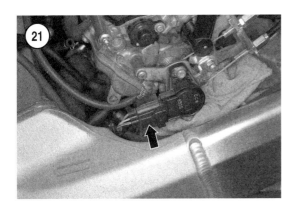

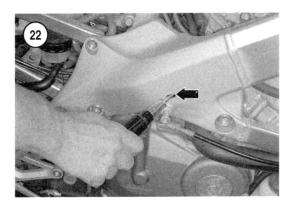

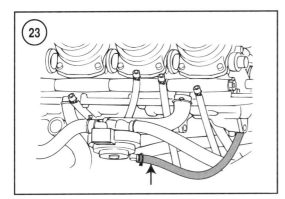

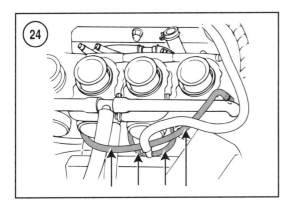

CARBURETOR ASSEMBLY

Removal/Installation

NOTE
There are numerous vacuum hoses on this carburetor assembly. Mark each hose and fitting to aid in installation.

Remove all four carburetors as an assembled unit.
1. Remove the seat as described in Chapter Sixteen.
2. Drain the cooling system (Chapter Three).
3. Remove the fuel tank as described in this chapter.
4. Remove the air filter housing as described in this chapter.
5. Disconnect the starter (chokc) cable from the cable holder (A, **Figure 18**) and disconnect it from the starter control arm (B).
6. Provide slack in the throttle cables as follows:
    a. At the hand throttle control, loosen the locknut (A, **Figure 19**) and turn the cable adjuster (B) all the way in to provide cable slack.
    b. At the carburetor throttle wheel, loosen the locknut (A, **Figure 20**) and turn the adjuster (B) in all the way to provide cable slack.
7. Disconnect the throttle position sensor electrical connector (**Figure 21**). Move the wiring harness out of the way.
8. On each side of the frame, insert a long Phillips screwdriver through the opening (**Figure 22**) and loosen the clamp screw on the four intake manifolds on the cylinder head.
9. On California models, perform the following:
    a. Disconnect the No. 11 tube (**Figure 23**) from the EVAP purge control valve.
    b. Disconnect the four No. 11 tubes (**Figure 24**) from the carburetor assembly.
10. Disconnect the air chamber front hose (**Figure 25**) from the T-fitting.

11. Disconnect the air chamber rear hose (**Figure 26**) from the T-fitting.

12. Pull the carburetor assembly upward and disengage it from the intake manifolds.

13. Cover the cylinder head intake openings with clean shop cloths (A, **Figure 27**).

14. Disconnect and drain the coolant hose from the float bowls on the No. 1 and No. 4 carburetors (B, **Figure 27**).

15. Disconnect the throttle cables from the throttle wheel and cable mounting bracket.

16. Partially remove the carburetor assembly from the engine and frame while guiding the throttle adjust cable (A, **Figure 28**) out from the frame.

17. Disconnect the throttle cables from the throttle wheel (B, **Figure 28**).

18. Install by reversing these removal steps while noting the following:

   a. Make sure all four carburetors are fully seated forward in the intake manifolds on the cylinder head. A solid bottoming out will be felt when they are correctly seated.

   b. Make sure each carburetor clamp screw is tight to avoid a vacuum loss and possible valve damage due to a lean fuel mixture.

   c. Make sure all hoses are connected to the correct fittings.

   d. Adjust the throttle cables as described in Chapter Three.

CARBURETOR OVERHAUL

Disassembly

Disassemble only one carburetor at a time to prevent the accidental interchange of parts.

> *CAUTION*
> *The throttle position sensor is pre-set by the manufacturer. Do not remove the throttle position sensor (**Figure 29**) from the bracket unless it requires replacement. Removal of the sensor may cause the sensor to move out of position, resulting in improper ignition timing. Refer all testing and replacement of the sensor to a Honda dealership.*

Refer to **Figure 30**.

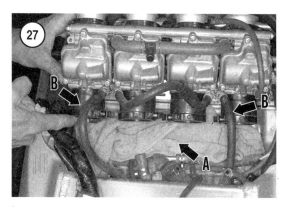
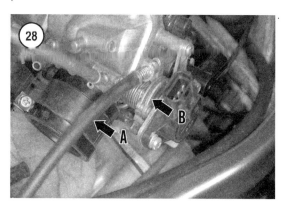
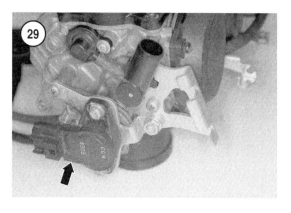

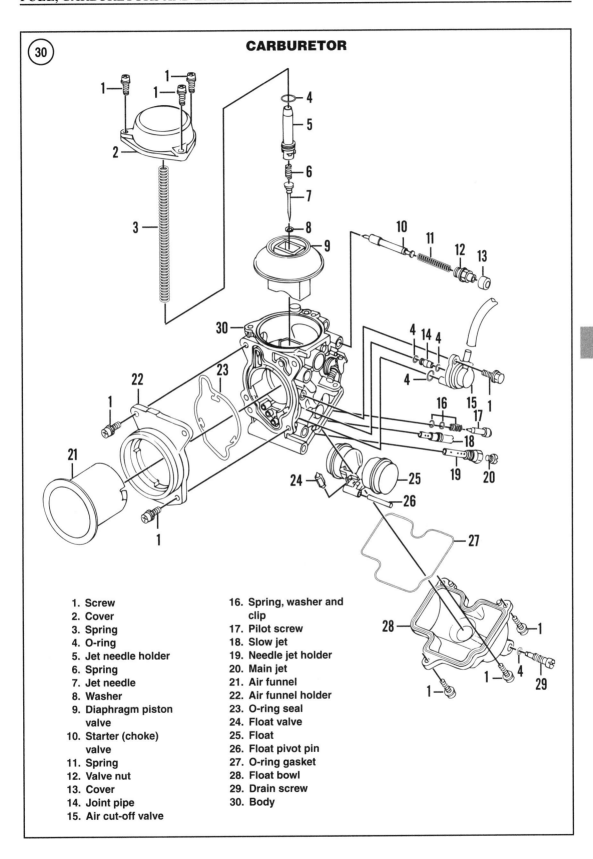

CARBURETOR

1. Screw
2. Cover
3. Spring
4. O-ring
5. Jet needle holder
6. Spring
7. Jet needle
8. Washer
9. Diaphragm piston valve
10. Starter (choke) valve
11. Spring
12. Valve nut
13. Cover
14. Joint pipe
15. Air cut-off valve
16. Spring, washer and clip
17. Pilot screw
18. Slow jet
19. Needle jet holder
20. Main jet
21. Air funnel
22. Air funnel holder
23. O-ring seal
24. Float valve
25. Float
26. Float pivot pin
27. O-ring gasket
28. Float bowl
29. Drain screw
30. Body

8

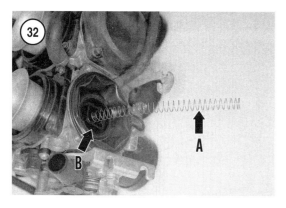

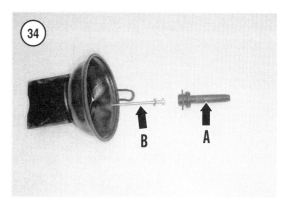

1. Remove the mounting screws and the cover (**Figure 31**).

2. Remove the spring (A, **Figure 32**) and the diaphragm/piston valve assembly (B)

3. Disassemble the diaphragm/piston valve as follows:

   a. Install a 4 mm screw (**Figure 33**) into the holder.

   b. Pull straight out on the 4 mm screw and remove the holder (A, **Figure 34**) securing the jet needle assembly. Remove the 4 mm screw.

   c. Withdraw the spring, jet needle (B, **Figure 34**) and washer.

4. Remove the mounting screws and remove the air funnel holder and funnel (**Figure 35**).

5. Remove the mounting screw (**Figure 36**) and remove the air cut-off valve assembly (**Figure 37**).

6. Disconnect the vent hose (**Figure 38**).

7. Remove the float bowl screws (A, **Figure 39**) and remove the float bowl (B). Discard the float bowl O-ring.

8. Push out and remove the float pin (A, **Figure 40**).

9. Pull straight up and remove the float assembly (B, **Figure 40**). Do not lose the needle valve hanging on the float tang.

10. Unscrew and remove the main jet (**Figure 41**) from the end of the needle jet holder.

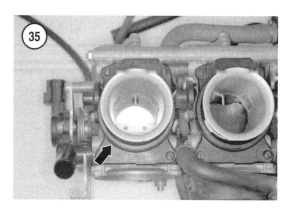

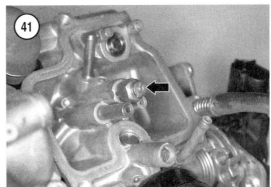

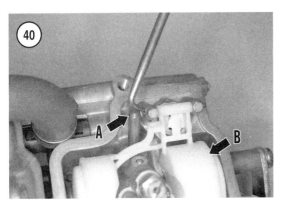

11. Unscrew and remove the slow jet (A, **Figure 42**).

12. Screw the pilot screw (B, **Figure 42**) in until it *lightly* seats while counting and recording the number of turns. The pilot screw must be reinstalled to this same position during assembly. Unscrew and remove the pilot screw, spring, washer and O-ring.

13. Remove the needle jet holder (C, **Figure 42**).

14. If necessary, remove the starter (choke) valves as follows:

    a. Remove the screws (**Figure 43**) and washers (**Figure 44**) securing the starter arm.

b. Disconnect the starter arm (**Figure 45**) from the starter valves. Do not lose the spring (**Figure 46**) located at the left end of the arm.

c. Unscrew the starter valve (**Figure 47**) from the carburetor body.

> *NOTE*
> *Further disassembly is neither necessary nor recommended. Do not remove the throttle shaft and butterfly assemblies (**Figure 48**). If these parts are damaged, the carburetor must be replaced, as these items are not available separately.*

15. Clean and inspect all parts as described in this chapter.

Assembly

1. If removed, install the starter (choke) valves as follows:

a. Screw the starter valve (**Figure 49**) into the carburetor body and tighten securely.

b. Connect the starter arm (**Figure 45**) onto the starter valves. Make sure to install the spring (**Figure 46**) at the left end of the arm.

c. Install the washers (**Figure 44**) and the screws (**Figure 43**) securing the starter arm. Tighten the screws securely, but do not overtighten.

2. Assemble the spring, washer and O-ring onto the pilot screw. Install the pilot screw (B, **Figure 42**) to this same position as noted during *Removal* Step 12.

3. Install the slow jet (**Figure 50**) and tighten securely.

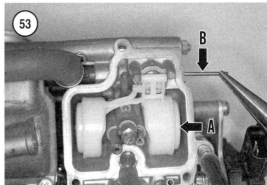

8

4. Install the needle jet holder (**Figure 51**) and tighten securely.

5. Install the main jet (**Figure 52**) into the end of the needle jet holder.

6. Install the float valve onto the float assembly (A, **Figure 53**) while indexing the needle valve into the housing.

7. Install the float pin (B, **Figure 53**) and push it in until it seats.

8. Check and adjust the float height as described in this chapter.

9. Install a *new* float bowl O-ring gasket.

10. Install the float bowl (B, **Figure 39**) and tighten the screws (A) securely.

11. Connect the vent hose (**Figure 38**).

12. Make sure the joint pipe and O-ring seals (**Figure 54**) are in place and install the air cut-off valve assembly. Install the mounting screw (**Figure 36**) and tighten securely.

13. If removed, install the air funnel and holder O-ring seal (**Figure 55**) onto the carburetor body.

14. Assemble the air funnel (A, **Figure 56**) onto the air funnel holder (B).

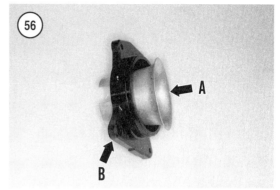

15. Install the air funnel and holder assembly onto the carburetor body. Align the air funnel cutouts (A, **Figure 57**) with the lugs (B) in the carburetor body. Carefully push the assembly into place (**Figure 35**) and install the mounting screws. Tighten the screws securely.

16. Assemble the diaphragm/piston valve (A, **Figure 58**) as follows:

a. Insert the jet needle/washer (A, **Figure 58**) into the diaphragm/piston valve. Carefully push the needle in until it seats (**Figure 59**).

b. Install a *new* O-ring seal onto the holder and apply a light coat of clean engine oil to the new O-ring.

c. Install the spring (B, **Figure 58**) and holder (**Figure 60**) into the diaphragm/piston valve and push it down until it bottoms.

17. Install the diaphragm/piston valve assembly into the body while guiding the jet needle into the needle jet holder (**Figure 61**).

18. Make sure the diaphragm is seated correctly in the sealing groove and that the loop aligns with the vent hole (**Figure 62**).

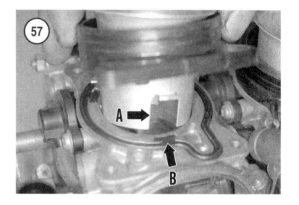

NOTE
The piston valve spring is very long and is difficult to install while keeping it straight. Use the method listed in Step 19 to avoid having the spring getting misaligned within the top cover.

19. Install the top cover and spring as follows:

a. Insert the upper end of the spring into the receptacle in the top cover (A, **Figure 63**) and into the piston valve receptacle (B).

b. Hold onto the top cover with one hand, raise the piston valve with a finger, and correctly

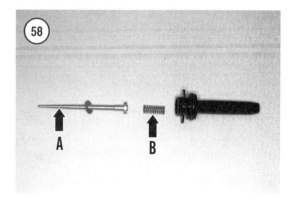

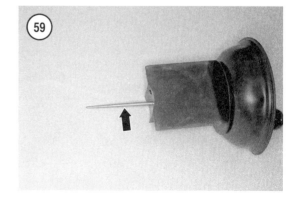

8

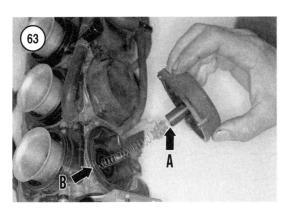

compress the spring between these two parts.

c. Hold the piston valve in the raised position and install the top cover onto the top of the carburetor.

d. Lower the piston valve and temporarily install the top cover screws.

e. Insert a finger into the venturi area and move the piston valve up in the carburetor body (**Figure 64**). The piston valve should rise all the way up into the bore and slide back down immediately with no binding. If it binds or if the movement is sluggish, chances are the diaphragm did not seat correctly, or the spring is misaligned to one side or not centered within the top cover. If necessary, remove the top cover and reposition the spring.

f. If the spring is installed correctly, tighten the top cover screws (**Figure 65**) securely.

20. After the assembly and installation are completed, adjust the carburetors as described in this chapter and in Chapter Three.

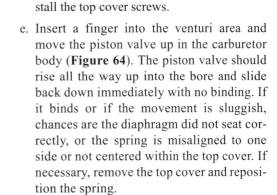

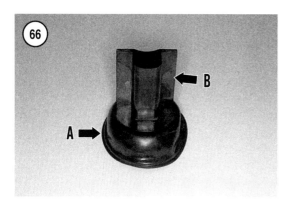

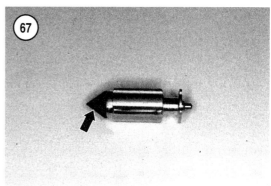

Cleaning and Inspection

> *CAUTION*
> *The carburetor bodies are equipped*
> *with plastic parts that cannot be re-*
> *moved. Do not dip the carburetor body,*
> *O-rings, float assembly, needle valve or*
> *diaphragm/piston valve into carburetor*
> *cleaner or other harsh solutions that*
> *can damage these parts. Honda does*
> *not recommend the use of a caustic car-*
> *buretor cleaning solvent. Instead, clean*
> *the carburetors and related parts in a*
> *petroleum-based solvent.*

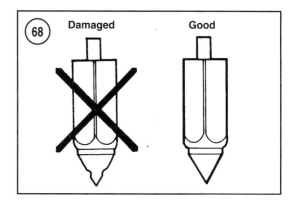

1. Initially clean all parts in a mild petroleum-based cleaning solution. Wash the parts in hot
soap and water and rinse them with cold water.
Blow-dry the parts with compressed air.

> *CAUTION*
> *If compressed air is not available, al-*
> *low the parts to air-dry or use a clean*
> *lint-free cloth. Do **not** use a paper*
> *towel to dry carburetor parts. The*
> *small paper particles could plug open-*
> *ings in the carburetor housing or jets.*

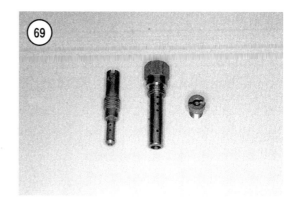

2. Allow the carburetor body and components to
dry thoroughly before assembly. Blow out the jets
and the needle jet holder with compressed air.

> *CAUTION*
> *Do **not** use wire or drill bits to clean*
> *jets. Even minor gouges in a jet can*
> *alter flow rate and upset the air/fuel*
> *mixture.*

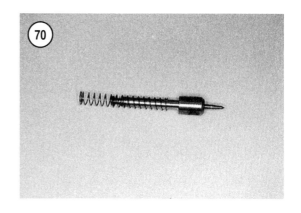

3. Make sure the float bowl drain screw is in good
condition and does not leak. Replace the drain
screw if necessary.

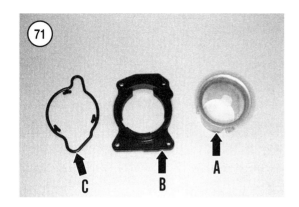

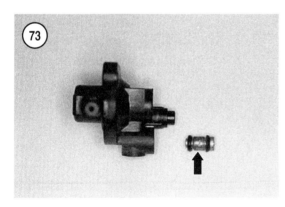

4. Inspect the diaphragm (A, **Figure 66**) for cracks, deterioration or other damage. Check the sides of the piston valve (B) for excessive wear. Install the piston valve into the carburetor body and move it up and down in the bore. The piston valve should move smoothly with no binding or excessive play. Replace the piston valve and/or carburetor body if necessary.

5. Inspect the tapered end of the needle valve (**Figure 67**) for steps, uneven wear or damage (**Figure 68**).

6. Inspect the needle valve seat for steps, uneven wear or other damage. Insert the needle valve into the valve seat, and slowly move it back and forth and check for smooth operation. If either part is worn or damaged, replace both parts as a pair for maximum performance.

7. Inspect the float for deterioration or damage. Place the float in a container of water and push it down. If the float sinks or if bubbles appear (indicating a leak), replace the float.

8. Inspect all of the jets (**Figure 69**). Make sure all holes are open and no part is worn or damaged. Replace the worn or unserviceable parts.

9. Inspect the jet needle taper (A, **Figure 58**) for steps, uneven wear or other damage. Install a *new* O-ring (**Figure 60**) on the holder.

10. If removed, inspect the pilot screw O-ring. Replace the O-ring if it has become hard or is starting to deteriorate.

11. Inspect the choke (starter) valve (**Figure 70**) for wear and make sure the spring has not sagged.

12. Inspect the air funnel (A, **Figure 71**) and holder (B) for contamination. Replace the O-ring seal (C, **Figure 71**) if it has hardened or deteriorated.

13. Inspect the air cut-off valve assembly (**Figure 72**) for damage. Make sure all openings are clear.

14. Inspect the air cut-off valve joint pipe (**Figure 73**). Install *new* O-ring seals.

15. Make sure all openings in the carburetor housing are clear. Refer to **Figure 74** and **Figure 75**.

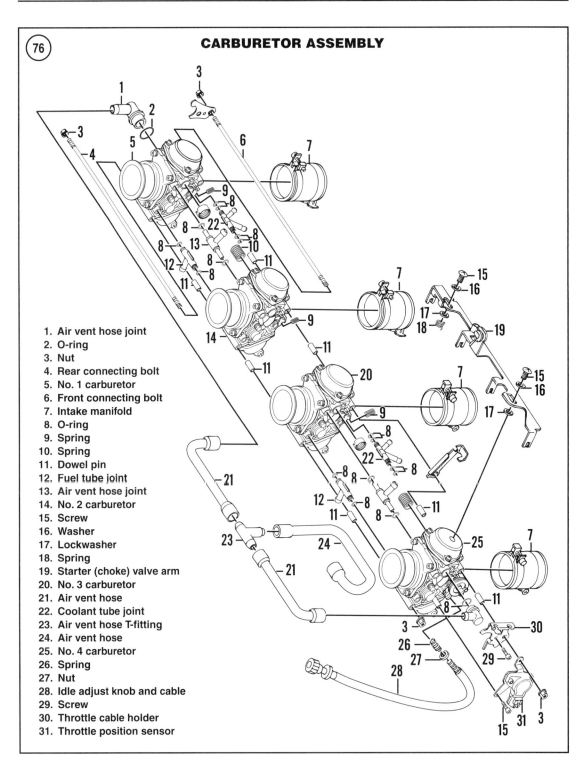

CARBURETOR ASSEMBLY (76)

1. Air vent hose joint
2. O-ring
3. Nut
4. Rear connecting bolt
5. No. 1 carburetor
6. Front connecting bolt
7. Intake manifold
8. O-ring
9. Spring
10. Spring
11. Dowel pin
12. Fuel tube joint
13. Air vent hose joint
14. No. 2 carburetor
15. Screw
16. Washer
17. Lockwasher
18. Spring
19. Starter (choke) valve arm
20. No. 3 carburetor
21. Air vent hose
22. Coolant tube joint
23. Air vent hose T-fitting
24. Air vent hose
25. No. 4 carburetor
26. Spring
27. Nut
28. Idle adjust knob and cable
29. Screw
30. Throttle cable holder
31. Throttle position sensor

Clean them out if they are plugged in any way, and then apply compressed air to all openings.

16. Check the top cover for cracks or damage, and replace if necessary.

17. Make sure the throttle plate screws (**Figure 48**) are tight.

18. Inspect the carburetor body for internal or external damage. If damaged, replace the carburetor

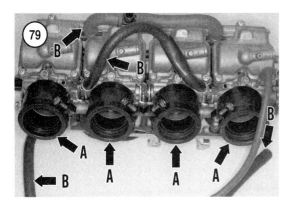

assembly. The body cannot be replaced separately.

19. Move the throttle wheel back and forth from stop to stop. The throttle lever should move smoothly and return under spring tension. If it does not move freely or if it sticks in any position, replace the carburetor.

CARBURETOR SEPARATION

Refer to **Figure 76**.

> *CAUTION*
> *The throttle position sensor is pre-set by the manufacturer. Do not remove the throttle position sensor (**Figure 77**) from the bracket unless it requires replacement. Removal of the sensor may cause the sensor to move out of position, resulting in improper ignition timing. Refer all testing and replacement to a Honda dealership.*

1. Remove the carburetor assembly as described in this chapter.

2. Remove the idle adjust knob and cable (**Figure 78**).

3. Loosen the screws and remove the intake manifolds (A, **Figure 79**).

4. If still installed, remove all fuel, air and vacuum hoses (B, **Figure 79**) from the carburetors. Label each hose and fitting so the hoses can be reinstalled in their original locations during assembly.

5. Remove the starter (choke) valves as follows:

   a. Remove the screws (**Figure 80**) and washers (**Figure 81**) securing the starter arm.

b. Disconnect the starter arm (**Figure 82**) from the starter valves. Do not lose the spring (**Figure 83**) located at the left end of the arm.

c. Unscrew the starter valve (**Figure 84**) from the carburetor body.

6. Loosen the synchronization adjusting screws (**Figure 85**) and remove the synchronization springs. Although only one screw is visible, loosen all screws.

7. On the right side of the carburetor assembly, perform the following:

a. Remove the nut (A, **Figure 86**) on the front carburetor connecting bolt.

b. Remove the nut (**Figure 87**) on the rear carburetor connecting bolt.

8. On the left side of the carburetor assembly, perform the following:

a. Remove the nut on the front carburetor connecting bolt.

b. Remove the nut (A, **Figure 88**) on the rear carburetor connecting bolt. Remove the bracket and the air joint (B).

9. Withdraw the front and rear connecting bolts from the carburetors.

CAUTION
*Do not remove the throttle position sensor (**Figure 77**) from the bracket unless it requires replacement. Removal of the sensor may cause the sensor to move out of position, resulting in improper ignition timing.*

10. Remove the screw (B, **Figure 86**), and if necessary, remove the throttle position sensor and bracket (C).

11. Remove the screw (D, **Figure 86**) and the throttle cable holder (E).

12. Pull straight out and remove the air vent hose joint and O-ring (F, **Figure 86**).

13. Carefully separate the No. 1 and No. 2 carburetors from the No. 3 and No. 4 carburetors. Remove the dowel pins between the two carburetor sets.

14. On the No. 1 and No. 2 carburetors, perform the following:

a. Remove the thrust spring.

b. Remove the fuel tube joint, air vent hose joint, water tube joint and the dowel pins.

15. On the No. 3 and No. 4 carburetors, perform the following:

a. Remove the starter (choke) cable holder.

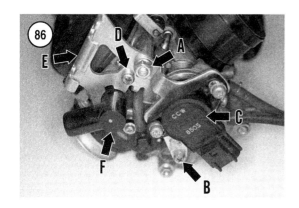

b. Remove the joint collar, fuel tube joint, air vent hose joint, water tube joint and the dowel pins.

16. Assemble the carburetors by reversing these disassembly steps, noting the following:

a, Install *new* O-rings on the fuel joints and air vent joints connecting the carburetors.

b. Place the carburetor assembly on a piece of plate glass.

c. Install the front and rear connecting bolts through all four carburetors.

d. Install and tighten the connccting bolt nuts securely while pressing down on all four carburetors to maintain proper alignment between all four carburetors.

e. Connect the air, fuel and vacuum hoses to the proper fittings as noted during disassembly.

f. When installing the intake manifolds, position the manifolds with the *CARB* mark facing the carburetors and with the clamp band screws facing toward the outside of the carburetor assembly. Align the clamping band hole with the manifold boss and tighten each clamp screw until the clearance between the band ends is 11-13 mm (0.4-0.5 in.).

CARBURETOR ADJUSTMENTS

Pilot Screw Adjustment
(Idle Drop Procedure)

The pilot screws are pre-set by the manufacturer and do not require adjustment unless the carburetor(s) is overhauled or the pilot screw(s) replaced.

Tool requirements

1. A tachometer able to detect 50 rpm changes is required for this procedure.

2. The following pilot screw wrench, or an equivalent:

a. U.S. and Canada models: Honda part No. 07KMA-MN90100 or 07KMA-MS60101.

b. Switzerland models: Honda part No. 07KMA-MN90100 or 07KMA-MS0101.

c. Other than U.S., Canada and Switzerland models: Honda part No. 07908-4730002 or 07908-4220201.

Procedure

1. Raise and support the fuel tank as described at the beginning of this chapter.

CAUTION
Do not tighten the pilot screw against the seat, as the pilot screw will be damaged.

8

2. Using the special tool, turn each pilot screw *clockwise* (**Figure 89**) until it *lightly* seats, then back it out the number of initial opening turns (**Table 1** or **Table 2**).

3. Start the engine and warm it to normal operating temperature (10 minutes of stop and go riding), then turn off the engine.

4. Connect the tachometer to the engine, following the manufacturer's instructions.

5. Start the engine. Adjust the idle speed with the idle adjust knob (**Figure 90**) to the idle speed listed in **Table 1** or **Table 2**.

6. Turn the No. 4 carburetor (right side) pilot screw in or out slowly to obtain the highest engine speed.

7. Repeat Step 6 for the remaining three carburetors.

8. Lightly open the throttle two or three times, then adjust the idle speed. See Step 5.

9. Turn the No. 4 carburetor pilot screw in until the engine speed drops by 50 rpm.

10. From the pilot screw opening position achieved in Step 9, turn the No. 4 carburetor pilot screw out to the *Final Opening* listed in **Table 1** or **Table 2**.

11. Adjust the idle speed. See Step 5.

12. Repeat Steps 8-11 for the remaining three carburetors.

13. Disconnect the tachometer and lower the fuel tank.

Float Height Inspection

1. Remove the carburetor assembly as described in this chapter.

2. Remove the screws (A, **Figure 91**) securing the float bowl and remove the bowl (B).

3. Hold the carburetor assembly so that the float arm just touches the float needle but is not pushing it down. Use a float level gauge (Honda part No. 07401-001000 or an equivalent) and measure the distance from the carburetor body to the bottom surface of the float body (**Figure 92**). The correct float height is listed in **Table 1** or **Table 2**.

4. If the float height is incorrect, replace the float(s).

> *NOTE*
> *All models use non-adjustable floats. Do not attempt to adjust the float, as the fuel level will be incorrect.*

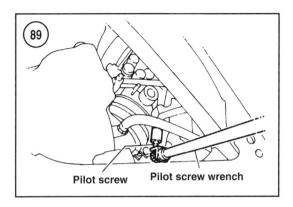

Pilot screw   Pilot screw wrench

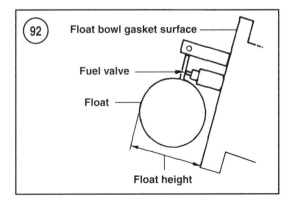

Float bowl gasket surface

Fuel valve

Float

Float height

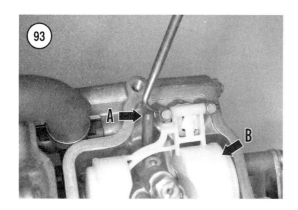

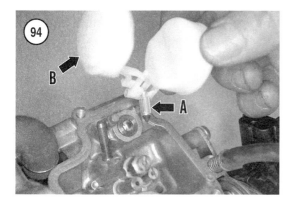

NOTE
If the fuel level is too high, the mixture will be rich. If the fuel level is too low, the mixture will be lean.

5. If necessary, replace the float(s) as follows:
   a. Push out and remove the float pin (A, **Figure 93**).
   b. Pull straight up and remove the float assembly (B, **Figure 93**). Do not lose the needle valve hanging on the float tang.
   c. Install the float valve (A, **Figure 94**) onto the new float assembly (B) while indexing the needle valve into the housing.
   d. Install the float pin (**Figure 95**) and push it in until it seats.
6. Install a *new* float bowl O-ring gasket.
7. Install the float bowl (B, **Figure 91**) and tighten the screws (A) securely.
8. Install the carburetor assembly as described in this chapter.

Needle Jet Adjustment

The needle jet is *non-adjustable* on all models.

High-Altitude Adjustment (U.S. and Canada Models)

If the motorcycle is going to be ridden for any sustained period of time at an elevation higher than 2000 m (6500 ft.), the carburetors must be readjusted to improve performance and decrease exhaust emissions.

NOTE
*If this adjustment has been performed by a Honda dealership, there should be a **Motorcycle Emission Control Information Update** label attached to the top surface of the rear fender next to the standard **Motorcycle Emission Control** label (**Figure 96**).*

The following pilot screw wrench, (Honda part No. 07KMA-MN90100 or 07KMA-MS60101), or an equivalent, is required for this procedure.
1. Remove the carburetor assembly as described in this chapter.
2. Remove the screws (A, **Figure 91**) securing the float bowl and remove the bowl (B).

3. Unscrew and remove the main jet (**Figure 97**) from the end of the needle jet holder (B).

4. Install a new main jet as follows:

   a. 49-state and Canada models No. 1 and No. 4 carburetor: No. 130.

   b. 49-state and Canada models No. 2 and No. 3 carburetor: No. 132.

   c. California models: No. 125.

5. Install the float bowl (B, **Figure 91**) and tighten the screws (A) securely.

6. Install the carburetor assembly as described in this chapter.

7. Raise and support the fuel tank as described at the beginning of this chapter.

> *CAUTION*
> *Do not tighten the pilot screw against the seat, as the pilot screw will be damaged.*

8. Connect the tachometer to the engine, following the manufacturer's instructions.

9. Start the engine and warm it to normal operating temperature (ten minutes of stop and go riding), then turn off the engine.

10. Start the engine and use the special tool to turn each pilot screw *clockwise* (**Figure 89**) 1/2 turn.

11. Adjust the idle speed with the idle adjust knob (**Figure 90**) to the idle speed listed in **Table 1** or **Table 2**.

12. Disconnect the tachometer and lower the fuel tank.

13. Attach a *Motorcycle Emission Control Information Update* label to the top surface of the rear fender next to the standard *Motorcycle Emission Control* label (**Figure 96**).

14. When the motorcycle is returned to lower elevations (near seal level), the pilot screws *must be returned to their original positions*, the original main jets installed and the idle speed readjusted to the specification in **Table 1** or **Table 2**.

Carburetor Rejetting

1. Do not attempt to solve a poor engine running condition by rejetting the carburetors. Make sure all other systems are operating correctly before considering the carburetors as the source of the problem. If the following list of conditions hold true, carburetor rejetting is most likely not the problem.

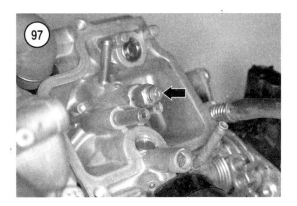

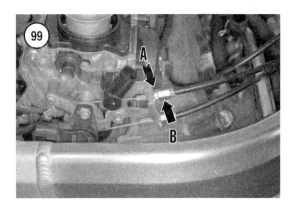

   a. The engine has held a good tune in the past with the standard jetting.

   b. The engine has not been modified.

   c. The motorcycle is being operated in the same geographical region under the same general climatic conditions as in the past.

   d. The motorcycle was and is being ridden at average highway speeds.

2. The following are conditions under which carburetor rejetting may be required:

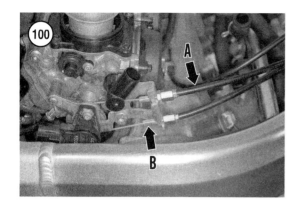

a. A non-standard type of air filter element is being used.

b. A non-standard exhaust system is installed.

c. Any type of upper end components in the engine (pistons, camshafts, valves, compression) have been modified.

d. The motorcycle is in use at considerably higher or lower elevation or in a considerably hotter or colder climate than in the past. See *High-Altitude Adjustment* in this chapter.

e. The motorcycle is being operated at considerably higher speeds than before and changing to a colder spark plug heat range does not solve the problem.

f. Someone has previously changed the carburetor jetting. Original equipment jet sizes are listed in **Table 1** and **Table 2**.

g. The motorcycle has never held a satisfactory engine tune.

3. If it is necessary to rejet the carburetors, check with a Honda dealership or motorcycle performance specialist for recommendations on the size of jets to install for specific conditions.

4. If the jets are going to be replaced, do so only one size at a time. After rejetting, test ride the motorcycle and inspect the spark plugs as described in Chapter Three.

THROTTLE CABLE REPLACEMENT

Always replace both throttle cables as a set.

1. Support the motorcycle on a swing arm safety stand. Block the front wheel so the motorcycle will not roll in either direction while on the safety stand (or centerstand on U.K. models).

2. Remove the seat as described in Chapter Sixteen.

3. Remove the fuel tank as described in this chapter.

4. Remove the air filter housing assembly as described in this chapter.

5. Remove both side fairing panels as described in Chapter Sixteen.

6. Partially remove the carburetor assembly sufficiently to gain access to the throttle wheel arm on the right side. It is not necessary to completely remove the carburetor assembly for this procedure.

7. Make a drawing of the cable routing from the right hand throttle housing to the carburetor assembly. Record this information for proper cable routing and installation.

8. Provide slack in the throttle cables as follows:

   a. At the hand throttle control, loosen the locknut (A, **Figure 98**) and turn the cable adjuster (B) all the way in to provide cable slack.

   b. At the carburetor throttle wheel, loosen the locknut (A, **Figure 99**) and turn the adjuster (B) all the way in to provide cable slack.

NOTE
*The throttle cables are different. Use masking tape to label the old cables before removing them. The upper cable (A, **Figure 100**) opens the throttle wheel arm. The lower cable (B) closes the throttle wheel arm.*

9. Open the right hand switch housing and disconnect the throttle cable ends as described under *Handlebar* in Chapter Thirteen.

10. At the carburetor assembly, disconnect the throttle cables from the throttle wheel. The pull cable is located on the top portion of the throttle wheel (**Figure 101**) and the push cable is located on the lower portion.

11. Remove the cables from the throttle cable holder.

12. Remove the cables from around the front of the right side fork tube and the frame (A, **Figure 102**). Note the position of any cable clamps for installation.

13. Compare the new and old cables.

14. If cables without nylon liners are used, lubricate them as described in Chapter Three.

15. Route the new cables through the same path as the old cables.

> *WARNING*
> *The throttle cables are the push/pull type and must not be interchanged. Attach the cables following the identification labels made on the old cables.*

16. Attach the new cables to the throttle and install the right-hand switch housing as described under *Handlebars* in Chapter Thirteen.

17. Install the throttle cables onto the throttle cable holder.

18. Connect the throttle cable ends onto the throttle wheel. The pull cable is located on the top portion of the throttle wheel (**Figure 101**) and the push cable is located on the lower portion.

19. Open the throttle and release it. The throttle should snap back smoothly. If operation is incorrect, carefully check that the cables are attached correctly and there are no tight bends in the cables. Repeat this check with the front wheel pointing straight ahead and then with the wheel turned full left and full right.

20. Adjust the throttle cables as described in Chapter Three.

21. Install the carburetor assembly as described in this chapter.

22. Install both side fairing panels as described in Chapter Sixteen.

23. Install the air filter housing assembly as described in this chapter.

24. Install the fuel tank as described in this chapter.

25. Install the seat as described in Chapter Sixteen.

26. Operate the throttle lever and make sure the throttle lever and throttle body linkage operates correctly. If the operation worked correctly in Step 19 but there is now a problem, check the cable routing as well as the air filter and fuel tank installation. Locate and repair the problem before continuing.

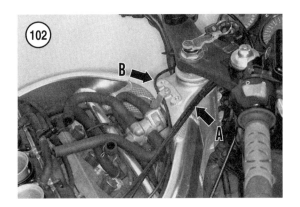

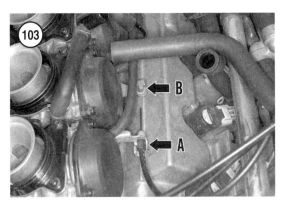

27. When the throttle is operating correctly, start the engine and run it at idle speed with the transmission in NEUTRAL. Turn the handlebar from side to side, making sure the idle speed does not increase. If it does, the throttle cables are improperly installed. If the idle speed did not increase, test ride the motorcycle slowly at first. If there is any problem with the throttle, stop the motorcycle and make the necessary repairs.

> *WARNING*
> *An improperly adjusted or incorrectly routed throttle cable can cause the throttle to stick in the open position. This could cause a loss of control. Do not ride the motorcycle until the throttle cable operation is correct.*

STARTER (CHOKE) CABLE REPLACEMENT

1. Support the motorcycle on a swing arm safety stand. Block the front wheel so the motorcycle will not roll in either direction while on the safety stand (or centerstand on U.K. models).

2. Remove the seat as described in Chapter Sixteen.

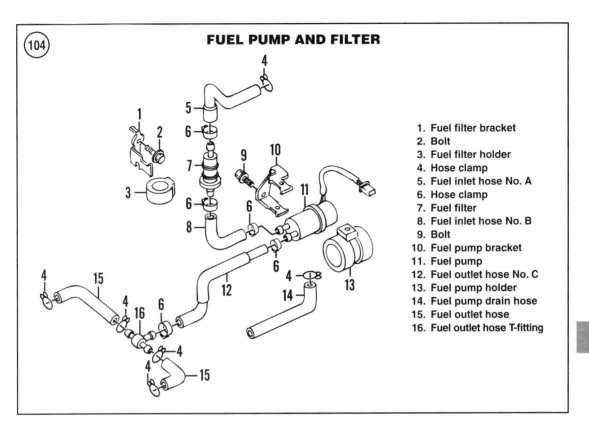

FUEL PUMP AND FILTER

(104)

1. Fuel filter bracket
2. Bolt
3. Fuel filter holder
4. Hose clamp
5. Fuel inlet hose No. A
6. Hose clamp
7. Fuel filter
8. Fuel inlet hose No. B
9. Bolt
10. Fuel pump bracket
11. Fuel pump
12. Fuel outlet hose No. C
13. Fuel pump holder
14. Fuel pump drain hose
15. Fuel outlet hose
16. Fuel outlet hose T-fitting

8

3. Remove the fuel tank as described in this chapter.

4. Remove the air filter housing assembly as described in this chapter.

5. Remove both side fairing panels as described in Chapter Sixteen.

6. Make a drawing of the starter (choke) cable routing from the left hand grip and switch assembly grip to the carburetor assembly. Record this information for proper cable routing and installation.

7. Open the left hand switch housing and disconnect the starter (choke) cable end from the choke lever as described under *Handlebar* in Chapter Thirteen.

8. Disconnect the starter (choke) cable from the cable holder (A, **Figure 103**) and disconnect it from the starter control arm (B).

9. Remove the cable from around the front of the left side fork tube and the frame (B, **Figure 102**). Note the position of any cable clamps for installation.

10. Compare the new and old cables.

11. Route the new cable through the same path as the old cable. Be sure to locate the cable *under* the bracket (B, **Figure 102**) on the frame by the steering stem.

12. Attach the new cable to the choke lever and install the left-hand switch housing as described under *Handlebars* in Chapter Thirteen.

13. Connect the starter (choke) cable onto the starter control arm (B, **Figure 103**) and the cable holder (A).

14. Operate the choke lever and make sure the carburetor linkage is operating correctly with no binding. If the cable operation is incorrect, check that the cable is attached correctly and that there are no tight bends in the cable.

15. Install both side fairing panels as described in Chapter Sixteen.

16. Install the air filter housing assembly as described in this chapter.

17. Install the fuel tank as described in this chapter.

18. Install the seat as described in Chapter Sixteen.

FUEL PUMP ASSEMBLY

Removal/Installation

Refer to **Figure 104**.

1. Support the motorcycle on a swing arm safety stand. Block the front wheel so the motorcycle will

not roll in either direction while on the safety stand (or centerstand on U.K. models).

2. Remove the seat as described in Chapter Sixteen.

3. Disconnect the negative battery cable as described in Chapter Ten.

4. Remove the fuel tank as described in this chapter.

5. On the right side, disconnect the two-pin black electrical connector from the fuel pump.

6. Loosen the hose clamps and disconnect the two fuel hoses (A, **Figure 105**) from the fuel pump. Plug the ends of both hoses.

7. Remove the fuel pump from the rubber mount (B, **Figure 105**) and remove the fuel pump.

8. Install by reversing these removal steps. Make sure all hose clamps are tight.

Fuel Flow Test

> *NOTE*
> *Prior to running this test, make sure the fuel filter has been replaced recently. If in doubt, install a new filter at this time to ensure an accurate fuel pump test.*

1. Raise the fuel tank and support it as described in this chapter.

2. Remove the rear cowl as described in Chapter Sixteen.

3. Use a jumper wire and connect it between the black/white and the black/blue wires of the six-pin electrical connector at the fuel pump transfer relay (**Figure 106**).

4. Disconnect the fuel hose from the three-way joint that goes to the carburetor.

5. Position this fuel hose in a graduated beaker.

6. Turn the engine stop switch to the RUN position.

7. Turn the ignition switch to the ON position (engine not running) and let the fuel flow into the beaker for five seconds.

8. Turn the ignition switch to the OFF position.

9. Multiply the amount of fuel in the beaker by 12 to establish the fuel pump flow capacity for one minute.

10. The minimum fuel flow for one minute is 700 cc (23.7 U.S. oz./24.6 Imp. oz.).

11. If the fuel flow is less than specified, replace the fuel pump as described in this chapter.

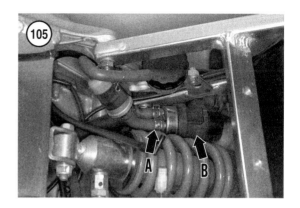

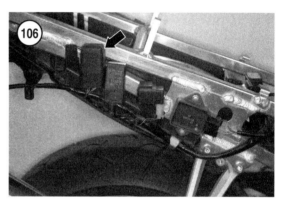

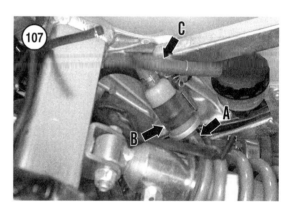

12. Disconnect the jumper wire from the fuel pump transfer relay electrical connector.

13. Install the rear cowl as described in Chapter Sixteen.

14. Lower and secure the fuel tank and support it as described in this chapter.

FUEL FILTER REPLACEMENT

1. Support the motorcycle on a swing arm safety stand. Block the front wheel so the motorcycle will

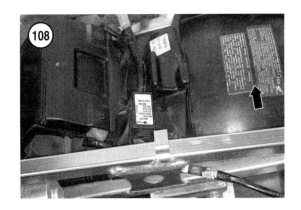

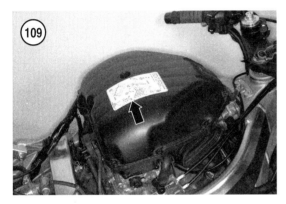

not roll in either direction while on the safety stand (or centerstand on U.K. models).

2. Remove the seat as described in Chapter Sixteen.

3. Disconnect the negative battery cable as described in Chapter Ten.

4. Remove the fuel tank as described in this chapter.

5. Loosen the hose clamps and disconnect the remaining fuel hose from the fuel filter (A, **Figure 107**).

6. Remove the fuel filter and rubber holder (B, **Figure 107**) from the mounting tab on the frame and remove the fuel filter.

7. Remove the fuel filter-to-fuel tank hose (C, **Figure 107**) from the old fuel filter and install it onto the new fuel filter.

8. Install the fuel filter by reversing these steps.

EMISSION CONTROL SYSTEM LABELS

Emission control information labels are mounted on the rear fender (**Figure 108**). On California mod-els, a vacuum hose routing diagram label is mounted on the air filter housing cover (**Figure 109**).

On most models, the hoses and fittings are labeled with identification numbers that correspond with the numbers listed on the vacuum hose routing diagram label. If these identification numbers have deteriorated or are missing, mark the hoses and their fittings with a piece of masking tape for proper installation. There are many vacuum hoses on these models. Reconnecting them can be confusing if they are not properly identified.

CRANKCASE BREATHER SYSTEM

All models are equipped with a crankcase breather system (**Figure 110**). The system re-circulates crankcase vapors into the air/fuel mixture so they can be burned.

NOTE
Figure 110 *shows a typical crankcase breather system that is used both on carbureted and fuel injected models.*

EVAPORATIVE EMISSION CONTROL SYSTEM (CALIFORNIA MODELS ONLY)

An evaporative emission control system (EVAP) is installed on all models sold in California. Refer to **Figure 111** for carbureted models or **Figure 112** for fuel injected models.

A vacuum hose routing diagram label is mounted on the air filter cover (**Figure 113**, typical). Fuel vapor from the fuel tank is routed into a charcoal canister, where it is stored when the engine is not running. When the engine is running, these vapors are drawn into the EVAP purge control solenoid valve and through the carburetor assembly or the throttle body and into the engine to be burned. Make sure all hose clamps are tight. Check all hoses for deterioration and replace as necessary.

Charcoal Canister Removal/Installation

1. Support the motorcycle on a swing arm safety stand. Block the front wheel so the motorcycle will not roll in either direction while on the safety stand (or centerstand on U.K. models).

8

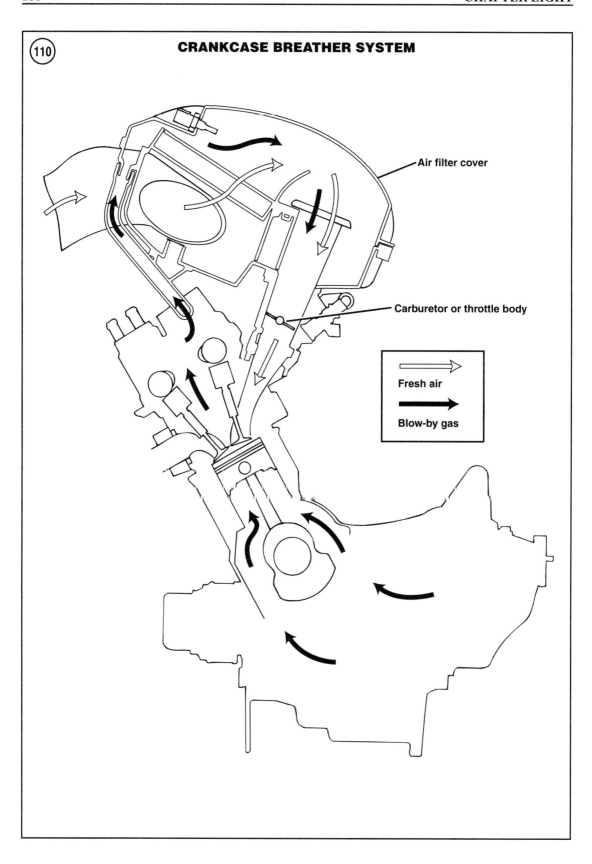

CRANKCASE BREATHER SYSTEM

(110)

Air filter cover

Carburetor or throttle body

Fresh air

Blow-by gas

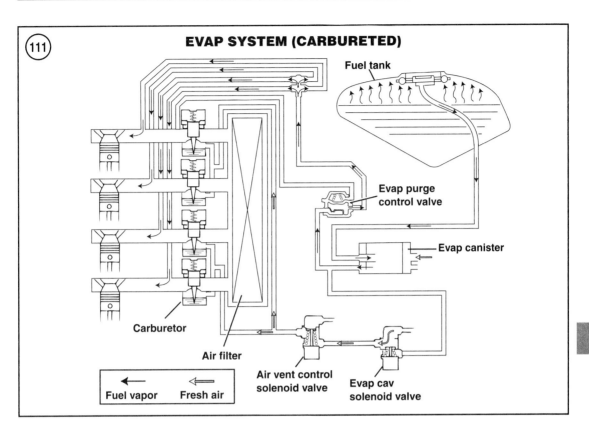

EVAP SYSTEM (CARBURETED)

Fuel tank

Evap purge control valve

Evap canister

Carburetor

Air filter

Air vent control solenoid valve

Evap cav solenoid valve

← Fuel vapor ⇐ Fresh air

8

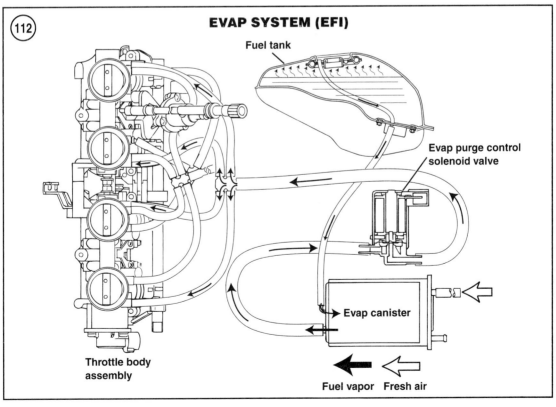

EVAP SYSTEM (EFI)

Fuel tank

Evap purge control solenoid valve

Evap canister

Throttle body assembly

Fuel vapor   Fresh air

2. Remove both side fairing panels as described in Chapter Sixteen.

3. Remove the bolt and nut securing the charcoal canister (**Figure 114**) and lower it from the frame.

4. Label the hoses at the charcoal canister, then disconnect them (A, **Figure 115**, typical).

5. Check all hoses for cuts, damage or soft spots. Replace any damaged hoses.

6. Install by reversing these removal steps. Make sure all hose fittings are tight.

Evaporative Purge Control Valve Removal/Installation

Carbureted models

1. Remove the fuel tank as described in this chapter.

2. Label the vacuum hoses at the control valve (**Figure 116**) for proper installation.

3. Remove the control valve from the mounting bracket on the air filter housing and remove the control valve.

4. Check all hoses for cuts, damage or soft spots. Replace any damaged hoses.

5. Install by reversing these removal steps. Make sure all hose fittings are tight.

Fuel injected models

1. Support the motorcycle on a swing arm safety stand. Block the front wheel so the motorcycle will not roll in either direction while on the safety stand (or centerstand on U.K. models).

2. Remove both side fairing panels as described in Chapter Sixteen.

3. Remove the bolt and nut securing the charcoal canister (**Figure 114**) and lower it from the frame.

4. Disconnect the electrical connector (B, **Figure 115**) from the purge control valve.

5. Remove the screws securing the purge control valve to the charcoal canister and remove it.

6. Install by reversing these removal steps. Tighten the screws securely.

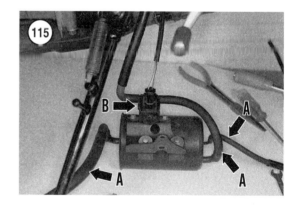
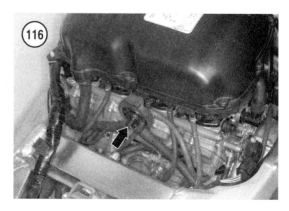

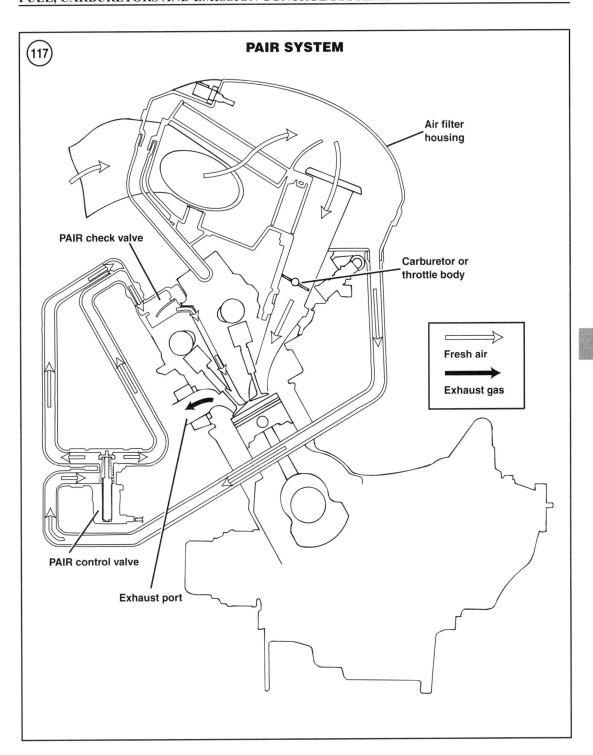

(117)

PAIR SYSTEM

Air filter
housing

PAIR check valve

Carburetor or
throttle body

Fresh air

Exhaust gas

PAIR control valve

Exhaust port

8

PAIR SYSTEM

The PAIR system, or the pulsed secondary air injection system, lowers emissions output by introducing secondary air into the exhaust ports (**Figure** 117). The introduction of air raises the exhaust temperature, which consumes some of the unburned fuel in the exhaust. Reed valves installed in the cylinder head cover prevent a reverse flow of air through the system.

PAIR Control Valve Testing

Carbureted models

1. Start the engine and warm it to normal operating temperature (ten minutes of stop and go riding), then turn off the engine.

2. Raise and support the fuel tank as described in this chapter.

3. Disconnect the four vacuum hoses (**Figure 118**) from the air filter housing.

4. Remove the screws securing the air filter cover and remove the cover (**Figure 119**).

5. Check that the secondary air intake port (A, **Figure 120**) is clean and free of carbon deposits.

6. If the secondary air intake port is carbon fouled, remove the PAIR reed valves from the cylinder head cover as described in this chapter.

7. Disconnect the air supply (air filter housing-to-PAIR control valve) hose from the air filter housing (B, **Figure 120**).

8. Partially remove the radiator from the engine as follows:

    a. Remove the lower bolt, nut and washer (**Figure 121**) securing the bottom of the radiator to the lower frame bracket.

    b. On the left side, remove the upper bolt and washer (**Figure 122**) securing the top of the radiator to the frame.

    c. Cover the radiator with a towel to prevent damage to the cooling fins.

    d. Swing the radiator forward so the lower mounting stay will not interfere with the radiator.

    e. Slide the radiator to the right side and remove it from the frame boss.

    f. Move the radiator forward and secure it to the front forks. Do not disconnect any of the coolant hoses from the radiator.

9. Disconnect the vacuum hose from the PAIR control valve. Plug the vacuum hose fitting on the control valve.

10. Connect a vacuum pump to the vacuum hose disconnected in Step 9.

11. Start the engine and slightly open the throttle to make sure that air is being drawn in through the air supply hose. If air is not drawn in, check for clogged air supply hoses. Clean out if necessary.

12. With the engine running, gradually apply vacuum (Step 9) of 400 mm Hg (15.7 in. Hg) and hold

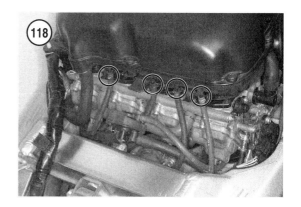

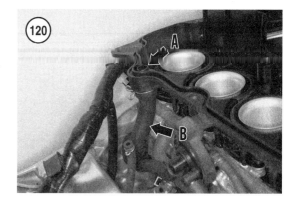

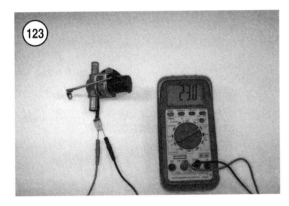

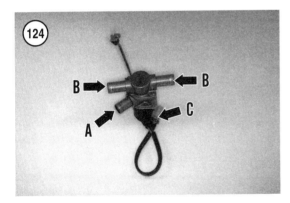

16. Remove the vacuum pump and reconnect the vacuum hose to the PAIR control valve.

17. Install the air filter cover and screws and tighten securely.

18. Connect the four vacuum hoses (**Figure 118**) onto the housing.

19. Lower the fuel tank and secure it as described in this chapter.

Fuel injected models

1. Remove the PAIR solenoid valve as described in this section.

2. Set an ohmmeter to R × 1 and measure resistance across the PAIR solenoid valve terminals (**Figure 123**). The specified resistance is 20-24 ohms (at 20° C/68° F). Replace the solenoid if the resistance is not as specified.

3. Connect an air pressure pump to port A in **Figure 124** and apply pressure through the port. Air should flow through the two separate B ports. Connect the leads from a 12-volt battery across the PAIR solenoid valve terminals (C, **Figure 124**) and apply pressure through port A. Air should not flow through either of the B ports when battery voltage is applied to the valve.

4. Replace the PAIR solenoid valve if it failed either test.

PAIR Solenoid Valve Removal/Installation

Carbureted models

1. Partially remove the radiator from the engine as follows:

    a. Remove the lower bolt, nut and washer (**Figure 121**) securing the bottom of the radiator to the lower frame bracket.

    b. On the left side, remove the upper bolt and washer (**Figure 122**) securing the top of the radiator to the frame.

    c. Cover the radiator with a towel to prevent damage to the cooling fins.

    d. Swing the radiator forward so the lower mounting stay will not interfere with the radiator.

    e. Slide the radiator to the right side and remove it from the frame boss.

it. Check that the air supply hose stops drawing air and that the vacuum does not bleed off.

13. If air is drawn in, or if the specified vacuum is not maintained, the PAIR control valve is defective and must be replaced.

14. Turn off the engine.

15. If after-burn occurs on deceleration, even when the secondary air supply system is normal, the air cut-off valve on the carburetor assembly may be defective.

f. Move the radiator forward and secure it to the front fork. Do not disconnect any of the coolant hoses from the radiator.

2. Label and disconnect the air hoses and vacuum tube from the PAIR solenoid valve and the cylinder head cover.

3. Remove the PAIR solenoid valve.

4. Install by reversing these removal steps. Make sure all hoses are correctly seated on the PAIR valve.

Fuel injected models

1. Remove the air filter housing as described in this chapter.

2. Remove the PAIR solenoid valve mounting screw (A, **Figure 125**).

3. Disconnect the PAIR solenoid valve two-pin black electrical connector.

4. Label and disconnect the air hoses (B, **Figure 125**) from the PAIR solenoid valve.

5. Remove the PAIR solenoid valve (C, **Figure 125**).

6. Install by reversing these removal steps. Make sure all hoses are correctly seated on the PAIR valve.

PAIR Reed Valves Removal/Installation

> *NOTE*
> *This procedure is shown with the cylinder head cover remove to better illustrate the steps.*

1. Remove the air filter housing as described in this chapter.

2. Remove the bolts and remove the PAIR reed valve cover (**Figure 126**).

3. Remove the reed valves (**Figure 127**) and the port plates (**Figure 128**).

4. Inspect each reed valve for fatigue or damage.

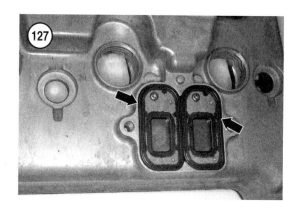

> *NOTE*
> *The reed valves must not be serviced or disassembled. Do not try to bend the stopper. If any part of the valve is defective, the valve assembly must be replaced.*

5. Install the port plates (**Figure 128**) and the reed valves (**Figure 127**).

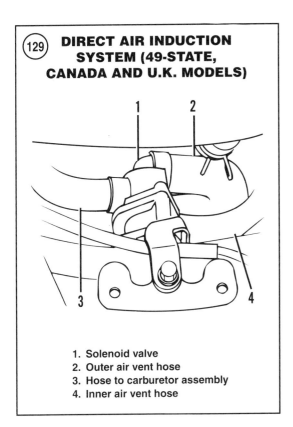

DIRECT AIR INDUCTION SYSTEM (49-STATE, CANADA AND U.K. MODELS)

1. Solenoid valve
2. Outer air vent hose
3. Hose to carburetor assembly
4. Inner air vent hose

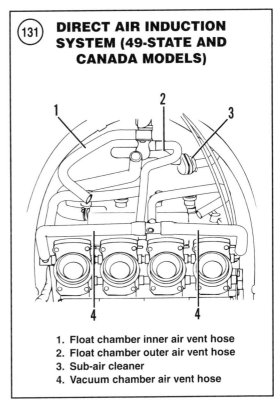

DIRECT AIR INDUCTION SYSTEM (49-STATE AND CANADA MODELS)

1. Float chamber inner air vent hose
2. Float chamber outer air vent hose
3. Sub-air cleaner
4. Vacuum chamber air vent hose

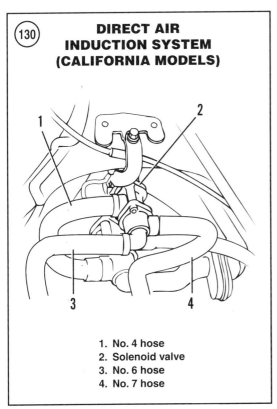

DIRECT AIR INDUCTION SYSTEM (CALIFORNIA MODELS)

1. No. 4 hose
2. Solenoid valve
3. No. 6 hose
4. No. 7 hose

6. Install the PAIR reed valve cover (**Figure 126**) and tighten the mounting screws securely.

7. Install the air filter housing as described in this chapter.

DIRECT AIR INDUCTION (CARBURETED MODELS)

Refer to **Figure 129** and **Figure 130**.

Inspection

1. Remove the front fairing as described in Chapter Sixteen.

2. Remove the air filter housing as described in this chapter.

3. Refer to **Figure 131** and inspect all of the hoses connected to the solenoid valve. Check for cracks, deterioration and/or loose connections. Replace any damaged hose.

4. Check the sub-air filter for damage.

5. Disconnect the air vent hose (Calif. No. 6) from the three-way joint that goes to the carburetor.

6. On California models, disconnect the No. 4 hose from the solenoid valve.

7. Turn the ignition switch to the OFF position. Blow air into the inner air vent hose (Calif. No. 7). Air should flow through the solenoid valve and out the air vent hose (Calif. No. 6) that goes to the carburetor.

8. Turn the ignition switch to the ON position. Blow air into the outer air vent hose (Calif. No. 4). Air should flow through the solenoid valve and out the air vent hose (Calif. No. 6) that goes to the carburetor.

9. If the solenoid valve fails either of these tests, it must be replaced.

10. Connect all hoses and make sure they are secure on the solenoid valve.

11. Install the air filter housing as described in this chapter.

12. Install the front fairing as described in Chapter Sixteen.

Solenoid Valve Removal/Installation

1. Remove the air filter housing as described in this chapter.

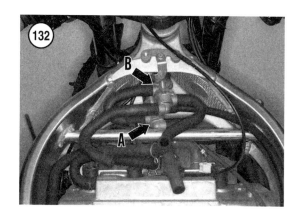

2. Disconnect the electrical connector from the vent solenoid (A, **Figure 132**) located below the upper solenoid (B).

3. Remove the upper solenoid valve mounting screw.

4. Label and disconnect the hoses from both solenoids and remove both solenoids.

5. Install by reversing these removal steps. Make sure all hoses are correctly seated on both solenoids.

Table 1 CARBURETOR SPECIFICATIONS (U.S. AND CANADA MODELS)	
Item	**Specification**
Carburetor I.D.	
49-state and Canada models	VP64C
California models	VP64B
Main jet[1]	
49-state and Canada models	
No. 1 and No. 4 carburetor	No. 132
No. 2 and No. 3 carburetor	No. 135
California models (all four carburetors)	No. 128
Slow jet	No. 40
Pilot screw	
Initial opening	
49-state and Canada models	3 1/8 turns out
California models	2 3/8 turns out
Final opening[2]	
49-state and Canada models	3/4 turns out
California models	1 turn out
Idle speed	
49-state and Canada models	1200-1400 rpm
California models	1300-1500 rpm
Float height	13.2-14.2 mm (0.52-0.56 in.)
Throttle cable free play	2-6 mm (1/12-1/4 in.)
1. Refer to text for high altitude adjustment.	
2. See text.	

Table 2 CARBURETOR SPECIFICATIONS (OTHER THAN U.S. AND CANADA MODELS)

Item	Specification
Carburetor identification	
Brazil models	VP64G
Mexico models	VP64H
Switzerland models	VP64E
Other than Brazil, Mexico and Switzerland	VP64A
Main jet[1]	
Brazil models	
No. 1 and No. 4 carburetor	No. 138
No. 2 and No. 3 carburetor	No. 140
Mexico models	
No. 1 and No. 4 carburetor	No. 128
No. 2 and No. 3 carburetor	No. 130
Other than Brazil and Mexico models	
No. 1 and No. 4 carburetor	No. 130
No. 2 and No. 3 carburetor	No. 132
Slow jet	No. 40
Brazil models	No. 45
Other than Brazil models	No. 40
Pilot screw	
Initial opening	
Brazil models	2 7/8 turns out
Mexico models	2 1/4 turns out
Switzerland models	3 1/4 turns out
Other than Brazil, Mexico and Switzerland	3 turns out
Final opening[2]	
Switzerland models	1/2 turn out
Other than Switzerland models	3/4 turn out
Idle speed	
Switzerland models	1150-1250 rpm
Other than Switzerland models	1100-1300 rpm
Float height	13.2-14.2 mm (0.52-0.56 in.)
Throttle cable free play	2-6 mm (1/12-1/4 in.)
PAIR solenoid valve resistance (EFI models)	20-24 ohms

1. Refer to text for high altitude adjustment.
2. See text.

FUEL AND ELECTRONIC
FUEL INJECTION SYSTEMS

This chapter describes procedures for the programmed fuel injection (PGM-FI) system.

Emission control systems for both carbureted and fuel injected models are covered in Chapter Eight.

Specifications are in **Tables 1-5** at the end of the chapter.

FUEL INJECTION
SYSTEM PRECAUTIONS

Electronic fuel injection (EFI) (**Figure 1**) service/testing requires caution to prevent damage to the throttle body and the engine control module (ECM).

1. The fuel system is pressurized. See *Depressurizing the Fuel System* in this chapter.

2. Do not clean the throttle bore inside diameter surfaces with any type of commercial carburetor cleaner, as it will damage the molybdenum surface coating.

3. Except for servicing the fuel injectors and starter valve assembly, do not disassemble the throttle body. Refer to *Throttle Body Service Precautions* in this chapter.

4. Make sure the ignition switch is off before disconnecting any components. ECM damage may occur if electrical components are disconnected/ connected with the ignition on.

5. Two Honda test harnesses are required to throughly test the EFI system. The manufacturer's test specifications using these harnesses provide a voltage reading. However, by refering to the MIL codes (**Table 5**) and testing the possible causes for continuity, when appropriate, or shorts to ground the problem can be isolated to a component or circuit/connector.

6. Refer to *Electrical Component Replacement* in Chapter Ten.

HOSE AND WIRING
HARNESS IDENTIFICATION

The fuel system uses a number of fuel and vacuum hoses. To allow easier assembly, develop a system to identify the hoses and connection points before disconnecting them. A vacuum hose identifier kit (Lisle part No. 74600) is used in the following procedures.

DEPRESSURIZING
THE FUEL SYSTEM

The fuel system is under pressure at all times, even when the engine is not operating. The fuel system is equipped with a service check bolt at the base

FUEL INJECTION SYSTEM (2001-ON MODELS)

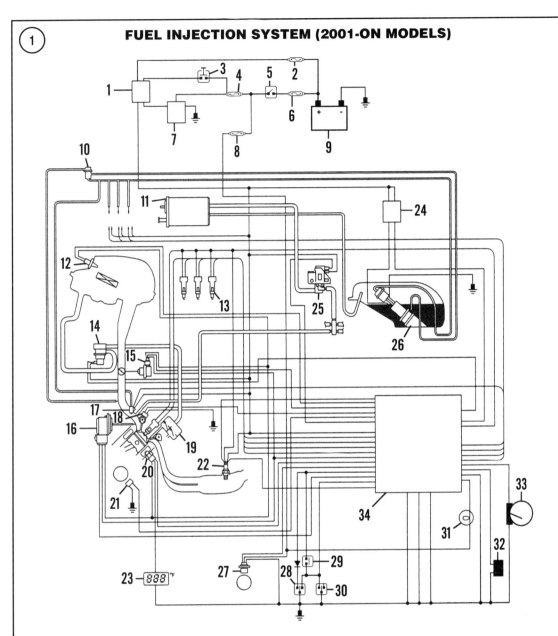

1. Engine stop relay
2. PGM-FI fuse (20 amp)
3. Engine stop switch
4. Sub-fuse (10 amp)
5. Ignition switch
6. Main fuse A (30 amp)
7. Bank angle sensor
8. Sub-fuse (10 amps)
9. Battery
10. Pressure regulator
11. EVAP canister (Calfornia models only)
12. IAT sensor
13. Direct ignition coil and spark plug
14. PAIR solenoid valve
15. TP sensor
16. MAP sensor
17. Injector
18. Cam pulse generator
19. PAIR check valve
20. ECT sensor
21. Ignition pulse generator
22. Oxygen sensor (California models only)
23. Water temperature LCD
24. Fuel cut-off relay
25. EVAP purge control solenoid valve (California models only)
26. Fuel pump
27. Vehicle speed sensor
28. Neutral switch
29. Clutch switch
30. Sidestand switch
31. Malfunction indicator lamp (MIL)
32. Service check connector
33. Tachometer
34. Engine control module (ECM)

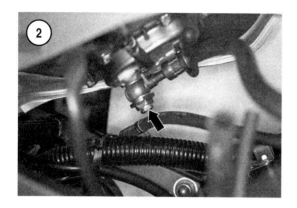

of the fuel tank for relieving the fuel pressure. Whenever a fuel line or fitting is loosened or removed, gasoline will spray out unless the system is depressurized first. Before disconnecting any fuel line or fitting, perform the following steps.

WARNING
Always wear eye protection when working on the fuel system.

WARNING
The engine must be turned off when depressurizing the fuel system.

1. Open and secure the fuel tank as described under *Fuel Tank* in this section.

2. Place several shop cloths under the fuel hose banjo bolt.

WARNING
Some fuel may spill and fuel vapors will be present when depressurizing the fuel system. Because gasoline is extremely flammable, perform this procedure away from all open flames, including appliance pilot lights and sparks. Do not smoke or allow someone who is smoking in the work area, as an explosion and fire may occur. Always work in a well-ventilated area. Wipe up spills immediately.

3. Loosen the fuel service check bolt (**Figure 2**) and allow fuel to run out until the pressure is released. Securely tighten the service check bolt at this time.

4. After performing the required service and before returning the motorcycle to service, install a *new* sealing washer and tighten the fuel service check bolt to 15 N•m (133 in.-lb.).

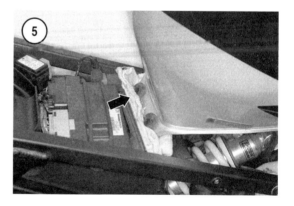

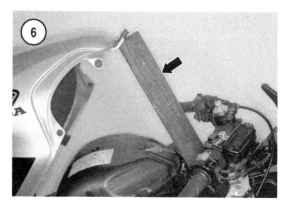

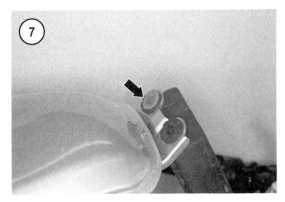

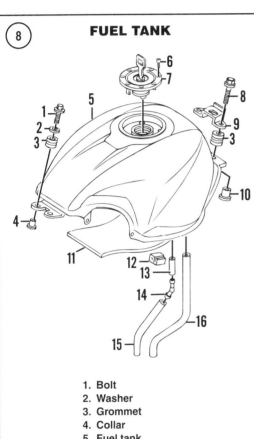

FUEL TANK

1. Bolt
2. Washer
3. Grommet
4. Collar
5. Fuel tank
6. Allen bolt
7. Fuel cap
8. Bolt
9. Seat bracket
10. Collar
11. Heat shield
12. Rubber cushion
13. Air vent tube
14. Air vent tube fitting
15. Air vent tube
16. Overflow hose

5. Properly dispose of any fuel-soaked rags. Wipe up any spilled fuel not caught by the shop cloths.

FUEL TANK

Open and Secure Fuel Tank

The fuel tank can be opened and secured in a raised position to access the air filter and fuel hoses.
1. Remove the seat as described in Chapter Sixteen.
2. Remove the air duct cover as described in Chapter Sixteen.
3. Remove the front two fuel tank mounting bolts and washers (**Figure 3**). Remove the collar from each mounting rubber grommet.
4. Remove the rear two fuel tank mounting bolts and washers (**Figure 4**). Remove the seat bracket, then remove the collar from each mounting rubber grommet.
5. Place a shop rag at the rear of the fuel tank mounting area (**Figure 5**) to protect the finish.

CAUTION
In Step 6, lift the fuel tank slowly, being careful not to overextend the fuel hose.

6. Lift the fuel tank all the way and support it with a piece of wood (**Figure 6**). Secure the wood to the front tank mount with a wood screw and washer (**Figure 7**).
7. Reverse the previous steps to close the fuel tank while noting the following:
   a. Make sure not to pinch or damage the overflow and air vent hoses when closing the fuel tank.
   b. Tighten the four fuel tank mounting bolts securely.

Removal/Installation

Refer to **Figure 8**.
Read this procedure through before starting work. Make sure all of the necessary equipment is on hand to keep from damaging the fuel tank.

WARNING
Some fuel may spill and fuel vapors will be present when removing the fuel tank. Because gasoline is extremely flammable, perform this procedure away from all open flames, including appliance pilot lights and sparks. Do not smoke or allow someone who is smoking in the work area, as an explosion and fire may

occur. Always work in a well-ventilated area. Wipe up spills immediately.

> *WARNING*
> *Gasoline is extremely flammable and must not be stored in an open container. Store gasoline in a sealed gasoline storage container, away from heat, sparks or flames.*

1. Depressurize the fuel system as described under *Depressurizing the Fuel System* in this chapter.

2. Remove the side fairing panels as described in Chapter Sixteen.

3. Remove the air duct cover (**Figure 9**) as described in Chapter Sixteen.

4. If the fuel tank is more than one-quarter full, siphon the fuel into a container approved for gasoline storage. This reduces the weight of the tank before having to remove and turn the tank over when disconnecting the fuel hoses later in this procedure. To do this, perform the following:

 a. Open the fuel cap.

 b. Place a siphon hose into the fuel tank. Place the other end of the siphon hose into a fuel storage can.

 c. Operate the siphon to drain as much fuel from the tank as possible.

 d. When the siphon shuts off, remove it from the fuel tank and storage can. Close the fuel cap and place the storage can in a safe place, away from all flames and sparks. Drain the siphon of all gasoline before putting it away.

5. Remove the front two fuel tank mounting bolts and washers (**Figure 3**). Remove the collar from each mounting rubber grommet.

6. Remove the rear two fuel tank mounting bolts and washers (**Figure 4**). Remove the seat bracket, then remove the collar from each mounting rubber grommet.

7. Place a shop rag at the front of the fuel tank mounting area (**Figure 10**) to protect the finish.

8. Raise the front of the fuel tank. On the left side, disconnect the fuel pump/reserve sensor electrical connector (**Figure 11**).

9. Loosen and disconnect the fuel hose banjo bolt and sealing washers (A, **Figure 12**) from the base of the fuel pump fitting on the fuel tank.

10. On the right side, disconnect the fuel tank air vent hose and overflow hose from the fuel tank (**Figure 13**).

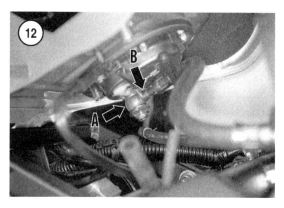

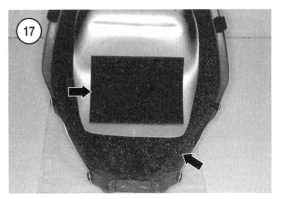

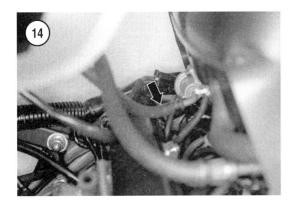

11. On the right side, disconnect the fuel return hose (**Figure 14**) from the pressure regulator on the throttle body fuel pipe. Avoid excessive force on the fuel pipe.

12. Plug the fuel pump opening to prevent fuel from leaking out of the tank.

13. Install the fuel tank by reversing these removal steps while noting the following:

   a. Connect the fuel hose to the fuel pump using two *new* washers (**Figure 15**). Align the fuel hose fitting through the stopper bracket (B, **Figure 12**) on the fuel pump. Install the fuel hose banjo bolt and tighten to 22 N•m (16 ft.-lb.).

   b. Make sure the return hose is properly routed.

   c. Tighten the rear fuel tank mounting bolts securely.

   d. After reconnecting the fuel tank air vent and overflow hoses to the fuel tank, clamp the hoses securely in place.

   e. Tighten the front fuel tank mounting bolts securely.

   f. Turn the ignition switch to the ON position and allow the fuel pump to pressurize the system. Check the fuel tank hoses for leaks.

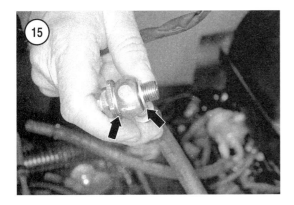

Inspection

1. Inspect all of the hoses for cracks, deterioration and other damage. Replace damaged hoses with the same Honda type and size materials. The hoses must be flexible and strong enough to withstand fuel pressure, engine heat and vibration.

2. Inspect the front, side and rear grommets (**Figure 16**) for deterioration or other damage. Replace if necessary. Make sure the metal collars are in place within the grommets.

3. Check all of the heat shields (**Figure 17**) for damage or deterioration. Replace as necessary.

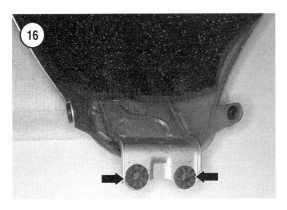

4. Use the ignition key and open the fuel filler cap. Inspect the fuel filler cap gaskets (**Figure 18**). If damaged or starting to deteriorate, replace the filler cap assembly.

AIR FILTER HOUSING

Removal/Installation

Refer to **Figure 19**.

1. Remove the fuel tank as described in this chapter.

> *NOTE*
> *Identify the hoses when disconnecting them from the air filter housing in the following steps. Refer to **Hose And Wiring Harness Identification** in this chapter.*

> *NOTE*
> *Hoses can be difficult to remove, especially when they have become bonded to their fittings. If a hose is stuck, twist the hose to break its seating bond. Pulling hard against a stuck hose may damage the hose or fitting end.*

2. Disconnect the two-pin gray electrical connector from the IAT sensor (**Figure 20**).

3. On the right side, carefully remove the rubber cover (**Figure 21**) from the air filter housing.

4. Remove the screws securing the air filter cover and remove the cover (**Figure 22**).

5. Remove the air filter element (**Figure 23**) from the housing.

6. Remove the screws (**Figure 24**) securing the air funnels and the housing to the throttle body assembly.

7. Remove the air funnels (**Figure 25**).

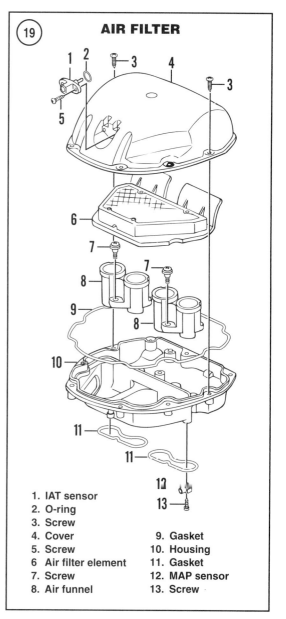

AIR FILTER

1. IAT sensor
2. O-ring
3. Screw
4. Cover
5. Screw
6 Air filter element
7. Screw
8. Air funnel

9. Gasket
10. Housing
11. Gasket
12. MAP sensor
13. Screw

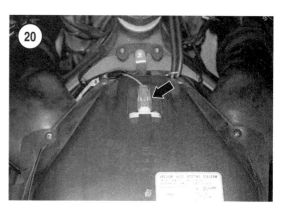

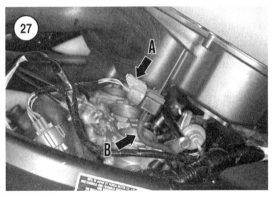

9

NOTE
The two vacuum hoses are connected to blind posts on the housing, not vacuum fittings. The purpose is to keep the vacuum hoses plugged and in place.

8. Disconnect the intake vacuum hoses (A, **Figure 26**) and the PAIR control valve air suction hose (B) from the housing.

9. Lift up the front of the housing and disconnect the four-pin MAP sensor (A, **Figure 27**) and vacuum hose (B) from the housing.

10. Disconnect the crankcase breather hose (**Figure 28**) from the housing.

11. Slowly pull the housing back and disconnect the air inlets from the fittings on the front fairing. Remove the housing assembly.

12. Cover the intake side of each injector body opening to prevent contamination or small parts from entering the throttle bores.

13. If necessary, remove the following components from the air filter housing as described in the appropriate procedure described in this chapter:

    a. MAP sensor.

    b. IAT sensor.

14. Install the air filter assembly by reversing these removal steps while noting the following:

    a. Inspect the housing gaskets and replace if necessary.

    b. Route and connect all of the hoses correctly. Make sure all hose clamps, where used, are positioned correctly on the hose ends.

Inspection

1. Visually check all of the exposed vacuum hoses for damage that may have occurred when disconnecting them. Replace damaged hoses with the correct size replacement hose.

2. Check the air inlets (A, **Figure 29**) for cracks or deterioration.

3. Inspect the base of the housing (B, **Figure 29**) where it attaches to the throttle body for damage.

4. Inspect the air funnels (**Figure 30**) for damage.

THROTTLE BODY

Service Precautions

Before servicing the throttle body assembly, note the following:

1. The throttle body is pre-set by the manufacturer. Do not disassemble or adjust the throttle body in any way other than as described in this section.

2. Do not loosen or tighten the white painted bolts and screws on the throttle body. Refer to **Figures 31-34**. Doing so may cause throttle and idle valve synchronization failure.

3. Tighten all bolts and screws to the specification in **Table 4**.

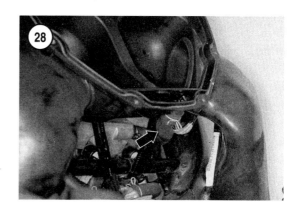

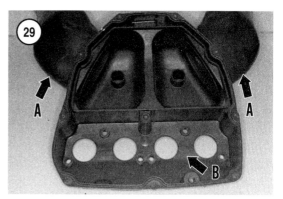

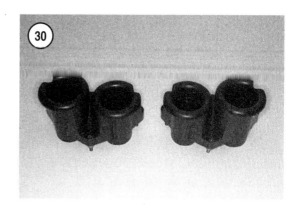

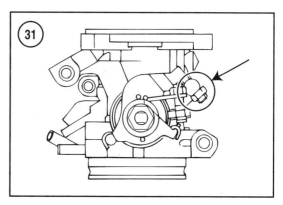

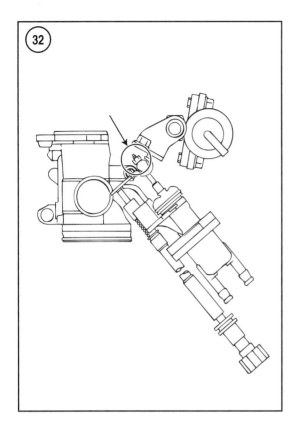

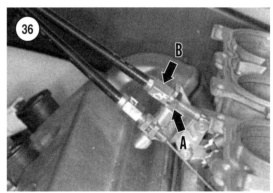

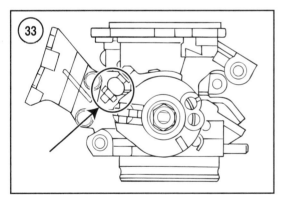

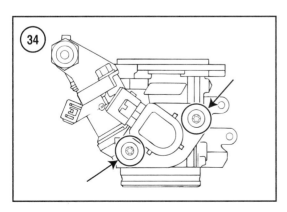

9

Removal

1. Depressurize the fuel system as described under *Depressurizing the Fuel System* in this chapter.

2. Remove the fuel tank as described in this chapter.

3. Remove the air filter housing as described in this chapter.

4. Drain the cooling system as described in Chapter Eleven.

5. To allow slack in the throttle cables, perform the following:

    a. At the throttle grip, loosen the locknut (A, **Figure 35**) and turn the adjuster (B) in to allow slack in the cable.

    b. At the throttle body, loosen the cable locknut (A, **Figure 36**) and turn the cable adjuster (B) to allow slack in the throttle cable.

6. On the left side, disconnect the ten-pin gray electrical connector (**Figure 37**) from the throttle body sub-harness. Push the tabs on both sides of the connector to disconnect it.

7. On the right side, disconnect the three-pin electrical connector (**Figure 38**) from the throttle position sensor.

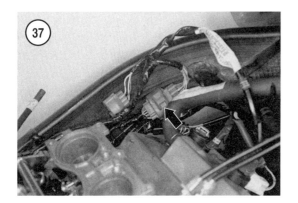

8. Disconnect the hose (**Figure 39**) from the pressure regulator.

9. On California models, disconnect the EVAP purge control solenoid hose from the throttle body connector (**Figure 40**).

10. On the left side, disconnect the throttle idle adjust knob (**Figure 41**) from the frame bracket.

11. Insert a long Phillips screwdriver through the frame hole (**Figure 42**) on each side, and loosen the clamping bands on all four intake manifolds.

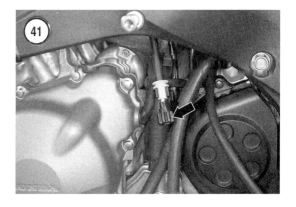

CAUTION
In Step 12, do not hold onto the fuel pipe
during throttle body assembly removal,
as the fuel pipe will be damaged.

12. Partially remove the throttle body assembly while carefully routing the sub-harness gray connector through the frame and around mounting hardware.

13. Place a clean shop cloth under the throttle body to prevent any debris from falling into the cylinder head intake openings.

14. Loosen the hose clamps securing the coolant hoses (**Figure 43**) to the fast idle wax unit. Disconnect the coolant hoses and plug them.

NOTE
After removing the throttle cables, do not snap the throttle valve from its full open to close position. Doing so may change or damage the idle adjustment, causing an incorrect engine idle operation.

15. Remove the throttle cables from the bracket (A, **Figure 44**).

16. Note the location of the throttle pull and push cables, then disconnect them from the throttle drum (B, **Figure 44**).

17. Remove the throttle body assembly from the engine and frame.

18. Tape or plug the intake ports (**Figure 45**) to prevent debris from falling into the cylinder head.

Installation

1. Lubricate the inside surface of each intake manifold with clean engine oil.

2. Remove the tape or plugs covering the intake ports.

3. Install the throttle cables onto the throttle drum as follows:

   a. Place a clean shop cloth onto the cylinder head intake ports, then place the throttle body onto the cylinder head.

   b. Attach the throttle pull and push cables onto the throttle drum (**Figure 46**) location as noted in *Removal* Step 16.

   c. Install the pull cable onto the throttle bracket (**Figure 47**) and temporarily tighten the locknut.

   d. Install the push cable onto the throttle bracket.

4. Connect the coolant hoses (**Figure 43**) onto the fast idle wax unit and tighten the hose clamps securely.

5. Correctly position the throttle body assembly while carefully routing the sub-harness gray connector through the frame and around other mounting hardware.

CAUTION
In Step 6, do not push on the fuel pipe during throttle body assembly installation, as the fuel pipe will be damaged.

6. Align the throttle body and intake manifolds with the cylinder head ports and push the throttle body assembly down firmly until they bottom. Tighten the manifold clamp screws (**Figure 42**) until the gap between the ears on the bands is 3-5 mm (0.12-0.20 in.).

7. On California models, connect the EVAP purge control solenoid hose onto the throttle body connector (**Figure 40**).

8. Connect the hose (**Figure 39**) onto the pressure regulator.

9. On the right side, connect the three-pin electrical connector (**Figure 38**) onto the throttle position sensor.

10. On the left side, connect the ten-pin gray electrical connector (**Figure 37**) onto the throttle body sub-harness.

11. On the left side, connect the throttle idle adjust knob (**Figure 41**) onto the frame bracket.

12. Refill the cooling system as described in Chapter Eleven.

13. Install the air filter housing and fuel tank as described in this chapter.

FUEL INJECTORS

Testing

The injectors can be tested without removing them from the throttle body.

1. Remove the seat as described in Chapter Sixteen.

2. Remove the air duct cover as described in Chapter Sixteen.

3. Remove the fuel tank front two mounting bolts and washers (**Figure 48**). Remove the collar from each mounting rubber grommet.

4. Remove the fuel tank rear two mounting bolts and washers (**Figure 49**). Remove the seat bracket, then remove the collar from each mounting rubber grommet.

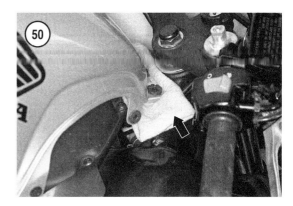

5. Place a shop rag at the front of the fuel tank mounting area (**Figure 50**) to protect the finish.

CAUTION
In Step 6, lift the fuel tank slowly, being careful not to overextend the fuel hose.

6. Lift up on the rear of the fuel tank sufficiently to gain access to the fuel injectors.

7. Start the engine and allow it to idle.

8. Use a mechanic's stethoscope and listen for operating sounds at each fuel injector.

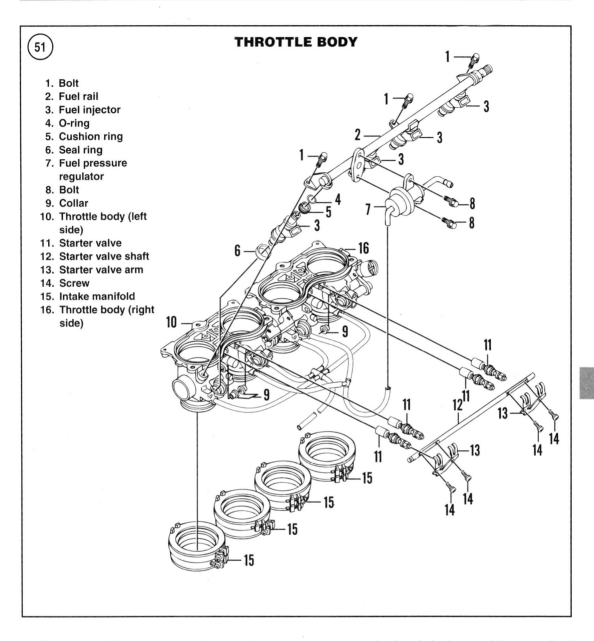

THROTTLE BODY

(51)

1. Bolt
2. Fuel rail
3. Fuel injector
4. O-ring
5. Cushion ring
6. Seal ring
7. Fuel pressure
   regulator
8. Bolt
9. Collar
10. Throttle body (left
    side)
11. Starter valve
12. Starter valve shaft
13. Starter valve arm
14. Screw
15. Intake manifold
16. Throttle body (right
    side)

9. If there is a difference in operating sound at one or more injectors, replace the faulty fuel injector(s) as described in this chapter.

10. If necessary, test the injector(s) resistance, and compare it to the specification in **Table 3**.

11. If necessary, test the injector wiring for continuity and shorts to ground

12. Install all components removed.

Removal

Refer to **Figure 51**.

1. Remove the throttle body assembly as described in this chapter.

2. Remove the three bolts (A, **Figure 52**) and remove the fuel injector and fuel pipe assembly (B) from the throttle body assembly.

NOTE
Identify and label each fuel injector
*(**Figure 53**), starting with the No. 1 on*
the left end. The left end has the pres-
sure regulator.

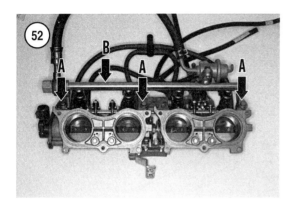

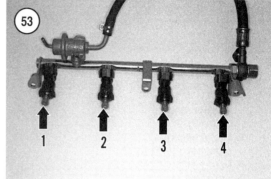

3. Carefully remove the fuel injector from the fuel pipe.

4. Remove the seal ring, cushion ring and O-ring from the fuel injector (**Figure 54**). All three parts must be replaced with new ones every time a fuel injector is removed from the fuel rail.

5. Repeat for each fuel injector.

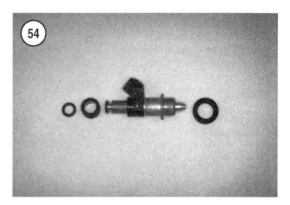

Inspection

1. Visually inspect the fuel injectors for damage.

2. Inspect the spray nozzle (**Figure 55**) for carbon buildup or damage. Replace if necessary.

3. Repeat for each fuel injector.

4. Inspect the injector ports in the throttle body (**Figure 56**) for contamination.

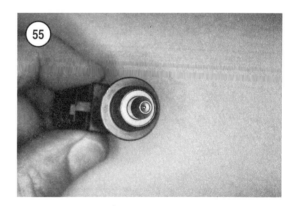

Installation

1. Install a *new* seal ring (**Figure 57**) into each injector port in the throttle body or onto the fuel injector (A, **Figure 58**).

2. Install a *new* cushion ring (B, **Figure 58**) onto the fuel injector.

> *CAUTION*
> *Be careful not to damage the new O-ring when installing it into the fuel rail.*

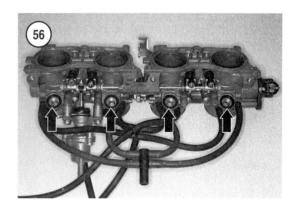

3. Apply a thin coat of clean engine oil to a *new* injector O-ring.

4. Install the O-ring (C, **Figure 58**) into the groove in the injector body.

5. Install each fuel injector (**Figure 59**) onto the fuel rail in the correct location. Make sure each fuel injector is correctly seated in the fuel rail.

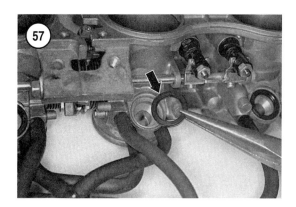

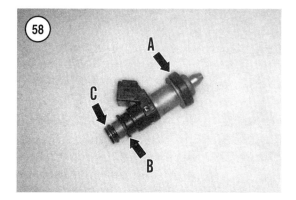

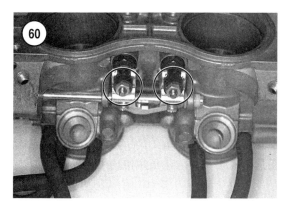

> *CAUTION*
> *Do not tear the seal rings when installing the fuel injectors into the throttle body.*

6. Push the fuel injector and fuel pipe assembly (B, **Figure 52**) evenly and straight into the throttle body to avoid damaging the seal ring. Do not turn the injectors during installation.

7. Check that the fuel pipe seats evenly over the throttle body.

> *CAUTION*
> *In Step 8, do not use the bolts to align or center the fuel pipe and the fuel injectors over the throttle body. Make sure the fuel pipe seats evenly over each fuel injector before installing and tightening the bolts.*

8. Install the three fuel pipe Allen bolts (A, **Figure 52**) and tighten securely.

9. Install the throttle body as described in this chapter.

STARTER VALVES

Disassembly

Refer to **Figure 51**.

1. Remove the throttle body as described in this chapter.

2. Remove the fuel injector and fuel pipe assembly as described in this chapter.

3. Turn each starter valve adjusting screw (**Figure 60**) in, counting the number of turns until it lightly seats. Record the number of turns.

4. On the No. 3 and 4 starter valves, remove the screws securing the starter valve arm (**Figure 61**).

5. On the No. 1 and 2 starter valves, perform the following:

    a. Remove the fast idle wax unit (A, **Figure 62**) as described in this chapter.

    b. Remove the screws securing the starter valve arm (B, **Figure 62**).

    c. Remove the screw and the fast idle wax unit link arm.

6. Loosen the locknut and remove the starter valve assembly.

7. Clean the starter valve bypass channels with compressed air.

> *CAUTION*
> *Do not clean the throttle bore inside diameter surfaces with any commercial carburetor cleaner, as it will damage the molybdenum surface coating.*

8. If necessary, remove the starter valve shaft (C, **Figure 62**) and three collars.

Assembly

1. If removed, install the starter valve shaft (C, **Figure 62**) and three collars.

2. Install the starter valve assembly into the valve hole.

3. Tighten the starter valve locknut to 2 N•m (18 in.-lb.).

4. On the No. 3 and 4 starter valves, perform the following:

    a. Compress the thrust spring and install the No. 3 and 4 starter valve arm onto the starter valves.

    b. Install and tighten the starter valve arm mounting screws to 1 N•m (8.8 in.-lb.).

5. On the No. 1 and 2 starter valves, perform the following:

    a. Compress the thrust spring and install the No. 1 and 2 starter valve arm onto the starter valves.

    b. Install and tighten the starter valve arm mounting screws to 1 N•m (8.8 in.-lb.).

6. Install the starter valve arm and tighten the screws securely.

7. Install the fast idle wax unit as described in this chapter.

8. Turn the starter valve adjusting screw (**Figure 60**) until it lightly seats. Then back out the number of turns recorded during disassembly. Repeat for each screw.

9. Install the throttle body as described in this chapter.

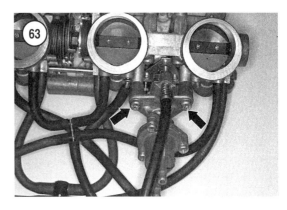

10. Check and adjust the starter valve synchronization as described in Chapter Three.

FAST IDLE WAX UNIT

Removal/Installation

1. Remove the throttle body as described in this chapter.

2. Remove the screws (**Figure 63**) securing the fast idle wax unit.

3. Release the wax unit shaft joint piece from the wax unit link arm (D, **Figure 62**). Remove the assembly.

4. Install by reversing these removal steps. Tighten the screws to the specification in **Table 4**.

Disassembly/Assembly

    Refer to **Figure 64**.

1. Using a crisscross pattern, and in two to three steps, loosen the three screws securing the cover to the base. Remove the screws.

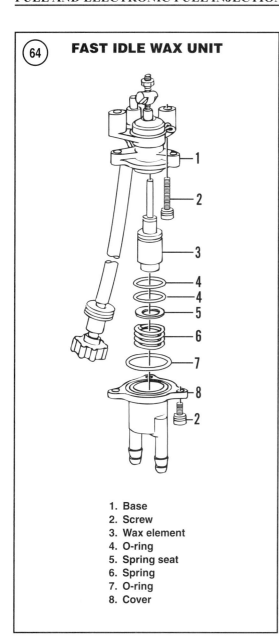

FAST IDLE WAX UNIT

1. Base
2. Screw
3. Wax element
4. O-ring
5. Spring seat
6. Spring
7. O-ring
8. Cover

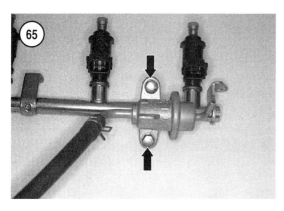

2. Remove the cover, O-ring, spring, spring seat and wax element.
3. Inspect the wax element for damage. Check the spring for fatigue or damage.
4. Replace any worn or damaged parts.
5. Install *new* O-rings onto the wax element and onto the cover.
6. Install the wax element, spring seat and spring into the base.
7. Install the cover onto the base and compress the spring. Install the screws and tighten in a crisscross pattern and in two to three steps. Tighten the screws securely.

PRESSURE REGULATOR

Removal/Installation

1. Remove the throttle body as described in this chapter.
2. Disconnect the vacuum hose from the pressure regulator.

CAUTION
In Step 3 and Step 4, do not push on the fuel pipe during pressure regulator removal and installation, or the fuel pipe will be damaged.

3. Hold onto the fuel pipe and remove the bolts securing the pressure regulator (**Figure 65**) to the fuel pipe.
4. Remove the pressure regulator and O-ring.
5. Install a *new* O-ring onto the base of the pressure regulator.
6. Install the pressure regulator and mounting bolts onto the fuel pipe. Hold onto the fuel pipe and tighten the bolts to 10 N•m (88 in.-lb.).
7. Connect the vacuum hose onto the pressure regulator.
8. Install the throttle body as described in this chapter.

FUEL PRESSURE CHECK

A Honda fuel pressure gauge (part No. 07406-0040002) is required to check the fuel pressure.

WARNING
Some fuel may spill and fuel vapors are present when measuring the fuel pressure. Because gasoline is extremely flammable, perform this procedure away from all open flames,

9

including appliance pilot lights and sparks. Do not smoke or allow someone who is smoking in the work area, as an explosion and fire may occur. Always work in a well-ventilated area. Wipe up spills immediately.

1. Disconnect the negative battery cable as described in Chapter Ten.

2. Open and support the fuel tank as described in this chapter.

3. Disconnect the vacuum hose from the pressure regulator (**Figure 66**).

4. Depressurize the fuel injection system as described in this chapter.

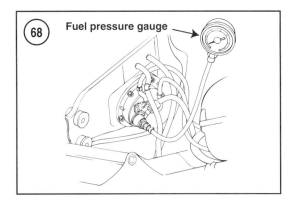

Fuel pressure gauge

5. Place several shop cloths under the fuel hose banjo bolt to catch any spilled fuel in the following steps.

6. Remove the service check bolt (**Figure 67**).

7. Install the fuel pressure gauge and sealing washer into the fuel hose banjo bolt in place of the service check bolt (**Figure 68**). Tighten securely.

8. Reconnect the negative battery cable at the battery as described in Chapter Ten.

9. Start the engine and read the fuel pressure gauge with the engine running at idle speed. See **Table 3** for the standard fuel pressure specification.

10. Turn the engine off.

11. If the fuel pressure reading is lower than specified in **Table 3**, check for the following:

    a. Leaking fuel line.

    b. Clogged fuel filter.

    c. Damaged fuel pump.

    d. Damaged pressure regulator.

12. If the fuel pressure reading is higher than specified in **Table 3**, check for the following:

    a. Pinched or plugged fuel return line.

    b. Damaged fuel pump.

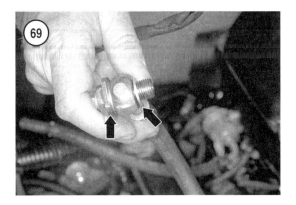

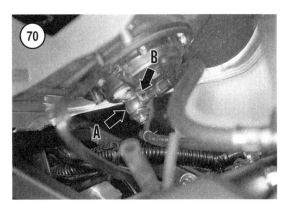

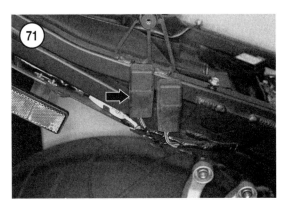

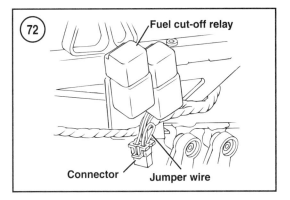

Fuel cut-off relay

Connector   Jumper wire

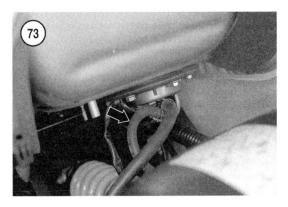

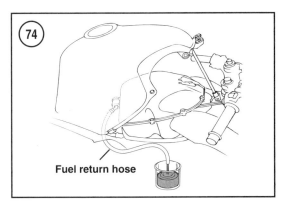

Fuel return hose

c. Damaged pressure regulator.

13. Disconnect the negative battery cable at the battery as described in Chapter Ten.

14. Remove the fuel pressure gauge.

15. Install the fuel service check bolt (**Figure 67**) and tighten to 15 N•m (133 in.-lb.).

16. If the fuel hose was removed, install two *new* washers (**Figure 69**) and connect the fuel hose to the fuel tank (A, **Figure 70**). Align the fuel hose fitting through the stopper bracket (B, **Figure 70**) on the fuel tank.

17. Tighten the banjo bolt to 22 N•m (16 ft.-lb.).

18. Connect the vacuum hose onto the pressure regulator (**Figure 66**).

19. Close and secure the fuel tank as described in this chapter.

FUEL FLOW TEST

WARNING
Some fuel may spill and fuel vapors are present when checking the fuel flow. Because gasoline is extremely flammable, perform this procedure away from all open flames, including appliance pilot lights and sparks. Do not smoke or allow someone who is smoking in the work area, as an explosion and fire may occur. Always work in a well-ventilated area. Wipe up spills immediately.

1. Open and secure the fuel tank as described in this chapter.

2. Remove the rear cowl as described in Chapter Sixteen.

3. Disconnect the connector at the fuel cut relay (**Figure 71**).

4. Connect a jumper wire across the wiring harness connector brown and black/white terminals (**Figure 72**).

CAUTION
Fuel will spill from the fuel return hose when it is disconnected. Catch the fuel in a plastic jar and dispose of it properly.

5. Place several shop cloths under the fuel return hose to catch any spilled fuel in the following steps.

6. Disconnect the fuel return hose (**Figure 73**) at the fuel tank. Plug the fuel tank hose joint.

7. Place the loose end of the fuel return hose into a large plastic graduated beaker (**Figure 74**).

9

8. Turn the ignition switch ON for ten seconds, then shut it OFF.

9. The specified fuel flow for ten seconds is listed in **Table 3**. Pour the measured fuel into an approved gasoline storage container.

10. If the fuel flow is less than specified, check for the following:

    a. Plugged fuel hose or fuel return hose.

    b. Clogged fuel filter.

    c. Damaged fuel pump.

    d. Damaged pressure regulator.

11. Reconnect the fuel return hose and secure it with its hose clamp.

12. Disconnect a jumper wire from the wiring harness connector brown and black/white terminals.

13. Reconnect the connector to the fuel cut relay (**Figure 71**).

14. Install the rear cowl as described in Chapter Sixteen.

15. Close and secure the fuel tank as described in this chapter.

FUEL PUMP ASSEMBLY

The fuel pump assembly is mounted on the base of the fuel tank.

Operation Test

1. Turn the ignition switch ON and listen for fuel pump operation. If the fuel pump does not operate within a few seconds, turn the ignition switch to the OFF position and continue with Step 2.

2. Open and secure the fuel tank as described in this chapter.

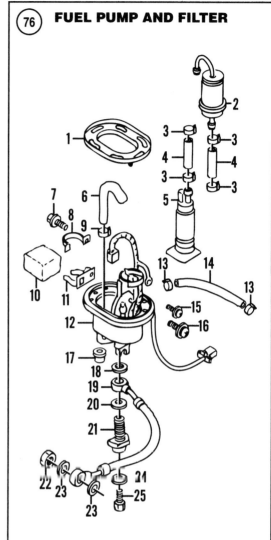

FUEL PUMP AND FILTER

1. Base gasket	15. Screw
2. Fuel filter	16. Screw
3. Hose clamp	17. Nut
4. Fuel inlet hose	18. Sealing washer
5. Fuel pump	19. Fuel pressure
6. Fuel pump return	hose
hose	20. Sealing washer
7. Bolt	21. 12 mm banjo bolt
8. Band	22. Sealing nut
9. Hose clamp	23. Sealing washer
10. Fuel return filter	24. Sealing washer
11. Bracket	(fuel service
12. Fuel pump	check bolt)
bracket	25. Service check
13. Hose clamp	bolt
14. Fuel return hose	

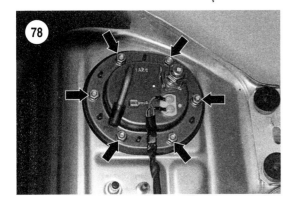

3. Disconnect the fuel pump electrical connector (**Figure 75**) at the fuel pump.

4. Connect a voltmeter between the brown (+) and green (-) connector terminals on the wiring harness side.

5. Turn the ignition switch to the ON position while reading the voltmeter. It should read 13.0-13.2 volts (battery voltage) for a few seconds.

6. If there is battery voltage, replace the fuel pump.

7. If there is no battery voltage, check the following:

   a. 30 amp main fuse as described in Chapter Ten.

   b. 10 amp sub-fuse as described in Chapter Ten.

   c. Engine stop switch as described in Chapter Ten.

   d. Fuel cut-off relay as described in this chapter.

   e. Engine stop relay as described in this chapter.

   f. Bank angle sensor as described in this chapter.

   g. ECM as described in this chapter.

8. Disconnect the voltmeter and connect the fuel pump connector (**Figure 75**) at the fuel pump.

9. Close and secure the fuel tank as described in this chapter.

Removal/Installation

> *WARNING*
> *Some fuel may spill and fuel vapors are present when removing and installing the fuel pump. Because gasoline is extremely flammable, perform this procedure away from all open flames, including appliance pilot lights and sparks. Do not smoke or allow someone who is smoking in the work area, as an explosion and fire may occur. Always work in a well-ventilated area. Wipe up spills immediately.*

Refer to **Figure 76**.

1. Remove the fuel tank as described in this chapter.

> *NOTE*
> *Note that the fuel pump electrical harness (**Figure 77**) is positioned toward the right side of the fuel tank. It must be reinstalled in the same location.*

2. Remove the fuel pump mounting nuts (**Figure 78**) and remove the fuel pump module and base gasket.

3. If necessary, refer to *Fuel Filter Replacement* in this chapter.

4. Inspect the gasket mating surface (**Figure 79**) on the fuel tank for damage. Clean off any old gasket residue to ensure a leak-free sealing surface.

9

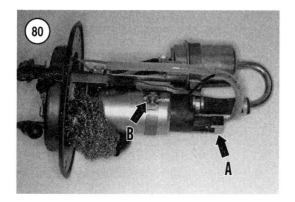

5. If pump replacement is necessary, perform the following:

   a. Disconnect the electrical connector (A, **Figure 80**).

   b. Remove the screws and lockwashers (B, **Figure 80**) and clamp securing the fuel pump to the bracket.

   c. Remove and replace the fuel pump.

6. Install a *new* base gasket (**Figure 81**) onto the fuel pump module mounting flange. Push it into position until it seats correctly (**Figure 82**) around the perimeter of the flange.

7. Correctly position the fuel pump assembly onto the fuel tank with the electrical harness (**Figure 77**) toward the right side.

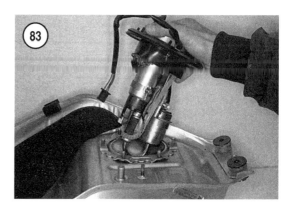

8. Carefully install the fuel pump assembly into the fuel tank (**Figure 83**), making sure not to damage the base gasket.

9. Install the mounting nuts (**Figure 78**) and tighten in the order shown in **Figure 84** and to 12 N•m (106 in.-lb.).

10. Install the fuel tank as described in this chapter.

Inspection

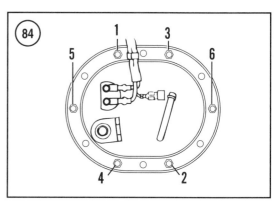

1. Inspect the fuel return filter (**Figure 85**) for deterioration; replace if necessary.

2. Inspect the electrical wires going to the fuel pump (A, **Figure 86**) and fuel level sensor (B) for deterioration or damage. If damaged, replace the fuel pump module.

3. Make sure the electrical harness is clamped into position on the mounting flange (**Figure 87**).

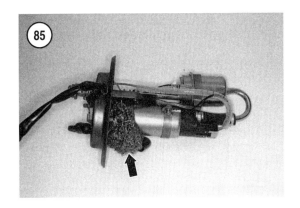

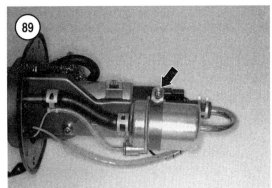

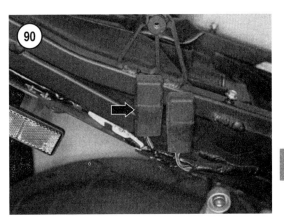

FUEL FILTER REPLACEMENT

1. Remove the fuel pump assembly as described in this chapter.

2. Loosen the hose clamps (A, **Figure 88**) and disconnect the fuel hoses from the fuel filter.

3. Remove the screw (**Figure 89**) and lockwasher on the clamping band. Remove the fuel filter (B, **Figure 88**) from the bracket.

4. Install the fuel filter by reversing these steps.

FUEL CUT RELAY

Testing

1. Turn the ignition switch to the OFF position.

2. Remove the rear cowl as described in Chapter Sixteen.

3. Disconnect the four-pin electrical connector from the fuel cut relay and remove the relay (**Figure 90**).

4. Connect an ohmmeter to the relay brown and black/white terminals (**Figure 91**).

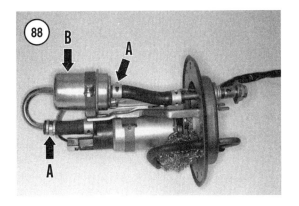

5. Connect the positive battery lead to the relay black/white terminal and the negative battery lead to the brown/black terminal. The ohmmeter should show continuity with the battery leads connected to the relay.

6. Replace the fuel cut relay switch if it failed this test.

7. Disconnect the battery leads and the ohmmeter.

8. Connect the four-pin electrical connector onto the fuel cut relay and install the relay (**Figure 90**).

9. Install the rear cowl as described in Chapter Sixteen.

Replacement

1. Remove the rear cowl as described in Chapter Sixteen.

2. Disconnect the electrical connector from the fuel cut relay (**Figure 90**).

3. Remove the fuel cut relay from the frame.

4. Install by reversing these removal steps.

MANIFOLD ABSOLUTE PRESSURE (MAP) SENSOR

Removal/Installation

1. Partially remove the air filter housing to gain access to the lower surface of the housing as described in this chapter.

2. Lift up the front of the housing and disconnect the four-pin connector (A, **Figure 92**) and vacuum hose (B) from the MAP sensor.

3. Remove the mounting screw and remove the MAP sensor.

4. Install by reversing these removal steps.

Testing

1. Make sure the vacuum hose is secure and in good condition.

2. Make sure the electrical connector is secure and that the pin terminals and wiring are in good condition.

3. Refer to the wiring diagram and test the MAP sensor wiring for continuity and shorts to ground.

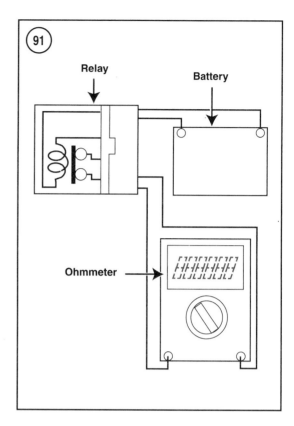

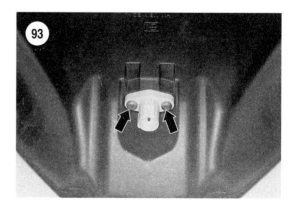

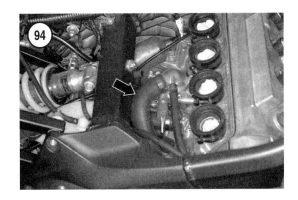

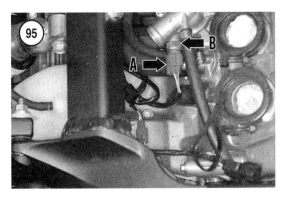

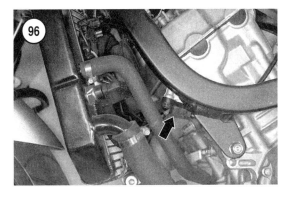

INTAKE AIR TEMPERATURE (IAT) SENSOR

Removal/Installation/Testing

1. Remove the cover from the air filter housing as described in this chapter.
2. Remove the screws and remove the IAT sensor (**Figure 93**) from the air filter housing.
3. Install by reversing these removal steps.
4. If necessary, test the IAT sensor resistance and compare it to the specification in **Table 3**.
5. If necessary, test the IAT wiring for continuity or shorts to ground.

ENGINE COOLANT TEMPERATURE (ECT) SENSOR

NOTE
The ECT sensor is also the sensor for the water temperature LCD.

Removal/Installation/Testing

1. Remove the throttle body as described in this chapter.
2. Remove the coolant hose (**Figure 94**) from the thermostat housing.
3. Disconnect the electrical connector (A, **Figure 95**) from the ECT sensor.
4. Unscrew and remove the ECT sensor (B, **Figure 95**) and the sealing washer from the thermostat housing.
5. Install a *new* sealing washer and the ECT sensor onto the thermostat housing. Tighten the ECT sensor to 23 N•m (17 ft.-lb.).
6. If necessary, test the ECT sensor resistance and compare it to the specification in **Table 3**.
7. If necessary, test the ECT sensor wiring for continuity or shorts to ground.
8. Reconnect the electrical connector (A, **Figure 95**) onto the ECT sensor.
9. Install the throttle body as described in this chapter.

CAMSHAFT PULSE GENERATOR

Removal/Installation/Testing

1. Remove the left side fairing as described in Chapter Sixteen.
2. Disconnect the camshaft pulse generator two-pin electrical connector (**Figure 96**).
3. Remove the mounting bolt and remove the camshaft pulse generator from the front surface of the cylinder head.
4. Install a *new* O-ring onto the camshaft pulse generator. Lubricate the O-ring with engine oil before installing the camshaft pulse generator.
5. Install the camshaft pulse generator onto the cylinder head and tighten the mounting bolt securely.
6. Install the left side fairing as described in this chapter.
7. If necessary, test the peak voltage output before removing the sensor. Compare the results to the specification in **Table 3**. Refer to *Ignition Pulse Generator Peak Voltage Test* in Chapter Ten. When performing the test on the camshaft pulse generator,

9

the gray wire terminal is positive and both sensors share the same yellow/white ground circuit.

THROTTLE POSITION (TP) SENSOR

Testing/Replacement

The TP sensor (**Figure 97**) is mounted on the right side of the throttle body assembly and cannot be replaced separately. If the TP sensor is damaged, replace the throttle body assembly. If necessary, test the sensor's wiring for continuity or shorts to ground.

BANK ANGLE SENSOR

Testing/Replacement

1. Support the motorcycle on level ground.
2. Block the front wheel so the motorcycle will not roll in either direction while on the jack or swing arm stand (or centerstand on U.K. models).

NOTE
*This procedure is shown with the front fairing removed to better illustrate these steps. Do **not** remove it for this test procedure, as the electrical connector must be connected.*

3. Remove the windshield and rear cowl as described in Chapter Sixteen.

NOTE
Do not disconnect the bank angle sensor connector when performing the following test.

4. Locate the bank angle sensor three-pin black electrical connector (A, **Figure 98**) but do not disconnect it.
5. Turn the ignition switch ON. Connect a voltmeter and measure voltage between the following bank angle sensor connector terminals:
   a. White/black (+) and green (–): Battery voltage.
   b. Red/white (+) and green (–): 0-1 volt.
6. Turn the ignition switch to the OFF position.
7. Remove the mounting screws (B, **Figure 98**) and remove the bank angle sensor (C).
8. Hold the bank angle sensor in its normal operating position (horizontal) and turn the ignition switch

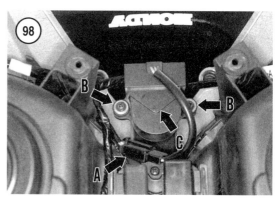

to the ON position. The engine stop relay (**Figure 99**) should click and the power supply is closed.
9. Turn the ignition switch to the OFF position.
10. Turn the bank angle sensor approximately 60° to either the left or right, then turn the ignition switch ON. The engine stop relay (**Figure 99**) should click and the power supply is open.
11. Turn the ignition switch OFF and disconnect the voltmeter.
12. If the bank angle sensor fails any part of this test, replace the bank angle sensor.

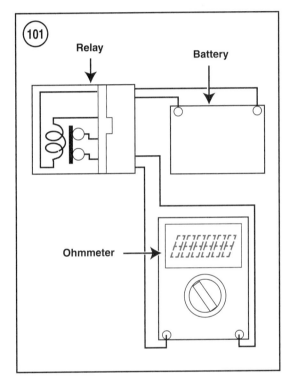

1. Remove the right side fairing as described in Chapter Sixteen.

2. Loosen and remove the oxygen sensors from the catalytic converter and washer (**Figure 100**).

3. Trace the oxygen sensor wire to its mating electrical connector, then disconnect the connector and remove the oxygen sensor and washer.

4. Install by reversing these steps. Tighten the oxygen sensors securely.

EMISSION CONTROL SYSTEM

Refer to Chapter Eight.

ENGINE STOP RELAY

Testing

1. Turn the ignition switch to the OFF position.

2. Remove the rear cowl as described in Chapter Sixteen.

3. Disconnect the four-pin electrical connector from the engine stop relay and remove the relay (**Figure 99**).

4. Connect an ohmmeter to the relay red/white and black/white terminals (**Figure 101**). The ohmmeter should show no continuity. Leave the ohmmeter leads connected as described and continue with Step 5.

5. Connect a positive battery lead to the relay red/white terminal and the negative battery lead to the black terminal. The ohmmeter must read continuity.

6. Replace the engine stop relay switch if it failed this test.

7. Disconnect the battery leads and the ohmmeter.

8. Connect the four-pin electrical connector onto the engine stop relay and install the relay (**Figure 99**).

9. Install the rear cowl as described in Chapter Sixteen.

13. Install by reversing these removal steps while noting the following:
    a. Install the bank angle sensor with its UP mark facing up.
    b. Install the rear cowl and windscreen as described in Chapter Sixteen.

OXYGEN SENSOR (CALIFORNIA MODELS)

Removal/Installation

The oxygen sensor (**Figure 100**) is mounted in the catalytic converter portion of the muffler.

Replacement

1. Remove the rear cowl as described in Chapter Sixteen.

2. Disconnect the electrical connector from the engine stop relay (**Figure 99**).

3. Remove the engine stop relay from the frame.

4. Install by reversing these removal steps.

9

ENGINE CONTROL MODULE (ECM)

Testing

Refer all ECM testing to a Honda dealership.

> *NOTE*
> *Most motorcycle dealerships and parts suppliers will not accept returns on electrical components. Do not attempt to troubleshoot a malfunction by replacing an expensive electrical component, such as an ECM.*

Removal/Installation

1. Remove the seat and the rear cowl as described in Chapter Sixteen.
2. Remove the band (**Figure 102**) securing the ECM.
3. Carefully lift the ECM (A, **Figure 103**) up off the battery tray cover and disconnect the 22-pin black and 22-pin light gray electrical connectors (B) from the ECM.
4. Remove the ECM and place it in a reclosable plastic bag to keep it clean. Store the ECM in a safe place to avoid damage to this expensive component.
5. Install by reversing these removal steps.

MALFUNCTION INDICATOR LIGHT (MIL)

The fuel injection system is equipped with diagnostic capability. Under normal operating conditions, the MIL (**Figure 104**) on the instrument cluster lights for a few seconds and then goes off when the ignition switch is turned on with the engine stop switch in the run position. If there is a fault in the system, the MIL illuminates and stays on until the ignition switch is turned off. The indicator blinks when the engine is running below 5000 rpm with the sidestand down. Under most conditions, the motorcycle will continue to run when the MIL is illuminated. However, the motorcycle should be taken to a Honda dealership as soon as possible for troubleshooting and repair.

Reading MIL Codes

To read the MIL codes, perform the following:
1. Support the motorcycle on level ground.

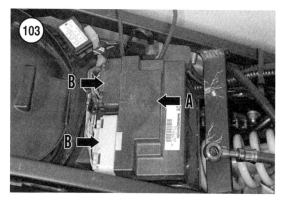

2. Block the front wheel so the motorcycle will not roll in either direction while on the jack or swing arm stand (or centerstand on U.K. models).
3. Start the engine and let it idle.
4A. If the malfunction indicator lamp does not light or blink, the system indicates that there is no problem data in the memory. Shut off the engine.
4B. If the malfunction indicator lamp blinks, the system indicates that there is problem data in the memory. Shut off the engine.
5. Place the sidestand in the DOWN position.
6. Turn the ignition switch to the OFF position.
7. Remove the seat as described in Chapter Sixteen.
8. Locate the service check connector on the left side of the battery area. Jump the connector terminals (**Figure 105**) with a jumper wire.
9. Turn the ignition switch to the ON position and the engine stop switch to the RUN position and note the following:
  a. If the ECM has no stored MIL codes, the MIL indicator will illuminate when the ignition switch is turned to the ON position.

b. If the ECM has stored MIL code(s), the MIL indicator will start blinking when the ignition switch is turned to the ON position.

10. Determine the MIL code(s) as follows:

a. The system indicates codes with a series of long (1.3 second) and short (0.5 second) flashes. Each long flash equals 10. Each short flash equals 1. For example, a long flash (1.3 second × 10 = 10) followed by three short flashes (0.5 second × 3 = 3) indicates a code of 13 (10 + 3).

b. When more than one MIL code occurs, the system will display the codes from lowest to highest. A short gap separates individual codes.

c. Refer to **Table 5** for MIL code identification.

11. After reading the MIL codes, turn the ignition switch to the OFF position and disconnect the jumper wire. Troubleshoot the affected system as follows:

a. Make sure the electrical connectors are secure and free of corrosion.

b. Check the wiring harness for damage such as frayed wiring or breaks. Refer to the wiring diagrams at the back of the manual and trace the appropriate circuit(s).

c. If the affected system has a vacuum function, make sure the hose(s) are securely attached and in good condition (no leaks).

d. If a code(s) refers to a particular component(s), refer to the tests in this chapter, or Chapter Ten, to determine if further testing is possible.

12. If the above tests fail to locate the problem, refer troubleshooting and repair to a Honda dealership.

> *NOTE*
> *If no start condition exists, the engines must be cranked for 10 seconds to generate a MIL code.*

Erasing MIL Codes

After MIL codes have been read and the system repaired, erase the failure codes from the ECM's memory as follows. If the motorcycle was repaired at a Honda dealership, the codes will be erased at the dealership.

> *NOTE*
> *Do not use this procedure if the motorcycle has not been serviced by a Honda dealership. The code must remain in the memory until the problem has been corrected.*

1. Support the motorcycle on level ground.

2. Block the front wheel so the motorcycle will not roll in either direction while on the jack or swing arm stand (or centerstand on U.K. models).

3. Place the sidestand in the DOWN position.

4. Turn the ignition switch to the OFF position and the engine stop switch to the RUN.

5. Remove the seat as described in Chapter Sixteen.

> *NOTE*
> *Read the following steps through once, then perform the procedure.*

6. Perform the following:

9

a. Locate the service check connector on the left side of the motorcycle. Jump the connector terminals with a jumper wire (**Figure 105**).

b. Turn the ignition switch to the ON position and perform the following:

c. Disconnect the jumper wire (**Figure 105**) from the service check connector.

d. The malfunction indicator lamp will illuminate for five seconds. During the time the indicator is illuminated, jump the service connector terminals with a jumper wire (**Figure 105**) to erase the memory.

NOTE
The service check connector must be jumped when the malfunction indicator lamp indicator is illuminated.

NOTE
If two long flashes (code 20) are indicated, the memory was not erased. Repeat Step 4.

7. Turn the ignition switch to the OFF position and remove the jumper wire from the service check connector.

NOTE
The diagnosis memory cannot be erased if the ignition switch is turned OFF before the malfunction indicator lamp illuminates.

THROTTLE CABLE REPLACEMENT

Always replace both throttle cables as a set.

1. Support the motorcycle on level ground.

2. Block the front wheel so the motorcycle will not roll in either direction while on the jack or swing arm stand (or centerstand on U.K. models).

3. Remove the seat as described in Chapter Sixteen.

4. Remove the fuel tank as described in this chapter.

5. Remove the air filter housing as described in this chapter.

6. At the throttle grip, loosen the locknut (A, **Figure 106**) and turn the adjuster (B) all the way in to allow maximum pull cable slack.

7. Make a drawing of the throttle cable routing from the right hand throttle housing to the throttle

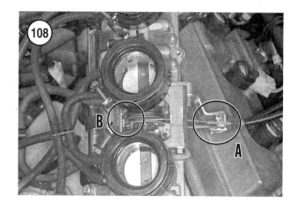

body. Record this information for proper cable routing and installation.

NOTE
*The throttle cables are different. Use masking tape to label the old cables before removing them. The upper cable (A, **Figure 107**) opens the throttle arm. The lower cable (B) closes the throttle arm.*

8. Open the right hand switch housing and disconnect the upper throttle cable ends as described under *Handlebar* in Chapter Thirteen.

NOTE
After removing the throttle cables, do not snap the throttle valve from its full open to close position. Doing so may change or damage the idle adjustment, causing an incorrect engine idle operation.

9. Partially remove the throttle body assembly, as described in this chapter, sufficiently to gain access to the lower portion of the throttle wheel.

10. At the throttle body, loosen the pull cable locknut securing the throttle cable to the cable

bracket. Remove the throttle cables from the bracket (A, **Figure 108**).

11. Note the location of the throttle pull and push cables, then disconnect them from the throttle drum (B, **Figure 108**).

12. Remove the cables from under the upper fork bridge (**Figure 109**). Note the position of any cable clamps for assembly.

13. Compare the new and old cables.

14. If cables without nylon liners are used, lubricate them as described in Chapter Three.

15. Route the new cables through the same path as the old cables.

CAUTION
The throttle cables are the push/pull type and must not be interchanged. Attach the cables following the identification labels made on the old cables.

16. Attach the new cables to the throttle and install the right-hand switch housing as described under *Handlebars* in Chapter Thirteen.

17. Install the throttle cables onto the throttle drum as follows:

   a. Place a clean shop cloth onto the cylinder head intake ports, then place the throttle body onto the cylinder head.

   b. Attach the throttle pull and push cables onto the throttle drum (**Figure 110**) locations as noted in Step 11.

   c. Install the pull cable onto the throttle bracket (**Figure 111**) and temporarily tighten the locknut.

   d. Install the push cable onto the throttle bracket.

18. Open the throttle and release it. The throttle should snap back smoothly. If operation is incorrect, carefully check that the cables are attached correctly and there are no tight bends in the cables. Repeat this check with the front wheel pointing straight ahead and then with the wheel turned full left and full right.

19. Adjust the throttle cables as described in Chapter Three.

20. Install all of the parts previously removed.

21. Operate the throttle lever and make sure the throttle lever and throttle body linkage operates correctly. If the operation worked correctly in Step 18 but there is now a problem, check the cable routing as well as the air filter housing and fuel tank instal-

lation. Locate and repair the problem before continuing.

22. When the throttle is operating correctly, start the engine and run it at idle speed with the transmission in NEUTRAL. Turn the handlebar from side to side, making sure the idle speed does not increase. If it does, the throttle cables are improperly installed. If the idle speed did not increase, test-ride the motorcycle slowly at first. If there is any prob-

lem with the throttle, stop immediately and make the necessary repairs.

WARNING
An improperly adjusted or incorrectly routed throttle cable can cause the throttle to stick in the open position. This could cause a loss of control. Do not ride the motorcycle until the throttle cable operation is correct.

Table 1 FUEL INJECTION SYSTEM TECHNICAL ABBREVIATIONS

Engine control module	ECM
Engine coolant temperature sensor	ECT sensor
Intake air temperature sensor	IAT sensor
Manifold absolute pressure sensor	MAP sensor
O2 sensor	Oxygen sensor
PGM-FI	Programmed fuel injection
Throttle position sensor	TP sensor

Table 2 FUEL INJECTION SYSTEM GENERAL SPECIFICATIONS

Fuel injection type	Programmed fuel injection (PGM-FI)
Throttle body identification number	
49-state and Canada models	GQ90C
California models	GQ90B
Germany models	GQ90D
All other models	GQ90A

Table 3 FUEL INJECTION SYSTEM TEST SPECIFICATIONS*

Item	Specification
Cam pulse generator peak voltage	0.7 volt minimum
Engine coolant temperature (ECT)	
sensor resistance	2300-2600 ohms
Fuel injector resistance	11.1-12.3 ohms
Fuel pressure at idle	343 kPa (50 psi)
Fuel pump flow (at 12 volts) minimum	188 cc (6.4 U.S. oz./6.6 Imp. oz.)
Idle speed	1200-1400 rpm
Intake air temperature (IAT) sensor resistance	1000-4000 ohms
Manifold absolute pressure at idle	150-250 mm Hg
Starter valve vacuum synchronization difference	20 mm Hg (see Chapter Three)
base throttle valve	No. 1 throttle body
PAIR solenoid valve resistance	20-24 ohms
Throttle grip free play	2-6 mm (1/16-1/4 in.)
*All voltage and resistance readings taken at 20° C (68° F)	

Table 4 FUEL INJECTION SYSTEM TORQUE SPECIFICATIONS

Item	N•m	in.-lb.	ft.-lb.
ECT sensor	23	–	17
Fast idle wax unit			
Link plate screw	1	8.8	–
Link plate mounting screw	5	44	–
Fuel filler cap bolt	2	18	–
Fuel pressure hose			
Banjo bolt (fuel tank side)	22	–	16
Sealing nut			
(throttle body side)	22	–	16
Service check bolt	15	133	–
Fuel pump mounting nuts	12	106	–
O2 sensor (California models)	25	–	19
Pressure regulator			
mounting bolts	10	88	–
Starter valve			
Locknut	2	18	–
Arm mounting screw	1	8.8	–
Throttle cable bracket			
mounting screw	3	27	–
Vacuum joint for			
synchronization	3	27	–

9

Table 5 MALFUNCTION INDICATOR LIGHT (MIL) CODES

MIL blink	Symptoms	Cause(s)
No blinks	Engine does not start*	Open circuit at power input wire of the ECM Faulty bank angle sensor Open circuit in bank angle sensor related circuit Faulty engine stop relay Open circuit in engine stop relay related wires Faulty engine stop switch Open circuit in engine stop switch related wires Faulty ignition switch Faulty ECM Blown FI 20 amp fuse Open circuit in engine stop switch ground
No blinks	Engine operates normally	Open or short in MIL wire Faulty ECM
Light stays on	Engine operates normally	Short circuit in service (check connector) Faulty ECM Short circuit in service (check connector wire)
1	Engine operates normally	Loose or poor contacts on MAP sensor connector Open or short circuit in MAP sensor wire Faulty MAP sensor

(continued)

Table 5 MALFUNCTION INDICATOR LIGHT (MIL) CODES (continued)

MIL blink	Symptoms	Cause(s)
2	Engine operates normally	Loose or poor connection of the MAP sensor vacuum hose Faulty MAP sensor
7	Hard start at low temperature	Loose or poor contacts on ETC sensor Open or short in ECT sensor wire Faulty ECT sensor
8	Poor engine response when operating the throttle quickly	Loose or poor contact on TP sensor Open or short circuit in TP sensor wire Faulty TP sensor
9	Engine operates normally	Loose or poor contact on IAT sensor Open or short circuit in IAT sensor wire Faulty IAT sensor
11	Engine operates normally	Loose or poor contact on vehicle speed sensor connector (Chap. 10) Open or short circuit in vehicle speed sensor connector (Chap. 10) Faulty vehicle speed sensor
12	Engine does not start	Loose or poor contact on No. 1 fuel injector connector Open or short circuit in No. 1 fuel injector wire Faulty No. 1 fuel injector
13	Engine does not start	Loose or poor contact on No. 2 fuel injector connector Open or short circuit in No. 2 fuel injector wire Faulty No. 2 fuel injector
14	Engine does not start	Loose or poor contact on No. 3 fuel injector connector Open or short circuit in No. 3 fuel injector wire Faulty No. 3 fuel injector
15	Engine does not start	Loose or poor contact on No. 4 fuel injector connector Open or short circuit in No. 4 fuel injector wire Faulty No. 4 fuel injector
18	Engine does not start*	Loose or poor contact at camshaft pulse generator connector Open or short circuit in camshaft pulse generator Faulty camshaft pulse generator
19	Engine does not start*	Loose or poor contact on ignition pulse generator connector (Chap. 10) Open or short circuit in ignition pulse generator (Chap. 10)
21	Engine operates normally	Faulty oxygen sensor (California)
23	Engine operates normally	Faulty oxygen sensor heater (California)
33	Engine operates normally Does not hold self diagnostic data	Faulty E2-PROM in ECM

*Engine must be cranked for ten seconds with stop switch in run position to generate a MIL code(s).

CHAPTER TEN

ELECTRICAL SYSTEM

This chapter contains service and test procedures for the following systems/components:

1. Charging system.
2. Ignition system.
3. Starting system.
4. Lighting system.
5. Electrical components.
6. Switches.
7. Fuses.

Refer to **Tables 1-9** at the end of the chapter for specifications.

ELECTRICAL COMPONENT REPLACEMENT

Most motorcycle dealerships and parts suppliers will not accept the return of any electrical part. If you cannot determine the *exact* cause of any electrical system malfunction, have a Honda dealership retest that specific system to verify your test results. If you purchase a new electrical component(s), install it, and then find that the system still does not work properly, you will probably not be able to return the unit for a refund.

Consider any test results carefully before replacing a component that tests only *slightly* out of specifcation, especially resistance. A number of variables can affect test results dramatically. These include the testing meter's internal circuitry, ambient temperature and conditions under which the machine has been operated. All instructions and specifications have been checked for accuracy; however, successful test results depend to a great extent upon individual accuracy.

ELECTRICAL CONNECTORS

All models are equipped with numerous electrical components, connectors and wires. Corrosion-causing moisture can enter these electrical connectors and cause poor electrical connections, leading to component failure. Troubleshooting an electrical circuit with one or more corroded electrical connectors can be time-consuming and frustrating.

When reconnecting electrical connectors, pack them in a dielectric grease compound. Dielectric grease is specially formulated for sealing and waterproofing electrical connections without interfering with current flow. Use only this compound or an equivalent designed for this specific purpose. Do not use a substitute that may interfere with the current flow within the electrical connector. Do not use silicone sealant.

After cleaning both the male and female connectors, make sure they are thoroughly dry. Apply dielectric grease to the interior of one of the connectors prior to connecting the connector halves. For best results, the compound should fill the entire inner area of the connector. On multi-pin connectors, also pack the backside of both the male and female side with the compound to prevent moisture from entering the connector. After the connector is fully packed, wipe all excessive compound from the exterior.

Get into the practice of cleaning and sealing all electrical connectors every time they are disconnected. This may prevent a breakdown on the road and also save time when troubleshooting a circuit.

BATTERY

A sealed, maintenance-free battery is installed on all models. The battery electrolyte level cannot be serviced. When replacing the battery, use a sealed type; do not install a non-sealed battery. Never attempt to remove the sealing caps from the top of the battery. The battery does not require periodic electrolyte inspection or refilling. Refer to **Table 1** for battery specifications.

To prevent accidental shorts that could blow a fuse when working on the electrical system, always disconnect the negative battery cable from the battery.

WARNING
Even though the battery is a sealed type, protect eyes, skin and clothing; electrolyte is corrosive and can cause severe burns and permanent injury. The battery case may be cracked and leaking electrolyte. If electrolyte gets into the eyes, flush both eyes thoroughly with clean, running water and get immediate medical attention. Always wear safety goggles when servicing the battery.

WARNING
While batteries are being charged, highly explosive hydrogen gas forms

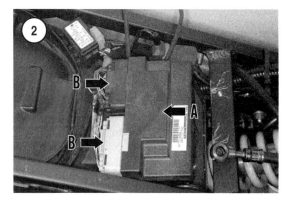

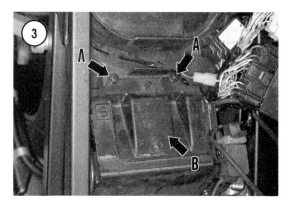

in each cell. Some of this gas escapes through filler cap openings and may form an explosive atmosphere in and around the battery. This condition can persist for several hours. Sparks, an open flame or a lighted cigarette can ignite the gas, causing an internal battery explosion and possible serious personal injury.

NOTE
Recycle the old battery. When replacing the old battery, be sure to turn in the old

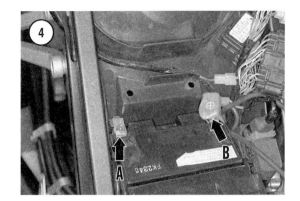

battery at that time. The lead plates and the plastic case can be recycled. Most motorcycle dealerships accept old batteries in trade when purchasing a new one. Never place an old battery in household trash; it is illegal, in most states, to place any acid or lead (heavy metal) contents in landfills.

Safety Precautions

Take the following precautions to prevent an explosion.

1. Do not smoke or permit any open flame near any battery being charged or which has been recently charged.

2. Do not disconnect live circuits at the battery. A spark usually occurs when a live circuit is broken.

3. Take care when connecting or disconnecting a battery charger. Turn the power switch OFF before making or breaking connections. Poor connections are a common cause of electrical arcs, which cause explosions.

4. Keep children and pets away from the charging equipment and the battery.

Removal/Installation

The battery is installed in the battery box, underneath the seat.

1. Read *Safety Precautions* in this section.

2. Turn the ignition switch to the OFF position.

3. Remove the seat as described in Chapter Sixteen.

4. On 2001-on models, perform the following:
   a. Remove the rear cowl as described in Chapter Sixteen.
   b. Remove the band (**Figure 1**) securing the electronic control module (ECM).
   c. Carefully lift the ECM (A, **Figure 2**) up off the battery tray cover and move it out of the way. If necessary, disconnect the 22-pin black and 22-pin light gray electrical connectors (B, **Figure 2**) from the ECM and remove the ECM.

5. Release the locking clips (A, **Figure 3**) and remove the battery tray (B).

6. First disconnect the negative battery cable (A, **Figure 4**), then the positive cable (B), from the battery terminals.

7. Insert a finger up through the hole in the bottom of the battery box (**Figure 5**) and push up on the battery. Grab the battery from the top and remove it from the battery box.

NOTE
On 2001-on models, if the battery is going to be removed from the frame for a long period of time, move the ECM back into position to eliminate stress on the wiring harness.

8. After the battery has been serviced or replaced, install it by reversing these removal steps while noting the following:
   a. Install the battery into the frame with the negative terminal on the right side of the frame.
   b. Always connect the positive battery cable first (B, **Figure 4**), then the negative cable (A).

CAUTION
Be sure the battery cables are connected to their proper terminals. Connecting the battery backward reverses the polarity and damages the rectifier and ignition system.

   c. Coat the battery leads with dielectric grease or petroleum jelly.

10

Cleaning/Inspection

The battery electrolyte level cannot be serviced. Never attempt to remove the sealing bar cap from the top of the battery. The battery does not require periodic electrolyte inspection or refilling.

1. Read *Safety Precautions* in this section.
2. Remove the battery from the motorcycle as described in the previous section. Do not clean the battery while it is mounted in the motorcycle.
3. Clean the battery case (**Figure 6**) with a solution of warm water and baking soda. Rinse thoroughly with clean water.
4. Inspect the physical condition of the battery. Look for bulges or cracks in the case, leaking electrolyte or corrosion buildup.
5. Check the battery terminal bolts, spacers and nuts for corrosion and damage. Clean parts with a solution of baking soda and water, and rinse thoroughly. Replace if damaged.
6. Check the battery cable clamps for corrosion and damage. If corrosion is minor, clean the battery cable clamps with a stiff brush. Replace excessively worn or damaged cables.

Testing

The maintenance-free battery can be tested while mounted in the motorcycle. A digital voltmeter is required for this procedure. See **Table 1** for battery voltage readings for the maintenance free battery.

1. Read *Safety Precautions* in this section.

NOTE
To prevent false test readings, do not test the battery if the battery terminals are corroded. Remove and clean the battery and terminals as described in this chapter, then reinstall it.

2. Connect a digital voltmeter between the battery negative and positive leads. Note the following:
   a. If the battery voltage is 13.0-13.2 volts (at 20° C [68° F]), the battery is fully charged. See **Table 3**.
   b. If the battery voltage is below 12.8 volts (at 20° C [68° F]), the battery is undercharged and requires charging. See **Table 3**.
3. If the battery is undercharged, recharge it as described in this chapter. Then test the charging system as described in Chapter Two.

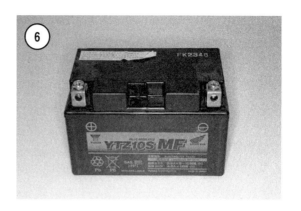

Charging

Refer to *Battery Initialization* in this chapter it the battery is new.

To recharge a maintenance-free battery, a digital voltmeter and a charger (**Figure 7**) with an adjustable or automatically variable amperage output are required. If this equipment is not available, have the battery charged by a shop with the proper equipment. Excessive voltage and amperage from an unregulated charger can damage the battery and shorten service life.

The battery should only self-discharge approximately one percent of its given capacity each day. If a battery not in use, without any loads connected, loses its charge within a week after charging, the battery is defective.

If the motorcycle is not used for long periods of time, an automatic battery charger with variable voltage and amperage outputs is recommended for optimum battery service life.

WARNING
During the charging process, highly explosive hydrogen gas is released from

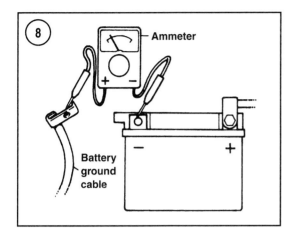

Ammeter

Battery ground cable

− +

the battery. Charge the battery only in a well-ventilated area away from any open flames (including pilot lights on home gas appliances). Do not allow any smoking in the area. Never check the charge of the battery by connecting screwdriver blades or other metal objects between the terminals; the resulting spark can ignite the hydrogen gas.

CAUTION
Always remove the battery from the motorcycle before connecting the battery charger. Never recharge a battery in the frame; corrosive gasses emitted during the charging process will damage surfaces.

1. Remove the battery as described in this chapter.
2. Connect the positive charger lead to the positive battery terminal and the negative charger lead to the negative battery terminal.
3. Set the charger at 12 volts and switch it on. Normally, a battery should be charged at a slow charge rate of 1/10 its given capacity. **Table 1** lists the battery capacity and charge rate for all models.
4. After the battery has been charged, turn the charger OFF, disconnect the leads and check the battery with a digital voltmeter. It should be within the limits specified in **Table 3**. If it is, and remains stable for one hour, the battery is charged.

Battery Initialization

A new battery must be fully charged before installation. Failure to do so reduces the life of the battery. Using a new battery without an initial charge causes permanent battery damage. That is, the battery will never be able to hold more than an 80% charge. Charging a new battery after it has been used will not bring its charge to 100%. When purchasing a new battery from a dealership or parts store, verify its charge status. If necessary, have them perform the initial or booster charge before accepting the battery.

CHARGING SYSTEM

The charging system consists of the battery, alternator and a voltage regulator/rectifier. A 30-amp main fuse protects the circuit. Refer to the main diagrams and individual circuit diagrams at the end of the manual.

Alternating current generated by the alternator is rectified to direct current. The voltage regulator maintains constant voltage to the battery and additional electrical loads (such as lights or ignition) despite variations in engine speed and load.

Troubleshooting

Refer to Chapter Two if the battery is discharging or overcharging.

Current Leakage (Draw) Test

Perform this test before performing the *Regulated Voltage Test*.
1. Turn the ignition switch to the OFF position.
2. Disconnect the negative battery cable as described under *Battery Removal/Installation* in this chapter.

CAUTION
Before connecting the ammeter into the circuit in Step 5, set the meter to its highest amperage scale. This prevents a large current flow from damaging the meter or blowing the meter's fuse.

3. Connect an ammeter between the negative battery cable and the negative battery terminal (**Figure 8**).
4. Switch the ammeter to its lowest scale and note the reading. The maximum current leakage (draw) must not exceed the specification in **Table 1**.
5. Dirt and/or electrolyte on top of the battery or a crack in the battery case can create a path for battery current to flow. If excessive current leakage is

10

noted, remove and clean the battery as described in this chapter, then repeat the leakage test.

6. If the current leakage is still excessive, consider the following probable causes:

   a. Faulty voltage regulator/rectifier.

   b. Damaged battery.

   c. Short circuit in the system.

   d. Loose, dirty or faulty electrical connectors in the charging circuit.

7. To find the short circuit that is causing excessive current leakage, refer to the wiring diagrams at the end of this book. Then continue to measure the current leakage while disconnecting different connectors in the electrical system one by one. When the current leakage returns to an acceptable level, the circuit is indicated. Test the circuit further to find the problem.

8. Disconnect the ammeter.

9. Reconnect the negative battery cable.

10. Reinstall the seat as described in Chapter Sixteen.

Regulated Voltage Test

This procedure tests charging system operation. It does not measure maximum charging system output. **Table 2** lists charging system test specifications.

To obtain accurate test results, the battery must be fully charged (13.0 volts or higher).

1. Start and run the engine until it reaches normal operating temperature, then turn the engine OFF

2. Connect a digital voltmeter to the battery terminals.

> *NOTE*
> *Do not disconnect either battery cable when making this test.*

3. Start the engine and allow it to idle. Turn the headlight switch to HI beam.

4. Gradually increase engine speed to 5000 rpm and read the voltage indicated on the voltmeter. Compare this with the regulated voltage reading in **Table 2**.

> *NOTE*
> *If the battery is often discharged but charging voltage tested normal during Step 4, the battery may be damaged.*

5. If the voltage reading is incorrect, perform the *Regulator/Rectifier Wiring Harness Test* in this chapter, while noting the following:

   a. If the regulated voltage is too low, check for an open or short circuit in the charging system

wiring harness, an open or short in the alternator or a damaged regulator/rectifier

   b. If the regulated voltage is too high, check for a poor regulator/rectifier ground, a damaged regulator/rectifier or a damaged battery.

Regulator/Rectifier Wiring Harness Test

This procedure tests the integrity of the wires and connectors attached to the regulator/rectifier.

1. Remove the rear cowl as described in Chapter Sixteen.

2A. On 1999-2000 models, disconnect the regulator/rectifier five-pin black electrical connector (**Figure 9**) on the right side.

2B. On 2001-on models, disconnect the regulator/rectifier six-pin black and three-pin white electrical connectors (**Figure 10**) located behind the fuel tank.

> *NOTE*
> *Make all of the tests (Steps 3-5) on the wiring harness connector side, not on the regulator/rectifier connector side.*

3. Check the battery charge lead as follows:

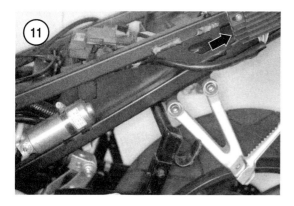

a. Connect a voltmeter to the red/white or red wire and a good engine ground.

b. With the ignition switch in the OFF position, read the voltmeter. It must be 13.0-13.2 volts (battery voltage).

c. If the voltage is less than specified, check the red/white or red wire for damage.

d. Disconnect the voltmeter leads.

4. Check the charge coil circuit as follows:

a. Switch an ohmmeter to R × 1.

b. Connect the ohmmeter alternately between the three yellow wires. Read the meter after each connection.

c. The ohmmeter must read 0.1-1.0 ohms (at 20° C [69° F]). If the resistance is excessive, inspect the wiring harness for loose or damaged wires.

5. Check the ground circuit as follows:

a. Switch an ohmmeter to R × 1.

b. Connect the ohmmeter to the green wire and a good engine ground.

c. The ohmmeter must read continuity.

d. If there is no continuity or high resistance, check the green wire for damage.

e. Disconnect the ohmmeter leads.

6. Reconnect the regulator/rectifier electrical connector(s).

7. Install the rear cowl as described in Chapter Sixteen.

Regulator/Rectifier Removal/Installation

1. Remove the rear cowl as described in Chapter Sixteen.

2. Disconnect the negative battery cable as described under *Battery Removal/Installation* in this chapter.

3A. On 1999-2000 models, perform the following:

a. Disconnect the regulator/rectifier five-pin black electrical connector (**Figure 9**) on the right side.

b. Remove the bolts securing the voltage regulator/rectifier to the frame and remove it.

3B. On 2001-on models, perform the following:

a. Disconnect the regulator/rectifier six-pin black and three-pin white electrical connectors (**Figure 10**) located behind the fuel tank.

b. Remove the bolts securing the voltage regulator/rectifier (**Figure 11**) to the frame and remove it.

4. Install by reversing these removal steps, while noting the following.

5. Make sure all electrical connectors are secure and corrosion-free.

STATOR COIL AND LEFT CRANKCASE COVER

Left Crankcase Cover Removal/Installation

1. Remove the rear cowl as described in Chapter Sixteen.

2. Disconnect the negative battery cable as described under *Battery Removal/Installation* in this chapter.

3. Follow the wiring harness from the crankcase cover to the alternator electrical connector (**Figure 12**, typical) on the left side of the frame. Disconnect the following:

a. On 1999-2000 models, disconnect the stator coil three-pin white electrical connector on the left side.

10

b. On 2001-on models, disconnect the three-pin white electrical connector (**Figure 12**) located behind the fuel tank.

4. Make a note of the alternator wiring harness routing from the left crankcase cover to where the connector plugs into the main wiring harness.

5. Carefully remove the alternator wiring harness from along the frame.

6. Place a clean drain pan underneath the left crankcase cover.

> *NOTE*
> *Some engine oil will drain when the left crankcase cover is removed.*

7. Remove the bolts and remove the left crankcase cover (**Figure 13**).

8. Remove the gasket and dowel pin (A, **Figure 14**).

9. If necessary, service the stator coil as described later in this section.

10. Do not clean the cover or stator coils in solvent. Wipe the cover with a clean rag.

> *NOTE*
> *If the cover is contaminated with oil sludge, remove the stator coil as described in the following procedure and then clean the cover.*

11. Install the left crankcase cover by reversing these removal steps, plus the following.

   a. Install the dowel pin (A, **Figure 14**) and a new gasket (B).

   b. Apply sealant to 10-15 mm (0.4-0.6 in.) on either side of the mating surface of the crankcase as shown in **Figure 15**.

   c. Install the left crankcase cover and tighten the mounting bolts securely.

   d. Make sure the electrical connector is free of corrosion. Check the wiring harness routing.

   e. Check the engine oil level as described in Chapter Three and add oil as required.

Stator Coil Resistance Test

The stator coil is mounted inside the left crankcase side cover. The stator coil can be tested while mounted on the engine.

1. Remove the rear cowl as described in Chapter Sixteen.

2. Disconnect the negative battery cable as described under *Battery Removal/Installation* in this chapter.

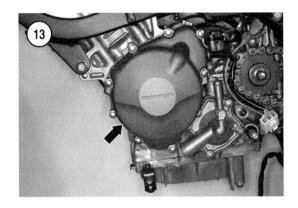

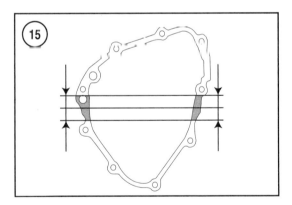

3. Follow the wiring harness from the crankcase cover to the alternator electrical connectors on the left side of the frame. Disconnect the following:

   a. On 1999-2000 models, disconnect the stator coil three-pin white electrical connector on the left side.

   b. On 2001-on models, disconnect the three-pin white electrical connector located behind the fuel tank.

4. Use an ohmmeter set at R × 1 and measure resistance between each yellow wire on the alternator

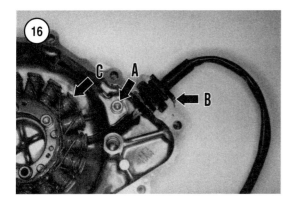

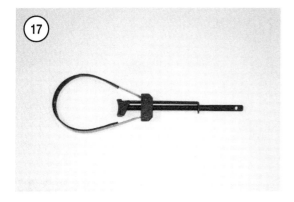

side of the connector (**Figure 12**, typical). **Table 2** lists the specified stator coil resistance.

5. Replace the stator if the resistance is not as specified.

6. Use an ohmmeter set at R × 1 to check continuity from each yellow stator wire to ground.

7. Replace the stator coil if any yellow terminal has continuity to ground. Continuity indicates a short within the stator coil winding.

NOTE
Before replacing the stator assembly, check the electrical wires to and within the electrical connector for any opens or poor connections.

8. If the stator coil fails either of these tests, replace it as described in this section.
9. Make sure the electrical connector is secure and corrosion-free.

Stator Coil Removal/Installation

1. Remove the left crankcase cover as described in this section.
2. Remove the wire harness bolt and clamp (A, **Figure 16**) and remove the clamp.
3. Pull the wire harness grommet (B, **Figure 16**) out of the cover.
4. Remove the stator coil mounting bolts and remove the stator coil (C, **Figure 16**).
5. Install the stator coil by reversing these steps, while noting the following:

   a. Apply Gasgacinch or an RTV sealer to the wiring harness rubber plug, then insert the plug into the cover notch (B, **Figure 16**).
   b. Apply a medium-strength threadlock onto all of the stator coil mounting bolts.
   c. Tighten the stator coil mounting bolts to 12 N•m (106 in.-lb.).

FLYWHEEL, STARTER CLUTCH AND STARTER REDUCTION GEAR

Special Tools

The following special tools or their equivalents are required to remove the flywheel (alternator rotor):
1. Flywheel puller, Honda part No. 07733-0020001 or 07933-3950000.
2. Flywheel holder (**Figure 17**), Honda part No. 07725-0040000.

Removal

1. Remove the left crankcase cover as described in this chapter.
2. Remove the starter reduction gear shaft and gear (**Figure 18**).

10

3. Hold the flywheel with a flywheel holder (**Figure 17**) and loosen the bolt (**Figure 19**). Then remove the bolt and washer.

4. Screw the flywheel puller into the flywheel.

> *CAUTION*
> *Do not try to remove the flywheel without the correct puller. Any attempt to do so may damage the flywheel and crankshaft.*

> *CAUTION*
> *If normal flywheel removal attempts fail, do not force the puller. Excessive force will strip the flywheel threads, causing expensive damage. Take the engine to a dealership for flywheel removal.*

5. Hold the flywheel with the flywheel holder and gradually tighten the flywheel puller until the flywheel pops off the crankshaft taper.

6. Remove the flywheel and needle bearing (A, **Figure 20**) from the crankshaft.

7. Do not remove the Woodruff key (B, **Figure 20**) from the crankshaft unless it is loose.

8. Remove the puller from the flywheel.

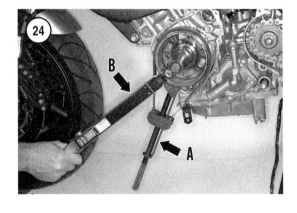

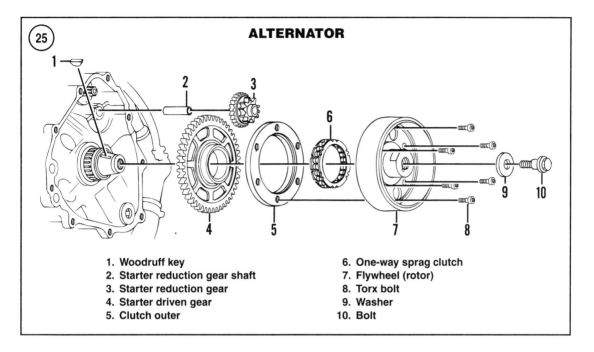

ALTERNATOR

1. Woodruff key
2. Starter reduction gear shaft
3. Starter reduction gear
4. Starter driven gear
5. Clutch outer
6. One-way sprag clutch
7. Flywheel (rotor)
8. Torx bolt
9. Washer
10. Bolt

Inspection

1. Clean the flywheel in solvent and dry with compressed air.

2. Check the flywheel for cracks or breaks.

WARNING
Replace a cracked or chipped flywheel. A damaged flywheel can fly apart at high engine speeds, throwing metal fragments into the engine. Do not attempt to repair a damaged flywheel.

3. Check the flywheel tapered bore and the crankshaft taper for damage.

4. Check the Woodruff keyway (A, **Figure 21**) for wear or damage. If damage is severe, replace the flywheel.

5. Inspect the inside of the flywheel (B, **Figure 21**) for metal debris picked up by the magnet. Remove all debris to avoid damage to the stator assembly.

6. Inspect the starter reduction gear and shaft (**Figure 22**) for excessive wear or damage. Replace if necessary.

7. Inspect the one-way sprag clutch roller cage (**Figure 23**) for damage.

8. Replace damaged parts as required.

Installation

1. Degrease both the crankshaft taper and the flywheel inner taper with aerosol parts cleaner. Allow both tapers to dry before installing the flywheel.

2. Install the needle bearing (A, **Figure 20**) onto the crankshaft. Apply engine oil to the bearing.

3. If removed, install the Woodruff key (B, **Figure 20**) onto the crankshaft. Make sure it is correctly seated.

4. Align the flywheel with the Woodruff key and install the flywheel onto the crankshaft taper.

5. Lubricate the flywheel bolt threads and washer with clean engine oil, then install and tighten finger-tight (**Figure 19**).

6. Hold the flywheel with the flywheel holder (A, **Figure 24**) and tighten the flywheel (alternator rotor) bolt (B, **Figure 24**) to 103 N•m (76 ft.-lb.).

7. Remove the flywheel holder from the flywheel.

8. Install the starter reduction gear and shaft (**Figure 18**). Push the shaft in until it bottoms.

9. Install the left crankcase cover as described in this chapter.

Starter Clutch Disassembly/Assembly

Refer to **Figure 25**.

10

1. Hold the alternator with one hand, then turn the starter driven gear clockwise and counterclockwise. The gear should only turn *counterclockwise* (**Figure 26**). If the gear turns clockwise, replace the starter clutch assembly.

2. Hold the alternator with one hand, then turn the starter driven gear counterclockwise (**Figure 26**) and pull up at the same time to remove it.

3. To remove the starter clutch assembly, perform the following:

   a. Install the Honda flywheel holder (**Figure 17**), Honda part No. 07725-0040000, or an equivalent onto the flywheel. Loosen the six Torx bolts (**Figure 27**) securing the starter clutch outer.

   b. Remove the bolts, turn the assembly over and remove the starter clutch outer and the sprag clutch (**Figure 28**).

4. Clean the starter clutch and driven gear in solvent and dry with compressed air.

5. Remove all threadlocking compound from the Torx bolts.

6. Inspect the starter driven gear teeth (A, **Figure 29**) for damage.

7. Inspect the starter driven gear boss (B, **Figure 29**) where the needle bearing rides for wear or damage.

8. Measure the starter driven gear boss outside diameter (**Figure 30**) and compare to dimension in **Table 5**. Replace if necessary.

9. Install the starter clutch as follows:

   a. Lubricate the one-way sprag clutch with engine oil.

   b. Position the one-way sprag clutch with the flange side going on last and install it into the flywheel.

   c. Install the clutch outer.

   d. Apply a medium strength threadlocking compound to the starter clutch Torx bolts and install them.

   e. Secure the flywheel with the Honda flywheel holder and tighten the Torx bolts (**Figure 27**) to 16 N•m (12 ft.-lb.).

   f. Turn the one-way clutch counterclockwise and install it into the clutch housing.

   g. Recheck the one-way sprag clutch operation. Hold the clutch housing with one hand and turn the starter driven gear. The gear should turn *counterclockwise* (**Figure 26**) but not clockwise.

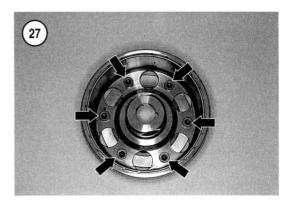

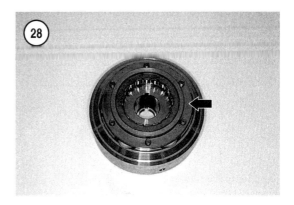

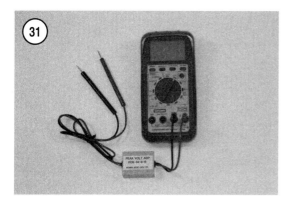

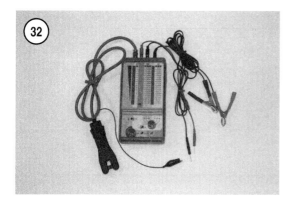

IGNITION SYSTEM

All models have a digital ignition system. The system includes the coil-integrated spark plug cap (direct ignition coil), where the ignition coil is in the spark plug cap, eliminating the spark plug secondary wire.

Refer to the main diagrams and individual circuit diagrams at the end of the manual.

Troubleshooting

Refer to Chapter Two.

Peak Voltage Tests and Equipment

WARNING
High voltage is present during ignition system operation. Do not touch ignition components, wires or test leads while cranking or running the engine.

Peak voltage tests check the voltage output of the ignition coil and pulse generator at normal cranking speed by using a peak voltage tester. These tests make it possible to accurately test the voltage output under operating conditions.

The peak voltage specifications listed in **Table 4** are minimum values. If the measured voltage meets or exceeds the specification, the test results are satisfactory. In some cases the voltage may greatly exceed the minimum specification.

One of the following testers, or an equivalent, is necessary to perform peak voltage tests. Refer to the manufacturer's instructions when using these tools.

1. Honda Peak voltage adapter (part No. 07HGJ-0020100). This tool (**Figure 31**) must be used in combination with a digital multimeter with a minimum impedance of 10M ohms/DCV.

2. Ignition Mate (**Figure 32**) (Motion Pro part No. 08-0193).

Ignition Coil Primary Peak Voltage Test

1. Check the battery to make sure it is fully charged and in good condition. A weak battery results in a slow engine cranking speed and an inaccurate peak voltage test.

2. Check engine compression as described in Chapter Three. If the compression is low in one or more cylinders, the following test results will be inaccurate.

3. Remove the fuel tank as described in Chapter Eight or Nine.

4. Remove the air filter assembly as described in Chapter Eight or Nine.

5. Remove both side fairing panels and the front inner faring as described in Chapter Sixteen.

6. Check all of the ignition component electrical connectors and wiring harnesses. Make sure the connectors are clean and properly connected.

7. Refer to *Spark Plugs* in Chapter Three and remove all four direct ignition coils (**Figure 33**) from

10

the spark plugs. Leave the spark plugs in place in the cylinder head.

8. Connect four known good test spark plugs to the direct ignition coils and ground all four against the cylinder head cover or cylinder heads (**Figure 34**).

9. If using the Honda peak voltage adapter (**Figure 31**), connect it to the multimeter.

NOTE
*If using the Ignition Mate (**Figure 32**) tester or a similar peak voltage tester, follow the manufacturer's instructions for connecting the tester to the direct ignition coils.*

NOTE
Do not disconnect the ignition coil six-pin black connector when performing Step 12.

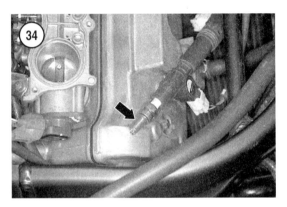

10. The ignition coil six-pin black connector location is as follows:

 a. 1999-2000 models: below the left side frame rail, next to the cylinder head (**Figure 35**).

 b. 2001-on models: under the fuel tank on the left side, above the cylinder head cover (**Figure 36**).

11. Connect the peak voltage adapter (**Figure 37**) to the backside of the ignition coil six-pin black electrical connector as follows:

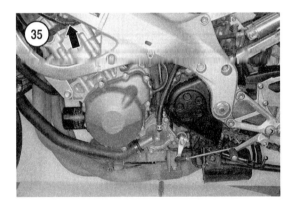

 a. No. 1 ignition coil. Connect the positive test lead to the blue/black terminal and the negative lead to a good ground.

 b. No. 2 ignition coil: Connect the positive test lead to the yellow/white terminal and the negative lead to a good ground.

 c. No. 3 ignition coil: Connect the positive test lead to the red/blue terminal and the negative lead to a good ground.

 d. No. 4 ignition coil: Connect the positive test lead to the red/yellow terminal and the negative lead to a good ground.

12. Turn the ignition switch to the ON position and the engine stop switch to the RUN position.

13. Read the voltage on the meter's scale and note the following:

 a. If there is no battery voltage, refer to the *No Spark at All Four Spark Plugs* procedure under *Ignition Troubleshooting* in Chapter Two. Perform the steps in order to find the problem.

 b. If there is battery voltage, continue with Step 18.

14. Shift the transmission into NEUTRAL.

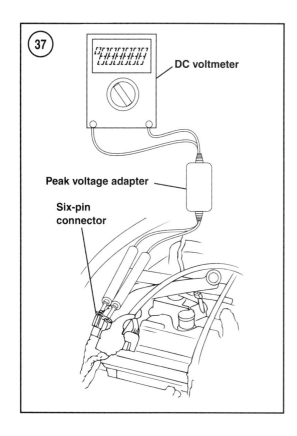

DC voltmeter

Peak voltage adapter

Six-pin connector

WARNING
High voltage is present during ignition system operation. Do not touch spark plugs, ignition components, connectors or test leads while cranking the engine.

15. Press the starter button while reading the meter.

16. Release the starter button, then connect the test lead to the other ignition coil primary leads. Repeat Step 15 for each ignition coil.

17. Interpret the test results as follows:

NOTE
The peak voltage specification is the minimum voltage. If the measured voltage meets or exceeds the specification, consider the test results satisfactory. On some components, the voltage may greatly exceed the minimum specification.

a. The minimum peak voltage reading is 100 volts.
b. The individual peak voltage reading recorded for each ignition coil can vary as long as the voltage readings are higher than the specified minimum value.
c. If the peak voltage reading for one or both ignition coils is less than 100 volts, perform the *No Spark at All Four Spark Plugs* procedure under *Ignition Troubleshooting* in Chapter Two. Perform the steps in order to find the problem.

18. Disconnect the test leads.

19. Remove the test spark plugs from the direct ignition coils.

20. Carefully push straight down on the direct ignition coils and engage it with the top of the correct spark plug still installed in the cylinder head. Push down until it seats completely on the spark plug and the cylinder head cover.

21. Connect the direct ignition coil two-pin electrical connector (**Figure 33**).

22. Repeat for each spark plug.

23. Install the air filter housing as described in Chapter Nine.

24. Install the fuel tank as described in Chapter Nine.

25. Install both side fairing panels and the front inner faring as described in Chapter Sixteen.

Ignition Pulse Generator Peak Voltage Test

1. Check the battery to make sure it is fully charged and in good condition. A weak battery results in a slow engine cranking speed and an inaccurate peak test reading.

2. Check engine compression as described in Chapter Three. If the compression is low in one or more cylinders, the following test results will be inaccurate.

3. Remove the seat and rear cowl as described in Chapter Sixteen.

4A. On 1999-2000 models, disconnect the 22-pin electrical connector from the ignition control module (**Figure 38**).

10

4B. On 2001-on models, perform the following:

   a. Remove the band (**Figure 39**) securing the electronic control module (ECM).

   b. Carefully lift the ECM up off the battery tray cover and disconnect the 22-pin light gray electrical connector from the ECM (**Figure 40**).

5. If using the Honda peak voltage adapter (**Figure 31**), connect it to the multimeter.

> *NOTE*
> *If using the Ignition Mate (**Figure 32**) tester or a similar peak voltage tester, follow its manufacturer's instructions for connecting the tester to the ignition coil.*

6. Shift the transmission into NEUTRAL.

> *WARNING*
> *High voltage is present during ignition system operation. Do not touch spark plugs, ignition components, connectors or test leads while cranking the engine.*

7A. On 1999-2000 models, connect the positive test lead to the yellow terminal and the negative lead to the white/yellow terminal.

7B. On 2001-on models, connect the positive test lead to the yellow terminal and the negative lead to ground (**Figure 41**).

8. On all models, perform the following:

   a. Turn the ignition switch to ON and the engine stop switch to the RUN position.

   b. Press the starter button while reading the meter.

> *NOTE*
> *The peak voltage specification is the minimum voltage. If the measured voltage meets or exceeds the specification, consider the test results satisfactory. On some components, the voltage may greatly exceed the minimum specification.*

   c. The minimum peak voltage reading is 0.7 volts.

   d. Release the starter button and turn the ignition switch to the OFF position.

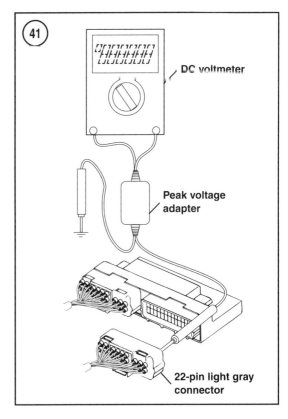

DC voltmeter

Peak voltage adapter

22-pin light gray connector

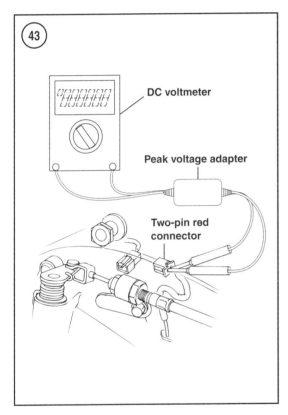

DC voltmeter

Peak voltage adapter

Two-pin red connector

e. If the peak voltage reading was incorrect, continue with Step 9 to measure the peak voltage at the ignition pulse generator connector.

9. Perform the following:

a. Disconnect the ignition pulse generator two-pin red electrical connector (**Figure 42**) located behind the clutch release cable.

b. Connect the tester to the ignition pulse generator connector yellow and white/yellow terminals (**Figure 43**).

c. Turn the ignition switch to the ON position and the engine stop switch to the RUN position.

d. Press the starter button while reading the meter.

e. The minimum peak voltage reading is 0.7 volts.

f. Release the starter button and turn the ignition switch to the OFF position.

10. If the peak voltage reading in Step 9 is 0.7 volts but the reading in Step 8 is less than 0.7 volts, check the wire harness for an open circuit or loose connector. If both voltage readings (Step 8 and Step 9) are less than 0.7 volts, perform the *No Spark at All Four Spark Plugs* procedure under *Ignition System Troubleshooting* in Chapter Two.

11. Disconnect the test leads and install all parts removed.

Direct Ignition Coil Removal/Installation

1. Remove the air filter housing as described in Chapter Eight or Nine.

> *NOTE*
> ***Figure 44*** *is shown with the carburetor or fuel injection assembly removed to better illustrate this step. Do not remove the assembly for this procedure.*

2. Carefully disconnect the two-pin electrical connector from the top of each direct ignition coil (**Figure 44**).

3. Clean the cylinder head cover and frame surfaces with compressed air. Check for and remove all loose debris or small parts that could fall into the spark plug receptacles in the cylinder head cover.

4. Carefully pull straight up on the direct ignition coil and disengage it from the top of the spark

10

plug(s). Remove it from the cylinder head cover and spark plug.

5. Repeat for any remaining direct ignition coil(s).

6. Install by reversing these removal steps. Make sure all electrical connections are secure and corrosion-free.

Ignition Pulse Generator
Removal/Installation

The ignition pulse generator is on the right side of the engine and can be removed with the engine mounted in the frame.

1. Remove the right crankcase cover as described in Chapter Six.

2. Remove the rubber grommet (A, **Figure 45**) from the cover.

3. Remove the bolts and remove the ignition pulse generator (B, **Figure 45**).

4. Remove all sealer residue from the grommet and its notch in the cover.

5. Install the ignition pulse generator (B, **Figure 45**) and tighten the bolts securely.

6. Apply a clear RTV to the grommet and install it into the notch in the cover (**Figure 46**).

7. Install the right crankcase cover as described in Chapter Six.

Ignition Pulse Generator Rotor
Removal/Installation

The ignition pulse generator rotor is mounted on the right side of the engine and can be removed with the engine mounted in the frame. This procedure is shown with the engine and clutch assembly removed to better illustrate the steps.

1. Remove the right crankcase cover as described in Chapter Six.

2. Shift the transmission into sixth gear.

3. Have an assistant apply the rear brake to keep the crankshaft from rotating in the next step.

4. Loosen and remove the bolt (A, **Figure 47**) securing the pulse generator rotor.

5. Remove the bolt, washer and the rotor (B, **Figure 47**).

6. To install the rotor, align the flat (**Figure 48**) with the special spline on the crankshaft and install the rotor (**Figure 49**).

7. Install the bolt and washer (A, **Figure 47**) and tighten the bolt to 59 N•m (44 ft.-lb.).

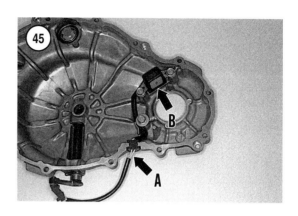

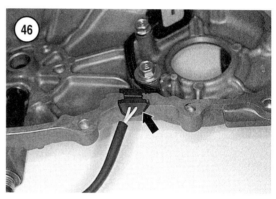

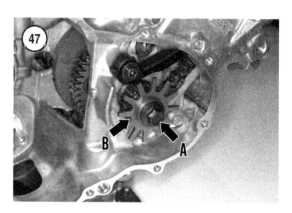

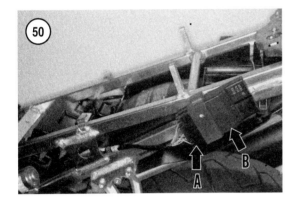

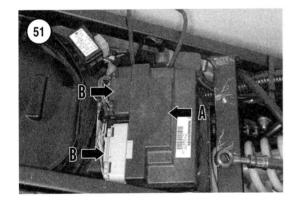

8. Install the right crankcase cover as described in Chapter Six.

Ignition Control Module (ICM) Removal/Installation (1999-2000 Models)

1. Remove the seat and the rear cowl as described in Chapter Sixteen.

2. Disconnect the negative battery cable as described in this chapter.

3. Disconnect the 22-pin electrical connector (A, **Figure 50**) from the ICM.

4. Remove the ICM (B, **Figure 50**) from the mounting bracket on the frame.

5. Place the ICM in a reclosable plastic bag to keep it clean. Store it in a safe place to avoid damage to this expensive component.

6. Install by reversing these removal steps. Refer to *Electrical Connectors* at the beginning of this chapter and pack the connector with dielectric grease compound.

Engine Control Module (ECM) Removal/Installation (2001-On Models)

1. Remove the seat and rear cowl as described in Chapter Sixteen.

2. Remove the band (**Figure 39**) securing the electronic control module (ECM).

3. Carefully lift the ECM (A, **Figure 51**) up off the battery tray cover and move it out of the way. Disconnect the 22-pin black and 22-pin light gray electrical connectors (B, **Figure 51**) from the ECM.

4. Remove the ECM and place it in a reclosable plastic bag to keep it clean. Store it in a safe place to avoid damage to this expensive component.

5. Install by reversing these removal steps. Refer to *Electrical Connectors* at the beginning of this chapter and pack the connector with dielectric grease compound.

STARTER

The starting system consists of the starter, starter gears, starter relay switch, various safety switches and the starter button. Refer to the main diagrams and individual circuit diagrams at the end of the manual.

Table 5 lists starter specifications.

CAUTION
Do not operate the starter for more than five seconds at a time. Wait approximately ten seconds between starting attempts.

Troubleshooting

Refer to Chapter Two.

10

Removal/Installation

1. Remove the seat as described in Chapter Sixteen.
2. Remove the side fairing panels and the front inner fairing in Chapter Sixteen.
3. Disconnect the negative battery cable as described in this chapter.
4. Drain the cooling system as described in Chapter Eleven.
5A. On 1999-2000 models, remove the carburetor assembly as described in Chapter Eight.
5B. On 2001-on models, remove the throttle body assembly as described in Chapter Nine.
6. Remove the thermostat housing as described in Chapter Eleven.
7. Move the rubber cap (A, **Figure 52**) aside and disconnect the starter cable (**Figure 53**) from the starter.
8. Remove the two starter mounting bolts (B, **Figure 52**). Note the location of the ground cable (A, **Figure 54**) secured by the rear bolt.
9. Move the starter toward the right side and remove the starter (B, **Figure 54**).
10. Install by reversing these removal steps, plus the following:

    a. Lubricate the starter O-ring (**Figure 55**) with engine oil.

    b. Remove all corrosion from the starter cable.

    c. Tighten the starter mounting bolts securely. Be sure to install the ground cable (A, **Figure 54**) under the rear bolt.

Disassembly

Refer to **Figure 56**.

NOTE
*Before disassembling the starter, locate the alignment marks on the starter housing and both end covers (**Figure 57**) for assembly. To maintain the correct alignment and position of the parts during disassembly, store each part in order and in a divided container (**Figure 58**).*

1. Loosen the starter case through bolts (A, **Figure 59**) and remove them.

NOTE
Record the number, type and thickness of the shims and washer used on both

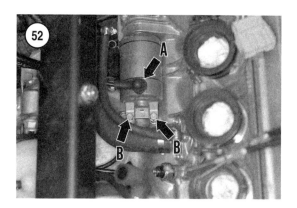

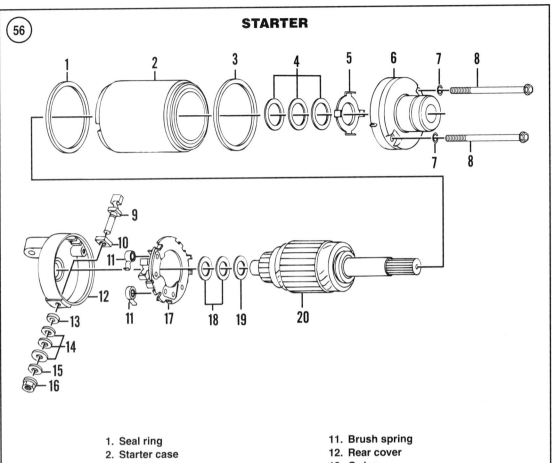

STARTER

1. Seal ring
2. Starter case
3. Seal ring
4. Shims
5. Lockwasher
6. Front cover
7. O-ring
8. Through bolt
9. Positive terminal bolt
10. Insulator bar
11. Brush spring
12. Rear cover
13. O-ring
14. Insulators
15. Washer
16. Nut
17. Negative brush holder
18. Shims
19. Shim
20. Armature

10

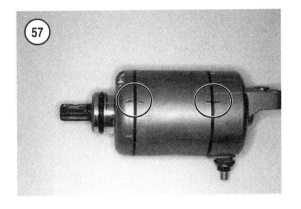

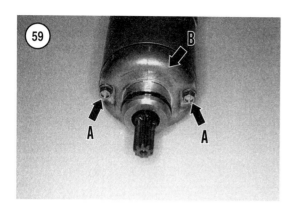

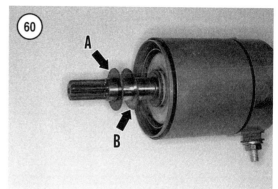

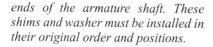

ends of the armature shaft. These shims and washer must be installed in their original order and positions.

NOTE
The number of shims used in the starter motor varies.

2. Slide the front cover (B, **Figure 59**) off of the armature shaft, then remove the insulated washer (A, **Figure 60**) and the shim(s) (B).

3. Remove the lockwasher (**Figure 61**) from the front cover.

4. Slide the rear cover (A, **Figure 62**) off the armature shaft and remove the shims.

5. Slide the starter case (B, **Figure 62**) off of the armature (C),

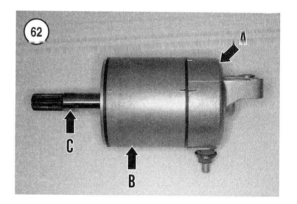

CAUTION
Do not immerse the armature coil or starter case in solvent, as the insulation may be damaged. Wipe the windings with a cloth lightly moistened in solvent and dry with compressed air.

6. Clean all grease, dirt and carbon from the components.

7. Inspect the starter as described in this chapter.

Inspection

NOTE
Before removing the nuts and washers in Step 1, record their description and order. They must be reinstalled in the same order to insulate this set of brushes from the case.

1. Remove the nut (**Figure 63**), washer and insulators securing the positive terminal bolt to the rear

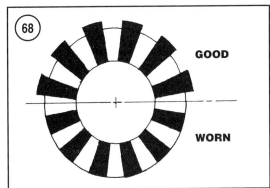

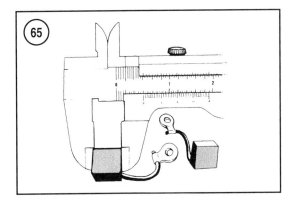

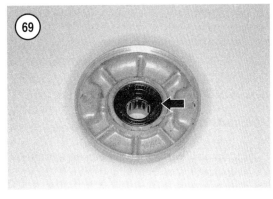

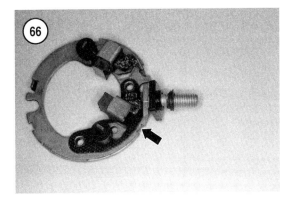

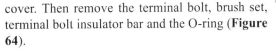

10

cover. Then remove the terminal bolt, brush set, terminal bolt insulator bar and the O-ring (**Figure 64**).

2. Measure the length of each brush (**Figure 65**) with a vernier caliper. If any brush is too short, replace both brushes as a set.

3. Inspect the brush springs for fatigue, cracks or other damage. Replace the brush plate (**Figure 66**) if the springs are severely worn or damaged.

4. Inspect the commutator (**Figure 67**) for abnormal wear or discoloration; neither condition can be repaired and requires replacement of the armature.

5. The mica in a good commutator is below the surface of the copper bars. On a worn commutator the mica and copper bars may be worn to the same level (**Figure 68**). If necessary, undercut the mica between each pair of bars.

6. Inspect the oil seal (**Figure 69**) and needle bearing (**Figure 70**) in the front cover for wear or damage.

7. Inspect the bushing (**Figure 71**) in the rear cover for severe wear or damage.

8. Replace the seal rings if they are worn or damaged.

9. Use an ohmmeter to make the following tests:

   a. Check for continuity between the commutator bars (**Figure 72**); there should be continuity between pairs of bars.

   b. Check for continuity between the commutator bars and the shaft (**Figure 73**); there should be no continuity.

   c. If the commutator fails either of these tests, replace the starter assembly. The armature is not available separately.

10. Check for continuity between the positive terminal and rear cover (**Figure 74**); there should be no continuity.

11. Check for continuity between the cable positive terminal and the brush wire (**Figure 75**); there should be continuity.

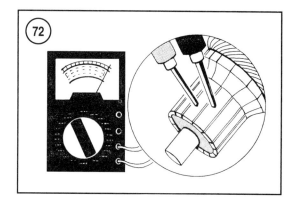

Assembly

1. Install the seal rings (**Figure 76**) into the case grooves.

2. If removed, set the brushes onto the brush holder (**Figure 66**).

3. Install the brush holder assembly into the rear cover (A, **Figure 77**). Align the boss on the brush holder with the groove in the starter case (**Figure 75**).

4. Install the O-ring (B, **Figure 77**) over the positive terminal bolt and seat it into the hole in the rear cover.

5. Install the following parts in order:

   a. Three insulators (C, **Figure 77**).

   b. Washer (D, **Figure 77**) and nut (E). Tighten the nut securely.

6. Install the shims (**Figure 78**) onto the armature shaft.

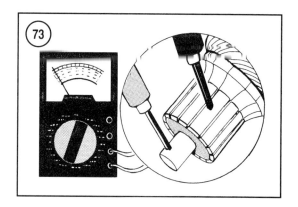

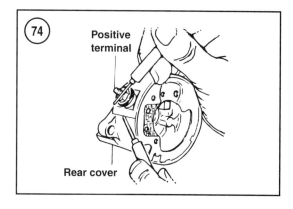

Positive terminal

Rear cover

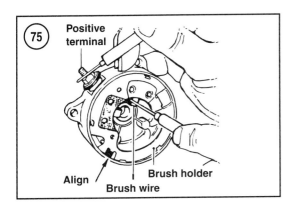

Positive terminal

Align

Brush wire

Brush holder

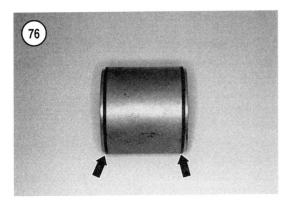

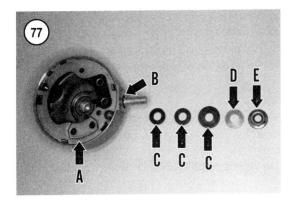

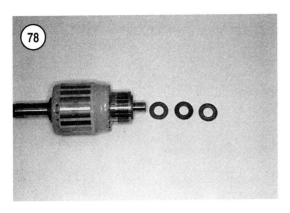

7. Install the armature into the rear cover (**Figure 79**) so the commutator contacts the brushes.

8. Install the starter case (B, **Figure 62**) over the armature. Align the index marks.

9. Install the shim(s) (B, **Figure 60**) and the insulated washer (A) over the armature shaft.

10. Install the lockwasher (**Figure 61**) into the front cover slots.

11. Install the front cover (B, **Figure 59**) and seat it against the starter case.

12. Align the index marks (**Figure 57**) on all three components.

13. Install the throughbolts (A, **Figure 59**) and tighten securely.

> *NOTE*
> *If a throughbolt does not pass through the starter, the end covers and/or brush plate, the components are installed incorrectly.*

STARTER RELAY SWITCH

Testing

1. Remove the seat and rear cowl as described in Chapter Sixteen.

2. Shift the transmission into NEUTRAL.

3. Turn the ignition switch to the ON position and press the starter button. The starter relay switch should click when the starter button is pressed. If a click is not heard, continue with Step 4.

4. Test the starter relay switch ground circuit as follows:

    a. Disconnect the starter relay switch electrical connector (**Figure 80**).

    b. Shift the transmission into NEUTRAL.

10

c. Using an ohmmeter set on R × 1, check for continuity between the green/red starter relay wire and a good engine ground.

d. The ohmmeter must read continuity.

NOTE
Normally the ohmmeter reads 0 ohm when making a ground test. However, because of the diode in the circuit, it is normal for the ohmmeter to show a slight resistance reading.

e. Disconnect the ohmmeter leads.

5. Check for voltage at the starter relay switch as follows:

a. Reconnect the starter relay switch electrical connector (**Figure 80**).

b. Shift the transmission into NEUTRAL.

c. Connect the positive voltmeter lead to the starter relay switch yellow/red wire and the negative voltmeter lead to a good engine ground.

d. Turn the ignition switch ON and press the starter button while reading the voltmeter.

e. The voltmeter must show battery voltage.

f. Turn the ignition switch OFF and remove the voltmeter leads.

6. Check the starter relay switch operation as follows:

a. Disconnect the starter relay switch electrical connector (**Figure 80**).

b. Disconnect the two large cable leads at the starter relay switch.

c. Switch an ohmmeter to the R × 1 scale and connect its test leads between the two large leads on the starter relay switch. The ohmmeter should show no continuity.

d. Connect a fully charged 12-volt battery to the starter relay switch. Connect the positive battery terminal to the yellow/red wire terminal and the negative battery terminal to the green/red wire terminal (**Figure 81**). The ohmmeter should now read continuity.

e. Disconnect the battery and ohmmeter leads.

7. Replace the starter relay switch if it failed any part of this test.

8. Reconnect the two cable leads and the connector at the starter relay switch.

9. Install the rear cowl and seat as described in Chapter Sixteen.

Removal/Installation

1. Remove the seat as described in Chapter Sixteen.

2. Disconnect the negative battery cable as described in this chapter.

3. Disconnect the starter relay switch electrical connector (**Figure 80**).

4. Slide the rubber boot (A, **Figure 82**) off the two large cable leads.

5. Disconnect the two large cable leads (B, **Figure 82**) at the starter relay switch.

6. Remove the starter relay switch from the frame.

7. Transfer the 30-amp main fuse (and spare) to the new starter relay switch.

8. Install by reversing these removal steps.

CLUTCH DIODE

The clutch diode is part of the starter circuit. This circuit prevents the starter from operating with the transmission in gear without pulling in the clutch lever. When troubleshooting the clutch diode, note the following:

1. The neutral indicator light should only come on when the transmission is in NEUTRAL. If the neutral light comes on when the transmission is in gear and the clutch is disengaged, suspect a faulty clutch diode.

2. If the starter does not operate when the transmission is in NEUTRAL, check for dirty or loose clutch diode terminal connections.

Testing/Replacement

1. Remove the seat as described in Chapter Sixteen.

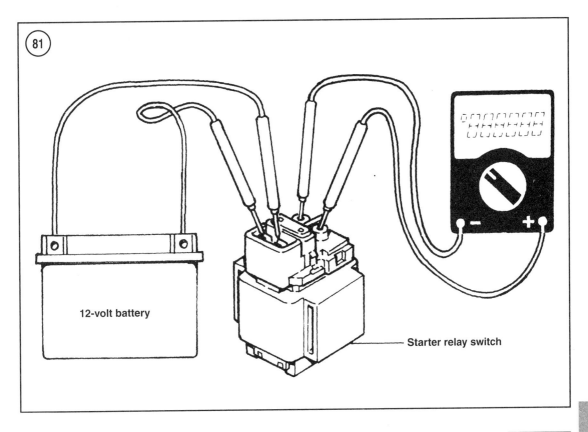

12-volt battery

Starter relay switch

10

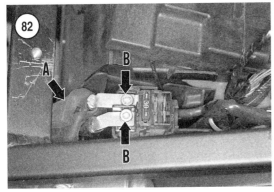

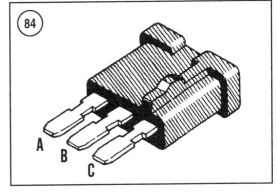

2. Open the fuse box cover (A, **Figure 83**) and disconnect the diode (B) from the fuse box.

3. Set an ohmmeter to the R × 1 scale.

4. Check for continuity between the three terminals on the diode (**Figure 84**). There must be continuity between A and B; C and B (in one direction) and no continuity with the test leads reversed. Replace the diode if it fails this test.

5. Reverse Step 2 to install the clutch diode.

6. Install the seat as described in Chapter Sixteen.

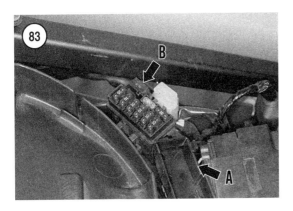

LIGHTING SYSTEM

The lighting system consists of a headlight, tail-light, turn signals and indicator lights. **Table 6** lists replacement bulbs for these components.

Always use the correct wattage bulb listed in **Table 6**. Using the wrong size bulb gives a dim light or causes the bulb to burn out prematurely.

Headlight Bulb Replacement

> *WARNING*
> *If the headlight just burned out or it was just turned off, it will be hot! Do not touch the bulb until it cools off.*

> *CAUTION*
> *All models use a quartz-halogen bulb(s). Traces of oil on this type of bulb reduce the life of the bulb. Do not touch the bulb glass. Clean any oil or other chemicals from the bulb with an alcohol-moistened cloth.*

> *NOTE*
> *This procedure is shown with the front fairing removed from both models to better illustrate the steps. There is sufficient room within the front suspension and front fairing (**Figure 85**) to replace the headlight bulb(s) with the front fairing in place.*

1. On 2001-on models, perform the following:

> *NOTE*
> *Remove the air duct cover and resonator from the side with the defective headlight bulb.*

 a. Remove the air duct cover(s) as described in Chapter Sixteen.

 b. Remove the resonator(s) from the air duct(s)

2. Disconnect the headlight bulb connector (**Figure 86**).

3. Remove the dust cover (**Figure 87**) from around the bulb.

4A. On 1999-2000 models, unhook and push the bulb retainer down (**Figure 88**) and remove the bulb (**Figure 89**).

4B. On 2001-on models, unhook and push the bulb retainer to the side (A, **Figure 90**) and re-

move the bulb/socket (B). Remove the bulb from the socket.

5. Check the connector for dirty or loose-fitting terminals.

6. Align the tabs on the new bulb (**Figure 91**) with the notches in the bulb holder (**Figure 92**) and install the bulb. Secure the bulb with the bulb retainer.

7. Install the dust cover (**Figure 87**) so its TOP mark is at the top of the housing. Make sure the dust cover fits snugly around the bulb and the housing.

8. Plug the connector (**Figure 86**) into the back of the bulb. Press it on until it bottoms.

9. On 2001-on models, repeat for the opposite side, if necessary.

10. Start the engine and check the headlight operation. If necessary, perform the *Headlight Adjustment* in this section.

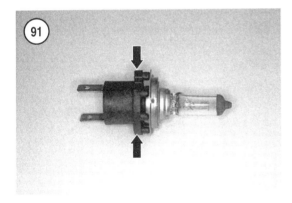

Headlight Adjustment

Proper headlight beam adjustment is critical to both the rider and to oncoming drivers. Adjust the headlight horizontally and vertically according to local Department of Motor Vehicle regulations. If necessary, refer this adjustment to a Honda dealership.

1. On 1999-2000 models, perform the following:
   a. To adjust the headlight horizontally, turn the upper screw (A, **Figure 93**).
   b. To adjust the headlight vertically, turn the lower screw (B, **Figure 93**).

2. On 2001-on models, perform the following:
   a. To adjust the headlight horizontally, turn the upper screw(s) (A, **Figure 94**).
   b. To adjust the headlight vertically, turn the lower screw(s) (B, **Figure 94**).

10

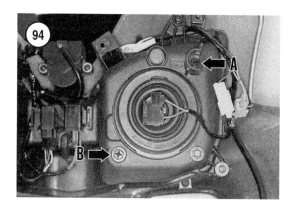

Headlight Housing Removal/Installation (1999-2000 Models)

Refer to **Figure 95**.

1. Remove the front fairing (Chapter Sixteen).

2. Remove the two headlight housing upper mounting screws and washers (A, **Figure 96**).

3. Remove the two headlight housing lower mounting screws, washers and cable clamps (B, **Figure 96**).

4. Remove the headlight housing.

5. Install by reversing these removal steps.

6. Start the engine and check the headlight operation. If necessary, perform the *Headlight Adjustment* in this section.

Headlight Housing Removal/Installation (2001-On Models)

Refer to **Figure 97**.

1. Remove the front fairing as described in Chapter Sixteen.

2. Disconnect the headlight relay (A, **Figure 98**) and turn signal relay (B) electrical connectors from the headlight housing.

3. Disconnect the electrical connector, then remove the screws securing the bank angle sensor (C, **Figure 98**) and remove the sensor.

4. Disconnect the turn signal/running light electrical connectors (A, **Figure 99**) from the headlight housing.

5. Remove the headlight housing four mounting screws (B, **Figure 99**) and remove the headlight housing (D, **Figure 98**).

6. Install by reversing these removal steps.

7. Start the engine and check the headlight operation. If necessary, perform the *Headlight Adjustment* in this section.

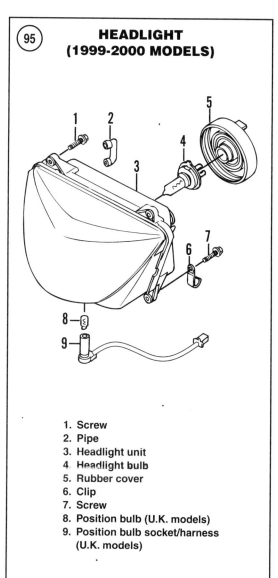

HEADLIGHT (1999-2000 MODELS)

1. Screw
2. Pipe
3. Headlight unit
4. Headlight bulb
5. Rubber cover
6. Clip
7. Screw
8. Position bulb (U.K. models)
9. Position bulb socket/harness (U.K. models)

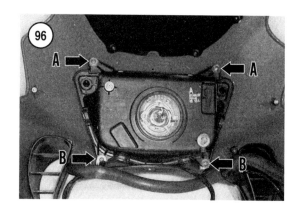

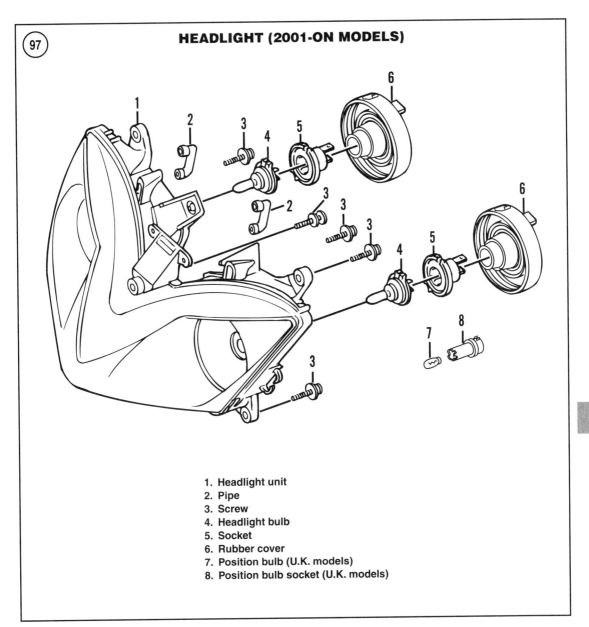

HEADLIGHT (2001-ON MODELS)

1. Headlight unit
2. Pipe
3. Screw
4. Headlight bulb
5. Socket
6. Rubber cover
7. Position bulb (U.K. models)
8. Position bulb socket (U.K. models)

10

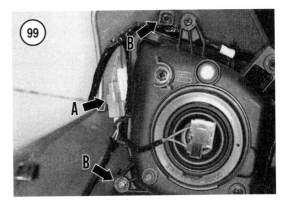

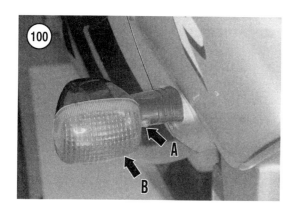

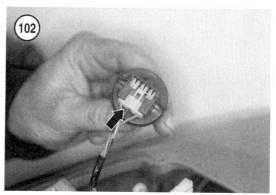

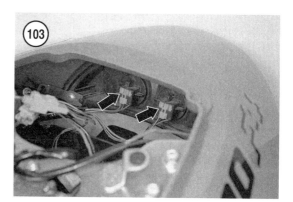

Position Bulb Replacement (U.K. Models)

1. On 1999-2000 models, refer to **Figure 95** and perform the following.
   a. Pull straight out and remove the bulb and socket from the base of the headlight unit at the lower portion of the front fairing.
   b. Remove the bulb from the socket and install a new bulb.
   c. Insert the bulb and socket into the base of the headlight unit. Press it in until it bottoms.

2. On 2001-on models, refer to **Figure 97** and perform the following:
   a. Turn the handlebar all the way to the left.
   b. Disconnect the electrical connector from the backside of the bulb socket.
   c. Pull straight out and remove the bulb and socket from the lower left side of the front fairing assembly.
   d. Remove the bulb from the socket and install a new bulb.
   e. Insert the bulb and socket into the base of the headlight unit. Press it in until it bottoms.
   f. Connect the electrical connector to the bulb socket.

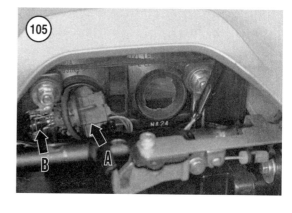

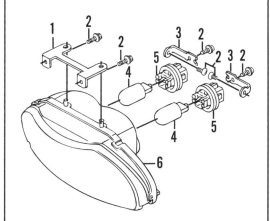

106 **TAILLIGHT/BRAKE LIGHT (1999-2000 U.S., 1999-ON U.K. MODELS)**

1. Upper mounting bracket
2. Screw
3. Side mounting bracket
4. Bulb
5. Socket
6. Taillight/brake light unit

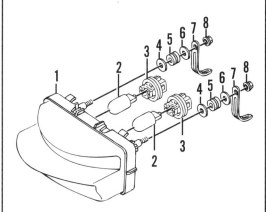

107 **TAILLIGHT/BRAKE LIGHT (2001-ON U.S. MODELS)**

1. Taillight/brake light unit
2. Bulb
3. Socket
4. Washer
5. Rubber grommet
6. Washer
7. Cable strap
8. Nut

Front and Rear Turn Signal Light Replacement

1. Remove the screw (A, **Figure 100**) securing the lens (B) and remove the lens.
2. Push the bulb (**Figure 101**) and turn it counterclockwise to remove it.
3. Install the new bulb and lens by reversing these steps.
4. Turn the ignition switch on and check the turn signal light operation.

Taillight/Brake Light Replacement

1. Remove the seat, or the pillion seat, as described in Chapter Sixteen.
2A. On 1999-2000 models, perform the following:
   a. Pull straight down and disconnect the electrical connectors (**Figure 102**) at the back of the bulb holders.
   b. Turn the bulb socket (**Figure 103**) counterclockwise and remove it.
   c. Pull the bulb straight out and remove it from the socket.
   d. Push a new bulb into the socket until it bottoms.
2B. On 2001-on models, perform the following:
   a. Pull down and disconnect the electrical connectors (**Figure 104**) at the back of the bulb holders.
   b. Turn the bulb holder counterclockwise and remove it (A, **Figure 105**).
   c. Push in on the bulb (B, **Figure 105**), turn it counterclockwise and remove it.
   d. Install the new bulb by reversing these steps.
3. Turn the ignition switch on and check the taillight and brake light operation.

Taillight/Brake Light Housing Removal/Installation

Refer to **Figure 106** and **Figure 107**.
1A. On 1999-2000 U.S. models and 1999-on U.K. models, perform the following:
   a. Remove the rear cowl as described in Chapter Sixteen.
   b. Remove the screws securing the mounting brackets (A, **Figure 108**).
   c. Remove the mounting brackets and remove the housing (B, **Figure 108**) from the rear cowl.
1B. On 2001-on U.S. models, perform the following:

10

a. Remove the seat and pillion seat as described in Chapter Sixteen.

b. Disconnect the electrical connectors at the back of the bulb holders (A, **Figure 109**).

c. Remove the nuts (B, **Figure 109**) securing the taillight/brake light assembly to the rear cowl.

d. Remove the cable straps and washers from the threaded studs on the housing.

e. Pull the housing (A, **Figure 110**) straight back out of the rear cowl.

2. Install by reversing these removal steps.

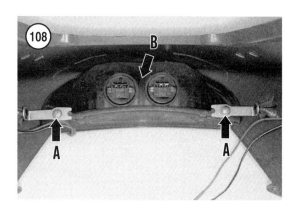

License Plate Light Replacement

1. Remove the license plate (B, **Figure 110**) from the bracket.

2. Remove the bolts, nuts and collars securing the license light assembly (C, **Figure 110**). Move the assembly off the rear fender.

3. On the backside of the assembly, remove the screws, license light cover and lens.

4. Push the bulb in and then turn it counterclockwise to remove it.

5. Install the bulb by reversing these steps.

6. Turn the ignition switch on and check the license plate light operation.

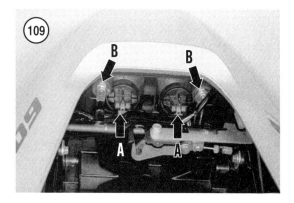

Combination Meter Indicator Light Bulb Replacement (1999-2000 Models)

> *NOTE*
> *On 2001-on models, the indicator lights are LED's and are not available separately. If one of the LED's fails, the printed circuit board must be replaced.*

1. Remove the combination meter as described in this chapter.

2. Carefully pry up and remove the bulb hole cap.

3. Using a flat blade screwdriver, turn the bulb 45° counterclockwise. Remove the bulb from the lower case.

4. Install a new bulb, turn it 45° clockwise and lock it into place.

5. Install the bulb hole cap and press it in until it bottoms.

6. Repeat for any remaining bulbs.

7. Install the combination meter as described in this chapter.

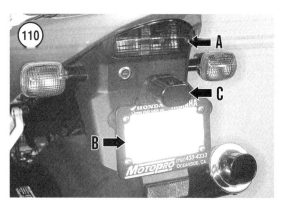

8. Turn the ignition switch on and check the indicator light operation.

COMBINATION METER

Removal/Installation

Refer to **Figure 111** and **Figure 112**.

1. Remove the seat and the front fairing as described in Chapter Sixteen.

2. Disconnect the negative battery cable as described in this chapter.

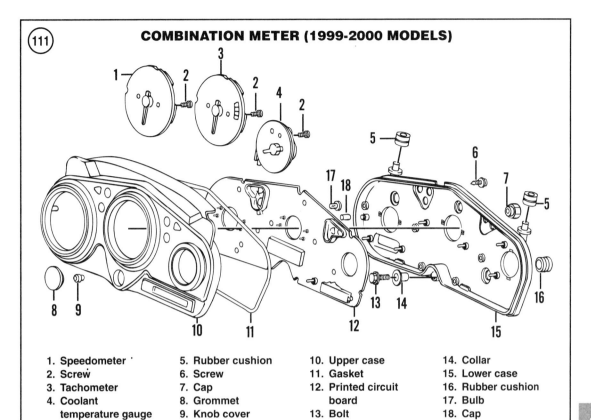

COMBINATION METER (1999-2000 MODELS)

1. Speedometer
2. Screw
3. Tachometer
4. Coolant temperature gauge
5. Rubber cushion
6. Screw
7. Cap
8. Grommet
9. Knob cover
10. Upper case
11. Gasket
12. Printed circuit board
13. Bolt
14. Collar
15. Lower case
16. Rubber cushion
17. Bulb
18. Cap

10

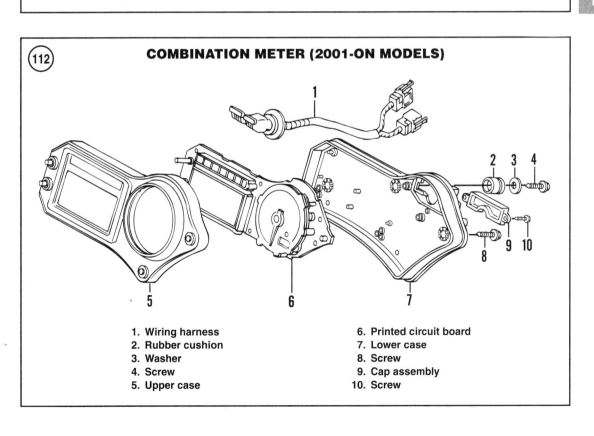

COMBINATION METER (2001-ON MODELS)

1. Wiring harness
2. Rubber cushion
3. Washer
4. Screw
5. Upper case
6. Printed circuit board
7. Lower case
8. Screw
9. Cap assembly
10. Screw

3A. On 1999-2000 models, perform the following:
  a. Remove the bolt cap and the meter mounting bolt.
  b. Disconnect the multi-pin electrical connector (**Figure 113**).
  c. Move the combination meter (**Figure 114**) away from the fairing mounting bracket and remove it.

3B. On 2001-on models, perform the following:
  a. Follow the combination meter wiring harness (**Figure 115**) on the left side and locate the nine-pin natural color and nine-pin black electrical connectors. Disconnect both connectors.
  b. Remove the three screws (**Figure 116**) securing the combination meter to the fairing mounting bracket.
  c. Remove the combination meter.

4. Install the combination meter by reversing these removal steps while noting the following:
  a. When installing the combination meter, align the mounting boss on the meter with the rubber grommets.
  b. Check the routing of the air temperature sensor wire.
  c. Start the engine and check all of the illumination lights and gauges for proper operation.

Disassembly/Assembly

This section describes disassembly of the combination meter assembly and, on 1999-2000 models, the replacement of the gauges. On 2001-on models, if any of the gauges are faulty, the printed circuit board must be replaced.

Refer to **Figure 111** and **Figure 112**.

1. Remove the combination meter as described in this section.

2A. On 1999-2000 models, perform the following:
  a. Remove the screws and separate the upper case from the lower case.
  b. Remove the mounting screws and remove the speedometer, tachometer or coolant temperature gauge from the printed circuit board.

2B. On 2001-on models, perform the following:
  a. Remove the screws and separate the upper case from the lower case.
  b. Remove the printed circuit board assembly from the upper case.

3. Reverse these steps to assemble the combination meter assembly.

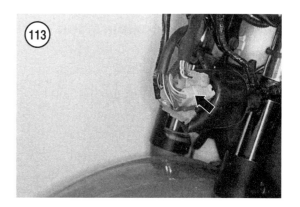

Voltage/Ground Inspection (All Models)

Disconnect the multi-pin electrical connector(s) from the combination meter assembly as previously described.

Voltage supply circuit

1. Connect a voltmeter positive lead to the black/brown wire terminal and the negative lead to ground. Turn the ignition switch to the ON position. There should be battery voltage.

2. If there is no battery voltage, check for an open circuit in the black/brown wire. Repair or replace the wiring harness.

3. Turn the ignition switch to the OFF position and disconnect the voltmeter.

Back-up voltage supply circuit

1. Connect a voltmeter positive lead to the red/green or red wire terminal and the negative lead to ground. There should be battery voltage at all times.

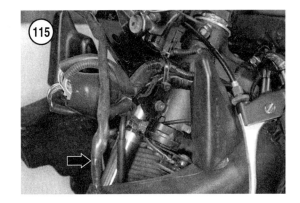

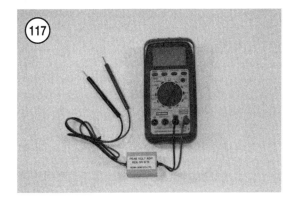

2. If there is no continuity, check for an open circuit in the red/green wire. Repair or replace the wiring harness.

3. Disconnect the ohmmeter.

Sensor ground circuit

1. Connect an ohmmeter to the green/black wire terminal and to ground. There should be continuity at all times.

2. If there is no continuity, check for an open circuit in the green/black wire. Repair or replace the wiring harness.

3. Disconnect the ohmmeter.

4. After the tests are completed, connect the multi-pin electrical connector(s) to the combination meter assembly.

TACHOMETER TEST

Testing (1999-2000 Models)

1. Disconnect the multi-pin electrical connector from the combination meter assembly as previously described.

2. Check that the speedometer and coolant temperature gauges function properly as described in this section.

3A. If they do not function properly, perform the *Voltage/Ground Inspection* in this chapter.

3B. If they function properly, perform the following:

    a. Disconnect the multi-pin electrical connector from the combination meter assembly as previously described.

    b. Connect a voltmeter positive lead to the yellow/green wire terminal and the negative lead to the green/black wire terminal. Turn the ignition switch to the ON position. There should be battery voltage.

    c. If there is battery voltage, replace the printed circuit board in the combination meter as described under *Combination Meter Disassembly/Assembly* in this chapter.

    d. If there is no battery voltage, check for an open circuit or short in the yellow/green wire. Repair or replace the wiring harness.

4. Turn the ignition switch to the OFF position and disconnect the voltmeter.

Testing (2001-On Models)

The Honda peak voltage adapter (part No. 07HGJ-0020100) and a digital multimeter (impedance 10M ohms/DCV minimum) are required for this test (**Figure 117**). Refer testing to a Honda dealership if these tools are not available.

NOTE
Refer to the manufacturer's instructions when using these tools.

10

1. Turn the ignition switch to the ON position and observe the tachometer needle. The needle should swing throughout the entire scale and then return to zero. If the needle does not move as indicated, perform the *Voltage/Ground Inspection* as described in this chapter.

2. Remove the front fairing as described in Chapter Sixteen.

3. Disconnect the nine-pin natural color and the nine-pin black electrical connectors from the main harness as previously described.

4. Check the combination meter electrical connectors and check for dirty or loose-fitting contacts.

5. Connect the positive peak voltage test lead to the tachometer yellow/green terminal in the nine-pin black connector and the negative lead to the green terminal in the nine-pin natural connector.

6. Start the engine and allow it to idle. Read the tachometer input voltage and note the following:

   a. If the reading is 10.5 volts minimum, and the tachometer is not working correctly, the tachometer is faulty and should be replaced.

   b. If the reading is below 10.5 volts, replace the engine control module (ECM) as described in this chapter.

   c. If the reading is 0 volts, continue with Step 7.

7. Disconnect the peak voltage adapter from the digital multimeter.

8. Remove the seat as described in Chapter Sixteen.

9. Disconnect the ECM 22-pin black connector (**Figure 118**).

10. Use an ohmmeter and check the yellow/green connector terminals for continuity between the tachometer and ECM. Continuity must be present between the tachometer and ECM.

   a. If there is no continuity, check for an open circuit in the wiring harness connecting the combination meter to the ECM unit.

   b. If there is continuity and the tachometer does not work correctly, the printed circuit board is faulty and should be replaced as described under *Combination Meter Disassembly/Assembly* in this chapter.

   c. Disconnect the ohmmeter.

11. Reconnect all electrical connectors.

12. Install the seat and the front fairing as described in Chapter Sixteen.

SPEEDOMETER/SPEED SENSOR

Removal/Installation

1. Remove the carburetor assembly or the throttle body assembly as described in Chapter Eight or Chapter Nine.

2. Follow the electrical cable from the speed sensor (**Figure 119**) and disconnect the three-pin black electrical connector from the harness.

3. Remove the bolts and remove the speed sensor from the upper surface of the crankcase. Refer to **Figure 119** and **Figure 120**.

4. Install by reversing these removal steps. Install a *new* O-ring seal on the sensor.

Speed System Inspection

1. Disconnect the multi-pin electrical connector from the combination meter assembly as previously described.

2. Check the combination meter electrical connector and check for dirty or loose-fitting contacts.

6. Disconnect the multi-pin electrical connector from the combination meter assembly as previously described.

7. Shift the transmission into NEUTRAL.

8. Turn the ignition switch to the ON position.

NOTE
In Step 9, connect the voltmeter leads to the connector terminals on the wiring harness side connector.

9. Connect a voltmeter positive lead to the pink/green wire terminal and the negative lead to the green/black wire terminal on the wire harness side of the connector.

10. Slowly rotate the rear wheel. There should be 0-5 pulse voltage.

11. If pulse voltage is present, replace the printed circuit board in the combination meter as described under *Combination Meter Disassembly/Assembly* in this chapter.

12. If there is no pulse voltage, check for an open circuit or short in the pink/green wire. Repair or replace the wiring harness.

13. If the pink/green wire is good, replace the speed sensor.

14. Turn the ignition switch to the OFF position and disconnect the voltmeter.

COOLANT TEMPERATURE GAUGE

System Inspection (1999-2000 Models)

NOTE
There is no system inspection procedure for the 2001-on models.

1. Check that the speedometer and tachometer gauges function properly as described in this section.

2A. If they do not function properly, perform the *Voltage/Ground Inspection* as described in this chapter.

2B. If they function properly, perform the following:
   a. Remove the left side faring as described in Chapter Sixteen.

NOTE
Figure 121 is shown with the carburetor assembly removed to better illustrate this step.

   b. Carefully reach through the opening in the left side of the frame (**Figure 122**) and dis-

3. Check that the tachometer and coolant temperature gauges function properly as described in this section.

4A. If they do not function properly, perform the *Voltage/Ground Inspection* as described in this chapter.

4B. If they function properly, proceed to Step 5.

5. Raise the rear wheel off the ground and support it on a swing arm stand (or centerstand on U.K. models).

connect the thermosensor wire connector (**Figure 121**) from the left side of the thermostat housing.

c. Use a jumper wire and ground the connector.

d. Turn the ignition switch to the ON position. The coolant temperature gauge needle should move to the *H* position.

e. If the needle moves as indicated, check the thermosensor as described in this section.

f. If the needle did not move, check for an open circuit in the green/blue wire.

g. If the green/blue wire is good, replace the printed circuit board in the combination meter as described under *Combination Meter Disassembly/Assembly* in this chapter.

h. Reconnect the thermosensor wire connector to the thermostat housing.

i. Install the left side faring as described in Chapter Sixteen.

THERMOSENSOR/ECT SENSOR (ALL MODELS)

On 1999-2000 models the thermosensor provides the signal for the coolant temperature gauge. On 2001-on models, with the advent of electronic fuel injection, the sensor is called the ECT sensor. The ECT sensor provides input for the engine control module (ECM) and the coolant temperature gauge. Sensor testing and replacement is identical to all models.

Testing/Replacement

The engine must be cold, preferably not operated for at least 12 hours, for this test.

1. Drain the engine coolant as described under *Coolant Change* in Chapter Three.

2. Remove the carburetor assembly or the throttle body assembly as described in Chapter Eight or Chapter Nine.

3A. On 1999-2000 models, perform the following:

a. Disconnect the connector from the thermosensor.

b. Unscrew and remove the thermosensor (**Figure 121**) from the left side of the thermostat housing.

3B. On 2001-on models, perform the following:

a. Disconnect the connector (A, **Figure 123**) from the ECT sensor.

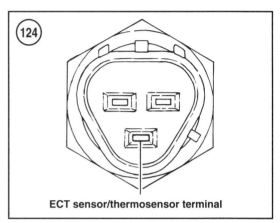

ECT sensor/thermosensor terminal

b. Unscrew and remove the ECT sensor (B, **Figure 123**) from the right side of the thermostat housing.

4. Place the sensor in a pan filled with a 50:50 mixture of coolant (water/antifreeze). Support the sensor so that the threads are not covered by the coolant and so that the bottom part of the sensor is at least 40 mm (1.57 in.) away from the bottom of the pan.

5. Place a shop thermometer in the pan. Use a thermometer that is rated higher than the test temperature.

6. Heat the coolant to the specified temperatures in **Table 7** and check the resistance between the terminal (**Figure 124**) on the sensor and ground (threads). Maintain the coolant at the specified temperature in **Table 7** for three minutes before testing.

7. If the resistance value is out of specification by more than 10%, replace the sensor.

8. Apply sealant to the threads of the sensor and install it into the thermostat housing. Tighten the sensor to the specification in **Table 9**.

9. Connect the electrical connector to the sensor.

10. Install all items removed.

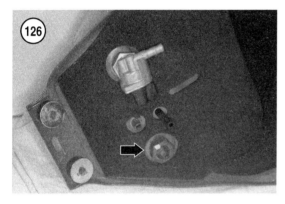

11. Refill the cooling system as described in Chapter Three.

LOW FUEL INDICATOR/FUEL RESERVE SENSOR (1999-2000 MODELS)

Testing

> *WARNING*
> *Some fuel may spill and fuel vapors are present when testing and replacing the fuel level sensor. Because gasoline is extremely flammable, perform this procedure away from all open flames, including appliance pilot lights and sparks. Do not smoke or allow someone who is smoking in the work area, as an explosion and fire may occur. Always work in a well-ventilated area. Wipe up spills immediately.*

Low fuel indicator does not go off

1. Raise and secure the fuel tank as described in Chapter Eight.

2. On the left side of the fuel tank, disconnect the fuel level sensor two-pin connector (one brown/black, one green/black).

3. Turn the ignition switch to the ON position and check the following:

    a. If the indicator on the combination meter (**Figure 125**) does not come on, replace the fuel level sensor as described in this chapter.

    b. If the indicator comes on, check for a short circuit in the brown/black wire.

Low fuel indicator does not come on

1. Check that the speedometer, tachometer and coolant temperature gauges function properly as described in this section.

2A. If they do not function properly, perform the *Voltage/Ground Inspection* as described in this chapter.

2B. If they function properly, perform the following:

    a. Raise and secure the fuel tank as described in Chapter Eight.

    b. Disconnect the fuel reserve level sensor two-pin connector.

    c. On the connector side, connect a jump wire between the two wires.

    d. Turn the ignition switch to the ON position and check the low fuel indicator.

    e. If the indicator comes on, replace the fuel reserve sensor as described in this chapter.

    f. If the indicator does not come on, check for an open circuit in the brown/black and green/black wires. If they are good, replace the printed circuit board in the combination meter as described in this chapter.

Removal/Installation

1. Remove the fuel tank as described in Chapter Eight. Drain the fuel out of the tank.

2. Place several heavy towels or a blanket on the workbench and turn the fuel tank upside down.

3. Unscrew and remove the fuel level indicator/fuel reserve sensor (**Figure 126**) from the base of the fuel tank. Remove the O-ring and discard it.

4. Install a *new* O-ring onto the sensor and install the sensor onto the fuel tank. Tighten the sensor to the specification in **Table 9**.

10

5. Install the fuel tank as described in Chapter Eight.

FUEL RESERVE SENSOR
(2001-ON MODELS)

Testing

WARNING
Some fuel may spill and fuel vapors are present when testing and replacing the fuel level sensor. Because gasoline is extremely flammable, perform this procedure away from all open flames, including appliance pilot lights and sparks. Do not smoke or allow someone who is smoking in the work area, as an explosion and fire may occur. Always work in a well-ventilated area. Wipe up spills immediately.

1. Turn the ignition switch to the ON position and make sure the fuel reserve indicator comes on.
2. If the fuel reserve indicator does not come on, perform the following:
   a. Remove the seat as described in Chapter Sixteen.
   b. Disconnect the fuel reserve three-pin black electrical connector (**Figure 127**).
   c. On the connector side, connect a jumer wire between the brown/black and green/black wires.
   d. Turn the ignition switch to the ON position and raise the sidestand. Check the fuel reserve indicator (**Figure 128**).

NOTE
The fuel reserve sensor is an integral part of the fuel pump assembly and cannot be replaced separately.

   e. If the indicator comes on, replace the fuel pump assembly as described in Chapter Nine.
   f. If the indicator does not come on, check for an open circuit in the brown/black and green/black wires.

TURN SIGNAL RELAY

Testing (1999-2000 Models)

1. Before troubleshooting the turn signal system, perform the following:

   a. Check the battery to make sure it is fully charged and in good condition. Refer to *Battery* in this chapter.
   b. Check for a burned-out bulb. Clean the bulb sockets of any corrosion.
   c. Make sure the bulb is the correct type and wattage. See **Table 6** for replacement bulbs.
   d. Check for a burned-out fuse.
   e. Check for loose connections in the circuit.
2. Remove the rear cowl as described in Chapter Sixteen.
3. Disconnect the three-pin black electrical connector from the turn signal relay (**Figure 129**).
4. On the wiring harness side of the connector, connect a jumper wire between the black/brown and gray wires.
5. Turn the ignition switch to the ON position.
6. Operate the turn signal switch and check the operation of the turn signals.
7. If the light does not come on, check for an open circuit in the black/brown and gray wires.
8. If the light comes on, use an ohmmeter and check for continuity between the green wire terminal and ground. Note the following:

Testing (2001-On Models)

1. Before troubleshooting the turn signal system, perform the following:

   a. Check the battery to make sure it is fully charged and in good condition. Refer to *Battery* in this chapter.

   b. Check for a burned-out bulb. Clean the bulb sockets of any corrosion.

   c. Make sure the bulb is the correct type and wattage. See **Table 6** for replacement bulbs.

   d. Check for a burned-out fuse.

   e. Check for loose connections in the circuit.

2. Place several heavy towels on the front fender to protect the finish.

3. Partially remove the front fairing as described in Chapter Sixteen to gain access to the turn signal relay located between the two headlight assemblies. Secure the fairing in this position.

4. Disconnect the three-pin black electrical connector from the turn signal relay (**Figure 130**).

5. Connect a jumper wire between the turn signal relay connector white/green and gray terminals.

6. Start the engine and operate the turn signal switch. Note the following:

   a. If the turn signal indicator light comes on, check the connector terminals for a loose or poor contact. If the connector terminals re okay, replace the turn signal relay.

   b. If the turn signal indicator light does not come on, check for an open wire in the wiring harness.

7. Connect the three-pin black electrical connector onto the turn signal relay (**Figure 130**).

10

HORN

Testing

1. Remove the front fairing as described in Chapter Sixteen.

2. Disconnect the electrical connectors from the horn (**Figure 131**, typical).

3. Connect a 12-volt battery across the horn terminals. The horn must sound loudly.

4. Replace the horn if it did not sound loudly in Step 3.

   a. If there is no continuity, check for an open circuit in the green wire.

   b. If there is continuity, check the connector terminals for a loose or poor contact. If the connector terminals are good, replace the turn signal relay.

9. Connect the three-pin black electrical connector onto the turn signal relay (**Figure 129**).

10. Install the rear cowl as described in Chapter Sixteen.

Removal/Installation

1. Remove the front fairing as described in Chapter Sixteen.

2. Disconnect the electrical connectors (**Figure 131**, typical) from the horn.

3. Remove the bolt and washer securing the horn to its mounting bracket and remove the horn.

4. Install by reversing these removal steps. Make sure the electrical connections are secure and corrosion-free.

5. Check the horn operation. If the horn does not work properly, perform the *Horn Testing* procedure in this section.

WARNING
Do not ride the motorcycle until the horn is working properly.

SWITCHES

Testing

Test the switches for continuity using an ohmmeter (see Chapter One) or a self-powered test light. Operate the switch in each of its operating positions and compare the results with the switch continuity diagram included with the wiring diagrams at the end of the manual. For example, **Figure 132** shows the continuity diagram for the horn switch. When the horn button is pressed, there should be continuity between the light green and black/brown terminals. The line joining the two terminals shows continuity (**Figure 132**). An ohmmeter connected between these two terminals should indicate continuity or a test light should illuminate. When the horn button is free, there should be no continuity between the same terminals.

1. Check the fuse as described under *Fuse* in this chapter.

2. Check the battery as described under *Battery* in this chapter. Charge the battery to the correct state of charge, if required.

3. Disconnect the negative battery cable at the battery if the switch connectors are not disconnected from the circuit.

CAUTION
Do not attempt to start the engine with the battery disconnected.

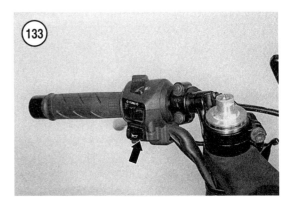

(132)	HORN SWITCH (TYPICAL)	
	Ho	BATS
FREE		
PUSH	●———————————●	
COLOR	Light green	Black/Brown

4. When separating two connectors, pull on the connector housings and not the wires.

5. After locating a defective circuit, check the connectors to make sure they are clean and properly connected. Check all wires going into a connector housing to make sure each wire is properly positioned and that the wire end is not loose.

6. Before disconnecting two connectors, check them for any locking tabs or arms that must be pushed or opened. If two connectors are difficult to separate, do not force them, as damage may occur.

7. When reconnecting electrical connector halves, push them together until they click or snap into place.

8. If the switch is operating erratically, chances are the contacts are oily, dirty or corroded. Disassemble the switch housing as described in this section to access the switch contacts. Clean the contacts as required.

9. If a switch or button does not perform properly, replace the switch as described in its appropriate section.

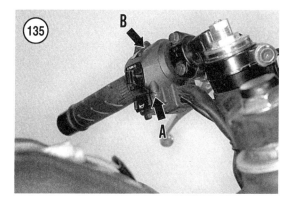

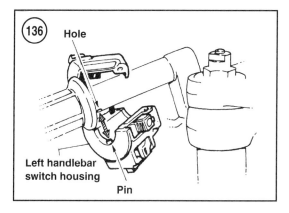

Hole

Left handlebar
switch housing

Pin

Left Handlebar Switch
Housing Replacement

The left handlebar switch housing (**Figure 133**) contains the dimmer, passing (U.K. models), horn and turn signal switches.

NOTE
The individual switches are not available separately. If one switch is damaged, replace the switch housing assembly.

1A. On 1999-2000 models, perform the following:
  a. Remove the front fairing and the left side air intake duct as described in Chapter Sixteen.
  b. Follow the wire harness from the left handlebar switch to the front of the steering stem. Locate the 13-pin black electrical connector and disconnect it.
1B. On 2001-on models, perform the following:
  a. Remove the front fairing as described in Chapter Sixteen.
  b. Follow the wire harness from the left handlebar switch to the front of the steering stem. Locate the nine-pin black electrical connector and disconnect it.
2. Disconnect the two wires from the clutch interlock switch (**Figure 134**) and the two wires from the horn.
3. Remove or cut any clamps securing the switch wiring harness to the handlebar. Do not cut the wiring harness.
4. Remove the handlebar switch housing screws (A, **Figure 135**) and open the switch assembly (B).
5. Remove the switch assembly from the handlebar.
6. Remove the wiring harness through the frame, then remove the switch housing from the handlebar.
7. Install the new switch housing, making sure to route the wiring harness along its original path.
8. Mount the left side handlebar switch housing onto the handlebar as follows:
  a. Install the left handlebar switch onto the handlebar.
  b. On 1999-2000 models, install the switch housing over the choke lever.
  c. Insert the switch housing pin into the hole in the handlebar (**Figure 136**). Try to twist the switch; it must not turn.
9. Install the front and rear switch housing screw. Tighten the front screw, then the rear screw. Tighten both screws securely.
10. Reconnect the switch housing electrical connectors.
11. Start the engine and check the operation of each switch.
12A. On 1999-2000 models, install the front fairing and the left side air intake duct as described in Chapter Sixteen.
12B. On 2001-on models, install the front fairing as described in Chapter Sixteen.

WARNING
Do not ride the motorcycle until each switch function is working properly.

10

Right Handlebar Switch
Housing Replacement

The right handlebar switch housing (**Figure 137**) contains the starter, engine stop and lighting switch (U.K. models).

NOTE
The switches mounted in the right handlebar switch housing are not available separately. If one switch is damaged, replace the switch housing assembly.

1A. On 1999-2000 models, perform the following:
    a. Remove the front fairing and the right side air intake duct as described in Chapter Sixteen.
    b. Follow the wire harness from the right handlebar switch to the front of the steering stem. Locate the three-pin red and four-pin red electrical connectors and disconnect them.
1B. On 2001-on models, perform the following:
    a. Remove the front fairing as described in Chapter Sixteen.
    b. Follow the wire harness from the right handlebar switch to the front of the steering stem. Locate the nine-pin black electrical connector and disconnect it.
2. Disconnect the two wires from the front brake light switch (**Figure 138**)
3. Remove or cut any clamps securing the switch wiring harness to the handlebar. Do not cut the wiring harness.
4. Remove the handlebar switch housing screws (A, **Figure 139**) and separate the switch housing (B) from around the handlebar and throttle grip.
5. Remove the wiring harness through the frame, then remove the switch housing from the handlebar.
6. Install the new switch housing, making sure to route the wiring harness along its original path.
7. Install the right side handlebar switch housing as follows:
    a. Align the switch housing locating pin with the hole in the handlebar and close the switch halves around the handlebar. Try to twist the switch; it must not turn.
    b. Install the front and rear switch housing screws and tighten securely.
8. Reconnect the switch housing electrical connectors.
9. Start the engine and check the operation of each switch.

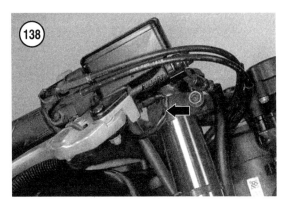

10A. On 1999-2000 models, install the front fairing and the left side air intake duct as described in Chapter Sixteen.

10B. On 2001-on models, install the front fairing as described in Chapter Sixteen.

WARNING
Do not ride the motorcycle until each switch and both throttle cables are working properly.

Ignition Switch Replacement

1A. On 1999-2000 models, remove the front fairing as described in Chapter Sixteen.

1B. On 2001-on models, remove the upper fork bridge as described under *Steering Stem Removal/Installation* in Chapter Thirteen.

2. Disconnect the ignition switch (**Figure 140**) four-pin electrical connector (**Figure 141**).

3. Remove the wire clamp from the switch wiring harness.

4A. On 1999-2000 models, perform the following:

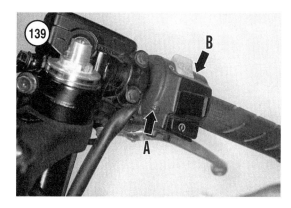

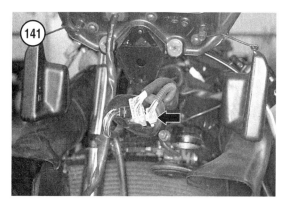

a. Remove the two T-40 Torx bolts securing the ignition switch to the bottom surface of the upper fork bridge.

b. Remove the ignition switch and wiring harness from the frame.

4B. On 2001-on models, perform the following:

a. Remove the two bolts securing the ignition switch to the top surface of the upper fork bridge.

b. Remove the ignition switch and wiring harness from the frame.

5. Install the new switch by reversing these removal steps while noting the following:

a. Apply a threadlocking compound onto the ignition switch mounting bolt threads and tighten the bolts securely.

b. Check the operation of the ignition switch.

Clutch Interlock Switch Testing/Replacement

The clutch interlock switch (**Figure 134**) is mounted in the clutch lever mounting bracket.

1. Disconnect the two electrical connectors at the clutch switch.

2. Switch an ohmmeter to the R × 1 scale, and then connect the ohmmeter leads across the two clutch switch terminals.

3. Read the ohmmeter scale while pulling in and then releasing the clutch lever. Note the following:

a. There must be continuity with the clutch lever pulled in and no continuity with the lever released.

b. Replace the clutch interlock switch if it fails to operate as described.

4. Remove the clutch interlock switch mounting screw and clutch switch.

5. Install a new clutch switch by reversing these removal steps.

Front Brake Light Switch Testing/Replacement

The front brake switch (**Figure 138**) is mounted on the front master cylinder assembly.

1. Disconnect the two electrical connectors at the front brake light switch.

2. Switch an ohmmeter to the R × 1 scale, then connect the ohmmeter leads across the two front brake light switch terminals.

3. Read the ohmmeter scale while pulling in and releasing the front brake lever. Note the following:

a. There must be continuity with the front brake lever pulled in and no continuity with the lever released.

b. Replace the front brake light switch if it fails to operate as described.

4. Remove the brake switch mounting screw and brake switch.

5. Reconnect the two electrical connectors at the front brake light switch.

10

6. Turn on the ignition switch and apply the front brake lever. Make sure the brake light illuminates.

WARNING
Do not ride the motorcycle until the rear brake light and front brake light switch work correctly.

Rear Brake Light Switch Testing/Replacement

The rear brake switch is mounted on the rear brake pedal assembly.

1. Remove the seat as described in Chapter Sixteen.

2. Follow the rear brake light switch wires (**Figure 142**) from the switch to the two-pin black electrical connector. Disconnect the connector.

3. Switch an ohmmeter to the R × 1 scale and connect the ohmmeter leads between the two rear brake light switch terminals.

4. Read the ohmmeter scale while applying and releasing the rear brake pedal. Note the following:

    a. There must be continuity with the rear brake pedal applied and no continuity with the pedal released.

    b. Replace the rear brake light switch if it fails to operate as described.

5. Remove the bolts (**Figure 143**) securing the right side footpeg bracket to frame. Move the bracket away from the frame.

NOTE
The following steps are shown with the right side footpeg bracket completely removed from the frame to better illustrate the steps.

6. Disconnect the return spring (A, **Figure 144**) from the rear brake light switch and remove the switch (B) from its mounting bracket and replace it with a new one.

7. Reconnect the spring and the rear brake light switch electrical connector.

8. Install the right side footpeg bracket to the frame and tighten the bolts to 26 N•m (19 ft.-lb.).

9. Adjust the rear brake light switch as described in Chapter Three.

10. Turn the ignition switch to the ON position and apply the rear brake pedal. Make sure the rear brake light operates correctly.

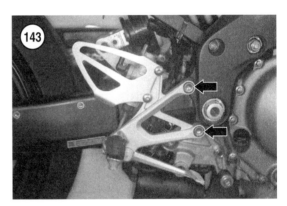

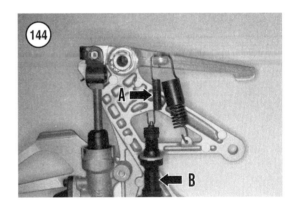

WARNING
Do not ride the motorcycle until the rear brake light and switch work correctly.

Oil Pressure Switch Testing/Replacement

The oil pressure switch is mounted in the back-side crankcase next to the coolant hose joint. If the oil pressure indicator light stays on when the engine is running, stop the engine and check the oil pressure (Chapter Three). If the oil pressure is within specification, perform the following.

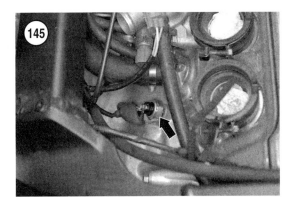

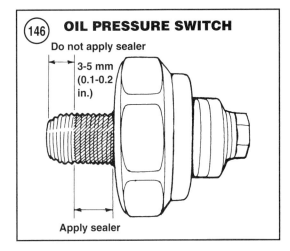

OIL PRESSURE SWITCH

Do not apply sealer

3-5 mm
(0.1-0.2
in.)

Apply sealer

damage. If the light does come on, replace the oil pressure switch.

4. Loosen and remove the oil pressure switch (**Figure 145**).

5. Wipe the switch threads in the lower crankcase to remove all oil and sealer residue.

6. Install the oil pressure switch as follows:

    a. Apply ThreeBond 1207B or an equivalent RTV sealant onto the oil pressure switch threads as shown in **Figure 146**. Do not apply sealant within 3-5 mm (0.1-0.2 in.) from the end of the switch threads.

NOTE
Allow the sealant to set for 10-15 minutes before installing the oil pressure switch.

    b. Install the oil pressure switch (**Figure 145**) and tighten it securely.

    c. Reconnect the wire onto the switch and slide the rubber boot back into place.

CAUTION
Do not overtighten the switch to correct an oil leak, as this may strip the crankcase threads. If oil leaks from the switch after installing it, remove the switch and clean all sealer residue from the oil switch and crankcase threads. Reseal and reinstall the switch.

7. Install the carburetor assembly or the throttle body as described in Chapter Eight or Chapter Nine.

8. Start the engine and observe the oil pressure indicator light. The light must go out within two seconds after starting the engine. If not, stop the engine and check for the cause of the low oil pressure.

Neutral Switch Testing/Replacement

The neutral switch is mounted in the lower left side of the crankcase beside the water pump assembly.

1. Remove the left side fairing panel as described in Chapter Sixteen.

2. Shift the transmission into NEUTRAL.

3. Disconnect the wire connector from the neutral switch (**Figure 147**).

1. Remove the carburetor assembly or the throttle body as described in Chapter Eight or Chapter Nine.

2. Remove the dust cover from the oil pressure switch (**Figure 145**).

3. Connect a jumper wire between the switch wire and a good engine ground. The oil pressure indicator should light when the ignition switch is turned ON. If the light does not come on, check the sub-fuse. Then check the wiring to the fuse box for

10

4. Switch an ohmmeter to the R × 1 scale. Connect one lead to the neutral switch terminal and the other ohmmeter lead to a good engine ground.

5. Read the ohmmeter scale with the transmission in NEUTRAL, and then in gear. Note the following:

    a. The ohmmeter must read continuity with the transmission in NEUTRAL.

    b. The ohmmeter must read infinity with the transmission in gear.

    c. If either reading is incorrect, check the wiring harness for damage or dirty or loose-fitting terminals. If the wiring harness is good, replace the neutral switch.

6. Loosen and remove the neutral switch (**Figure 148**) and washer.

7. Install the neutral switch with a *new* washer and tighten to 12 N•m (106 in.-lb.). Reconnect the wire onto the switch.

8. Start the engine and check the neutral switch indicator light operation with the transmission in NEUTRAL and in gear.

9. Install the left side fairing panel as described in Chapter Sixteen.

Sidestand Switch Testing/Replacement

The sidestand switch is mounted on the outer surface of the sidestand.

1. Support the motorcycle on level ground.

2. Block the front wheel so the motorcycle will not roll in either direction while on the jack or swing arm stand (or centerstand on U.K. models).

3A. On 1999-2000 models, remove the right side fairing panel as described in Chapter Sixteen.

3B. On 2001-on models, remove the fuel tank as described in Chapter Nine.

4. Trace the sidestand switch wire from the switch to the two-pin green connector. Disconnect the connector.

5. Switch an ohmmeter to the R × 1 scale. Connect the ohmmeter leads across the sidestand switch terminals in the connector.

6. Operate the sidestand in its up and down positions while reading the ohmmeter scale. Note the following:

    a. The ohmmeter must read continuity with the sidestand up.

    b. The ohmmeter must read infinity with the sidestand down.

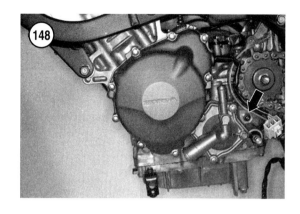

    c. If either reading is incorrect, check the wiring harness for damage or dirty or loose-fitting terminals. If the wiring harness is good, replace the sidestand switch.

7. Release the sidestand switch wiring harness from the frame hooks.

NOTE
Figure 149 *is shown with the sidestand removed to better illustrate the step.*

8. Remove the bolt and sidestand switch (**Figure 149**).

9. Clean the switch mounting area on the sidestand.

10. Align the switch pin with the hole in the sidestand and install the sidestand switch.

11. Install a new sidestand switch mounting bolt and tighten to 10 N•m (88 in.-lb.).

12A. On 1999-2000 models, install the right side fairing panel as described in Chapter Sixteen.

12B. On 2001-on models, install the fuel tank as described in Chapter Nine.

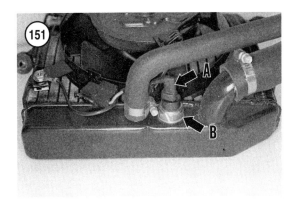

Cooling Fan Motor Switch Testing

The cooling fan motor switch is mounted on the left side of the radiator (**Figure 150**). It controls the radiator fan according to engine coolant temperature.

When troubleshooting the cooling fan motor switch, check the fan motor fuse. Also clean any rust or corrosion from the electrical terminals on the fan motor switch. If these items are good, refer to the appropriate failure.

Fan motor does not stop

1. Remove the left side fairing as described in Chapter Sixteen.
2. Turn the ignition switch to the OFF position and disconnect the fan motor switch connector (**Figure 150**), then turn the ignition switch ON again and note the operation of the fan motor.
3. If the fan motor stops, replace the fan motor switch as described in this section.
4. If the fan motor did not stop, check for a short circuit in the wire between the ignition switch and fan switch.

Fan motor does not start

1. Start the engine and warm it up to normal operating temperature.
2. Disconnect the connector at the fan motor switch (**Figure 150**).
3. Connect a jumper wire between the fan motor switch connector and ground. Then turn the ignition switch to the ON position and check the fan motor operation. Note the following:
    a. If the fan motor starts, perform Step 4.
    b. If the fan motor did not start, go to Step 5.
4. Check the connector at the fan motor switch for a dirty or loose fitting terminal. If the connector is in good condition, replace the fan motor switch and retest.
5. Using a voltmeter, check for voltage between the fan motor switch connector and ground. Note the following:
    a. If there is battery voltage, the fan motor is damaged. Replace the fan motor as described in Chapter Nine.
    b. If there is no voltage reading, perform Step 6.
6. Check for the following conditions:
    a. Damaged fan circuit wiring harness.
    b. Blown fuse. See *Fuses* in this chapter.

10

Fan Motor Switch Replacement

1. Drain the cooling system as described in Chapter Three.

> *NOTE*
> *Figure 151 is shown with the radiator removed to better illustrate the step. The switch can be replaced with the radiator in the frame.*

2. Disconnect the electrical connector (A, **Figure 151**) at the fan motor switch.
3. Remove the fan motor switch (B, **Figure 151**) and O-ring.
4. Install a *new* O-ring onto the fan motor switch.
5. Install the fan motor switch and tighten to 18 N•m (13 ft.-lb.).

FUSES

Whenever a fuse blows, determine the cause before replacing the fuse. Usually, the trouble is a short circuit in the wiring. Worn-through insulation or a short to ground from a disconnected wire may cause this.

> *CAUTION*
> *If replacing a fuse, make sure the ignition switch is turned to the OFF position. This lessens the chance of a short circuit.*

> *CAUTION*
> *Never substitute any metal object for a fuse. Never use a higher amperage fuse than specified. An overload could cause a fire and the complete loss of the motorcycle.*

Main Fuse

The 30-amp main fuse is mounted on the starter relay switch. The starter relay switch is mounted underneath the seat. To check or replace the main fuse, perform the following:

1. Turn the ignition switch to the OFF position.
2. Remove the seat and the rear cowl as described in Chapter Sixteen.
3. Disconnect the electrical connector (**Figure 152**) from the starter relay switch.
4. Remove the main fuse (**Figure 153**) and inspect it. Replace the fuse if it has blown (**Figure 154**).

> *NOTE*
> *A spare 30-amp main fuse is stored in the bottom of the starter relay switch rubber holder.*

5. Reconnect the starter relay switch electrical connector.
6. Reinstall the starter relay switch onto its mounting brackets.
7. Reinstall the rear cowl and the seat as described in Chapter Sixteen.

Fuse Box

The fuse box is mounted underneath the seat. To identify an individual fuse and its amperage, refer to the decal mounted on the top of the fuse box cover and the wiring diagram at the end of this book.

If a fuse in the fuse box blows, perform the following:

1. Turn the ignition switch to the OFF position.

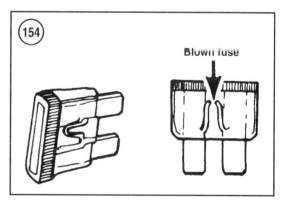

Blown fuse

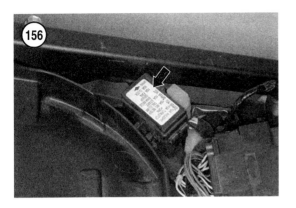

2. Remove the seat as described in Chapter Sixteen.

3. Remove the fuse box cover. Refer to **Figure 155** for 1999-2000 models or **Figure 156** for 2001-on models.

4. Remove and inspect the fuse (**Figure 157**). Replace the fuse if it has blown (**Figure 154**).

NOTE
A spare 10- and 20-amp fuse is stored in the fuse box.

5. Install the fuse box cover.

6. Install the seat as described in Chapter Sixteen.

WIRING DIAGRAMS

Color wiring diagrams for all models are located at the end of this manual.

10

Table 1 BATTERY SPECIFICATIONS

Type	Maintenance-free (sealed)*
Capacity	
1999-2000 models	12 volt 8 amp hour
2001-on models	12 volt 8.6 amp hour
Current leakage (draw)	
1999-2000 models	0.1 mA maximum
2001-on models	2.0 mA maximum
Voltage (at 20° C [68° F])	
Fully charged	13.0-13.2 volts
Need charging	Below 12.3 volts
Charging current	
Normal	0.9 amps at 5-10 hours
Quick	
1999-2000 models	4.0 amps at 1 hour
2001-on models	4.5 amps at 1/2 hour

*A maintenance-free battery is installed on all models described in this manual. Because this type of battery requires a high-voltage charging system, do not install a standard type battery.

Table 2 ALTERNATOR AND CHARGING SYSTEM SPECIFICATIONS

Alternator	
Type	Three-phase AC

(continued)

Table 2 ALTERNATOR AND CHARGING SYSTEM SPECIFICATIONS (continued)

Alternator (continued)	
Capacity	
1999-2000 models	343 watts at 5000 rpm
2001-on models	433 watts at 5000 rpm
Regulated voltage	13.5-15.5 V at 5000 rpm
Stator coil resistance	0.1-1.0 ohm*

*Test must be made at an ambient temperature of 20° C (68° F). Do not test when the engine or component is hot.

Table 3 MAINTENANCE-FREE BATTERY VOLTAGE READINGS

State of charge	Voltage reading
100%	13.0-13.2
75%	12.8
50%	12.5
25%	12.2
0%	12.0 volts or less

Table 4 IGNITION SYSTEM SPECIFICATIONS*

Ignition coil peak voltage	100 volts minimum
Ignition pulse generator peak voltage	0.7 volt minimum
Ignition timing (F mark)	
1999-2000 models	10° BTDC at idle
2001-on models	13° BTDC at idle

* Testing must be performed with a peak voltage tester. See text for further information.

Table 5 STARTER SPECIFICATIONS

Item	New	Service limit
Starter motor brush length	12.0-13.0 mm (0.47-0.51 in.)	6.5 mm (0.26 in.)
Starter driven gear boss outside diameter	51.699-51.718 mm (2.0354-2.0361 in.)	51.684 mm (2.0348 in.)

Table 6 REPLACEMENT BULBS

Item	Wattage × quantity
Headlight (high/low beam)	
1999-2000 models	60/55W × 2
2001-on models	55/55W × 2
Position light*	5W
Front turn signal/running light	
(U.S. and Canada models)	23/8W × 2
Front turn signal, front and rear (U.K. models)	21W × 2
Rear turn signal	23W × 2
(U.S. and Canada models)	23/8W × 2
Rear turn signal, front and rear (U.K. models)	21W × 2

(continued)

Table 6 REPLACEMENT BULBS (continued)

Item	Wattage × quantity
Tail/brake light	5/21W
License plate light	5W
Instrument illumination light	
1999-2000 models	1.1W × 3
2001-on models	LED
Turn signal indicator light	
1999-2000 models	1.1W × 2
2001-on models	LED
High beam indicator light	
1998-2000 models	1.1W
2001-on models	LED
Neutral indicator light	
1998-2000 models	1.1W
2001-on models	LED
Oil pressure indicator light	
1998-2000 models	1.1W
2001-on models	LED
Low pressure indicator	LED
MIL-FI warning indicator (2001-on models)	LED

*Position light on models so equipped.

Table 7 SENSOR AND SWITCH TEST READINGS

Item	Test readings
Coolant temperature gauge thermosensor	
1999-2000 models	
At 80° C (176° F)	47-57 ohms
At 120° C (248° F)	14-18 ohms
ECT sensor	
2001-on models	
At 80° C (176° F)	2100-2600 ohms
At 120° C (248° F)	650-730 ohms
Fan motor switch	
Starts to close (ON)	98-102° C (208-216° F)
Stops opening (OFF)	93-97° C (199-207° F)

10

Table 8 FUSE SPECIFICATIONS

Main fuse	30 amp
FI fuse (2001-on models)	20 amp
Sub-fuse (1999-2000 models)	
Headlight, passing	10 amp
Ignition, starter, fuel solenoid	10 amp
Turn signals, tail/brake light, horn, meters	10 amp
Cooling fan motor	10 amp
Sub-fuse (2001-on models)	
Headlight	10 amp
Neutral, oil, temp, tachometer, speedometer, position, horn, tail/brake light	10 amp
Turn signals, engine stop, horn and passing	10 amp
Starter, bank angle sensor	10 amp
Combination meter	10 amp
Cooling fan motor	10 amp

Table 9 ELECTRICAL SYSTEM TORQUE SPECIFICATIONS

Item	N•m	in.-lb.	ft.-lb.
Alternator			
Rotor bolt	103	–	76
Stator coil bolts	12	106	–
Starter clutch Torx bolts	16	–	12
Cooling fan motor switch*	18	–	13
ECT sensor (2001-on models)	23	–	17
Fuel reserve sensor			
(1999-2000 models)	23	–	17
Ignition switch bolts	25	–	18
Neutral switch	12	106	–
Pulse generator rotor bolt	59	–	44
Right side footpeg bracket bolts	26	–	19
Side stand switch bolt	10	88	–
Thermosensor (1999-2000 models)*	10	88	–
*Apply sealant to sensor threads.			

CHAPTER ELEVEN

COOLING SYSTEM

This chapter describes the repair and replacement of cooling system components. **Table 1** and **Table 2** at the end of the chapter list cooling system specifications. For electrical test procedures, refer to Chapter Ten. For routine cooling system maintenance, refer to Chapter Three.

COOLING SYSTEM INSPECTION

The pressurized cooling system consists of the radiator, water pump, radiator cap, thermostat, electric cooling fan and coolant reserve tank.

WARNING
*Do not remove the radiator cap (**Figure 1**) when the engine is hot. The coolant is very hot and is under pressure. Severe scalding could result if the coolant contacts skin.*

WARNING
The radiator fan and fan switch are connected directly to the battery. Whenever the engine is warm or hot, the fan may start even with the ignition switch turned OFF. Never work around the fan or touch the fan until the engine is completely cool.

CAUTION
Drain and flush the cooling system at the interval listed in Chapter Three. Refill with a mixture of ethylene glycol antifreeze (formulated for aluminum engines) and distilled water. Do not reuse the old coolant, as it deteriorates with use. Do not operate the cooling system with only distilled water, even in climates where antifreeze protection is not required; doing so

*will promote internal engine corrosion. Refer to **Coolant Change** in Chapter Three.*

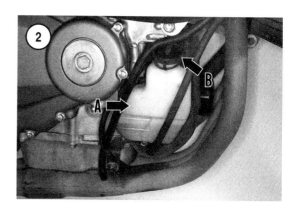

> *NOTE*
> *Waste antifreeze is toxic and may never be discharged into storm sewers, septic systems, or onto the ground. Place used antifreeze in the original container and dispose of it according to local regulations. Do not store coolant where it is accessible to children or pets.*

It is important to keep the coolant level to the FULL mark on the coolant reserve tank. Refer to A, **Figure 2** for 1999-2000 models or A, **Figure 3** for 2001-on models.

1. Check the level with the engine at normal operating temperature and the motorcycle held upright.

2. If the level is low, remove the reservoir tank cap and add coolant to the reserve tank, not to the radiator. Refer to B, **Figure 2** or B, **Figure 3**.

3. Check the coolant hoses and clamps for looseness or damage.

4. Start the engine and allow it to idle. If steam is observed at the muffler, a head gasket might be damaged. If enough coolant leaks into the cylinder, the cylinder could hydrolock, thus preventing the engine from being cranked. Coolant may also be present in the engine oil. If the oil on the dipstick is foamy or milky-looking, there is coolant in the oil. If so, correct the problem before returning the motorcycle to service.

> *CAUTION*
> *If the engine oil is contaminated with coolant, change the oil and filter after performing the repair.*

5. Check the radiator for clogged or damaged fins. Refer radiator repair to a Honda dealership or a radiator repair shop.

6. Check all coolant hoses for cracks or damage. Replace all questionable parts. Make sure the hose clamps are tight, but not so tight that they cut the hoses. Refer to *Hoses and Hose Clamps* in this chapter.

7. When troubleshooting the cooling system for loss of coolant, pressure test the system as described in Chapter Three.

HOSES AND HOSE CLAMPS

Hoses deteriorate with age. Replace them periodically or whenever they show signs of cracking or leakage. To be safe, replace the hoses every two years. The spray of hot coolant from a cracked hose can injure the rider and passenger. Loss of coolant can also cause the engine to overheat and cause damage.

Whenever any component of the cooling system is removed, inspect the hoses and clamps to determine if replacement is necessary.

Inspection

1. With the engine cool, check the cooling hoses for brittleness, hardness or cracks. Replace hoses in this condition.

2. With the engine hot, examine the hoses for swelling along the entire hose length. Replace hoses that show signs of swelling.

3. Check the area around each hose clamp. Signs of rust around clamps indicate possible hose leakage from a damaged or over-tightened clamp.

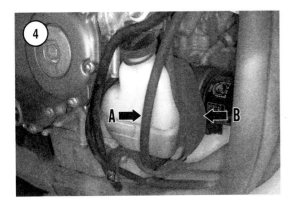

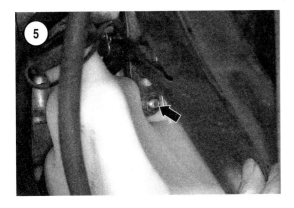

Replacement

Perform hose replacement when the engine is cool.

1. Drain the cooling system as described under *Coolant Change* in Chapter Three.

2. Loosen the hose clamps from the hose to be replaced. Slide the clamps along the hose and out of the way.

3. Twist the hose end to break the seal and remove it from the connecting joint. If the hose has been on for some time, it may have become fused to the joint. If so, insert a small screwdriver or pick tool between the hose and joint. While working the tool around the joint, carefully pry the hose loose with a thin screwdriver.

> *CAUTION*
> *Do not apply excessive force to a hose when attempting to remove it. Many of the hose connectors are fragile and can be easily damaged.*

4. Examine the connecting joint for cracks or other damage. Repair or replace parts as required. Remove rust and corrosion with a wire brush.

5. Inspect the hose clamps and replace if necessary. The hose clamps are as important as the hoses. If they do not hold the hose in place tightly, coolant will leak.

6. Slide the hose clamp over the outside of the hose and then install the hose over its connecting joint. Make sure the hose clears all obstructions and is routed properly.

> *NOTE*
> *If it is difficult to install a hose on a joint, apply some antifreeze into the end of the hose where it seats onto its connecting joint. This usually aids installation.*

7. With the hose positioned correctly on the joint, position the clamp back away from end of the hose slightly. Tighten the clamp securely, but not so much that the hose is damaged.

> *NOTE*
> *If installing coolant hoses onto the engine while it is removed from the frame, check the position of the hose clamp(s) to make sure it can be loosened when installed in the frame.*

8. Refill the cooling system as described under *Coolant Change* in Chapter Three. Start the engine and check for leaks. Retighten hose clamps as necessary.

COOLANT RESERVE TANK

Removal/Installation (1999-2000 Models)

1. Park the motorcycle on level ground.

2. Remove the right side fairing panel as described in Chapter Sixteen.

3. Slide the rubber heat guard away from the reserve tank.

4. Disconnect the siphon tube (A, **Figure 4**) at the bottom of the reserve tank and drain the antifreeze. Plug the hose opening.

5. Remove the breather hose from the frame bracket.

6. Pull back on the rubber heat guard (B, **Figure 4**) and remove the bolt (**Figure 5**) securing the reserve tank to the frame. Remove the reserve tank and heat guard.

7. Install the coolant reserve tank by reversing these removal steps while noting the following:

11

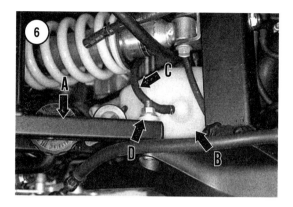

a. Install the mounting bolt but do not overtighten.

b. Refill the coolant reserve tank with a 50:50 mixture of antifreeze and distilled water as described in Chapter Three.

c. Check the hoses for leaks.

Removal/Installation (2001-On Models)

1. Remove the seat rail (A, **Figure 6**) as described in Chapter Sixteen.

2. Pull the reserve tank up and off the engine hanger collar.

3. Disconnect the siphon tube at the bottom of the reserve tank and drain the antifreeze. Plug the hose opening.

4. Remove the reserve tank (B, **Figure 6**) from the frame.

5. Disconnect the radiator overflow hose (C, **Figure 6**) and the siphon hose from the reserve tank. Plug the hose openings.

6. Inspect the coolant reserve tank and replace if it is leaking or damaged.

7. Install the coolant reserve tank by reversing these removal steps while noting the following:

a. Install the reserve tank mounting tab over the frame engine hanger collar (D, **Figure 6**).

b. Refill the coolant reserve tank with a 50:50 mixture of antifreeze and distilled water as described in Chapter Three.

c. Check the hoses for leaks.

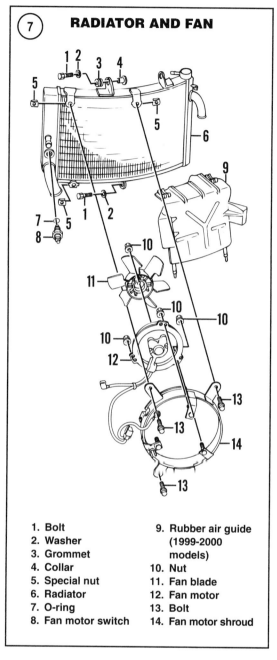

RADIATOR AND FAN

1. Bolt	9. Rubber air guide
2. Washer	(1999-2000
3. Grommet	models)
4. Collar	10. Nut
5. Special nut	11. Fan blade
6. Radiator	12. Fan motor
7. O-ring	13. Bolt
8. Fan motor switch	14. Fan motor shroud

RADIATOR

WARNING
The radiator fan and fan switch are connected to the battery. Whenever the engine is warm or hot, the fan may start with the ignition switch turned off. Never work around the fan or touch the fan until the engine is completely cool. If work is required in the

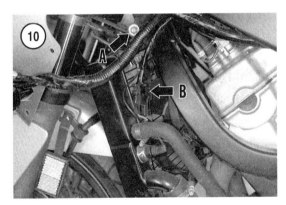

fan area when the engine is hot, disconnect the negative battery cable.

Removal/Installation

The radiator and fan are removed as an assembly. Refer to **Figure 7**.

1. Park the motorcycle on level ground. Support the rear of the motorcycle securely on a swing arm motorcycle stand.

2. Disconnect the negative battery cable at the battery as described in Chapter Ten.

3. Remove both side fairing panels and the front inner fairing panel as described in Chapter Sixteen.

4. Drain the cooling system as described in Chapter Three.

5. Disconnect the siphon hose (A, **Figure 8**) and the air bleed hose (B) from the radiator.

6. On the right side, disconnect the upper hose (**Figure 9**) from the radiator.

7. On the left side, loosen the upper bolt (A, **Figure 10**) securing the top of the radiator to the frame.

8. On the left side, disconnect the lower radiator hose (A, **Figure 11**) and the oil cooler hose (B) from the radiator.

9. Disconnect the radiator fan sub-harness two-pin black electrical connector (B, **Figure 10**).

10. Remove the lower bolt, nut and washer (**Figure 12**) securing the bottom of the radiator to the lower frame bracket.

11. On the left side, remove the upper bolt and washer (A, **Figure 10**) securing the top of the radiator to the frame.

12. Pull the radiator toward the right side and disengage the upper mount and release the radiator from the frame boss grommet.

11

13. Carefully remove the radiator down and out of the frame. Do not make contact with the lower frame bracket. Remove the radiator.

14. On 1999-2000 models, carefully remove the rubber air guide from the frame.

15. Install by reversing these removal steps, plus the following:

    a. Make sure the rubber grommets and flange collars are in place in the mounting holes in the radiator. These help to prevent road shocks and vibration from damaging the mounting brackets.

    b. When installing the radiator, align the grommet on top of the radiator with the mounting boss on the right side of the frame.

    c. Make sure the fan motor electrical connector is free of corrosion, then reconnect.

    d. Refill the cooling system with the recommended type and quantity of coolant as described in Chapter Three.

    e. Check the hoses for leaks.

Inspection

1. Inspect the radiator cap top and bottom seals (**Figure 13**) for deterioration or damage. Check the spring for damage. Pressure test the radiator cap as described under *Cooling System Inspection* in Chapter Three. Replace the radiator cap if necessary.

2. Flush off the exterior of the radiator with a water hose on low pressure. Spray both the front and the back to remove all dirt and debris. Carefully use a whiskbroom or stiff paintbrush to remove any stubborn debris.

> *CAUTION*
> *Do not press too hard on the cooling fins and tubes, as they may be damaged and cause a leak.*

3. Carefully straighten out any bent cooling fins with a broad-tipped screwdriver.

4. Check for cracks or coolant leakage (usually a moss-green colored residue) at the filler neck (**Figure 14**), the various hose fittings (A, **Figure 15**) and the upper and lower tank seams (**Figure 16**).

5. Check the mounting bracket (**Figure 17**) and locating tabs (**Figure 18**) for cracks or damage.

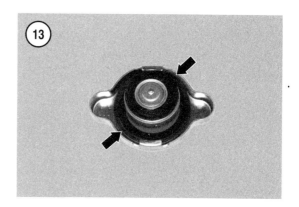

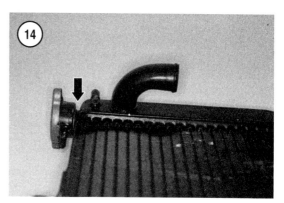

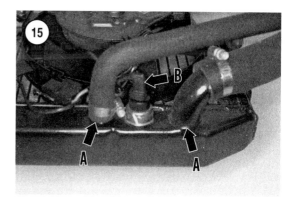

6. To prevent oxidation to the radiator, touch up any area where the black paint is worn off. Use a good-quality spray paint. Do not apply heavy coats, as this cuts down on the cooling efficiency of the radiator.

COOLING FAN

The cooling fan is mounted on the backside of the radiator.

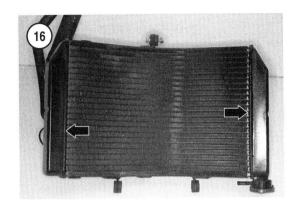

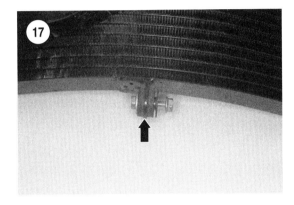

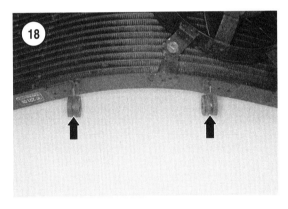

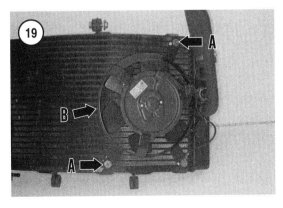

Testing

To test the fan motor and switch, refer to *Fan Motor Switch Testing* in Chapter Ten.

Removal/Installation

Refer to **Figure 7**.
1. Remove the radiator as described in this chapter.
2. Disconnect the fan motor switch connector (B, **Figure 15**) at the switch.
3. Remove the bolts (A, **Figure 19**) and then remove the fan motor/shroud assembly (B) from the radiator.
4. To remove the fan blade, remove the nut securing the fan blade to the fan motor. Then remove the fan blade.
5. Remove the nuts and remove the fan motor from the shroud.
6. Install by reversing these removal steps while noting the following.
7. If the fan blade was removed, install it as follows:

    a. Align the flat surface in the fan blade with the fan motor shaft flat and install the fan blade.

    b. Apply a threadlocking compound to the cooling fan blade nut and tighten to 3 N•m (27 in.-lb.).

    c. Install the fan motor nuts and tighten to 5 N•m (44 in.-lb.).

Fan Motor Switch

To replace the cooling fan motor switch, refer to *Fan Motor Switch Testing* in Chapter Ten.

THERMOSTAT

Removal/Installation

Refer to **Figure 20**.
1. Drain the cooling system as described under *Coolant Change* in Chapter Three.
2A. On 1999-2000 models, remove the carburetor assembly as described in Chapter Eight.
2B. On 2001-on models, remove the throttle body assembly as described in Chapter Nine.

> *NOTE*
> *If necessary, loosen the hose clamps and disconnect the two hoses from the thermostat housing cover.*

11

3. Remove the bolts securing the thermostat housing cover (**Figure 21**). Lift off and remove the thermostat housing cover from the housing.

4. Remove the thermostat and the rubber seal (A, **Figure 22**).

5. If necessary, test the thermostat as described in this chapter.

6. Install a *new* new rubber seal onto the thermostat.

7. Install the thermostat and rubber seal into the thermostat housing. Align the thermostat with the air bleed hole (B, **Figure 22**) facing toward the rear of the frame.

8. Install the thermostat housing cover onto the thermostat housing. Tighten the bolts to 12 N•m (106 in.-lb.).

9. Refill the cooling system with the recommended type and quantity of coolant as described under *Coolant Change* in Chapter Three.

Inspection

Test the thermostat to ensure proper operation as follows:

NOTE
Do not allow the thermometer or thermostat to touch the sides or bottom of the pan, or a false reading will result.

1. Suspend the thermostat in a pan of water (**Figure 23**) and place a thermometer in the pan of water. Use a thermometer that is rated higher than the test temperature.

2. Gradually heat the water and continue to gently stir the water until it reaches the temperature specified in **Table 1**. At this temperature, the thermostat should start to open.

3. Continue to heat the water to the *fully open* temperature. The minimum valve lift is 8 mm (0.3 in.) at 95° C (203° F).

4. Replace the thermostat if it remains open at normal room temperature or stays closed after the specified temperature has been reached during the test procedure. Make sure the replacement thermostat has the same temperature rating.

NOTE
After the specified temperature is reached, it may take three to five minutes for the valve to open completely.

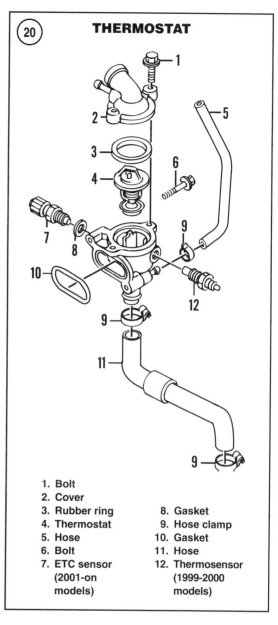

THERMOSTAT

1. Bolt
2. Cover
3. Rubber ring
4. Thermostat
5. Hose
6. Bolt
7. ETC sensor (2001-on models)
8. Gasket
9. Hose clamp
10. Gasket
11. Hose
12. Thermosensor (1999-2000 models)

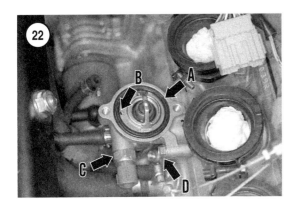

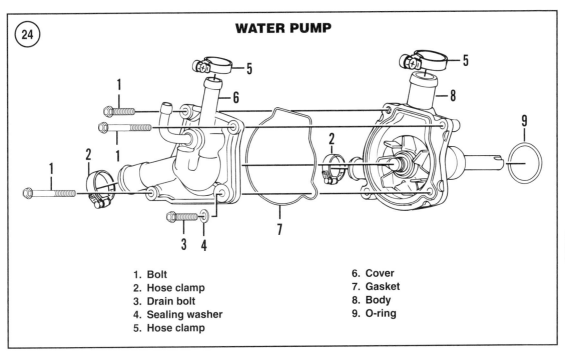

WATER PUMP

1. Bolt
2. Hose clamp
3. Drain bolt
4. Sealing washer
5. Hose clamp
6. Cover
7. Gasket
8. Body
9. O-ring

11

THERMOSTAT HOUSING

Removal/Installation

1. Remove the thermostat as described in this chapter.

2A. On 1999-2000 models, perform the following:

  a. Disconnect the thermosensor connector from the left side of the housing.

  b. Unscrew and remove the thermosensor from the left side of the thermostat housing.

2B. On 2001-on models, perform the following:

  a. Disconnect the ECT sensor (C, **Figure 22**) connector from the right side of the thermostat housing.

  b. Disconnect the fast idle wax unit coolant hose and bypass hose from the housing.

3. Remove the bolts (D, **Figure 22**) and remove the thermostat housing from the cylinder head.

4. Thoroughly clean the mating surface on the cylinder head of all residue.

5. Install a *new* O-ring seal onto the groove in the thermostat housing.

6. Install the thermostat housing onto the cylinder head and tighten the bolts securely.

7. Install the thermostat as described in this chapter.

WATER PUMP

The water pump (**Figure 24**) is mounted on the left side of the engine.

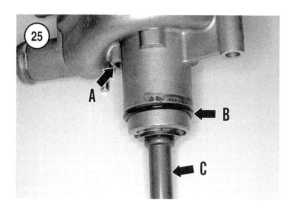

The water pump requires no routine maintenance and replacement parts are unavailable. Replace the complete unit if it is defective.

Pre-inspection

NOTE
The following photographs are shown with the water pump removed to better illustrate the steps. These pre-inspection steps can be performed with the water pump installed on the engine.

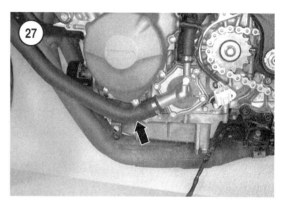

Check the water pump inspection hole (A, **Figure 25**) for leakage. If coolant leaks from the passage, an internal seal is damaged; replace the water pump unit. If there is no indication of coolant leakage from the inspection hole, pressure test the cooling system as described under *Cooling System Inspection* in Chapter Three.

Check the drain bolt and sealing washer (**Figure 26**) for leakage. If necessary, replace the sealing washer and tighten the bolt securely.

Removal

1. Remove the left side fairing as described in Chapter Sixteen.
2. Drain the engine oil as described under *Engine Oil and Filter Change* in Chapter Three.
3. Drain the cooling system as described under *Coolant Change* in Chapter Three.
4. Disconnect the lower radiator hose (**Figure 27**) from the water pump inlet fitting.
5. Disconnect the oil cooler hose (**Figure 28**) from the water pump outlet fitting.
6. Disconnect the bypass hose (**Figure 29**) from the water pump inlet fitting.

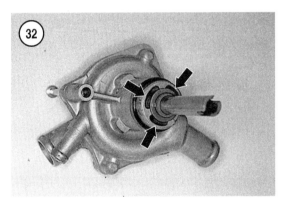

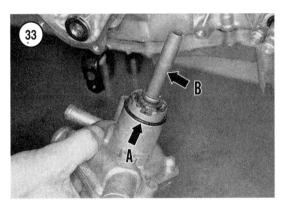

7. Disconnect the hose (**Figure 30**) from the water pump outlet fitting.

8. Remove the two mounting bolts (**Figure 31**) securing the water pump.

9. Withdraw the water pump from the crankcase.

10. Inspect the water pump as described in this chapter.

Installation

1. Apply a molybdenum oil solution into the holes (**Figure 32**) in the water pump body.

2. Install a *new* water pump body O-ring (A, **Figure 33**).

3. Lubricate the O-rings with water-resistant grease.

4. Align the groove in the impeller shaft (B, **Figure 33**) with the oil pump shaft and install the water pump. If necessary, slightly rotate the impeller to align the water pump shaft with the oil pump shaft.

5. Push the water pump body onto the crankcase until it bottoms. Do not install any mounting bolts until the body is seated flush onto the crankcase.

6. Align the water pump mounting bolt holes with the crankcase bolt holes. Install and tighten the bolts (**Figure 31**) to 12 N•m (106 in.-lb.).

7. Connect the hose (**Figure 30**) onto the water pump outlet fitting.

8. Connect the bypass hose (**Figure 29**) onto the water pump inlet fitting.

9. Connect the oil cooler hose (**Figure 28**) onto the water pump outlet fitting.

10. Connect the lower radiator hose (**Figure 27**) onto the water pump inlet fitting.

11. Refill the engine with oil as described in Chapter Three.

12. Refill the cooling system with the recommended type and quantity of coolant as described in Chapter Three.

Disassembly/Inspection/Assembly

NOTE
The water pump cover and the two water pump O-rings are available separately, but no other replacement parts are available. If any part of the water pump is defective, it must be replaced as a unit.

11

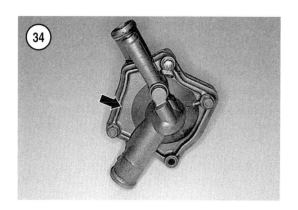

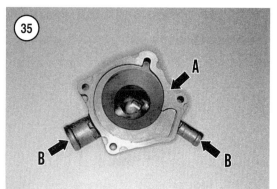

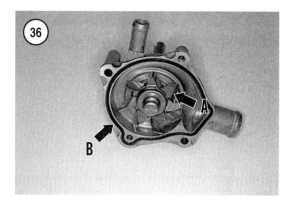

1. Remove the water pump assembly as described in this section.

2. If still attached, remove the bolts securing the cover (**Figure 34**) and remove the cover.

3. Inspect the water pump cover (A, **Figure 35**) for corrosion and damage. Make sure the inlet and outlet fittings are clear (B, **Figure 35**).

4. Check the impeller blades (A, **Figure 36**) for corrosion or damage. If corrosion is minor, clean the blades. If corrosion is severe or if the blades are cracked or broken, replace the water pump assembly.

5. Turn the impeller shaft (B, **Figure 33**) and check the bearing for excessive noise or roughness. If the bearing turns roughly or is damaged, replace the water pump unit.

6. Replace the water pump body O-ring (B, **Figure 36**) and the body O-ring (A, **Figure 33**) every time the water pump is removed from the crankcase.

7. Lubricate both O-rings with water-resistant grease.

8. Install the cover (**Figure 34**) and bolts and tighten securely.

9. Install the water pump assembly as described in this section.

WATER PUMP OUTLET HOSE

The water pump outlet hose carries coolant from the water pump to the fitting on the back surface of the cylinder block.

Replacement

1. Drain the cooling system as described under *Coolant Change* in Chapter Three.

2A. On 1999-2000 models, remove the carburetor assembly as described in Chapter Eight.

2B. On 2001-on models, remove the throttle body assembly as described in Chapter Nine.

3. Remove the thermostat housing as described in this chapter.

4. Disconnect the hose (**Figure 30**) from the outlet fitting.

5. Remove the bolts securing the outlet hose fitting (**Figure 37**) to the cylinder block and remove the hose assembly.

6. Install by reversing these removal steps. Install a *new* O-ring (**Figure 38**) to the fitting and lubricate it with water-resistant grease.

Table 1 COOLING SYSTEM SPECIFICATIONS

Coolant type	Honda HP coolant or an equivalent*
Standard concentration	50% mixture coolant and purified water
Coolant capacity	
Radiator and engine	2.7 L (2.9 U.S. qt., 2.4 Imp. qt.)
Reserve tank	0.31 L (0.33 U.S. qt., 0.27 Imp. qt.)
Radiator cap relief pressure	108-137 kPa (16-20 psi)
Thermostat (1999-2000 models)	
Begins to open	73-77° C (163-171° F)
Fully open	90° C (194° F)
Minimum valve lift @ 95° C (203° F)	8 mm (0.3 in.)
Thermostat (2001-on models)	
Begins to open	80-84° C (176-183° F)
Fully open	90° C (194° F)
Minimum valve lift @ 95° C (203° F)	8 mm (0.3 in.)

*Use a high quality ethylene glycol coolant that does not contain silicate inhibitors as they can case premature wear to the water pump seals and cause blockage of radiator passages. See text for further information.

Table 2 COOLING SYSTEM TORQUE SPECIFICATIONS

Item	N•m	in.-lb.	ft.-lb.
ECT sensor (2001-on models)	23	–	17
Cooling fan			
Mounting bolt[2]	3	27	–
Motor mounting nuts	5	44	–
Motor switch[1]	18	–	13
Thermostat housing cover bolts	12	106	–
Thermosensor (1999-2000 models)[1]	10	88	–
Water pump mounting bolts	12	106	–

1. Apply sealant to the threads.
2. Apply a medium strength locking agent onto fastener threads.

11

CHAPTER TWELVE

WHEELS, TIRES AND DRIVE CHAIN

This chapter describes service procedures for the wheels, wheel bearings, tires, drive chain and sprockets.

Tire, wheel and drive train specifications are listed in **Tables 1-5** at the end of the chapter.

MOTORCYCLE STANDS

Many procedures in this chapter require that the front or rear wheel be lifted off the ground. While the centerstand (U.K. models only) can be used to lift the rear wheel, a motorcycle front end stand (**Figure 1**) is required to lift the front wheel. Before purchasing and using a front wheel stand, check the manufacturer's instructions to make sure the stand will work with the model being worked on. If any adjustments or accessories are required for the motorcycle and/or stand, perform the necessary adjustment or install the correct parts before lifting the front wheel. When using a front wheel stand, have an assistant standing by to help. After lifting the front wheel and supporting the motorcycle on a stand, make sure the motorcycle is properly supported before walking away from it.

On models without a centerstand, use a suitable size jack under the engine or use a swing arm safety stand to raise the rear wheel.

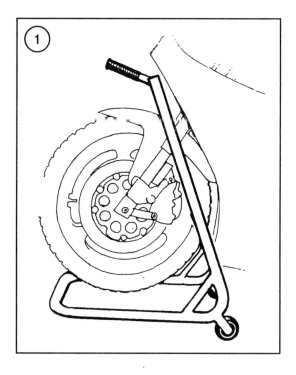

FRONT WHEEL

Removal

1. Support the motorcycle with the front wheel off the ground. See *Motorcycle Stands* in this chapter.

2. Remove both the right and left side brake calipers as follows:

   a. Push the brake caliper in (toward the wheel) by hand. Doing so pushes the caliper pistons into the caliper to provide additional brake pad clearance when reinstalling the caliper.

   b. Remove both brake calipers as described in Chapter Fifteen.

NOTE
Insert a spacer in the calipers to hold the brake pads in place. Then, if the brake lever is inadvertently squeezed, the pistons will not be forced out of the calipers. If this does happen, the calipers must be disassembled to reseat the pistons and the system will have to be bled.

3. Loosen the axle pinch bolts on the right side (A, **Figure 2**).

4. Loosen and remove the axle bolt (B, **Figure 2**).

5. Loosen the axle pinch bolts on the left side (A, **Figure 3**).

NOTE
Before removing the front wheel, note the direction of the rim and tire rotation arrows. The wheel must be reinstalled so the arrows point in the direction of forward rotation. The wheel can be installed in either direction.

NOTE
The wheel collars on the left and right sides are different. Identify the collars before removing them and mark them after wheel removal.

6. Withdraw the front axle from the left side (B, **Figure 3**) and lower the wheel to the ground.

7. Remove the left side short collar (**Figure 4**).

8. Remove the right side long collar (**Figure 5**).

CAUTION
Do not set the wheel down on the disc surface, as it may be damaged.

Inspection

  Replace worn or damaged parts as described in this section.

12

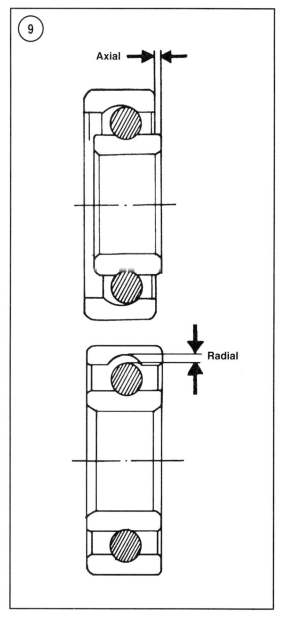

1. Clean the axle and collars in solvent to remove all grease and dirt.

2. Remove any corrosion on the front axle and collars with a piece of fine emery cloth.

3. Check the axle surface for any cracks or other damage. Check the axle operating areas for any nicks or grooves that can cut and damage the seals.

4. Check the axle bolt and axle threads for damage. Replace the axle and axle bolt if their corners are damaged.

5. Check the axle runout with a set of V-blocks and dial indicator (**Figure 6**). Replace the axle if its runout exceeds the service limit in **Table 2**.

6. Check the disc brake bolts (**Figure 7**) for tightness. Tighten the bolts to 20 N•m (15 ft.-lb.) if necessary. To service the brake disc, refer to Chapter Fifteen.

7. Clean the seals with a rag. Then inspect the seals (A, **Figure 8**) for wear, hardness, cracks or other damage. If necessary, replace the seals as described under *Front and Rear Hubs* in this chapter.

8. Turn each bearing inner race (B, **Figure 8**) by hand. The bearing must turn smoothly. Some axial play (side to side) is normal, but radial play (up and

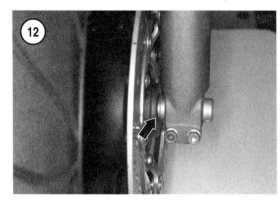

down) must be negligible. See **Figure 9**. If one bearing is damaged, replace both bearings as a set. Refer to *Front Hub* in this chapter.

9. Check wheel runout as described in this chapter.

Installation

1. Make sure the axle bearing surfaces of the fork sliders and axle are free from burrs and nicks.

2. Lightly coat the axle with bearing grease and set aside until installation.

3. Lubricate the seal lips (A, **Figure 8**) with waterproof grease.

NOTE
In Step 4 and Step 5, install the collars in their original mounting positions and facing in the same direction.

4. Install the long collar (**Figure 5**) into the right side.

5. Install the short collar (**Figure 4**) into the left side.

6. Install the wheel between the fork tubes with the wheel's rim (**Figure 10**) and tire arrow marks facing in the direction of forward rotation.

WARNING
The front wheel can be installed in either rotational direction. Make sure to install it correctly as noted in Step 6.

7. Position the front wheel between the fork sliders. Raise the wheel assembly up and align it with the front axle holes in the fork sliders.

8. Install the axle (B, **Figure 3**) from the left side and push it through until it bottoms.

9. Install the axle bolt (B, **Figure 2**) and tighten it finger-tight.

10. Hold the axle and tighten the front axle bolt (B, **Figure 2**) to 59 N•m (44 ft.-lb.).

11. Tighten the right axle pinch bolts (A, **Figure 2**) to 22 N•m (16 ft.-lb.).

12. Check that both the right side (**Figure 11**) and left side (**Figure 12**) axle spacer are correctly in place.

13. Install both the right and left side brake caliper as described in Chapter Fifteen. Spin the front wheel and apply the front brake to reposition the brake pads in both calipers.

14. Remove the stand from the motorcycle so both wheels are on the ground. Then apply the front brake and pump the fork several times to seat the axle.

15. Tighten the left axle pinch bolts (A, **Figure 3**) to 22 N•m (16 ft.-lb.).

WARNING
Step 16 determines if there is adequate brake disc to caliper clearance. Failure to provide adequate clearance may cause brake disc damage and reduced braking efficiency. Both conditions may cause brake failure.

12

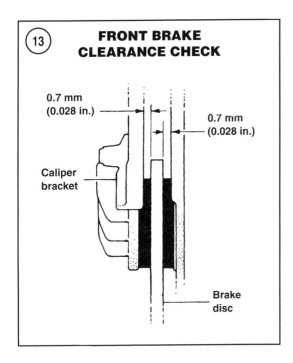

FRONT BRAKE
CLEARANCE CHECK

0.7 mm
(0.028 in.)

0.7 mm
(0.028 in.)

Caliper
bracket

Brake
disc

16. Check the brake disc clearance as follows:
   a. Insert a 0.7 mm (0.028 in.) feeler gauge between the side of each brake disc and fork axle bracket (slider) as shown in **Figure 13**.
   b. The feeler gauge should pass through the gap easily. If the clearance is too small, loosen the axle pinch bolts (A, **Figure 2** and A, **Figure 3**) and twist the slider(s) by hand to obtain the correct clearance. When the clearance is correct, tighten the axle pinch bolts to 22 N•m (16 ft.-lb.). Then recheck the clearance. Remove the feeler gauge.

WARNING
Do not ride the motorcycle until the brake disc clearance is correct and both front brake calipers operate correctly with full hydraulic advantage.

NOTE
If the correct clearance cannot be obtained, check the brake disc for loose mounting bolts or excessive runout (Chapter Fifteen).

REAR WHEEL

Removal

1. Support the motorcycle on level ground.

2. Block the front wheel so the motorcycle will not roll in either direction while on the jack or swing arm stand (or centerstand on U.K. models).

3. Remove the screws securing the drive chain guard (**Figure 14**). This allows for easy removal of the drive chain from the driven sprocket.

WARNING
If the motorcycle has just been run, the muffler will be very HOT. If possible, wait for the muffler to cool down. If not, wear heavy gloves.

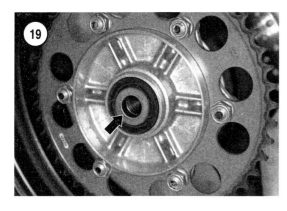

4. Have an assistant apply the rear brake, then loosen the rear axle nut (A, **Figure 15**).

5. Loosen the drive chain adjust bolt (B, **Figure 15**) on both sides of the swing arm to provide the maximum amount of slack in the drive chain.

CAUTION
If using a jack, place a piece of wood on the jack pad to protect the crankcase.

6A. If necessary, place a suitable size jack or wooden blocks under the crankcase to support the

motorcycle securely with the rear wheel off the ground.

6B. Raise the rear of the motorcycle with a safety stand.

7. Remove the rear axle nut (A, **Figure 15**) and washer.

8. Push the wheel forward and derail the drive chain from the rear sprocket.

9. Withdraw the rear axle (A, **Figure 16**) from the left side, then remove the drive chain adjuster plate (B).

10. On the right side, remove the drive chain adjuster plate.

11. Pull the wheel rearward and remove it from the swing arm. Secure the rear caliper to the swing arm (**Figure 17**).

12. Remove the spacer from the right side (**Figure 18**) and the left side (**Figure 19**) of the wheel.

CAUTION
Do not set the wheel down on the disc surface, as it may be damaged.

NOTE
Place a plastic or wooden spacer between the brake pads in place of the disc. Then, if the brake pedal is inadvertently pressed, the piston will not be forced out of the caliper. If this occurs, disassemble the caliper to reseat the piston.

13. Inspect the wheel as described in this chapter.

Installation

1. Make sure all contact surfaces on the axle, swing arm, drive chain adjuster plates and spacers are free of dirt and burrs.

2. Apply a light coat of grease to the axle, bearings, spacers and grease seals.

3. If removed, install the caliper assembly into place on the swing arm guide (**Figure 17**).

4. Remove the spacer from the rear caliper.

5. Install the drive chain adjuster plates onto both sides of the swing arm.

6. Partially position the wheel into place and roll it forward.

7. Install the spacer into the right side (**Figure 18**) and the left side (**Figure 19**) of the wheel.

12

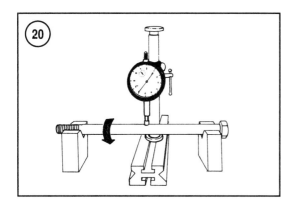

8. Move the wheel forward and onto the caliper assembly, being careful not to damage the leading edge of the brake pads.

9. Install the drive chain onto the rear sprocket.

10. Raise the rear wheel up and into alignment with the swing arm.

11. Install the rear axle (A, **Figure 16**) in from the left side. Push the rear axle through the swing arm, the wheel, the caliper bracket and through the other side of the swing arm.

12. Install the washer and the rear axle nut (A, **Figure 15**). Finger-tighten the nut at this time.

13. Adjust the drive chain as described in Chapter Three.

14. Tighten the rear axle nut to 93 N•m (69 ft.-lb.).

15. If used, remove the jack or wooden block(s) from under the crankcase. Remove the blocks from the front wheel.

16. Roll the motorcycle back and forth several times. Apply the rear brake as many times as necessary to make sure the brake pads are against the brake disc correctly.

Inspection

NOTE
The rear wheel hub is equipped with a single seal that is located on the right side of the hub. The other seal is located in the rear coupling assembly on the left side.

1. If still in place, remove the spacer from the right side (**Figure 18**) and the left side (**Figure 19**) from the hub.

2. Clean the axle and spacers in solvent to remove all old grease and dirt. Make sure all axle contact surfaces are clean and free of dirt and old grease prior to

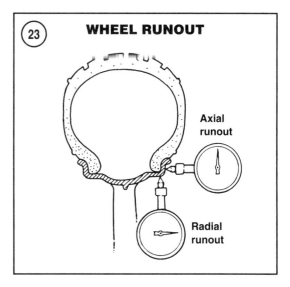

installation. If these surfaces are not cleaned, the axle may be difficult to remove later on.

3. Place the axle on V-blocks and place the tip of a dial indicator in the middle of the axle (**Figure 20**). Rotate the axle and check the runout. If axle runout exceeds specification, replace the axle; do not attempt to straighten it.

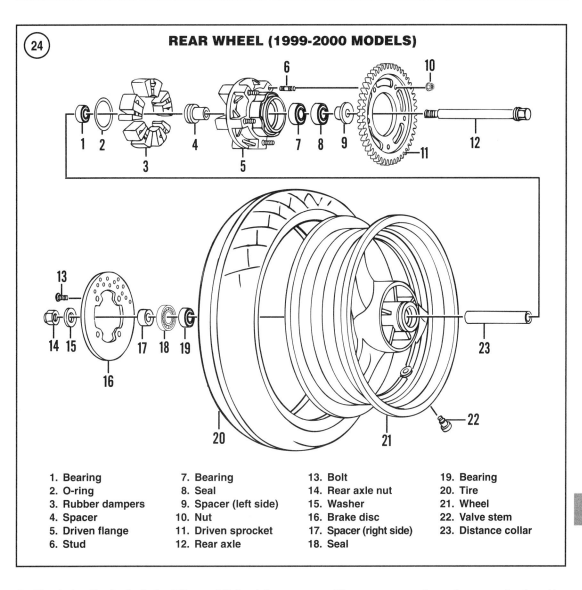

REAR WHEEL (1999-2000 MODELS)

1. Bearing	7. Bearing	13. Bolt	19. Bearing
2. O-ring	8. Seal	14. Rear axle nut	20. Tire
3. Rubber dampers	9. Spacer (left side)	15. Washer	21. Wheel
4. Spacer	10. Nut	16. Brake disc	22. Valve stem
5. Driven flange	11. Driven sprocket	17. Spacer (right side)	23. Distance collar
6. Stud	12. Rear axle	18. Seal	

4. Check the disc brake bolts (**Figure 21**) for tightness. Tighten the bolts to 40 N•m (30 ft.-lb.) if necessary.

5. Check the rear sprocket nuts (**Figure 22**) for tightness. Tighten the nuts to 88 N•m (65 ft.-lb.) if necessary.

6. Check rim runout as follows:

a. Measure the radial (up and down) runout of the wheel rim with a dial indicator (**Figure 23**). If runout exceeds specification, check the wheel bearings.

b. Measure the axial (side to side) runout of the wheel rim with a dial indicator (**Figure 23**). If runout exceeds specification, check the wheel bearings.

c. If necessary, replace the rear wheel and/or rear coupling bearings as described in *Front and Rear Hubs* in this chapter.

7. Inspect the wheel rim for dents, bending or cracks. Check the rim and rim sealing surface for scratches that are deeper than 0.5 mm (0.01 in.). If any of these conditions are present, replace the wheel.

8. Since the rear caliper is off the disc at this time, check the brake pads for wear. Refer to Chapter Fifteen.

REAR COUPLING
AND REAR SPROCKET

Refer to **Figure 24** and **Figure 25**.

12

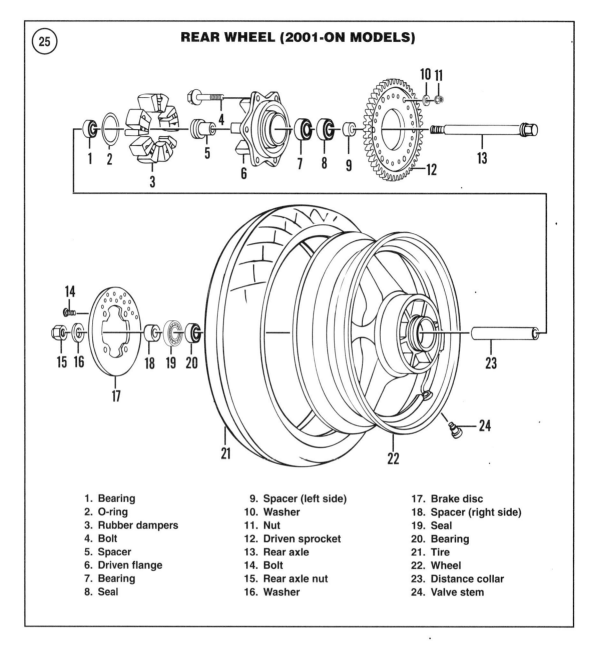

REAR WHEEL (2001-ON MODELS)

1. Bearing
2. O-ring
3. Rubber dampers
4. Bolt
5. Spacer
6. Driven flange
7. Bearing
8. Seal
9. Spacer (left side)
10. Washer
11. Nut
12. Driven sprocket
13. Rear axle
14. Bolt
15. Rear axle nut
16. Washer
17. Brake disc
18. Spacer (right side)
19. Seal
20. Bearing
21. Tire
22. Wheel
23. Distance collar
24. Valve stem

Removal/Disassembly/Assembly

1. Remove the rear wheel as described in this chapter.

2. If still in place, remove the left axle spacer.

3. If the rear sprocket is going to be removed, loosen and remove the nuts (**Figure 22**) securing the rear sprocket to the rear coupling at this time.

NOTE
If the rear coupling assembly is difficult to remove from the hub, tap on the

backside of the sprocket (from the opposite side of the wheel through the wheel spokes) with the wooden handle of a hammer. Tap evenly around the perimeter of the sprocket until the coupling assembly is free of the hub and the rubber dampers.

4. Pull straight up and remove the rear coupling assembly from the rear hub.

5. Remove the distance collar (**Figure 26**) from the rear coupling assembly.

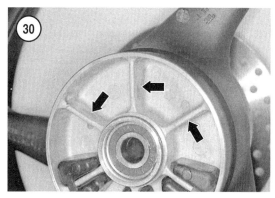

6. Inspect the rear sprocket-to-rear coupling area as described in this chapter.

7. Install by reversing these removal steps while noting the following:

    a. Align the rear coupling bosses (**Figure 27**) with the receptacles between the rubber damper (**Figure 28**) and install the rear coupling. Press it down until it bottoms.

    b. If removed, install the rear sprocket so the side with the stamping faces away from the rear coupling.

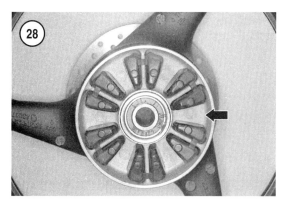

CAUTION
On a new motorcycle or after a new rear sprocket has been installed, check the torque on the rear sprocket nuts after ten minutes of riding and after each ten-minute riding period until the nuts have seated and remain tight. Failure to keep the sprocket nuts correctly tightened will cause the destruction of a very expensive rear hub.

    c. Tighten the rear sprocket nuts to 88 N•m (65 ft.-lb.) after the assembly has been reinstalled in the rear wheel.

Inspection

1. Remove and inspect the rubber dampers (**Figure 29**) for signs of damage or deterioration. If damaged, replace as a complete set.

2. Inspect the raised webs (**Figure 30**) in the rear hub. Check for cracks or wear. If any damage is visible, replace the rear wheel.

3. Inspect the rear coupling assembly for cracks or damage, replace if necessary.

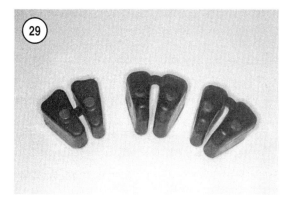

12

4. Inspect the rear sprocket teeth (**Figure 31**). If the teeth are visibly worn or undercut (**Figure 32**), replace the rear sprocket as described in this chapter.

CAUTION
If the rear sprocket requires replacement, also replace the engine drive sprocket and the drive chain. Never install a new drive chain over worn sprockets or a worn drive chain over new sprockets. The old part will wear out the new part prematurely.

5. If the rear sprocket requires replacement, also inspect the drive chain as described in Chapter Three and the engine sprocket as described in Chapter Seven. They also may be worn and need replacing.
6. Inspect the bearing (**Figure 33**) for excessive axial play and radial play (**Figure 34**). Replace the bearing if it has an excess amount of free play.
7. On a non-sealed bearing, check the balls for evidence of wear, pitting or excessive heat (bluish tint). Turn the inner race by hand. The bearing must turn smoothly without excessive play or noise. Replace questionable bearings. Ensure a perfect match by comparing the old bearing to the new one.

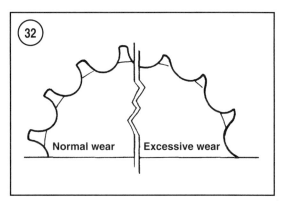

Normal wear | Excessive wear

NOTE
Fully sealed bearings are available from many bearing specialty shops. Fully sealed bearings provide better protection from dirt and moisture that passes through worn or damaged seals.

FRONT AND REAR HUBS

Pre-inspection

Inspect each wheel bearing as follows:
1. Support the motorcycle with either the front or rear wheel off the ground. Make sure the axle is tightened securely.

   a. Hold the wheel along its sides (180° apart) and try to rock it back and forth. If there is any noticeable play at the axle, the wheel bearings are worn or damaged and require replacement. Have an assistant apply the front or rear brake while rocking the wheel again. On severely worn bearings, play is detected at the bearings even though the wheel is locked in position.

   b. Push the front caliper(s) in by hand to move the brake pads away from the brake disc. This makes it easier to spin the wheel when performing substep c.

   c. Spin the wheel and listen for excessive wheel bearing noise. A grinding or catching noise indicates worn bearings.

   d. Apply the front or rear brake several times to reposition the brake pads in the calipers.

   e. To check any questionable bearing, continue with Step 2.

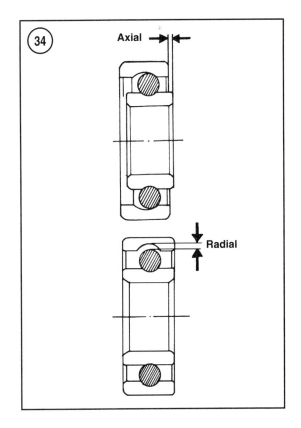

CAUTION
Do not remove the wheel bearings for inspection purposes, as they may be damaged during removal. Remove the wheel bearings only if they require replacement.

2A. Remove the front wheel as described in this chapter.

2B. Remove the rear wheel as described in this chapter.

CAUTION
When handling the wheel assembly in the following steps, do not lay the wheel down where it is supported by the brake disc, as this could damage the disc. Support the wheel on wooden blocks.

3. Pry the seals out of the hub (**Figure 35**). Support the tool with a rag to avoid damaging the hub or brake disc.

NOTE
*If a seal is hard to remove, do not damage the mounting bore by trying to force it out. Remove the seal with a seal removal tool as described under **Seals** in Chapter One.*

4. Remove any burrs created during seal removal. Use emery cloth to smooth the mounting bore. Do not enlarge the mounting bore.

NOTE
Before removing the wheel bearings, check the tightness of the bearings in the hub by pulling the bearing up and then from side to side. The outer bearing race should be a tight fit in the hub with no movement. If the outer bearing race is loose and wobbles, the bearing bore in the hub may be cracked or damaged. Remove the bearings as described in this procedure and check the hub bore carefully. If any cracks or damage are found, replace the wheel. It cannot be repaired.

5. Turn each bearing inner race by hand. The bearing must turn smoothly with no roughness, catching, binding or excessive noise. Some axial play (side to side) is normal, but radial play (up and down) must be negligible (**Figure 34**).

6. Check the bearing's outer seal (**Figure 36**) for buckling or other damage that would allow dirt to enter the bearing.

12

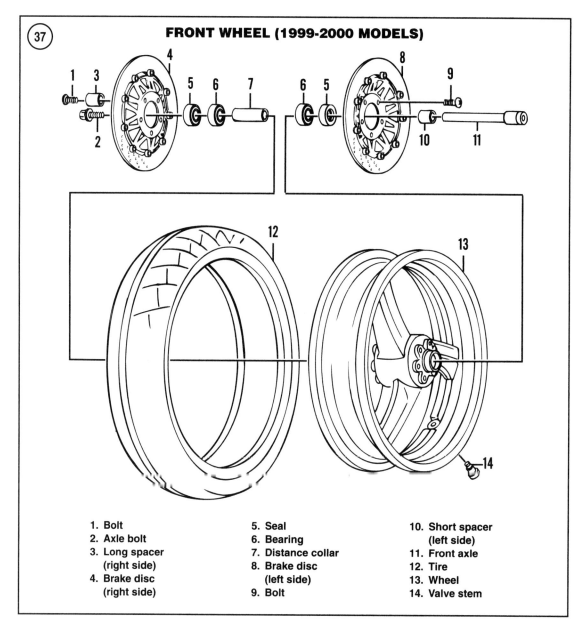

FRONT WHEEL (1999-2000 MODELS)

1. Bolt
2. Axle bolt
3. Long spacer
   (right side)
4. Brake disc
   (right side)
5. Seal
6. Bearing
7. Distance collar
8. Brake disc
   (left side)
9. Bolt
10. Short spacer
    (left side)
11. Front axle
12. Tire
13. Wheel
14. Valve stem

7A. On the front wheel, if one bearing is damaged, replace both bearings as a set.

7B. On the rear wheel, if the one bearing is damaged, also replace the bearing in the rear coupling as a set.

Disassembly

This section describes removal of the wheel bearings from the front and rear hub. Refer to **Figures 24, 25, 37** and **38**. If the bearings are intact, one of the removal methods described in this section can be used. To remove a bearing where the inner race assembly has fallen out, refer to *Removing Damaged Bearings* in this section.

CAUTION
When handling the wheel assembly in the following steps, do not lay the wheel down where it is supported by the brake disc because this could damage the disc. Support the wheel on two wooden blocks.

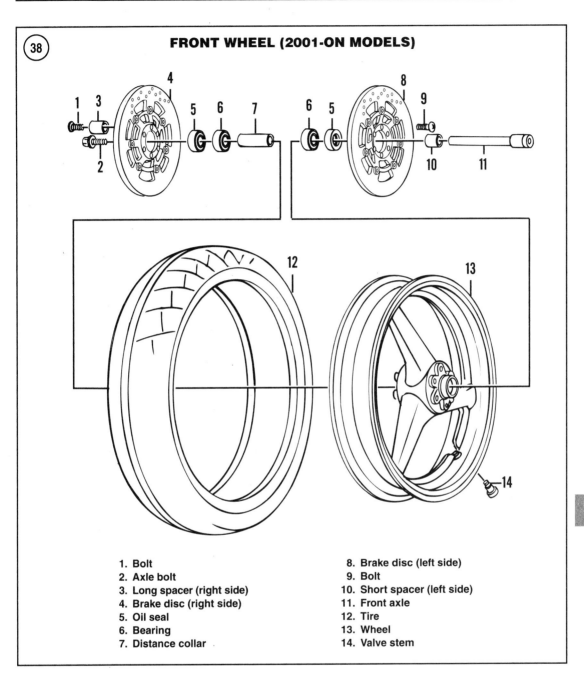

FRONT WHEEL (2001-ON MODELS)

1. Bolt
2. Axle bolt
3. Long spacer (right side)
4. Brake disc (right side)
5. Oil seal
6. Bearing
7. Distance collar

8. Brake disc (left side)
9. Bolt
10. Short spacer (left side)
11. Front axle
12. Tire
13. Wheel
14. Valve stem

1. Pry the seals out of the hub (**Figure 35**). Support the tool with a rag to avoid damaging the hub or brake disc.

> *NOTE*
> *If a seal is hard to remove, do not damage the mounting bore by trying to force the seal out. Remove the seal with a seal removal tool as described under **Seals** in Chapter One.*

2. Remove any burrs created during seal removal. Use emery cloth to smooth the mounting bore. Do not enlarge the mounting bore.

3. Examine the wheel bearings (**Figure 36**) for excessive damage, especially the inner race. If the inner race of one bearing is damaged, remove the other bearing first. If both bearings are damaged, try to remove the bearing with the least amount of damage first. On rusted and damaged bearings, applying

pressure against the inner race may cause the race to pop out, leaving the outer race in the hub.

WARNING
Safety glasses must be worn when removing the bearings in the following steps.

NOTE
Step 4 describes two methods of removing the wheel bearings. Step 4A requires the use of the Kowa Seiki Wheel Bearing Remover set. Step 4B describes how to remove the bearings without special tools.

NOTE
*The wheel bearing set consists of two remover shafts and a number of remover heads (expanding collets). The Kowa Seiki Wheel Bearing Remover set shown in **Figure 39** can be ordered through a Honda dealership from K & L Supply Co. in Santa Clara, CA.*

4A. To remove the wheel bearings with the Kowa Seiki Wheel Bearing Remover set:

  a. Select the correct size remover head tool and insert it into one of the bearings (**Figure 40**).

  b. From the opposite side of the hub, insert the remover shaft into the slot in the backside of the remover head (**Figure 41**). Then position the hub with the remover head tool resting against a solid surface and strike the remover shaft to force it into the slit in the remover head. This wedges the remover head tool against the inner bearing race. See **Figure 41**.

  c. Position the hub and strike the end of the remover shaft with a hammer to drive the bearing from the hub (**Figure 42**). Remove the bearing and tool. Release the remover head from the bearing.

  d. Remove the distance collar from the hub.

  e. Remove the opposite bearing the same way.

4B. To remove the wheel bearings without special tools:

CAUTION
The hub and bearings will be hot after heating them with a torch. Make sure to wear welding gloves when handling the parts.

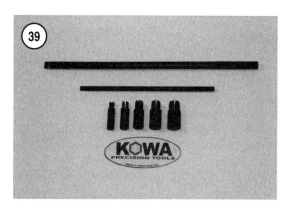

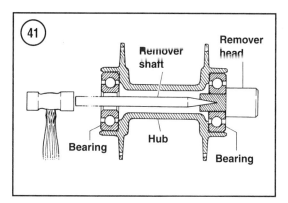

NOTE
Clean the hub of all chemical residue before heating it with a torch in this procedure.

  a. Heat one side of the hub with a propane torch. Work the torch in a circular motion around the hub, making sure not to hold the torch in one area. Then turn the wheel over and remove the bearing as described in the next step.

  b. Using a long drift, tilt the distance collar away from one side of the bearing (**Figure 43**).

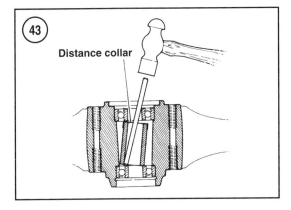

Distance collar

NOTE
Do not damage the distance collar when removing the bearing. If necessary, grind a clearance groove in the drift to enable it to contact the bearing while clearing the distance collar.

c. Tap the bearing out of the hub with a hammer, working in a circle around the bearing inner race.

d. Remove the distance collar from the hub.

e. Turn the hub over and heat the opposite side.

f. Drive out the opposite bearing, using a suitable driver.

g. Inspect the distance collar for burrs or dents created during removal.

5. Clean and dry the hub and distance collar.

Inspection

1. Check the hub mounting bore for cracks or other damage. If one bearing is a loose fit, the mounting bore is damaged. Replace the hub.

2. Inspect the distance collar for cracks, corrosion or other damage. Then check the distance collar ends. If the ends appear compressed or damaged, replace the distance collar. Do not try to repair the distance collar by cutting or grinding its end surfaces, as this shortens the distance collar.

NOTE
The distance collar operates against the wheel bearing inner races to prevent them from moving inward when the axle is tightened. If the ends of the distance collar are damaged, shortened, or if it is not installed in the hub, the inner bearing races move inward and bind as the axle is tightened, causing bearing damage and seizure.

Assembly

1. Before installing the new bearings and seals, note the following:

   a. Install both bearings with their closed side facing out. If a bearing is sealed on both sides, install the bearing with its manufacturer's marks facing out.

   b. Install the seals with their closed side facing out.

   c. When grease is specified in the following steps, use water-resistant bearing grease.

2. Remove any dirt or debris from the hub before installing the bearings.

3. Pack the open side of each bearing with grease.

NOTE
When installing the bearings, install the right side bearing first, then the left side bearing.

4. Place the right side bearing squarely against the bore opening with its closed side facing out. Select a driver or socket (**Figure 44**) with an outside diame-

ter slightly smaller than the bearing's outside diameter. Then drive the bearing into the bore until it bottoms out.

5. Turn the wheel over and install the distance collar. Center it against the first bearing's inner race.

6. Place the left side bearing squarely against the bore opening with its closed side facing out. Using the same driver, drive the bearing partway into the bearing bore. Then stop and make sure the distance collar is centered in the hub. If not, install the axle through the hub to align the distance collar with the bearing. Then remove the axle and continue installing the bearing until it bottoms in the hub.

7. Insert the axle through the hub and turn it by hand. Check for any roughness or binding, indicating bearing damage.

NOTE
If the axle will not go in, the distance collar is not aligned correctly with one of the bearings.

8. Pack the lip of each seal with grease.

9. Place a seal squarely against one of the bore openings with its closed side facing out. Then drive the seal in the bore until it is flush with the outside of the hub's mounting bore (**Figure 45**).

10. On the front hub, repeat Step 9 for the other seal.

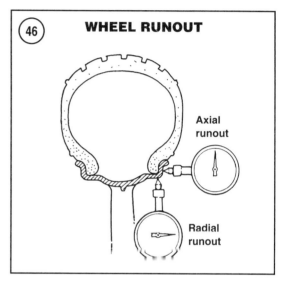

WHEEL RUNOUT

Axial runout

Radial runout

Removing Damaged Bearings

When worn and rusted wheel bearings are used too long, the inner race can break apart and fall out of the bearing, leaving the outer race pressed in the hub. Because the outer race seats against a shoulder inside the hub, its removal is difficult because only a small part of the race is accessible above the hub's shoulder. This presents a small and difficult target to drive against. To remove a bearing's outer race under these conditions, first heat the hub evenly with a propane torch. Then drive out the outer race with a drift and hammer. Grind a clearance tip on the end of the drift, if necessary, to avoid damaging the hub's mounting bore. Check this before heating the hub. When removing the race, apply force at opposite points around the race to prevent it from rocking and binding in the mounting bore once it starts to move. After removing the race, inspect the hub mounting bore carefully for cracks or other damage.

WHEEL RUNOUT AND BALANCE

Proper wheel inspection includes visual inspection, checking rim runout and wheel balance. Checking runout and wheel balance requires a truing or wheel balancing stand. If these tools are not available, refer the service to a Honda dealership.

Replace the wheel if it is dented or damaged in any way. While a new wheel is not cheap, its cost does not compare to the personal injury that could occur if a damaged wheel becomes unstable or fails while riding. If there is any doubt as to wheel condition, take it to a Honda dealership or sportmotorcycle specialist and have them inspect the wheel. It is also a good idea to have a specialist inspect any used wheels that may be considered for purchase.

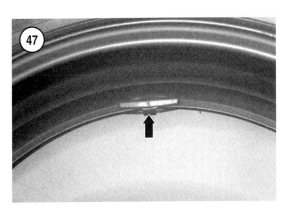

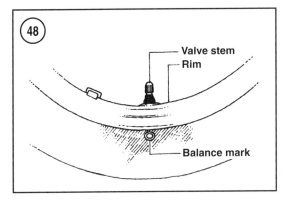

Wheel Runout Inspection

1. Clean the wheel rim to remove all road grit, chain lube and other debris. Any material left on the rim affects the runout measurement. This includes any surface roughness caused by peeled or uneven paint and corrosion.

2. Inspect the wheel rim for dents, bending or cracks. Check the rim and rim sealing surface for scratches that could cause the tire to leak air.

NOTE
The runout check can be performed
with the tire mounted on the wheel.

3. Mount the wheel on a truing stand. See **Figure 46** for the dial indicator inspection points.

4. Spin the wheel slowly by hand and measure the radial (up and down) runout with a dial indicator as shown in **Figure 46**. If the runout is excessive (**Table 2**), go to Step 6.

5. Spin the wheel slowly by hand and measure the axial (side to side) runout with a dial indicator as shown in **Figure 46**. If the runout is excessive (**Table 2**), go to Step 6.

6. If the runout is excessive, remove the wheel from the truing stand and turn each bearing inner race by hand. If necessary, remove the seal (**Figure 45**) to check the bearings closely. Each bearing must turn smoothly and be a tight fit in its mounting bore. Some axial play (side to side) is normal, but radial play (up and down) must be negligible. Then check the bearing for visual damage. If a bearing turns roughly, replace both bearings as a set. If a bearing is loose in its mounting bore, the hub is probably damaged. Remove the bearings and check the mounting bore for any cracks, gouges or other damage.

7. If the wheel bearings and hub are in good condition but the runout is out of specification, replace the damaged wheel.

Wheel Balance Inspection

A wheel that is not balanced is unsafe because it seriously affects the steering and handling of the motorcycle. Depending on the degree of unbalance and the speed of the motorcycle, anything from a mild vibration to a violent shimmy may occur, which may result in loss of control. An imbalanced wheel also causes abnormal tire wear.

Motorcycle wheels can be checked for balance either statically or dynamically with spin balancing. This section describes how to static balance the wheels using a wheel inspection stand. To obtain a higher degree of accuracy, take both wheels to a dealership and have them balanced with a dynamic wheel balancer. This machine spins the wheel to accurately detect any imbalance.

Balance weights are used to balance the wheel and are attached to the rim. Weight kits are available from motorcycle dealerships. Purchase the crimp type that can be attached to the raised ridge along the center of the rim (**Figure 47**).

The wheel must be able to rotate freely when checking wheel balance. Because excessively worn or damaged wheel bearings affect the accuracy of this procedure, check the front wheel bearings as described in this chapter. Check the wheel hub for cracks and other damage. Also confirm that the tire balance mark, a paint mark on the tire, is aligned with the valve stem (**Figure 48**). If not, break the tire loose from the rim and align the balance mark

12

with the valve stem. See *Tire Changing* in this chapter.

NOTE
When balancing the wheel, leave the brake disc(s) attached to the wheel.

1. Remove the wheel as described in this chapter.
2. Clean the seals and inspect the wheel bearings as described under in this chapter.
3. Clean the tire and rim. Remove any stones or pebbles stuck in the tire tread.
4. Mount the wheel on an inspection stand (**Figure 49**).

NOTE
To check the original balance of the wheel, leave the existing weights in place on the wheel.

5. Spin the wheel by hand and let it coast to a stop. Mark the tire at its bottom point with chalk.
6. Spin the wheel several more times. If the same spot on the tire stops at the bottom each time, the wheel is out of balance. This is the heaviest part of the tire. When an unbalanced wheel is spun, it always comes to rest with the heaviest spot at the bottom.
7. Attach a test weight to the wheel at the point opposite the heaviest spot and spin the wheel again
8. Experiment with different weights until the wheel, when spun, comes to rest at a different position each time. When a wheel is correctly balanced, the weight of the tire and wheel assembly is distributed equally around the wheel.
9. Remove the test weight and install the correct size weight to the rim. Make sure it is crimped tightly to the rim's surface (**Figure 47**).
10. Record the number and position of weights on the wheel. Then, if the motorcycle experiences a handling or vibration problem at a later time, first check for any missing weights.
11. Install the wheel as described in this chapter.

TIRE CHANGING

Tire changing is an important part of the motorcycle's safety and operation. Changing sportbike tires, due to the size of the tire and tight bead/rim seal, can be extremely difficult. Incorrect installation due to a lack of patience, skill or equipment can damage

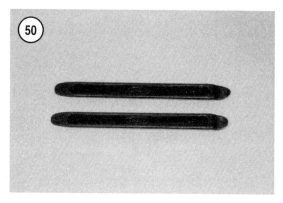

both the tire and the wheel. Many experienced owners who do most or all of their own maintenance and service choose to have their tires changed by a professional technician with specialized tire changing equipment designed for alloy wheels.

The following procedure is provided for those who choose to do the work.

Tools

NOTE
Before purchasing a bead breaker, make sure it will work on CBR600F tire sizes.

To change the tires, the following tools are required:

1. A set of tire levers or flat-handled tire irons with rounded ends (**Figure 50**).
2. Bead breaker.
3. Spray bottle filled with soapy water.
4. Plastic rim protectors for each tire iron.

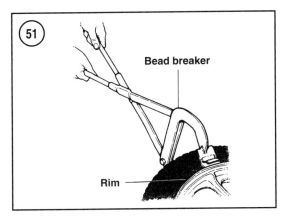

Bead breaker

Rim

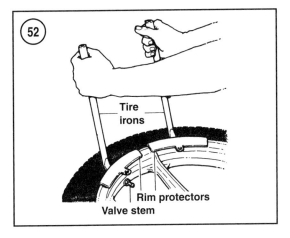

Tire irons

Rim protectors

Valve stem

Removal

WARNING
The original equipment cast wheels are designed for use with tubeless tires. Do not install a tube inside of a tubeless tire, as excessive heat may build up in the tire and cause the tube to burst.

WARNING
The wheels can be damaged easily during tire removal. Work carefully to avoid damaging the tire beads, inner liner of the tire or the wheel rim flange that form the sealing surfaces. As described in the text, insert rim protectors between the tire irons and rim to protect the rim from damage.

NOTE
Tires are harder to replace when the rubber is hard and cold. If the weather is hot, place the wheels and new tires in the sun or in a closed automobile.

The heat helps soften the rubber, easing removal and installation. If the weather is cold, place the tires and wheels inside a warm building.

NOTE
It is easier to replace tires when the wheel is mounted on some type of raised platform. A popular item used by many home mechanics is a metal drum. Before placing the wheel on a drum, cover the drum edge with a length of garden or heater hose, split lengthwise and secured in place with plastic ties. When changing a tire at ground level, support the wheel on two wooden blocks to prevent the brake disc from contacting the floor.

1. If the tire is going to be reused, mark the valve stem location on the tire (**Figure 48**) so the tire can be installed in the same position for easier balancing.

2. Remove the valve core to deflate the tire.

CAUTION
The inner rim and tire bead areas are sealing surfaces on a tubeless tire. Do not scratch the inside of the rim or damage the tire bead. Do not attempt to force the bead off the rim with any type of leverage, such as a long tire iron. It is very easy to damage the tire bead surface on the tire and rim. It is also possible to crack or break the alloy wheel. Removing tubeless tires from their rims can be difficult because of the exceptionally tight bead and rim seal. If unable to break the tire bead with a bead breaker, take the wheel to a motorcycle dealership and have them change the tire.

3. Use a bead breaker and break the bead all the way around the tire (**Figure 51**). Do not try to force the bead with tire irons. Make sure that both beads are clear of the rim beads.

4. Lubricate the tire beads with soapy water on the side to be removed first.

CAUTION
*Always use rim protectors (**Figure 52**) between the tire irons and the rim to protect the rim from damage.*

12

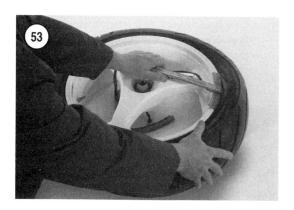

5. Insert the tire iron under the bead (**Figure 53**). Force the bead on the opposite side of the tire into the center of the rim and pry the bead over the rim with the tire iron.

6. Insert a second tire iron next to the first (no more than 8 in. [20.3 cm] apart) to hold the bead over the rim. Then work around the tire with the first tool prying the bead over the rim (**Figure 54**). Work slowly by taking small bites with the tire irons. Taking large bites or using excessive force can damage the tire bead or rim.

> *NOTE*
> *If the tire is tight and hard to pry over the rim, use a third tire iron and a rim protector. Use one hand and arm to hold the first two tire irons, then use the other hand to operate the third tire iron when prying the tire over the rim.*

7. Turn the wheel over. Insert a tire iron between the second bead and the same side of the rim that the first bead was pried over (**Figure 55**). Force the bead on the opposite side from the tool into the center of the rim. Pry the second bead off the rim, working around the wheel with the two rim protectors and tire irons.

8. Remove the valve stem and discard it. Remove all rubber residue from the valve stem hole (**Figure 56**) and inspect the hole for cracks and other damage.

9. Remove old balance weights from the rim surface.

10. Carefully clean the rim bead with a brush; do not use excessive force or damage the rim sealing surface. Then inspect the sealing surface for any cracks, corrosion or other damage.

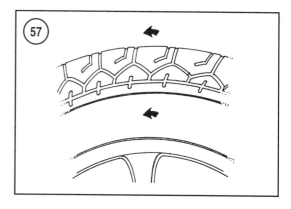

> *NOTE*
> *If there is any doubt as to wheel condition, take it to a Honda dealership or*

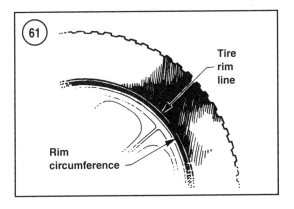

sportmotorcycle specialist for a thorough inspection.

Installation

1A. If installing the original tire, carefully inspect the tire for any damage.

1B. If installing a new tire, remove all stickers from the tire tread.

2. Lubricate both beads of the tire with soapy water.

3. Make sure the correct tire, either front or rear, is installed on the correct wheel and that the direction arrow on the tire faces in the direction of wheel rotation (**Figure 57**).

4. Align the paint spot (**Figure 48**) near the bead indicating the lightest point of the tire with the valve stem.

5. Place the backside of the tire into the center of the rim. The lower bead should go into the center of the rim and the upper bead outside (**Figure 58**). Use both hands to push the backside of the tire into the rim as far as possible. Use tire irons when it becomes difficult to install the tire by hand (**Figure 59**).

6. Press the upper bead into the rim opposite the valve. Pry the bead into the rim on both sides of the initial point with a tire tool, working around the rim to the valve (**Figure 60**).

7. Check the bead on both sides of the tire for an even fit around the rim.

8. Lubricate both sides of the tire with soapy water.

> *WARNING*
> *Always wear eye protection when seating the tire beads onto the rim. Never exceed 56 psi (4.0 k/cm²) inflation pressure as the tire could burst causing severe injury. Never stand directly over the tire while inflating it.*

9. Inflate the tire until the beads seat into place. A loud pop should be heard as each bead seats against its side of the rim.

10. After inflating the tire, check to see that the beads are fully seated and that the tire rim lines (**Figure 61**) are the same distance from the rim all the way around the tire. If one or both beads do not seat, deflate the tire, re-lubricate the rim and beads with soapy water and re-inflate the tire.

11. Inflate the tire to the required pressure listed in **Table 3**. Screw on the valve stem cap.

12

12. Balance the wheel as described in this chapter.

NOTE
After installing new tires, follow the tire manufacturer's instructions for breaking-in (scuffing) the tire.

TIRE REPAIRS

Only use tire plugs as an emergency repair. Refer to the manufacturer's instructions to install and note the motorcycle weight and speed restrictions. After performing an emergency tire repair with a plug, consider the repair temporary and replace the tire at the earliest opportunity.

Refer all tire repairs to a Honda dealership or other qualified motorcycle technician.

DRIVE CHAIN

Refer to **Table 4** for drive chain specifications. Refer to *Drive Chain* in Chapter Three for routine drive chain inspection and lubrication procedures.

This section describes how to replace the drive chain with the swing arm mounted on the motorcycle.

Replacement

All models are equipped with a chain that uses a staked master link (**Figure 62**). On these models, the chain can be replaced with the swing arm mounted on the motorcycle. The following section describes chain replacement using the Honda drive chain tool set (part No. 07HMH-MR1010A). When using the Honda tool, follow the instructions provided with the tool. If using an aftermarket drive chain tool, follow its operating instructions. Use the following steps to supplement the instructions provided with the chain tool.

1. Support the motorcycle on level ground.
2. Block the front wheel so the motorcycle will not roll in either direction while on the jack or safety stand (or centerstand on U.K. models).

WARNING
If the motorcycle has just been run, the muffler will be very HOT. If possible, wait for the muffler to cool down. If not, wear heavy gloves.

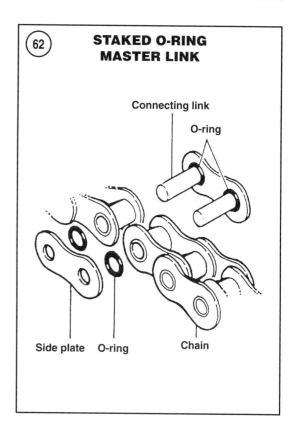

62

STAKED O-RING MASTER LINK

Connecting link

O-ring

Side plate   O-ring   Chain

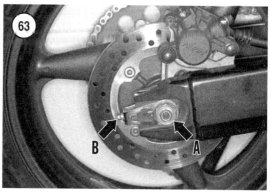

63

64

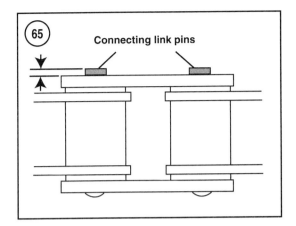

Connecting link pins

3. Loosen the rear axle nut (A, **Figure 63**).

4. Loosen the drive chain adjust bolt (B, **Figure 63**) on both sides of the swing arm to provide the maximum amount of slack in the drive chain.

CAUTION
If using a jack, place a piece of wood on the jack pad to protect the crankcase.

5A. If necessary, place a suitable size jack or wooden blocks under the crankcase to support the motorcycle securely with the rear wheel off the ground.

5B. Raise the rear of the motorcycle with a safety stand.

6. Rotate the rear wheel and chain to locate the crimped pin ends on the master link. Break the chain at this point.

7. Assemble the chain tool, following the manufacturer's instructions.

8. Install the chain tool across the master link, then operate the tool (**Figure 64**) and push the connecting link out of the side plate to break the chain. Remove the side plate, connecting link and O-rings (**Figure 62**).

WARNING
Never reuse the connecting link, side plate and O-rings, as they could break and cause the chain to separate. Reusing a master link may cause the chain to come apart and lock the rear wheel and cause a serious accident.

9. Remove the drive chain.

10. If installing a new drive chain, count the links of the new chain, and if necessary, cut the chain to length as described under *Cutting a Drive Chain to Length* in this section. See **Table 4** for the original equipment chain sizes.

11. Install the drive chain through the swing arm and around the drive sprocket.

NOTE
Always install the drive chain through the swing arm before connecting and staking the master link.

12. Assemble the new master link as follows:
   a. Install an O-ring on each connecting link pin (**Figure 62**).
   b. Insert the connecting link through the inside of the chain and connect both chain ends together.
   c. Install the remaining two O-rings (**Figure 62**) onto the connecting link pins.
   d. Install the side plate (**Figure 62** with its identification mark facing out (away from the chain).

13. Stake each connecting link pin as follows:

NOTE
*The master link specifications referred to in **Table 4** are for the original equipment DID and RK drive chains installed on all models. If installing a different drive chain, refer to its manufacturer's specifications.*

   a. Measure the height of the connecting link pins from the outer side plate surface to the top of each link pin (**Figure 65**). See **Table 4** for the standard connecting link pin height measurement. If the height measurement is incorrect, readjust the side plate's height position on the connecting link.
   b. Assemble the chain tool onto the master link and carefully stake each connecting link pin end (**Figure 66**) to the diameter specified in **Table 4**. Work carefully and do not exceed the

12

specified outside diameter measurement. Measure with a vernier caliper (**Figure 67**).

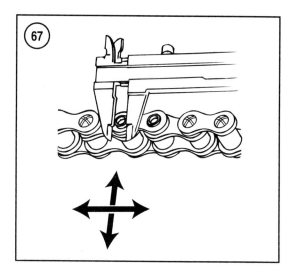

NOTE
If the diameter of one pin end is out of specification, remove the master link. Then install a new master link assembly.

14. Remove the chain tool and inspect the master link for any cracks or other damage. Check the staked area for cracks (**Figure 68**). Then make sure the master link O-rings were not crushed. If there are any cracks on the staked link surfaces or other damage, remove the master link and install a new one.

15. If there are no cracks, pivot the chain ends where they hook onto the master link. Each chain end must pivot freely. Compare by pivoting other links of the chain. If one or both drive chain ends cannot pivot on the master link, the chain is too tight. Remove and install a new master link assembly.

WARNING
An incorrectly installed master link may cause the chain to come apart and lock the rear wheel, causing a serious accident. If the tools to safely rivet the chain together are not available, take it to a Honda dealership. Do not ride the motorcycle unless absolutely certain the master link is installed correctly.

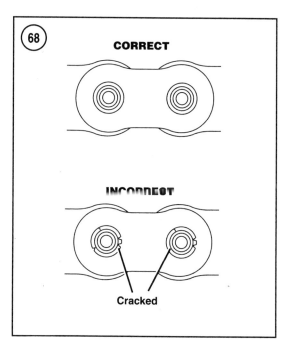

16. Adjust the drive chain and tighten the rear axle nut as described in Chapter Three.

Cutting a Drive Chain to Length

Table 4 lists the correct number of chain links required for original equipment gearing. If the replacement drive chain is too long, cut it to length as follows:

1. Stretch the new chain on a workbench. Set the master link aside for now.

2. If installing a new chain over original equipment gearing, refer to **Table 4** for the correct number of links for the new chain. If sprocket sizes were changed, install the new chain over both sprockets, with the rear wheel moved forward, to determine the correct number of links to remove. Make a chalk mark on the two chain pins to be cut. Count the chain links one more time or check the chain length before cutting.

WARNING
Using a hand or bench grinder as described in Step 3 will cause flying particles. Do not operate a grinding tool without proper eye protection.

3A. If using the Honda tool, use it to break the drive chain.

3B. If not using a chain tool, cut the chain as follows:

   a. Grind the head of two pins flush with the face of the side plate with a grinder or suitable grinding tool.

   b. Press the side plate out of the chain with a chain breaker; support the chain carefully while doing this. If the pins are still tight, grind more material from the end of the pins and then try again.

   c. Remove the side plate and push out the connecting link.

4. Install the new drive chain as described in this chapter.

Table 1 TIRE AND WHEEL SIZE SPECIFICATIONS

Item	Specification
Tire size	
Front	120/70 ZR 17 (58W)
Rear	180/55 ZR 17 (73W)
Tire tread minimum depth	
Front	1.5 mm (0.06 in.)
Rear	2.0 mm (0.08 in.)
Tire brands (1999-2000 models)	
Bridgestone	
Front	BT56F RADIAL E
Rear	BT56R RADIAL G
Dunlop	
Front	D207FJ
Rear	D207P
Michelin	
Front	TX15C
Rear	TX25
Tire brands (2001-on models)	
Bridgestone	
Front	BT10FF
Rear	BT010RF
Dunlop	
Front	D207FJ
Rear	D207P
Michelin	
Front	Pilot SPORT E
Rear	Pilot SPORT E

Table 2 WHEELS AND AXLE SERVICE SPECIFICATIONS

Item	Specification
Rim runout limit	
Axial	2.0 mm (0.08 in.)
Radial	2.0 mm (0.08 in.)
Axle runout limit	
Front	0.20 mm (0.008 in.)
Rear	0.20 mm (0.008 in.)
Wheel balance weight	60 g (2.1 oz.) maximum

12

Table 3 TIRE INFLATION PRESSURE*

	Front psi (kPa)	Rear psi (kPa)
Up to 90 kg (200 lbs.) load	36 (250)	42 (290)
Up to maximum weight capacity	36 (250)	42 (290)

*Tire inflation pressure is for OE tires. Aftermarket tires may require different inflation pressure. The use of tires other than those specified by Honda may cause instability.

Table 4 DRIVE CHAIN AND SPROCKET SPECIFICATIONS

Item	Specification
Drive chain (1999-2000 models)	DID525HV-112L (110 links)
	DID525HV-120ZB (110 links)
	RK525 R0Z1-112L (110 links)
	RK525 R0Z1-120LJ-F2 (110 links)
Drive chain (2001-on models)	DID525HV-112L (108 links)
	RK525 R0Z1-112L (108 links)
Master link*	
DID chains	
Connecting link pin height	1.15-1.55 mm (0.045-0.061 in.)
Connecting link pin end outside diameter	5.50-5.80 mm (0.217-0.228 in.)
RK chains	
Connecting link height	1.20-1.40 mm (0.047-0.055 in.)
Connecting link pin end outside diameter	5.45-5.85 mm (0.215-0.230 in.)
Chain slack	25-35 mm (1-1 3/8 in.)
Sprocket sizes	
Drive (front)	16 teeth
Driven (rear)	
1999-2000 models	45 teeth
2001-on models	46 teeth

*See text for service procedures on how to stake the master link.

Table 5 WHEEL TORQUE SPECIFICATIONS

Item	N•m	in.-lb.	ft.-lb.
Brake caliper			
mounting bolts*	30	–	22
Brake disc bolts*			
Front wheel	20	–	15
Rear wheel	40	–	30
Front axle bolt	59	–	44
Front axle pinch bolts	22	–	16
Rear axle nut	93		69
Rear sprocket nuts	88	–	65

*ALOC type bolt. Install new bolts during installation.

FRONT SUSPENSION AND STEERING

This chapter describes procedures for the repair and maintenance of the handlebar, front fork and steering components. See Chapter Twelve for front wheel and tire service. Front suspension and steering specifications are listed in **Table 1** and **Table 2** at the end of the chapter.

> *WARNING*
> *Replace all fasteners used on the front suspension and steering components with parts of the same type. Do not use a replacement part of lesser quality or substitute design; this may affect the performance of the system or result in failure of the part that leads to loss of motorcycle control. Careful attention to the torque specifications during installation is required to ensure proper retention of these parts.*

HANDLEBAR ASSEMBLIES

These models are equipped with separate handlebar assemblies that slip over the top of the fork tubes.

> *NOTE*
> *Before removing a handlebar(s), make a drawing of the appropriate control cables from the handlebar(s) and through the frame. This information proves helpful when reinstalling the handlebar(s) and cables.*

Left Handlebar Removal

This section describes the removal of the components from the left handlebar and then the handlebar from the left fork tube. If it is only necessary to remove the handlebar with all components intact, proceed to Step 7 and Step 8.

NOTE
If the front fairing is still in place, cover it with a heavy towel or blanket to protect the finish during this procedure. Also protect the fuel tank.

1. Disconnect the clutch interlock switch wire connectors from the clutch switch (**Figure 1**).
2. Remove the bolts (A, **Figure 2**) securing the clutch lever bracket. Remove the clutch lever assembly.
3. Remove the left handlebar switch housing screws (B, **Figure 2**) and open the switch assembly. On 1999-2000 models, disconnect the choke cable end from the choke lever. On all models, remove the switch assembly from the handlebar.
4. Remove the screw securing the handlebar weight (**Figure 3**) and remove the weight.
5. If necessary, remove the handlebar grip from the handlebar as described in this chapter.

NOTE
On 1999-2000 models, the handlebar grip must be removed before the choke lever can be removed.

6. On 1999-2000 models, if necessary remove the handlebar grip and choke lever assembly.
7. Remove the stop ring (C, **Figure 2**) from the groove in the top of the fork tube.
8. Loosen the handlebar clamp bolt (D, **Figure 2**) and remove the handlebar.

Left Handlebar Installation

1. Install the left handlebar over the fork tube. Align the top of the handlebar boss with the groove in the upper fork bridge and the stop ring groove in the fork tube (A, **Figure 4**).
2. Tighten the handlebar clamp bolt (B, **Figure 4**) securely.
3. Install the stop ring into the groove in the top of the fork tube (C, **Figure 2**). Make sure the stop ring seats in the groove completely.

NOTE
The following steps are only necessary if all of the components were removed from the handlebar.

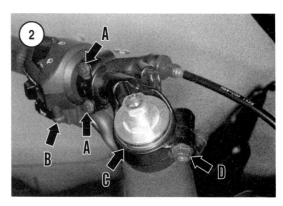

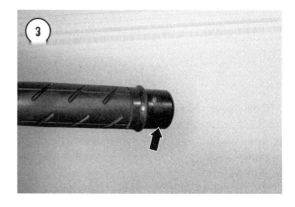

4A. On 1999-2000 models, if the handlebar grip was removed, perform the following:
   a. If removed, install the choke lever assembly.
   b. Apply grease onto the exposed choke cable wire and connect the cable end onto the choke lever.
   c. Install the handlebar grip as described in this chapter.
4B. On 2001-on models, if removed, install the handlebar grip as described in this chapter.
5. Install the left handlebar switch. On 1999-2000 models, install the switch housing over the choke

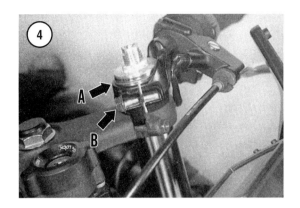

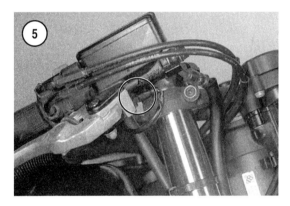

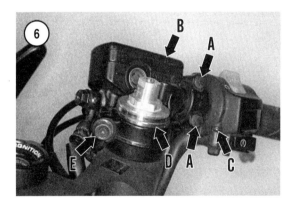

9. Remove the heavy towel or blanket from the front fairing.

Right Handlebar Removal

This section describes the removal of all the components from the right handlebar and then the handlebar from the left fork tube. If it is only necessary to remove the handlebar with all components intact, proceed to Step 7 and Step 8.

CAUTION
Cover the fairing and fuel tank with a heavy cloth or plastic tarp to protect it from brake fluid spills. Brake fluid damages plastic, painted and plated surfaces. Wash off spilled brake fluid immediately.

1. Remove the screw and handlebar outer weight (**Figure 3**) and remove the weight.
2. Disconnect the brake switch wire connector at the brake light switch (**Figure 5**).

NOTE
Do not disconnect the brake hydraulic line when removing the master cylinder in Step 2.

3. Remove the brake master cylinder holder mounting bolts (A, **Figure 6**) and holder and remove the brake master cylinder (B) from the handlebar. Secure the brake master cylinder to the frame with a bungee cord. Make sure the master cylinder is in an upright position.
4. Remove the handlebar switch housing screws (C, **Figure 6**) and separate the switch.
5. Slide the throttle pipe and switch assembly off the handlebar.

NOTE
Prior to disconnecting the throttle cables, note their location on the throttle grip. The cables must be installed in the same location during assembly.

6. Disconnect the throttle cable ends from the throttle grip and remove the switch housing.
7. Remove the stop ring (D, **Figure 6**) from the groove in the top of the fork tube.
8. Loosen the handlebar clamp bolt (E, **Figure 6**) and remove the handlebar.

13

lever. On all models, insert the switch housing pin into the hole in the handlebar. Install the switch housing screws. Tighten the front switch screws (B, **Figure 2**), then the rear screw.
6. Install the clutch lever bracket and align the end of the bracket with the punch mark on the handlebar. Install and tighten the bolts (A, **Figure 2**) securely.
7. Reconnect the electrical connectors at the clutch interlock switch (**Figure 1**).
8. Install the handlebar weight (**Figure 3**) and tighten the screw to 10 N•m (88 in.-lb.).

HANDLEBAR WEIGHT ASSEMBLY

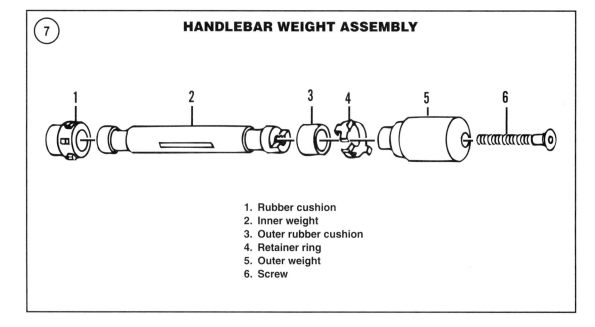

1. Rubber cushion
2. Inner weight
3. Outer rubber cushion
4. Retainer ring
5. Outer weight
6. Screw

Right Handlebar Installation

NOTE
Steps 5-6 and 12 are only necessary if all of the components were not removed from the handlebar.

1. Install the right handlebar over the fork tube. Align the top of the handlebar boss with the groove in the upper fork bridge and with the stop ring groove in the fork tube (D, **Figure 6**).

2. Tighten the handlebar clamp bolt (E, **Figure 6**) securely.

3. Install the stop ring into the groove in the top of the fork tube (D, **Figure 6**). Make sure the stop ring seats in the groove completely.

4. Clean the throttle grip of all old grease.

5. Lightly grease the right handlebar where the throttle grip operates.

6. Install the throttle grip over the right handlebar.

7. Lightly grease the throttle cable ends and connect them to the throttle grip.

8. Open the right handlebar switch assembly and connect the throttle cables onto the throttle grip.

9. Close the right handlebar switch over the throttle grip while aligning the switch housing locating pin with the hole in the handlebar. Install the switch housing screws (C, **Figure 6**), then tighten the upper screw and then the lower screw.

10. Open and release the throttle grip. It must open and close (snap back) without any binding or roughness.

11. Install the front master cylinder (B, **Figure 6**) as follows:

    a. Reconnect the brake switch wires at the switch (**Figure 5**).

    b. Install the master cylinder by aligning the end of its bracket with the punch mark on the handlebar.

    c. Install the master cylinder bracket holder with its UP mark facing up.

    d. Install the master cylinder lever bracket mounting bolts (A, **Figure 6**). Tighten the upper bolt first, then the lower bolt, to 12 N•m (106 in.-lb.).

12. Install the outer handlebar weight (**Figure 3**) and secure it with a new mounting screw. Tighten the handlebar weight mounting screw to 10 N•m (88 in.-lb.).

13. Open and release the throttle grip. Make sure it opens and closes (snaps back) without any binding or roughness. Then support the motorcycle on its centerstand and turn the handlebar from side to side, checking throttle operation at both steering lock positions.

WARNING
An improperly installed throttle grip assembly may cause the throttle to stick open. Failure to properly assem-

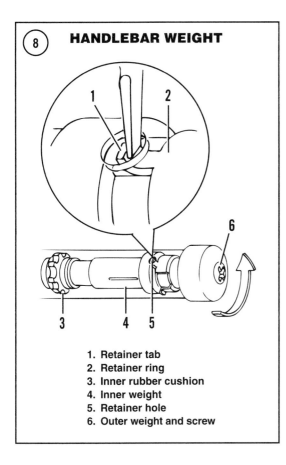

HANDLEBAR WEIGHT

1. Retainer tab
2. Retainer ring
3. Inner rubber cushion
4. Inner weight
5. Retainer hole
6. Outer weight and screw

ble and adjust the throttle cables and throttle grip could cause a loss of steering control. Do not start or ride the motorcycle until the throttle grip is correctly installed and snaps back when released.

Handlebar Grips Inspection

The handlebar grips must be secured tightly to the left handlebar and to the throttle grip (right side). Replace cut or damaged grips, as water may enter between the grip and its mounting surface and cause the grip to slip. This could cause a loss of steering control. Replace the handlebar grips as described under *Handlebar Weights* in this chapter.

Handlebar Weights

Each handlebar is equipped with an inner and outer handlebar weight assembly (**Figure 7**). The

handlebar weights can be serviced with the handlebars mounted on the motorcycle.

1. Remove the screw and handlebar outer weight (**Figure 3**, typical).

> *NOTE*
> *The left side hand grip must be removed before the left inner weight assembly can be removed from the handlebar. Do not remove the right-hand grip from the throttle unless it is going to be replaced.*

2. To remove the hand grips, perform the following:

> *NOTE*
> *If reusing the hand grips, remove them carefully to avoid puncturing or tearing them.*

  a. Carefully insert a thin flat-blade screwdriver between the handlebar or throttle housing and grip.

  b. Spray electrical contact cleaner into the space created by the screwdriver. Then remove the screwdriver and quickly twist the grip back and forth to break the cement bond between the hand grip and handlebar.

  c. Slide the hand grip off the handlebar.

3. When servicing the right side, remove the throttle grip as described under *Right-Handlebar Removal* in this chapter.

4. Insert a screwdriver into the retainer hole (1, **Figure 8**) and straighten the retaining ring tab. Make sure the tab clears the hole.

5. Reinstall the outer weight and its mounting screw.

6. Twist and pull the outer weight to remove it and the inner weight assembly (4, **Figure 8**) from the handlebar.

7. Remove the mounting screw and the outer weight. Discard the mounting screw.

8. Remove the retaining ring from the inner weight and discard it.

9. Replace the inner rubber cushion (3, **Figure 8**) if excessively worn or damaged.

10. Install a new retaining ring onto the inner weight.

11. Install the outer weight onto the inner weight. Align the outer weight boss with the slot in the inner

13

weight. Then install a new handlebar weight mounting screw (6, **Figure 8**) and tighten it securely.

12. Install the handlebar weight assembly into the handlebar. Hook the retainer tab on the retaining ring into the hole in the handlebar. Make sure the retainer tab engages the handlebar hole as shown in **Figure 8**.

13. Install the right handlebar switch/throttle assembly as described under *Right Handlebar Installation* in this chapter.

NOTE
When replacing the right-hand grip, reconnect the throttle cables and install the throttle housing onto the handlebar before installing the new grip. By having the throttle housing installed on the handlebar, the grip can be installed so that its shoulder does not contact the switch housing.

NOTE
Steps 14-19 describe how to cement the hand grips onto the handlebar and throttle housing. When using a grip cement (Honda Grip Cement or ThreeBond 1501C Griplock), follow the manufacturer's instructions carefully.

14. Clean and dry the handlebar and throttle housing surface.

15. On 1999-2000 models, install the choke lever onto the left handlebar, if removed.

16. If reusing the grips, use a contact cleaner to remove all old glue residue from inside the grips.

NOTE
If the original hand grips are torn or damaged, install new hand grips.

17. Apply the grip cement to the left handlebar, the outer surface of the throttle grip and inside the hand grips.

NOTE
The left and right side hand grips are different. Install the grip with the larger inside diameter over the throttle housing. Also, if the grip surfaces are not symmetrical, install the grips with their raised or directional hand pads positioned correctly.

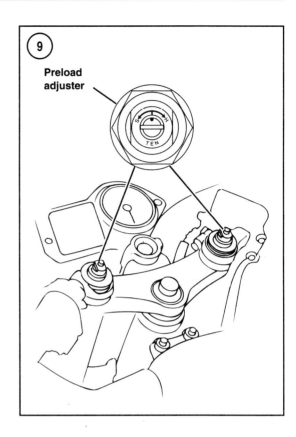

(9)

Preload adjuster

18. Install the hand grip over the handlebar or throttle housing. Make sure there is clearance between the end of the grip and the switch housing. Remove all excess grip cement from the end of each grip.

19. Follow the grip cement manufacturer's instructions regarding drying time before operating the motorcycle.

WARNING
Loose or damaged hand grips can slide off and cause loss of steering control. Make sure the hand grips are correctly installed and cemented in place before operating the motorcycle.

20. When the grip cement is dry, open the throttle grip and then release it. Make sure it opens and closes (snaps back) without any binding or roughness.

WARNING
An improperly installed throttle grip assembly may cause the throttle to stick open. Failure to properly assem-

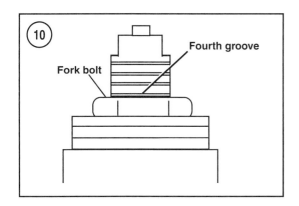

Fourth groove

Fork bolt

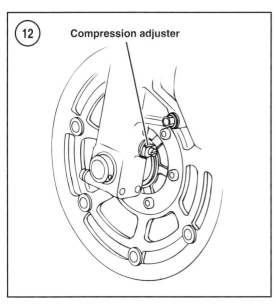

Compression adjuster

ble and adjust the throttle cables and throttle grip could cause a loss of steering control. Do not start or ride the motorcycle until the throttle grip is correctly installed and snaps back when released.

FRONT FORK

The following sections describe complete adjustment and service for the front fork. To prevent damaging the fork during service, note the following:

1. To avoid rounding off the shoulders on the fork caps, use a six-point socket when loosening and tightening the fork caps.

2. Do not overtighten the handlebar and fork bridge clamp bolts, as this can damage the fork bridge threads and fork tubes. Always refer to the torque specifications.

3. The fork sliders are easily scratched. Handle them carefully during all service procedures.

4. When holding the fork tubes in a vise, protect the tubes with soft jaws and do not overtighten.

Spring Preload Adjustment

Adjust the spring preload by turning the adjuster (**Figure 9**) in the top of each fork cap with a 14 mm open end wrench. The adjuster is marked with equally spaced alignment marks to ensure that both fork springs are adjusted equally.

The standard position is set when the fourth groove (**Figure 10**) is visible. The adjustable range, as measured from the top of the fork bolt is 6-21 mm (0.2-0.8 in.).

> *WARNING*
> *Both fork springs must be adjusted to the same setting. If the springs are set on different settings, it affects the motorcycle's handling and may cause a loss of steering control. Turn the spring adjuster (**Figure 11**) clockwise to increase spring preload or counterclockwise to decrease preload. Make certain that the preload is equal on both springs.*

Compression Adjustment

Adjust the spring compression by turning the adjuster screw (**Figure 12**) in the adjuster (**Figure 13**) at the base of the fork slider with a screwdriver.

1. Turn the compression adjuster clockwise until it lightly seats and no longer turns. This is the full hard mark H setting.

2. Turn the compression adjuster counterclockwise approximately 1 1/4 turns until the punch mark

13

aligns with the reference mark. This is the standard position.

3. To reduce compression damping, turn the adjuster counterclockwise toward the *S* mark.

4. To increase compression damping, turn the adjuster clockwise toward the *H* mark.

> *WARNING*
> *Both fork springs must be adjusted to the same setting. If the springs are set on different settings, it affects the motorcycle's handling and may cause a loss of steering control.*

Rebound Adjustment

Adjust the spring rebound by turning the adjuster screw (**Figure 14**) in the top of each fork cap with a screwdriver.

1. Turn the adjuster clockwise until it lightly seats and no longer turns. This is the full hard *H* setting.

2. Turn the rebound adjuster counterclockwise approximately 1 3/4 turns until the punch mark aligns with the reference mark. This is the standard position.

3. To reduce rebound damping, turn the adjuster counterclockwise toward the *S* mark.

4. To increase compression damping, turn the adjuster clockwise toward the *H* mark.

> *WARNING*
> *Both fork springs must be adjusted to the same setting. If the springs are set on different settings, it affects the motorcycle's handling and may cause a loss of steering control.*

Removal/Installation
(Fork Not To Be Serviced)

> *NOTE*
> *This procedure is shown with the front fairing removed. It is possible to remove the front fork with the front fairing in place, but removal allows additional working room.*

1. Remove the front wheel as described in Chapter Twelve.

2. Remove the front fender as described in Chapter Sixteen.

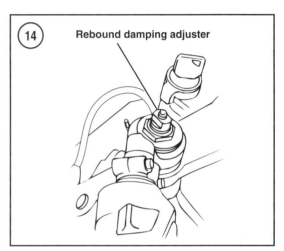

Rebound damping adjuster

3. Remove the side fairing panel from each side as described in Chapter Sixteen.

4. Remove the band(s) (**Figure 15**) securing the handlebar switch cables to the fork tube on each side.

5. If both fork tube assemblies are going to be removed, mark them with an R (right side) and L (left side) so the assemblies will be reinstalled on the correct side.

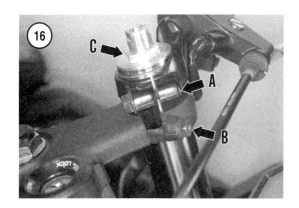

6. Remove the handlebar (A, **Figure 16**) from the fork tube as described in this chapter.

7. Loosen the upper (B, **Figure 16**) and lower (**Figure 17**) fork bridge clamp bolts, then slide the fork assembly down and out for both fork bridges. It may be necessary to rotate the fork tube slightly while pulling it down and out. Remove the fork assembly and take it to the workbench for service.

8. Repeat for the other fork assembly.

9. Install a fork tube through the lower fork bridge.

10. Continue to push the fork tube up through the upper fork bridge until the top surface of the fork tube is 33 mm (1.3 in.) above the top surface of the upper fork bridge (**Figure 18**). This dimension is necessary to make room for the handlebar assembly.

11. Tighten the upper clamp bolt (B, **Figure 16**) to 23 N•m (17 ft.-lb.).

12. Tighten the lower clamp bolt (**Figure 17**) to 39 N•m (29 ft.-lb.).

13. Install the handlebar as described in this chapter.

14. Install both side fairing panels as described in Chapter Sixteen.

15. Install the front fender as described in Chapter Sixteen.

16. Install the front wheel as described in Chapter Twelve.

Removal (Fork To Be Serviced)

NOTE
This procedure is shown with the front fairing removed. It is possible to remove the front fork with the front fairing in place, but removal allows additional working room.

1. Remove the front wheel as described in Chapter Twelve.

2. Remove the front fender as described in Chapter Sixteen.

3. Remove the side fairing panel from each side as described in Chapter Sixteen.

4. Remove the band(s) (**Figure 15**) securing the handlebar switch cables to the fork tube on each side.

5. If both fork tube assemblies are going to be removed, mark them with an R (right side) and L (left side) so the assemblies will be reinstalled on the correct side.

6. Remove the handlebar (A, **Figure 16**) from the fork tube as described in this chapter.

7. Use a six-point socket and loosen the fork cap (C, **Figure 16**).

8. Loosen the upper (B, **Figure 16**) and lower (**Figure 17**) fork bridge pinch bolts, then slide the fork assembly part way down and retighten the lower pinch bolt (**Figure 17**).

9. Place a drain pan under the fork slider to catch the fork oil.

13

10. Use an 8 mm Allen wrench and impact driver and loosen the fork damper 8 mm Allen bolt at the base of the slider.

11. Remove the Allen bolt and drain the fork oil. Pump the slider several times to expel most of the fork oil. Reinstall the Allen bolt to keep residual oil in the fork.

NOTE
Figure 19 is shown with the fork assembly removed for clarity.

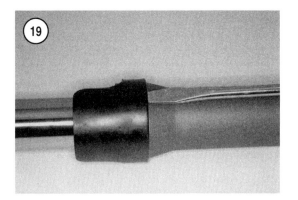

12. Use a wide flat blade screwdriver and carefully release the fork protector (**Figure 19**) from the slider groove. Slide the protector up onto the fork tube.

13. Slide the dust seal up on the fork tube.

14. Remove the stopper ring (**Figure 20**) from the fork slider.

15. Lower the fork slider on the fork tube.

NOTE
It may be necessary to slightly heat the area on the slider around the oil seal prior to removal. Use a rag soaked in hot water; do not apply a flame directly to the fork slider.

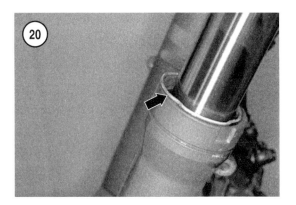

16. There is an interference fit between the bushing in the fork slider and the bushing on the fork tube. In order to remove the fork tube from the slider, pull hard on the fork tube using quick in and out strokes (**Figure 21**). Doing so will withdraw the bushing and the oil seal from the slider.

17. Remove the slider from the fork tube. If still in place, remove the oil lock piece from the damper rod.

18. Loosen the lower clamp bolt (**Figure 17**). Slide the fork tube (**Figure 22**) out of the lower fork bridge. It may be necessary to rotate the fork tube slightly while pulling it down and out. Remove the fork assembly and take it to the workbench for service.

19. Repeat for the other fork assembly.

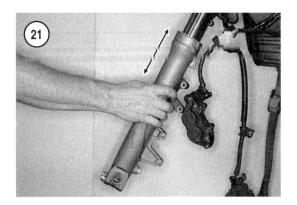

Installation (Fork Was Serviced)

1. Assemble the fork as described in this chapter.

2. Install a fork tube through the lower fork bridge.

3. Continue to push the fork tube up through the upper fork bridge until the top surface of the fork tube is 33 mm (1.3 in.) above the top surface of the upper fork bridge (**Figure 18**).

4. Tighten the upper clamp bolt (B, **Figure 16**) to 23 N•m (17 ft.-lb.).

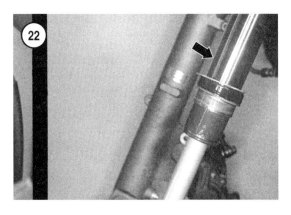

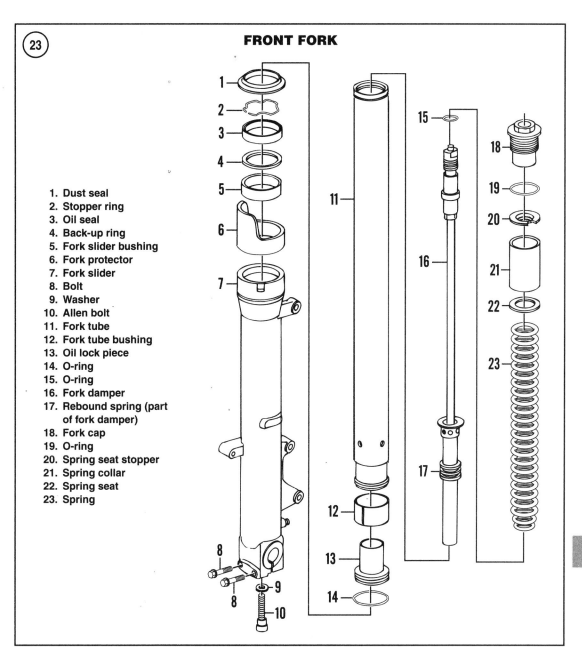

FRONT FORK

1. Dust seal
2. Stopper ring
3. Oil seal
4. Back-up ring
5. Fork slider bushing
6. Fork protector
7. Fork slider
8. Bolt
9. Washer
10. Allen bolt
11. Fork tube
12. Fork tube bushing
13. Oil lock piece
14. O-ring
15. O-ring
16. Fork damper
17. Rebound spring (part of fork damper)
18. Fork cap
19. O-ring
20. Spring seat stopper
21. Spring collar
22. Spring seat
23. Spring

5. Tighten the lower clamp bolt (**Figure 17**) to 39 N•m (29 ft.-lb.).

6. Install the fork cap (C, **Figure 16**) onto the top of the fork tube and tighten it to 23 N•m (17 ft.-lb.).

7. Install the handlebar (A, **Figure 16**) as described in this chapter.

8. Install the band(s) (**Figure 15**) securing the handlebar switch cables to the fork tube on each side.

9. Install both side fairing panels as described in Chapter Sixteen.

10. Install the front fender as described in Chapter Sixteen.

11. Install the front wheel as described in Chapter Twelve.

Disassembly

This section describes complete disassembly of the front fork (**Figure 23**). If only changing the fork oil and/or setting the oil level, perform Steps 1-10.

1. Hold the fork in a vertical position and completely unscrew the fork cap (**Figure 24**) from the fork tube. The fork cap cannot be removed at this time as it is still attached to the fork damper.

2. Turn the fork assembly upside down and drain the residual fork oil into a suitable container. Pump the fork several times by hand to expel most of the oil. Dispose of the fork oil properly.

3. Slide the fork tube down into the fork slider to expose the spring collar.

4. Install a 14 mm open end wrench on the damper rod cartridge nut (**Figure 25**) and another one on the flats on the fork cap (**Figure 26**).

5. Hold onto the fork cap and loosen the fork damper nut.

6. Use a six-point socket and completely unscrew the fork cap from the damper rod cartridge.

7. Remove the fork cap (**Figure 27**) and piston rod from the damper rod cartridge.

8. Remove the spring seat stopper, spring collar and spring seat from above the fork spring.

9. Withdraw the fork spring and fork damper.

10. Slide the slider bushing, backup ring, oil seal, stopper ring and dust seal off the fork tube. Keep them in the order of removal.

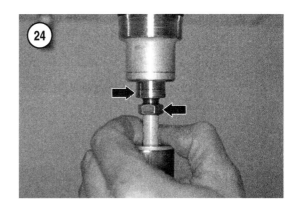

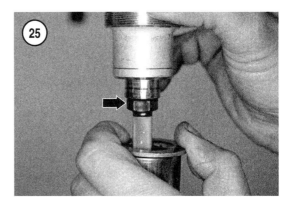

> *CAUTION*
> *The oil lock piece is long and has an O ring seal at the base of it. This piece is very difficult to remove from the slider unless it is loose. Do not try to remove the oil lock piece unless it is loose or is known to be faulty.*

11. *If loose*, remove the oil lock piece (**Figure 28**) from the slider.

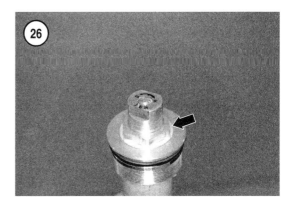

> *NOTE*
> *Do not remove the fork tube bushing unless it is going to be replaced. Inspect it as described in this chapter.*

12. Inspect the components as described in this chapter.

Inspection

Replace any damaged or excessively worn components. Repair damaged threads with an appropriate size metric tap or die. Simply cleaning and

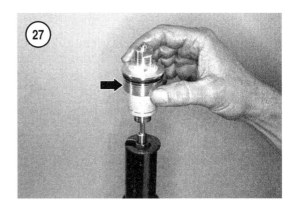

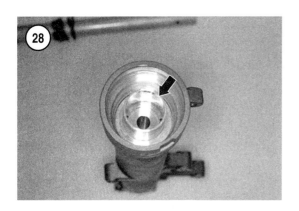

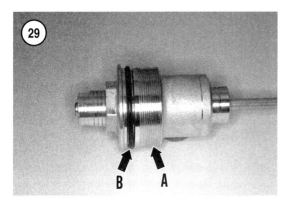

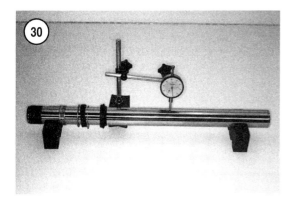

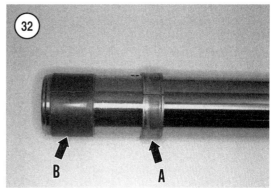

reinstalling unserviceable components will not improve performance of the front suspension.

1. Thoroughly clean the parts, except the fork damper, in solvent and dry them. Check the fork tube for signs of wear or scratches.

> *NOTE*
> *Cleaning the fork damper in solvent allows it to absorb some of the solvent that is difficult to remove. Solvent left in the fork damper will contaminate the fork oil. Instead, wipe the fork damper off with a clean cloth and set it aside for inspection and assembly.*

2. Inspect the fork cap threads (A, **Figure 29**) for wear or damage.

3. Install a *new* O-ring (B, **Figure 29**) on the fork cap.

4. Check the fork tube for severe wear or scratches. Check for chrome flaking or other damage that could damage the oil seal.

5. Check the fork tube for straightness. Place the fork tube on V-blocks and measure the runout with a dial indicator (**Figure 30**). If the runout is beyond the wear limit in **Table 1**, replace the fork tube.

6. Inspect the fork cap bolt threads in the fork tube (**Figure 31**) for wear or damage.

7. Make sure the oil hole in the fork tube is clear. Clean out if necessary.

8. Check the fork tube stopper ring and groove (**Figure 33**) for wear or damage. Replace the stopper ring if stretched or damaged.

9. Check the slider for dents or exterior damage that may cause the upper fork tube to stick.

13

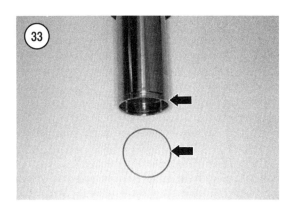

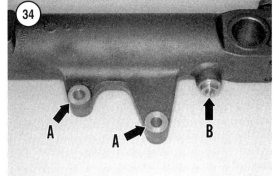

10. Inspect the brake caliper mounting bosses (A, **Figure 34**) on the slider for cracks or other damage.

11. Check the front axle bore (A, **Figure 35**) in the slider for burrs or damage.

12. Check the front axle clamp bolts (B, **Figure 35**) for thread damage.

13. Check the compression damping adjuster (B, **Figure 34**). Make sure it can be turned from one stop to the other.

14. Inspect the oil seal seating area (**Figure 36**) in the slider for damage or burrs.

15. Inspect the slider (A, **Figure 32**) and fork tube (B) bushings for scoring, excessive wear or damage. Check for discoloration and material coating damage. If the coating is worn off so that the copper base material is showing on approximately 3/4 of the total surface, the bushing is severely worn. Replace both bushings as a set.

16. To replace the fork tube bushing (B, **Figure 32**), open the bushing slot with a screwdriver and slide the bushing off the fork tube. Lubricate the new bushing with fork oil, then open its slot slightly and slide it into the fork tube slot. Spin the bushing to make sure it is centered in the slot.

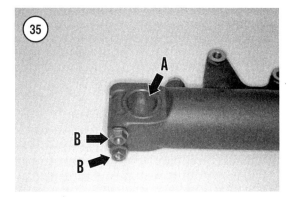

NOTE
*Do not remove the rebound adjuster (**Figure 37**) or the rebound spring, as they are an integral part of the fork damper and cannot be replaced separately. Doing so can damage the fork damper assembly. If either is faulty, replace the fork damper as an assembly.*

17. Inspect the fork damper assembly as follows:
   a. Check the fork damper housing for straightness.

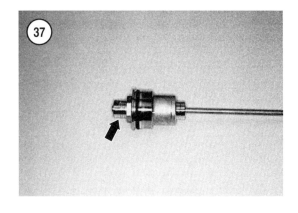

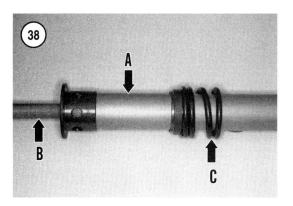

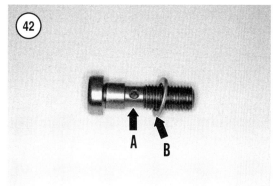

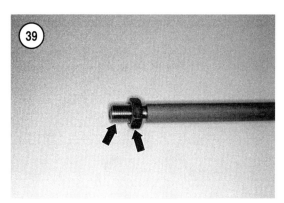

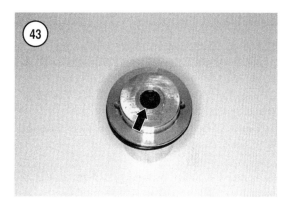

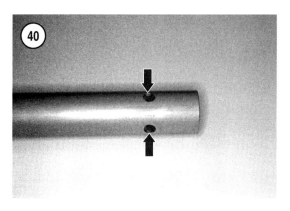

b. Hold the fork damper (A, **Figure 38**) and operate the piston rod (B) by hand. Make sure there is no binding or roughness, which indicates a bent piston rod or damaged fork damper.

c. Check the rebound spring (C, **Figure 38**) for cracks or other damage.

d. Check the threads and nut (**Figure 39**) at the top of the fork damper for damage.

e. Make sure the oil holes (**Figure 40**) are clear. Clean out if necessary.

f. Inspect the fork damper threads (**Figure 41**) for the Allen bolt for wear or damage.

g. Make sure the Allen bolt oil holes (A, **Figure 42**) are clear. Clean out if necessary.

18. If removed, check the threads (**Figure 43**) in the base of the oil lock piece for wear or damage.

19. Check the spring seat stopper and spring seat for cracks or distortion.

20. Measure the uncompressed length of the fork spring as shown in **Figure 44**. Replace the spring if it has sagged to the wear limit in **Table 1**. Replace both the right and left side springs if they are unequal in length.

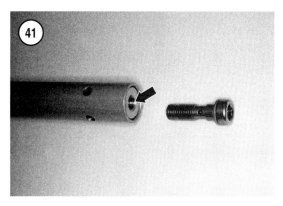

13

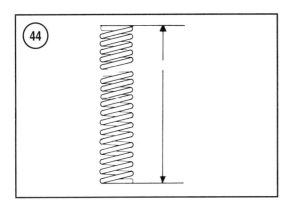

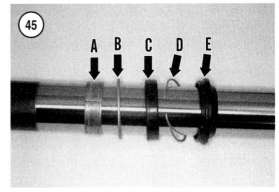

Assembly

1. Before assembling the parts, make sure there is no solvent residue remaining in the slider or on any component.

2. Install *new* O-rings where necessary. Then lubricate each O-ring with fresh fork oil.

3. Coat all parts with fresh fork oil prior to installation.

4. If removed, install a new bushing (B, **Figure 32**) onto the fork tube.

5. Install the slider bushing (A, **Figure 45**) and backup ring (B) down onto the fork tube.

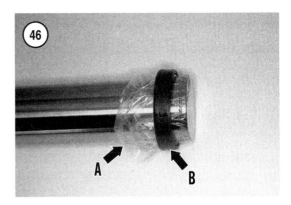

> *NOTE*
> *Place a clinging type of plastic wrap (A, **Figure 46**) over the end of the fork tube and coat it with fork oil. This will prevent damage to the dust seal and the oil seal lips when installing them over the top of the fork tube. These parts can then be carefully slid over the fork tube and plastic wrap without damaging the seals.*

6. Install a new fork seal as follows:
   a. Lubricate the seal lips with fork oil.
   b. Position the seal with the manufacturer's name and size code facing up.
   c. Slide the seal down the fork tube (B, **Figure 46**). Remove the plastic wrap.

7. Push the oil seal down the fork tube (C, **Figure 45**).

8. Install the stopper ring (D, **Figure 45**) and dust seal (E) onto the fork tube.

9. Install the fork tube into the fork slider (**Figure 47**).

10. Secure the fork tube in the vise so the fork tube faces straight up.

11. Move the dust seal, stopper ring and oil seal up the fork tube out of the way.

12. Install the fork slider bushing and backup ring as follows:

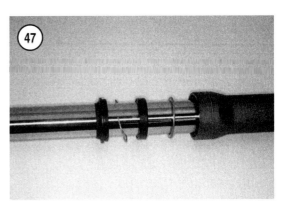

a. Slide the slider bushing and backup ring (B) down the fork tube. Make sure the backup ring is installed with its chamfered side facing down and set it on top of the bushing.

b. Use a fork oil seal driver (**Figure 48**) and drive the bushing into the fork slider until it bottoms out in the recess in the slider. The knocking sound made by the driver changes when the bushing bottoms.

c. Remove the special tool.

NOTE
Fork oil seal drivers can be purchased from aftermarket suppliers. To select a driver, first measure the outside diameter of one fork tube.

13. Install a new fork seal as follows:
   a. Push the oil seal down into position on the slider.
   b. Drive the oil seal into the slider with the same tool (**Figure 48**) used in Step 12.
   c. Continue to install the seal until the groove in the slider can be seen above the top surface of the seal (**Figure 49**).

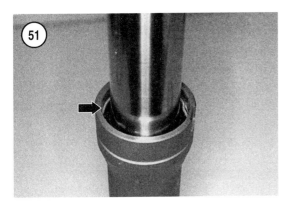

14. Slide the stopper ring over the fork tube (**Figure 50**) and install it into the groove in the slider. Make sure the stopper ring is completely seated in the slider groove (**Figure 51**).

NOTE
If the stopper ring cannot seat completely into the slider groove, the oil seal has not been installed far enough into the slider.

15. Slide the dust seal down the fork tube and seat it into the slider (**Figure 52**).

16. Install the fork protector onto the fork slider. Index it correctly with the slider notch (**Figure 53**).

13

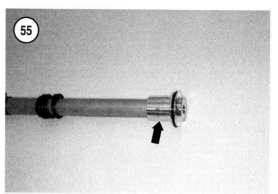

17. If the oil lock piece was removed, install a *new* O-ring (**Figure 54**) onto the oil lock piece, then install the oil lock piece (**Figure 55**) onto the end of the fork damper.

18. Insert the fork damper and oil lock piece into the fork tube (**Figure 56**). Slowly push the fork damper into the fork tube until it bottoms.

19. Install a *new* washer (B, **Figure 42**) onto the damper rod Allen bolt.

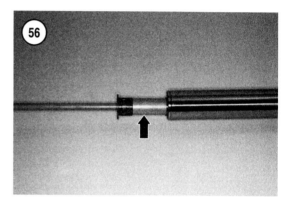

> *NOTE*
> *If the fork damper turns while tightening the Allen bolt in Step 20, temporarily install the fork spring, spring seat, spring collar, spring seat and fork cap. During this step, it is unnecessary to thread the fork cap onto the piston rod. Instead, push the fork damper down and bottom it out of the way. Installing these parts applies pressure against the fork damper and prevents it from turning. Remove these parts after tightening the Allen bolt.*

20. Apply a medium strength threadlocking compound onto the Allen bolt threads. Then thread the Allen bolt (**Figure 57**) into the bottom of the fork damper and tighten it to 34 N•m (25 ft.-lb.).

21. Fill the fork with oil, set the oil level and complete fork assembly as described under *Fork Oil Adjustment* in this section.

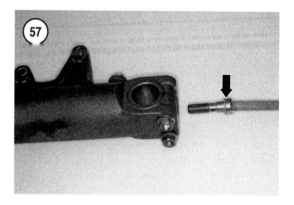

> *NOTE*
> *In the following steps, keep the fork assembly vertical to avoid the loss of fork oil installed in Step 21.*

22. Install the fork spring with the closer wound coils going in last (**Figure 58**).

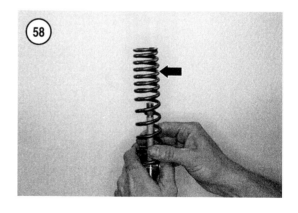

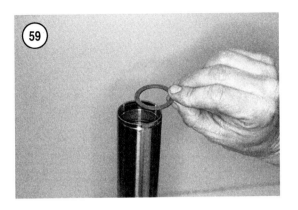

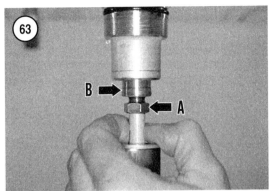

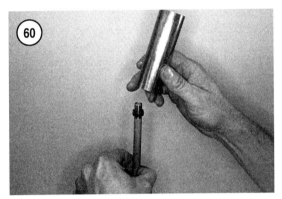

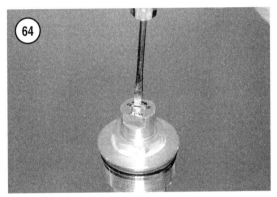

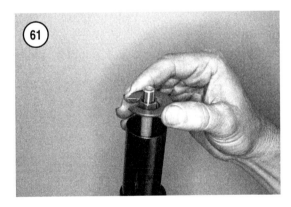

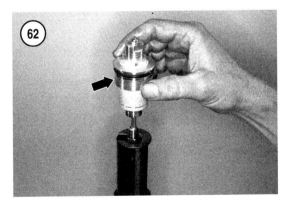

23. Install the spring seat (**Figure 59**) and the spring collar (**Figure 60**) onto the top of the fork spring.

24. Hold up the damper rod and install the spring seat stopper (**Figure 61**) under the damper rod nut.

25. Partially install the fork cap assembly (**Figure 62**) onto the damper rod threads.

13

CAUTION
The following adjustment must be made to the rebound adjuster. If positioned incorrectly within the fork cap, the rebound adjuster cannot be adjusted correctly after the fork has been assembled.

26. Reposition the rebound adjuster within the fork cap as follows:

    a. Turn the locknut all the way down on the damper rod until it stops (A, **Figure 63**).

    b. Use a small narrow blade screwdriver (**Figure 64**) and turn the adjuster *counterclockwise* until it lightly seats.

    c. Turn the adjuster *clockwise* three complete turns, then stop.

27. Screw the fork cap assembly (B, **Figure 63**) onto the fork damper until it seats against the damper rod, *not against the locknut.*

28. Install a 14 mm open end wrench on the damper rod locknut (**Figure 65**), and secure the fork cap (**Figure 66**). Tighten the locknut securely.

29. Pull the fork tube up against the fork cap (**Figure 67**) and screw the fork cap into the fork tube and tighten securely. Do not try to tighten to the correct torque at this time.

30. Install the fork assemblies as described in this chapter and tighten the fork cap to 23 N•m (17 ft.-lb.).

Fork Oil Adjustment

This section describes steps on filling the fork with oil, setting the oil level and completing fork assembly. See **Table 1** for the recommended type of fork oil.

NOTE
Steps 1-8 describe how to bleed the fork leg and set the oil level.

1. Perform Steps 1-20 of *Assembly* in the prior procedure.

2. Push the fork tube down and bottom out against the slider (A, **Figure 68**)

3. Position the fork vertically and slowly pour the recommended type and quantity of fork oil into the fork.

NOTE
As oil replaces air during the bleeding procedure (Steps 4-5), the oil level in the fork drops. Continue to add oil to maintain a high oil level in the fork. When bleeding the fork tube, do not be concerned with maintaining or achieving the proper oil capacity. Setting the oil level (Step 9) determines the actual amount of oil used in each fork tube.

4. Slowly pump the piston rod until fork oil flows out from the hole in the top of the damper rod hole (B, **Figure 68**). Continue to pump until all trapped air is expelled.

5. Hold the slider with one hand and slowly extend the fork tube. Repeat this until the fork tube moves smoothly with the same amount of tension through

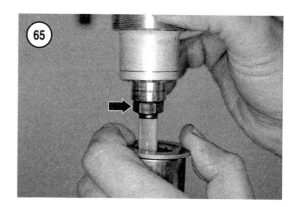
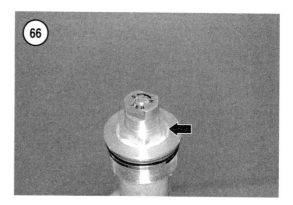

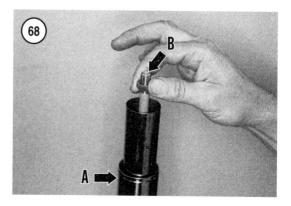

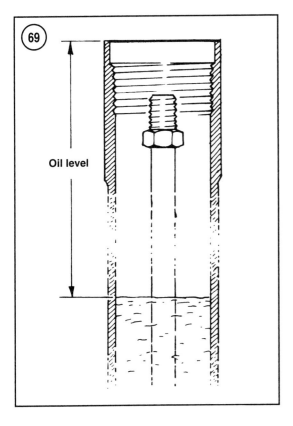

Oil level

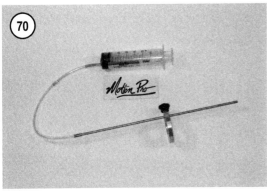

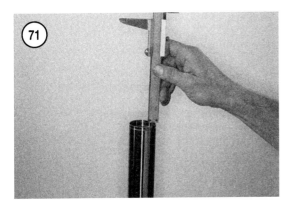

the compression and rebound travel strokes. Then stop with the fork tube bottomed out.

6. Set the fork tube aside for approximately five minutes to allow any suspended air bubbles in the oil to surface.

7. Set the oil level (**Figure 69**) as follows:

   a. Make sure the fork tube is bottomed against the slider and placed in a vertical position.

   b. Use an oil level gauge (**Figure 70**) or vernier caliper (**Figure 71**) and set the oil level to the specification in **Table 1**.

> *NOTE*
> *If no oil is drawn out when setting the oil level, there is not enough oil in the fork tube. Add more oil and reset the level.*

   c. If used, remove the oil level gauge.

8. Perform Steps 22-30 of *Assembly*.

STEERING HEAD AND STEM

The steering head assembly (**Figure 72**) uses retainer-type steel ball bearings. Each bearing consists of three pieces: upper race, lower race and ball bearing. The bearings can be lifted out of their operating positions after removing the steering stem. Do not remove the lower inner race that is pressed onto the steering stem or the bearing races that are pressed into the frame steering head unless they are to be replaced.

Regular maintenance consists of steering inspection, adjustment and bearing lubrication. When the steering cannot be adjusted correctly, the bearings may require replacement. However, to determine bearing condition, the steering assembly must be removed and inspected. Inspect the steering adjustment and lubricate the bearings at the intervals listed in the maintenance schedule in **Table 1** of Chapter Three.

This section describes complete service and adjustment procedures for the steering head assembly.

Special Tools

A Honda steering stem socket (part No. 07916-3710101) or equivalent is required to adjust the steering stem/bearing. Refer to *Steering Head Bearing Races* in this chapter for bearing race replacement procedures and special tools.

13

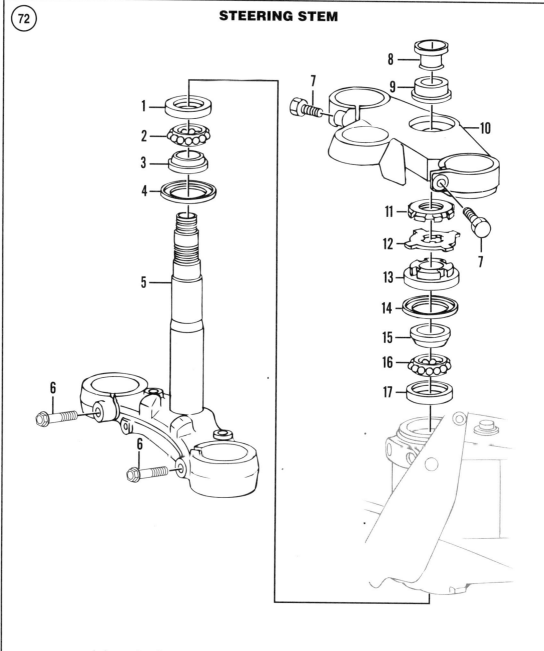

STEERING STEM

1. Lower bearing outer race
2. Lower bearing
3. Lower bearing inner race
4. Lower dust seal
5. Steering stem
6. Bolt
7. Bolt
8. Steering stem cap
9. Steering stem nut
10. Upper fork bridge
11. Locknut
12. Lockwasher
13. Steering stem adjust nut
14. Upper dust seal
15. Upper bearing inner race
16. Upper bearing
17. Upper bearing outer race

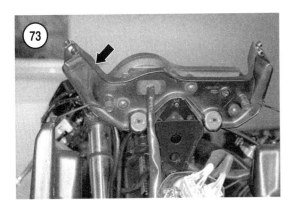

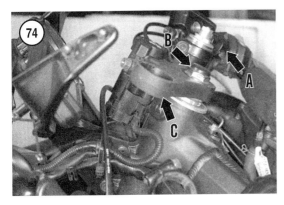

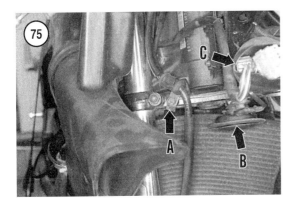

Removal

Refer to **Figure 72**.

1. Remove the fuel tank as described in Chapter Eight or Nine.

2. Remove the front wheel as described in Chapter Twelve.

3. Remove both side fairings and the front fairing assembly as described in Chapter Sixteen.

4. Remove the combination meter and mounting bracket (**Figure 73**).

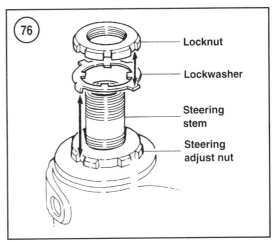

Locknut

Lockwasher

Steering stem

Steering adjust nut

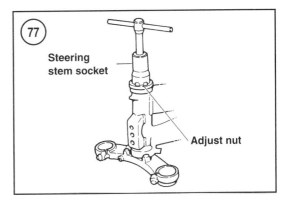

Steering stem socket

Adjust nut

5. Remove both handlebars (A, **Figure 74**) as described in this chapter.

6. Remove the bolt (A, **Figure 75**) securing the front brake hose and mounting bracket at the steering stem.

7. Disconnect the electrical connector at the horn. Remove the bolt securing the horn and remove the horn and bracket (B, **Figure 75**).

8. Release the wire band and the tie-wrap and disconnect the four-pin white electrical connector (C, **Figure 75**) at the steering stem.

9. Remove both front fork assemblies as described in this chapter.

10. Remove the steering stem cap, then remove the steering stem nut (B, **Figure 74**).

11. Remove the upper fork bridge (C, **Figure 74**).

12. Pry the lockwasher tabs away from the locknut groove. Then remove the locknut and lockwasher (**Figure 76**). Make sure a new lockwasher is installed during assembly.

13. Loosen the steering adjust nut with the Honda steering stem socket (part No. 07916-3710101) or equivalent (**Figure 77**).

13

14. Hold the lower end of the steering stem against the frame and remove the steering adjust nut and dust seal (**Figure 78**), then lower the steering stem down and out of the steering head.

15. Remove the upper inner race and the upper bearing.

16. Remove the lower bearing (**Figure 79**) from its race on the steering stem.

> *NOTE*
> *The upper outer race, lower outer race and lower inner race are installed with a press fit. Only remove these parts when replacing the bearing assembly.*

Inspection

Replace parts that show excessive wear or damage as described in this section.

> *WARNING*
> *The improper repair of damaged frame and steering components can cause the loss of steering control. If there is apparent frame, steering stem or fork bridge damage, consult with a Honda dealership or qualified frame shop for professional inspection and possible repair.*

1. Clean and dry all parts.
2. Check the frame for cracks and fractures.
3. Inspect the steering stem nut, locknut and steering adjust nut for excessive wear or damage.
4. Inspect the upper dust seal for tearing, deterioration or other damage.
5. Check the steering stem for:
   a. Cracked or bent stem.
   b. Damaged lower bridge.
   c. Damaged threads.
6. Check the upper fork bridge for cracks or other damage. Replace if necessary.
7. Inspect the bearing assemblies as follows:
   a. Inspect the bearing races (A, **Figure 80**) for severe wear, pitting, cracks or other damage. To replace the lower inner bearing race, refer to *Lower Inner Bearing Race Replacement* in this chapter. To replace the outer bearing races, refer to *Outer Bearing Race Replacement* in this chapter.

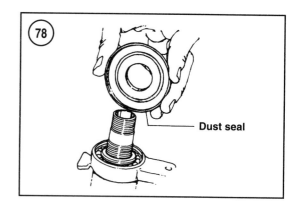

Dust seal

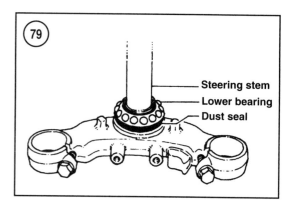

Steering stem
Lower bearing
Dust seal

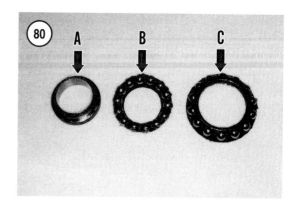

   b. Inspect the upper (B, **Figure 80**) and lower (C) bearings for pitting, excessive wear, corrosion, retainer damage or discoloration.

   c. Replace the upper and lower bearing assemblies at the same time.

> *NOTE*
> *Each bearing assembly consists of the bearing and an inner and outer race. Always replace the bearings in upper and lower sets.*

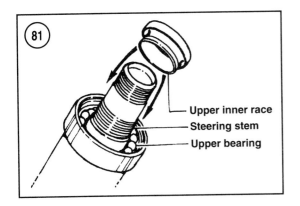

Upper inner race
Steering stem
Upper bearing

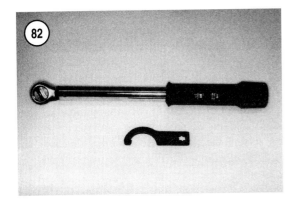

5. Install the steering stem into the steering head and hold it in place. Make sure the lower bearing is centered inside the lower outer race.

6. Install the upper bearing and seat it into its outer race (**Figure 81**).

7. Install the upper inner race (**Figure 81**) and seat it into the bearing.

8. Install the upper dust seal and seat it over the bearing assembly.

9. Apply oil to the steering adjust nut (**Figure 76**) threads and thread it onto the steering stem. Tighten finger-tight.

10. Tighten the steering adjust nut (**Figure 76**) as follows:

   a. Use the Honda steering stem socket (**Figure 77**) to seat the bearings in the following steps. See *Special Tools* in this section.

NOTE
*If the Honda tool is not available, use a spanner wrench and torque wrench (**Figure 82**) to seat the bearings. Refer to **Torque Wrench Adapters** in Chapter One for information on using these tools.*

   b. Tighten the steering stem adjust nut (**Figure 76**) to 25 N•m (18 ft.-lb.).

   c. Turn the steering stem from lock to lock several times to seat the bearings. The steering stem must pivot smoothly.

   d. If the steering stem pivots smoothly, loosen the steering stem adjust nut (**Figure 76**) and retighten to 25 N•m (18 ft.-lb.).

NOTE
If the steering stem does not pivot smoothly, one or both bearing assemblies may be damaged. Remove the steering stem and inspect the bearings.

   e. Turn the steering stem from lock to lock to recheck bearing play.

NOTE
Do not continue with Step 11 until the steering stem turns correctly. If there is any excessive play or roughness, recheck the steering adjustment.

11. Align the tabs of a *new* lockwasher with the grooves in the steering stem adjust nut and install

8. When reusing bearings, clean them thoroughly with a bearing degreaser and dry thoroughly. Repack each bearing with grease.

**Steering Stem Assembly
and Steering Adjustment**

1. Make sure the upper and lower bearing races are properly seated in the steering head. Then lubricate each bearing race with grease.

2. Thoroughly lubricate each bearing (B and C, **Figure 80**) with bearing grease.

3. Install the lower steering bearing (**Figure 79**) onto the lower inner bearing race.

4. Lubricate the upper dust seal lip with grease.

NOTE
Before installing the steering stem in Step 5, make sure the threads on the stem are clean. Any dirt, grease or other residue on the threads affects the steering stem tightening torque and adjustment.

13

the lockwasher. Bend the two shorter tabs (opposite each other) into the adjust nut grooves. See **Figure 76**.

WARNING
Never reinstall a used lockwasher, as the tabs may break off, making the lockwasher ineffective.

12. Install and tighten the locknut (**Figure 76**) as follows:
   a. Install the locknut and tighten finger-tight.
   b. Hold the steering stem adjust nut (to keep it from turning) and tighten the locknut approximately 1/4 turn (90°) to align its grooves with the outer lockwasher tabs.
   c. Bend the outer lockwasher tabs (**Figure 76**) up into the locknut grooves.

13. Install the upper fork bridge (C, **Figure 74**) and the steering stem head nut (B). Tighten the nut only finger-tight at this time.

14. Install both fork tubes as described in this chapter. Tighten the lower fork bridge clamp bolts to 39 N•m (29 ft.-lb.).

15. Tighten the steering stem head nut (B, **Figure 74**) to 103 N•m (76 ft.-lb.).

16. Turn the steering stem from lock-to-lock. Make sure it moves smoothly.

NOTE
If the steering stem is too tight after tightening the steering stem head nut, the bearings may be damaged or the steering stem adjust nut was tightened incorrectly. If the steering stem is too loose, the steering will become unstable.

17. Install the steering stem cap.

18. Install the horn mounting bracket and tighten the bolt (B, **Figure 75**) securely. Turn the ignition switch on and check the horn operation.

19. Install the front brake hose and mounting bracket and tighten the bolt (A, **Figure 75**) securely. Check the brake hose routing.

20. Connect the four-pin white electrical connector (C, **Figure 75**) at the steering stem. Secure the wires with the wire band and the tie wrap.

21. Install both handlebars (A, **Figure 74**) as described in this chapter.

22. Install the combination meter and mounting bracket (**Figure 73**).

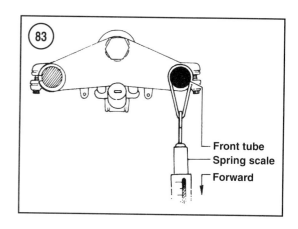

23. Install both side fairing panels and the front fairing assembly as described in Chapter Sixteen.

24. Install the front wheel as described in Chapter Twelve.

25. Inspect the steering bearing preload as described in this chapter.

26. Check the choke, clutch and throttle cables for proper operation. If necessary, adjust each cable as described in Chapter Three.

27. Install the fuel tank as described in Chapter Eight or Nine.

28. Check that the front brake works properly.

WARNING
Do not ride the motorcycle until the horn, control cables and front brake all work properly.

STEERING BEARING PRELOAD

The most common steering complaints are excessive steering play and slow or hard steering. Excessive steering play means there is excessive movement between the steering stem and frame. Hard steering requires the rider to make a greater steering effort when turning the handlebars. Both conditions are usually caused by an incorrect steering stem adjustment. However, dry or damaged bearings can cause similar conditions.

Check the steering head for looseness at the intervals specified in Chapter Three or whenever the following symptoms or conditions exist:

1. The handlebars vibrate more than normal.

2. The front fork makes a clicking or clunking noise when the front brake is applied.

3. The steering feels tight or slow.

4. The motorcycle does not steer straight on level road surfaces.

Inspection

A spring scale is required for this procedure.

1. Remove the front fairing assembly as described in Chapter Sixteen.

2. Secure the motorcycle with the front tire off the ground. See *Motorcycle Stands* in Chapter Twelve.

3. Attach a spring scale onto one of the fork tubes as shown in **Figure 83**.

> *NOTE*
> *When checking the steering play, make sure there is no interference from the control cables, brake hoses or wiring harness. Making adjustments to compensate for such interference leads to a loose steering adjustment.*

4. Center the wheel. Pull the spring scale and note the reading on the scale when the steering stem begins to turn. See **Table 1** for the correct steering preload reading. If any other reading is obtained, perform the adjustment procedure in this section.

5. If a spring scale is not available, check steering adjustment as follows:

   a. Center the front wheel. Push lightly against the left handlebar grip to start the wheel turning to the right, then let go. The wheel should continue turning under its own momentum until the fork hits its stop.

   b. Center the wheel, and push lightly against the right handlebar grip.

   c. If, with a light push in either direction, the front wheel turns all the way to the stop, the steering adjustment is good.

   d. If the front wheel does not turn all the way to the stop, the steering is too tight. Adjust the steering as described in this chapter.

   e. Center the front wheel and kneel in front of it. Grasp the bottoms of the two front fork sliders. Try to pull the fork forward, then try to push it toward the engine. If no play is felt, the steering adjustment is good.

   f. If the steering adjustment is too tight or too loose, adjust it as described in this chapter.

6. Install the front fairing assembly as described in Chapter Sixteen.

Adjustment

1. Secure the motorcycle with the front tire off the ground. See *Motorcycle Stands* in Chapter Twelve.

2. Remove the front fairing assembly as described in Chapter Sixteen.

3. Remove the fuel tank as described in Chapter Eight or Chapter Nine.

4. Recheck the steering as described under *Inspection* in this section.

5. If the bearing preload is incorrect, lower the front wheel to the ground. Then adjust the steering adjust nut (**Figure 84**) as described under *Steering Stem Assembly and Steering Adjustment* in this chapter.

6. Reverse Steps 1-3 to complete installation.

> *WARNING*
> *Do not ride the motorcycle until the steering stem is adjusted correctly and all of the cables work properly.*

STEERING HEAD BEARING RACES

Due to the aluminum frame design, several special tools are required to remove and install the steering head bearing races. Due to the expense of these tools, consider having a Honda dealership perform the procedure. Attempting to replace the bearing races without the proper tools may damage the frame.

13

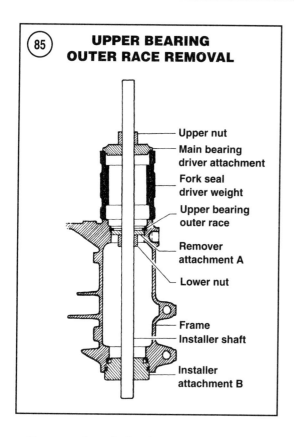

UPPER BEARING OUTER RACE REMOVAL

- Upper nut
- Main bearing driver attachment
- Fork seal driver weight
- Upper bearing outer race
- Remover attachment A
- Lower nut
- Frame
- Installer shaft
- Installer attachment B

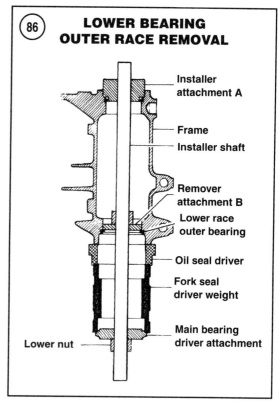

LOWER BEARING OUTER RACE REMOVAL

- Installer attachment A
- Frame
- Installer shaft
- Remover attachment B
- Lower race outer bearing
- Oil seal driver
- Fork seal driver weight
- Main bearing driver attachment
- Lower nut

Do not replace the bearing races unless they are worn or damaged. They are easily damaged during removal

The top and bottom bearing races are not the same size. Have the parts supplier identify the bearing kits and make sure the correct bearing race is installed in the correct end of the frame.

Special Tools

A hydraulic press and the following Honda special tools are required to replace the steering head races:

1. Main bearing driver attachment: 07946-ME90200.

2. Fork seal driver weight: 07947-KA50100.

3. Oil seal driver: 07965-MA60000.

4. Installer shaft: 07VMF-KZ30200.

5. Installer attachment A: 07VMF-MAT0100.

6. Installer attachment B: 07VMF-MAT0200.

7. Remover attachment A: 07VMF-MAT0300.

8. Remover attachment B: 07VMF-MAT0400.

Outer Bearing Race Replacement

Do not remove the upper and lower outer bearing races unless they are going to be replaced. The bearing/race assembly must be replaced in sets.

CAUTION
If any binding is observed when removing or installing the bearing races, stop and release all tension from the bearing race. Check the tool alignment to make sure the bearing race is moving evenly in its mounting bore. Otherwise, the bearing race may gouge the frame mounting bore and cause permanent damage.

1. To remove the upper outer race, perform the following:

    a. Assemble the tools onto the steering head as shown in **Figure 85**. Make sure to align the remover attachment *A* with the groove in the steering head.

    b. Hold the end of the installer shaft with a wrench and turn the upper nut slowly to remove the upper outer race.

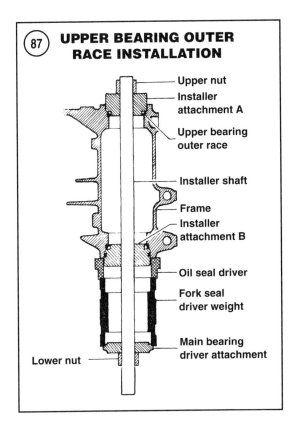

87 UPPER BEARING OUTER RACE INSTALLATION

Upper nut
Installer attachment A
Upper bearing outer race
Installer shaft
Frame
Installer attachment B
Oil seal driver
Fork seal driver weight
Main bearing driver attachment
Lower nut

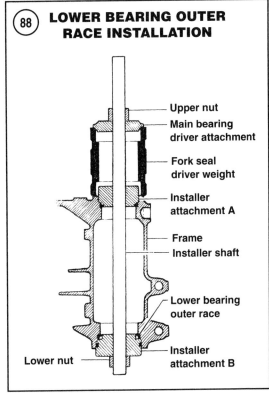

88 LOWER BEARING OUTER RACE INSTALLATION

Upper nut
Main bearing driver attachment
Fork seal driver weight
Installer attachment A
Frame
Installer shaft
Lower bearing outer race
Installer attachment B
Lower nut

c. Disassemble the tools from the steering head and bearing race.

2. To remove the lower outer race, perform the following:

a. Assemble the tools onto the steering head as shown in **Figure 86**. Make sure to align the remover attachment *B* with the groove in the steering head.

b. Hold the end of the installer shaft with a wrench and turn the lower nut slowly to remove the lower outer race.

c. Disassemble the tools from the steering head and bearing race.

3. Clean each bearing race bore, then check for cracks or other damage.

4. To install the new upper outer race, perform the following:

a. Place the new race squarely into the bore opening with its tapered side facing out. Then assemble the tools through the bearing race and steering head as shown in **Figure 87**. Recheck the bearing race and tool alignment before applying pressure to the race.

b. Hold the end of the installer shaft with a wrench and slowly turn the lower nut to align the groove in the installer attachment A with the upper mounting bore in the steering head. This ensures that the tool and bearing race are square with the steering head mounting bore.

c. Then hold the end of the installer shaft and turn the lower nut to press the bearing race into the steering head. Continue until the bearing race bottoms in the mounting bore.

d. Carefully remove the tools from the steering head.

5. To install the new lower outer race, perform the following:

a. Place the new race squarely into the bore opening with its tapered side facing out. Then assemble the tools through the bearing race and steering head as shown in **Figure 88**. Recheck the bearing race and tool alignment before applying pressure to the race.

b. Hold the end of the installer shaft with a wrench and slowly turn the upper nut to align the groove in the installer attachment B with the lower mounting bore in the steering head.

13

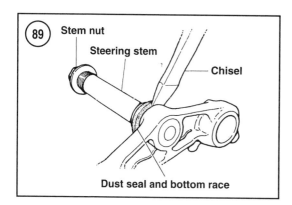

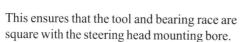

Dust seal and bottom race

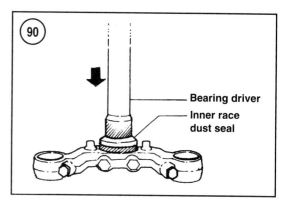

This ensures that the tool and bearing race are square with the steering head mounting bore.

c. Then hold the end of the installer shaft and turn the upper nut to press the bearing race into the steering head. Continue until the bearing race bottoms in the mounting bore.

d. Carefully remove the tools from the steering head.

6. Lubricate the upper and lower bearing races with grease.

Lower Inner Bearing Race Replacement

The lower inner race is a press fit on the steering stem. Replace the lower dust seal when replacing the lower inner race.

1. Thread the steering stem nut onto the steering stem (**Figure 89**).

WARNING
Striking a chisel with a hammer can cause flying chips. Wear safety glasses in Step 2 to prevent eye injury.

NOTE
Installing the steering stem nut as described in Step 1 helps prevent damaging the steering stem threads when removing the lower inner bearing race.

2. Remove the lower inner bearing race and dust seal with a chisel as shown in **Figure 89**. To prevent damaging the steering stem, remove the bearing race evenly by applying pressure against the bearing race a little at a time while working at different points around the bearing.

3. Discard the lower inner bearing race and dust seal.

4. Clean the steering stem with solvent and dry thoroughly.

5. Inspect the steering stem race surface for cracks or other damage. Replace the steering stem if necessary.

6. Install a new lower dust seal over the steering stem.

7. With the bearing surface facing up, slide the new lower inner bearing race onto the steering stem until it stops.

8. Install the steering stem in a press. Support the bottom of the steering stem with a bearing driver or piece of round metal. Then install a bearing driver (**Figure 90**) over the steering stem and seat it against the inner bearing race inside shoulder. Do not allow the bearing driver to contact the bearing race surface.

9. Press the lower inner race onto the steering stem until it bottoms.

10. Remove the steering stem from the press.

Table 1 FRONT SUSPENSION SPECIFICATIONS

Item	Specification	Wear limit
Front fork stroke	120 mm (4.7 in.)	–
Fork oil (1999-2000 models)		
Type	Pro-Honda Suspension Fluid SS-8	
Capacity	472.5-477.5 ml	
	(16.2-16.18 U.S. oz./16.61-16.79 Imp. oz.)	
Oil level	118 mm (4.65 in.)	
Fork oil (2001-on models)		
Type	Pro-Honda Suspension Fluid SS-8	
Capacity	459.5-464.5 ml	
	(15.52-15.68 U.S. oz./16.21-16.39 Imp. oz.)	
Oil level	116 mm (4.57 in.)	
Fork spring free length		
1999-2000 models	336 mm (13.23 in.)	329.3 mm (12.96 in.)
2001-on models	286 mm (11.26 in.)	280.3 mm (11.03 in.)
For tube runout	–	0.20 mm (0.008 in.)
Steering preload	10-15 kgf (2.2-3.3 lbf)	

Table 2 FRONT SUSPENSION AND STEERING TORQUE SPECIFICATIONS

Item	N•m	in.-lb.	ft.-lb.
Axle bolt	59	–	44
Axle pinch bolt	22	–	16
Brake hose			
clamp bolt	10	88	–
three-way joint bolt	10	88	–
Caliper mounting bolt[1]	30	–	22
Damper rod Allen bolt[2]	34	–	25
Fork bridge			
lower clamp bolt	39	–	29
upper clamp bolt	23	–	17
Fork cap bolt	23	–	17
Handlebar weight			
mounting screw	10	88	–
Master cylinder clamp bolt	12	106	–
Steering stem adjust nut	25	–	18
Steering stem head nut	103	–	76

1. ALOC type bolt. Install new bolts during installation.
2. Apply a medium strength threadlock to the threads.

13

CHAPTER FOURTEEN

REAR SUSPENSION

This chapter describes repair and replacement procedures for the rear suspension components. Refer to Chapter Eleven for rear wheel, driven flange, rear axle and tire service.

Rear suspension specifications are listed in **Table 1** and **Table 2** at the end of this chapter.

> *WARNING*
> *Replace all rear suspension fasteners with parts of the same type. Do not use a replacement part of lesser quality or substitute design, as this may affect the performance of the system or result in failure of the part, leading to loss of motorcycle control. The torque specifications listed must be used during installation to ensure proper component retention.*

SHOCK LINKAGE

Removal

Refer to **Figure 1**.

1. Support the motorcycle on level ground
2. Block the front wheel so the motorcycle will not roll in either direction while on the jack or safety stand (or centerstand on U.K. models).
3. Remove the rear wheel as described in Chapter Twelve.

> *WARNING*
> *Do not service the suspension linkage when the exhaust system is hot.*

> *NOTE*
> *Before removing the shock arm plates, locate the FR or arrow mark on each plate. These marks must face forward. If there are no marks, draw an arrow mark with a permanent marker on the outside of each shock arm plate pointing forward.*

4. Remove the lower bolt and nut (A, **Figure 2**) securing the shock absorber to the shock plates.
5. Remove the bolt and nut (B, **Figure 2**) securing the shock plates to the swing arm.

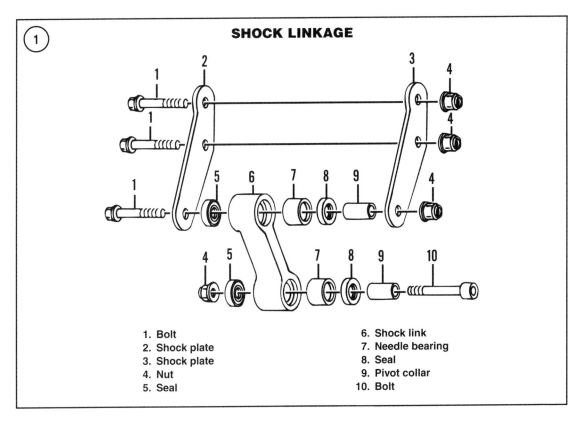

SHOCK LINKAGE

1. Bolt
2. Shock plate
3. Shock plate
4. Nut
5. Seal
6. Shock link
7. Needle bearing
8. Seal
9. Pivot collar
10. Bolt

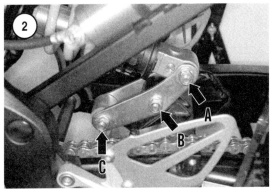

6. Remove the bolt and nut (C, **Figure 2**) securing the shock plates to the shock link.

7. Remove both shock plates.

8. Remove the bolt and nut (**Figure 3**) securing the shock link to the shock link brackets on the frame and crankcase.

NOTE
If the shock link cannot be removed, loosen the bolts and nuts securing the shock link bracket (A, Figure 4) to the

14

crankcase. This will allow clearance for shock link removal.

9. Remove the shock link (B, **Figure 4**) from the frame.

10. Inspect the shock linkage as described in this chapter.

Installation

Refer to **Figure 1**.

1. Apply a light coat of wheel bearing grease to all of the shock linkage mounting bolts. Do not apply grease to the mounting bolt threads or nuts. These must be tightened with dry threads.

NOTE
The shock link is symmetrical and can be installed in either direction.

2. Install the shock link (**Figure 4**) onto the shock link bracket. Install the shock link mounting bolt (**Figure 3**) from the left side. Install the nut finger-tight at this time.

3. Position the shock arm plates with their FR or arrow marks facing toward the front of the motorcycle. Install the shock arm plate mounting bolts from the left side as follows:

   a. Install the bolt and nut (C, **Figure 2**) securing the shock plates to the shock link.
   b. Install the bolt and nut (B, **Figure 2**) securing the shock plates to the swing arm.
   c. Install the lower bolt and nut (A, **Figure 2**) securing the shock absorber to the shock plates.
   d. Install the nuts finger-tight at this time.

4. If the shock link bracket (A, **Figure 4**) fasteners were loosened in Step 9, tighten the bolts and nuts to 44 N•m (32 ft.-lb.).

5. Tighten all of the suspension linkage fasteners to the specifications in **Table 2**.

6. Install the rear wheel as described in Chapter Twelve.

Inspection

Replace worn or damaged parts as described in this chapter.

1. Remove the pivot collars (**Figure 5**) from the shock link.

2. If necessary, pry the seals (A, **Figure 6**) out of the shock link.

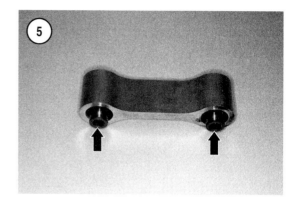

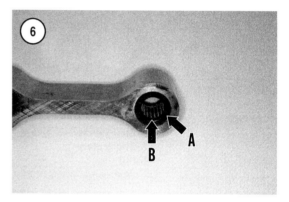

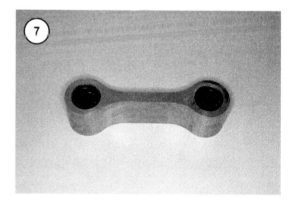

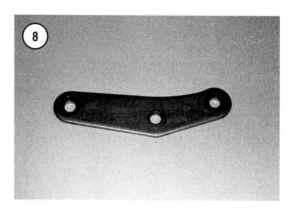

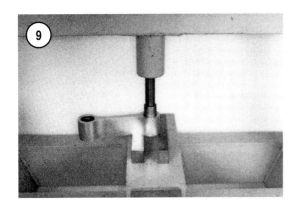

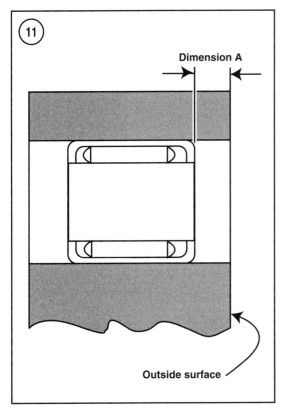

Dimension A

Outside surface

3. Clean and dry all parts and the mounting bolts and nuts. Replace damaged fasteners.

4. Clean the shock link pivot collars and check for wear.

5. Check the shock link (**Figure 7**) and shock arm plates (**Figure 8**) for cracks, bending or other damage.

6. Inspect the pivot collars for excessive wear, rust or damage. Check the collars for burrs or nicks that may damage the seals. Remove burrs or nicks with sandpaper or a fine cut file.

7. Check each needle bearing (B, **Figure 6**) for cracks, rust and other damage. Replace damaged bearings as described under *Needle Bearing Replacement* in this section.

> *CAUTION*
> *If the needle bearings do not require replacement, do not remove them for inspection or lubrication, as they may be damaged during removal and reinstallation.*

8. Clean the bearings once again in solvent and thoroughly dry them with compressed air.

9. Pack the bearings with water-resistant grease.

10. Pack the lips of the new seals with the same grease and install into position on the shock link. Install the seals (A, **Figure 6**) with the closed side facing out. Push them into place by hand.

11. Apply a thin film of the same grease to the outside of each collar and install the collars (**Figure 5**) into their original mounting position. Center them in their bearings.

Needle Bearing Replacement

A hydraulic press is required to replace the needle bearings.

1. Support the shock link in a press (**Figure 9**) and press out the needle bearings.

2. Clean and dry the shock arm.

3. Inspect each mounting bore for galling, cracks or other damage.

4. Support the shock link in a press (**Figure 10**) and press in the bearings so their outer surface is 5.2-5.7 mm (0.20-0.22 in.) below the outer edge of the shock link surface as shown in Dimension A in **Figure 11**.

5. Pack the new bearings with water-resistant grease.

14

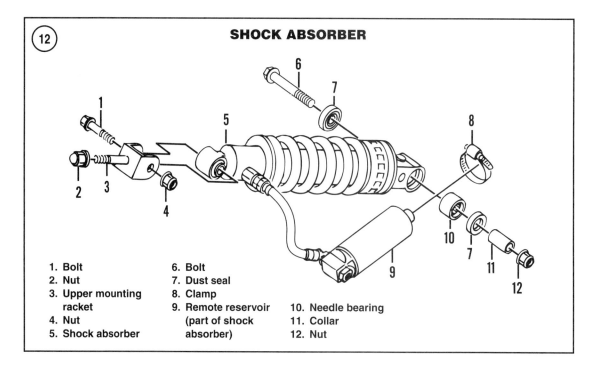

SHOCK ABSORBER

1. Bolt
2. Nut
3. Upper mounting
   racket
4. Nut
5. Shock absorber

6. Bolt
7. Dust seal
8. Clamp
9. Remote reservoir
   (part of shock
   absorber)

10. Needle bearing
11. Collar
12. Nut

6. Install a collar into each bearing and pivot it by hand. Each collar should pivot smoothly. If there is any roughness or binding, the bearing was damaged during installation.

SHOCK ABSORBER

A single rear shock absorber (**Figure 12**) with adjustable preload and rebound is used on all models.

Spring Preload Adjustment

Set the spring preload by adjusting the notched cam collar (A, **Figure 13**) with the pin spanner and extension tool provided in the motorcycle tool kit. Adjust the cam collar so a notch sets against the index tab on the shock absorber housing. The cam positions are numbered 1 (softest) through 7 (heaviest). **Table 1** lists the standard preload position.

Rebound Damping Adjustment

The rear shock absorber is equipped with a rebound damping adjuster (**Figure 14**) on the bottom right side of the shock housing (B, **Figure 13**). Turn the rebound adjuster screw with a screwdriver.

CAUTION
Do not turn the rebound damping adjuster past the point where it stops at its full clockwise or counterclockwise positions. Doing so damages the adjuster screw and requires replacement of the shock absorber.

1. To set the rebound damping adjuster to the standard position:

  a. Turn the rebound adjuster *clockwise* until it stops. This is the full hard position.

  b. Now turn the adjuster *counterclockwise* approximately 1 1/2 turns so the punch mark on the adjuster aligns with the punch mark on the

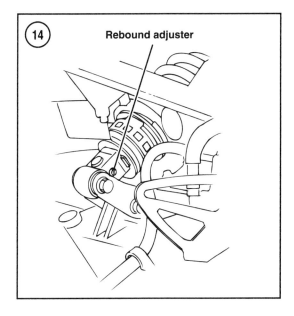

14 Rebound adjuster

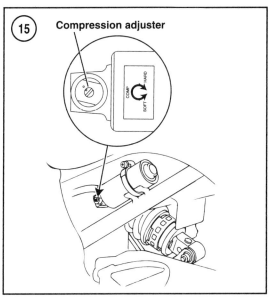

15 Compression adjuster

16

shock body. The rebound adjuster is now set at its standard position.

2. To reduce the rebound damping adjustment, turn the adjuster *counterclockwise* toward its *S* (soft) mark on the shock housing.

3. To increase the rebound damping adjustment, turn the adjuster *clockwise* toward its *H* (hard) mark on the shock housing.

Compression Damping Adjustment

The rear shock absorber is equipped with a compression damping adjuster (**Figure 15**) on the end of the shock reservoir (**Figure 16**). Turn the compression adjuster screw with a screwdriver.

> *CAUTION*
> *Do not turn the compression damping adjuster past the point where it stops at its full clockwise or counterclockwise positions. Doing so damages the adjuster screw and requires replacement of the shock absorber.*

1. To set the compression damping adjuster to the standard position:

    a. Turn the compound adjuster *clockwise* until it *lightly* seats. This is the full hard position.

    b. Now turn the adjuster *counterclockwise* approximately 1 1/2 turns so the punch mark on the adjuster aligns with the punch mark on the reservoir. The compression adjuster is now set at its standard position.

2. To reduce the compression damping adjustment, turn the adjuster *counterclockwise* toward its *S* (soft) mark on the shock housing.

3. To increase the compression damping adjustment, turn the adjuster *clockwise* toward its *H* (hard) mark on the shock housing.

Removal/Installation

1. Support the motorcycle on level ground.

2. Block the front wheel so the motorcycle will not roll in either direction while on the jack or safety stand (or centerstand on U.K. models).

> *CAUTION*
> *If using a jack, place a piece of wood on the jack pad to protect the crankcase.*

14

3A. If necessary, place a suitable size jack or wooden blocks under the crankcase to support the motorcycle securely with the rear wheel off the ground.

3B. Raise the rear of the motorcycle with a swing arm safety stand.

4. Remove the seat and rear cowl as described in Chapter Sixteen.

5. Loosen the reservoir clamp band screw (A, **Figure 17**) and remove the reservoir (B) from the seat rail.

6. Remove the bolt and nut (C, **Figure 17**) securing the lower portion of the shock absorber to the shock plates.

7. Remove the bolt and nut (**Figure 18**) securing the upper portion of the shock absorber to the frame mount under the seat.

8. Carefully guide the reservoir and hose out through the frame opening and remove the shock absorber assembly from the frame.

9. Apply a light coat of water-resistant grease to the shock absorber mounting bolts. Do not apply grease to the mounting bolt threads or nuts. These fasteners must be tightened with dry threads.

10. Install the shock absorber and reservoir into the frame with the reservoir facing toward the left side.

11. Install the upper and lower mounting bolts and nuts. Tighten the nuts to 44 N•m (32 ft.-lb.).

12. Install the reservoir into the seat rail and tighten the band screw securely.

Inspection

Replace the shock absorber if it is leaking oil or shows damage as described in this section.

WARNING
The shock absorber housing contains high-pressure nitrogen gas. Do not tamper with or attempt to open the shock housing. Do not place it near an open flame or other extreme heat. Do not dispose of the shock assembly. Take it to a dealership where it can be deactivated and disposed of properly.

CAUTION
The shock absorber is not serviceable. The only replacement parts available for the shocks are the lower mounting needle bearing, bushing and seals. Do not disassemble the shock absorber.

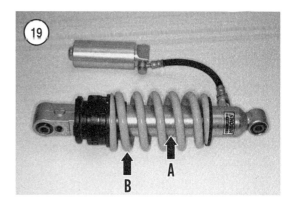
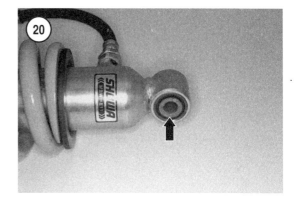

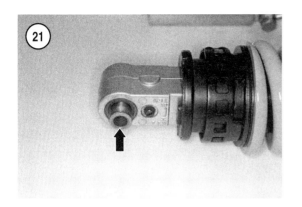

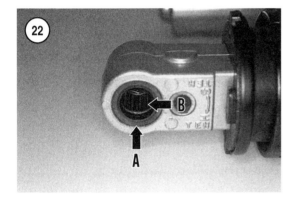

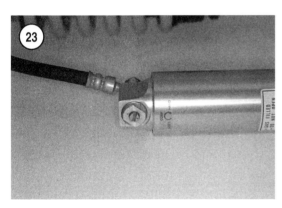

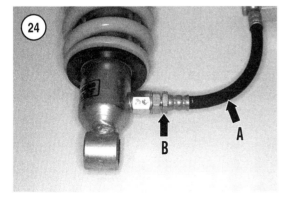

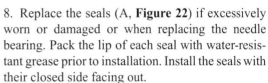

1. Check the shock housing (A, **Figure 19**) for dents, damage or oil leakage.

2. Check the spring (B, **Figure 19**) for cracks or other damage. Check the spring seats for damage. The spring is not removable. If damaged, replace the shock absorber.

3. Check the bushing (**Figure 20**) in the upper shock absorber joint for excessive wear or damage. The bushing must be a tight fit. If damaged, replace the shock absorber.

4. Push the collar (**Figure 21**) out of the lower shock joint.

5. Inspect the collar for scoring or excessive wear.

6. Pry the seals (A, **Figure 22**) out of the lower shock joint. The seals are easy to remove and can be reused if not damaged.

7. Check the shock absorber needle bearing (B, **Figure 22**) installed in the lower shock joint for rust, excessive wear or damage. If necessary, replace the bearing as described under *Shock Absorber Needle Bearing Replacement* in this section.

8. Replace the seals (A, **Figure 22**) if excessively worn or damaged or when replacing the needle bearing. Pack the lip of each seal with water-resistant grease prior to installation. Install the seals with their closed side facing out.

9. Inspect the remote reservoir (**Figure 23**) and interconnecting hose (A, **Figure 24**) and fittings (B) for leakage or damage. If any parts are damaged, replace the shock absorber assembly.

10. Check that the spring preload adjuster (**Figure 25**) rotates freely with the spanner wrench.

11. Replace the shock mounting bolts and nuts if damaged.

14

Needle Bearing Replacement

A press is required to replace the shock absorber needle bearing (B, **Figure 22**).

1. Remove the shock absorber seals by carefully prying them out with a screwdriver.

2. Support the shock absorber in a press with the rebound damping adjuster side facing up (**Figure 26**).

3. Press the needle bearing out of the lower joint.

4. Pack the new needle bearing with water-resistant grease.

5. Support the shock absorber in a press with the rebound damping adjuster side facing up. Press in the new needle bearing (**Figure 27**) and center it inside the mounting bore.

6. Install the collar into the needle bearing and turn it by hand. The collar should turn smoothly.

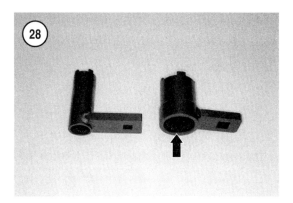

SWING ARM

Special Tools

A Honda locknut wrench (part No. 07908-4690003) (**Figure 28**), or an equivalent, is required to remove, install and tighten the left side pivot adjust bolt locknut.

After the swing arm pivot bolt has been removed for swing arm and/or engine removal, the alignment of all of the receptacles that the pivot bolt must pass through will have shifted slightly. Even the slightest amount of misalignment will make installation of the swing arm pivot bolt very difficult. The shoulder at the end of the threaded portion (**Figure 29**) on the pivot bolt will catch on the spacers, the crankcase and the swing arm pivot areas and make installation very difficult.

Obtain an additional swing arm pivot bolt and modify it. Cut off the threaded end and grind a slight

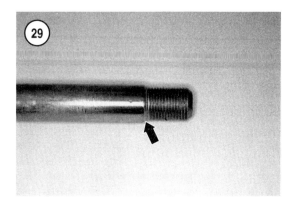

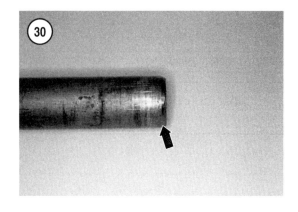

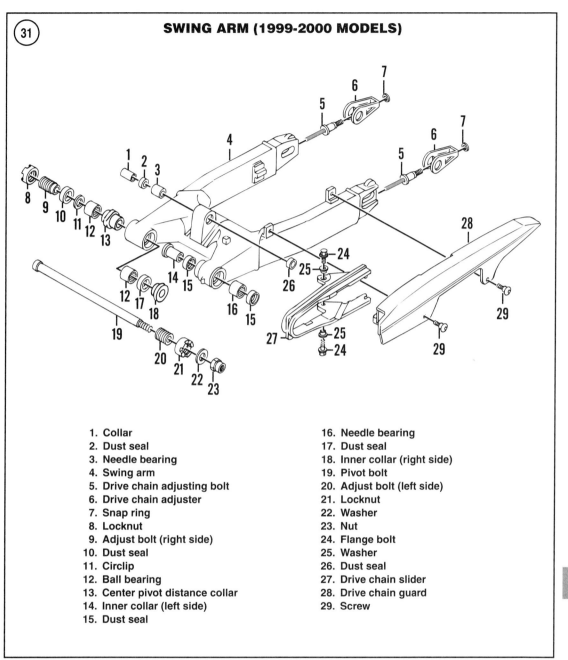

SWING ARM (1999-2000 MODELS)

1. Collar
2. Dust seal
3. Needle bearing
4. Swing arm
5. Drive chain adjusting bolt
6. Drive chain adjuster
7. Snap ring
8. Locknut
9. Adjust bolt (right side)
10. Dust seal
11. Circlip
12. Ball bearing
13. Center pivot distance collar
14. Inner collar (left side)
15. Dust seal
16. Needle bearing
17. Dust seal
18. Inner collar (right side)
19. Pivot bolt
20. Adjust bolt (left side)
21. Locknut
22. Washer
23. Nut
24. Flange bolt
25. Washer
26. Dust seal
27. Drive chain slider
28. Drive chain guard
29. Screw

chamfer on the end as shown in **Figure 30**. The chamfered bolt will then be able to pass through the various openings and align them. This modified bolt can also be used for engine removal and installation in Chapter Five.

This modified pivot bolt is installed from the left side to align all of the components and then pushed out by the standard pivot bolt from the right side.

Refer to **Figure 31** and **Figure 32**.

Removal

NOTE
The swing arm removal sequence is the same for all models. Installation is unique and is separated into two different procedures. Follow the correct installation procedure for the model year being worked on.

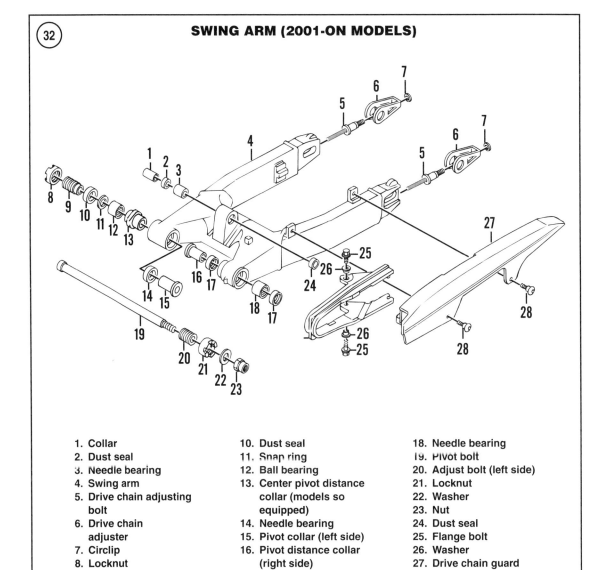

SWING ARM (2001-ON MODELS)

1. Collar
2. Dust seal
3. Needle bearing
4. Swing arm
5. Drive chain adjusting bolt
6. Drive chain adjuster
7. Circlip
8. Locknut
9. Adjust bolt (right side)
10. Dust seal
11. Snap ring
12. Ball bearing
13. Center pivot distance collar (models so equipped)
14. Needle bearing
15. Pivot collar (left side)
16. Pivot distance collar (right side)
17. Dust seal
18. Needle bearing
19. Pivot bolt
20. Adjust bolt (left side)
21. Locknut
22. Washer
23. Nut
24. Dust seal
25. Flange bolt
26. Washer
27. Drive chain guard
28. Screw

1. Remove the rear wheel (A, **Figure 33**) as described in Chapter Twelve.

2. If still in place, remove the screws securing the drive chain guard and remove the guard.

3. Remove the muffler from the exhaust system as described in Chapter Four.

4. Remove the bolts securing both brake hose guides (B, **Figure 33**) and remove both guides.

5. Remove the rear brake caliper (**Figure 34**) from the right side of the swing arm. Suspend the caliper to the seat rail with a Bungee cord or wire.

> *CAUTION*
> *The engine must be supported, since the swing arm pivot bolt goes through the swing arm and the engine crankcase.*

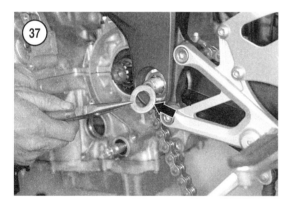

6. Secure the engine with a hydraulic jack. Place a wooden block between the engine and jack support. Operate the jack to place tension against the engine to support the engine and to aid with the removal of the swing arm pivot bolt.

7. Remove the bolt and nut (**Figure 35**) securing the shock plates to the swing arm.

8. On the left side, loosen and remove the swing arm pivot bolt locknut (**Figure 36**) and washer (**Figure 37**).

9. Withdraw the swing arm pivot bolt (**Figure 38**) from the right side.

10. Using the special locknut tool, loosen the left side pivot adjusting bolt locknut (**Figure 39**).

11. Using the special locknut tool, remove the right side pivot adjusting bolt locknut (**Figure 40**).

12. Support the swing arm on a box or with a tie down.

14

13. Loosen the right side pivot adjusting bolt (**Figure 41**) sufficiently to clear the swing arm pivot area.

14. Loosen the left side pivot adjusting bolt sufficiently to clear the swing arm pivot area.

15. Remove the swing arm from the frame.

16. Inspect the swing arm as described in this chapter.

Disassembly

Remove the roller bearings and needle bearings only if they require replacement. Do not remove them for normal inspection or lubrication as removal may damage them.

Keep all parts separated from the right and left side pivot areas. The seals and pivot collars are unique to each side and cannot be interchanged. Also the bearings on the right side on the 1999-2000 model differ from those on the 2001-on models. Refer to the year references made in the following text regarding the differences.

1. If necessary, remove the drive chain slider mounting bolts and collars (**Figure 42**). Then remove the drive chain slider. Discard the bolts, as new ones must be used during assembly.

> *NOTE*
> *The swing arm and shock link seals can usually be removed without damaging them. If the seals are hard, worn or damaged during removal, replace them during assembly.*

2A. On 1999-2000 models, perform the following:
   a. Remove the right and left side inner collars. The right side inner collar is short and the left side is long.
   b. Remove the dust seals from each side of both pivot areas.

2B. On 2001-on models, perform the following:
   a. Remove the pivot distance collar from the right side (A, **Figure 43**).
   b. Remove the pivot collar from the left side (B, **Figure 43**).
   c. Remove the dust seals (A, **Figure 44**) from each side of both pivot areas.

3. Remove the shock link pivot collar (**Figure 45**) and dust seals (A, **Figure 46**).

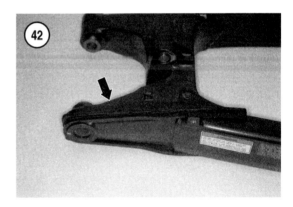

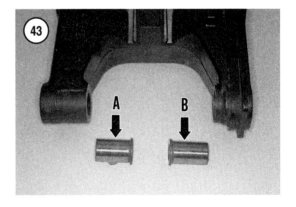

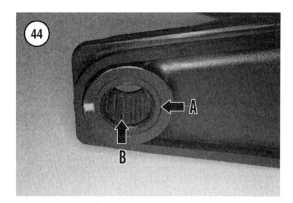

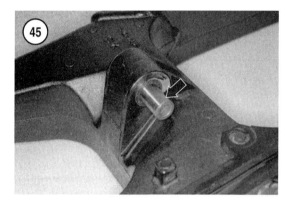

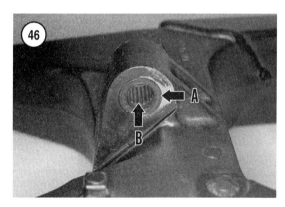

4. If still in place, remove the drive chain adjusters (**Figure 47**).

Inspection

Replace parts that show excessive wear or damage as described in this section.
1. Clean and dry all parts.
2. Inspect the pivot collars for excessive wear, rust or other damage. If the collar outer surface is excessively worn or damaged, the needle bearing is probably damaged.
3. Inspect the swing arm needle bearing (B, **Figure 44**) for overheating, rust, or broken or dented needles. Then check the bearing fit in its mounting bore. The bearing must be a tight fit. If the pivot collar was damaged, replace the pivot collar and needle bearing as a set at the same time.
4. Repeat Step 3 to inspect the shock link needle bearing (B, **Figure 46**) and collar.
5. On the right side, check the ball bearings for any visual damage. Then turn the bearing(s) by hand. The bearing(s) should turn smoothly. If a bearing turns roughly, replace the bearing(s). On 1999-2000 models, replace the ball bearings as a set.

NOTE
Replace damaged bearings as described under **Bearing Replacement** *in this section.*

Bearing Replacement (1999-2000 Models)

Remove the ball bearings and needle bearings only if the bearings must be replaced. The two right side ball bearings must be replaced as a set.

NOTE
For general information on bearing replacement, refer to **Bearing Replacement** *in Chapter One.*

1. If not previously removed, remove the collars and the dust seals as described under *Disassembly* in this section.

NOTE
In Step 2, the two ball bearings are identical with the same part number.

2. To replace the right side pivot bolt ball bearings, perform the following:

a. Remove the snap ring from the swing arm pivot groove (**Figure 48**).

b. Support the swing arm in a press so the left side faces down.

c. Press both ball bearings and the center pivot distance collar out of the swing arm and discard the bearings. The collar may be reused if not damaged.

d. Check the snap ring groove and bearing mounting bore for cracks or other damage.

e. Support the swing arm in a press with the right side facing up.

f. Pack both ball bearings with water-resistant wheel bearing grease.

g. Install both roller bearings with their manufacturer's marks facing out. Press in the inner ball bearing until it bottoms against the swing arm inner shoulder.

h. Install the center pivot distance collar against the inner ball bearing.

i. Press in the outer ball bearing until it is seated against the center pivot distance collar.

j. Install a *new* snap ring into the swing arm groove. Make sure the snap ring seats in the groove completely.

3. To replace the left side pivot bolt needle bearing, perform the following:

a. Support the swing arm in a press so the right side faces down.

b. Press the needle bearing out of the swing arm and discard it.

c. Check the bearing mounting bore for cracks or other damage.

d. Pack the needle bearing with water-resistant wheel bearing grease.

e. Support the swing arm in a press with the left side facing up.

f. Install the needle bearing with its manufacturer's marks facing out.

g. Press in the needle bearing until its outer surface is 5-6 mm (0.20-0.24 in.) below the inside swing arm surface as shown in Dimension A, **Figure 49**.

4. To replace the shock link pivot bearing, perform the following:

a. Assemble the Honda bearing remover set special tool (part No. 07LMC-KV30100) or an equivalent onto the needle bearing (A, **Figure 50**).

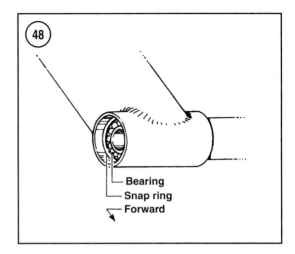

Bearing
Snap ring
Forward

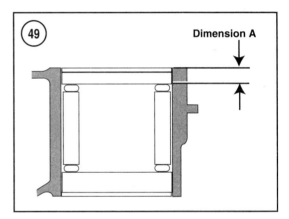

Dimension A

b. Hold onto the special tool (B, **Figure 50**), tighten the center bolt (C) and withdraw the needle bearing out of the pivot bore.

c. Check the mounting bore for cracks and other damage.

d. Pack the new bearing with water-resistant grease.

e. Assemble the special tool and install the needle bearing into the pivot bore. Position the bearing so it is 5.5-6.0 mm (0.22-0.24 in.) below the mounting bore surface as shown in Dimension A, **Figure 51**.

Bearing Replacement (2001-On Models)

Remove the ball bearing and needle bearings only if the bearings must be replaced.

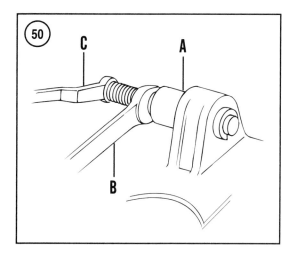

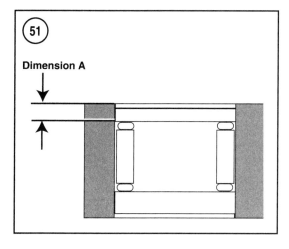

Dimension A

NOTE
*For general information on bearing replacement, refer to **Bearing Replacement** in Chapter One.*

1. If not previously removed, remove the collars and dust seals as described under *Disassembly* in this section.

2. To replace the right side ball bearing, perform the following:

    a. Remove the snap ring from the swing arm groove.

    b. Remove the ball bearing with a universal type bearing removal tool.

    c. Check the snap ring groove and bearing mounting bore for cracks or other damage.

    d. Support the swing arm in a press with the right side facing up.

    e. Pack the bearing with water-resistant wheel bearing grease.

    f. Install the ball bearing with their manufacturer's marks facing out. Press the ball bearing in until it bottoms against the needle bearing.

    g. Install the snap ring into the swing arm groove. Make sure the snap ring seats in the groove completely.

3. To replace the right side needle bearing, perform the following:

    a. Support the swing arm in a press with the right side facing down.

    b. Press the needle bearing out of the swing arm and discard it.

    c. Check the bearing mounting bore for cracks or other damage.

    d. Pack the needle bearing with water-resistant wheel bearing grease.

    e. Support the swing arm in a press with the right side facing up.

    f. Install the needle bearing with its manufacturer's marks facing out.

    g. Press in the needle bearing until it is seated against the shoulder of the bearing mounting bore.

    h. Install the ball bearing as previously described.

4. To replace the left side pivot bolt needle bearing, perform the following:

    a. Support the swing arm in a press so the left side faces down.

    b. Press the needle bearing out of the swing arm and discard it.

    c. Check the bearing mounting bore for cracks or other damage.

    d. Pack the bearing with water-resistant wheel bearing grease.

    e. Support the swing arm in a press with the left side facing up.

    f. Install the needle bearing with its manufacturer's marks facing out.

    g. Press in the needle bearing until its outer surface is 5.0-6.0 mm (0.20-0.24 in.) below the inside swing arm surface mounting bore surface as shown in Dimension A, **Figure 49**.

5. To replace the shock link pivot bearing, perform the following:

    a. Assemble the Honda bearing remover set special tool (part No. 07LMC-KV30100) or an equivalent onto the needle bearing (A, **Figure 50**).

14

b. Hold onto the special tool (B, **Figure 50**), tighten the center bolt (C) and withdraw the needle bearing out of the pivot bore.

c. Check the mounting bore for cracks and other damage.

d. Pack the new bearing with water-resistant grease.

e. Assemble the special tool and install the needle bearing into the pivot bore. Position the bearing so it is 5.5-6.0 mm (0.22-0.24 in.) below the mounting bore surface as shown in Dimension A, **Figure 51**.

Drive Chain Slider Inspection

Replace the drive chain slider if it is damaged or worn (**Figure 42**).

Assembly

Different size swing arm dust seals are used. Compare the manufacturer's marks from the new and used seals to identify them.

Refer to **Figure 31** and **Figure 32**.

1. Pack the open side of each dust seal with water-resistant grease. Pack grease between the dust seal lips.

2. Install the shock link pivot collar and dust seals as follows:

a. Install the shock link dust seals (A, **Figure 46**) with their closed side facing out.

b. Press in both dust seals until the outer surface is flush with the shock link bore outside surface.

c. Lubricate the pivot collar with grease and install it into the swing arm (**Figure 45**).

3A. On 1999-2000 models, install the inner collars and dust seals as follows:

a. Lubricate the collars with grease.

b. Install the left side outer dust seal until it is seated onto the bearing.

c. Install the left side inner dust seal until it is seated 4 mm (0.2 in.) from the outer surface of the pivot area.

d. Install the right side inner and outer dust seals until they are seated onto the bearing.

e. Position the collars with the flange side going in last.

f. Install the right side short inner collar and the left side long inner collar from the inner sur-

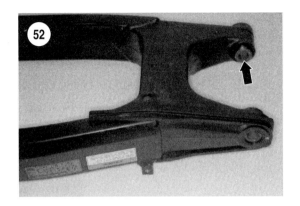

face. Push them until they are seated against the swing arm pivot areas.

3B. On 2001-on models, install the pivot collars and dust seals as follows:

a. Lubricate the collar with grease and install it into the swing arm.

b. Install the left side outer dust seal until it is seated onto the bearing.

c. Install the left side inner dust seal until it is seated 4 mm (0.2 in.) from the outer surface of the pivot area.

d. Install the right side inner and outer dust seals until they are seated onto the bearing.

NOTE
*The pivot collar and pivot distance collar must be installed on the correct side of the swing arm. The right side pivot distance collar (A, **Figure 43**) is identified by a groove on the flange.*

e. Position the collars with the flange side going in last and install both collars from the inner surface. Push them until they are seated against the swing arm pivot areas (**Figure 52**).

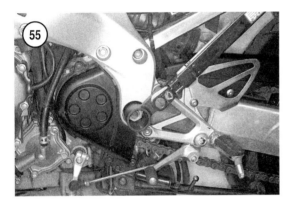

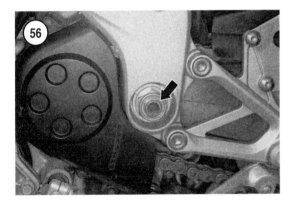

4. Install the drive chain slider as follows:

a. Install the drive chain slider onto the front of the swing arm and align the slit with the raised boss on the swing arm.

b. Insert the chain slider bosses into the swing arm holes.

c. Apply a medium-strength threadlocking compound onto the chain slider *new* bolt threads. Install the collars and bolts (**Figure 40**) and tighten to 9 N•m (80 in.-lb.).

Installation (1999-2000 Models)

WARNING
Tighten all swing arm fasteners to the specified torque and in the specified sequence. If the torque specification and/or correct sequence are not followed correctly, loosen all fasteners and start over. Failure to follow these instructions will result in component failure and possible unsafe riding conditions, such as a loss of control.

1. Install both the right and left side adjust bolts. Install them so they do not project past the frame inner surface.

2. Install the swing arm into position in the frame and shock arm plates. Support it on a box.

3. To temporarily hold the swing arm in place, use the modified swing arm pivot bolt previously described and insert it from the left side, through the frame, the swing arm, the crankcase, the swing arm and the frame on the other side. Make sure the swing arm is correctly aligned with the frame pivot points.

4. Tighten the right side pivot adjust bolt to 12 N•m (106 in.-lb.). Loosen the right side pivot adjust bolt, then tighten again to 7 N•m (62 in.-lb.).

5. Install the right side pivot bolt locknut, using the special locknut wrench (**Figure 53**). Tighten the locknut to the following. See *Engine Installation* in Chapter Five for a description of the *indicated* and *actual* specifications.

   a. Indicated torque specification: 58 N•m (43 ft.-lb.).

   b. Actual torque specification: 64 N•m (47 ft.-lb.).

6. From the right side, insert the actual swing arm pivot bolt, slowly pushing out the special tool pivot bolt installed in Step 3. Push it in all the way (**Figure 54**).

7. Tighten the left side pivot adjust bolt to 12 N•m (106 in.-lb.). Loosen the left side pivot adjust bolt, then tighten to 7 N•m (62 in.-lb.).

8. Install the left side locknut. Hold onto the pivot adjust bolt, using the special locknut wrench (**Figure 55**). Tighten the locknut to the following:

   a. Indicated torque specification: 58 N•m (43 ft.-lb.).

   b. Actual torque specification: 64 N•m (47 ft.-lb.).

9. Push the swing arm pivot bolt the remaining way in until it is seated.

10. On the left side, install the washer and locknut (**Figure 56**).

14

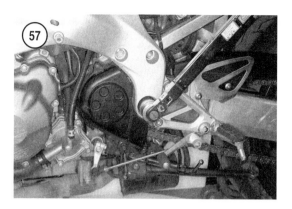

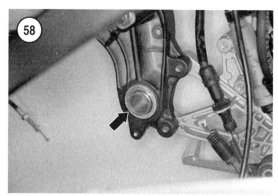

11. Have an assistant hold onto the swing arm pivot bolt, then tighten the locknut (**Figure 57**) to 93 N•m (69 ft.-lb.).

12. Remove the box from under the swing arm.

13. Install the shock plate to the swing arm bolt from the left side and install the nut. Tighten the nut to 44 N•m (32 ft.-lb.).

14. Move the swing arm up and down several times to make sure all swing arm components are properly seated. If the swing arm moves roughly, loosen the swing arm locknut nut and check for the problem.

15. Install the rear brake caliper onto the right side of the swing arm.

16. Move the rear brake hose onto position on the swing arm and install the hose guides and bolts. Tighten the bolts securely.

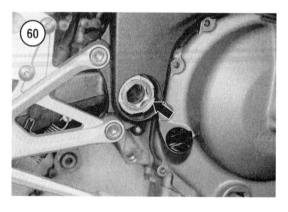

17. Install the muffler as described in Chapter Four.

18. Install the drive chain guard and tighten the screws securely.

19. Install the rear wheel (Chapter Twelve).

Installation (2001-On Models)

WARNING
Tighten all swing arm fasteners to the specified torque and in the specified sequence. If the torque specification and/or correct sequence are not followed correctly, loosen all fasteners and start over. Failure to follow these instructions will result in component failure and possible unsafe riding conditions, such as a loss of control.

1. Install both the right and left side adjust bolts. Install them so they do not project past the frame inner surface (**Figure 58**).

2. Install the swing arm into position in the frame and shock arm plates. Support it on a box.

3. To temporarily hold the swing arm in place, use the modified pivot bolt previously described and insert it from the left side, through the frame, the swing arm, the crankcase, the swing arm and the frame on the other side. Make sure the swing arm is correctly aligned with the frame pivot points.

4. Tighten the right side pivot adjust bolt (**Figure 59**) to 12 N•m (106 in.-lb.). Loosen the right side pivot adjust bolt, then retighten to 7 N•m (62 in.-lb.).

5. Install the right side pivot bolt locknut (**Figure 60**).

6. Hold onto the right side pivot adjust bolt (A, **Figure 61**), using the special locknut wrench (B). Tighten the locknut to the following. See *Engine Installation* in Chapter Five for a description of the *indicated* and *actual* torque specifications.

    a. Indicated torque specification: 58 N•m (43 ft.-lb.).

    b. Actual torque specification: 64 N•m (47 ft.-lb.).

7. From the right side, insert the actual swing arm pivot bolt, slowly pushing out the special tool installed in Step 3.

8. Tighten the left side adjust bolt (**Figure 62**) to 12 N•m (106 in.-lb.). Loosen the left side adjusting bolt, then retighten to 7 N•m (62 in.-lb.).

9. Install the left side locknut (**Figure 63**).

10. Hold onto the left pivot adjust bolt, using the special locknut wrench. Tighten the locknut to the following:

    a. Indicated torque specification: 58 N•m (43 ft.-lb.).

    b. Actual torque specification: 64 N•m (47 ft.-lb.).

11. Push the swing arm pivot bolt all the way in until it is seated.

12. On the left side, install the washer (**Figure 64**) and locknut (**Figure 65**).

13. Have an assistant hold onto the swing arm pivot bolt, then tighten the locknut to 64 N•m (47 ft.-lb.).

14. Remove the box from under the swing arm.

15. Install the shock plate to the swing arm bolt from the left side and install the nut (**Figure 66**). Tighten the nut to 93 N•m (69 ft.-lb.).

14

16. Move the swing arm up and down several times to make sure the swing arm components are properly seated. If the swing arm moves roughly, loosen the swing arm locknut nut and check for the problem.

17. Install the rear brake caliper onto the right side of the swing arm.

18. Move the rear brake hose onto position on the swing arm and install the hose guides and bolts. Tighten the bolts securely.

19. Install the muffler as described in Chapter Four.

20. Install the drive chain guard and tighten the screws securely.

21. Install the rear wheel (Chapter Twelve).

Table 1 REAR SUSPENSION SPECIFICATIONS

Item	Specification
Rear wheel travel	120 mm (4.7 in.)
Shock absorber standard preload position	No. 3

Table 2 REAR SUSPENSION TORQUE SPECIFICATIONS

Item	N•m	in.-lb.	ft.-lb.
Drive chain slider bolt[1]	9	80	–
Shock arm plates-to-			
swing arm bolt and nut	44	–	32
shock absorber	44	–	32
Shock absorber			
upper and lower nuts	44	–	32
Shock link-to-			
engine bolt and nut	44	–	32
shock absorber	44	–	32
shock arm plates bolt and nut	44	–	32
Shock link bracket nut	39	–	29
Swing arm[2]			
Adjust bolt (right and left)			
Initial	12	106	–
Final	7	62	–
Adjust bolt locknut (right and left)			
Indicated	58	–	43
Actual	64	–	47
Pivot bolt locknut	93	–	69

1. ALOC type bolt. Install a new bolt or nut during installation.
2. Refer to text for correct tightening sequence.

CHAPTER FIFTEEN

BRAKES

This chapter describes service procedures for the front and rear disc brakes. **Tables 1-4** at the end of the chapter list front and rear brake specifications.

BRAKE FLUID SELECTION

When adding brake fluid, use DOT 4 brake fluid from a sealed container. DOT 4 brake fluid is glycol-based and draws moisture, which greatly reduces its ability to perform correctly. Purchase brake fluid in small containers and discard any small leftover quantities. Do not store a container of brake fluid with less than 1/4 of the fluid remaining.

CAUTION
Do not intermix DOT 5 (silicone-based) brake fluid, as it can cause brake system failure.

PREVENTING BRAKE FLUID DAMAGE

Many of the procedures in this chapter require handling brake fluid. Be careful not to spill any fluid, as it stains or damages most surfaces. To prevent brake fluid damage, note the following:

1. Before performing any procedure in which there is the possibility of brake fluid contacting the motorcycle, cover the work area with a large piece of plastic. It only takes a few drops of brake fluid to damage the surface of an expensive part.

2. Before handling brake fluid or working on the brake system, fill a bucket with soap and water and keep it close to the motorcycle while working. If brake fluid contacts the motorcycle, clean the area and rinse it thoroughly.

3. To help control the flow of brake fluid when filling the reservoirs, punch a small hole into the seal of a new container next to the edge of the pour spout.

BRAKE SERVICE

WARNING
*When working on the brake system, do **not** inhale brake dust. It may contain asbestos, which is a known carcinogen. Do **not** use compressed air to*

blow off brake dust. Use an aerosol brake cleaner. Wear a facemask and wash thoroughly after completing the work.

The disc brake system transmits hydraulic pressure from the master cylinders to the brake calipers. This pressure is transmitted from the calipers to the brake pads, which grip both sides of the brake discs and slow the motorcycle. As the pads wear, the pistons move out of the caliper bores to automatically compensate for wear. As this occurs, the fluid level in the master cylinder reservoir goes down. This must be compensated for by occasionally adding fluid.

The proper operation of this system depends on a supply of clean brake fluid (DOT 4) and a clean work environment when any service is being performed. Any tiny particle of debris that enters the system can damage the components and cause poor brake performance.

Brake fluid is hygroscopic (easily absorbs moisture) and moisture in the system will reduce brake performance. Purchase brake fluid in small containers and properly discard any small quantities that remain. Small quantities of fluid will quickly absorb the moisture in the container. Use only fluid clearly marked DOT 4. If possible, use the same brand of fluid. Do not replace the fluid with a silicone (DOT 5) fluid. It is not possible to remove all of the old fluid. Other types are not compatible with DOT 5. Do not reuse drained fluid and discard old fluid properly. Do not combine brake fluid with fluids for recycling.

Perform brake service procedures carefully. Do not use any sharp tools inside the master cylinders or calipers or on the pistons. Damage of these components could cause a loss of system hydraulic pressure. If there is any doubt about the ability to correctly and safely service the brake system, have a professional technician perform the task.

Consider the following when servicing the brake system:

1. The hydraulic components rarely require disassembly. Make sure it is necessary.

2. Keep the reservoir covers in place to prevent the entry of moisture and debris.

3. Clean parts with an aerosol brake parts cleaner or isopropyl alcohol. Never use petroleum-based solvents on internal brake system components. They will cause seals to swell and distort.

4. Do not allow brake fluid to contact plastic, painted or plated parts. It will damage the surface.

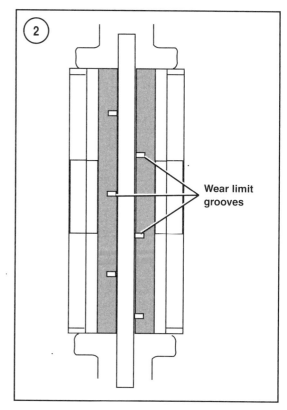

Wear limit grooves

5. Dispose of brake fluid properly.

6. If the hydraulic system, not including the reservoir cover, has been opened, bleed the system to remove air from the system. Refer to *Bleeding the System* in this chapter.

FRONT BRAKE PADS

There is no recommended mileage interval for changing the front brake pads. Pad wear depends greatly on riding habits and the condition of the brake

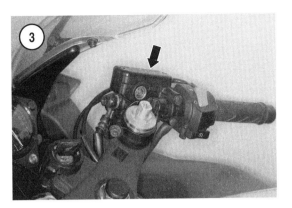

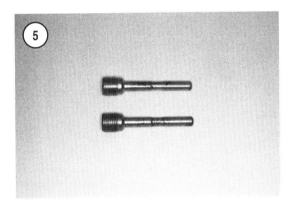

system. Inspect the front brake pads (**Figure 1**) for uneven wear, scoring, oil contamination or other damage. As the brake pads wear, the brake fluid level drops in the reservoir and automatically adjusts for wear. Replace the brake pads if the pad wear limit grooves are worn away (**Figure 2**).

Always replace the front brake pads in sets by servicing both front calipers at the same time. Never use one new brake pad with a used brake pad in a caliper. Never replace the brake pads in one brake caliper without replacing them in the other caliper.

Doing so results in an unbalanced braking condition.

> *CAUTION*
> *Due to the amount of pad material remaining after the wear limit grooves (**Figure 2**) are worn away, check the brake pads frequently. If pad wear is uneven, the backing plate may contact the disc and damage it.*

Replacement

> *NOTE*
> *Be sure order the correct set of brake pads for the model year being worked on. There are different Honda part numbers for the various models.*

1. Read the information listed under *Brake Service* in this chapter.
2. Remove the front master cylinder cover (**Figure 3**) and use a large syringe to remove and discard about 50 percent of the fluid from the reservoir. This prevents the master cylinder from overflowing when the caliper pistons are compressed for reinstallation. Do not drain the entire reservoir or air will enter the system.
3. Loosen both pad pins (**Figure 4**).
4. Carefully push, then pull, the caliper against the brake disc. This will press the pistons back into the caliper bores. This will allow room for the new brake pads.

> *CAUTION*
> *Do not allow the master cylinder reservoir to overflow when performing Step 6. Brake fluid damages most surfaces it contacts.*

> *CAUTION*
> *The pistons should move smoothly when compressing them in Step 4. If not, check the caliper for sticking pistons or damaged caliper bores, pistons and seals. Repair requires overhaul of the brake caliper assembly.*

5. Remove the pad pins and the pad spring.
6. Remove both brake pads.
7. Inspect the pad pins (**Figure 5**) for excessive wear, corrosion or damage. Use a wire-wheel to remove corrosion and dirt from the pad pin surface. A

15

dirty or damaged pad pin surface prevents the brake pads from sliding properly and results in brake drag and overheating of the brake disc.

8. Inspect the brake pads (**Figure 6**) as follows:

   a. Inspect the friction material for light surface dirt, grease and oil contamination. Remove light contamination with sandpaper. If the contamination has penetrated the surface, replace the brake pads.

   b. Inspect the brake pads for excessive wear or damage. Replace the brake pads when the wear limit grooves (**Figure 2**) are no longer visible.

   c. Inspect the brake pads for uneven wear. If one pad has worn more than the other, the brake caliper may not be working correctly. Refer to *Front Brake Caliper* in this chapter.

   d. Inspect the metal plates (**Figure 7**) on the backside of each pad for corrosion, tightness and damage.

> *NOTE*
> *If brake fluid is leaking from around the pistons, overhaul the brake caliper as described in this chapter.*

9. Service the brake disc as follows:

   a. Use brake cleaner and a fine-grade emery cloth to remove road debris and brake pad residue and any rust from the brake disc. Clean both sides of the disc.

> *NOTE*
> *Cleaning the brake disc is especially important if changing brake pad compounds. Many compounds are not compatible with each other.*

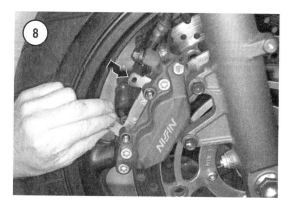

   b. Check the brake disc for wear as described in this chapter.

10. Make sure the metal plates (**Figure 7**) are in place on the backside of each brake pad.

11. Install the outboard brake pad (**Figure 8**) into the caliper.

12. Partially install the top pad pin (A, **Figure 9**) to hold the outboard brake pad in position.

13. Install the inboard brake pad (B, **Figure 9**) into the caliper.

14. Position the pad spring (A, **Figure 10**) into the caliper with the arrow mark facing up. Install and push the upper pad pin (B, **Figure 10**) through the spring's upper (A, **Figure 11**) and lower (B) inter-

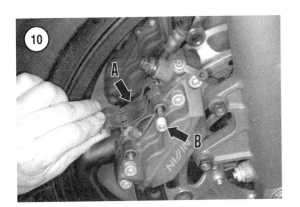

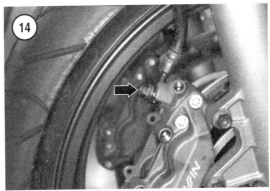

locking legs to secure the spring into place. Push the upper pad pin all the way in (**Figure 12**).

15. Press down on the pad spring, then install and push the lower pad pin through the spring's upper and lower interlocking legs to secure the spring into place. Push the lower pad pin all the way in (**Figure 13**).

16. Screw in the pad pins and tighten to 18 N•m (13 ft.-lb.).

17. Repeat for the opposite brake assembly.

18. Operate the front brake lever to seat the pads against the disc, then check the brake fluid level in the reservoir. If necessary, add new DOT 4 brake fluid as described in Chapter Three.

> *WARNING*
> *Do not ride the motorcycle until the front brakes operate correctly with full hydraulic advantage. If necessary, bleed the front brakes as described in this chapter.*

FRONT BRAKE CALIPER

Removal/Installation

1. If the caliper is going to be removed and serviced, perform the following:

    a. Drain the brake fluid from the front master cylinder as described under *Brake Fluid Draining* in this chapter.

    b. Remove the brake pads as previously described.

    c. Remove the brake hose banjo bolt and washers at the caliper (**Figure 14**). Plug the hose, then place it in a reclosable plastic bag (A, **Figure 15**) to prevent leakage and hose contamination.

15

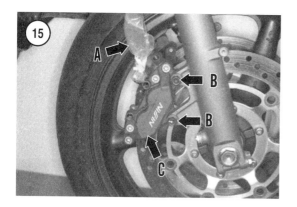

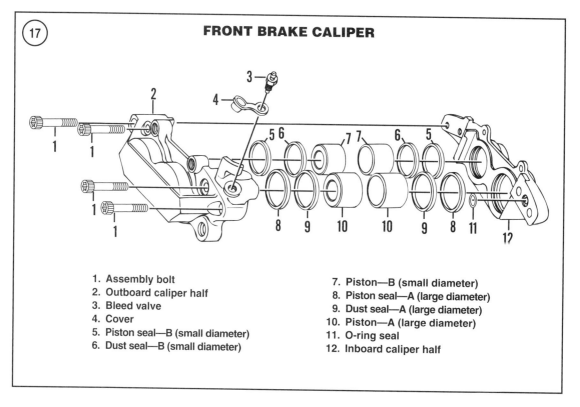

FRONT BRAKE CALIPER

1. Assembly bolt
2. Outboard caliper half
3. Bleed valve
4. Cover
5. Piston seal—B (small diameter)
6. Dust seal—B (small diameter)
7. Piston—B (small diameter)
8. Piston seal—A (large diameter)
9. Dust seal—A (large diameter)
10. Piston—A (large diameter)
11. O-ring seal
12. Inboard caliper half

2. Remove the caliper mounting bolts (B, **Figure 15**).

3. Slide the caliper (C, **Figure 15**) up and off the brake disc. If the brake pads are still in place, insert a block between the brake pads to keep them separated.

NOTE
The spacer block prevents the piston from being forced out of the caliper if the front brake lever is accidentally applied while the brake caliper is removed from the brake disc.

4. Install the brake caliper onto the brake disc and into position on the fork slider. If installed, be careful not to damage the leading edge of the brake pads.

5. Install the caliper mounting bolts (B, **Figure 15**) and tighten to 30 N•m (22 ft.-lb.).

6. If the caliper was serviced, install the brake pads as previously described.

7. If the caliper was serviced, perform the following:

   a. Remove the plastic bag (A, **Figure 15**) from the brake hose.

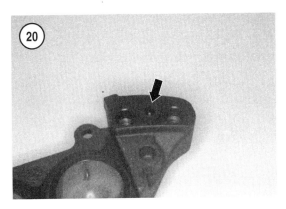

b. Place a *new* washer on each side of the brake hose. Then thread the banjo bolt (**Figure 14**) into the caliper and tighten to 34 N•m (25 ft.-lb.).

CAUTION
After tightening the banjo bolt, make sure the brake hose is correctly positioned against the caliper stoppers (Figure 16).

c. Refill the master cylinder and bleed the brake system as described in this chapter.

8. If the brake caliper was not removed from the motorcycle, remove the spacer block from between the brake pads.

9. Repeat for the opposite brake caliper assembly.

10. Roll the motorcycle back and forth and apply the front brake several times to reposition the brake pads in both calipers.

WARNING
Do not ride the motorcycle until both front brake calipers operate correctly with full hydraulic advantage.

Disassembly

Brake caliper service involves removing the pistons and separating the caliper body halves. An air compressor is required during the disassembly procedure.

Refer to **Figure 17**.

NOTE
Prior to removing the caliper from the fork slider, loosen the caliper assembly bolts (Figure 18).

1. Remove the brake caliper as described in this chapter.

2. Remove the brake pads as described in this chapter.

3. Remove the brake caliper assembly bolts (**Figure 19**) and separate the brake caliper halves. Note that there are two different length assembly bolts.

4. Remove the O-ring seal (**Figure 20**) from the inboard caliper half.

5. Remove the pistons as follows:

WARNING
Compressed air forces the pistons out of the caliper under considerable force. Do not cushion the pistons by hand, as injury could result.

a. Two different size pistons are used.

b. Support the caliper on a wooden block with the piston side facing down. Place a thick towel between the pistons and workbench. Make sure there is enough space underneath the caliper for the pistons to be removed completely.

c. Direct compressed air through the brake line port to remove the pistons.

15

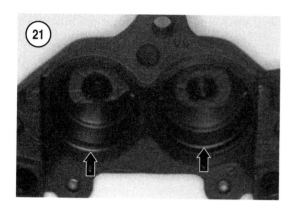

6. Use a small tool to carefully pry the dust and piston seals from the grooves in the cylinder bore. Repeat for each bore.

7. Repeat for the other caliper half.

8. If still in place, remove the bleed valve and its cover from the outboard caliper half.

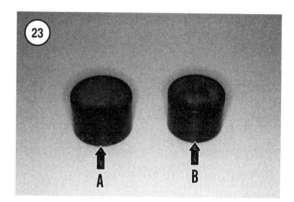

Inspection

When measuring the brake caliper components, compare the actual measurements to the specifications in **Table 1**. Replace worn or damaged parts as described in this section.

1. Clean and dry the caliper assembly as follows:
   a. Handle the brake components carefully when servicing them.
   b. Remove all threadlocking compound residue from the brake caliper body halves and their mounting bolt threads.
   c. Use only DOT 4 brake fluid or isopropyl alcohol to wash rubber parts in the brake system. Never allow any petroleum-based cleaner to contact the rubber parts. These chemicals cause the rubber to swell, requiring their replacement.
   d. Clean the dust and piston seal grooves (**Figure 21**) carefully to avoid damaging the caliper bore. Use a small pick or brush to clean the grooves. If a hard varnish residue has built up in the grooves, soak the caliper body halves in solvent to help soften the residue. Then wash the caliper halves in soapy water and rinse completely.
   e. If alcohol or solvent was used to clean the caliper, blow dry with compressed air.
   f. Check the fluid passages to make sure they are clean and dry.
   g. After cleaning the parts, place them on a clean lint-free cloth until assembly.

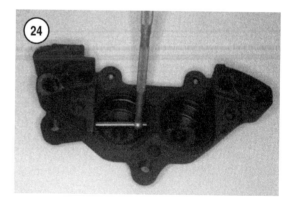

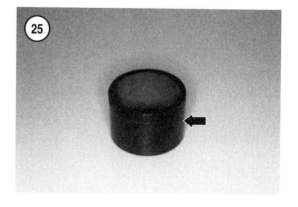

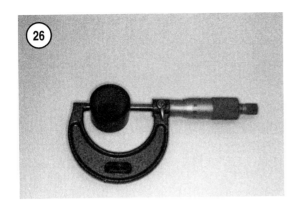

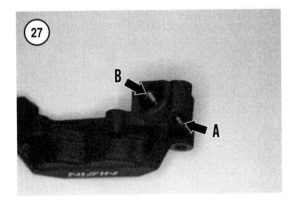

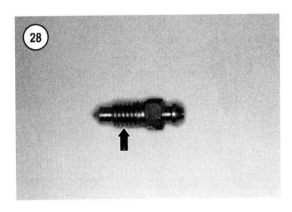

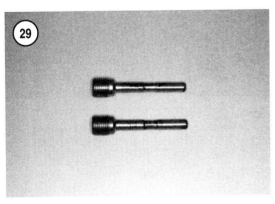

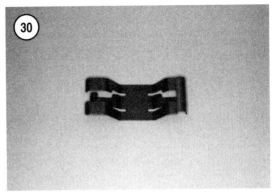

CAUTION
Do not get any oil or grease onto any of the brake caliper components. These chemicals cause the rubber parts in the brake system to swell, permanently damaging them.

2. Check the caliper body mating surfaces (**Figure 22**) for burrs or other damage.

3. Check each cylinder bore for corrosion, deep scratches and other wear marks. Do not hone the cylinder bores.

NOTE
*Each caliper uses two different bore diameters. The leading piston and bore have the larger diameter of the two (adjacent to the bleed valve). Refer to the leading (A, **Figure 23**) and trailing (B) piston and caliper diameter specifications in **Table 1** when measuring the parts in the following steps.*

4. Measure each caliper cylinder diameter (**Figure 24**).

5. Inspect the pistons (**Figure 25**) for pitting, corrosion, cracks or other damage.

6. Measure each piston outside diameter (**Figure 26**).

7. Inspect the bleed valve (A, **Figure 27**) and banjo bolt (B) threads for wear or damage.

8. Clean the bleed valve with compressed air. Check the valve threads (**Figure 28**) for damage. Replace the dust caps if missing or damaged.

9. Clean the banjo bolts with compressed air.

10. Inspect the pad pin bolts (**Figure 29**) for wear or damage.

11. Inspect the pad spring (**Figure 30**) for cracks or damage.

Assembly

Refer to **Figure 17**.

Use new DOT 4 brake fluid when lubricating the parts in the following steps.

> *NOTE*
> *Before soaking the new piston and dust seals in brake fluid, compare them to the old parts, determine their sizes and match them to their respective bores. Two different size seals are used. Refer to the brake caliper cylinder bore leading and trailing bore measurements in **Table 1**.*

1. Soak the new piston and dust seals in brake fluid.
2. Lubricate the pistons and cylinder bores with brake fluid.

> *NOTE*
> *The piston seals (A, **Figure 31**) are thicker than the dust seals (B).*

3. Install a new piston seal into each cylinder bore rear groove.
4. Install a new dust seal into each cylinder bore front groove.

> *NOTE*
> *Check that each seal fits squarely into its respective cylinder bore groove.*

5. Install each piston into its respective caliper bore with its open side facing out (**Figure 32**). To prevent the pistons from damaging the seals, turn them into the bore by hand. Install the pistons until they bottom.
6. Install a *new* O-ring seal (**Figure 33**) onto the inboard caliper body.
7. Make sure the rubber joint seal is still in place and assemble the caliper body halves.
8. Apply a medium strength threadlocking compound to the caliper mounting bolts prior to installation.
9. Install *new* brake caliper assembly bolts. Install the short bolts (A, **Figure 34**) in the outer two holes and the long bolts (B) in the inner two holes and tighten finger-tight. Then check the caliper body mating surfaces. Make sure the surfaces are flush all the way around the caliper halves.
10. Tighten the brake caliper assembly bolts sufficiently to hold the caliper halves together. After the

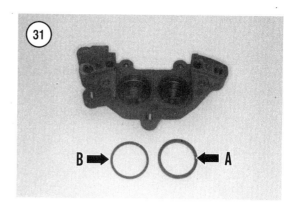

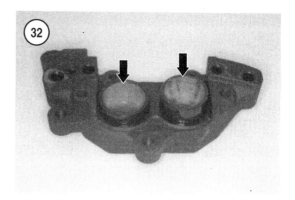

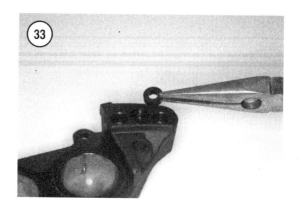

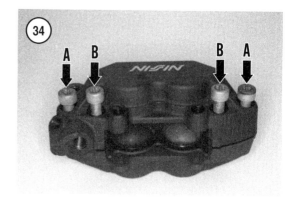

35

36

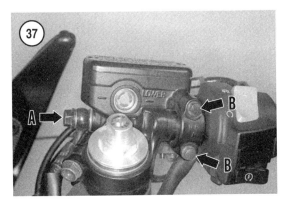

37

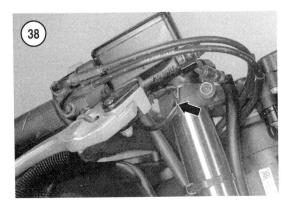

38

caliper is installed on the fork slider in Step 14, tighten the bolts (**Figure 35**) to 23 N•m (17 ft.-lb.).

11. Install the bleed valve and cover (**Figure 36**) into the outboard caliper. Tighten to 6 N•m (53 in.-lb.).

12. Install the brake pads as described in this chapter.

13. Install the brake caliper as described in this chapter.

14. Repeat for the other brake caliper.

FRONT MASTER CYLINDER

Read the information listed under *Brake Service* in this chapter before servicing the front master cylinder.

Removal/Installation

1. Support the motorcycle on level ground.

2. Block the front wheel so the motorcycle will not roll in either direction while on the swing arm stand (or centerstand on U.K. models).

3. Cover the fuel tank and front fairing with a heavy cloth or plastic tarp to protect them from accidental brake fluid spills.

> *CAUTION*
> *Wash brake fluid off any surface immediately, as it damages the finish. Use soapy water and rinse completely.*

4. Drain the front brake lever line as described under *Brake Fluid Draining* in this chapter.

5. Remove the banjo bolt (A, **Figure 37**) and washers securing the brake hose to the master cylinder. Plug the brake hose to prevent brake fluid from dripping out. Tie the loose end of the hose to the handlebar to prevent it from dripping brake fluid.

6. Plug the bolt opening in the master cylinder to prevent leakage when removing the master cylinder in the following steps.

7. Disconnect the brake switch wire connector at the brake light switch (**Figure 38**).

8. Remove the brake master cylinder holder mounting bolts (B, **Figure 37**) and holder, then remove the brake master cylinder from the handlebar.

9. If necessary, service the master cylinder as described in this chapter.

15

10. Clean the handlebar, master cylinder and clamp mating surfaces.

11. Mount the master cylinder onto the handlebar and align the end of the master cylinder and clamp mating surfaces with the punch mark on the handlebar.

12. Install the master cylinder holder and its mounting bolts (B, **Figure 37**). Install the holder with its UP mark (C) facing up.

13. Tighten the upper master cylinder clamp bolt first, then the lower bolt. Tighten both bolts to 9 N•m (80 in.-lb.).

NOTE
When the master cylinder clamp is correctly installed, the upper edge of the clamp touches the master cylinder, leaving a gap at the bottom.

14. Reconnect the front brake light switch connectors at the switch (**Figure 38**).

15. Secure the brake hose to the master cylinder with the banjo bolt (A, **Figure 37**) and two *new* washers on each side of the brake hose. Position the brake hose arm against the master cylinder bracket as shown in **Figure 39** and tighten the banjo bolt to 34 N•m (25 ft.-lb.).

16. Bleed the front brakes as described under *Brake Bleeding* in this chapter.

17. After bleeding the brakes and before riding the motorcycle, turn the ignition switch on and make sure the rear brake light comes on when operating the front brake lever. If not, check the front brake light switch and connectors.

WARNING
Do not ride the motorcycle until the front and rear brakes and brake light operate properly.

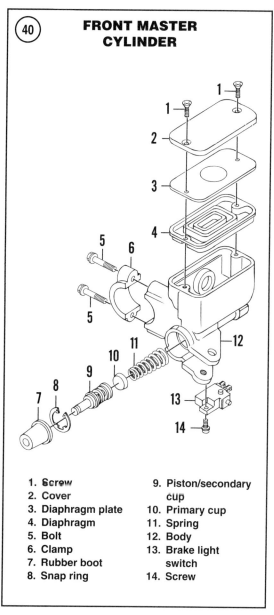

FRONT MASTER CYLINDER

1. Screw
2. Cover
3. Diaphragm plate
4. Diaphragm
5. Bolt
6. Clamp
7. Rubber boot
8. Snap ring
9. Piston/secondary cup
10. Primary cup
11. Spring
12. Body
13. Brake light switch
14. Screw

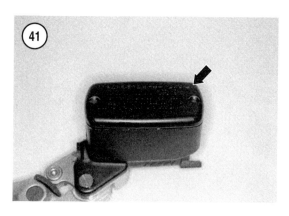

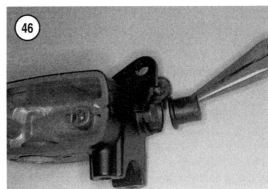

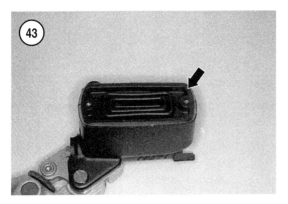

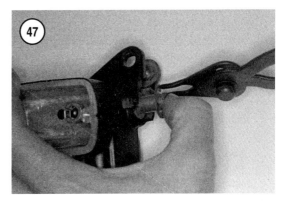

Disassembly

Refer to **Figure 40**.

1. Remove the master cylinder as described in this chapter.

2. If still in place, remove the master cylinder cover (**Figure 41**), diaphragm plate (**Figure 42**) and diaphragm (**Figure 43**). Pour out any remaining brake fluid and discard it.

3. Remove the screw and remove the front brake light switch (**Figure 44**).

4. Remove the nut and pivot bolt (A, **Figure 45**), then remove the front brake lever and its adjuster assembly (B).

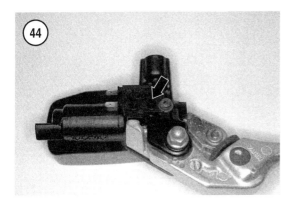

5. Remove the rubber boot (**Figure 46**) from the groove in the end of the piston.

> *WARNING*
> *If brake fluid is leaking from the piston bore, the piston cups are worn or damaged. Replace the piston assembly.*

6. Compress the piston and remove the snap ring (**Figure 47**) from the groove in the master cylinder.

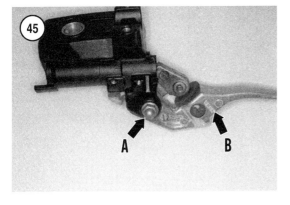

7. Remove the piston assembly and spring from the master cylinder bore. Do not remove the primary and secondary cups from the piston.

Inspection

When measuring the front master cylinder components, compare the actual measurements to the specifications in **Table 1**. Replace worn or damaged parts as described in this section.

1. Clean and dry the master cylinder assembly as follows:

    a. Handle the brake components carefully when servicing them.

    b. Use only DOT 4 brake fluid or isopropyl alcohol to wash rubber parts (rubber boot and piston assembly) in the brake system. Never allow any petroleum-based cleaner to contact the rubber parts. These chemicals cause the rubber to swell, requiring their replacement.

    c. Clean the master cylinder piston snap ring groove (A, **Figure 48**) carefully. Use a small pick or brush to clean the groove. If a hard varnish residue has built up in the groove, soak the master cylinder in solvent to help soften the residue. Then wash in soapy water and rinse completely.

    d. Blow the master cylinder dry with compressed air.

    e. Place cleaned parts on a clean lint-free cloth until assembly.

> *WARNING*
> *Do not get any oil or grease onto any of the master cylinder components. These chemicals cause the rubber parts in the brake system to swell, permanently damaging them.*

> *WARNING*
> *Do not remove the primary and secondary cups from the piston assembly for cleaning or inspection purposes.*

2. Check the piston assembly for the following defects:

    a. Broken, distorted or collapsed piston return spring (A, **Figure 49**).

    b. Worn, cracked, damaged or swollen primary (B, **Figure 49**) and secondary cups (C).

    c. Scratched, scored or damaged piston (D, **Figure 49**).

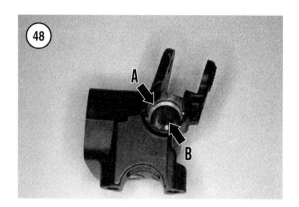

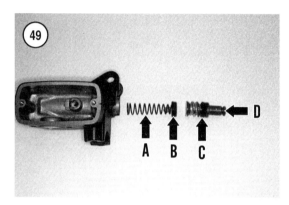

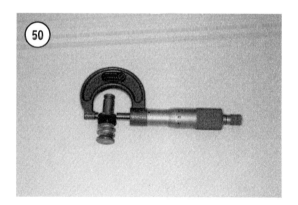

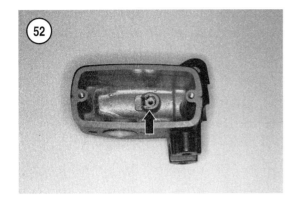

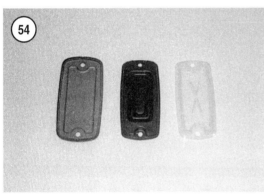

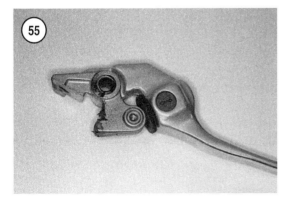

d. Corroded, weak or damaged snap ring.

e. Worn or damaged rubber boot.

If any of these parts are worn or damaged, replace the piston assembly.

3. Measure the piston outside diameter (**Figure 50**).

4. To assemble a new piston assembly, perform the following:

   a. If replacing the piston, install the new primary and secondary cups onto the piston. Use the original piston assembly as a reference when installing the new cups onto the piston.

   b. Before installing the new piston cups, lubricate them with brake fluid.

   c. Clean the new piston in brake fluid.

   d. Install the primary cup (B, **Figure 49**) onto the spring and then the secondary (C) cup onto the piston.

5. Inspect the master cylinder bore (B, **Figure 48**). Replace the master cylinder if its bore is corroded, cracked or damaged in any way. Do not hone the master cylinder bore to remove scratches or other damage.

6. Measure the master cylinder bore inside diameter (**Figure 51**).

7. Check for plugged supply and relief ports (**Figure 52**) in the base of the master cylinder. Clean with compressed air.

8. Check the banjo bolt threads (**Figure 53**) for damage.

9. Inspect the diaphragm plate, diaphragm and top cover (**Figure 54**) for deterioration and other damage.

10. Check the brake lever assembly (**Figure 55**) for the following defects:

   a. Damaged brake lever.

   b. Excessively worn or damaged pivot bolt.

   c. Damaged adjuster arm assembly.

Assembly

15

1. If installing a new piston assembly, assemble it as described under *Inspection* in this section.

2. Lubricate the piston assembly and cylinder bore with DOT 4 brake fluid.

3. Install the small end of the spring onto the primary piston as shown in B, **Figure 49**.

> *WARNING*
> *Do not allow the piston cups to tear or turn inside out when installing the piston into the master cylinder bore. Both cups are larger than the bore. To*

ease installation, lubricate the cups and piston with DOT 4 brake fluid.

4. Insert the spring and primary piston assembly into the master cylinder bore (**Figure 56**). Push it in, then install the piston assembly into the master cylinder bore (**Figure 57**).

5. Compress the piston assembly and install the snap ring (**Figure 58**) into the master cylinder bore groove.

> *WARNING*
> *The snap ring must seat in the master cylinder groove completely (**Figure 59**). Push and release the piston a few times to make sure it moves smoothly and that the snap ring does not pop out.*

6. Slide the rubber boot over the piston. Seat the outer dust cover lip into the groove in the end of the piston (**Figure 60**).

7. Install the brake lever assembly as follows:
   a. Lubricate the pivot bolt with silicone brake grease.
   b. Install the brake lever and adjuster assembly (B, **Figure 45**).
   c. Install and tighten the brake lever pivot bolt securely. Check that the brake lever moves freely. If there is any binding or roughness, remove the pivot bolt and brake lever and inspect the parts.
   d. Hold the pivot bolt, then install and tighten the brake lever pivot nut (A, **Figure 45**) to 6 N•m (53 in.-lb.). Check that the brake lever moves freely.

8. Install the front brake switch (**Figure 44**) and tighten it securely.

9. Install the diaphragm (**Figure 43**), the diaphragm plate (**Figure 42**) and the top cover (**Figure 41**). Do not tighten the screws, as brake fluid will be added later.

10. Install the master cylinder as described in this chapter.

REAR BRAKE PADS

There is no recommended mileage interval for changing the brake pads in the rear brake caliper. Pad wear depends on personal riding habits and the condition of the brake system. Inspect the rear brake pads (**Figure 61**) for uneven wear, scoring, oil con-

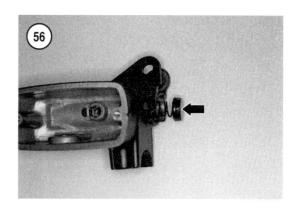

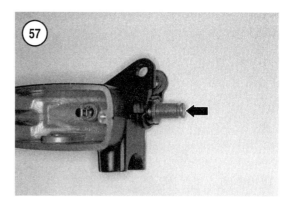

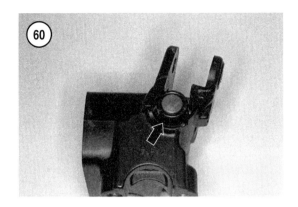

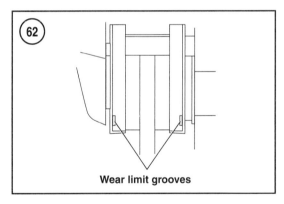

Wear limit grooves

tamination or other damage. Replace the brake pads if the wear limit grooves (**Figure 62**) are no longer visible. To maintain even brake pressure on the rear disc, replace both brake pads at the same time. Never use one new brake pad with a used brake pad in the caliper.

> *CAUTION*
> *Due to the amount of pad material re-maining after the wear limit grooves (**Figure 62**) are worn away, check the brake pads frequently. If pad wear is uneven, the backing plate may contact the disc and damage it.*

Replacement

> *NOTE*
> *The brake pads can be removed with the brake caliper mounted on the mo-torcycle. To inspect the piston and seals for leakage or damage, remove the brake caliper as described in this chapter.*

1. Read the information listed under *Brake Service* in this chapter.
2. Support the motorcycle on level ground.
3. Block the front wheel so the motorcycle will not roll in either direction while on the swing arm stand (or centerstand on U.K. models).
4. Remove the seat and the rear cowl as described in Chapter Sixteen.
5. Remove the bolt and nut (A, **Figure 63**) securing the master cylinder reservoir to the seat rail. Pull the master cylinder away from the seat rail and remove the cap (B, **Figure 63**).
6. Use a large syringe to remove and discard about 50 percent of the fluid from the reservoir. This prevents the master cylinder from overflow-ing when the caliper piston is compressed for re-installation. Do not drain the entire reservoir, or air will enter the system. Reinstall the cap and tighten securely.

> *CAUTION*
> *Do not allow the master cylinder res-ervoir to overflow when performing Step 9. Brake fluid damages most sur-faces it contacts.*

7. Unscrew and remove the pad pin plug (A, **Fig-ure 64**).

15

8. Remove the caliper rear mounting bolt (B, **Figure 64**).

9. Take hold of the caliper body (from the outside) and push it toward its brake disc (**Figure 65**). This pushes the piston into the caliper to make room for the new brake pads.

10. Pivot the caliper up and partially off the brake disc (**Figure 66**).

11. Loosen and remove the pad pin (A, **Figure 67**) and both brake pads (B).

12. Do not remove the pad spring (A, **Figure 68**), but make sure it is in good condition. Replace the pad spring if it appears weak or damaged.

13. Inspect the pad pin for excessive wear, corrosion or damage. Use a wire-wheel to remove corrosion and dirt from the pad pin surface. A dirty or damaged pad pin surface prevents the brake pads from sliding properly and results in brake drag and overheating of the brake disc.

14. Inspect the brake pads as follows:

   a. Inspect the friction material (**Figure 69**) for light surface dirt, grease and oil contamination. Remove light contamination with sandpaper. If the contamination has penetrated the surface, replace the brake pads.

   b. Inspect the brake pads for excessive wear or damage. Replace the brake pads when the friction material is worn down to the wear indicator line.

   c. Inspect the brake pads for uneven wear. If one pad is worn more than the other, the brake caliper may not be working correctly. Refer to *Brake Caliper* in this chapter.

NOTE
If brake fluid is leaking from around the piston, overhaul the brake caliper as described in this chapter.

   d. Inspect the metal plate (**Figure 70**) on the backside of each pad for corrosion, tightness and damage.

15. Service the brake disc as follows:

   a. Use brake cleaner and a fine grade emery cloth to remove all brake pad residue and any rust from the brake disc. Clean both sides of the disc.

NOTE
A thorough cleaning of the brake disc is especially important when changing brake pad compounds. Many

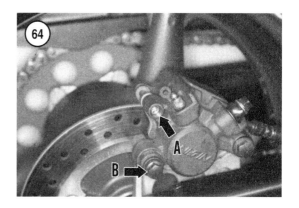

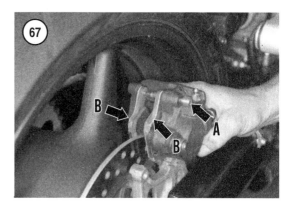

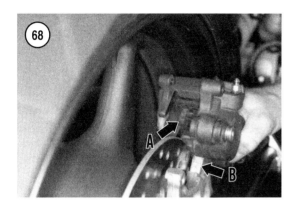

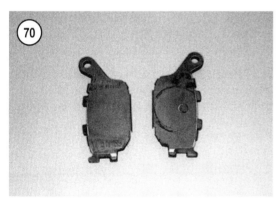

compounds are not compatible with each other.

   b. Check the brake disc for wear as described in this chapter.

16. Install the brake pads (B, **Figure 67**) into the caliper so the friction material on both brake pads faces toward the brake disc. Insert the extended arm on the end of each pad onto the pad retainer in the caliper bracket (B, **Figure 68**).

17. Push both brake pads against the pad spring and install the pad pin (A, **Figure 67**) through the brake caliper and brake pad holes. Tighten the pad pin to 18 N•m (13 ft.-lb.).

18. Install the caliper rear mounting bolt (B, **Figure 64**) and tighten to 23 N•m (17 ft.-lb.).

19. Install and tighten the pad pin (A, **Figure 64**) securely.

20. Operate the rear brake pedal several times to seat the pads against the disc, then check the brake fluid level in the reservoir. If necessary, add new DOT 4 brake fluid.

> *WARNING*
> *Do not ride the motorcycle until the front and rear brakes operate correctly with full hydraulic advantage. If necessary, bleed the brakes as described in this chapter.*

REAR BRAKE CALIPER

Removal/Installation

1. If the caliper is going to be removed and serviced, perform the following:

   a. Drain the brake fluid from the rear master cylinder as described under *Brake Fluid Draining* in this chapter.

   b. Remove the brake pads as previously described.

   c. Remove the brake hose banjo bolt and washers at the caliper (A, **Figure 71**). Plug the hose, then place it in a reclosable plastic bag to prevent leakage and hose contamination.

2. Remove the caliper mounting bolts (B, **Figure 71**).

3. Remove the caliper from the mounting bracket.

15

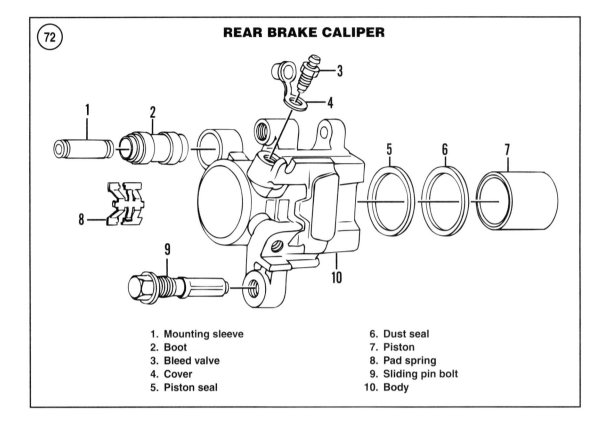

REAR BRAKE CALIPER

1. Mounting sleeve
2. Boot
3. Bleed valve
4. Cover
5. Piston seal
6. Dust seal
7. Piston
8. Pad spring
9. Sliding pin bolt
10. Body

4. If the brake hose was not disconnected at the caliper, insert a spacer block between the brake pads and support the caliper with a wire hook.

NOTE
The spacer block prevents the piston from being forced out of the caliper if the rear brake pedal is accidentally applied while the brake caliper is removed from the brake disc.

5. If necessary, service the brake caliper as described in this chapter.

6. Check that the brake pads were not contaminated with brake fluid. If so, replace the brake pads as described in this chapter.

7. If the brake caliper was not completely removed from the motorcycle, remove the spacer block from between the brake pads.

8. Install the caliper assembly over the brake disc. Be careful not to damage the leading edge of the pads.

9. Install *new* brake caliper mounting bolts (B, **Figure 71**) and tighten to 23 N•m (17 ft.-lb.).

10. Place a *new* sealing washer on each side of the brake hose. Then thread the banjo bolt (A, **Figure 71**) into the caliper and tighten finger-tight.

11. Position the brake hose against the caliper hose stoppers and tighten the banjo bolt to 34 N•m (25 ft.-lb.).

CAUTION
After tightening the banjo bolt, make sure the brake hose is routed against the caliper hose stoppers.

12. Refill the master cylinder and secure it to the seat rail. Tighten the bolt securely.

13. Bleed the brake lever and brake pedal lines as described in this chapter.

14. Operate the rear brake pedal to seat the pads against the brake disc.

WARNING
Do not ride the motorcycle until the rear brake operate with full hydraulic advantage.

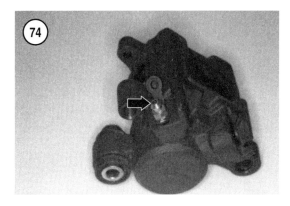

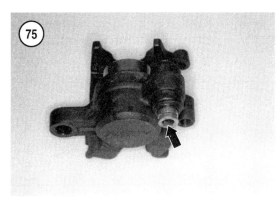

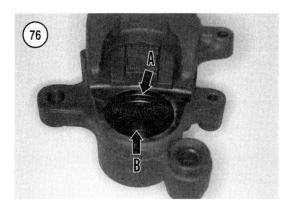

Disassembly

Refer to **Figure 72**.

1. If still in place, remove the brake pads as described in this chapter.

2. Remove the brake caliper as described in this chapter.

3. Remove the pad spring (**Figure 73**).

4. Remove the bleed valve and cover (**Figure 74**).

5. Remove the mounting sleeve (**Figure 75**) from the rubber boot.

6. Remove the piston as follows:

> *WARNING*
> *Compressed air forces the piston out of the caliper under considerable force. Do not cushion the piston by hand, as injury could result.*

a. Support the caliper on a wooden block with the piston side facing down. Place a thick towel between the piston and workbench. Make sure there is enough space underneath the caliper for the piston to be removed completely.

b. Direct compressed air through the brake line port and force the piston out of the caliper.

7. Use a small tool to carefully pry the dust and piston seals from the grooves in the cylinder bore.

Inspection

When measuring the brake caliper components, compare the actual measurements to the specifications in **Table 2**. Replace worn or damaged parts as described in this section.

1. Clean and dry the caliper assembly as follows:

a. Handle the brake components carefully when servicing them.

b. Use only DOT 4 brake fluid or isopropyl alcohol to wash rubber parts in the brake system. Never allow any petroleum-based cleaner to contact the rubber parts. These chemicals cause the rubber to swell, requiring their replacement.

c. Clean the dust and piston seal grooves (A, **Figure 76**) carefully to avoid damaging the caliper bore. Use a small pick or brush to clean the grooves. If a hard varnish residue has built up in the grooves, soak the caliper body in solvent to help soften the residue.

15

Then wash the caliper in soapy water and rinse completely.

d. If alcohol or solvent was used to clean the caliper, blow dry with compressed air.

e. Check the fluid passages to make sure they are clean and dry.

f. After cleaning the parts, place them on a clean lint-free cloth until assembly.

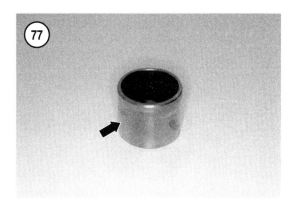

CAUTION
Do not get any oil or grease onto any of the brake caliper components. These chemicals cause the rubber parts in the brake system to swell, permanently damaging them.

2. Check the cylinder bore (B, **Figure 76**) for corrosion, deep scratches and other wear marks. Do not hone the cylinder bore.

3. Measure the caliper cylinder bore diameter.

4. Inspect the piston (**Figure 77**) for pitting, corrosion, cracks or other damage.

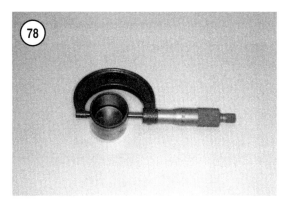

5. Measure the piston outside diameter (**Figure 78**).

6. Clean the bleed valve with compressed air. Check the valve threads for damage. Replace damaged dust cover.

7. Clean the banjo bolt with compressed air.

8. Inspect the spring (**Figure 79**) for damage.

9. Inspect the caliper mounting sleeve (**Figure 80**) and boot assembly as follows:

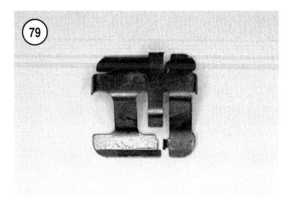

WARNING
A floating caliper is used on all models. The caliper mounting bolt goes through the mounting sleeve. These two components allow the brake caliper to slide or float during piston movement. The rubber boot installed over the mounting sleeve helps control caliper movement by preventing excessive mounting sleeve vibration and play, and prevents dirt from damaging the mounting sleeve operating surfaces. If the mounting sleeve is excessively worn or damaged, the caliper cannot slide smoothly. This condition causes uneven brake pad wear, resulting in brake drag and overheating. The caliper mounting bolt, sliding mounting bolt and rubber boot are an important part of the

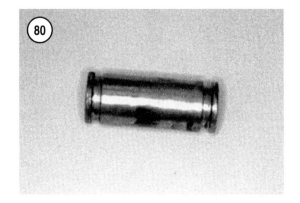

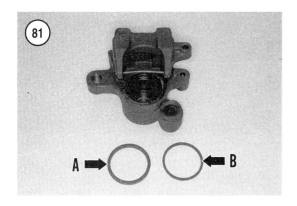

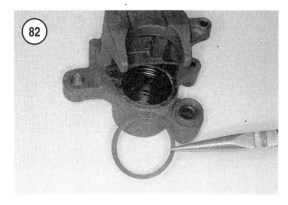

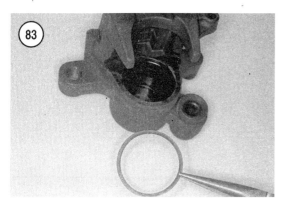

*brake caliper and must be maintained
to provide proper brake operation.*

a. Inspect the caliper mounting sleeve and boot for wear, deterioration and damage.
b. Inspect the caliper sliding pin rear mounting bolt for excessive wear, uneven wear (steps) and other damage.

Assembly

1. Install the bleed valve and cover into the caliper. Tighten finger-tight.
2. Soak the new piston and dust seals in DOT 4 brake fluid.
3. Lubricate the piston and cylinder bore with brake fluid.

NOTE
*The piston seal (A, **Figure 81**) is thicker than the dust seal (B).*

4. Install a new piston seal (**Figure 82**) into the lower groove of the cylinder bore.
5. Install a new dust seal (**Figure 83**) into the upper groove of the cylinder bore.

NOTE
Check that each seal fits squarely into its respective cylinder bore groove.

6. Install the piston into the caliper bore with its open side facing out (**Figure 84**). To prevent the piston from damaging the seals, turn them into the bore by hand. Install the piston until it bottoms out.
7. Install the mounting sleeve (**Figure 75**) into the rubber boot and center it within the boot.
8. Install the bleed valve and cover (**Figure 74**).
9. Install the pad spring (**Figure 73**).
10. Install the brake caliper as described in this chapter.
11. Install the brake pads as described in this chapter.
12. Install the rear brake caliper as described in this chapter.

REAR MASTER CYLINDER

Read the information listed under *Brake Service* in this chapter before servicing the rear master cylinder.

15

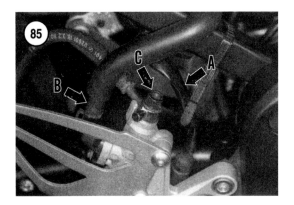

Removal

1. Support the motorcycle on level ground.
2. Block the front wheel so the motorcycle will not roll in either direction while on the swing arm stand (or centerstand on U.K. models).
3. Remove the seat, rear cowl and the right fairing panel as described in Chapter Sixteen.

> *CAUTION*
> *Wipe up any spilled brake fluid imme-diately, as it damages the finish of most plastic and metal surfaces. Use soapy water and rinse thoroughly.*

4. Drain the brake pedal line as described under *Brake Fluid Draining* in this chapter.
5. Disconnect the two-pin black connector (A, **Figure 85**) from the rear brake light switch.
6. Remove the bolt and nut (A, **Figure 86**) securing the master cylinder reservoir to the seat rail. Pull the master cylinder away from the seat rail (B, **Figure 86**).
7. Loosen the clamp and disconnect the reservoir hose (B, **Figure 85**) from the fitting on the rear master cylinder. Remove the reservoir assembly from the frame.
8. Remove the banjo bolt (C, **Figure 85**) and washers securing the rear brake hose to the top of the master cylinder. Plug the brake hose and place the end in a reclosable plastic bag to prevent brake fluid from leaking out.
9. Remove the bolts (**Figure 87**) securing the right side footpeg bracket assembly to the frame and remove the assembly.
10. Remove the bolts (A, **Figure 88**) securing the master cylinder and the guard to the footpeg bracket and remove the bracket (B).
11. If necessary, remove the cotter pin (A, **Figure 89**) and the brake pedal joint pin (B). Discard the

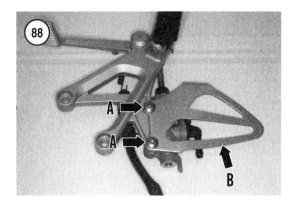

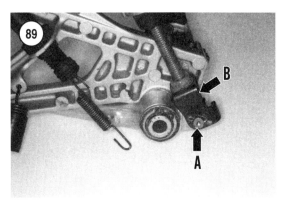

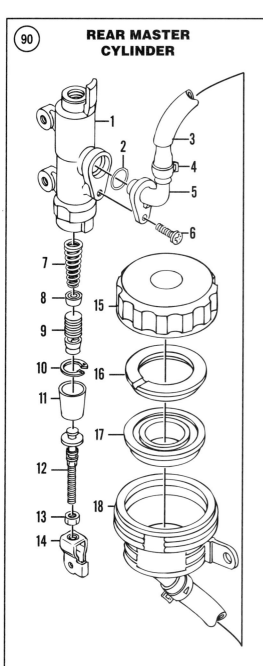

90 **REAR MASTER CYLINDER**

1. Body
2. O-ring seal
3. Interconnecting hose
4. Hose clamp
5. Reservoir joint
6. Screw
7. Spring
8. Primary cup
9. Piston/secondary cup
10. Snap ring
11. Rubber boot
12. Pushrod
13. Nut
14. Joint
15. Cap
16. Diaphragm plate
17. Diaphragm
18. Reservoir

cotter pin. Disconnect the master cylinder from the brake pedal.

Installation

1. If removed, install the master cylinder joint (B, **Figure 89**) onto the rear brake pedal mounting tab. Insert the joint pin in from the outside and install a *new* cotter pin (A, **Figure 89**) and bend the ends over completely.

2. Move the master cylinder into position on the footpeg bracket. Correctly position the guard (B, **Figure 88**) and install the bolts (A). Tighten the bolts securely.

3. Install the right side footpeg bracket assembly onto the frame and install the bolts (**Figure 87**) securing the assembly. Tighten the bolts to 26 N•m (19 ft.-lb.).

4. Remove the plastic bag and plug from the rear brake hose. Move the rear brake hose into position on top of the master cylinder.

5. Secure the brake hose to the master cylinder with the banjo bolt (C, **Figure 85**) and two *new* washers. Position the brake hose against the holder on the master cylinder and tighten the banjo bolt to 34 N•m (25 ft.-lb.).

6. Move the reservoir hose (B, **Figure 85**) into position and connect it to the master cylinder fitting. Tighten the clamp securely.

7. Hold the master cylinder reservoir next to the seat rail and refill the master cylinder with brake fluid. Install the top cap, then install the frame mounting bolt and nut (A, **Figure 86**) and tighten finger-tight at this time. The reservoir must be moved out to bleed the brakes.

8. Connect the two-pin black connector (A, **Figure 85**) onto the rear brake light switch.

9. Bleed the brakes as described in this chapter.

10. Turn the ignition switch on and check that the rear brake light comes on when the rear brake pedal is depressed.

15

WARNING
Do not ride the motorcycle until the front and rear brakes and brake light work properly.

Disassembly

Refer to **Figure 90**.

1. Slide the rubber boot (A, **Figure 91**) out of the master cylinder bore.

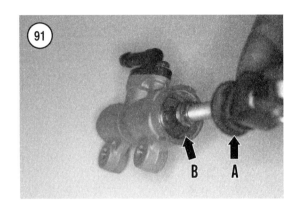

> *WARNING*
> *If brake fluid is leaking from the master cylinder bore, the piston cups are excessively worn or damaged. Replace the piston assembly.*

> *NOTE*
> *To aid in the removal/installation of the piston snap ring, thread a bolt and nut into the master cylinder and secure the nut and bolt in a vise.*

2. Compress the piston and remove the snap ring (B, **Figure 91**) from the groove in the master cylinder, then remove the pushrod/piston assembly (**Figure 92**).

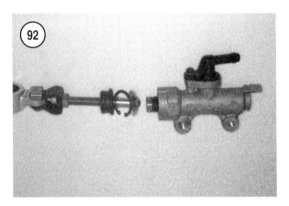

3. Remove the piston assembly and spring.
4. If necessary, remove the screw, the reservoir hose joint (**Figure 93**) and O-ring from the master cylinder body.
5. Inspect all components as described in this chapter.

Inspection

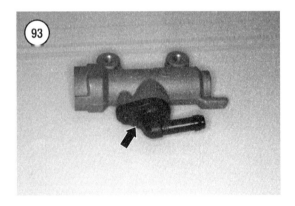

When measuring the master cylinder components, compare the actual measurements to the specifications in **Table 2**. Replace worn or damaged parts as described in this section.

1. Clean and dry the master cylinder assembly as follows:
   a. Handle the brake components carefully when servicing them.
   b. Use only DOT 4 brake fluid or isopropyl alcohol to wash rubber parts (piston seals and O-ring) in the brake system. Never allow any petroleum-based cleaner to contact the rubber parts. These chemicals cause the rubber to swell, requiring their replacement.
   c. Clean the master cylinder snap ring groove (A, **Figure 94**) carefully. Use a small pick or brush to clean the groove. If a hard varnish residue has built up in the groove, soak the master cylinder in solvent to help soften the residue. Then wash in soapy water and rinse completely.
   d. Dry the master cylinder with compressed air.
   e. After cleaning parts, place them on a clean lint-free cloth until assembly.

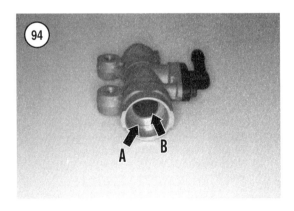

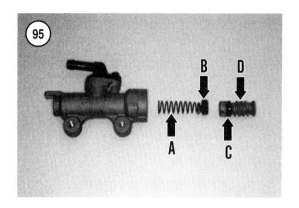

WARNING
Do not get any oil or grease onto any of the brake master cylinder components. These chemicals cause the rubber parts in the brake system to swell, permanently damaging them.

WARNING
Do not remove the primary and secondary cups from the piston assembly for cleaning or inspection purposes.

2. Check the piston assembly for the following defects:
   a. Broken, distorted or collapsed piston return spring (A, **Figure 95**).
   b. Worn, cracked, damaged or swollen primary (B, **Figure 95**) and secondary cups (C).
   c. Scratched, scored or damaged piston (D, **Figure 95**).
   d. Corroded, weak or damaged snap ring.
   e. Worn or damaged rubber boot.

If any of these parts are worn or damaged, replace the piston assembly.

3. Measure the piston outside diameter (**Figure 96**).

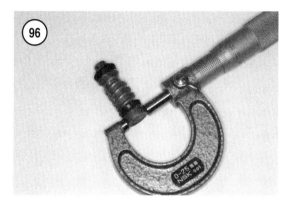

4. Measure the master cylinder bore inside diameter (**Figure 97**).

5. To assemble a new piston assembly, perform the following:
   a. When replacing the piston, install the new secondary cup (**Figure 98**) onto the piston. Use the original piston assembly as a reference when installing the new cup onto the piston.
   b. Before installing the new piston cups, lubricate them with brake fluid.
   c. Clean the new piston in brake fluid.
   d. Install the primary cup (B, **Figure 95**) onto the return spring.
   e. Install the secondary cup (**Figure 98**) onto the piston.

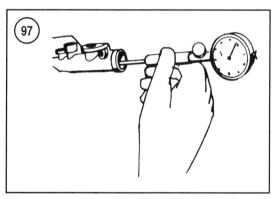

6. Inspect the master cylinder bore (B, **Figure 94**). Replace the master cylinder if its bore is pitted, corroded, cracked or damaged in any way. Do not hone the master cylinder bore to remove scratches or other damage.

7. Check for plugged supply and relief ports in the master cylinder. Clean with compressed air.

8. Check the pushrod assembly for the following defects:
   a. Corroded or damaged pushrod.

15

b. Damaged pushrod joint.
9. To service the pushrod, perform the following:
   a. Loosen the locknut and unscrew the pushrod joint from the pushrod.
   b. Replace worn or damaged parts.
   c. Assemble the pushrod in the order shown in **Figure 90**. Do not tighten the locknut. The pushrod length must be adjusted after reassembling the master cylinder.

Assembly

1. If installing a new piston assembly, assemble it as described under *Inspection* in this section.
2. Lubricate the piston assembly and cylinder bore with DOT 4 brake fluid.
3. Install the spring (large end first) into the cylinder as shown in **Figure 99**. The primary cup installed on the small spring end must be facing out, toward the bore opening.

> *CAUTION*
> *Do not allow the piston cups to tear or turn inside out when installing the piston into the master cylinder bore. Both cups are larger than the bore. To ease installation, lubricate the cups and piston with brake fluid.*

4. Insert the piston and secondary cup (**Figure 100**) into the master cylinder bore (**Figure 101**) and against the spring.

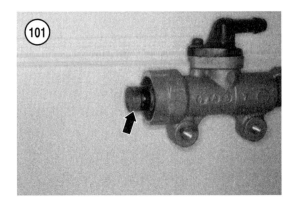

> *NOTE*
> *Before installing the snap ring, mount the master cylinder in a vise as described under **Disassembly** in this section.*

5. Use silicone brake grease to lubricate the end of the pushrod that contacts the piston.
6. Install the pushrod into the master cylinder bore and seat it against the piston.
7. Push the pushrod to compress the piston assembly and position the washer below the snap ring groove, then install the snap ring (B, **Figure 91**) into the master cylinder groove.

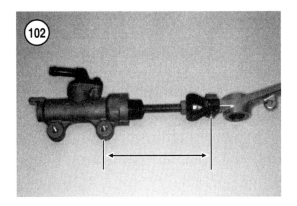

> *CAUTION*
> *The snap ring must seat in the master cylinder groove completely. Push and release the piston a few times to make*

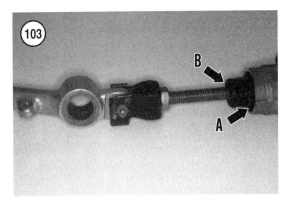

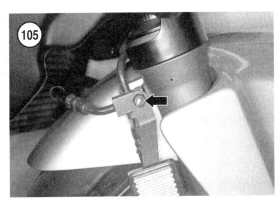

sure it moves smoothly and that the circlip does not pop out.

8. Turn the brake joint to adjust the pushrod length (**Figure 102**) to 100 mm (3.94 in.). Then tighten the master cylinder pushrod locknut against the brake joint to 18 N•m (13 ft.-lb.).

9. Slide the dust cover (A, **Figure 91**) down the pushrod and seat it against the washer (A, **Figure 103**). Seat the outer end of the boot onto the pushrod (B, **Figure 103**).

10. Install the master cylinder as described in this chapter.

BRAKE HOSE REPLACEMENT

Check the brake hoses at the brake inspection intervals listed in Chapter Three. Replace the brake hoses if they show signs of wear or damage, or if they have bulges or signs of chafing.

To replace a brake hose, perform the following:

1. Drain the brake system as described under *Brake Fluid Draining* in this chapter.

2. Use a plastic drop cloth to cover areas that could be damaged by spilled brake fluid.

3. When removing a brake hose or brake line, note the following:

    a. Record the hose or line routing on a piece of paper.

    b. Remove any bolts or brackets securing the brake hose to the frame or suspension component. Refer to **Figure 104** and **Figure 105** for the front and **Figure 106** for the rear.

    c. Before removing the banjo bolts, note how the end of the brake hose is installed or indexed against the part it is threaded into. The hoses must be installed facing in their original position.

4. Replace banjo bolts with damaged hex-heads.

5. Always install *new* washers with the banjo bolts.

6. Reverse these steps to install the new brake hoses, while noting the following:

    a. Compare the new and old hoses to make sure they are the same.

    b. Clean the new washers, banjo bolts and hose ends to remove any contamination.

    c. Referring to the notes made during removal, route the brake hose along its original path.

    d. Install a *new* banjo bolt washer on each side of the brake hose.

15

e. Tighten the banjo bolts to 34 N•m (25 ft.-lb.).

f. After replacing a front brake hose, turn the handlebars from side to side to make sure the hose does not rub against any part or pull away from its brake unit.

g. Refill the master cylinders and bleed the brakes as described in this chapter.

WARNING
Do not ride the motorcycle until the front and rear brakes operate correctly with full hydraulic advantage and the brake light works properly.

BRAKE DISC

Inspection

The front brake discs can be inspected while installed on or removed from the motorcycle. Small marks on the disc are not important, but deep scratches or other marks may reduce braking effectiveness and increase brake pad wear. If these grooves are evident and the brake pads are wearing rapidly, replace the brake disc.

The minimum (MIN) disc thickness if stamped on the disc. Refer to **Table 1** and **Table 2** for disc specifications.

1. Support the motorcycle on level ground.

2. Block the front wheel so the motorcycle will not roll in either direction while on the swing arm stand (or centerstand on U.K. models).

3. Measure the thickness around the disc at several locations with a micrometer (**Figure 107**). Replace the disc if its thickness at any point is less than the marked MIN thickness on the disc. Also refer to the service limit specified in **Table 1** or **Table 2**.

4. Install a dial indicator and position its stem against the brake disc (**Figure 108**, typical). Then zero the dial gauge. Slowly turn the front wheel or rear axle/brake disc and measure runout. If the runout exceeds the service limit in **Table 1** or **Table 2**, first check for loose brake disc mounting bolts. If the bolts are tight, inspect the front wheel bearings (Chapter Thirteen) or the rear axle bearings in the bearing holder (Chapter Fourteen). Then check the brake disc mounting surface for damage. If the bearings and disc mounting surfaces are in good condition, replace the brake disc.

5. Clean the disc of any rust or corrosion and wipe clean with brake cleaner. Never use an

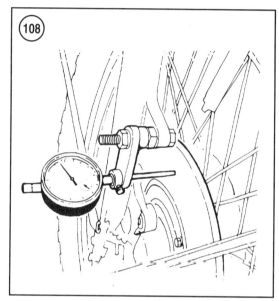

oil-based solvent that may leave an oil residue on the disc.

6. Check the floating disc fasteners (**Figure 109**) for damage or looseness. If any are damaged, replace the disc.

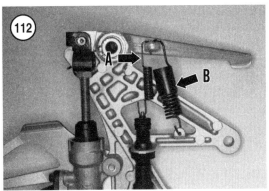

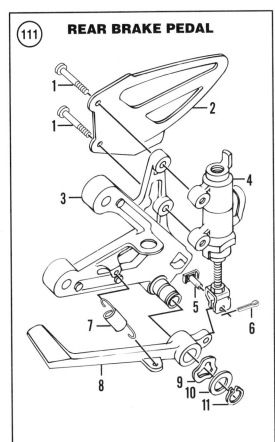

REAR BRAKE PEDAL

1. Bolt
2. Guard
3. Footpeg bracket
4. Rear master cylinder
5. Joint pin
6. Cotter pin
7. Return spring
8. Brake pedal
9. Wave washer
10. Thrust washer
11. Snap ring

Removal/Installation

1A. Remove the front wheel as described in Chapter Eleven.

1B. Remove the rear wheel as described in Chapter Eleven.

2. Remove the bolts (**Figure 110**) securing the brake disc to the wheel and remove the disc.

3. Perform any necessary service to the front hub (wheel bearing or tire replacement) before installing the brake discs.

4. Clean the brake disc threaded holes in the hub.

5. Clean the brake disc mounting surface on the hub.

6. Install the brake disc with its directional arrow facing toward the wheel's normal rotating direction.

> *WARNING*
> *The bolts securing the brake disc must*
> *be replaced every time they are removed.*

7. Install *new* brake disc mounting bolts and tighten to the specification in **Table 3** or **Table 4**.

8. Clean the disc of any rust or corrosion and spray clean with brake cleaner. Never use an oil-based solvent that may leave an oil residue on the disc.

9. Install the front or rear wheel as described in Chapter Eleven.

15

REAR BRAKE PEDAL

Removal

Refer to **Figure 111**.

1. Remove the right footpeg bracket assembly as described under *Rear Master Cylinder Removal* in this chapter.

2. Disconnect the brake light switch spring (A, **Figure 112**) and brake pedal return spring (B) from the brake pedal.

3. Remove the snap ring (**Figure 113**), the thrust washer (**Figure 114**) and the wave washer (**Figure 115**) securing the brake pedal to the footpeg bracket.

4. Remove the cotter pin and clevis pin (**Figure 116**) and disconnect the master cylinder from the rear brake pedal. Discard the cotter pin.

5. Remove the rear brake pedal from the pivot post on the footpeg bracket.

6. Clean the footpeg, brake pedal and footpeg holder pivot surfaces.

7. Inspect the brake pedal assembly and replace worn or damaged parts.

Installation

1. Apply a water-resistant grease onto the brake pedal and footpeg pivot surfaces.

2. Reconnect the master cylinder pushrod to the brake pedal with the clevis pin and a new cotter pin (**Figure 116**). Spread the cotter pin arms over to lock it.

3. Install the brake pedal, wave washer and the thrust washer onto the footpeg shaft. Install the snap ring (**Figure 113**) into the footpeg shaft groove. Make sure the snap ring seats completely in the groove.

4. Reconnect the brake pedal return spring (B, **Figure 112**).

5. Install the brake light switch into its holder and reconnect the brake light switch return spring (A, **Figure 112**).

6. Install the right footpeg holder assembly as described under *Rear Master Cylinder Installation* in this chapter.

7. Operate the rear brake pedal, making sure it moves without any binding or roughness.

8. Adjust the rear brake light switch as described in Chapter Three.

> *WARNING*
> *Do not ride the motorcycle until the rear brake, brake pedal and brake light work properly.*

BRAKE BLEEDING

Bleeding the brakes removes air from the brake system. Air in the brake system increases brake lever or pedal travel while causing it to feel spongy

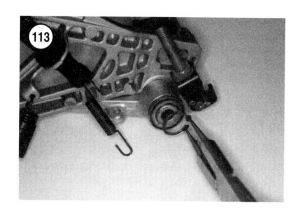

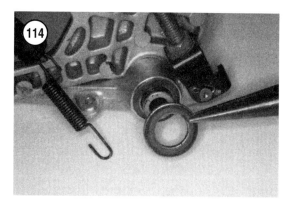

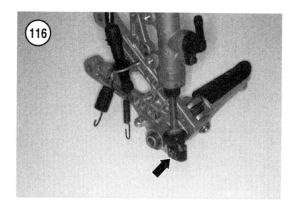

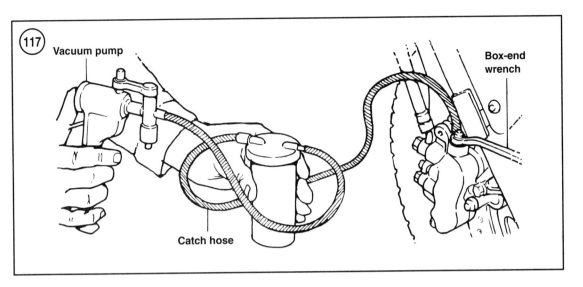

(117)

Vacuum pump

Box-end wrench

Catch hose

and less responsive. Under extreme braking (heat) conditions, it can cause complete loss of brake action.

The brake hose systems can be filled manually or with the use of a vacuum pump. Both methods are described in this section. When the brake lines are full of brake fluid, the brakes are bled manually. Both procedures are described in this section.

When adding brake fluid during the bleeding process, use DOT 4 brake fluid. Do not reuse brake fluid drained from the system or use DOT 5 (silicone based) brake fluid. Brake fluid damages most surfaces, so wipe up any spills immediately with soapy water and rinse completely.

NOTE
When bleeding the brakes, check the fluid level in the front and rear master cylinders frequently to prevent them from running dry, especially when using a vacuum pump. If air enters the system it must be bled again.

General Bleeding Tips

When bleeding the brakes, note the following:

1. Clean the bleed valves and the area around the valves of all dirt and debris. Make sure the passageway in the end of the valve is open and clear.

2. Use a box-end wrench to open and close the bleed valves. This prevents damage to the hex-head, especially if the valve is rusted in place.

3. Install the box-end wrench (**Figure 117**) on the bleed valve before installing the catch hose. This allows operation of the wrench without having to disconnect the hose.

NOTE
*The catch hose (**Figure 117**) is the hose installed between the bleed valve and catch bottle.*

4. Replace bleed valves that have damaged hex-head surfaces. If rounded off, the valves cannot be tightened fully and are also difficult to loosen.

5. Use a clear catch hose to allow visible inspection of the brake fluid as it leaves the caliper. Air bubbles visible in the catch hose indicate that there still may be air trapped in the brake system.

6. Depending on the play of the bleed valve when it is loosened, it is possible to see air exiting through the catch hose even through there is no air in the brake system. A loose or damaged catch hose also causes air leaks. In both cases, air is being introduced into the bleed system at the bleed valve threads and catch hose connection, and not from within the brake system itself. This condition can be misleading and cause excessive brake bleeding when there is no air in the system.

7. Open the bleed valve just enough to allow fluid to pass through the valve and into the catch bottle.

15

The farther the bleed valve is opened, the looser the valve becomes. This allows air to be drawn into the system from around the valve threads.

> *WARNING*
> *Do not apply an excessive amount of grease to the bleed valve threads. This can block the bleed valve passageway and contaminate the brake fluid.*

8. If air is suspected of entering the bleed system from around the bleed valve threads, remove the bleed valve and apply silicone brake grease to the valve's threads to prevent air from passing by them. Then reinstall the bleed valve into the brake caliper.

9. If the system is difficult to bleed, tap the banjo bolt on the master cylinder as well as the brake caliper and connecting hoses a few times. It is not uncommon for air bubbles to become trapped in the hose connection where the brake fluid exits the master cylinder and caliper. When a number of bubbles appear in the master cylinder reservoir after tapping the banjo bolt, air was trapped in this area. Also, tap the other hole and line connection points at the calipers and other brake units.

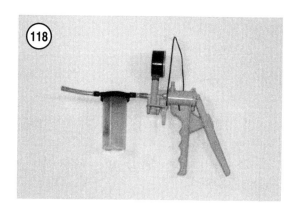

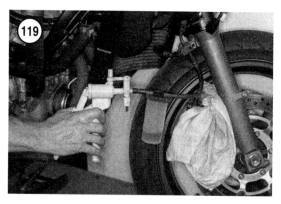

BLEEDING THE SYSTEM

> *NOTE*
> *These procedures are shown on the front wheel and apply to the rear wheel as well.*

Brake Bleeder Procedure

This one-person procedure uses the Mityvac hydraulic brake bleeding kit (**Figure 118**). This tool and equivalents are available from automotive or motorcycle supply stores or from mail order outlets.

1. Remove the dust cap from the caliper bleed valve.

2. Place a clean shop cloth over the caliper to protect it from accidental brake fluid spills.

3. Assemble the Mityvac tool according to its manufacturer's instructions. Secure it to the caliper bleed valve (**Figure 119**).

4. Clean the top of the master cylinder of all dirt and foreign matter.

5. Turn the handlebars to level the front master cylinder (**Figure 120**) and remove the screws, reservoir cover (B), diaphragm plate and diaphragm.

6. Fill the reservoir almost to the top with DOT 4 brake fluid and reinstall the diaphragm and cover. Leave the cover in place during this procedure to prevent the entry of dirt.

7. Operate the pump several times to create a vacuum in the line. Brake fluid will quickly draw from the caliper into the pump's reservoir. Open the bleed valve and then tighten the caliper bleed valve before the fluid stops flowing through the hose. To prevent air from being drawn through the master cylinder, add fluid to maintain its level at the top of the reservoir.

> *NOTE*
> *Do not allow the master cylinder reservoir to empty during the bleeding operation or more air will enter the system. If this occurs, the procedure must be repeated.*

8. Continue the bleeding process until the fluid drawn from the caliper is bubble free. If bubbles are withdrawn with the brake fluid, more air is trapped in the line. Repeat Step 7, making sure to refill the master cylinder to prevent air from being drawn into the system.

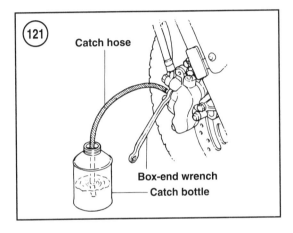

Catch hose

Box-end wrench
Catch bottle

9. When the brake fluid is free of bubbles, tighten the bleed valve and remove the brake bleeder assembly. Reinstall the bleed valve dust cap.

WARNING
Dispose of the brake fluid expelled during the bleeding process. Do not reuse the brake fluid.

10. If necessary, add fluid to correct the level in the master cylinder reservoir. When topping off the front master cylinder, turn the handlebar until the reservoir is level; add fluid until it is level with the reservoir gasket surface. The fluid level in the rear master cylinder must be slightly below the upper gasket surface.
11. On front brakes, repeat Steps 1-9 for the other caliper.
12. Reinstall the reservoir diaphragm and cover. Install the screws and tighten securely.
13. Test the feel of the brake lever or pedal. It must be firm and offer the same resistance each time it is operated. If it feels spongy, it is likely that there is still air in the system and it must be bleed again. Af-

ter bleeding the system, check for leaks and tighten all fittings and connections as necessary.

WARNING
Do not ride the motorcycle until the front and/or rear brake are operating correctly with full hydraulic advantage.

14. Test ride the motorcycle slowly at first to make sure that the brakes are operating properly.

Manual Procedure

NOTE
Before bleeding the brake, check that all brake hoses and lines are tight.

1. Connect a length of clear tubing to the bleed valve on the caliper. Place the other end of the tube into a clean container (**Figure 121**). Fill the container with enough fresh DOT 4 brake fluid to keep the end of the tube submerged. The tube must be long enough so that a loop can be made higher than the bleeder valve to prevent air from being drawn into the caliper during bleeding.
2. Clean the top of the master cylinder of all dirt and foreign matter.
3. Remove the screws securing the master cylinder top cover and remove the cover, diaphragm plate and the diaphragm.
4. Fill the reservoir almost to the top with DOT 4 brake fluid and reinstall the diaphragm and cover. Leave the cover in place during this procedure to prevent the entry of dirt.

NOTE
During this procedure, it is important to check the fluid level in the master cylinder reservoir often. If the reservoir runs dry, more air will enter the system.

5. Slowly apply the brake lever several times. Hold the lever in the applied position and open the bleed valve about 1/2 turn. Allow the lever to travel to its limit. When the limit is reached, tighten the bleed valve, then release the brake lever. As the brake fluid enters the system, the level will drop in the master cylinder reservoir. Maintain the level at the top of the reservoir to prevent air from being drawn into the system.

15

6. Continue the bleeding process until the fluid emerging from the hose is completely free of air bubbles. If the fluid is being replaced, continue until the fluid emerging from the hose is clean.

NOTE
If bleeding is difficult, allowing the fluid to stabilize for a few hours. Repeat the bleeding procedure when the tiny bubbles in the system settle out.

7. Hold the lever in the applied position and tighten the bleed valve. Remove the bleed tube and install the bleed valve dust cap.

WARNING
Dispose of the brake fluid expelled during the bleeding process. Do not reuse the brake fluid.

8. If necessary, add fluid to correct the level in the master cylinder reservoir. When topping off the front master cylinder, turn the handlebar until the reservoir is level; add fluid until it is level with the reservoir gasket surface. The fluid level in the rear master cylinder must be slightly below the upper gasket surface.

9. On front brakes, repeat Steps 1-8 for the other caliper.

10. Install the diaphragm, diaphragm plate and the top cover and tighten the screws securely.

11. Test the feel of the brake lever or pedal. It must be firm and offer the same resistance each time it is operated. If it feels spongy, it is likely that there is still air in the system and it must bleed it again. After bleeding the system check for leaks and tighten all fittings and connections as necessary.

WARNING
Do not ride the motorcycle until the front and/or rear brake are operating correctly with full hydraulic advantage.

12. Test ride the motorcycle slowly at first to make sure that the brakes are operating properly.

BRAKE FLUID DRAINING

Before disconnecting a brake hose from the front or rear brake, drain the brake fluid as described in this section. Doing so reduces the amount of brake fluid that can spill out when disconnecting the brake hoses and lines from the system.

Front Brake Lever Line

1. Read the information listed under *Brake Bleeding* in this chapter.
2. Support the motorcycle on level ground.
3. Block the front wheel so the motorcycle will not roll in either direction while on the swing arm stand (or centerstand on U.K. models).
4. Turn the handlebars to level the front master cylinder and remove the screws (**Figure 120**), reservoir cover, diaphragm plate and diaphragm.
5. Connect a brake bleeder to the front brake caliper bleed valve (**Figure 119**) as described under *Bleeding the System* in this chapter. Operate the bleeder tool to remove as much brake fluid from the system as possible.
6. Close the bleed valve and disconnect the brake bleeder tool.
7. Repeat for the other caliper.
8. Service the brake components as described in this chapter.

Rear Brake Pedal Line

1. Read the information listed under *Brake Bleeding* in this chapter.
2. Support the motorcycle on level ground.
3. Remove the seat, rear cowl and the right side cover as described in Chapter Sixteen.
4. Block the front wheel so the motorcycle will not roll in either direction while on the swing arm stand (or centerstand on U.K. models).
5. Connect a brake bleeder to the rear brake caliper bleed valve (**Figure 123**) as described under *Bleeding the System* in this chapter. Operate the bleeder tool to remove as much brake fluid from the system as possible.

123

CAUTION
Wipe up any spilled brake fluid imme-
diately, as it damages the finish of
most plastic and metal surfaces. Use
soapy water and rinse thoroughly.

6. Remove the bolt and nut (A, **Figure 122**) securing the master cylinder reservoir to the seat rail. Pull the master cylinder away from the seat rail.

7. Remove the rear master cylinder reservoir cap (B, **Figure 122**) and diaphragm.

8. Connect a brake bleeder to the rear brake caliper bleed valve (**Figure 123**) as described under

Bleeding the System in this chapter. Operate the bleeder tool to remove as much brake fluid from the system as possible.

9. Disconnect the brake bleeder and remove it from the brake caliper.

10. Service the brake components as described in this chapter.

FLUSHING THE BRAKE SYSTEM

When flushing the brake system, use DOT 4 brake fluid as a flushing fluid. Flushing consists of pulling new brake fluid through the system until the new fluid appears at the caliper and without the presence of any air bubbles. To flush the brake system, follow one of the bleeding procedures described under *Bleeding The System* in this chapter.

WARNING
Never reuse old brake fluid. Properly
discard all brake fluid flushed from
the system.

Table 1 FRONT BRAKE SPECIFICATIONS

Item	Standard mm (in.)	Wear limit mm (in.)
Brake fluid	DOT 4	
Brake disc runout	–	0.20 (0.008)
Brake disc thickness	4.4-4.6 (0.17-1.8)	3.5 (0.14)
Front master cylinder		
Cylinder diameter	15.870-15.913 (0.6248-0.6265)	15.925 (0.6270)
Piston diameter	15.827-15.854 (0.6231-0.6242)	15.815 (0.6226)
Front caliper		
Cylinder diameter		
Leading bore A	33.96-34.01 (1.337-1.339)	34.02 (1.339)
Trailing bore B	32.030-32.080 (1.2610-1.2630)	32.09 (1.263)
Piston diameter		
Leading bore A	33.802-33.835 (1.3308-1.3321)	33.794 (1.3305)
Trailing bore B	31.877-31.910 (1.2550-1.2563)	31.869 (1.255)

15

Table 2 REAR BRAKE SPECIFICATIONS

Item	Standard mm (in.)	Wear limit mm (in.)
Brake fluid	DOT 4	
Brake disc runout	–	0.30 (0.012)
Brake disc thickness	4.8-5.2 (0.19-0.21)	4.0 (0.16)
Rear master cylinder		
Cylinder diameter	14.000-14.043 (0.5512-0.5529)	14.055 (0.5533)
Piston diameter	13.957-13.984 (0.5495-0.5506)	13.945 (0.5490)
Rear caliper		
Cylinder diameter	38.18-38.23 (1.503-1.505)	38.24 (1.506)
Piston diameter	38.098-38.148 (1.4999-1.5019)	38.09 (1.500)
Brake pedal height	Rider preference	
Master cylinder		
pushrod length	100 (3.94)	–

Table 3 FRONT BRAKE TORQUE SPECIFICATIONS

Item	N•m	in.-lb.	ft.-lb.
Brake disc bolts[1]	20	–	15
Brake hose banjo bolt	34	–	25
Brake lever pivot nut	6	53	–
Caliper bleed valve	6	53	–
Caliper assembly bolts[2]	23	–	17
Caliper mounting bolts	30	–	22
Caliper pad pins	18	–	13
Master cylinder			
cover screws	2	18	–
mounting bolts	9	80	–

1. ALOC type bolt. Install new bolts during installation.
2. Apply a medium strength threadlock to the threads.

Table 4 REAR BRAKE TORQUE SPECIFICATIONS

Item	N•m	in.-lb.	ft.-lb.
Brake disc bolts*	42	–	31
Brake hose banjo bolt	34	–	25
Caliper bleed valve	6	53	–
Caliper mounting bolts	23	–	17
Caliper pad pin	18	–	13
Master cylinder			
mounting bolt	9	80	–
pushrod joint nut	18	–	13
Right side footpeg			
bracket bolts	26	–	19

*ALOC type bolt. Install new bolts during installation.

BODY PANELS

This chapter contains removal and installation procedures for the fairing components.

It is suggested that as soon as a body part is removed from the frame, all mounting hardware (small brackets, bolts, nuts, rubber bushings and metal collars) be reinstalled onto the removed part. Honda makes frequent changes, so the part and the way it is attached to the frame may differ slightly from the described service procedure in this chapter. Also, if working on a used machine, some of the fasteners may be missing, incorrectly installed or different from the original equipment.

The plastic fairing and frame side cover parts are very expensive to replace. After each part is removed from the frame, wrap it in a towel or blanket and store it in a safe area where it will not be damaged.

PLASTIC TRIM CLIPS

Plastic trim clips are used at various locations on different body panels. The trim clips degenerate with heat, age and use. Refer to A, **Figure 1** for a new trim clip and to B, **Figure 1** for a worn trim clip. It is very difficult, or even sometimes impossible, to install a worn trim clip through the mounting hole(s). The ends may break off, or get distorted so they will not close down sufficiently to allow insertion into the body panel mounting holes.

16

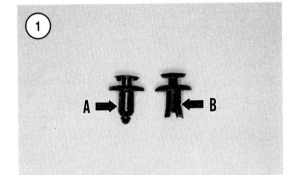

A ➡   ⬅ B

These clips are very inexpensive and should be replaced as necessary. Purchase at least a dozen if all of the body panels are going to be removed.

SEAT (1999-2000 U.S. AND CANADA, 1999-ON U.K. MODELS)

Removal/Installation

1. Use the ignition key and unlock the seat lock (**Figure 2**).

2. Pull up on the rear of the seat (A, **Figure 3**) and pull the seat back (B) while disconnecting the front seat hook from the fuel tank bracket.

3. To install, push the front of the seat down and lock it into the fuel tank bracket. Push the rear of the seat down to lock it.

> *WARNING*
> *After the seat is installed, pull up on it firmly and move it from side to side to make sure it is securely mounted in place. If the seat is improperly installed, it could lead to loss of control and a possible accident.*

RIDER'S SEAT (2001-ON U.S. AND CANADA MODELS)

Removal/Installation

1. Pull the rear corner of the seat up and remove the mounting bolt (**Figure 4**).

2. Repeat for the other side, then pull the seat back up (**Figure 5**) while disconnecting the front seat hook from the fuel tank bracket.

3. To install, push the front of the seat down and lock it into the fuel tank bracket. Push the rear of the seat down and install both mounting bolts. Tighten the bolts securely.

> *WARNING*
> *After the seat is installed, pull up on it firmly and move it from side to side to make sure it is securely mounted in place. If the seat is improperly installed, it could lead to loss of control and a possible accident.*

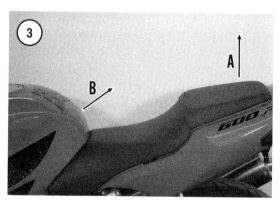

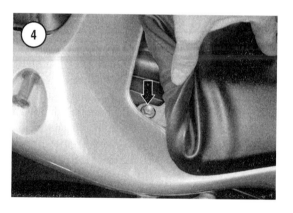

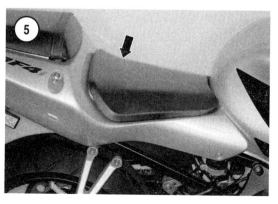

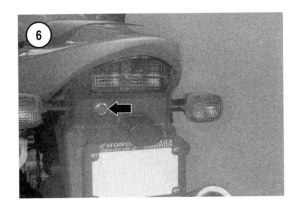

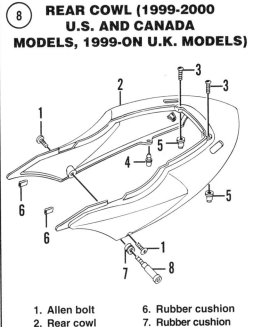

1. Allen bolt
2. Rear cowl
3. Screw
4. Trim clip
5. Nut
6. Rubber cushion
7. Rubber cushion
   (U.K. models only)
8. Shoulder bolt
   (U.K. models only)

PILLON SEAT (2001-ON U.S. AND CANADA MODELS)

Removal/Installation

1. Use the ignition key and unlock the seat lock (**Figure 6**).

2. Pull up on the rear of the seat (**Figure 7**), pivot it forward and unhook the front brackets and remove the seat.

3. To install, hook the seat brackets on the rear cowl bracket, pivot it down and lock the seat in place.

> *WARNING*
> *After the seat is installed, pull up on it firmly and move it from side to side to make sure it is securely mounted in place. If the seat is improperly installed, it could lead to the passenger sliding to one side and a possible accident.*

REAR COWL (1999-2000 U.S. AND CANADA, 1999-ON U.K. MODELS)

Removal/Installation

Refer to **Figure 8**.

1. Remove the seat as described in this chapter.

2A. On U.S. and Canada models, remove the Allen bolt (**Figure 9**) on each side of the cowl.

2B. On U.K. models, remove the shoulder bolt and rubber cushion on each side of the cowl.

3. Remove both top screws (**Figure 10**) at the rear of the cowl.

4. Remove the lower trim clip (**Figure 11**) on each side of the cowl.

16

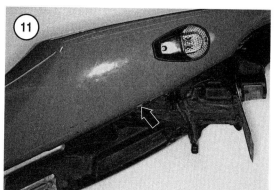

5. Disconnect the electrical connectors (**Figure 12**) from the tail/brake lights.

6. Carefully pull out on the front of the rear cowl, then pull it straight back and off the tail/brake light unit attached to the seat rail. Remove the rear cowl.

7. Install by reversing these removal steps while noting the following:

   a. Push the rear cowl mating surfaces against the seat rail prior to installing and tightening the mounting bolts and screws.

   b. Tighten the bolts and screws securely.

REAR COWL (2001-ON U.S. AND CANADA MODELS)

Removal/Installation

Refer to **Figure 13**.

1. Remove both seats as described in this chapter.

2. Remove the two plastic trim clips (**Figure 14**) on each side.

3. Remove the rear special hook bolt and washer (**Figure 15**) on each side.

4. Remove the front screws (**Figure 16**) on each side.

5. Pull out on the sides, then move toward the rear (**Figure 17**) and remove the rear cowl.

6. Install by reversing these removal steps.

SIDE FAIRING (ALL MODELS)

Removal/Installation

Refer to **Figure 18**.

1. Remove the seat as described in this chapter.

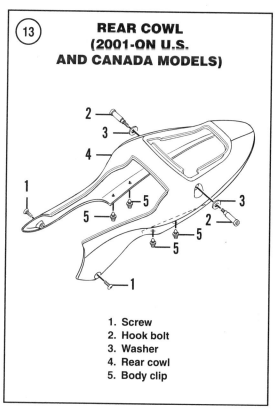

REAR COWL (2001-ON U.S. AND CANADA MODELS)

1. Screw
2. Hook bolt
3. Washer
4. Rear cowl
5. Body clip

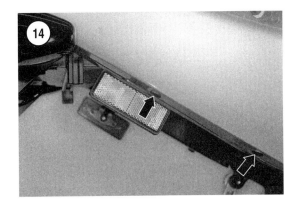

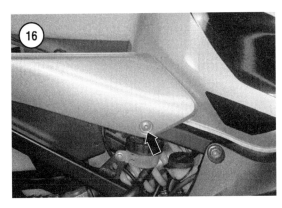

2. Remove the fuel tank as described in Chapter Nine.

3. Remove the front inner fairing as described in this chapter.

4. Remove the two lower trim clips (A, **Figure 19**).

5. Remove the lower short Allen bolt (B, **Figure 19**).

6. Remove the rear lower long Allen bolt (**Figure 20**).

7. Remove the rear upper short Allen bolt (**Figure 21**).

8. Secure the side fairing and remove the three front long Allen bolts (A, **Figure 22**).

9. Pull straight out at the upper rear corner (B, **Figure 22**) and unhook the fairing mounting boss from the rubber grommet on the frame mount.

10. Remove the side fairing from the frame.

11. Install by reversing these removal steps while noting the following:

    a. Moisten the frame mount rubber grommet with a wetting agent like Windex. Do not use any type of lubricant.

    b. Install the short and long Allen bolts in the correct locations.

    c. Tighten the bolts securely.

FRONT INNER FAIRING (ALL MODELS)

Removal/Installation

Refer to **Figure 18**.

> *WARNING*
> *Do not remove this fairing panel after the motorcycle has been run. The exhaust system is HOT. Protect hands accordingly.*

1. Remove the two Allen screws (**Figure 23**) on each side.

2. Remove the trim clip (**Figure 24**) on each side.

3. At the top of the fairing on each side, carefully release the locating slots from the locating tabs on the front fairing.

4. Pull the upper portions away from the front fairing, and pull it straight down and away from the front and side fairing panels.

5. Install by reversing these removal steps. Tighten the screws securely.

16

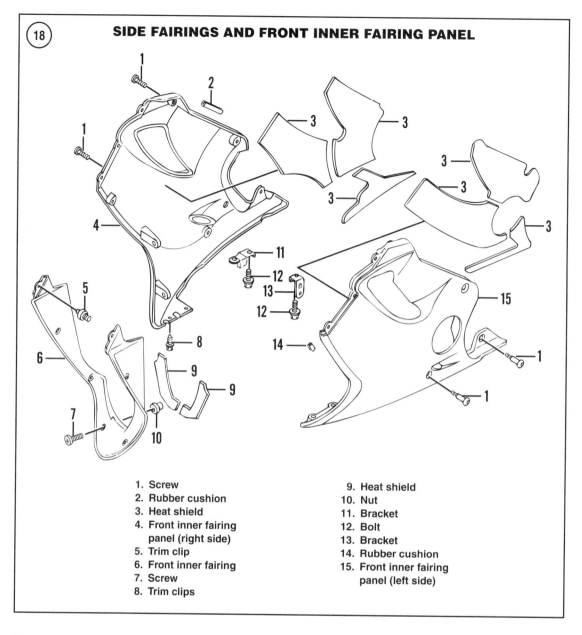

SIDE FAIRINGS AND FRONT INNER FAIRING PANEL

1. Screw
2. Rubber cushion
3. Heat shield
4. Front inner fairing panel (right side)
5. Trim clip
6. Front inner fairing
7. Screw
8. Trim clips
9. Heat shield
10. Nut
11. Bracket
12. Bolt
13. Bracket
14. Rubber cushion
15. Front inner fairing panel (left side)

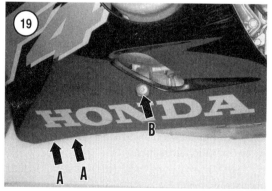

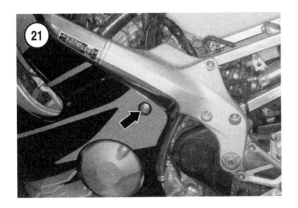

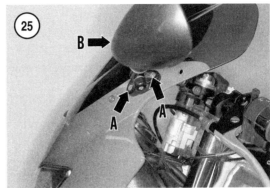

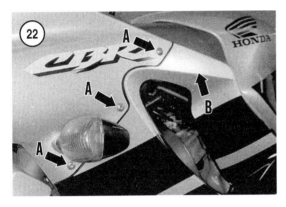

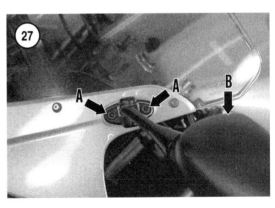

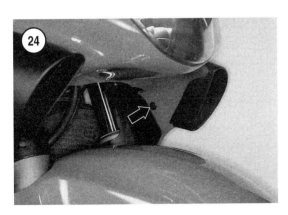

MIRRORS (ALL MODELS)

Removal/Installation

16

1. On 1999-2000 models, remove the Allen bolts (A, **Figure 25**), then remove the mirror (B) from the front fairing and the fairing mounting bracket. Do not lose the cushion washer (**Figure 26**) at each bolt location.

2. On 2001-on models, remove the Allen bolts (A, **Figure 27**), then remove the mirror (B) from the front fairing and the fairing mounting bracket.

3. Repeat for the other side if necessary.

4. Install the mirror(s) and tighten the bolts securely.

5. Sit on the seat and readjust the mirrors before riding the motorcycle.

WINDSHIELD (1999-2000 MODELS)

Removal/Installation

1. Remove the left and right side mirrors (A, **Figure 28**) as described in this chapter.

2. Remove the two front screws, plastic washers and rubber washers (B, **Figure 28**) on each side.

3. Remove the rear long Allen shoulder bolt and nut (C, **Figure 28**) on each side. Remove the collar from the mounting hole to avoid misplacing it.

4. Carefully remove the windshield (D, **Figure 28**) from the front faring.

5. Install by reversing these steps while noting the following:

   a. Align the groove in the front of the windshield with the locating lug on the front fairing.

   b. Install the collar into the rear mount hole prior to installing the long Allen shoulder bolt on each side.

   c. Install the rubber washers and the plastic washers in the correct order prior to installing the mounting screws.

   d. Tighten the screws securely.

WINDSHIELD (2001-ON MODELS)

Removal/Installation

1. Remove the three screws, plastic washers, rubber washers and nut (**Figure 29**) on each side securing the windshield to the front fairing.

2. Carefully remove the windshield from the front fairing.

3. Install by reversing these steps while noting the following:

   a. Install the rubber washers and the plastic washers in the correct order prior to installing the mounting screws.

   b. Tighten the screws securely.

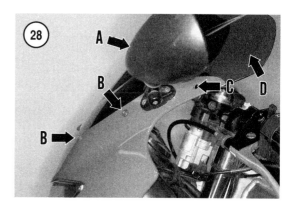

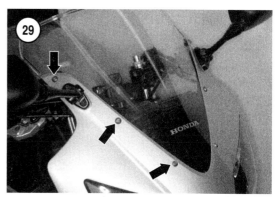

FRONT FAIRING AND AIR DUCTS (1999-2000 MODELS)

Removal/Installation

Refer to **Figure 30**.

1. Remove the fuel tank as described in Chapter Eight.

2. Remove the left and right side fairing panels and front inner fairing panel as described in this chapter.

3. Remove the mirrors as described in this chapter.

4. Remove the combination meter trim panel on each side as follows:

   a. In front of the steering head and directly below the combination meter, remove the trim clip (**Figure 31**) securing the trim panels together.

   b. Remove the screws (**Figure 32**) securing the trim panel to the front fairing.

   c. Carefully pull the trim panel out to the side and from under the combination meter. Remove the panel.

   d. Repeat for the trim panel on the other side.

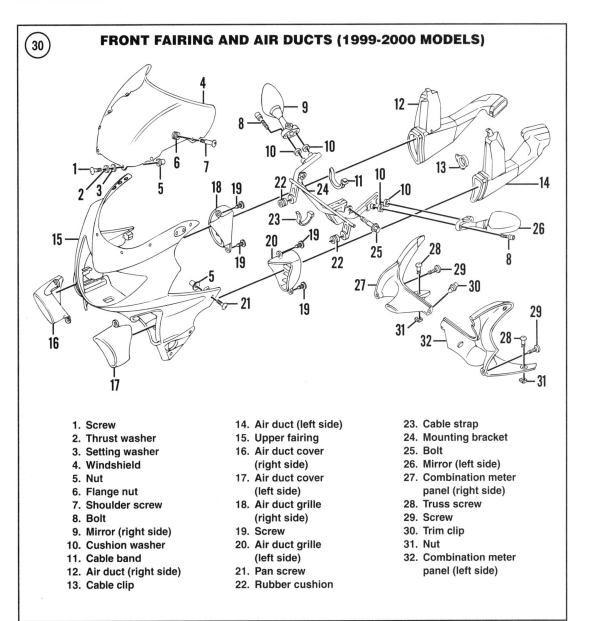

FRONT FAIRING AND AIR DUCTS (1999-2000 MODELS)

30

1. Screw
2. Thrust washer
3. Setting washer
4. Windshield
5. Nut
6. Flange nut
7. Shoulder screw
8. Bolt
9. Mirror (right side)
10. Cushion washer
11. Cable band
12. Air duct (right side)
13. Cable clip

14. Air duct (left side)
15. Upper fairing
16. Air duct cover (right side)
17. Air duct cover (left side)
18. Air duct grille (right side)
19. Screw
20. Air duct grille (left side)
21. Pan screw
22. Rubber cushion

23. Cable strap
24. Mounting bracket
25. Bolt
26. Mirror (left side)
27. Combination meter panel (right side)
28. Truss screw
29. Screw
30. Trim clip
31. Nut
32. Combination meter panel (left side)

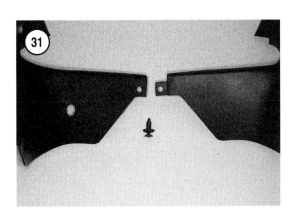

31

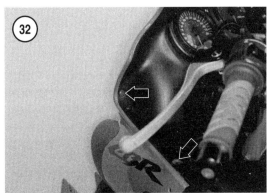

32

16

5. Place several heavy towels (**Figure 33**) on the front fender to protect the finish on both the fender and the front fairing.

6. Have an assistant release the front fairing from the mounting boss on each side, the mirror mounting hole raised bosses on each side and both air ducts, and then pull the front fairing slightly forward and rest it on the front fender (**Figure 34**).

7. Disconnect the following:

    a. Release the electrical connector from the headlight (**Figure 35**) and disconnect the additional electrical connectors (**Figure 36**).

    b. On the right side, disconnect the air vent hose (A, **Figure 37**) from the fitting (B).

8. Remove the front fairing assembly.

9. Disconnect the air duct (**Figure 38**) from the air filter housing and remove both air ducts.

10. Install by reversing these removal steps while noting the following:

    a. Moisten the mount rubber grommets with a wetting agent like Windex. Do not use any type of lubricant.

    b. Check the headlight and turn signal connectors for corrosion. Clean if necessary.

    c. Make sure the air duct hook is secure on the mounting bracket post (**Figure 39**) and that the air duct is seated correctly in the air filter housing (**Figure 40**).

    d. Align the front faring mounting bosses with the rubber grommets on the fairing mounting grommets and push the fairing into place.

    e. Align the front of the air duct with the fitting on the front fairing.

    f. Check the operation of the headlight and front turn signals.

FRONT FAIRING AND AIR DUCTS (2001-ON MODELS)

Removal/Installation

Refer to **Figure 41**.

1. Remove the fuel tank as described in Chapter Nine.

2. Remove the left and right side fairing panels and the front inner fairing panel as described in this chapter.

3. Remove the air duct cover as follows:

    a. Remove the upper screw (**Figure 42**) securing the air duct cover to the front fairing.

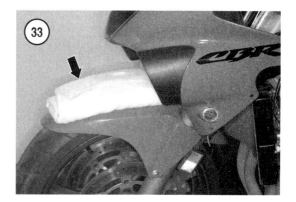

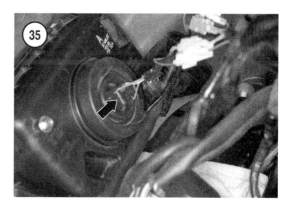

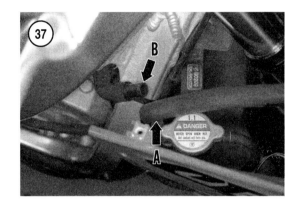

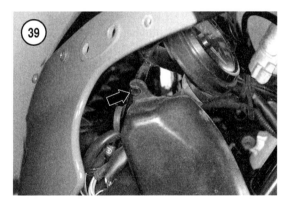

b. Remove the screw (A, **Figure 43**) securing the air duct cover to the fuel tank.

c. Pull straight out at the upper rear corner (B, **Figure 43**) and unhook the air duct cover from the rubber grommet on the fuel tank.

d. Move the air duct cover straight back and release the locating tab from the slot on the front fairing.

e. Remove the air duct cover.

f. Repeat for the air duct cover on the other side.

4. Remove the mirrors as described in this chapter.

5. Place several towels on the front fender to protect the finish on both the fender and the front fairing.

6. Have an assistant release the front fairing from the mounting boss on each side, the mirror mounting hole raised bosses on each side and both air ducts (**Figure 44**), and then pull the front fairing slightly forward and rest it on the front fender.

7. Disconnect the following:

a. Release the electrical connector from the headlight (A, **Figure 45**).

b. Disconnect the sub-harness electrical connector (B, **Figure 45**).

8. Remove the front fairing assembly.

9. If necessary, remove the air ducts from the front fairing.

10. Install by reversing these removal steps while noting the following:

a. Moisten the fuel tank mount rubber grommets with a wetting agent like Windex. Do not use any type of lubricant.

b. On the left side, correctly position the main wiring harness between the front fairing and the air duct as shown in **Figure 46**. Do not pinch the harness.

c. Check the headlight and turn signal connectors for corrosion. Clean if necessary.

d. Make sure the air ducts are secure on the inside surface of the front fairing air intake cover (**Figure 47**) and that they are seated correctly in the air filter housing air duct (**Figure 44**).

e. Hook the air duct resonator chamber onto the metal stay (**Figure 48**).

f. Check the operation of the headlight and front turn signals.

16

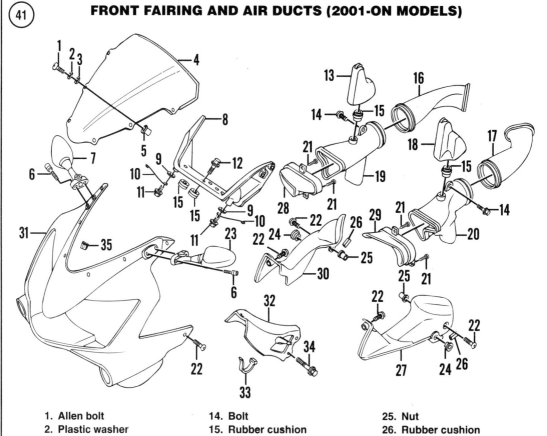

(41) FRONT FAIRING AND AIR DUCTS (2001-ON MODELS)

1. Allen bolt
2. Plastic washer
3. Rubber washer
4. Windshield
5. Nut
6. Bolt
7. Mirror (right side)
8. Mounting bracket
9. Washer
10. Resonator support wire
11. Nut
12. Bolt
13. Resonator chamber
14. Bolt
15. Rubber cushion
16. Air filter air duct (right side)
17. Air filter air duct (left side)
18. Resonator chamber
19. Air duct (right side)
20. Air duct (left side)
21. Screw
22. Pan screw
23. Mirror (left side)
24. Rubber grommet
25. Nut
26. Rubber cushion
27. Air duct cover (left side)
28. Air duct grille (right side)
29. Air duct grille (left side)
30. Air duct cover (right side)
31. Upper fairing
32. Bracket
33. Cable strap
34. Bolt
35. Clip

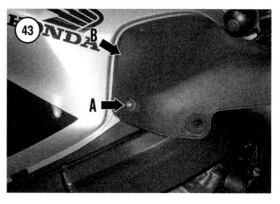

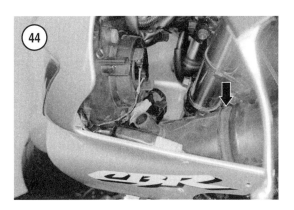

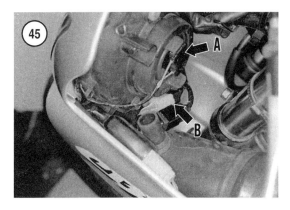

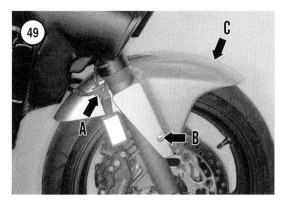

FRONT FENDER

Removal/Installation

1. On the right side, remove the Allen bolt and brake line bracket (A, **Figure 49**).
2. On the left side remove the Allen bolt and reflex reflector.
3. Remove the lower bolt (B, **Figure 49**) on each side.
4. Pull the front fender (C, **Figure 49**) forward and remove it.
5. Install by reversing these removal steps.

REAR FENDER AND SEAT RAIL (1999-2000 MODELS)

Removal/Installation

1. Remove the rear cowl (A, **Figure 50**) as described in this chapter.
2. Remove the battery (A, **Figure 51**) as described in Chapter Ten.
3. In the area below the seat, refer to Chapter Ten and disconnect and remove the following:

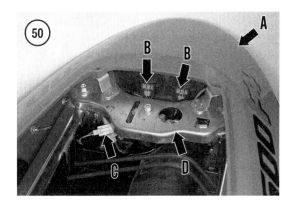

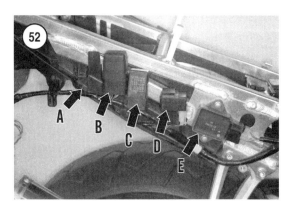

a. Remove the starter relay switch (B, **Figure 51**).

b. Remove the fuse box (C, **Figure 51**).

4. Remove the fuel tank as described in Chapter Eight.

5. Disconnect the following:

a. Tail/brake light (B, **Figure 50**), turn signal and license plate light electrical connectors (C).

b. Seat lock cable from the seat latch on the frame cross member (D, **Figure 50**).

6. On the right side, disconnect the electrical connectors and remove the following components from the mounting tabs on the seat rail.

a. Air vent control valve solenoid valve relay (49-state, Canada and U.K. models) (A, **Figure 52**).

b. Fuel pump transfer relay (B, **Figure 52**).

c. Turn signal relay (C, **Figure 52**).

d. Fuel cut-off relay (D, **Figure 52**).

e. Regulator/rectifier (E, **Figure 52**).

7. On the left side, disconnect the electrical connector (A, **Figure 53**) and remove the ignition control module (B).

8. On the left side, loosen the clamp band and remove the shock absorber reservoir (**Figure 54**) from the seat rail. Secure the reservoir (A, **Figure 55**) in the upright position.

9. Remove the bolts, washers and nuts securing the rear fender to the seat rail.

10. Slide the rear fender part way toward the rear, then remove the collars between the seat rail and the rear fender.

11. Check that all components and fasteners have been removed, then slide the rear fender toward the rear and remove it.

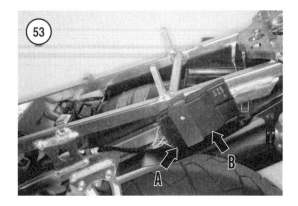

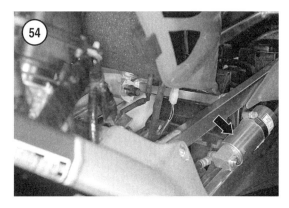

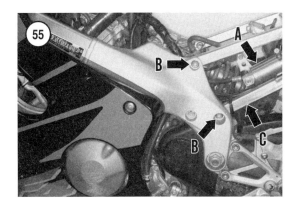

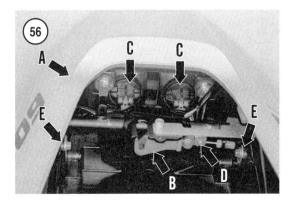

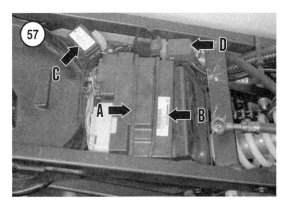

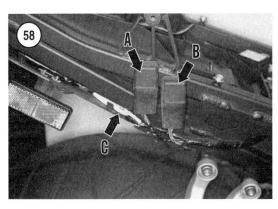

12. Remove all clamps securing all wiring harnesses to the seat rail.

13. Remove the bolts securing the passenger right side footpeg to the seat rail.

14. Remove the two bolts (B, **Figure 55**) and nuts on each side securing the seat rail to the frame. Remove the seal rail (C, **Figure 55**).

15. Install by reversing these removal steps while noting the following:

    a. Install all of the electrical components onto the seat rail mounting tabs.

    b. Make sure all electrical connectors are secure.

    c. Secure all electrical wiring harnesses to the seat rail in the correct location.

    d. Tighten the seat rail mounting bolts to 49 N•m (36 ft.-lb.) and the footpeg bolts to 26 N•m (19 ft.-lb.).

REAR FENDER AND SEAT RAIL (2001-ON MODELS)

1. Remove the seat and rear cowl (A, **Figure 56**) as described in this chapter.

2. Remove the fuel tank as described in Chapter Eight.

3. In the area below the seat, refer to Chapter Ten and disconnect and remove the following:

    a. Remove the engine control module (A, **Figure 57**).

    b. Remove the battery (B, **Figure 57**).

4. Release the bosses from the rear fender and remove the battery tray.

5. Unhook the retaining tab and remove the fuse box (C, **Figure 57**).

6. Remove the starter relay switch (D, **Figure 57**) from the mounting boss.

7. At the rear of the seat rail, disconnect the connectors from the rear turn signals, license plate light (B, **Figure 56**) and tail/brake lights (C).

8. Unhook the seat lock cable from the mechanism (D, **Figure 56**).

9. Remove the fuel cut-off relay (A, **Figure 58**) and engine stop relay (B) from the seat rail bosses.

10. Unhook the rear electrical sub-harness (C, **Figure 58**) from the guides on the rear fender.

11. Remove the two bolts and washers (E, **Figure 56**) securing the rear fender to the seat rail.

16

12. Slide the rear fender partially toward the rear. Check that all components and fasteners have been removed, then slide the rear fender toward the rear and remove it.

13. Loosen the clamp band and move the shock absorber reservoir (A, **Figure 59**) off the seat rail. Secure it in the upright position.

14. Remove the bolt and nut (A, **Figure 60**) securing the rear master cylinder reservoir to the seat rail bracket. Move the reservoir out of the way.

15. Remove the plastic band (B, **Figure 60**) securing the rear brake light wire harness to the seat rail.

16. Remove the bolts securing the voltage regulator/rectifier (B, **Figure 59**) to the frame and remove it.

17. Remove the bolts securing the passenger right side footpeg (**Figure 61**) to the seat rail.

18. Remove the bolts securing the passenger left side footpeg (C, **Figure 59**) to the seat rail.

19. Remove the two bolts (C, **Figure 60**) on each side securing the seat rail to the frame. Remove the seal rail (D).

20. Install by reversing these removal steps while noting the following:

   a. Install all of the electrical components onto the seat rail mounting tabs.

   b. Make sure all electrical connectors are secure.

   c. Secure all electrical wiring harnesses to the seat rail in the correct location.

   d. Tighten the seat rail mounting bolts to 49 N•m (36 ft.-lb.) and the foot peg bolts to 26 N•m (19 ft.-lb.).

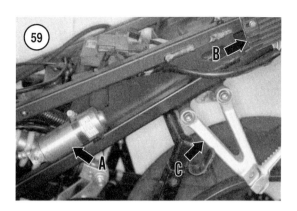

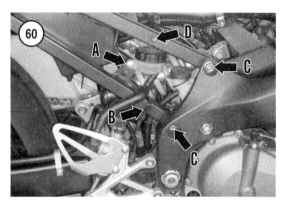

INDEX

17

17

17

17

WIRING
DIAGRAMS

CHARGING SYSTEM (1999-2000 MODELS)

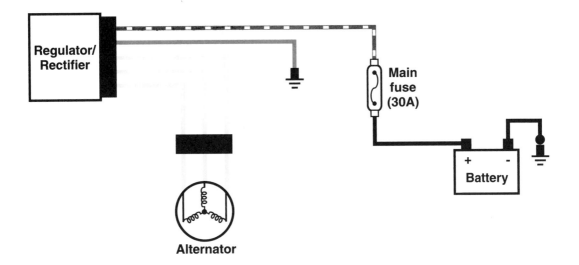

Regulator/
Rectifier

Main
fuse
(30A)

+ -
Battery

Alternator

18

CHARGING SYSTEM (2001-ON MODELS)

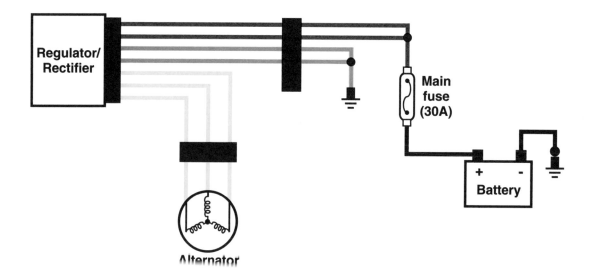

IGNITION SYSTEM (1999-2000 MODELS)

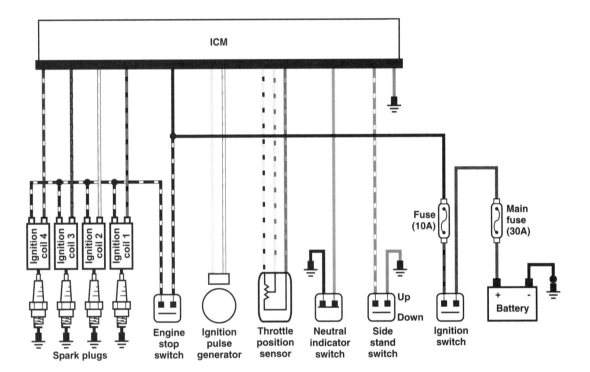

IGNITION SYSTEM (2001-ON MODELS)

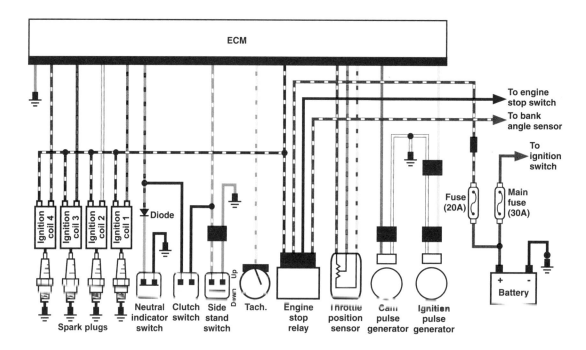

STARTING SYSTEM (ALL MODELS)

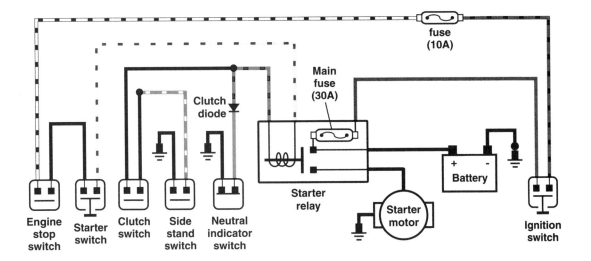

1999-2000 CBR600F4 (49-STATE AND CANADA MODELS)

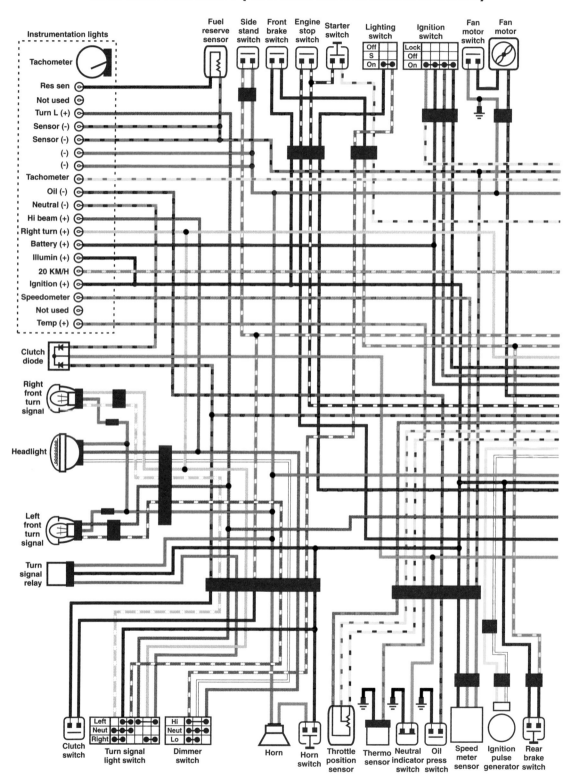

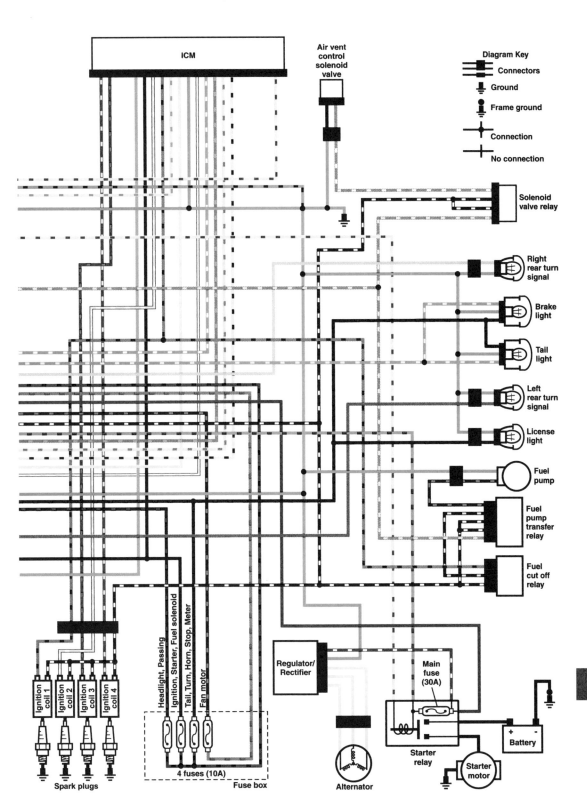

18

1999-2000 CBR600F4 (CALIFORNIA MODELS)

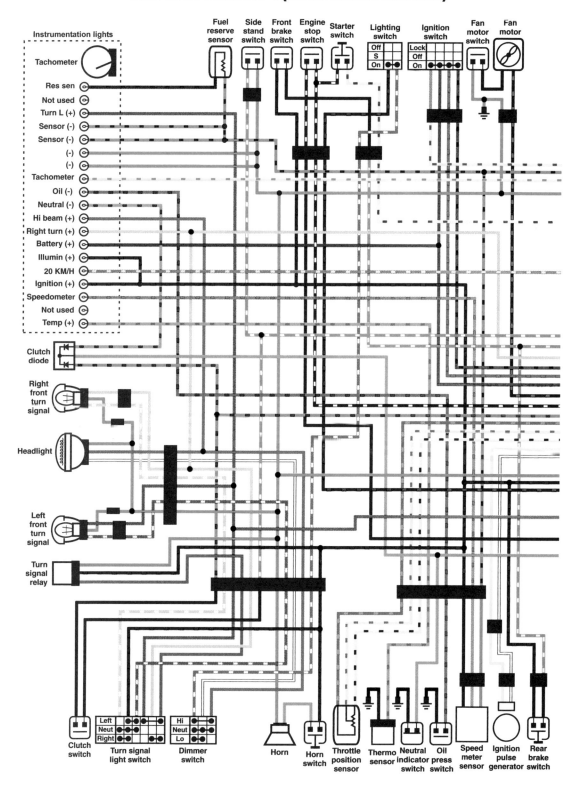

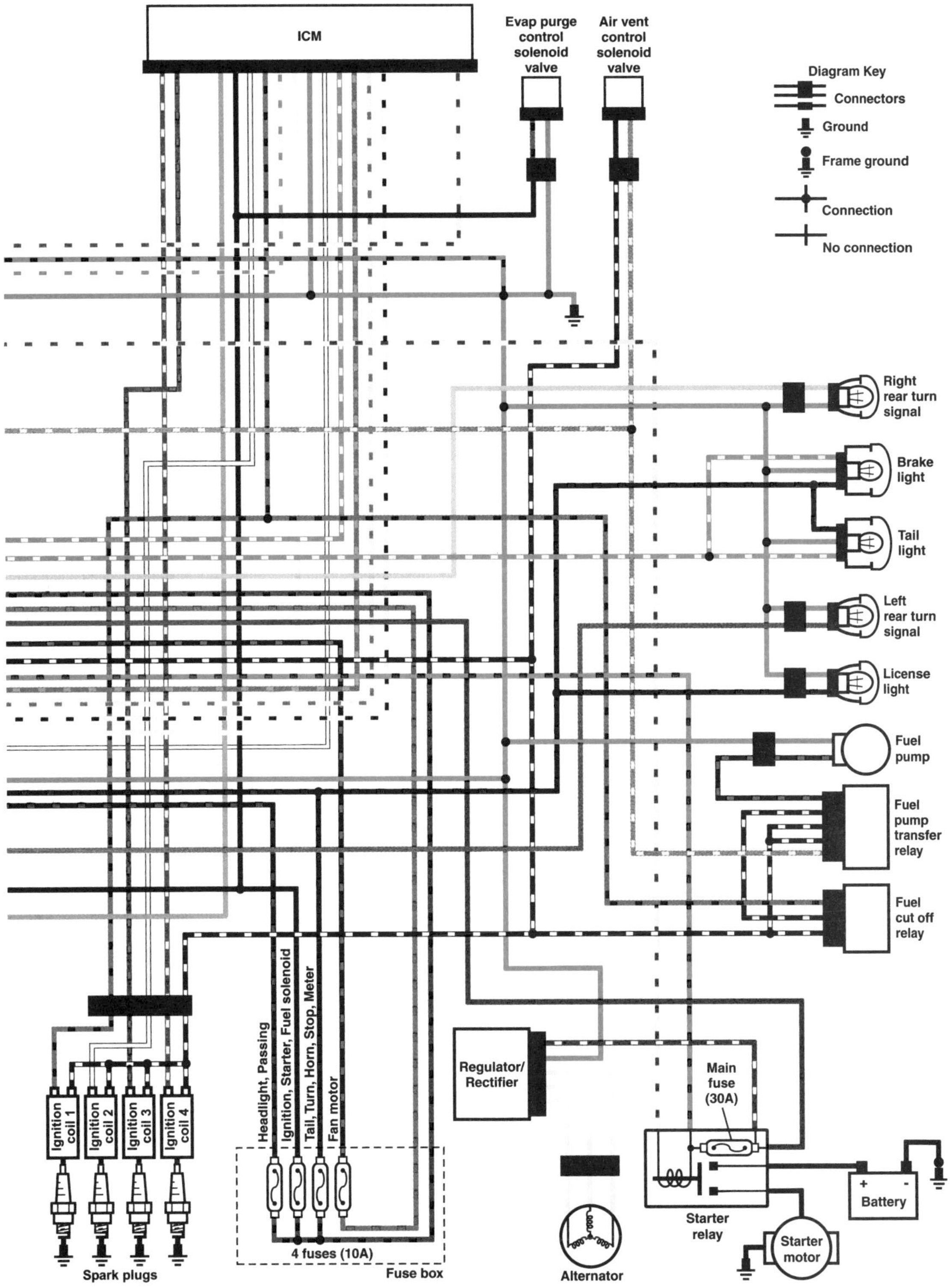
ICM
Evap purge control solenoid valve
Air vent control solenoid valve
Diagram Key
Connectors
Ground
Frame ground
Connection
No connection
Right rear turn signal
Brake light
Tail light
Left rear turn signal
License light
Fuel pump
Fuel pump transfer relay
Fuel cut off relay
Ignition coil 1
Ignition coil 2
Ignition coil 3
Ignition coil 4
Spark plugs
Headlight, Passing
Ignition, Starter, Fuel solenoid
Tail, Turn, Horn, Stop, Meter
Fan motor
4 fuses (10A)
Fuse box
Regulator/ Rectifier
Alternator
Main fuse (30A)
Starter relay
Battery
Starter motor

1999-2000 CBR600F (AUSTRALIA, BRAZIL AND MEXICO MODELS)

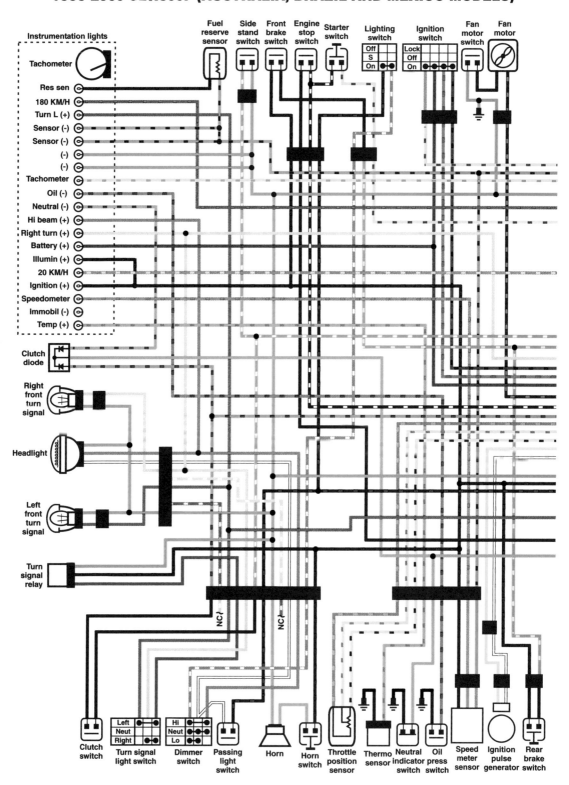

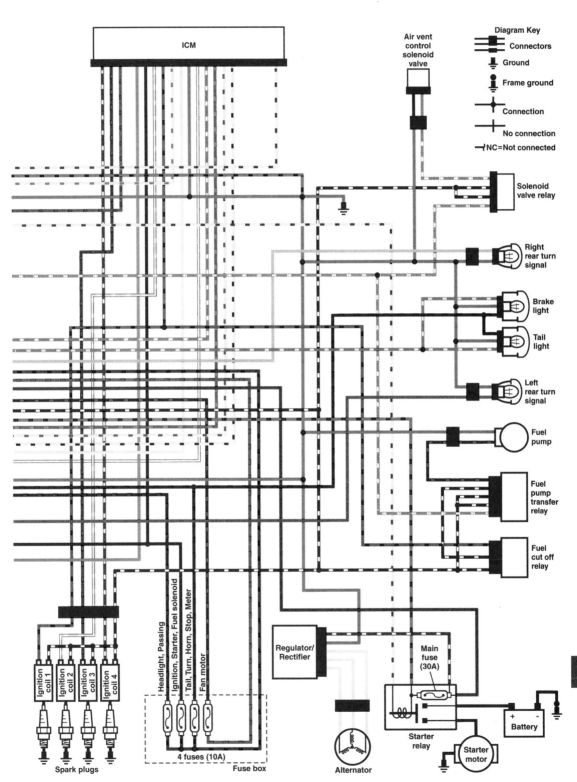

1999-2000 CBR600F (ALL MODELS EXCEPT AUSTRALIA, BRAZIL AND MEXICO)

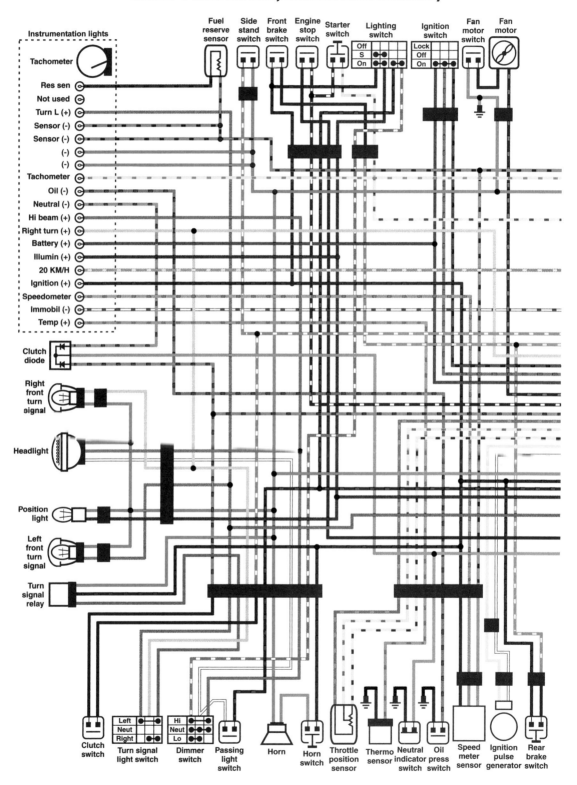

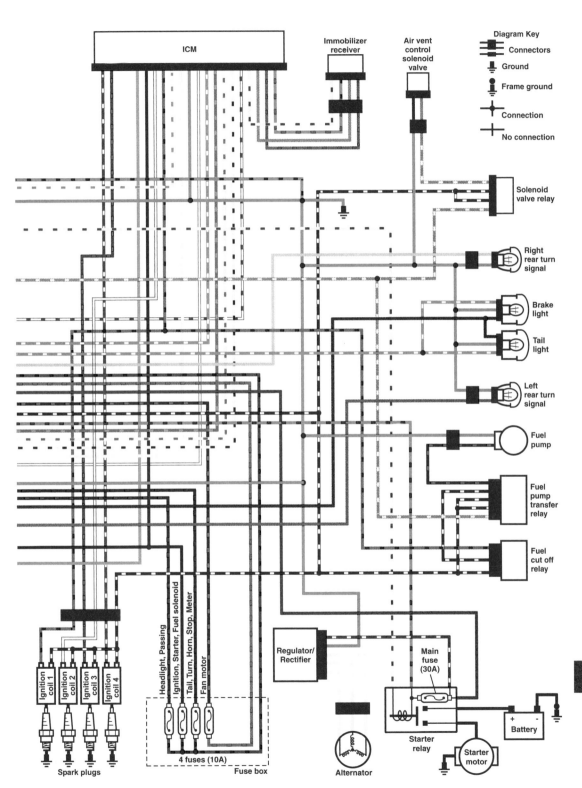

18

2001-ON CBR600F4i (U.S. MODELS)

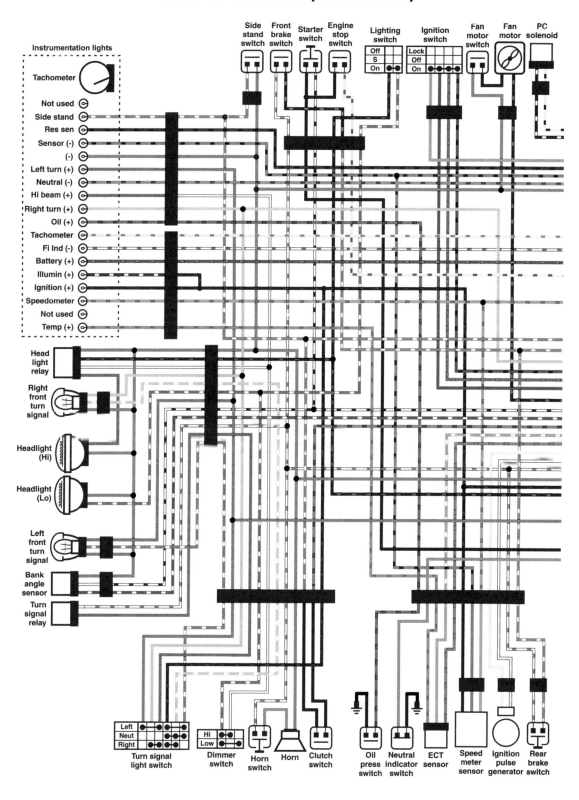

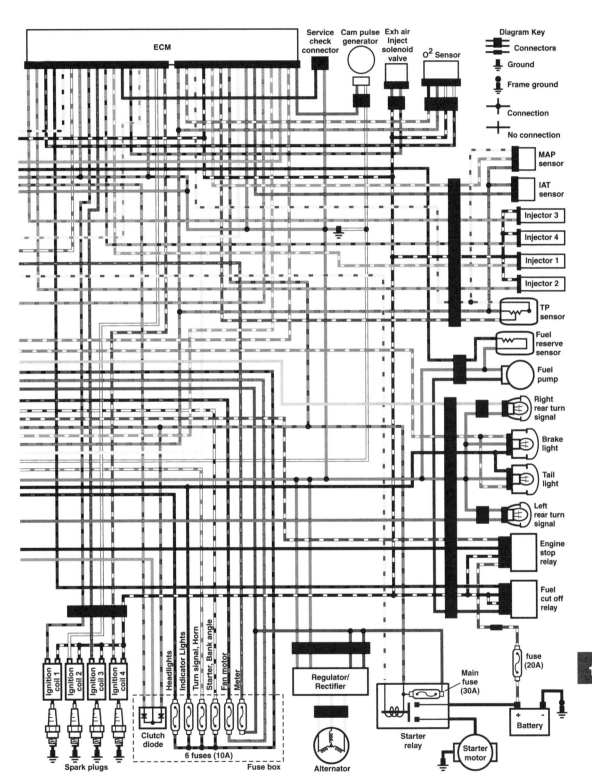

2001-ON CBR600F SPORT (GERMANY MODELS)

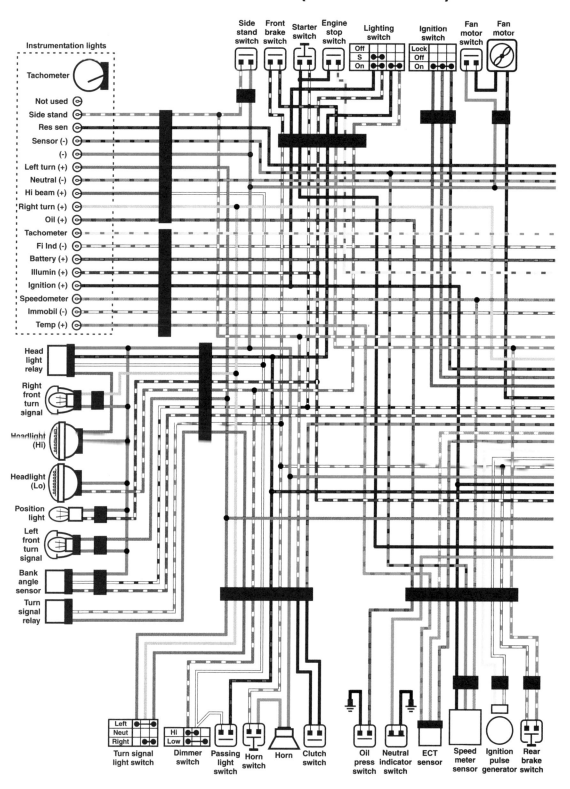

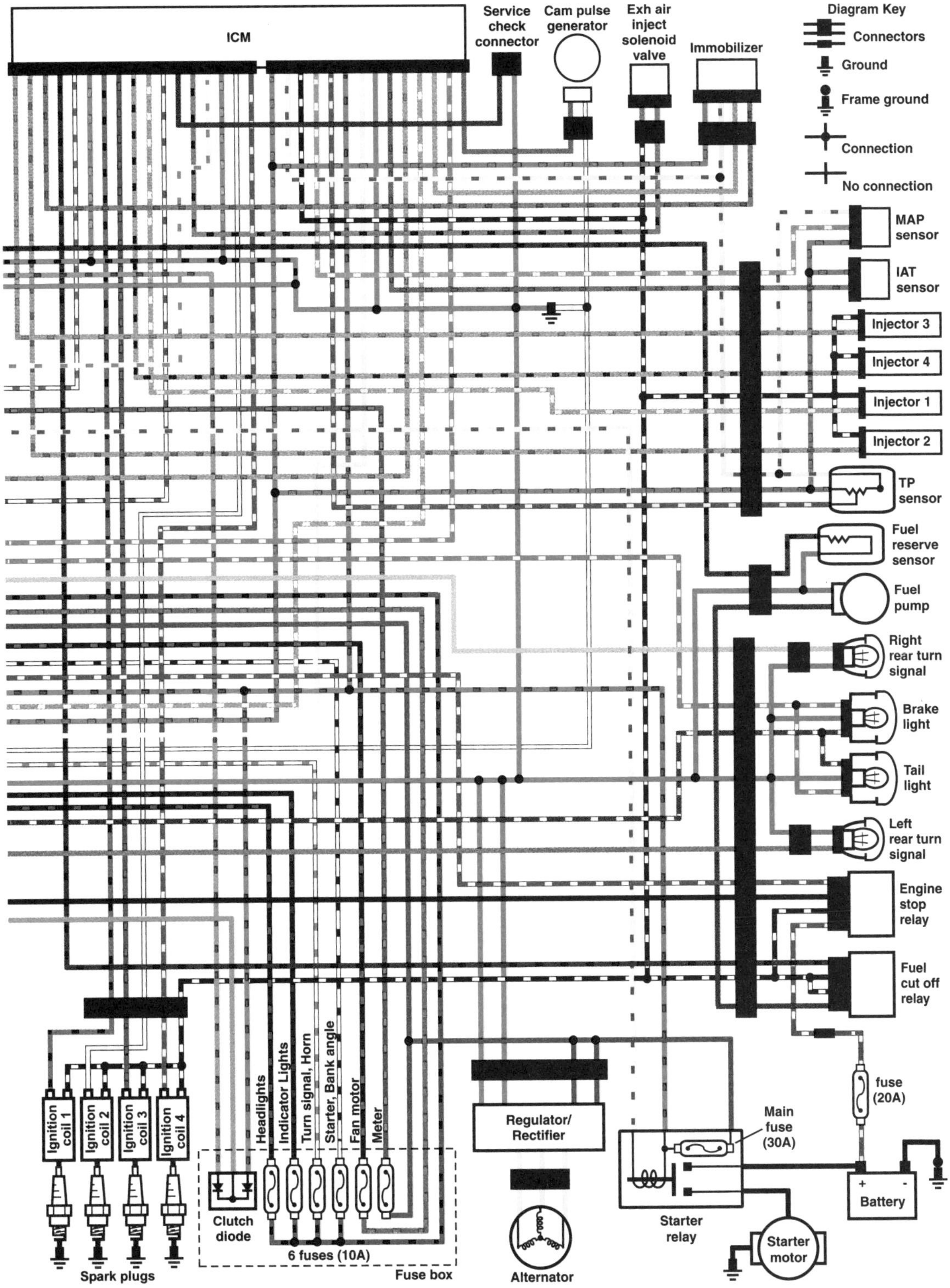

Diagram Key

- Connectors
- Ground
- Frame ground
- Connection
- No connection

2001-ON CBR600F SPORT (FRANCE MODELS)

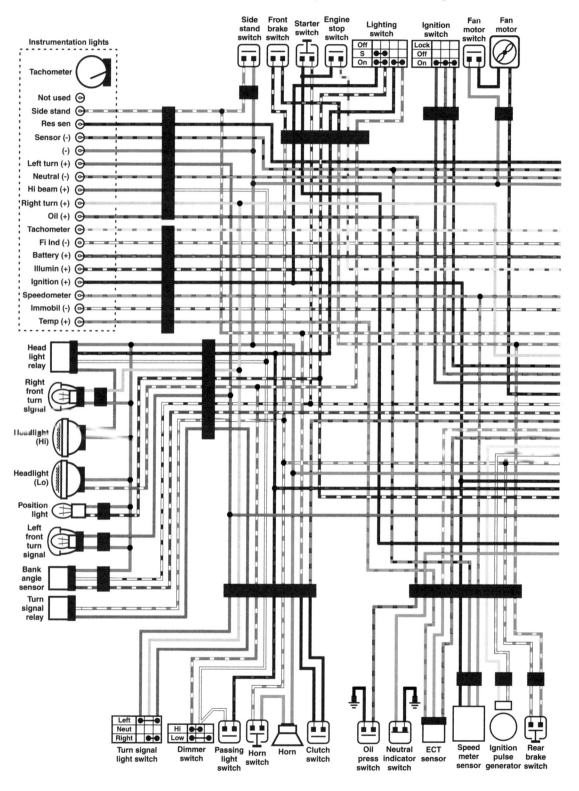

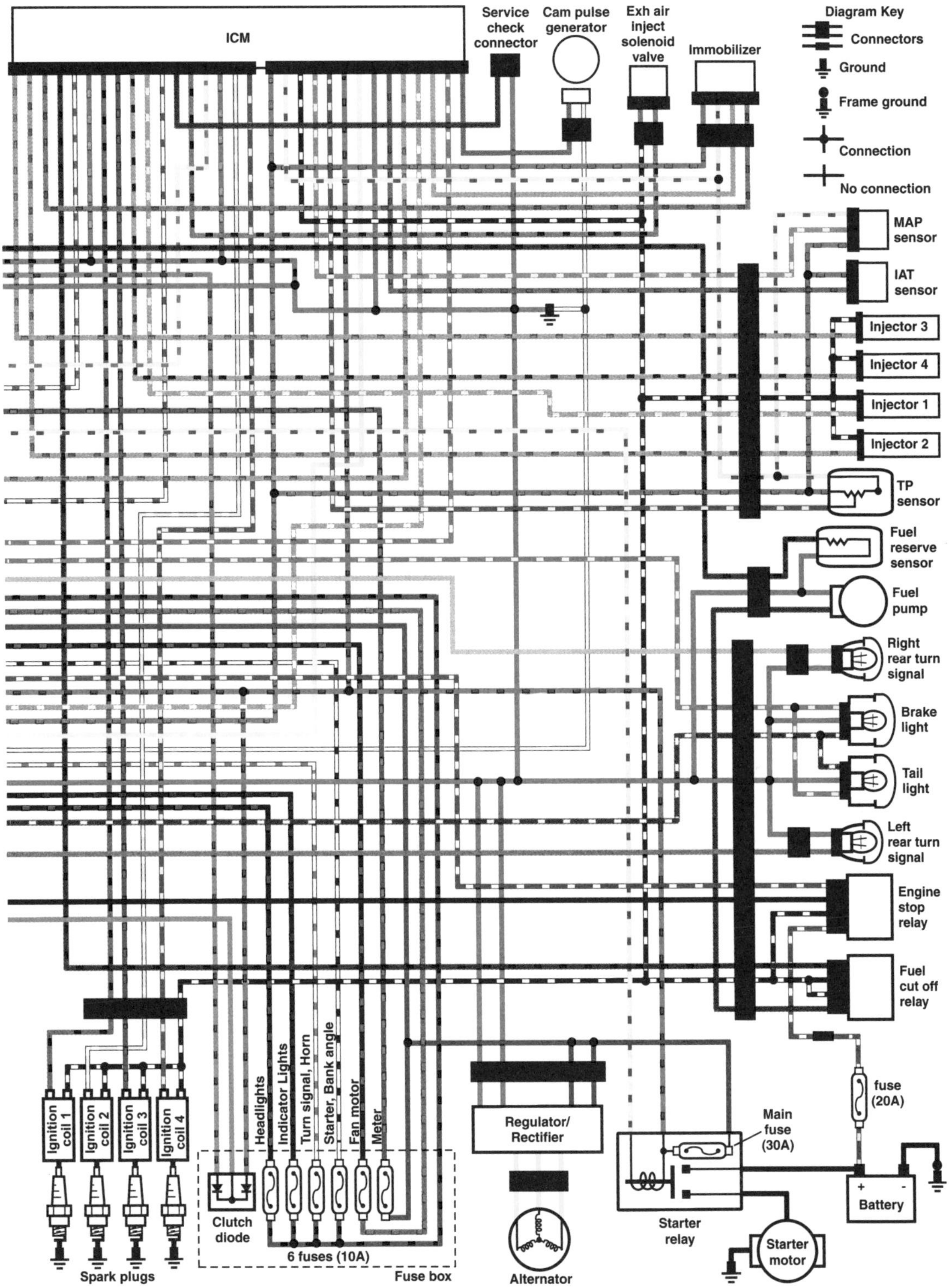

Diagram Key

- Connectors
- Ground
- Frame ground
- Connection
- No connection

ICM

Service check connector

Cam pulse generator

Exh air inject solenoid valve

Immobilizer

MAP sensor

IAT sensor

Injector 3

Injector 4

Injector 1

Injector 2

TP sensor

Fuel reserve sensor

Fuel pump

Right rear turn signal

Brake light

Tail light

Left rear turn signal

Engine stop relay

Fuel cut off relay

fuse (20A)

Ignition coil 1

Ignition coil 2

Ignition coil 3

Ignition coil 4

Headlights

Indicator Lights

Turn signal, Horn

Starter, Bank angle

Fan motor

Meter

Clutch diode

6 fuses (10A)

Fuse box

Spark plugs

Regulator/ Rectifier

Alternator

Main fuse (30A)

Starter relay

Starter motor

Battery

18

2001-ON CBR600F SPORT (ALL MODELS EXCEPT FRANCE AND GERMANY)

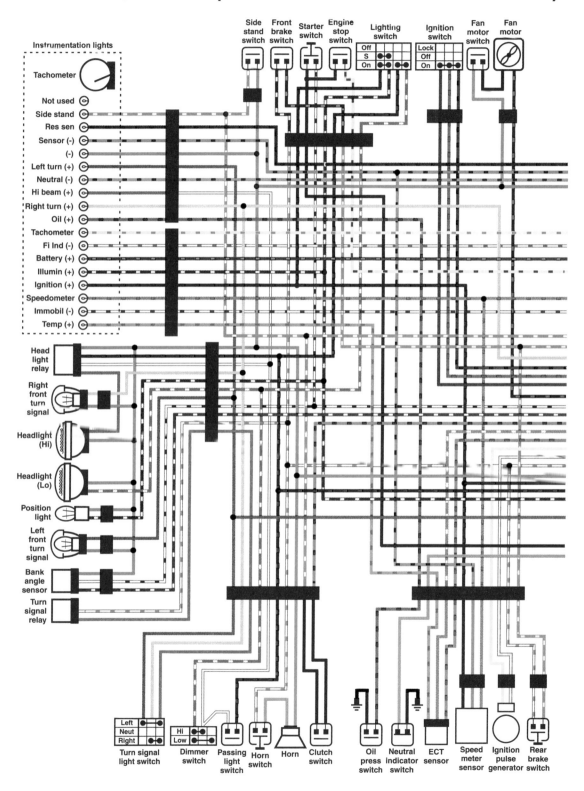

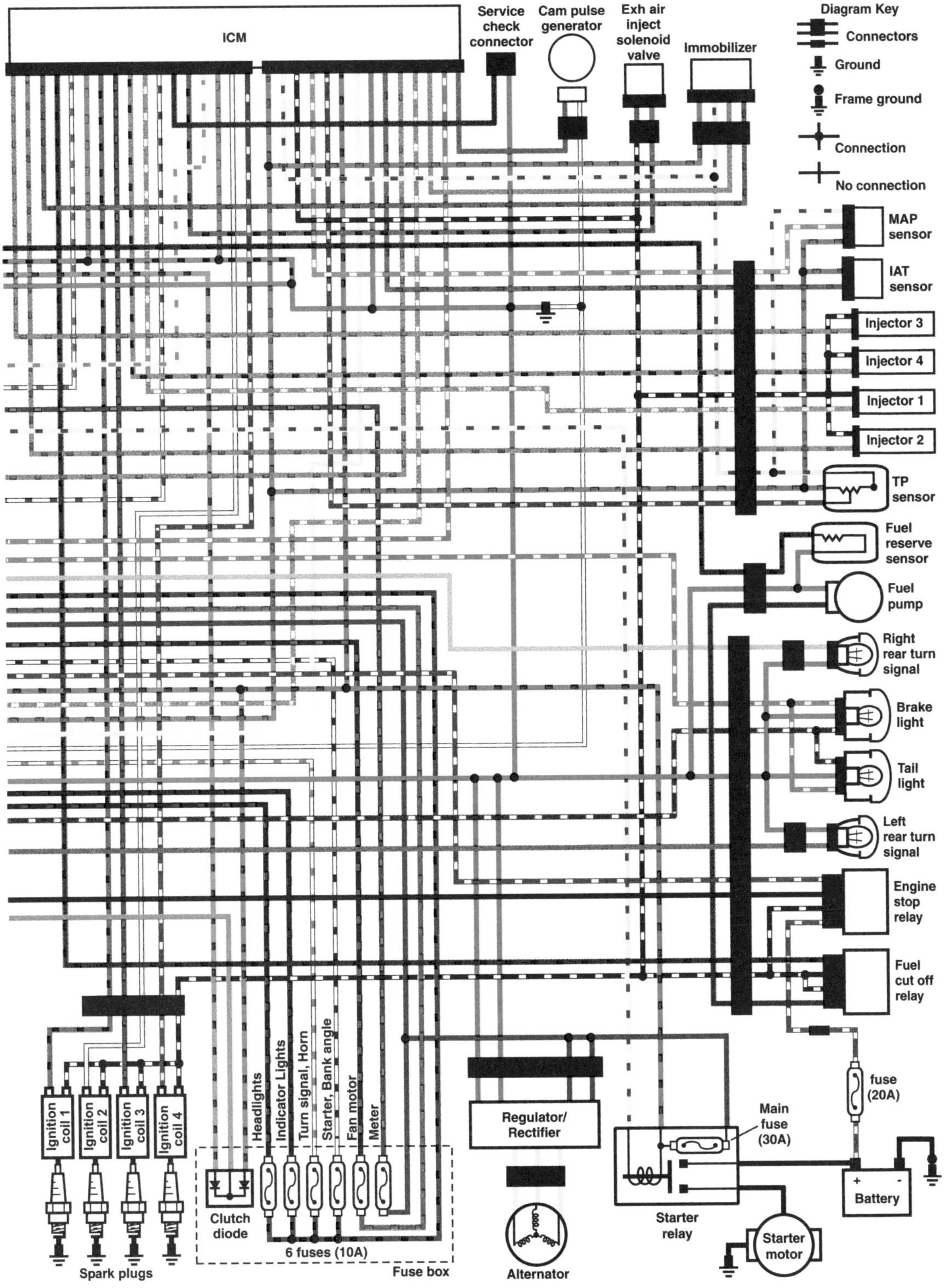

ICM

Service check connector

Cam pulse generator

Exh air inject solenoid valve

Immobilizer

Diagram Key

Connectors

Ground

Frame ground

Connection

No connection

MAP sensor

IAT sensor

Injector 3

Injector 4

Injector 1

Injector 2

TP sensor

Fuel reserve sensor

Fuel pump

Right rear turn signal

Brake light

Tail light

Left rear turn signal

Engine stop relay

Fuel cut off relay

fuse (20A)

Ignition coil 1

Ignition coil 2

Ignition coil 3

Ignition coil 4

Headlights

Indicator Lights

Turn signal, Horn

Starter, Bank angle

Fan motor

Meter

Clutch diode

6 fuses (10A)

Fuse box

Spark plugs

Regulator/ Rectifier

Alternator

Main fuse (30A)

Starter relay

Starter motor

Battery

18

NOTES

NOTES

NOTES

NOTES

NOTES

MAINTENANCE LOG

Date	Miles	Type of Service

Check out *clymer.com* for our full line of powersport repair manuals.

BMW

M308	500 & 600 CC Twins, 55-69
M309	F650, 1994-2000
M500-3	BMW K-Series, 85-97
M501	K1200RS, GT & LT, 98-05
M502-3	BMW R50/5-R100 GSPD, 70-96
M503-3	R850, R1100, R1150 and R1200C, 93-05

HARLEY-DAVIDSON

M419	Sportsters, 59-85
M428	Sportster Evolution, 86-90
M429-4	XL/XLH Sportster, 91-03
M427-1	Sportster, 04-06
M418	Panheads, 48-65
M420	Shovelheads, 66-84
M421-3	FLS/FXS Evolution, 84-99
M423-2	FLS/FXS Twin Cam, 00-05
M422-3	FLH/FLT/FXR Evolution, 84-99
M430-4	FLH/FLT Twin Cam, 99-05
M424-2	FXD Evolution, 91-98
M425-3	FXD Twin Cam, 99-05

HONDA

ATVs

M316	Odyssey FL250, 77-84
M311	ATC, TRX & Fourtrax 70-125, 70-87
M433	Fourtrax 90 ATV, 93-00
M326	ATC185 & 200, 80-86
M347	ATC200X & Fourtrax 200SX, 86-88
M455	ATC250 & Fourtrax 200/ 250, 84-87
M342	ATC250R, 81-84
M348	TRX250R/Fourtrax 250R & ATC250R, 85-89
M456-3	TRX250X 87-92; TRX300EX 93-04
M215	TRX250EX, 01-05
M446-2	TRX250 Recon & ES, 97-04
M346-3	TRX300/Fourtrax 300 & TRX300FW/Fourtrax 4x4, 88-00
M200-2	TRX350 Rancher, 00-06
M459-3	TRX400 Foreman 95-03
M454-3	TRX400EX 99-05
M205	TRX450 Foreman, 98-04
M210	TRX500 Rubicon, 98-04

Singles

M310-13	50-110cc OHC Singles, 65-99
M319-2	XR50R, CRF50F, XR70R & CRF70F, 97-05
M315	100-350cc OHC, 69-82
M317	Elsinore, 125-250cc, 73-80
M442	CR60-125R Pro-Link, 81-88
M431-2	CR80R, 89-95, CR125R, 89-91
M435	CR80, 96-02
M457-2	CR125R & CR250R, 92-97
M464	CR125R, 1998-2002
M443	CR250R-500R Pro-Link, 81-87
M432-3	CR250R, 88-91 & CR500R, 88-01
M437	CR250R, 97-01
M352	CRF250, CRF250X & CRF450R, CRF450X, 02-05
M312-13	XL/XR75-100, 75-03
M318-4	XL/XR/TLR 125-200, 79-03
M328-4	XL/XR250, 78-00; XL/XR350R 83-85; XR200R, 84-85; XR250L, 91-96
M320-2	XR400R, 96-04
M339-7	XL/XR 500-650, 79-03

Twins

M321	125-200cc, 65-78
M322	250-350cc, 64-74
M323	250-360cc Twins, 74-77
M324-5	Twinstar, Rebel 250 & Nighthawk 250, 78-03
M334	400-450cc, 78-87
M333	450 & 500cc, 65-76
M335	CX & GL500/650 Twins, 78-83
M344	VT500, 83-88
M313	VT700 & 750, 83-87
M314-2	VT750 Shadow (chain drive), 98-05
M440	VT1100C Shadow , 85-96
M460-3	VT1100C Series, 95-04

Fours

M332	CB350-550cc, SOHC, 71-78
M345	CB550 & 650, 83-85
M336	CB650, 79-82
M341	CB750 SOHC, 69-78
M337	CB750 DOHC, 79-82
M436	CB750 Nighthawk, 91-93 & 95-99
M325	CB900, 1000 & 1100, 80-83
M439	Hurricane 600, 87-90
M441-2	CBR600F2 & F3, 91-98
M445-2	CBR600F4, 99-06
M434-2	CBR900RR Fireblade, 93-99
M329	500cc V-Fours, 84-86
M438	Honda VFR800, 98-00
M349	700-1000 Interceptor, 83-85
M458-2	VFR700F-750F, 86-97
M327	700-1100cc V-Fours, 82-88
M340	GL1000 & 1100, 75-83
M504	GL1200, 84-87
M508	ST1100/PAN European, 90-02

Sixes

M505	GL1500 Gold Wing, 88-92
M506-2	GL1500 Gold Wing, 93-00
M507-2	GL1800 Gold Wing, 01-05
M462-2	GL1500C Valkyrie, 97-03

KAWASAKI

ATVs

M465-2	KLF220 & KLF250 Bayou, 88-03
M466-4	KLF300 Bayou, 86-04
M467	KLF400 Bayou, 93-99
M470	KEF300 Lakota, 95-99
M385	KSF250 Mojave, 87-00

Singles

M350-9	Rotary Valve 80-350cc, 66-01
M444-2	KX60, 83-02; KX80 83-90
M448	KX80/85/100, 89-03
M351	KDX200, 83-88
M447-3	KX125 & KX250, 82-91 KX500, 83-04
M472-2	KX125, 92-00
M473-2	KX250, 92-00
M474-2	KLR650, 87-06

Twins

M355	KZ400, KZ/Z440, EN450 & EN500, 74-95
M360-3	EX500, GPZ500S, Ninja R, 87-02
M356-4	Vulcan 700 & 750, 85-04
M354-2	Vulcan 800 & Vulcan 800 Classic, 95-04
M357-2	Vulcan 1500, 87-99
M471-2	Vulcan Classic 1500, 96-04

Fours

M449	KZ500/550 & ZX550, 79-85
M450	KZ, Z & ZX750, 80-85
M358	K7650, 77-83
M359-3	900-1000cc Fours, 73-81
M451-3	1000 &1100cc Fours, 81-02
M452-3	ZX500 & 600 Ninja, 85-97
M453-3	Ninja ZX900-1100 84-01
M468-2	Ninja ZX-6, 90-04
M469	ZX7 Ninja, 91-98
M453-3	Ninja ZX900, ZX1000 & ZX1100, 84-01
M409	Concours, 86-04

POLARIS

ATVs

M496	Polaris ATV, 85-95
M362	Polaris Magnum ATV, 96-98
M363	Scrambler 500, 4X4 97-00
M365-2	Sportsman/Xplorer, 96-03

SUZUKI

ATVs

M381	ALT/LT 125 & 185, 83-87
M475	LT230 & LT250, 85-90
M380-2	LT250R Quad Racer, 85-92
M343	LTF500F Quadrunner, 98-00
M483-2	Suzuki King Quad/ Quad Runner 250, 87-98

Singles

M371	RM50-400 Twin Shock, 75-81
M369	125-400cc 64-81
M379	RM125-500 Single Shock, 81-88
M476	DR250-350, 90-94
M384-3	LS650 Savage, 86-04
M386	RM80-250, 89-95
M400	RM125, 96-00
M401	RM250, 96-02

Twins

M372	GS400-450 Twins, 77-87
M481-4	VS700-800 Intruder, 85-04
M482-2	VS1400 Intruder, 87-01
M484-3	GS500E Twins, 89-02
M361	SV650, 1999-2002

Triple

M368	380-750cc, 72-77

Fours

M373	GS550, 77-86
M364	GS650, 81-83
M370	GS750 Fours, 77-82
M376	GS850-1100 Shaft Drive, 79-84
M378	GS1100 Chain Drive, 80-81
M383-3	Katana 600, 88-96 GSX-R750-1100, 86-87
M331	GSX-R600, 97-00
M478-2	GSX-R750, 88-92 GSX750F Katana, 89-96
M485	GSX-R750, 96-99
M377	GSX-R1000, 01-04
M338	GSF600 Bandit, 95-00
M353	GSF1200 Bandit, 96-03

YAMAHA

ATVs

M499	YFM80 Badger, 85-01
M394	YTM/YFM200 & 225, 83-86
M488-5	Blaster, 88-05
M489-2	Timberwolf, 89-00
M487-5	Warrior, 87-04
M486-5	Banshee, 87-04
M490-3	Moto-4 & Big Bear, 87-04
M493	YFM400FW Kodiak, 93-98
M280-2	Raptor 660R, 01-05

Singles

M492-2	PW50 & PW80, BW80 Big Wheel 80, 81-02
M410	80-175 Piston Port, 68-76
M415	250-400cc Piston Port, 68-76
M412	DT & MX 100-400, 77-83
M414	IT125-490, 76-86
M393	YZ50-80 Monoshock, 78-90
M413	YZ100-490 Monoshock, 76-84
M390	YZ125-250, 85-87 YZ490, 85-90
M391	YZ125-250, 88-93 WR250Z, 91-93
M497-2	YZ125, 94-01
M498	YZ250, 94-98 and WR250Z, 94-97
M406	YZ250F & WR250F, 01-03
M491-2	YZ400F, YZ426F, WR400F WR426F, 98-02
M417	XT125-250, 80-84
M480-3	XT/TT 350, 85-00
M405	XT500 & TT500, 76-81
M416	XT/TT 600, 83-89

Twins

M403	650cc, 70-82
M395-10	XV535-1100 Virago, 81-03
M495-4	V-Star 650, 98-05
M281-2	V-Star 1100, 99-05
M282	Road Star, 99-05

Triple

M404	XS750 & 850, 77-81

Fours

M387	XJ550, XJ600 & FJ600, 81-92
M494	XJ600 Seca II, 92-98
M388	YX600 Radian & FZ600, 86-90
M396	FZR600, 89-93
M392	FZ700-750 & Fazer, 85-87
M411	XS1100 Fours, 78-81
M397	FJ1100 & 1200, 84-93
M375	V-Max, 85-03
M374	Royal Star, 96-03
M461	YZF-R6, 99-04
M398	YZF-R1, 98-03
M399	FZ1, 01-05

VINTAGE MOTORCYCLES

Clymer® Collection Series

M330	Vintage British Street Bikes, BSA, 500–650cc Unit Twins; Norton, 750 & 850cc Commandos; Triumph, 500-750cc Twins
M300	Vintage Dirt Bikes, V. 1 Bultaco, 125-370cc Singles; Montesa, 123-360cc Singles; Ossa, 125-250cc Singles
M301	Vintage Dirt Bikes, V. 2 CZ, 125-400cc Singles; Husqvarna, 125-450cc Singles; Maico, 250-501cc Singles; Hodaka, 90-125cc Singles
M305	Vintage Japanese Street Bikes Honda, 250 & 305cc Twins; Kawasaki, 250-750cc Triples; Kawasaki, 900 & 1000cc Fours